THE**GREEN**GUIDE
Germany

Sony Centre, Potsdamer Platz, Berlin © P. & G. Bowater/Tips Images/Photononstop

MICHELIN

General Manager   Cynthia Clayton Ochterbeck

THEGREENGUIDE **GERMANY**

Editorial Manager	Jonathan Gilbert
Editor	Rachel Mills
Principal Writer	Andrea Schulte-Peevers
Production Manager	Natasha G. George
Cartography	Stéphane Anton
Photo Editor	Yoshimi Kanazawa
Proofreader	Liz Jones
Interior Design	Chris Bell
Cover Design	Chris Bell, Christelle Le Déan
Layout	Michelin Apa Publications Ltd., John Heath
Cover Layout	Michelin Apa Publications Ltd.

Contact Us

The Green Guide
Michelin Maps and Guides
One Parkway South
Greenville, SC 29615, USA
www.michelintravel.com

Michelin Maps and Guides
Hannay House
39 Clarendon Road
Watford, Herts WD17 1JA, UK
℘01923 205240
www.ViaMichelin.com
travelpubsales@uk.michelin.com

Special Sales

For information regarding bulk sales,
customized editions and premium sales,
please contact our Customer Service
Departments:
USA   1-800-432-6277
UK   01923 205240
Canada 1-800-361-8236

Note to the reader Addresses, phone numbers, opening hours and prices published in this guide are accurate at the time of press. We welcome corrections and suggestions that may assist us in preparing the next edition. While every effort is made to ensure that all information printed in this guide is correct and up-to-date, Michelin Apa Publications Ltd. accepts no liability for any direct, indirect or consequential losses howsoever caused so far as such can be excluded by law.

HOW TO USE THIS GUIDE

PLANNING YOUR TRIP

The blue-tabbed PLANNING YOUR TRIP section gives you **ideas for your trip** and **practical information** to help you organize it. You'll find tours, practical information, a host of outdoor activities, a calendar of events, information on shopping, sightseeing, kids' activities and more.

INTRODUCTION

The orange-tabbed INTRODUCTION section first explores **The Country Today**. The **History** section guides the reader through 500 000 years, touching on the earliest evidence of human life right up to reunification and the 21C. The **Architecture**, **Art**, **Literature**, **Music** and **Cinema** sections explore Germany's culture. **Nature** delves into the country's Geology and Landscape.

DISCOVERING

The green-tabbed DISCOVERING section features Principal Sights by region, featuring the most interesting local **Sights**, **Walking Tours**, nearby **Excursions**, and detailed **Driving Tours**. Admission prices shown are normally for a single adult.

ADDRESSES

We've selected the best hotels, restaurants, cafés, shops, nightlife and entertainment to fit all budgets. See the Legend on the cover flap for an explanation of the price categories. See the back of the guide for an index of hotels and restaurants.

Sidebars

Throughout the guide you will find blue, orange and green-coloured text boxes with lively anecdotes, detailed history and background information.

😊 A Bit of Advice 😊

Green advice boxes found in this guide contain practical tips and handy information relevant to the sight in the Discovering section.

STAR RATINGS★★★

Michelin has given star ratings for more than 100 years. If you're pressed for time, we recommend you visit the ★★★ or ★★ sights first:

★★★ **Highly recommended**

★★   **Recommended**

★   **Interesting**

MAPS

- 🗺 Regional Driving Tours map and Principal Sights map.
- 🗺 Region maps.
- 🗺 Maps for major cities and villages.
- 🗺 Local tour maps.

All maps in this guide are oriented north, unless otherwise indicated by a directional arrow. The term "Local Map" refers to a map within the chapter or Tourism Region. A complete list of the maps found in the guide appears at the back of this book.

T. Krieger/MICHELIN

PLANNING YOUR TRIP

INTRODUCTION TO GERMANY

DISCOVERING GERMANY

CONTENTS

Welcome to Germany

Germany is a rich quilt of dynamic cities, awe-inspiring scenery and spirit-lifting culture. Although it only became a nation in 1871, its influence on history goes back at least a couple of millennia. No matter your itinerary, you will inevitably stumble upon intriguing relics of the past, from Roman ruins to mighty cathedrals and dazzling palaces. Be sure to venture off the main tourist trail for those extra-special personal discoveries.

BERLIN AND BRANDENBURG
(p100–141)

Sassy, confident and irreverent, Berlin is a sly seductress who tempts you with her explosive creativity, vibrant cultural landscape and keen sense of history. Visit major landmarks such as Checkpoint Charlie and the Brandenburg Gate, then soak up the city's idiosyncratic spirit by drifting about its distinct neighbourhoods. For a break from urbanity, hop on a train to Brandenburg, a timelessly beautiful rural area shaped by water and accented by the dreamy palaces and parks of Potsdam.

THE BALTIC COAST AND INLAND *(p142–173)*

Germany's Baltic Coast once revelled in the wealth of its Hanseatic League towns. The proud red-brick buildings of Lübeck, Wismar, Stralsund and Greifswald still hark back to those medieval glory days. Fringing the coast is a landscape of often startling beauty; a pastiche of bays, islands and cliffs accented by beach-fringed seaside resorts whose dazzling white spa architecture has drawn royalty and the rich for over a century.

THE NORTHWEST *(p174–241)*

Germany's northwest stretches from the wind-battered beaches of the Frisian Islands to the historic towns of Münster, Goslar and Celle and the fairytale cities of Bremen and Hamelin. Take a day in the slow lane roaming

around the Harz Mountains, or opt for an urban jolt in maritime Hamburg, which will charm you with cutting-edge couture, culture and cuisine.

THE WEST *(p242–337)*

This region wraps culturally vibrant conurbations and laid-back countryside into one attractive package. Get a dose of world-class art and architecture in Düsseldorf, Cologne and Frankfurt, then make a date with the Romans in Trier and with Charlemagne in Aachen. Whatever you do, do not miss a trip down the Rhine or Moselle rivers to explore a startlingly beautiful mosaic of vine-clad slopes, dreamy half-timbered villages and medieval hilltop fortresses.

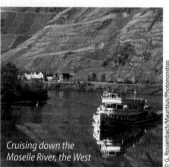

Cruising down the Moselle River, the West

© G. Rossenbach/Mauritius/Photononstop

THE SOUTHWEST *(p338–405)*

Nowhere does Germany feel more radiantly old-world than in the Black Forest, a rustic landscape of "Hansel-and-Gretel" woods, undulating hills, gushing waterfalls and snow-dusted mountaintops. Along with nearby

Lake Constance, it has long been a favourite holiday playground. Key cities include the elegant spa town of Baden-Baden, Freiburg with its vibrant student scene and Stuttgart, which is a must-see not only for those who worship at the altar of the automobile.

MUNICH AND SOUTHERN BAVARIA (p406–471)

Few cities in Germany exude the contagious energy that you'll find bubbling away in the streets and legendary beer halls of Munich. Outside of the city, natural and manmade beauty is all around. Crane your neck while marvelling at the sky-etching Alps, explore higgledy-piggledy villages where ancient traditions still thrive, or visit Ludwig II's fantasy castles. This is truly a land of superlatives ready to deliver a lifetime of memories.

NORTHERN BAVARIA (p472–507)

One of Germany's most iconic drives is along the Romantic Road, which runs through soul-stirring scenery from Würzburg and its wine country past the cobblestoned perfection of Rothenburg ob der Tauber as far as peaceful Füssen near the Alps. Slow down – this region wants to be savoured. History buffs should point the compass towards Nuremberg, music lovers at Bayreuth and architecture fans at Bamberg.

CENTRAL GERMANY (p508–547)

Though cradling the natural splendours of the Thuringian Forest, central Germany's appeal rests mostly in its contributions to literature, music, the arts, philosophy and religion. This is where you can walk in the footsteps of Luther and Bach, Goethe and Gropius, Herder and Nietzsche who

Dom, Magdeburg, Central Germany
© Christina Hanck/iStockphoto.com

all lived and worked in such towns as Weimar, Erfurt, Dessau-Rosslau, Magdeburg and Wittenberg.

THE EAST (p548–577)

Since reunification, the German East has shaken off its Cold War-era brooding and blossomed into a dynamic, prolific and forward-looking region. Endowed with a stunning city skyline, Dresden draws cultural types with its architectural landmarks and stunning art collections. The mighty Elbe courses right through town, linking it with the fairytale landscape of Saxon Switzerland and the porcelain hub of Meissen. Youthful and progressive Leipzig has shaped German history since the Middle Ages, most recently as the city that sparked the "peaceful revolution" of 1989, precipitating the fall of the East German regime.

Bastei, Saxon Switzerland, the East
© Fox497/Dreamstime.com

Beach with wicker chairs, Fischland peninsula, the Baltic Coast
T. Krieger/MICHELIN

Michelin Driving Tours

GRAND TOURS

1 HAMBURG AND SCHLESWIG-HOLSTEIN

550km/342mi tour leaving from Hamburg.

This tour through the *Länder* (states) of Hamburg and Schleswig-Holstein meanders through the far north of Germany, a region with a glorious Hanseatic past. The country's second largest city, **Hamburg** is a bustling port set on the banks of the Elbe estuary; its central districts are ideal for a stroll and the richly endowed museums will be much appreciated by art lovers. A mere 70km/43mi from Hamburg is **Lübeck**. This delightful town in northern Germany has been on UNESCO's World Heritage list since 1987. Remarkably preserved, it boasts an exceptional collection of houses and monuments from many different periods. Not far from Lübeck, **Travemünde**, on the shores of the Baltic Sea, is renowned for its sandy beaches, extensive seafront promenade and its casino. The tour continues northwards with the next port of call being **Kiel**, the gateway to Scandinavia. Capital of Schleswig-Holstein, Kiel combines a long maritime tradition with a modern atmosphere. The route then takes a northwesterly direction along the

Salzspeicher, Lübeck

J. Bouraly/MICHELIN

Baltic coast to **Schleswig**, an ideal place to relax and explore. Heading westwards, from one sea to the other, takes you to the island of **Sylt** and the other North Frisian islands. Their fragile sandy shores are pitted against the North Sea in a constant battle against marine erosion. Lastly, the peaceful seaside town of **Husum**, birthplace of the writer Theodor Storm, offers all the attractions of a modern tourist resort.

2 BALTIC SEA, MECKLENBURG-VORPOMMERN

650km/380mi tour leaving from Neubrandenburg.

This itinerary will give you a glimpse of a region of Germany that is wild and captivating and little known among foreign visitors. The town of **Neubrandenburg** has a surprise in store with its imposing medieval ramparts, miraculously spared by the Second World War. The journey continues westwards through the **Mecklenburg lake district**, a well-preserved region and one of the least populated in Germany. With countless lakes and a wide range of activities, it is of particular appeal to nature-lovers. **Schwerin** is without a doubt one of the most pleasant towns in northern Germany. Its refined architecture and the majestic charm of its castle set atop an island facing the old town add to the appeal of this city, the state capital of Mecklenburg-Vorpommern. Our itinerary then takes us north to the coast where **Wismar**, with its trove of red-brick buildings, provides an excellent introduction to the Baltic Coast. The town's historic centre was classed a UNESCO World Heritage Site in 2002, along with that of **Stralsund**. Along with **Rostock** and **Bad Doberan**, Stralsund is well worth a visit on your way to the island of **Rügen**. Here, an astonishing variety of landscapes awaits: bands of sandy dunes, land reclaimed from the sea, salt meadows, cultivated fields, endless mudflats (Watt, or Wadden) and prehistoric tumuli. Rügen, like the neighbouring island of **Usedom**, is a very popular vacation destination with delightful seaside, health and spa resorts and unique late 19C spa architecture. Last stop on the itinerary is **Greifswald**, whose very old architecture reveals a Scandinavian influence.

③ BREMEN, HAMBURG AND LOWER SAXONY

550km/342mi tour leaving from Bremen.

The bustling town of **Bremen** is a true delight. A large port and city of artistic interest where the Weser Renaissance style flourished, it has a number of parks and a charming riverside promenade. After a stop in **Hamburg**, 125km/78mi to the northeast (*see description in itinerary ①*), the tour next takes you to **Lüneburg**, which owes its longstanding prosperity to salt and marks the gateway to the vast expanse of the **Lüneburg Heath**. In the face of the increasing advances of agriculture, attempts are being made to preserve this wild environment which is characterized by picturesque copses of birch, pine and juniper. From mid-August to mid-September, the purple carpet of heather in bloom will have you burning up the pixels in your digicam. South of the heath awaits the dignified city of **Celle**. There are many reasons to stop here; treasures from the old city, a magnificently restored ducal palace and a folklore and history museum to name but a few. For car fanatics, a detour to Wolfsburg's **Autostadt** – a vast complex set up by Volkswagen – is a must. You can tour the plant, visit a strikingly designed science museum and roam around landscaped areas of park and water. A stop in **Braunschweig** is followed by a leisurely look around the beautiful city of **Wolfenbüttel** with its exceptional collection of Renaissance houses. Further west, after **Hildesheim**, **Hannover** awaits with its famous Herrenhausen gardens.

④ BERLIN AND BRANDENBURG

600km/373mi tour leaving from Neubrandenburg.

After a look around **Neubrandenburg** (*see description in itinerary ②*), head south to explore Schloss **Rheinsberg** where Frederick the Great, by his own account, spent the happiest years of his life as a young man. **Berlin**, Germany's vibrant capital, is a mere 90km/56mi further south. The buzzing city offers a wealth of culture and an after-dark scene not only night-owls will love. It is an amazing metropolis that will captivate you with its world-class museums and art galleries, a lively café scene, monumental landmarks, huge parks and gardens and the easy-going attitude of the locals. Another town marked by the personality of Frederick the Great, who held a brilliant and cosmopolitan court here, **Potsdam** is a genuine "Rococo treasure" of universal appeal. Carry on westwards and, after the small town of **Brandenburg** in the heart of the Havelland lake region, stop off at **Tangermünde**, which is still enclosed within its late 14C ramparts. **Stendal**, just a few kilometres away, was until the mid-16C the most important town in the Brandenburg March before the ravages of the Thirty Years' War sent it on a downward spiral. Several monuments typical of the Gothic brick architecture still attest to this former

Berliner Dom by the Spree

© René Mattes/hemis.fr

period of prosperity. Further north you can admire the beautiful cathedral of **Havelberg**, a pretty town set on the banks of the River Havel.
The itinerary ends with a foray into the picturesque **Mecklenburg lake district**.

5 HARZ, THURINGIA, SACHSEN-ANHALT AND LEIPZIG

750km/466mi tour leaving from Leipzig.
This route is tailor-made for culture vultures, taking you into a region where – particularly in the 18C – literature and music flourished. **Leipzig** is a city of artistic interest that can be proud of its exceptional musical heritage; Bach, Wagner and Mendelssohn all lived here at one time and the city remains very much in the foreground of the German music scene. Around 60km/37mi south, **Naumburg** stands among hills cloaked in vineyards and forests. The town is particularly renowned for its cathedral, which is an exceptional blend of Romanesque and Gothic style elements. **Weimar**, **Jena**, **Erfurt** and **Eisenach** are all names with strong connotations in German culture through their association with such key figures as Luther, Goethe and Schiller. Offering a pleasant distraction from the "cultural pilgrimage", the Thuringian Forest and, further north, the Harz mountains take you right to the very heart of nature.
Steeped in legend, the latter offers a limitless menu of year-round outdoor pursuits. Next, steer towards **Magdeburg** for a look at its fantastic Gothic cathedral before heading to **Wittenberg**, where Martin Luther posted his 95 Theses against church corruption. For this reason, the town is considered the cradle of the Reformation. The route continues via **Dessau**, famous for its Bauhaus legacy and a gateway to the Garden Realm, a 18C wonderland of landscaped gardens with **Wörlitzer Park** as its finest jewel.

6 DRESDEN AND ERZGEBIRGE

650km/380mi tour leaving from Dresden.
Saxony is a region that has played a key role in Germany's history. A city of art and culture, **Dresden** has undergone extensive restorations of its Baroque treasures (most famously the complete rebuilding of the Frauenkirche), making it once again "the Florence of the Elbe". Southeast of here, the **Sächsische Schweiz** charms with its whimsically eroded sandstone formations and winding gorges gouged from the rock – this region is truly one of Germany's most spectacular natural wonders. The towns of **Bautzen** and **Görlitz** provide an opportunity to sample the culture of the Sorbs. An ethnic German minority, their homeland today straddles the *Länder* (states) of Saxony and Brandenburg. Not only do the Sorbs still speak their own language, but they have also kept alive many traditions. These include the decoration of eggs at Easter and the wearing of the Sorbian national costume and tall embroidered headdresses. Heading northwards takes you to **Branitz**, a stone's throw from Cottbus, where Prince Hermann von Pückler-Muskau built a palace and – indulging his passion for garden design – a fabulous park. Heading back to Dresden, make a stop at **Schloss Moritzburg** and **Meissen**, renowned for its porcelain. If you have the time, extend your tour with a trip through the **Erzgebirge**, a wooded region with a long tradition in both mining and toy making. Make **Annaberg-Buchholz** with its impressive Flamboyant Gothic church a key stop before heading back to Dresden.

7 PFALZ, RHINE VALLEY AND MOSELLE VALLEY

950km/570mi tour leaving from Cologne.
Not far from the borders with Belgium, Luxembourg and France,

Karl Theodor Bridge towards Church of the Holy Spirit, Heidelberg

© R. Schmid/Sime/Photononstop

this extensive loop takes in key sights in western Germany. The Rhine valley is full of surprises; with its steeply terraced vineyards and rocky outcrops dominated by lofty castles, the route from **Koblenz** to **Rüdesheim** or **Bingen** affords some magnificent views. Take a stroll around the historic centre of **Mainz** with its maze of alleyways and old houses. After **Darmstadt**, take the **Bergstraße** southwards to historic **Heidelberg**, a symbol of German Romanticism, whose hillside castle leaves a lasting impression. The route continues west to **Speyer**, whose enormous Romanesque cathedral is the burial place of several Holy Roman Emperors. Heading north takes you along the German Wine Route through the **Pfalz**, a region blessed with a mild microclimate conducive to the cultivation of exotic fruits. Next up is **Worms**, which competes with **Trier** for the title of oldest town in Germany; both were founded by the Romans. From Trier to Koblenz, the winding course of the **Moselle** takes you past picturesque villages, castles and vineyards. Cruises, hiking and cycling are among the activities that beckon along here. **Aachen**, on the border with Belgium and Holland, is next on the agenda. The town is indelibly associated with Charlemagne, who made it capital of his Frankish

Empire. Nearly three dozen princes were crowned king or emperor in its cathedral between 936 and 1531. From Aachen it won't be long before the famous twin spires of the cathedral of **Cologne** come into view. This delightful city on the Rhine is also known for its Romanesque churches, colourful historic houses, top-notch art museums and raucous beer taverns serving the local brew called Kölsch.

8 NUREMBERG AND FRANKEN
650km/380mi-tour leaving from Nuremberg.
This itinerary provides a chance to explore the age-old sights of northern Bavaria. It begins with **Nuremberg**, an old bronze casters' and goldbeaters' town and one of the most beautiful medieval cities in Germany. Further south, **Eichstätt** is distinguished by a harmonious mix of Rococo and contemporary architecture. West of here join the **Romantische Straße** (Romantic Road), Germany's most popular holiday route, in Nördlingen. It links some fantastic medieval cities, including **Dinkelsbühl** and **Rothenburg ob der Tauber**, before reaching its northern terminus in Würzburg, where the mid-17C grandeur of the powerful prince-bishops of the Schönborn family is reflected in the splendid Residenz

Fischerviertel, Ulm
© Dirk Homburg/Ulm/ Neu-Ulm Touristik GmbH

Palace. Next up is **Bamberg** with its pretty-as-a-penny historic quarter (a UNESCO World Heritage Site since 1993) and imposing hilltop cathedral. Our route then continues via **Coburg** to the nearby **Wallfahrtskirche Vierzehnheiligen**. This pilgrimage church is a Baroque masterpiece by Balthasar Neumann with a truly captivating wealth of decoration. **Bayreuth**, the last stop on the tour, is a high point for fans of the composer Richard Wagner as well as the Rococo architectural style.

⑨ BADEN-WÜRTTEMBERG AND BODENSEE

850km/510mi tour leaving from Freiburg.
Southwest Germany has an astonishing number of remarkable tourist attractions. The easy-going atmosphere of the old university town of **Freiburg** is infectious and its paved alleyways beg to be explored. The town is the southern gateway to the **Schwarzwald**, a region steeped in legend and endowed with great variety of scenery. Add to that its picturesque villages, a passion for cuckoo clocks and the possibilities of hiking in summer and skiing in winter, and it is easy to see why this mountainous region is one of Germany's most popular tourist

destinations. Passing through towns such as the elegant spa resort of **Baden-Baden**, which attracts a wealthy clientele all year round, and **Karlsruhe**, the route takes you up to **Bruchsal** whose sumptuous 18C palace houses a museum devoted to mechanical musical instruments. A short distance southeast of here looms **Kloster Maulbronn**; built in 1147, it was one of the earliest Cistercian abbeys in Germany. The school established here during the Reformation (1557) has seen the flowering of many scientific, literary and philosophical talents, including Kepler, Hölderlin and Hermann Hesse. The road south leads to **Tübingen** and **Ulm**. Tübingen's maze of narrow sloping streets lined with half-timbered houses, combined with its animated student life, create a relaxed and lighthearted atmosphere. In Ulm, you can stroll between the canals and the Danube and admire the town's extraordinary cathedral.

The Upper Swabian Plateau is dotted with Baroque churches famous for their dazzling decoration and architecture. **Zwiefalten** and **Weingarten** are two superb illustrations of the Baroque style that flourished so extensively in southern Germany. The tour ends with the magnificent **Bodensee**, a vast lake that also borders Switzerland and Austria. It is regarded by Germans as their very own "Riviera".

⑩ MUNICH AND THE BAVARIAN ALPS

650km/380mi tour leaving from Munich.
A tour through this far southern region, with its magnificent alpine scenery and wealth of culture, will undoubtedly be a high point in your exploration of Germany.

The country's second most popular tourist destination after Berlin, **Munich** – Bavaria's vibrant capital – is a prosperous and lively city. Art lovers will delight in its fabulous museums and Baroque churches.

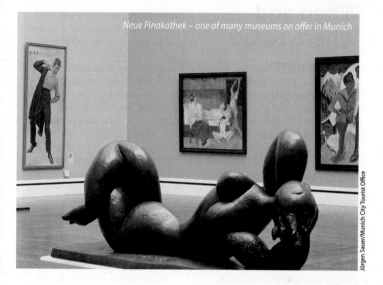

Neue Pinakothek – one of many museums on offer in Munich

Jürgen Sauer/Munich City Tourist Office

A little over 100km/62mi to the east, on the Austrian border, **Burghausen** is crowned with the biggest medieval fortress in Germany. Its defence system, reinforced at the beginning of the 16C in the face of a threatening invasion by the Turks, stretches for around 1km/0.6mi. The much-travelled **Deutsche Alpenstraße** kicks off in **Berchtesgaden**, where you can explore underground salt mines, hike in the shadow of the mighty Watzmann mountain or take a cruise on the magical Königssee. The Alpenstraße is an intensely scenic route passing dreamy villages, bucolic meadows as well as famous ski resorts such as **Garmisch-Partenkirchen**, which is lorded over by the Zugspitze, Germany's tallest mountain. When the Alpenstraße reaches Füssen, be sure to make a side trip to **Neuschwanstein**, the famous fantasy castle of "fairytale king" Ludwig II. Füssen is also the southern terminus of the equally fabled Romantische Straße, which you follow as far as **Augsburg**, an attractive city founded by the Romans.

REGIONAL TOURS

In the *DISCOVERING* section you will find local driving tours (with cor-responding maps, or you can find the route plotted on the region map) for the following Principal Sights:

- ◆ **RÜGEN ISLAND**
- ◆ **MECKLENBURG LAKE DISTRICT**
- ◆ **GOSLAR**
- ◆ **HANN. MÜNDEN**
- ◆ **EIFEL**
- ◆ **TRIER**
- ◆ **MOSELLE VALLEY**
- ◆ **RHINE VALLEY**
- ◆ **FRANKFURT AM MAIN**
- ◆ **HEIDELBERG**
- ◆ **PFALZ**
- ◆ **BLACK FOREST**
- ◆ **BADEN WINE ROUTE**
- ◆ **LAKE CONSTANCE**

- ◆ **BAD WIMPFEN**
- ◆ **SWABIAN JURA**
- ◆ **UPPER SWABIAN PLATEAU**
- ◆ **MUNICH**
- ◆ **GERMAN ALPINE ROAD**
- ◆ **BERCHTESGADEN**
- ◆ **PASSAU**
- ◆ **ROMANTIC ROAD**
- ◆ **WÜRZBURG**
- ◆ **NUREMBERG**
- ◆ **BAYREUTH**
- ◆ **JENA**
- ◆ **EISENACH**
- ◆ **DRESDEN**
- ◆ **ANNABERG-BUCHHOLZ**

When and Where to Go

WHEN TO GO

Whatever the season, the weather in Germany is subject to enormous variation. The period when you are most likely to find good weather extends from May to October (🙂 it can get very hot during high summer in Baden-Württemberg and Bavaria). Spring and autumn, when tourist crowds are thinner, can be the perfect time to discover the country. It is sensible to pack some waterproof clothing whenever you plan to go. Before you leave, don't forget to find out about any holidays, festivals, fairs or other events that may considerably increase the number of visitors in certain towns and make finding a room difficult (🔎 see Calendar of Events). Skiers will find snow-covered slopes from the end of November until late February.

WHERE TO GO
CITY BREAKS

Hamburg

Germany's second-largest city is also one of its most beautiful, laced by rivers and canals, characterised by great architecture and endowed with a spirit of openness that harks back to its Hanseatic League days.

Wherever you go, it's imbued with maritime flair, from its vast container port, which can be toured by boat, to its riverside promenades that invite strolling. Must-sees include the canal-laced Speicherstadt with its elegant red-brick warehouses, and the Hafen City, which is the largest urban construction project in Europe.

Cologne

"Why is it so lovely on the Rhine?" asks a popular German song. You'll quickly find the answer in Cologne. With its famous Gothic cathedral, lively beer halls, lovely river promenades, world-class museums and superb shopping, this is a city that's easy to love. If possible, visit in February during Carnival, a raucous pre-Lent celebration, when locals don fancy dress and demonstrate their legendary joie de vivre at parties and street parades.

Munich

Beer, lederhosen and Oktoberfest – the Bavarian capital certainly conjures plenty of cliches. But what about BMW, high-tech and world-class music and fashion? Revel in Munich's contradictions as you stroll around the vast English Garden, pick up gourmet treats at the Viktualienmarkt and hoist a mug of foamy beer at an atmosphere-charged beer hall.

Schildergasse – main shopping street of Cologne

© www.koelntourismus.de

For culture, report to the amazing Pinakothek museums or tour the royal splendour of the Residenz. In the end you'll find that a weekend is not enough to explore this great city.

Berlin

Germany's most populous city is also its most popular. Keenly aware of its unique past, the country's capital has shed its dour Cold War demeanour and grown into a confident, sassy and modern city with flourishing art, music and fashion scenes. Take the exciting pulse of a city that's forever in the state of "becoming" as you explore landmarks old and new – the Brandenburg Gate and Checkpoint Charlie to the Holocaust Memorial and Potsdamer Platz. Whether you stand in awe of ancient treasures on Museum Island, explore the park and building at Charlottenburg Palace or sample the famed Berlin nightlife, you'll make memories to last a lifetime.

TOURIST ROUTES

Clearly signposted, these "thematic" itineraries provide a handy means of crisscrossing the country and getting to know it better. They include:

- ◆ **Badische Weinstraße (Baden Wine Route)**, from Baden-Baden to Lörrach *(170km/105.6mi)*. Breathtaking scenery, superb cuisine, plenty of sunshine and some of the finest wines in the country await in Germany's southwestern corner.
- ◆ **Burgenstraße (Castle Road)**, from Mannheim to Bayreuth and then on to Prague *(975km/605mi)*. Plunge back into medieval times as you skirt the 70 legend-shrouded castles of this meandering route.
- ◆ **Bocksbeutelstrasse (Middle Franconian Wine Route)**, southeast of Würzburg *(50km/31mi)*. Sample delicious Franconian wines bottled in their signature flagons called *"Bockbeutel"* at time-honoured wine estates.

- ◆ **Deutsche Alleenstraße (German Tree-lined Road)**, from Rügen Island to Lake Constance *(2 900km/1 812mi)*. Let nature embrace you as you travel beneath a shady canopy of mature beeches, chestnuts and oaks arching over Germany's longest holiday route.
- ◆ **Deutsche Ferienstraße Ostsee-Alpen (Baltic Sea to the Alps)**, from the Fehmarn Island to Berchtesgaden *(1 738km/1 086mi)*. From dune-fringed beaches to snowy mountains, the entire quilt of Germany's varied landscapes unfolds on this epic north–south journey.
- ◆ **Deutsche Weinstraße (German Wine Road)**, from Bockenheim/Palatinate to Wissembourg/Alsace *(91km/56.5mi)*. Spring arrives early along this sweet, unhurried route dotted with charming villages steeped in history and hemmed in by rambling vineyards.
- ◆ **Deutsche Fachwerkstraße (Route of Half-timbered Buildings)**, nine routes through Lower Saxony, Hessen and Baden-Württemberg. There is an undeniable fairytale quality to these centuries-old higgledy-piggledy half-timbered houses, each of which is decorated with individual fancy and artistry.
- ◆ **Alte Salzstraße (Old Salt Road)**, from Lüneburg to Lübeck *(100km/62mi)*. Horsecarts needed three weeks to transport salt – the "White Gold" – along this historic trading route. You can do it in just a day or two!
- ◆ **Straße der Romanik (Romanesque Road)**, loops through Sachsen-Anhalt, leaving from Magdeburg *(about 1 000km/625mi)*. European history was made 1 000 years ago in towns along this route of dignified cathedrals, fierce fortresses and rambling abbeys.
- ◆ **Romantische Straße (Romantic Road)**, from Würzburg to

Füssen *(315km/196mi)*. On this dreamy route you can check off many of Germany's most famous destinations, including Rothenburg ob der Tauber and Neuschwanstein.

♦ **Silberstraße (Silver Route)**, from Zwickau to Dresden *(115km/71.4mi)*. This enchanting "ribbon of riches" winds through rural, mountainous countryside steeped in ancient traditions.

♦ **Klassikerstraße Thüringen (Thuringian Classical Route)**, Goethe to Gropius *(300km/186.4mi)*. Germany's legacy as a land of poets, thinkers and innovators is confirmed along this intensely cultural route.

♦ **Oberschwäbische Barockstraße (Upper Swabian Baroque Route)**, from Ulm to Lake Constance (Bodensee) *(455m/282.7mi)*. This route links the "greatest hits" (churches, abbeys, libraries) of the wonderfully exuberant southern German Baroque and Rococo styles.

♦ **Straße der Weser-Renaissance (Weser Renaissance Route)**, Münden to Bremen *(400km/248.5mi)*. In the 16C, merchants and the nobility expressed their prosperity in large manors festooned with frilly turrets, gables, oriels and balconies.
This route preserves some of the style's finest examples.
See www.germany-tourism.de

IDEAS FOR YOUR VISIT
NATIONAL PARKS
Germany's 14 national parks are wonderful playgrounds for nature-lovers and active types. Further information is available from **Europarc Deutschland**, Friedrichstraße 60, 10117 Berlin, *(030) 28 87 88 20, www.europarc-deutschland.de.

♦ **Bavaria:** Bavarian Forest (Bayerischer Wald), Berchtesgaden.
♦ **Schleswig-Holstein:** Schleswig-Holstein mudflats (Wattenmeer).
♦ **Lower Saxony:** Lower Saxon mudflats (Niedersächsisches Wattenmeer), Harz.
♦ **North Rhine-Westphalia:** Eifel.
♦ **Hamburg:** Hamburg mudflats (Wattenmeer).
♦ **Hessen:** Kellerwald-Edersee.
♦ **Saxony-Anhalt:** Harz.
♦ **Mecklenburg-Western Pomerania:** Jasmund, Müritz, Vorpommersche Boddenlandschaft.
♦ **Saxony:** Saxon Switzerland (Sächsische Schweiz).
♦ **Brandenburg:** Lower Oder valley (Unteres Odertal).
♦ **Thuringia:** Hainich.

LAKES AND MOUNTAINS
If you want to stand on the top of Germany, you have to travel to Garmisch-Partenkirchen, where the Zugspitze soars 2 964m/9 724ft skywards. Though not as high, many other mountains are steeped in legend, such as the Watzmann in Berchtegaden and the Brocken in the Harz National Park.
The largest lake is the Bodensee (Lake Constance), which shares borders with Austria and Switzerland. Nearby, Lake Chiemsee is popular for swimming and sailing, while the Mecklenburger Seenplatte lake district is best explored by canoe or kayak.

COASTLINE
Relax on sandy beaches, connect with nature on a walk across the mudflats and feel the brisk wind in your face along the 1 000km/625mi of Germany's windswept coastline. In the west, the North Sea is rougher and punctuated with numerous islands, including glamorous Sylt and the family-friendly East Frisian Islands. The Baltic Sea in the east is comparatively shallow and calm, it is home to Rügen, Germany's largest island with its famous chalk cliffs.

What to See and Do

OUTDOOR FUN

For nature-lovers and outdoor sports fans alike, Germany's varied landscapes provide an ideal setting for all sorts of activities. Some very useful information in this respect can be found at www.germany-tourism.de (under Nature, Activity and Recreation).

CANOEING AND KAYAKING

Those interested in canoeing and kayaking or rafting should get in touch with **Bundesvereinigung Kanutouristik,** Hannah-Arendt-Straße 3–7, 35037 Marburg, ℰ(06421) 168 91 60, www.kanutouristik.de.

CYCLING

Cycling can be a very practical, healthy, economical and "green" way to explore the German countryside. There are about 200 long-distance routes as well as dedicated bike paths in many cities. Information is available from the **Allgemeiner Deutscher Fahrad Club** (ADFC, ℰ0421 34 62 90, www.adfc.de). The ADFC also publishes the Bett & Bike directory of bicycle-friendly lodging (www.bettundbike.de). The German National Tourist Office offers a free route finder with maps and planning tips at www.germany-tourism. de/cycling.

FISHING

A German fishing license is required. For information contact:
- **Deutscher Anglerverband**, Weißenseer Weg 110, 10369 Berlin, ℰ(030) 97 10 43 79, www.anglerverband.com
- **Verband Deutscher Sportfischer,** Siemensstraße 11–13, 63071 Offenbach, ℰ(069) 857 06 95, www.vdsf.de.

GOLF

High-quality golf courses are abundant in both metropolitan areas and the German countryside. For

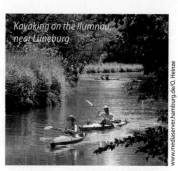
Kayaking on the Ilumnau, near Lüneburg

www.mediaserver.hamburg.de/O. Heinze

information, contact the **Deutscher Golf Verband**, Viktoriastraße 16, 65189 Wiesbaden, ℰ(0611) 99 02 00, www.golf.de. Greens fees range from 40€ to 90€ for a one-day pass during the week, rising to about 55€ to 110€ on weekends.

HORSE RIDING

Lists of equestrian centres can be obtained from regional and local tourist offices, or contact the **Deutsche Reiterliche Vereinigung**, Freiherr von Langen-Straße 13, 48231 Warendorf, ℰ(02581) 636 20, www.pferd-aktuell.de.

HUNTING

For information on hunting in Germany, contact **Jagdschutz-Verband**, Johannes-Henry-Straße 26, 53113 Bonn, ℰ(0228) 94 90 620, www.jagd-online.de.

SAILING AND WINDSURFING

Sail sports are hugely popular all along the North Sea and Baltic Sea coast as well as on such lakes as Lake Constance, Lake Müritz and Lake Starnberg, near Munich. Information can be obtained from the German Sailing Federation, **Deutscher Seglerverband**, Gründgensstraße 18, 22309 Hamburg, ℰ(40) 632 00 90, www.dsv.org.

WALKING

The **Deutscher Wanderverband**, Wilhelmshöher Allee 157–159, 34121 Kassel, ℰ(0561) 93 87 30, www. dt-wanderverband.de can provide details on hikes organised by regional

PARK/PLACE	☎/WEBSITE	NEAREST MOTORWAY EXIT
Bavaria-Filmstadt/ Geiselgasteig (Bayern)	(089) 64 99 20 00 www.bavaria-filmstadt.de	A 99: Oberhaching (4)
Churpfalzpark Loifling/ Cham (Bayern)	(099 71) 303 40 www.churpfalzpark.de	A 3: Straubing (106)
Erlebnispark Schloß Thurn/ Heroldsbach (Bayern)	(091 90) 92 98 98 www.schloss-thurn.de	A 73: Baiersdorf Nord (10)
Erlebnispark Tripsdrill/ Cleebronn-Tripsdrill (Baden-Württemberg)	(071 35) 99 99 www.tripsdrill.de	A 81: Mundesheim (13)
Erlebnispark Ziegenhagen/ Witzenhausen (Hessen)	(055 45) 246 www.erlebnispark-ziegenhagen.de	A 75: Hann. Münden (75)
Europa-Park/Rust (Baden-Württemberg)	(01805) 77 66 88 www.europapark.de	A 5: Ettenheim (57)
Fränkisches Wunderland/ Plech (Bayern)	(092 44) 98 90 www.wunderland.de	A 9: Plech (46)
Freizeit-Land/Geiselwind (Bayern)	(095 56) 921 10 www.freizeitlandgeiselwind.de	A 3: Geiselwind (76)
Filmpark Babelsberg/ Potsdam (Brandenburg)	(0331) 721 27 50 www.filmpark-babelsberg.de	A 115: Potsdam– Babelsberg (5)
Fort Fun Abenteuerland/ Bestwig-Wasserfall (Nordrhein-Westfalen)	(029 05) 811 23 www.fortfun.de	A 46: Bestwig (71)
Hansa-Park/Sierksdorf (Schleswig-Holstein)	(045 63) 47 40 www.hansapark.de	A 1: Eutin (15)
Heide-Park/Soltau (Niedersachsen)	(01805) 91 91 01 www.heidepark.de	A 7: Soltau-Ost (44)
Holiday Park/Haßloch (Rheinland-Pfalz)	(0180) 500 32 46 www.holidaypark.de	A 65: Neustadt-Süd (13)
Phantasialand/Brühl (Nordrhein-Westfalen)	(01805) 366 200 www.phantasialand.de	A 553: Brühl-Süd (2)
Potts Park/Minden-West (Nordrhein-Westfalen)	(0571) 510 88 www.pottspark-minden.de	A 2: Porta Westfalica (33)
Ravensburger Spieleland/ Meckenbeuren	(075 42) 40 00 www.spieleland.de	A 96: Wangen-West (5)
Hollywood-und Safaripark/ Schloß Holte-Stukenbrock (Nordrhein-Westfalen)	(052 07) 95 24 25 www.safaripark.de	A 2, then A 33: Stukenbrock-Senne (23)
Legoland (Günzburg)	(01805) 70 07 57 01 www.legoland.de	A 7, then A 8: exit Günzburg
Serengetipark/Hodenhagen (Niedersachsen)	(05164) 979 90 www.serengeti-park.com	A 7: Westenholz (7)
Taunus-Wunderland/ Schlangenbad (Hessen)	(061 24) 40 81 www.taunuswunderland.de	A 66: Wiesbaden– Frauenstein (2)
Vogelpark Walsrode/ Walsrode (Niedersachsen)	(051 61) 60 440 www.vogelpark-walsrode.de	A 27: Walsrode-Süd (28)
Movie Park Germany/ Bottrop-Kirchhellen (Nordrhein-Westfalen)	(020 45) 89 90 www.movieparkgermany.de	A 31: Kirchhellen– Feldhausen (40)

associations and also publishes guides and maps, many of them online at www.wanderbares-deutschland.de. Another source of information on mountain trails, shelters and overnight huts is the **Deutscher Alpenverein** (DAV, German Alpine Club), Von-Kahr-Straße 2–4, 80997 München, ℘(089) 14 00 30, www.alpenverein.de.
For up-to-the-minute details on refuge opening times, weather reports, trail conditions, etc., contact the DAV's **Alpine Information Centre** (Alpine Auskunft) at ℘(089) 29 49 40, Mon–Fri 9am–noon, Mon–Wed 1pm–4pm and Thu 1pm–6pm. For the Alpine weather forecast, call ℘(089) 29 50 70.

WINTER SPORTS

Although the Alps and the Black Forest remain the most popular skiing areas in Germany, snow sport is also possible in the central upland regions of the Harz mountains, the Thuringian Forest and the Sauerland.

SPAS

Spa treatments have been around since Roman times and Germans still consider them an important component of a healthy lifestyle. The frantic pace of modern life is driving an increasing number of visitors to follow suit at one of Germany's many spa resorts. Not only are spas used for the treatment or prevention of certain illnesses, they are also an ideal place to recharge your batteries.
Spa resorts have access to mineral water with medicinal properties and offer proper facilities for applying the necessary treatments. They are usually found in beautiful natural settings and are an interesting alternative for those wishing to have a quiet vacation, enjoy nature and enhance their well-being. Information on all of the country's spa resorts can be obtained from the German Spa Association, the **Deutscher Heilbäderverband**, Reinhardstraße 46, 10117 Berlin, ℘(030) 24 63 69 20,

www.deutscher-heilbaederverband.de. Another useful website is www.baederkalender.de.

ACTIVITIES FOR KIDS

In this guide, sights of particular interest to children are indicated with a KIDS symbol. Some attractions may offer discount fees for children.

ZOOS AND ANIMAL PARKS

Kids love animals, of course, and Germany has plenty of places to meet cuddly koalas, pet a sheep or marvel at tiger teeth. An excellent online resource with detailed information about more than 800 zoos throughout the country is www.zoo-infos.de.

DEUTSCHE SPIELZEUGSTRASSE (GERMAN TOY ROAD)

This enchanting tourist route travels for 300km/186mi from Waltershausen in Thuringia to Schwabach in Franconia, passing through 30 towns where toys, dolls, teddy bears and other playthings are being produced, often in traditional fashion.
For the full scoop, contact Deutsche Spielzeugstraße, Lauterer Straße 60, 96450 Coburg, ℘(095 61) 51 43 22, www.spielzeugstrasse.de.

KINDERLAND BAYERN

The Kinderland initiative in Bavaria is a network of more than 350 lodging properties, restaurants and leisure facilities such as theme parks, fun pools, museums, cable-cars and zoos. Members are classified with three, four or five "bears" according to their family-friendliness.
For more information, see Kinderland Bayern, Leopoldstraße 146, 80804 Munich, ℘(0 89) 212 39 70, www.kinderland.by.

THEME PARKS

For a list of the best known and most popular amusement parks in Germany, see http://www.germany-tourism.de/ENG/infocenter/theme_parks.htm.

SHOPPING

Germany is a shopper's paradise with shopping centres, department stores, boutiques and specialist shops often conveniently clustering in pedestrianised city centres. Most towns also have weekly farmers' markets selling whatever fruit and vegetables are in season. Flea markets, meanwhile, are great for picking up some offbeat souvenirs.

Generally, though, souvenirs are best purchased directly in the region where they hail from. So in the Black Forest you might acquire a cuckoo clock, in Bavaria a beer stein or a pair of lederhosen, in the Rheingau a bottle of excellent Riesling wine, in Meissen handpainted porcelain, in Nuremberg spicy gingerbread, in Lübeck delicious marzipan and in Berlin an authenticated piece of the Wall. Other popular items to bring back home include natural cosmetics by Dr. Hauschka, Birkenstock sandals, stuffed toys made by Steiff, collectible Käthe Kruse dolls and Solingen-made cutlery. Dedicated shoppers might want to visit in December, when you can stock up on enchanting ornaments and beautiful decorations at dozens of Christmas markets lighting up nearly every town square.

SIGHTSEEING

The *DISCOVERING GERMANY* section gives the opening times and admission charges for monuments, museums, churches, etc. On account of the ever-increasing cost of living and frequent variations in the opening times of these monuments, this information should only be used as a rough guide. It is intended for tourists who are travelling on their own and are not entitled to any reduction. With prior agreement, groups can obtain special conditions as regards both times and charges. Enquire at the ticket office before purchasing your tickets; age-related reductions, in particular, are often available.

It is always a good idea to make enquiries by phone before setting off, since certain monuments may be temporarily closed for restoration. Visiting conditions for churches are only specified if the interior is of particular interest, if there are set opening times or if there is an admission charge. Churches can generally not be visited during services. If a church is open only during services, visitors should behave respectfully.

BOOKS
HISTORY AND BIOGRAPHY

A Concise History of Germany – Mary Fulbrook
The Reformation – Owen Chadwick
The Thirty Years' War – Veronica Wedgwood
The Rise and Fall of the Third Reich – William Shirer
The Last Days of Hitler – Hugh Trevor-Roper
The Wall: The People's Story – Christopher Hilton
Stasiland – Anna Funder

THE ARTS

Bauhaus – Frank Whitford
The Expressionists – Wolf Dieter Dube
The Weimar Years: A Culture Cut Short – John Willett

LITERATURE

Nibelungenlied – Anonymous
The Lost Honour of Katharina Blum – Heinrich Böll
Caucasian Chalk Circle; The Threepenny Opera; Mother Courage – Bertolt Brecht
The Tin Drum; The Flounder; From the Diary of a Snail; My Century – Günter Grass
The Glass Bead Game; Narcissus and Goldmund; Steppenwolf – Hermann Hesse
Runaway Horse – Martin Walser

The Reader – Bernhard Schlink
Buddenbrooks; The Magic Mountain –
    Thomas Mann
The Wall Jumper –
    Peter Schneider
All Quiet on the Western Front –
    Erich Maria Remarque
A Model Childhood –
    Christa Wolf
Berlin Alexanderplatz –
    Alfred Döblin

TRAVEL AND MODERN GERMAN SOCIETY

A Time of Gifts –
    Patrick Leigh Fermor
A Traveller's Wine Guide to Germany –
    Kerry Brady Stewart et al
A Tramp Abroad – Mark Twain
Deutschland: A Winter's Tale –
    Heinrich Heine
Germany and the Germans –
    John Ardagh
Goodbye to Berlin –
    Christopher Isherwood
*The Simon & Schuster Guide to the
    Wines of Germany* – Ian Jamieson
The Germans – Gordon A Craig
The Origins of Modern Germany –
    Geoffrey Barraclough
Vanishing Borders – Michael Farr

FILMS

Baader-Meinhof Complex (2008) –
    Academy Award-nominated film
    tells the story of the formation
    and early years of the Red Army
    Faction 1970s terrorist gang.
The Lives of Others (2006) –
    Academy Award-winner zeroes
    in on the all-pervasiveness of the
    East German secret police,
    the Stasi.
Sophie Scholl – The Final Days (2005)
    A dramatisation of the final days
    of Sophie Scholl, co-founder of
    the Nazi resistance group, The
    White Rose.
Downfall (2004) –
    A gripping account of Hitler's final
    days cooped up in a Berlin bunker.
Goodbye, Lenin! (2003) –
    A son must protect his sick
    mother from learning that her
    beloved GDR has vanished while
    she lay in a coma.
Run Lola Run (1998) –
    Fast-paced movie about a
    woman who has 20 minutes
    to find and bring 100 000
    Deutschmarks to her boyfriend
    so he does not rob a supermarket.
Wings of Desire (1987) –
    An angel in postwar Berlin falls
    in love with a trapeze artist and
    decides to become human and
    thus mortal.
Das Boot (1981) – Blood, sweat,
    fear, claustrophia and cameraderie
    experienced by a German
    World War II submarine crew
    under attack.
The Enigma of Kaspar Hauser (1974) –
    True story set in 1820s Nuremberg
    about a young man who emerges
    after being held captive in a
    dungeon since birth.
Ludwig (1973) – The tragic life and
    mysterious death of King Ludwig II
    of Bavaria.
Triumph of the Will (1935) –
    Leni Riefenstahl's infamous
    propaganda film of the 1934
    Nazi Party rally in Nuremberg.
The Blue Angel (1930) –
    A nerdy professor's life goes
    on a downward spiral after he
    marries a sexy lounge singer
    (Marlene Dietrich).
Metropolis (1927) – Fritz Lang's silent
    epic about the uprising of a
    proletarian class working
    underground.

Calendar of Events

Listed below are some of the major events and festivals held throughout the year in Germany. More details can be obtained from tourist offices and at www.germany-tourism.com.
👆*See also under "Festivals" in some Address Books in the DISCOVERING GERMANY section.*

1 JANUARY
New Year's Day International Ski Jump, part of the Vierschanzentournee (Four Hills Tournament) – **Garmisch-Partenkirchen**

TWO WEEKS IN FEBRUARY
International Film Festival (Berlinale): – **Berlin**

SUNDAY BEFORE SHROVE TUESDAY
"München Narrisch" Carnival – **Munich**

SHROVE MONDAY
Rosenmontagszug: procession and street carnival – **Cologne, Düsseldorf**, **Mainz**, **Munich**

SHROVE MONDAY AND TUESDAY
Narrensprung Carnival (Dance of the Fools): elaborate traditional costumes and expressive wooden masks – **Rottweil**

MAUNDY THURSDAY TO EASTER MONDAY
Traditional Sorbian Easter Egg Market – **Bautzen**

30 APRIL/1 MAY
Walpurgisnacht: Witches' Sabbath Festival – **Various towns in the Harz region**

MAY TO MID-SEPTEMBER EVERY SUNDAY AT NOON
Rattenfängerspiel: pageant retracing the legend of the Pied Piper – **Hameln**

ASCENSION DAY
Leipzig Bach Festival – **Leipzig**

FRIDAY AFTER ASCENSION
Blutritt: equestrian cavalcade in honour of the Holy Blood relic – **Weingarten**

EARLY MAY TO EARLY JUNE
Festival of Classical Music – **Schwetzingen**

FIVE DAYS FROM MAY 7
Hafengeburtstag: the world's largest harbour festival – **Hamburg**

SECOND HALF OF MAY
International horse racing at Iffezheim – **Baden-Baden**

Four Hills Tournament, Garmisch-Partenkirchen

© Daniel Karmann/EPA/Photoshot

Hafengeburtstag, Hamburg

www.mediaserver.hamburg.de/C. Spahrbier

WHITSUN
Kuchen und Brunnenfest: dance of the salt workers in traditional 16C costume – **Schwäbisch Hall**

Meistertrunk: performance of the legend of the "Long Drink" during the Thirty Years' War by locals in period costume – **Rothenburg ob der Tauber**

Carnival of Cultures: colourful street festival with international music, dancing and parades – **Berlin**

WHIT MONDAY
Pfingstritt: equestrian parade – **Kötzting**

WHIT TUESDAY
Historische Geißbockversteigerung: auctioning of a goat in period costumes with folk dancing and a local fair – **Deidesheim**

CORPUS CHRISTI
Solemn procession through the decorated town – **Munich**
Mülheimer Gottestracht: procession of boats along the Rhine – **Cologne**
Procession through flower-decked street – **Hüfingen**

LAST SATURDAY OF MAY
Wildpferdefang: capture and auction of young stallions – **Merfelder Bruch**

14 DAYS AFTER WHITSUN, FROM FRIDAY TO MONDAY
Salatkirmes (Salad Fair): commemorates the introduction of the potato to the Hessen region; traditional local costumes – **Schwalmstadt**

1ST WEEKEND IN JUNE AND SEPTEMBER, 2ND WEEKEND IN JULY
Castle illuminations (firework displays) – **Heidelberg**

THREE DAYS IN MID-JUNE
Luther's Wedding: celebration of the reformer's marriage with historical costume parade – **Lutherstadt Wittenberg**

LATE JUNE
Christopher Street Day: gay pride parades – **Berlin, Cologne, Hamburg, Dresden, Munich**

JUNE TO AUGUST
Summer Music Festival: classical music in the Cistercian abbey – **Chorin**
Festival of Drama and Opera in the abbey ruins; theatre, opera – **Bad Hersfeld**

**JUNE TO SEPTEMBER
(EVERY 5 YEARS, NEXT: 2012)**
Documenta: world's largest
international exhibition of
contemporary art – **Kassel**

LAST WEEK OF JUNE
Kiel Week: international sailing
regatta; city-wide festival – **Kiel**

LAST WEEKEND OF JUNE
Bergstadtfest: parade in historical
costumes – **Freiberg**

**FOUR SUNDAYS FROM END OF JUNE
(EVERY 4 YEARS, NEXT: 2013)**
Fürstenhochzeit (Landshut Royal
Wedding): historical pageant in period
costume – **Landshut**

DURING SUMMER MONTHS
Mecklenburg-Vorpommern Summer
Music Festival, held in historic mansions,
castles and churches – **throughout
Mecklenburg-Vorpommern**

JULY TO AUGUST
Schleswig-Holstein Music Festival –
throughout Schleswig-Holstein
Festival on the cathedral steps –
Erfurt

Der Rhein in Flammen (The Rhine in
Flames): fireworks and illuminated
casteles and boats along the Rhine
valley between Koblenz and Bingen –
Koblenz-Oberwesel, **St. Goar**

1ST WEEKEND IN JULY
Spreewald Festival: Sorbian folklore
and traditions – **Lübbenau**

EARLY JULY
Archers' Festival: procession of archers
– **Hannover**

**MID-JULY (EVERY 4 YEARS,
NEXT: 2013)**
Fischerstechen (Fishermen's Festival)
– **Ulm**

**3RD WEEKEND IN JULY
(SATURDAY TO MONDAY)**
Kinderzeche: commemorating the
saving of the town by a deputation of
children (historical costumes) –
Dinkelsbühl

PENULTIMATE MONDAY IN JULY
Schwörmontag: river procession on
the Danube – **Ulm**

3RD SUNDAY AND MONDAY IN JULY
Tänzelfest: historical procession by
school children – **Kaufbeuren**

**LAST SATURDAY IN JULY AND
1ST SUNDAY IN AUGUST**
Summer music festival – **Hitzacker**

END OF JULY TO END OF AUGUST
Bayreuther Festspiele: Wagner
Opera Festival – **Bayreuth**

Fischerstechen, Ulm

© Horst Hörger/Ulm/Neu-Ulm Touristik GmbH

Bremer Freimarkt

Jochen Mönch/BTZ Bremer Touristik-Zentrale

2ND SATURDAY IN AUGUST
Seenachtsfest: evening lakeside festival – **Constance**

2ND WEEK IN AUGUST
Further Drachenstich (Slaying of the Dragon): pageant of the legend of St. George, in period costume – **Furth im Wald**

SATURDAY AFTER 24 AUGUST
Schäferlauf: shepherds' race (barefoot over a field of stubble) – **Markgröningen**

LAST WEEK IN AUGUST
International horse racing at Iffezheim – **Baden-Baden**

END OF SEPTEMBER TO EARLY OCTOBER
Cannstatter Volksfest: popular local fair – **Bad Cannstatt**

MID-SEPTEMBER TO MID-OCTOBER
Beethoven Fest: International music festival in composer's home town – **Bonn**

TWO WEEKS PRECEDING FIRST SUNDAY IN OCTOBER
Oktoberfest: beer festival. The largest popular festival in the world attracts around 6 million people to the Bavarian capital every year – **Munich**

FIVE DAYS IN EARLY OR MID-OCTOBER
Frankfurt Book Fair: the world's largest book fair with 1 800 exhibitors from 100 countries – **Frankfurt am Main**

1ST AND 2ND WEEKEND IN OCTOBER
Weinlesefest: wine fair and election of the Queen of Wine – **Neustadt an der Weinstraße**

LAST 10 DAYS IN OCTOBER
Bremer Freimarkt: largest popular fair in northern Germany – **Bremen**

SUNDAY BEFORE 6 NOVEMBER
Leonhardifahrt: similar celebration to that at Bad Tölz (🕯 *see below*) – **Benediktbeuern**

6 NOVEMBER
Leonhardifahrt: gaily decorated horse-drawn carts process through town to celebrate Mass in honour of St. Leonard – **Bad Tölz**

ADVENT
Christmas markets – throughout Germany (🕯 *see p28*) but especially in **Nuremberg**, **Munich**, **Dresden**

24 DECEMBER AND NEW YEAR'S EVE
Weihnachtsschießen und Neujahrsschießen: Christmas and New Year shooting matches – **Berchtesgaden**

Christmas pyramids at Striezelmarkt, Dresden

© Landeshauptstadt Dresden/Sylvio Dittrich

Christmas Markets

A stroll through a German Christmas market is a delightful assault on the senses. The aroma of cinnamon-roasted almonds mingles with that of steaming mulled wine and sausage smoke wafting from beechwood fires. Each stall is festively adorned and laden with tempting arrays of wooden toys, shiny ornaments, filigree lace, Christmas pyramids, adorable little smoking men, hand-blown glass, fragrant candles and other seasonal decorations. Stop for a minute to listen to the local choir singing "Oh Tannenbaum" while standing below a massive fir tree covered in thousands of sparkling lights. Watch the excitement in children's eyes as they wait for their turn on Santa's lap and the glee as they bite into a candied apple. Pure magic!

Dresden holds the claim for Germany's oldest Christmas market with a tradition going back to 1434. The most famous in the country, though, is the one in Nuremberg, but there are dozens of others in cities, towns and villages. They're almost always held on the central market square with stalls spilling out into surrounding streets. The nicest markets are in historic settings, backed by cathedrals, half-timbered houses and stately town halls. Most start in late November and run through 24 December, with stalls open daily, including Sundays. For a full list, see www.germany-christmas-market.org.uk.

- ◆ **Nuremberg** (26 Nov–24 Dec)
- ◆ **Rothenburg ob der Tauber** (26 Nov–23 Dec)
- ◆ **Munich** (26 Nov–24 Dec)
- ◆ **Dresden** (26 Nov–24 Dec)
- ◆ **Hamburg** (23 Nov–31 Dec)
- ◆ **Cologne** (22 Nov–23 Dec)
- ◆ **Berlin** (22 Nov–31 Dec)

Nuremberg Christmas market

Uli Kowatsch/Stadt Nürnberg

Know Before You Go

USEFUL WEBSITES

www.romantischestrasse.de
One of Germany's most popular tourist destinations is the *Romantische Straße*, the Romantic Road. Half-timbered houses, medieval fortresses and city walls, Alpine vistas and art-filled churches stretch along the route. The website offers detailed travel information and maps for each of the towns and cities along the way.

www.burgenstrasse.de
Some of Germany's most romantic castles are on the *Burgenstraße,* or Castle Road, that travels from Mannheim to Prague. For maps and details about the route, visit the website.

www.deutsche-weinstrasse.de
The website of the German Wine Institute offers information about each of Germany's wines and wine regions as well as a listing of the nation's wine festivals.

www.naturpark.de
Germany is home to 14 national parks, 15 biosphere reserves and 101 nature parks. The site offers detailed information and maps for each of Germany's parks.

www.deutscher-heilbaederverband.de
Spas and wellness centres have long been considered by Germans an important part of healthy living. A visit to The German Spa Association's website provides links to spas nationwide, including lists of those with English-speaking therapists.

www.zoo-infos.de
Parents travelling with young children may want to visit the website prior to arriving in Germany. This comprehensive site includes information about and links to all of the zoos and animal parks in the country.

www.oktoberfest.de
Oktoberfest is one of the world's most famous festivals. Visitors to Munich interested in up-to-date festival information can visit the site.

CULTURAL ORGANISATIONS
The Goethe-Institut websites for each of the cities below can be accessed via **www.goethe.de**.

* **Goethe-Institut Johannesburg**, 119 Jan Smuts Ave, Parkwood 2193, Johannesburg, ℘(011) 442 3232, fax (011) 442 3738.
* **Goethe-Institut London**, 50 Princes Gate, Exhibition Road, London SW7 2PH, ℘(020) 7596 4000, fax (020) 7594 0240.
* **Goethe-Institut New York**, 72 Spring St., 11th Floor, New York, NY 10012, ℘(212) 439 8700, fax (212) 439 8705.
* **Goethe-Institut Ottawa**, Saint Paul University, 223 Main St., Suite 128, Ottawa, ON, K1S 1C5, ℘613 2329000, fax (613) 232 9000.
* **Goethe-Institut Sydney**, 90 Ocean Street, Woollahra, NSW 2025, ℘(02) 8356 8333, fax (02) 8356 8314.

TOURIST OFFICES
Information on travel arrangements and accommodation and a variety of brochures are available from the **German National Tourist Office**. For online information refer to www.germany-tourism.de, the German National Tourist Office website. Every destination featured in the *DISCOVERING GERMANY* section of this guide has specific tourist office details. Local tourist offices are marked on town plans with the 🛈 symbol.

CHICAGO
- **German National Tourist Office Chicago**, PO Box 59594, Chicago, IL 60659-9594, ✆(773) 539-6303, fax (773) 539-6378, info@gntoch.com, www.cometogermany.com

JOHANNESBURG
- **German National Tourist Office**, c/o Lufthansa German Airlines, PO Box 412246, Craighall, 2024 Johannesburg ✆(011) 325 1927, fax (011) 325 0867

LONDON
- **German National Tourist Office**, PO Box 2695, London W1A 3TN ✆(020) 7317 0908, fax (020) 7317 0917, gntolon@d-z-t.com, www.germany-tourism.co.uk

NEW YORK
- **German National Tourist Office**, 122 East 42nd Street, New York, NY 10168-0072 ✆(212) 661-7200, fax (212) 661-7174, office-usa@germany.travel, www.cometogermany.com

INTERNATIONAL VISITORS
GERMAN EMBASSIES AND CONSULATES ABROAD

IN AUSTRALIA
- **Embassy of the Federal Republic of Germany**, Canberra, 119 Empire Circuit, Yarralumla ACT 2600, ✆(02) 6270 1911 fax (02) 6270 1951, info@canberra.diplo.de, www.canberra.diplo.de
- **Consulate General of the Republic of Germany**, Sydney, 13 Trelawney Street, Woollahra NSW 2025, ✆(02) 9328 7733, fax (02) 9327 9649, info@sydney.diplo.de www.sydney.diplo.de

IN CANADA
- **Embassy of the Federal Republic of Germany**, 1 Waverley Street, Ottawa, ON, K2P 0T8 ✆(613) 232 1101, fax (613) 594 9330, info@ottawa.diplo.de, www.ottawa.diplo.de
  Postal address: PO Box 379, Postal Station "A", Ottawa, ON, K1N 8V4
- **Consulate General of the Federal Republic of Germany**, 2 Bloor Street East, 25th Floor, Toronto, Ontario, M4W 1A8. ✆(416) 925 28 13, fax (416) 925 28 18, info@toronto.diplo.de, www.toronto.diplo.de

IN SOUTH AFRICA
- **Embassy of the Federal Republic of Germany**, 180 Blackwood Street, Arcadia, Pretoria 0083, ✆(012) 427 89 00, fax (012) 343 94 01, Info@pretoria.diplo.de, www.pretoria.diplo.de
  Postal address: PO Box 2023, Pretoria 0001
- Consulate-General of the Federal Republic of Germany, 19th Floor, Safmarine House, 22 Riebeek Street, Cape Town 8001 ✆(021) 405 30 00, fax (021) 421 04 00, info@ kapstadt.diplo.de, www.kapstadt.diplo.de
  Postal address: PO Box 4273, Cape Town 8000

IN THE UNITED KINGDOM
- **Embassy of the Federal Republic of Germany**, 23 Belgrave Square, London SW1X 8PZ, ✆(020) 7824 1300, fax (020) 7824 1435, info@london.diplo.de, www.london.diplo.de
- **Consulate General of the Federal Republic of Germany**, 16 Eglinton Crescent, Edinburgh EH12 5DG, Scotland ✆(0131) 337 2323, fax (0131) 346 1578,

info@edinburgh.diplode,
www.edinburgh.diplo.de

IN THE UNITED STATES

♦ **Embassy of the Federal Republic of Germany**, 4645 Reservoir Road NW, Washington, DC 20007-1998 ℘(202) 298 4000, fax (202) 298 42 49, info@washington.diplo.de, www.washington.diplo.de

♦ **Consulate General of the Federal** Republic of Germany, 871 United Nations Plaza (1st Avenue @ 49th Street), New York, NY 10017 ℘(212) 610 9700, fax (212) 940 04 02, info@newyork.diplo.de, www.new-york.diplo.de

FOREIGN EMBASSIES AND CONSULATES IN GERMANY

♦ **American** Embassy
American Embassy, Pariser Platz 2, 10117 Berlin, ℘030 830 50, fax 030 83 05 10 50

♦ **American** Consulate-General
Willi-Becker-Allee 10, 40227 Düsseldorf, ℘0211 7 88 89 27, fax 0211 7 88 89 36

♦ **Australian** Embassy
Wallstraße 76–79, 10179 Berlin, ℘030 88 00 88 0, fax 030 88 00 88 210, www.germany.embassy.gov.au

♦ **Australian** Consulate-General
Neue Mainzer Straße 52–58, 60322 Frankfurt am Main, ℘069-90 55 80, fax 069-90 55 81 19

♦ **British** Embassy Berlin
Wilhelmstraße 70-71, 10117 Berlin, ℘030 20 45 7-0, fax 030- 20 45 7 579, www.britischebotschaft.de

♦ **British** Consulate-General
Yorckstraße 19, 40476 Düsseldorf, ℘0211 94 48-0, fax 0211 48 81 90

♦ **Canadian** Embassy
Leipziger Platz 17, 10117 Berlin, ℘030 20 31 20, fax 030 20 31 25 90, www.kanada-info.de

♦ **Canadian** Consulate-General
Benrather Straße 8, 40213 Düsseldorf, ℘0211-17 21 70, fax 0211-35 91 65

♦ **South African Embassy,**
Tiergartenstraße 18, 10785 Berlin, ℘030 22 07 30, fax 030 22 07 31 90, www.suedafrika.org

♦ **South African Consulate-General,**
Sendlinger-Tor-Platz 5, 80336 München, ℘089 2 31 16 30, fax 089 23 11 63 63

ENTRY REQUIREMENTS
PASSPORTS AND VISAS

Citizens of European Union countries need a national identity card or a passport to visit Germany; there is no limit to the length of their stay. Under the visa-waiver program, citizens of certain nations (including Australia, Canada, New Zealand and the US) require only a passport, but no visa, in order to be admitted to Germany as tourists for up to three months within a six-month period. Citizens of all other countries, including South Africa, need to apply for a Schengen Visa at the German consulate in their home country. Regulations change from time to time. Check www.auswaertiges-amt.de for up-to-the-minute details.

DRIVING LICENCE

A valid national driving licence is required to drive in Germany. Third-party insurance cover is compulsory; it is advisable to carry an International Motor Insurance Certificate (Green Card), which serves as proof of third-party insurance. If you are bringing your own car into the country, you will need the vehicle registration papers as well as proof of insurance.

CUSTOMS REGULATIONS

In order find out the latest customs allowances when returning to your country from Germany, **UK citizens** should contact the Customs Office or check online at www.ukba.homeof-fice.gov.uk/travellingtotheuk/cus-toms. For **US citizens**, the US Customs Service offers a publication called *Know Before You Go*, which is available as a downloadable pdf http://www.

cbp.gov/linkhandler/cgov/travel/
vacation/kbyg/kbyg_regulations.ctt/
kbyg_regulations.pdf.

Most articles that you take to Germany
for your personal use don't incur duty
and tax. If you're arriving from a non-
EU country, the following duty-free
allowances apply to people over 17: 1L
of strong liquor or 2L of less than 22 per-
rcent alcohol by volume plus 4L of wine
plus 16L of beer and ether 200 cigarettes
or 100 cigarillos or 50 cigars or 250g of
loose tobacco.

HEALTH

Be sure to obtain adequate travel
health insurance before going on
your trip. European Union citizens
are entitled to free or reduced-cost
emergency medical treatment while
visiting Germany. You should carry
your European Health Insurance
Card (EHIC), available free of charge
through your national health
authority. Applications can usually
be made online. Contact your local
office or see http://ec.europa.eu for
full details.

Citizens from countries outside the
EU should check with their health
insurance provider if they are
covered for medical emergencies
while travelling in Germany. If not,
definitely obtain travel insurance,
preferably one that covers emergency
repatriation to your home country.
Many German doctors and hospitals
require visitors to pay at the time of
service. Make sure you understand
what kind of documentation your
insurance requires for reimbursement.
For referrals to an English-speaking
doctor, contact your embassy or
consulate in Germany. If you take
regular medication, bring a sufficient
supply as well as a letter from your
doctor stating that they are required
to treat your medical condition.

ACCESSIBILITY

Germany is generally a well-equipped
country for disabled visitors, and many
of the sights described in this guide
are accessible to people with special
needs. Sights marked with the symbol
♿ offer access for wheelchairs. Still, it
is always best to call ahead to discuss
your particular needs.

Access ramps and/or lifts can be found
in most public buildings as well as
train stations, museums, theatres and
cinemas. In historic towns, though,
cobblestone streets may present a
challenge in getting around. Newer
hotels have lifts and rooms equipped
for wheelchair-users. Trains, trams,
underground trains and buses are
becoming increasingly accessible.
Guide dogs are allowed on all forms of
public transport.

An excellent reference source is the
annually updated guide *Handicapped-
Reisen Deutschland* (16.80€),
published by Escales Verlag. It lists
specifics about 400 wheelchair-
friendly hotels, apartments and youth
hostels and is available at bookshops,
online (e.g. at www.handicapped-
reisen.de) and directly from the
publisher (☎07841 684 11 33; fax
07841 684 11 45; info@escales-verlag.
de). Barrier-free travel planning
assistance is also provided by Natko
(☎0211-336 8001; www.natko.de).
Disabled motorists need to be aware
that a disabled car badge/sticker
does not entitle them to unrestricted
parking (local disabled residents are
granted special parking permits only
in exceptional circumstances).

Getting There and Getting Around

BY PLANE

Numerous airlines operate regular services to Germany's airports, the busiest of which are Frankfurt and Munich. Others are in Berlin, Bremen, Dresden, Düsseldorf, Hamburg, Hannover, Cologne/Bonn, Leipzig, Nuremberg, Saarbrücken and Stuttgart. The German national carrier **Lufthansa** can be contacted on the following numbers:

- **Australia**: ☏1300 655 727
- **Canada**: ☏1-800 563 5954
- **South Africa**: ☏0861 842538
- **UK**: ☏0871 945 9747
- **USA**: ☏800 645 3880

Information about flights to and within Germany can also be obtained, and reservations made, at www.lufthansa.com.

Several budget airlines, including Ryanair, easyJet and Germanwings also fly to several German destinations from throughout Europe. **Ryanair** serves Berlin, Bremen, Weeze (near Düsseldorf), Hamburg-Lübeck, Altenburg (near Leipzig), Memmingen and Karlsruhe/Baden-Baden.

For information and reservations, visit www.ryanair.com or contact one of their call centres. Dial ☏0871 246 0000 (£0.10/min) from within the UK, ☏0900 116 0500 (0.62€/min) in Germany and ☏+353 1 248 0856 from the rest of the world.

The route network of **EasyJet** includes Berlin, Köln/Bonn, Dortmund, Dresden, Düsseldorf, Hamburg and Munich from various airports in the UK. For information and reservations, visit www.easyjet.com, or call ☏0871 244 2366 (£0.10/min) in the UK.

Germanwings flies to Berlin, Köln/Bonn, Dortmund, Dresden, Friedrichshafen, Hamburg, Hannover, Leipzig/Halle, Munich, Stuttgart and Zweibrücken. Contact them on www.

germanwings.com or ☏0906 294 1918 (£0.25/min) in the UK.

Inland Flights

There are numerous internal flights in Germany, most of them operated by **Lufthansa** (☏0180 583 84 26, www.lufthansa.com). Other carriers with domestic services include **Air Berlin** (☏01805-73 78 00 in Germany, www.airberlin.com, 0.14€/min) and **Germanwings** (☏0900-191 91 00 in Germany, www.germanwings.com, 0.99€/min).

BY SHIP

There are no longer any direct ferry services between the UK and Germany. Check www.ferrybooker. com, a single site covering all sea-ferry routes and operators. The principal routes to the continent are:

- Dover to Calais, France (sailing: 1hr 15min);
- Harwich to Hoek van Holland, Netherlands (sailing: 3hrs 45min);
- Hull to Zeebrugge, Belgium (13hrs 30min);
- Newcastle to Amsterdam (15hrs)

BY TRAIN

International high-speed rail links from London St. Pancras to Aachen and Cologne (Eurostar to Brussels, then Thalys) can make the train an attractive alternative to plane, coach or car in terms of time, price and convenience. Visitors leaving London

Berlin Hauptbahnhof

© Jon Arnold/hemis.fr

can reach Aachen in just 3hrs 30min and Cologne in just over 4hrs.

TICKETS AND FARES

Deutsche Bahn (DB), Germany's leading railway, offers quick and comprehensive service around the country. Major cities are served by DB's high-speed InterCityExpress (ICE) trains or InterCity/EuroCity (IC/EC) services; regional centres are connected by a fleet of RegionalExpress (RE), RegionalBahn (RB) and S-Bahn trains.

Special tickets: **German Rail Pass** (www.raileurope.com) – valid for four to ten days of intra-Germany travel within one month (available only to non-European residents); **Bahncards** (www.bahn.de) – 25 percent or 50 percent discount for frequent travellers within Germany; **InterRail One Country Pass** (www.railpassshop.com) which buys unlimited rail travel within Germany for three, four, six or eight days of travel within one month (available only to European but not to German residents).

In addition, various saver tickets, seasonal promotions and discounted fares for children, seniors, students and groups are also available.

For further information and reservations, contact:
Deutsche Bahn UK Booking Centre, ℘08718 808 066 (🕐open Mon–Fri 9am–5pm, Sat–Sun 9am–1pm), www.bahn.co.uk. Information can also be obtained from Deutsche Bahn's main website, www.bahn.com.
Alternatively, try Rail Europe, 178 Piccadilly, London W1, ℘08448 484 064. For their brochure, call ℘08448 484 055 or download it from www.raileurope.co.uk.

BY COACH

Eurolines serves many cities in Germany from the UK. Coaches are equipped with air conditioning, WC, TV/video, reclining seats, etc. Journey times can be quite long (from London Victoria it takes around 19hrs to Berlin, 20hrs to Munich and 13hrs to Cologne), but tickets are inexpensive, especially when booked in advance (a 30-day advance return costs around 82€). For information and reservations, call ℘08717 818 181 in the UK, or visit the Eurolines website at www.eurolines.co.uk.

The **Eurolines Pass**, valid for 15 or 30 days, allows you to travel for a set price between a choice of 43 cities across Europe, with numerous internal connections available within Germany (low/high season prices for adults £179/289 for a 15-day pass and £279/389 for a 30-day pass). There are discounts for children, youths (under 26) and senior citizens. Children under four travel free. For further details, call ℘08717 818 177 in the UK or visit www.eurolines-pass.com.

BY BUS

Bus can be useful for travel within Germany, especially in areas where train service is sporadic or non-existent. Bus stations tend to be located next to railway stations. For prices and timetables, contact **Deutsche Touring** (℘069-790 35 01; www.touring.de).

BY CAR

Coming from the UK, the fastest and easiest way to Germany is via the Eurotunnel. These shuttle trains whisk cars, motorbikes, bicycles and coaches from Folkestone through the Channel Tunnel to Coquelles (near Calais, France) in about 35 minutes.
From there you can be in Germany in about 3hrs. Check fares and details with your travel agent, call ℘08705-353 535 in the UK or visit www.eurotunnel.com.
With no direct ferry services from the UK to Germany, the closest port to the German border is Hoek van Holland in the Netherlands (served from Harwich). 🕭 *See By Ship, above, for additional routes.* From these ports numerous routes using autobahns and national roads lead into Germany. Michelin offers drivers and motorcyclists a free online route

planning service at www.viamichelin.
com. You can determine stopovers
between departure point and
destination and define your route
using various criteria (such as time,
distance, use of motorways, road
tolls, etc.). You are given information
on mileage, journey time, hotels and
restaurants along the way (selected
from the *Michelin Guide Germany*), and
map extracts that can be printed out.

DISTANCES

- Calais to Frankfurt via
  Cologne 600km/374mi.
- Hoek van Holland to Munich
  via Bonn, Mainz, Stuttgart and
  Augsburg 845km/525mi.
- Zeebrugge to Munich via
  Karlsruhe, Stuttgart and
  Augsburg 853km/530mi.
- Calais to Cologne via Aachen
  417km/259mi.

DRIVING REGULATIONS

Traffic in Germany drives on the right.
Drivers in cities with trams should
be especially careful before crossing
tramlines. The maximum speed in
built-up areas is 50kph/31mph. On the
open road the maximum increases
to 100kph/62mph. There is no official
limit on motorways (signposted "A"
for *Autobahn*), but there are many
stretches where slower speeds must
be observed; watch for signs. In any
case, it's safest not to exceed speeds of
130kph/81mph. There is a compulsory
speed limit of 80kph/50mph on roads
and motorways for vehicles with
trailers. Careless or reckless driving
is considered a serious offence in
Germany and fines can be stiff. The
maximum limit for alcohol in the blood
is 0.05%.

German motorways are toll-free
and well equipped with 24hr service
areas providing: petrol, spare parts
and accessories, washrooms, toilets,
public telephones, refreshments,
accommodation and first-aid
equipment.

In some city centres car traffic is
banned, but there are usually plenty

IMPORTANT WARNING SIGNS:	
Anfang	beginning
Ausfahrt	exit
Baustelle	roadworks, building site
Einbahnstraße	one-way street
Einfahrt	entrance
Ende	end
Gefahr	danger
LKW	HGV; truck
PKW	private car
Rechts einbiegen	turn right
Links einbiegen	turn left
Rollsplitt	gravel chippings
Stau	hold-up, traffic jam
Unfall	accident
Umleitung	diversion
Verengte Fahrbahn	road narrows
Vorfahrt	priority
Vorsicht	look out!

of signposted parking garages
(*Parkhaus*).

Seatbelt usage is compulsory in the
back as well as the front of the car.
Children under age 12, or less than
1.5m/4ft 11in tall, are required by
law to be fastened in a suitable child
car seat; there are fines for non-
compliance. It is a legal requirement
to carry the regulation red emergency
triangle, for warning other motorists
of a breakdown or enforced roadside
halt, and a first-aid box (including
disposable gloves and rescue blanket).
In Germany emergency services are
always given priority and drivers
should pull over to the side of the road.

BREAKDOWN SERVICE

For 24-hour service on motorways and
main roads, call the German motoring
association ADAC at ✆0180/2 22
22 22 (or ✆22 22 22 from mobile
phones; www.adac.de). If you don't
have a mobile phone, use the orange
emergency phones spaced about

2km/1.2mi apart. Small arrows on the roadside posts indicate the direction of the nearest one.

On-the-spot repairs are free, as only the cost of replacement parts or towing is charged. Motorists ringing this service should ask specifically for the *"Straßenwachthilfe"* (road patrol assistance). The *Michelin Guide Deutschland* lists the numbers to use to contact the ADAC service in all big towns.

PETROL

The following grades of petrol are generally available in Germany:

- *Super Plus Bleifrei*:
  Super unleaded (98 octane)
- *Super Bleifrei*:
  Standard unleaded (95 octane)
- Diesel

Leaded petrol is no longer available. A lead substitute can be added to the fuel tank of those vehicles that require it; the additive can be purchased at petrol stations.

CAR HIRE

The minimum age for car hire is 25, although some companies may rent to drivers ages 21 to 24 at a surcharge. You also need to have had your driving licence for more than one year.

The major car hire firms have offices at airports and main railway stations and in large towns, but it is generally cheaper to arrange car hire before travelling to Germany. Some useful numbers (in Germany) include:

- **Avis**: ℘01805 21 77 02, www.avis.com
- **Europcar**: ℘01805 80 00, www.europcar.com
- **Hertz**: ℘01805 33 35 35, www.hertz.com
- **Budget/Sixt**: ℘01805 24 43 88, www.budget.com

Where to Stay and Eat

WHERE TO STAY

Hotel recommendations are located in the Address Books throughout the *DISCOVERING GERMANY* section of this guide. For coin ranges and for a description of the symbols used in the Address Books, see the Legend on the cover flap.

ADDRESSES IN THE GUIDE

We have selected accommodations for their value, location or character, trying to cater for all budgets. However, popular tourist regions, resorts and big cities are more expensive than others. Likewise, there is often a significant price difference between high and low season. During festivals and other cultural events last-minute accommodations are very hard to find.

Tourist information offices have lists of local lodging in hotels, inns *(Gasthof* or *Gasthaus)*, guesthouses, farms, castles, hostels and holiday flats. Room rates always include tax and service charges. There may be an extra charge for breakfast. Many tourist office and hotel websites let you check for room availability and make advance reservations or consult www.booking.com, www.venere.com, www.hotels.com, www.expedia.com and www.opodo.de. Hotels catering specifically for families are at www.familotel.de. For last-minute bargains, check HRS (℘0870 243 0003 in the UK, ℘0221 2077 600 in Germany, www.hrs.com).

HOLIDAY FLATS AND HOMES

Furnished holiday flats and homes are widely available in Germany, increasingly so in the cities as well. Local tourist offices normally have information on availability. Also check www.deutschertourismusverband.de.

Bed and Breakfast

Tourist offices keep lists of private room rentals *(Privatzimmer)*, or look for a sign saying *Zimmer frei* outside private houses.

For advance reservations try www.bed-and-breakfast.de or www.bedandbreakfast.de.

CAMPING

With around 2 500 campsites, Germany has plenty of scope for camping. Most are closed between November and March, but a few remain open all year. Fees are usually composed of a charge per person (2.50€ to 7€), for your tent (4€ to 8€) and for your car (2€ to 5€). More information is available from **Bundesverband der Campingwirtschaft in Deutschland (BVCD)**, www.bvcd.de and from **ADAC**, ✆01805 10 11 12, www.adac.de. The latter publishes an annually updated guide called *ADAC Camping and Caravaning Führer*. Online sources include www.eurocampings.de and www.alanrogers.com.

HOSTELS

Germany has almost 600 **Hostelling International-affiliated (HI) youth hostels**, which are managed by the Deutsches Jugendherbergswerk (DJH, www.djh.de) and open to people of all ages. Staying at a hostel requires membership of an HI association. Non-members can obtain cards directly at the hostels. Advance booking is recommended during the holiday season and at city centre youth hostels. Bookings can be made by phone, fax, email and online at www.hihostels.com.

There is also a growing number of independent **backpacker hostels** that don't require membership. They are especially prevalent in big cities, Berlin in particular, and generally cater more to individual travellers than groups or families. Standards vary widely. For information go to www. backpackernetwork.de. For online reservations, try www.gomio.com,

www.hostelworld.com, www.hostels. com and www.hostels.net.

ECONOMY CHAIN HOTELS

Both domestic and international budget chains are becoming increasingly prevalent, even in city centres. Rooms are usually small but have a TV and private bathroom; there's often an extra charge for breakfast. The German National Tourist Office has put together a list of hotels charging 40€ at www.germany-tourism.de/ENG/ infocenter/holidays_on_a_small_ budget.htm.

◆ **Holiday Inn Express**: www.hiexpress.com
◆ **Meininger**: www.meininger-hotels.com
◆ **Motel One**: www. motel.one
◆ **Novotel**: www.novotel.com

FARMS

Farm stays are popular with families especially in Bavaria and in the wine-growing regions. For details, check www.landtourismus.de or www. bauernhofurlaub-deutschland.de.

HISTORIC BUILDINGS

For information about hotels and restaurants in castles and other historic buildings, contact your country's German National Tourist office or try **Histohotels**, ✆036 43-493 39 25, www.histohotels.de.

Farm stay in Seebach, Black Forest

© TI Seebach/Schwarzwald Tourismus GmbH

Nürnberger Rostbratwürste

© Karl-Friedrich Hohl/iStockphoto.com

Regional Specialities

Bavaria and Franconia
- **Leberknödel:** Dumplings of liver, bread and onion, sometimes in broth.
- **Leberkäs:** Minced beef and pork (no liver), cooked in the form of a loaf.
- **Knödel:** Dumplings of potato or soaked bread.
- **Steckerlfisch:** Skewered grilled mackerel, often served at festivals such as Oktoberfest.
- **Rostbratwürste:** Small sausages grilled over beechwood charcoal.

Baden-Württemberg
- **Schneckensuppe:** Soup with snails.
- **Spätzle:** Egg-based handmade pasta in long strips.
- **Maultaschen:** Pasta stuffed with a mixture of veal and spinach.
- **Geschnetzeltes:** Thinly sliced veal in a cream sauce.

Rhineland-Palatinate
- **Sauerbraten:** Beef marinated in wine vinegar, served with potato dumplings.
- **Reibekuchen:** Potato pancakes served with apple or blueberry sauce.
- **Saumagen:** Stuffed pork belly with pickled cabbage.
- **Schweinepfeffer:** Highly seasoned pork ragout, thickened with blood.
- **Federweißer:** Partially fermented new wine accompanied by an onion tart.

Hessen and Westphalia
- **Töttchen:** Ragout of brains and calf's head, cooked with herbs.
- **Pfefferpothast:** Stew cooked with pepper, lemon and capers.

Thuringia
- **Linsensuppe mit Thüringer Rotwurst:** Lentil soup with Thuringian sausages.

Saxony
- **Leipziger Allerlei:** Vegetable medley e.g. of peas, carrots and asparagus.
- **Dresdener Stollen:** Dense butter cake with dried fruits.

Lower Saxony and Schleswig-Holstein
- **Aalsuppe:** Sweet-and-sour eel soup with prunes, pears, vegetables and bacon.
- **Labskaus:** Traditional sailor's dish; beef, pork and salted herrings with potatoes and beetroot, served with gherkins and fried egg.
- **Grünkohl mit Pinkel:** Minced kale cooked with smoked sausage and onion.

The Michelin Guide Deutschland
For a more exhaustive list of hotels and restaurants consult the *Michelin Guide Deutschland*.

WHERE TO EAT
Restaurant recommendations are located in the Address Books throughout the *DISCOVERING GERMANY* section of this guide. For coin ranges and for a description of the symbols used in the Address Books, see the Legend on the cover flap.

German Cuisine
German food is more varied and balanced than is generally supposed. Breakfast **(Frühstück)** is usually a generous spread including cold meats, cheese and an assortment of fresh bread and rolls. Lunch **(Mittagessen)** is traditionally a hot meal consisting of soup and a main course revolving around fish or meat. Many modern Germans, though, eat their main meal at dinnertime, preferring a light one at midday. Snack stands are called **Imbisse** and are ubiquitous. Sausages, especially the grilled **Bratwurst** are a staple and often paired with potato salad or sauerkraut. Choices are greater and more international in the big cities, where the Turkish doner kebab is a popular tummy filler. Many Germans still indulge in an afternoon coffee break in a café. Most offer a large selection of cakes, such as **Schwarzwälder Kirschtorte** (Black Forest gâteau) or **Käsekuchen** (cheesecake) alongside lighter fruit tarts and the famous **strudel** (fruit wrapped in crisp pastry). The evening meal **(Abendessen)** is either a cold supper of meats, cheese and bread or a cooked dinner.

Useful Words and Phrases

ja, nein yes, no
danke thank you
bitte please
Hallo (informal) Hello
Tschüss (informal) Bye
Guten Tag (formal) Good day
Auf Wiedersehen (formal) Goodbye
eins, zwei, drei one, two, three
vier, fünf, sechs four, five, six
sieben, acht seven, eight
neun, zehn nine, ten
links, rechts left, right
Wie geht es Ihnen? How are you?
Sprechen Sie Englisch? Do you speak English?
Ich spreche kein Deutsch. I don't speak German.
Was kostet das? How much is it?
Das ist zu teuer That's too expensive.
Wo ist...? Where is...?
Ich heisse... My name is...
Wieviel Uhr ist es? What time is it?
Ist der Tisch frei? Is that table taken?
Die Rechnung, bitte. The bill, please.
Haben Sie ein Zimmer frei? Are there any rooms available?
Wo ist die Toilette? Where is the loo?
Hilfe! Help!
Entschuldigung Sorry
Montag Monday
Dienstag Tuesday
Mittwoch Wednesday
Donnerstag Thursday
Freitag Friday
Samstag Saturday
Sonntag Sunday
Ein Bier, bitte A beer, please.
Frühstück Breakfast
Mittagessen Lunch
Abendessen Dinner
Imbiss Snack
Polizei Police
Krankenhaus Hospital
Rufen Sie einen Arzt! Call a doctor!
Es ist ein Notfall! Emergency!
gut good
schlecht bad
Ich habe mich verirrt. I'm lost.
Wie weit ist es...? How far is it?

Basic Information

BUSINESS HOURS
BANKS

Banks are open from 8.30am to 4pm Monday to Friday (sometimes to 6pm on Thursday) and are closed on weekends. Branches in rural and suburban areas usually close for lunch between noon and 1pm. Bureaux de change *(Wechselstuben)* tend to keep longer hours.

SHOPPING

German shopkeepers are able to keep any hours they want, but most stick with the traditional pattern of opening around 9am or 10am and closing between 6.30pm and 8pm Monday to Friday and around 2pm or 4pm on Saturday. In major cities, some central supermarkets and shopping centres now stay open until 9pm or 10pm, sometimes daily, sometimes only on Friday and Saturday. Only bakeries and flower shops open for a few hours on normal Sundays. All stores are allowed to open on up to 10 pre-determined Sundays per year, including throughout December. Petrol stations and shops at big city train stations are your main options for stocking up on basics after hours.

MUSEUMS

Museums are usually closed on Mondays. Art museums often have a late-night opening one evening per week. Ticket offices usually close between 30 minutes and one hour before closing time.

COMMUNICATIONS

The international dialling code for Germany is **49**, so from the UK, for example, you would dial 00 49 + local dialling code **omitting** the initial 0 + subscriber's number.

International dialling codes from Germany:
- ✆ 00 44 for the UK
- ✆ 00 353 for Ireland
- ✆ 00 1 for the USA and Canada
- ✆ 00 61 for Australia
- ✆ 00 27 for South Africa

National directory enquiries:
- ✆ 11 833

International directory enquiries:
- ✆ 11 834

Public telephones: phonecards *(Telefonkarten)* for the largely card-operated public telephones are sold at post offices and newspaper kiosks. Some phones also take bank cards. *Note that phone calls from hotel rooms are generally expensive.*

Mobile phones operate on the GSM900/1800 network. If you have an unlocked phone, you can easily obtain a local German number by buying a SIM card at a telecom store or in such supermarkets as Aldi and Lidl. SIMs cost about 15€ and come with pre-paid airtime that can be recharged by buying scratchcards at newsagents or supermarkets. If your phone is not unlocked, you can buy a pre-paid phone for around 30€ at a major electronics stores such as Saturn or Media Markt. *Please note that it is illegal to use your phone while driving.*

ELECTRICITY

Voltage is 220V and appliances use two-pin plugs. Appliances operating on 110V, such as those from North America, require a transformer. Most electric shavers and laptops run on both 110V and 220V.

EMERGENCIES

Police: ✆ 110
Fire brigade: ✆ 112
Medical emergencies: ✆ 112
Traffic accidents: ✆ 110

POST

Yellow is the trademark colour of the Deutsche Post, as the German postal service is called. Most post offices are open Mondays to Fridays from 8am to 6pm and on Saturdays from 8am to noon. Smaller and rural branches may observe a lunch break, while those in city centres may keep slightly longer hours. Postal rates are 0.55€ for standard letters (up to 20g) sent within Germany, 0.70€ to countries within Europe and 1.70€ for letters destined for overseas.

MEDIA
NEWSPAPERS

Regional daily newspapers are widely read in Germany. The conservative *Frankfurter Allgemeine* and Munich's centrist *Süddeutsche Zeitung* enjoy a broad readership throughout Germany. Berlin's most popular daily is the *Tagesspiegel*, but the *Berliner Zeitung* and the *taz* are also popular with readers in the capital. Among the national newspapers, the sensationalist daily *Bild* is the most widely read. *Die Welt* offers better quality news. *Focus* and *Der Spiegel* are respected weekly news magazines, while *Stern* and *Bunte* belong more in the tabloid category.

The main foreign newspapers are available at airports, train stations and many kiosks and newsagents.

TELEVISION

Germany has two national state television channels, **ARD** and **ZDF**. There are also public regional channels such as Cologne's Westdeutscher Rundfunk (WDR) and Munich's Bayerischer Rundfunk (BR) and the Franco-German cultural television channel **Arte**.

In addition, many private channels feature a mix of soap operas, sitcoms, game shows and films. Although most of them target the general public (RTL 2, PRO 7, SAT 1), there are some theme channels, such as the music channel VIVA and the sports channel DSF.

MONEY

The euro has been the unit of currency in Germany since the beginning of 2002. Foreign currency can be exchanged at the airports, in banks, at hotels and at exchange offices such as those operated by Reisebank and usually located in major train stations.

To check on the latest currency exchange rates, consult www.xe.com or www.oanda. com.

CREDIT CARDS

Cash is still the dominant method of payment in Germany, especially in rural areas, although credit cards are slowly gaining in popularity. You can usually whip out your plastic at petrol stations, travel agents, international hotels and better restaurants and boutiques, but it is always best to check first.

In the event of loss or theft of your card, call the following numbers immediately:

* **Visa** ℘(0800) 814 91 00,
* **Eurocard-Mastercard** ℘(069) 79 33 19 10,
* **American Express** ℘(069) 97 97 10 00.

ATMS

Generally, the easiest and most convenient way to obtain cash is by using your bank card at a local ATM in Germany. Most are linked to such international networks as Cirrus, Maestro and Star. Credit cards may also be used but fees for cash advances can be steep.

PUBLIC HOLIDAYS

1 Jan, **6 Jan** (in Baden-Württemberg, Bayern and Sachsen-Anhalt only).
Good Friday, **Easter Sunday**, **Easter Monday**, **1 May**, **Ascension**, **Whit Sunday and Monday (Pentecost)**, **Corpus Christi** (in Baden-Württemberg, Bayern, Hessen, Nordrhein-Westfalen, Rheinland-Pfalz, Saarland, Sachsen, Thüringen and those communities with a predominantly Roman Catholic population only).
15 Aug (in Roman Catholic communities in Saarland and Bayern only).
3 Oct (Day of German Unity).
31 Oct (Reformation Day, in Brandenburg, Mecklenburg-Vorpommern, Sachsen, Sachsen-Anhalt and Thüringen).

1 Nov (in Baden-Württemberg, Bayern, Nordrhein-Westfalen, Rheinland-Pfalz and Saarland only). **Buß- und Bettag** (Day of Repentance and Prayer, usually **third Wed in Nov**, observed in Sachsen only), **24**, **25**, **26** and **31 Dec**.

DISCOUNTS

Discounts are widely available for seniors, children, families and the disabled, for instance for local attractions, public transport and tours. Many city and regional tourist offices issues Welcome Cards, which offer discounts or free access to participating local attractions as well as unlimited public transport during the period of their validity. Students should get an International Student Identity Card (ISIC) which is good for a host of discounts, including air fare, and travel insurance.

BY TRAIN

See *Getting Around: Tickets and Fares* for information on special ticket offers available through Deutsche Bahn.

BY AIR

For flying between European cities, discount carriers such as easyJet, Germanwings and Ryanair usually offer the best fares. If you are under 26 or a student, you may qualify for cheaper fares with major carriers. Check with such travel agents as STA Travel or Flight Centre. Children under the age of two usually travel free.

SMOKING

Germany was the last major European country to succumb, but in January 2008 strict anti-smoking laws kicked in even in this final bastion of nicotine. Confusingly, there is no national policy with each of the *Länder* (states) making its own rules. Generally, smoking is no longer allowed in public buildings, hospitals, trains and train stations. It is also not permitted in restaurants, cafés, bars and nightclubs. In some regions, smoking is permitted if an establishment has a separate room designated for smokers or if it's smaller than 75sq m/800sq ft, serves no food and does not allow anyone under 18. Smoking is usually possible at outdoor tables in restaurants and cafés.

TAXES

The national Value Added Tax *(Mehrwertsteuer)* is 19 percent for goods and services and 7 percent for food and books. It is always included in the price.

TIME

German clocks are set to Central European Time, which is Greenwich Mean Time + 1 hour.

WHEN IT IS NOON IN GERMANY, IT IS	
3am	in Los Angeles
6am	in New York
11am	in Dublin
11am	in London
7pm	in Perth
9pm	in Sydney
11pm	in Auckland

In Germany "am" and "pm" are not used but the 24-hour clock is widely applied.

TIPPING

In restaurants, cafés and bars tipping is not compulsory but most people generally add about 10 percent for good service. Don't leave the tip on the table; pay the waiter in person. Taxi drivers typically receive a 5 percent tip. In better hotels, porters and others assisting with your luggage expect 2€ per bag. Room cleaning staff should be tipped about 1€ or 2€ per person per day. Cleaners at public toilets or in some bars restaurants get about 0.50€.

CONVERSION TABLES

Weights and Measures

1 kilogram (kg)	**2.2 pounds (lb)**	**2.2 pounds**	*To convert*
6.35 kilograms	14 pounds	1 stone (st)	*kilograms*
0.45 kilograms	16 ounces (oz)	16 ounces	*to pounds,*
1 metric ton (tn)	**1.1 tons**	**1.1 tons**	*multiply by 2.2*
1 litre (l)	**2.11 pints (pt)**	**1.76 pints**	*To convert litres*
3.79 litres	1 gallon (gal)	0.83 gallon	*to gallons, multiply*
4.55 litres	1.20 gallon	1 gallon	*by 0.26 (US)*
			or 0.22 (UK)
1 hectare (ha)	**2.47 acres**	**2.47 acres**	*To convert*
1 sq kilometre	**0.38 sq. miles**	**0.38 sq. miles**	*hectares to*
(km²)	**(sq mi)**		*acres, multiply*
			by 2.4
1 centimetre (cm)	**0.39 inches (in)**	**0.39 inches**	*To convert metres*
1 metre (m)	**3.28 feet (ft) or 39.37 inches**		*to feet, multiply*
	or 1.09 yards (yd)		*by 3.28; for*
			kilometres to miles,
1 kilometre (km)	**0.62 miles (mi)**	**0.62 miles**	*multiply by 0.6*

Clothing

Women					Men			
	35	4	2½			40	7½	7
	36	5	3½			41	8½	8
	37	6	4½			42	9½	9
Shoes	38	7	5½		Shoes	43	10½	10
	39	8	6½			44	11½	11
	40	9	7½			45	12½	12
	41	10	8½			46	13½	13
	36	6	8			46	36	36
	38	8	10			48	38	38
Dresses	40	10	12		Suits	50	40	40
& suits	42	12	14			52	42	42
	44	14	16			54	44	44
	46	16	18			56	46	48
	36	6	30			37	14½	14½
	38	8	32			38	15	15
Blouses &	40	10	34		Shirts	39	15½	15½
sweaters	42	12	36			40	15¾	15¾
	44	14	38			41	16	16
	46	16	40			42	16½	16½

Sizes often vary depending on the designer. These equivalents are given for guidance only.

Speed

KPH	10	30	50	70	80	90	100	110	120	130
MPH	6	19	31	43	50	56	62	68	75	81

Temperature

Celsius (°C)	0°	5°	10°	15°	20°	25°	30°	40°	60°	80°	100°
Fahrenheit (°F)	32°	41°	50°	59°	68°	77°	86°	104°	140°	176°	212°

To convert Celsius into Fahrenheit, multiply °C by 9, divide by 5, and add 32.
To convert Fahrenheit into Celsius, subtract 32 from °F, multiply by 5, and divide by 9.
NB: Conversion factors on this page are approximate.

View from the Mount Belchen, Black Forest
© Erich Spiegelhalter/Schwarzwald Tourismus GmbH

The Country Today

Germany is a highly decentralised federal state whose human, political and administrative facets reflect very individual traits that are rooted in its history. This brief, factual portrait highlights some of the aspects peculiar to the German nation and to life in Germany today.

21C GERMANY

POPULATION

With over 82 million inhabitants, Germany is the most highly populated country in the European Union and the second-most populous in Europe after Russia. It has been in demographic decline for about 25 years and is experiencing an accelerated ageing of the population (the average age – over 44.3 – is the highest in Europe). By 2030 the population is projected to have dropped to 77 million.

About 6.7 million foreigners live in Germany, with the five largest groups being Turks (1.7 million), Italians (530 000), Poles (385 000) , Serbian/Montenegrin (330 000) and Greek (295 000).

German society is highly urbanised. The most densely populated areas are Greater Berlin, the Ruhr region, the Frankfurt-am-Main area, Wiesbaden and Mainz, and another region taking in Mannheim and Ludwigshafen.

LIFESTYLE

Although a thoroughly modern society, many Germans still place a lot of importance on traditions. Having *"Kaffee und Kuchen"* (coffee and cake) on Sunday afternoons is as time-honoured as popping down to a beer garden with friends or screaming your lungs out at football matches. Children and the elderly are well respected, as are dogs and the rights of bicyclists on their dedicated paths. Although the car is a bit of a sacred cow, most Germans use public transport or a bicycle for getting around town. They tend to be culturally curious and regularly patronise museums, theatres, opera, festivals and other such events and institutions. A staggering 70 percent of all Germans older than 14 years are active members of groups, clubs or organisations. Some 36 percent undertake voluntary duties. Even lesser educated or less wealthy individuals tend to be extraordinarily well travelled. German food overall has become lighter and healthier in recent years and many Germans are willing to spend extra for organic products. Recycling is *de rigeur*.

RELIGION

Germany is predominantly a Christian country, although adherence has dwindled considerably in the past two decades. The main denominations are Roman Catholic (25 million members) and Lutheran (26 million). Both churches levy a church tax, which the state collects, to fund social services. Citizens can opt out of paying this tax. There are also about 4 million Muslims, most of them from among the Turkish immigrant population. The Jewish community has been growing steadily since reunification, replenished mostly by emigrants from the former Soviet Union. It now stands at about 106 000 members in more than 100 congregations.

SPORT

Sport is very popular in Germany. There are around 90 000 sports clubs with 27 million members. In a nation that has hosted the FIFA World Cup twice and won it three times, football is predictably the most popular activity, followed by gymnastics and tennis. Germany has produced such legendary sports figures as Max Schmeling, Michael Schumacher, Boris Becker, Franz Beckenbauer, Dirk Novitzki, Katarina Witt and Steffi Graf.

MEDIA

Germany has two public TV channels, the Allgemeiner Deutscher Rundfunk (ARD) and the Zweites Deutsches Fernsehen (ZDF). Both are financed largely through public licensing fees. In addition, there are numerous private TV stations, including some specialising in

Traditions and Festivities

Germany is a thoroughly modern society but one with strong roots in the past. Some time-honoured festivals have been celebrated for decades or even centuries.

Bavarian maypole
© ra-photos/iStockphoto.com

Karneval – Also known as Fasching in Bavaria and Fasnacht in Baden-Württemberg, the pre-Lent season culminates in the week before Ash Wednesday. Street parties and costume parades take over many cities, primarily Düsseldorf, Cologne, Mainz and Munich, as well as the Black Forest villages.

Maifest – Throughout Germany, this end-of-winter celebration on 1 May culminates in dancing and singing around the *Maibaum* (May tree), which is often painted, carved and decorated.

St. Martinstag – This festival, held on 10–11 November, honours a 4C saint known for his humility and generosity with a lantern procession, followed by feasting on stuffed roasted goose.

Nikolaus – On the eve of 5 December, German children put their shoes outside the door, which St. Nick will fill with sweets and toys by dawn – provided they were well-behaved during the year!

Advent – The four weeks before Christmas are celebrated by counting down the days with an advent calendar, hanging up Christmas decorations and lighting an additional candle every Sunday on the four-candle advent wreath.

Christmas – Celebrations start on Christmas Eve with dinner, presents and a church visit. Christmas Day itself is usually spent with close family; the 26th ("second" Christmas Day) visiting friends and more distant family.

Alemannic carnival – Fasnet – in Gengenbach, Black Forest
© Gengenbach Kultur-und Tourismus und Tourismus/Schwarzwald Tourismus

47

The War on Smoking

Change comes slowly in Germany, which in 2008 became one of the last countries in Europe to introduce a smoking ban. Because of the federalised nature of the country it was left to each of the 16 *Länder* (states) to come up with its own regulations, resulting in confusion. Most states agreed that smoking should be *verboten* in schools, hospitals, airports, train stations and government buildings. Lighting up in restaurants is also a no-no, but bars, nightclubs and festival tents are a different story. Laws generally allow establishments to build separate, closed-off smoking areas. However, small pub owners, who did not have sufficient space to create such a room, felt discriminated against and brought their case before Germany's highest court. It ruled in their favour: one-room bars or pubs smaller than 75sq m/800sq ft may decide to permit smoking provided they don't serve food and don't admit anyone under 18. Only easy-going Berlin made use of this ruling. Other states, in particular Bavaria, are going the other way. In 2010, the southern state held a referendum in which 61 percent voted in favour of banning smoking in all pubs, restaurants and beer tents. No exceptions, not even at Oktoberfest!

sports or music. The largest-circulation national newspaper is *Bild*, which is known for its sensationalist, gossipy reporting. Well-respected, nationally-read regional papers include Munich-based *Süddeutsche Zeitung* and the *Frankfurter Allgemeine*. *Der Spiegel* and *Focus* are the most widely read weekly news magazines.

LANGUAGE

The German language has Indo-European origins and is spoken by about 100 million people. Besides "High German" regional dialects are alive and well, especially in Bavaria, Swabia and Hesse. The purest form of German is spoken in the Hannover region in Lower Saxony.

FOOD AND DRINK

See also PLANNING YOUR TRIP, Where to Stay and Eat

Although there is some regional variation, German food is generally rather rich and hearty. Typical dishes pair potatoes with a piece of meat (most likely pork – often sausages) and a cooked vegetable (e.g. sauerkraut or red cabbage). Of late, though, a new generation of chefs has been busy modernising traditional menus by using fresh, locally sourced and seasonal ingredients and thus making dishes lighter and healthier. Thanks to Germany's large immigrant

population, especially in the cities, you are never far from pizza, doner kebabs, Thai or Chinese food.

Each region has its own specialities, but some dishes are served all over the country, including **Schnitzel** (breaded and pan-fried pork cutlet), **Schweinebraten** (roast pork) **Sauerbraten** (vinegar-marinated braised beef) and **Gulasch** (either in the form of soup or as a stew).

BEER AND WINE

Germans are justifiably proud of their national beverage, produced by nearly 1 200 breweries throughout the country. Although no longer required by law, most German brewers still adhere to a purity law *(Reinheitsgebot)* decreed in 1516, whereby nothing but barley, hops

Ph. Gajic/MICHELIN

and plain water may be used in the making of beer (with the addition, today, of yeast).

German vineyards cover 102 000ha/ 252 000 acres, extending from Lake Constance to the Saaletal, and from Trier to Dresden. Growers produce a variety of wines from a wide range of grapes. The most famous German grape is the noble Riesling, which accounts for 22 percent of vineyard area, followed by Müller-Thurgau with 13.5 percent . Wines from the Middle Rhine, Moselle, Saar and Ruwer rivers are aromatic and refreshing, those from the Rheingau delicate and from the Nahe full-bodied and elegant. Also try the potent, dry wines of Franconia and the varied wines of Baden and Württemberg.

Among the **red wines**, choice examples come from Rheinhessen and Württemberg. The Palatinate and the Ahr are known for their well-balanced reds, especially the Spätburgunder, which accounts for 11.5 percent of total output, making it the third-most popular grape varietal in Germany.

ECONOMY

After the Second World War, the economy of West Germany made a spectacular recovery, generally referred to as an **"economic miracle"** *(Wirtschaftswunder)*. The system instituted was the so-called **"social market economy"**, which combined private enterprise with government regulation with the multi-pronged goal of keeping inflation and unemployment in check, setting standards for working conditions, and providing for social welfare. The **reunification** of the two Germanies in 1990 presented an enormous challenge.

The high cost of the economic integration of the former German Democratic Republic severely impacted on the competitiveness of the Federal Republic. To this day, the modernisation of the new *Länder* (states) and social support for employees continues to put a great strain on the federal budget with annual transfers from west to east amounting to about 9.5€ billion in 2009.

Today, Germany has the fifth-largest economy in the world based on GDP, after the US, China, Japan and India. Along with the rest of the world, the country was hard hit by the worldwide economic downturn of 2008. Government measures taken to rev up the economic engine included multi-billion Euro rescue packages for banks, stimulus packages for business and industry and tax cuts.

Although these actions significantly increased the country's budget deficit, they may have had their intended result: in mid-2010 Germany posted a 2.2 percent economic growth rate for the second quarter of the year, its fastest quarterly growth since reunification.

INDUSTRY

Industry remains the cornerstone of Germany's economic strength, representing around one third of Gross Domestic Product (GDP). About 30 major corporations with a global presence (Thyssen-Krupp, Bayer, Hoechst, Siemens, Bosch, BMW, Volkswagen, etc.) are listed on the German share index (DAX).

The true backbone of the economy, though, are the tens of thousands of small and mid-size companies (up to 500 employees) which collectively provide over 25 million jobs. Key industries are vehicles, mechanical engineering, electrical engineering and chemicals. About 29 million people work in the service sector, especially banking and insurance.

TRADE

"Made in Germany" is still considered a seal of quality and the country remains the world's largest exporter (mostly cars, machinery, metals). The most important trading partners are France, the Netherlands, the USA and Great Britain. In 2009, goods and services worth 82€ billion were exported to France, 54€ billion to the Netherlands and the USA, 53€ billion to Great Britain.

Of late, demand has been especially great for solar-powered products, where Germany has shown to be especially innovative. In fact, the country is the

Solar plant in Eberswalde-Finow, Brandenburg

© Patrick Pleul/Picture Alliance/Photoshot

largest producer of wind turbines and solar power technology.

GOVERNMENT AND ADMINISTRATION

Since 1949, two parties – The centre-right Christian Democratic Union (CDU) with its Bavarian sister party (CSU) and the centre-left Social Democratic Party (SPD) – have dominated political life in the Federal Republic. There are also three minor parties: the liberal Free Democratic Party (FDP); The Left, which is essentially the successor party of the defunct East German Socialist Unity Party, and the environmentalist Alliance '90/The Greens. The federal government usually consists of a coalition between one of the big political parties and one of the smaller ones.

In 1949, the year West Germany was founded, the CDU/CSU joined with the FDP to elect **Adenauer** as chancellor. The party returned to power under the aegis of **Helmut Kohl**, who was elected Chancellor four times (1983, 1987, 1991 and 1994). The SPD came to power for the first time in 1969 led by **Willy Brandt**. In 1974 it allied with the FDP under **Helmut Schmidt**. The SPD also claimed victory in the 1998 elections under the leadership of **Gerhard Schröder** who governed in a coalition with the Alliance '90/The Greens. This marked the first time the environmental party achieved power on national level. The government introduced a variety of social and economic reforms intended to adapt Germany's social market economy to the demands of globalisation. Although the opposition parties made some gains, the Schröder-led coalition government was re-elected in 2002.

RECENT DEVELOPMENTS

Continued frustration with high unemployment, high taxes and slow economic growth led to an impatience with the SPD/Green coalition and early federal elections in September 2005. When neither SPD and CDU/CSU emerged as a clear winner, the two formed a grand coalition with **Angela Merkel** as Chancellor. Despite hopes that the coalition members would be able to tackle Germany's problems jointly, the liaison ultimately led to stagnation. During the 2009 the CDU/CSU emerged as a strongest party and formed a coalition with the FDP, with Angela Merkel staying on as chancellor and FDP party chief Guido Westerwelle becoming vice-chancellor and foreign minister.

A FEDERAL STATE

Germany has a federated governmental structure whose 16 *Länder*, or states, enjoy considerable powers. The **Basic Law** established in 1949 guarantees individual liberties and defines the institutions of a democratic republic. The Federal Parliament is composed of two chambers: the **Bundestag**, a national assembly of approximately 600

The Länder Regions

The Federal Republic comprises 16 *Länder* (states), 11 of which formed the old West Germany and five of which were added in 1990, reconstituted from the 15 districts of the former East German Democratic Republic. Each state organises its constitution within the terms of the Basic Law. The *Länder* have a legislative assembly (**Landtag**) elected by universal suffrage and an executive body consisting of a council of ministers with a President (**Ministerpräsident**). Areas involving the sovereignty of the state, such as foreign affairs, defence or monetary policy, fall under the responsibility of the Federal Government, but the *Länder* possess broad powers; they have exclusive jurisdiction over education and culture, and are actively involved in the areas of justice and the economy.

members elected by universal suffrage, has legislative powers and chooses the chancellor; and the **Bundesrat**, a federal council with members drawn from the *Länder* governments, which also has some legislative powers, particularly concerning the *Länder*.

The **chancellor** holds executive power and is elected by the Bundestag, to whom he/she is accountable. The chancellor sets the broad lines of government policy, introduces laws (adopted by the Bundestag) and is responsible for their implementation. The role of the federal president (**Bundespräsident**) is essentially representative. He/she concludes foreign treaties, and appoints or removes judges and federal ministers as suggested by the chancellor.

The supreme judicial authority rests with the **Constitutional Court** (Verfassungsgericht), which ensures compliance with the Basic Law, guards constitutional principles and acts as arbitrator in disputes between the Federal Government and the *Länder*.

History

Long divided into a number of autonomous states, Germany was slow to achieve unity. This nation of great diversity, which was for a long time marked by feudalism and whose regions still hold considerable powers, is today one of the main spearheads of European unity.

TIMELINE
GERMANS AND ROMANS

The earliest evidence of human life on German territory today is the lower jawbone dating back over 500 000 years of the so-called *Homo heidelbergensis*, which was discovered near Heidelberg in 1907. The Middle Paleolithic Age (200 000–40 000 BC) is considered the age of Neanderthal man (🔾 *see DÜSSELDORF: Excursions*). The first "modern people", the *Homo sapiens*, who survived on fishing, hunting and gathering, lived during the Late Paleolithic, an epoch of the Stone Age within the last Ice Age. During the Neolithic Era, people began to settle in village-like communities, where they lived for a while, grew plants and began raising animals.

The last prehistoric period, the Iron Age, began around 1 000 BC, following

La Tène Culture

The name for this cultural epoch supported by Celtic tribes (5C–1C BC) originated at an excavation site on Switzerland's Neuenburg Lake. Over 2 500 objects were found, including grave furnishings and treasures. The La Tène culture was located primarily in southwestern Germany, along the northern edge of the Alps and in the Main-Moselle area. Fortifications expanded into settlements, the first north of the Alps. The advance of Germanic tribes and the expansion of the Roman Empire brought the La Tène culture to an end.

the Bronze Age, thus named because that material was widely used to make implements, weapons and jewellery. The Iron Age is divided up into the La Tène culture and the Hallstatt culture. Economic and political power started becoming more concentrated; evidence from graves suggests a stratified social system.

In the first millennium BC, Germanic tribes began resettling towards Central Europe. The occurrence and extent of this movement was under the auspices of numerous population groups of various origins and cultural levels living in the area between the northern German flatlands and the central mountain ranges. The first written reference to "Germania" is in the works of the Roman author Poseidonius (1C BC). Julius Caesar, too, used this term in his *De Bello Gallico* to describe the non-Gallic regions north of the Alps.

The wars conducted by the Kimbers and the Teutons against the Romans around 100 BC were the first military conflicts between German tribes and the Roman civilisation. The expansion of the western German tribes was stopped by Caesar's conquest of Gaul (58–55 BC). The aims of foreign policy until Emperor Augustus also covered the inclusion of Germania into the Roman Empire all the way to the Elbe, an objective that was never met.

During the 1C AD, the **Limes** was built: A 550km/341.7mi fortified line that sealed the Roman sphere of influence from the Rhine to the Danube. Skirmishes did break out every now and then, but there were also alliances, trade and cultural exchanges. New towns arose where Roman camps stood and at river crossings (e.g. Cologne, Koblenz, Regensburg).

In the 2C–3C AD, large tribes like the Franks, the Saxons and the Alemanni joined forces. The military kingdoms of the age of mass migration gave way to early medieval states.

AD 9 Three Roman legions under General Varus are annihilated by Germanic troops under prince **Arminius**, resulting

Charlemagne crowned as Emperor on Christmas Day AD 800, in Chroniques de France ou de Saint Denis *(14C)*

©2008 Hip/Scala, Florence

in Roman relinquishment of bastions on the Rhine.

314 One year after announcing the Edict of Tolerance, Emperor Constantine establishes the first German bishopric, in Trier.

375 Beginning of the *Völkerwanderung*, the "movement of the peoples": the Huns drive the Goths (eastern Germans) to the west. The former *Imperium Romanum* breaks into partial empires.

800 End of the West Roman Empire brought about by German general Odoaker, who is in turn murdered by the Ostrogoth Theodorich.

THE FRANKISH EMPIRE

The tribal union of the Franks expanded slowly south. Their king, Clovis I, eliminated the remains of the West Roman Empire and adopted Christianity. In the 7C, the Merovingians lost their hegemony to the Carolingians, formerly the highest royal officials under the Merovingians. Since the 8C, the general term *thiutisk* developed from a derivation of the word for "tribe" to describe the peoples speaking Germanic languages. There was still no supra-regional language spoken to the east of the Rhine, the area of the Franks, until the 11C. In the 10C, the term *Regnum Teutonicorum* appeared for the first time in relation to the Eastern Frankish tribes. During the 11C and 12C it slowly established itself as a term.

Charlemagne's Empire

After being crowned Emperor in St. Peter's Basilica in Rome in 800, Charlemagne followed the lead of the Roman emperors. His empire stretched from Spain to the Elbe, from Rome to the English Channel. Charlemagne's reign introduced the "Carolingian Renaissance" as well as a new administrative structure. The emperor instituted a county constitution, disposing of independent duchies and tribal states. Each administrative district was governed by an officer chosen from the Frankish aristocracy, thus ensuring the coherence of the empire. Vulnerable borders were secured by border marches under authorised margraves. And emissaries with royal powers watched over the imperial administration. The king constantly travelled his empire, visiting the *Pfalzen*, which grew into major economic and cultural centres, and overnighting in Imperial abbeys.

751   Pope Zacharias agrees to the deposition of the last of the Merovingian kings, Childeric III, in favour of the palatine Pippin. Three years later the Pope places Rome under the protection of the Frankish kings.

768   Charlemagne becomes ruler. He conquers, among others, the Lombards, divides up Bavaria and defeats the Saxons after a long war.

800   Coronation of Charlemagne in Rome. The emperor legally assumes sovereignty over the former empire.

843   The Treaty of Verdun divides the Carolingian Empire among Charlemagne's grandchildren. The East Frankish Kingdom is given to Ludwig the German. The final division, determined by the treaties of Mersen (870) and Verdun/Ribemont (879–80), would evolve into Germany and France.

911   The East Franks elect the Frankish duke Konrad to become their king, separating themselves from the West Franks.

THE HOLY ROMAN EMPIRE

The Holy Roman Empire consisted of an elective monarchy in which the king was crowned emperor by the pope. From the 11C onwards, the emperor could rely on being king of not only Germany and Italy, but also of Burgundy. An especially "German" Imperial concept gave way to a Roman-universal idea of an emperor, a fact underscored in 1157 by the additional title *sacrum Imperium*.

During the time of the Staufer dynasty, in the mid-13C, the claim to rule in Italy came to an end. In the 15C, the term "Holy Roman Empire of the German Nation" was finally established, implying the politically active community of the German Imperial estates, who acted as a counterweight to the emperor.

Ruling this empire, which during the High Middle Ages stretched from Sicily to the Baltic, was difficult without central administration and technical, financial and military wherewithal. By granting land and privileges (e.g. customs rights), administrative responsibility, security and imperial expansion were domains of the aristocracy.

Beginning in the second half of the 11C, the **Investiture Controversy** pitted the Pope against the Emperor on the issue of the right to invest bishops. This weakened the empire and shook up Christianity. The dispute ended with the Concordat of Worms (1122), declaring that ecclesiastical dignitaries had to be separated from worldly goods. The position of the bishops became similar to that of the princes, since they became vassals of the empire.

These vassals gradually accumulated more power owing to the heredity laws of the fiefs and regalia. In the long term this weakened the empire, paving the way for the rise of numerous territorial states. The regional princely territorial states replaced the personal union state.

962   In Rome, Otto the Great, having been crowned king in 936, is crowned emperor by the Pope. The Ottonian dynasty rules until the death of Henry II in 1024, and is followed by that of the Salians (Franks).

1073   Pope Gregory VII elected. The reformer disputes the role of secular power in the church. The crux of the conflict was the penitent journey to Canossa (1077) by King Heinrich IV to receive absolution from the Pope, who had excommunicated him.

1152–90   Rule of the Staufer emperor Frederick I Barbarossa, who strengthens Imperial power *(restauratio Imperii)* and captures the duchies of Bavaria and Saxony from the Guelph duke Henry the Lion (*see BRAUNSCHWEIG*). He also strives to limit papal power.

1212–50   Frederick II stays in southern Italy and Sicily for much of his reign, holding little interest in the area north of the

Alps. Two Imperial edicts (1220–31) confirm the power over the territories of the secular and religious princes.

1254–73 The years between the death of Konrad IV and the election of Rudolf of Habsburg are known as the **Interregnum**. It is a time of lawlessness under "foreign" kings and anti-kings, finally eliminating the empire's power in the High Middle Ages.

THE LATE MIDDLE AGES

After the Interregnum, the power of the Habsburgs grew. Building up and consolidating family power by the 15C though the Luxembourg, Nassau and Wittelsbach families occasionally won the throne. The emperors tried to have a son elected king during their lifetime in order to maintain the ranking of their own dynasties. But during the Renaissance, the Imperial crown surrendered its holiness.

In the Late Middle Ages, the *Hoftage*, or Imperial meetings, became the **Reichstag**, a meeting of 350 secular and religious Imperial estates, foreshadowing a sharp dualism between the emperor and his estates. At the Reichstag in Worms (1495), fundamental reforms created the preconditions for transforming the Reich into a unified legal and pacified territory. The proclamation of the *Ewiger Landfrieden* (eternal peace in the land) prohibited personal feuds, favouring a new legal basis. A permanent Imperial Chamber Court ensured com-

Engraved frontspiece to Luther's Bible (1648)

©2005 Hip/Scala, Florence

pliance. After a long debate, financial reform was pushed through raising the *Common Penny*, a combination of wealth tax, income tax and poll tax. Later *Reichstage* divided up the empire into administrative units – the *Reichskreise*, or Imperial districts. In 1663, the Permanent Reichstag was set up in Regensburg.

Inspired by the Humanists, the concept of a "German nation" began to arise politically as well as culturally, legitimised by the rediscovery of literary monuments such as "Germania" by Tacitus. Until around 1500, Europeans spoke of the *Deutsche Lande* (German lands); after 1500 the term "Deutschland" in the singular became common.

The Golden Bull

Beginning in the 10C, the number of electors for the king began to decline. At the same time the election process became more regulated and formalised. In 1356, the Golden Bull promulgated an Imperial law regulating royal election, defining an institutional framework and limiting the power of the empire. From now on, the king would be elected by three religious electors (the archbishops of Mainz, Cologne and Trier) and four secular ones (the king of Bohemia, the margrave of Brandenburg, the duke of Saxony and the Palatine of the Rhine) and then crowned emperor. The election was set in Frankfurt/Main, and the coronation in Aachen; papal confirmation was no longer necessary. This law, announced by the Luxembourg emperor **Charles IV**, is considered the empire's first constitution and a basis for a federal system of state.

The Hanseatic League

The Hanseatic League existed between the 12C and the 17C. Its basic structure was established by about 1300. Thirty larger and numerous smaller cities joined to safeguard their shipping and trade interests. This union went through its Golden Age in the 14C: over 100 cities, under Lübeck's leadership, formed the most significant economic force in northern Germany. After the Thirty Years' War, the Hanseatic tradition only continued in Hamburg, Lübeck and Bremen.

1273 After a warning from the Pope, electors choose as king Count Rudolf of Habsburg (dynastic power in the Breisgau, Alsace and Aargau).

1346–78 Charles IV of Luxembourg emerges as the most important ruler of the Late Middle Ages.

1386 Founding of the University of Heidelberg, Germany's first.

1414–18 Council of Constance; the largest church meeting of the Middle Ages to date.

1438 After the death of the last Luxembourg emperor, the electors choose the Habsburg duke Albrecht V to become King Albrecht II.

c. 1450 Invention of movable type printing by Johann Gutenberg from Mainz; flourishing and spread of Humanism.

1452 During a military campaign by Frederick III, the last imperial coronation takes place in Rome.

1493 Maximilian I becomes king. As of 1508 he is the "elected Roman Emperor". His successors adopt the Imperial title immediately after the royal coronation in Aachen, avoiding the difficult and dangerous journey to Rome.

1519–56 Emperor Charles V, Maximilian's grandchild, gathers more power during his term than any ruler since the Carolingians.

THE REFORMATION AND THE THIRTY YEARS' WAR

In 1503, **Martin Luther** (1483–1546) entered the Augustinian monastery of Erfurt. A dedicated cleric, he was tormented by the problem of salvation. Appointed Professor of Theology in Wittenberg (1512–17), he found in the Holy Scriptures his answer: "We cannot earn forgiveness for our sins through our deeds, only God's mercy justifies us in our faith in it." Man's salvation, Luther argued, lies entirely within the grace of God. This concept led him to attack the Church's dealing in indulgences. On 31 October 1517, he nailed to the doors of Wittenberg Church his "95 Theses" condemning such practices and reminding the faithful of the importance of Christ's sacrifice and the Grace of God. Luther disagreed with Catholicism's prescribed acts of atonement (confession, monetary contributions) as the only way to achieve salvation. He condemned the priest's role as "mediator" between man and God, advocating instead the "direct line" approach: man and God alone.

Luther was denounced in the court of Rome, refused to recant, and in 1520 burned the Papal Bull, threatening him with excommunication. Subsequently he attacked the institutions of the Church. He objected to the primacy of the clergy in spiritual matters, arguing the universal priesthood of Christians conferred by baptism.

Refusing again to recant before the Diet of Worms (1521), where he had been summoned by Charles V, Luther was placed under a ban of the Empire and his works were condemned.

The patronage of Frederick the Wise, Duke of Saxony, enabled the reformer to seek refuge in Wartburg Castle where he translated the Bible from Latin into "everyday" German, making God's Word available to the German-speaking layperson. Indeed, his translation of the Bible is considered the first literary work in modern German. Luther's Bible and 95 Theses were a direct cause

Prussian Reforms: The Revolution from Above

The reforms already prepared by the General Land Law of 1794 were initially set in motion by Baron von Stein and, after his dismissal, by Baron von Hardenberg. The two men went about installing new structures for government and society virtually by decree and with almost revolutionary energy. Abolition of serfdom by the Edict of 1807 was of particular importance, as was the lifting of guild compulsion and the introduction of a free crafts market. Educational reforms followed, resulting in the founding of the university in Berlin by Wilhelm von Humboldt (1810) and military reform. Other reforms included the emancipation of Jews and the modernisation of the administration.

of the ensuing split of the Protestants from Roman Catholicism.

The Council of Trent (1545–63) resulted in the renewal of Catholicism and the Counter Reformation, which was resolutely supported by the emperor. The internal struggles of the Protestants and the feud between Rudolf II and his brother Matthias ended the Peace of Augsburg. The Protestant Union led by the Electorate of the Palatinate now faced the Catholic League with the Duchy of Bavaria at its head. The Bohemian Rebellion of 1618 led to the outbreak of the Thirty Years' War, which began as a religious conflict and soon engulfed all of Europe.

The war, which was almost exclusively fought on German territory, devastated the land, caused general havoc, left cities in rubble and ruined economic life in the countryside. By the end of the war, only individual territorial states showed some gain in authority; the empire's significance dwindled.

1530 Invited by Charles V to Augsburg, theologians of the opposing faiths fail to agree. Luther's assistant, Melanchthon, draws up the "Confession of Augsburg", the charter of Protestantism.

1555 The Peace of Augsburg establishes a compromise, and Lutheran Protestantism is recognised as equal to Catholicism. The empire loses its sovereignty over religious matters to the territories.

1618 The Bohemian estates refuse to recognize Archduke Ferdinand, the successor of Emperor Matthias, as the Bohemian king. Instead, they elect the Protestant Elector Frederick V from the Palatinate to be their ruler. After the Defenestration of Prague in May (when the Bohemian king's representatives were thrown out of a window by nobles protesting reduced privileges), the situation intensifies and leads to the Thirty Years' War.

1618–23 The first phase of the war (Bohemian-Palatinate War) is decided by the defeat of Frederick V at the battle of Weißer Berg in 1620 against an army commanded by Tilly.

1625–29 Phase two (the Danish-Dutch War) ends with Denmark's Protestant soldiers defeated by Imperial troops under Wallenstein.

1630–35 Sweden enters the war on the Protestant side (Swedish War). King Gustav Adolph II dies in battle near Lützen.

1635–48 France, under the leadership of Richelieu, participates in the alliance with Bernhard von Weimar (French-Swedish War).

1648 Peace of Westphalia: peace treaty in Münster and Osnabrück after five years of negotiations (see MÜNSTER).

1688–97 Palatinate War of Succession. Louis XIV lays claim to the left bank of the Rhine; French troops under Louvois devastate the Palatinate.

The Deutscher Bund

The Deutscher Bund, or German Confederation, a loose federation with little authority, was founded in 1815. The confederation included 39 politically autonomous states; four free cities; the kings of Holland, Denmark and the Low Countries; and portions of Prussia and Austria. The Bundestag (Parliament) included 11 governmentally-appointed representatives who met in Frankfurt and were led by Austria. Prince Metternich, who came from the Rhineland, played a decisive role in this union after he became Austrian chancellor. In collaboration with Prussia, he mercilessly crushed the libertarian and national movements.

The restoration policies of the Bundestag gave rise to a period of extreme calm (Biedermeier period).

THE RISE OF PRUSSIA

In 1415, Burgrave Frederick of Hohenzollern was granted the Electorate of Brandenburg. The Duchy of Prussia, 203 years later, also came under the authority of his dynasty. Frederick William (1640–1688), the Great Elector, turned the small country into the strongest, best-governed northern German state thanks to successful power policies, deprivation of the estates' power, a centralised administration and the creation of a standing army. He also expanded the country, adding eastern Pomerania, which he received in the Peace of Westphalia: two peace treaties which ended the Thirty Years' War. After the revocation of the Edict of Nantes in France, thousands of Huguenots fled to Brandenburg and built up the economic basis of Berlin.

His grandson, King Frederick William I continued his efforts by laying the foundations of a Prussian military and official state. Fulfilment of one's duty, industriousness, economy and strict discipline were aspects inspired by the

"Soldier King". His son, **Frederick the Great** (1740–1786), took the throne in a country with an exemplary administration, and within a few years it became the second Imperial power. The Silesian War and the Seven Years' War won him Silesia, and the division of Poland extended his power eastwards.

This connoisseur of music and literature, the friend and correspondent of Voltaire, was considered an "enlightened ruler" and had a high reputation among European scholars. The rule of "Old Fritz" left Prussia with a well organised administration and a close relationship between the king and the nobles, all cornerstones of Prussian power.

1701 Elector Frederick III is crowned Frederick I King of Prussia in Königsberg.

1740–48 War of Austrian Succession/ Silesian Wars: the legality of the Pragmatic Sanction (1713) pronounced by Charles VI is disputed. The war is triggered by Frederick II's troops marching into Silesia.

1756–63 Prussia joins forces with England against the Emperor during the Seven Years' War. By the end of the war, Prussia is the fifth European power; the system of power will guide Europe until World War I.

THE WAY TO A GERMAN NATIONAL STATE

Since 1792, war had raged between France and the other powers of Europe. The Peace of Lunéville, signed in 1801, resulted in the loss of German territories on the left bank of the Rhine. The Decision of the Deputation of German Estates (1803) destroyed the political and legal foundations of the old Empire. Bavaria, Prussia, Baden and Württemberg benefited, gaining territory, while the latter two received Elector ranking. Sixteen of the southern and western German states left the Imperial Union and founded the Confederation of the Rhine in 1806 in Paris under the protection of France. At the **Congress of Vienna** (1814–15) leaders discussed the geographical reorganisation, including restoration of the political status quo of 1792, legitimisation of the *Ancien Régime*, and solidarity among the princes in combating revolutionary ideas and movements.

Since the 18C, literature, philosophy, art and music had melded, giving rise to a single German culture that preceded patriotism. The ideals of the French Revolution, the end of the Holy Roman Empire, the experience of French occupation and other reforms led to the growth of a 19C movement towards a free, unified German national state. One important stage on the way to unity was an economic one: the foundation of the German *Zollverein* (Customs Union) at the behest of Prussia.

On 31 March 1848, a pre-Parliament met in Frankfurt and held a National Convention, which opened on 18 May in the Paulskirche in Frankfurt. The aim was to pass a liberal constitution and consideration of the future German state. On the table were the Greater German Solution, with the Habsburg empire under Austrian leadership; and the Smaller German Solution, i.e. without Austria, but with a Hohenzollern emperor at the

top. The latter was finally voted in. However, Prussian King Frederick William IV refused the Imperial crown brought to him by a delegate from the Paulskirche Parliament.

Otto von Bismarck, appointed Minister-President of Prussia in 1862, needed only eight years to bring about unification under Prussian rule. With the loyalty of an elite bourgeoisie created by the advances of industry and science, and aided by the neutrality of Napoleon III, he pursued a policy of war aggres-

Otto von Bismarck

©2008 Hip/Scala, Florence

sively. After joining forces with Austria in defeating Denmark in 1864, Prussia declared war on her German ally and defeated the Imperial troops at the battle of Sadowa, thus ending Austrian-Prussian dualism for good.

A year later, Bismarck created the North German Alliance, including all German states north of the River Main; Hannover, Hessen and Schleswig-Holstein already belonged to Prussia. The Franco-Prussian War of 1870–71 completed the task of unification.

1806 Napoleon marches into Berlin. Emperor Francis II of Austria surrenders the Imperial Crown ending the Holy Roman Empire going back to Charlemagne.

1813 Prussia commands the Coalition in the Wars of Liberation against Napoleon, who is defeated in the Battle of Nations at Leipzig.

1814–15 Congress of Vienna establishes the German Confederation; Holy Alliance between Russia, Prussia and Austria.

1819 The Decisions of Karlsbad include press censorship, prohibitions of fraternities and monitoring of universities.

1833–34 Founding of the German Customs Union *(Zollverein)*, an economic unification of most German states – except Austria – led by Prussia.

1835 First German railway line opens between Nuremberg and Fürth.

1848 Unrest in France in February spreads to Mannheim and then, in March, to all German states. But the "March Revolution" quickly turns into a bourgeois reform movement.

THE GERMAN EMPIRE (1871–1918)

The immediate cause of the Franco-Prussian War of 1870–71 was the claim by the House of Hohenzollern (Leopold von Hohenzollern-Sigmaringen) to the Spanish throne. Bismarck succeeded in kindling national pride on both sides of the border. France then declared war on Prussia.

The southern states united with the states of the North German Union led by Prussia. The German princes all stood against France as they had signed secret alliances with Prussia. After the victory of Sedan (2 September), the southern states opened negotiations with Prussia on the issue of German unification. The first years following the founding of the German Reich in 1871 were marked by an exceptional economic boom, the **Gründerzeit**, financed in part by the receipt of 5 billion francs in French war reparations. The advantages of the larger boundary-free economic area and efforts to standardise coins, measures and weights combined to create rapid growth in the financial, industrial, construction and traffic sectors.

1871 On 18 January, William I is crowned German Emperor in the Mirror Room of Versailles. Imperial Germany, enlarged by the acquisition of Alsace-Lorraine, remains in theory a federation, but is in fact under Prussian domination. Germany is transformed from an agricultural to an industrial economy.

1888 William II succeeds his father Frederick III's brief reign.

1890 After numerous altercations, the Emperor forces Bismarck's resignation. The Emperor's unabashed expansionary policies and dangerous foreign policy provokes the enmity of England, Russia and France.

WORLD WAR I AND THE WEIMAR REPUBLIC

The assassination of the Austrian Archduke Franz Ferdinand and his wife at Sarajevo on 28 June 1914 unleashed an intense international reaction. Austria-Hungary's declaration of war against Serbia mobilised the great powers of Europe. Germany launched into wars on two fronts: German troops moved into France, halting only once they reached the River Marne; in the east, German troops invaded large sections of Russian territory.

1914 Germany declares war on France and Russia on 3 August.

1917 The armistice agreed with Russia is shattered by revolution. The USA enters the war after Germany declares indiscriminate submarine warfare.

1918 On 28–29 October, the sailors of the German naval fleet at Wilhelmshaven raise up in mutiny. Revolution erupts in Germany, with workers' and soldiers' councils springing up throughout the land. The revolution is suppressed by the provisional government under Friedrich Ebert with the support of military supreme command. On 9 November, William II abdicates and Philipp Scheidemann proclaims the German Republic in Berlin. Two days later, Matthias Erzberger signs the armistice at Compiègne.

After the November revolution, which dwindled in early 1919 due to the unrest caused by the Spartacists, the model of a liberal democratic state with a strong president was established. On 11 August 1919, Germany adopted a Republican Constitution in Weimar, where the National Convention was meeting. This "republic without republicans" shouldered the burden of the Treaty of Versailles, which took effect in 1920: acceptance of responsibility for the war, diminution of national territory (including important agricultural and industrial areas), loss of colonies, demilitarisation and high reparations.

The only truly republican parties accepting the constitution, the SPD (Social Democrats), the Centre Party and the DDP (German Democratic Party) had a parliamentary majority after 1920. The Weimar Republic had 16 government changes, an average of one every eight-and-a-half months. Galloping inflation erupted, brought about by economic crisis, difficulties in relaunching the industrial sector and by high government debt: the bourgeoisie was ruined, and all financial assets except real estate were worthless.

Germany experienced an economic upswing and relative tranquillity from 1924 to 1929 in spite of major economic burdens and high unemployment. The Dawes Plan can be credited with these successes; it managed German reparations, ended the French occupation of the Ruhr and committed to capital investment. Germany was even accepted into the League of Nations (1926) during the incumbency of Chancellor and Foreign Minister Gustav Stresemann. A year earlier in Locarno, Germany and France signed a pact pledging not to use violent means to revise borders – a corresponding agreement could not be signed for the eastern borders.

However, the world economic crisis hit the Weimar Republic in 1929. High foreign debt, sharp export declines, inflation and dramatic unemployment all led to the rise of radical political parties, especially the German National Socialist Worker's Party, after 1930. They presented a theory that solving social problems would require a people's community, or *Volksgemeinschaft*, based on race.

Nazi storm-troops and Communist groups increasingly fought in the street. Social elites and the business community saw in **Adolf Hitler** a bulwark against Communism: on 30 January 1933, Hitler was named Chancellor of the Reich by President Von Hindenburg; it was the end of the Weimar Republic.

1919 The National Convention meets in Weimar; Friedrich Ebert (SPD) is named its first president (11 February); Versailles Peace Treaty is signed (28 June).

1923 Occupation of the Ruhr region on 11 January by France, because of Germany's failure to make reparation payments. The NSDAP (the National Socialist German Workers' Party) attempts a coup in Munich on 8–9 November led by Adolf Hitler, who had joined the party in 1919. The coup is foiled, Hitler is jailed but released in 1924.

1925 After the death of Friedrich Ebert, former Field Marshall General Paul von Hindenburg is elected President of the Republic.

1930 An electoral defeat in the Reichstag (Parliament) ushers in several presidial cabinets (Brüning, Von Papen, Von Schleicher), i.e. governments without parliamentary majorities.

1932 At the Reichstag elections in July, the NSDAP assumes leadership with almost 38 percent of the votes. Together with the Communists, the Nazis have an absolute majority, which lets the radical parties block all other parliamentary minorities.

THE NAZI DICTATORSHIP AND WORLD WAR II

No sooner had the NSDAP taken power under Hitler than it began to organise a totalitarian dictatorship and eliminate all democratic rules. In a climate of propaganda, intimidation and terror on the part of the SA, SS and Gestapo, all parties, associations and social organisations were liquidated or dissolved, with the exception of the churches. The NSDAP was declared the sole legal party. Opponents were thrown into concentration camps and murdered. Their power and societal control allowed the party to penetrate every level of state government. Competing authorities and rivalries quietly co-existed, but art and literature were subjected to censorship, forcing numerous artists into exile.

The Nuremberg Laws promulgated at the Reich party rally (September 1935) codified Jewish persecution on racist grounds; prohibitions, loss of civil rights and mass arrests were the instruments of the anti-Semitic ideology. As early as 1 April 1933, the NSDAP had ordered a "boycott of the Jews", initiating the gradual exclusion of Germany's 500 000 Jews from public life. On the night of 9–10 November 1938, the Nazis organised a pogrom *(Reichskristallnacht)* during which synagogues, Jewish homes and shops were damaged or destroyed. The improved worldwide economic situation helped reduce unemployment as did a program of public works (autobahns, drainage schemes), a policy of re-armament and the recruitment of youth into para-governmental organisations. The National Socialist Reich stood at the zenith of its power: materially speaking and otherwise, many Germans had profited up until that point.

The assault on Poland on 1 September 1939, launched **World War II**. German preparations for an annihilation war had been underway since 1936 in the hopes of eliminating other peoples and creating a European area dominated by Aryan Eurasians. But the war reached German civilians as soon as the British and the Americans began dropping explosive and incendiary bombs on war-related and residential targets. By the end of the war, Germany lay in ruins, the bulk of the inhabitants suffered from under-nourishment and millions had been driven out of the eastern regions. With the liberation of the concentration camps, the world discovered with what cruelty and meticulousness the Nazis had carried out their policy of genocide against the Jews.

GERMANY FROM POSTWAR 1945 TO THE PRESENT

1945 Germany and Berlin are divided into four zones of occupation. According to the agreement, American and British forces pull out of Saxony, Thuringia and Mecklenburg and redeploy in the western sector of Berlin. At the Potsdam Conference (*see POTSDAM*) the victorious powers decide to demilitarise and democratise Germany and administer it jointly.

1946 Amalgamation of the British and American zones.

1948 End of the Four-Power administration of Germany after the Soviet delegate leaves

Dresden in ruins, 1945
©UPPA/Photoshot

the Allied Control Council (20 March). Soviet blockade of the western sectors of Berlin, the city is supplied by the airlift.

1949 Creation (23 May) of the Federal Republic in the three western zones. The Soviet zone becomes (7 October) the German Democratic Republic. Under Konrad Adenauer, chancellor until 1963, and Ludwig Erhard, minister of economic affairs, the Federal Republic enjoys a spectacular economic rebirth and re-establishes normal international relations.

1952 Soviet leadership offers to create a single, neutral, democratic Germany, a reunification initiative which fails.

1961 Construction of the "Berlin Wall" begins (12–13 August).

1972 Signature of a treaty between the two Germanies (East and West), a milestone in Chancellor Willy Brandt's policy of openness towards the East *(Ostpolitik)*.

Willy Brandt
©UPPA/Photoshot

Germany in the EU

The European Union is the result of a decades-long process of economic and political integration. It began in the 1950s with the goal of putting an end to centuries of bloody wars pitting neighbouring nations against each other and culminating in World War II. Germany was one of the six founding countries, along with Italy, France, Belgium, Holland and Luxembourg.

The EU currently has 27 members, 15 of which share a common currency, the euro. Germany, which held the EU Council Presidency in the first half of 2007, is a strong supporter of the 2007 Treaty of Lisbon that promotes collaboration among EU members on global challenges such as climate change, security and sustainable development.

REUNIFICATION: THE FALL OF THE BERLIN WALL

1989 Citizens of East Germany occupy West German embassies in Prague, Budapest and Warsaw with the aim of travelling to West Germany. The opening of the border between Austria and Hungary launches an East German mass migration. On 4 November the largest demonstration ever brings together over 1 million people in East Berlin. On the night of 9–10 November, the internal German border is opened, the Wall is breached. On 7 December, the Round Table meets for the first time as an institution of public control, with representatives from the political parties and the citizens' movements.

1990 Treaty of reunification drawn up; on 3 October the German Democratic Republic (DDR) joins the Federal Republic of Germany (BRD) according to Article 23 of the Basic Law. On 2 December, the first joint German parliamentary elections take place.

2005 Angela Merkel is elected German Chancellor.

2005 Bavaria-born Cardinal Joseph Ratzinger is elected Pope Benedikt XVI, becoming the first German pope since 1523.

2009 Federal elections result in a coalition government between the centre-right CDU and the liberal FDP. Angela Merkel stays on as Chancellor.

Keen to achieve rapid reunification, on 28 November 1989, West German Chancellor **Helmut Kohl** put forward a ten-point plan providing for the initial constitution of a confederation. On 3 October 1990 (now one of Germany's national holidays) the parliament sitting in the Reichstag in Berlin ratified the treaty of reunification. Helmut Kohl won the elections in December 1990 and, in 1991, the Bundestag chose Berlin

as capital of the reunified country. With the withdrawal of the last Allied troops in 1994, Germany became a sovereign state. It set its sights on the construction of a unified Europe. After the Federal President's move to Berlin, Parliament followed suit in 1999. On 19 April the new Plenary Room of the Reichstag building, crowned by a dome designed by British architect Lord Norman Foster, was inaugurated.

Reunification caused considerable economic and social problems: a drop in competitiveness, high unemployment in the new *Länder* and high taxes in the West to finance the modernisation of the East fuelled growing discontent. These problems eventually led to the loss of Helmut Kohl's CDU-CSU party in the 1998 elections and the ascendancy of Social Democrat **Gerhard Schröder** in coalition with the Green Party.

Under Schröder, Germany succeeded in reclaiming a post-World War leadership role within Europe and on the international stage. Germany is considered a leading political and economic force within the European Union, and its military has played an active peace-keeping role in war-torn Kosovo (1999) and also sent troops to Afghanistan.

But while the country has re-emerged as a positive force internationally, economic stresses continued to take their toll, resulting in Schröder's ousting in the 2005 federal elections. With neither of the big parties able to reach a majority, the two formed a rare Grand Coalition, with the role of Chancellor going to **Angela Merkel**. Merkel's election reflected several historical milestones for Germany. She was the country's first female chancellor; the first former citizen of East Germany to head a reunified German government; and was the youngest person to be chancellor since World War II.

The Grand Coalition was marked by compromise and stagnation, which was not helped by the global fiscal crisis of 2008. In the 2009 elections, voters nevertheless returned the CDU/CSU with Merkel at the helm into power, this time in an alliance with the liberal FDP.

Architecture

Germany's geographical location and history have left it open to the influence of artistic currents from the rest of Europe – mainly French in the Gothic period and Italian in the Renaissance period. Each style has been interpreted and adapted according to regional tastes.

This inventiveness has allowed Germany to develop an originality that is reflected in the sumptuous decoration of the Baroque abbeys in Bavaria and in the Expressionism of the inter-war years.

ROMANESQUE
CAROLINGIAN ARCHITECTURE (9C AND EARLY 10C)

Under the impetus of the emperor and the great prelates, a large number of religious buildings were built in Germany on a basilical or central plan (Palatine Chapel at Aachen), both inherited from Antiquity. Carolingian architecture is marked by the building of churches with two chancels: at the west end, a particular form emerged, the **Westwerk**, a tall square structure attached to the nave and often flanked by two towers, like at Corvey, for instance. The Westwerk constitutes almost a church in itself, where the emperor may have worshipped and where a special liturgy developed. It had a long-lasting effect on German Romanesque architecture.

OTTONIAN ARCHITECTURE (10C AND EARLY 11C)

The restoration of Imperial power by Otto I in 962 was accompanied by a revival of religious architecture in Saxony and in the regions of the Meuse and Lower Rhine. The huge churches of this period, characterised by deeply projecting transepts and wide aisles, feature wooden roofs that were usually painted. The alternation of piers and columns broke up the uniformity of the central portion, and east and west choirs were linked by the nave, with a skillful use of proportion giving a harmonious effect. The churches of St. Michaelis at Hildesheim and St. Cyriacus at Gernrode date back to this period.

RHINELAND ROMANESQUE STYLE

At Cologne and in the surrounding countryside, several churches feature a distinctive ground plan with a triple apse designed in the form of a cloverleaf, a style dating back to the 11C. A fine example can be seen at the church of St. Maria im Kapitol in Cologne. These trefoil extensions are adorned on the outside with blind arcades and a "dwarf gallery" (*Zwerggalerie*) – a motif of Lombard origin.

In the Middle Rhine region, the style achieves its full splendour in the majestic "Imperial" cathedrals of Speyer (the first church to be entirely vaulted), Mainz and Worms. Typical of these cathedrals are floor plans with a double chancel and no ambulatory, but sometimes a double transept. The exterior features numerous towers, blind arcades and Lombard bands. A characteristic of these Rhineland towers is a pointed roof in the form of a bishop's mitre, the base decorated with a lozenge pattern.

The churches of Limburg and Andernach and the cathedral at Naumburg, which were built early in the 13C, mark the transition between two periods. They are built in a style which combines Romanesque aesthetics and Gothic structures, with pointed rib vaulting and triforia.

GOTHIC
THE GRADUAL EMERGENCE OF THE GOTHIC STYLE (13C)

The French style of Gothic architecture, which attempted to free itself of Romanesque austerity, did not flourish in Germany until the mid-13C. Architecture then reached new heights of refinement, producing such masterpieces as the cathedral in Cologne with its vast interior, two tall slender towers framing the façade in the French style and its soaring pointed vaulting. Also inspired by the French Gothic style are the cathedrals of Regensburg, Freiburg im Breisgau, Magdeburg and Halberstadt. A fur-

Mainz Cathedral

D. Scherf/MICHELIN

ther manifestation of the predominance of French architecture can be seen in the establishment of Cistercian monasteries between 1150 and 1250.

Their churches, usually without towers or belfries and often later modified in the Baroque manner, were habitually designed with squared-off chancels flanked by rectangular chapels. The abbey of Maulbronn is one of very few Cistercian complexes preserved almost in its entirety still extant in Europe.

THE ORIGINALITY OF GERMAN ARCHITECTURE

The German imprint first emerged in the use of brick. In the north of the country the most imposing edifices were brick, complete with buttresses and flying buttresses. Typical of this brick Gothic style (known in German as *Backsteingotik*) are the Nikolaikirche at Stralsund, the Marienkirche in Lübeck, the town halls of those two cities, Schwerin Cathedral and the abbey church at Bad Doberan. Also unique to Gothic German architecture is the adoption of a new layout inspired by Cistercian architecture and manifested in the **hall-churches** *(Hallenkirche)*. In these buildings, the aisles are now the same height as the nave, which therefore has no clerestory windows, and are separated from it only by tall columns.

In the Elisabethkirche in Marburg, the three aisles are separated by thin supports, giving an impression of space and homogeneity.

LATE GOTHIC ARCHITECTURE

The lengthy Late Gothic period (14C, 15C and 16C) witnessed the widespread construction of hall-churches, including Freiburg Cathedral, the Frauenkirche in Munich and the Georgskirche, Dinkelsbühl. The vaulting features purely decorative ribs forming networks in the shape of stars or flowers in stark contrast to the austerity of the walls. St. Annenkirche at Annaberg-Buchholz epitomises this artistic virtuosity, free of all constraints.

Secular Architecture in the Late Middle Ages – Commercial prosperity among merchants and skilled craftsmen in the 14C and 15C led to the construction in town centres of impressive town halls and beautiful gabled and half-timbered private houses, frequently adorned with painting and sculpture. Examples of such architecture are still to be seen in the old town centres of Regensburg, Rothenburg ob der Tauber, Goslar and Tübingen.

THE RENAISSANCE

The Renaissance (1520–1620) is no more than a minor episode in the history of German architecture. Long held at bay by the persistence of the Gothic style, it was finally eclipsed by the troubles of the Reformation. Renaissance-style buildings are therefore rare in German towns. Augsburg is the lone exception. Its beautiful mansions lining Maximilianstraße and its town hall were designed by **Elias Holl** (1573–1646), Germany's most important Renaissance builder.

Southern Germany shows a marked Italian influence: elegant Florentine arcading was used by Jakob Fugger the Rich as decoration for his funerary chapel at Augsburg (1518); the Jesuits, building the Michaelskirche in Munich (1589), were clearly inspired by their own Sanctuary of Jesus (Gesù) in Rome; and in Cologne, the town hall with its two-tier portico reflects Venetian influence.

Northern Germany, on the other hand, was influenced by Flemish and Dutch design. In the rich merchants' quarters, many-storeyed gables, such as those of the Gewandhaus in Brunswick, boast rich ornamentation in the form of obelisks, scrollwork, statues, pilasters, etc. The castles at Güstrow and Heidelberg and the old town of Görlitz are important examples of Renaissance architecture, while the buildings of Wolfenbüttel, Celle, Bückeburg and Hameln are steeped in the particular charm of the so-called "Weser Renaissance" (&see HAMELN).

BAROQUE

After the disruption of the Thirty Years' War (1618–48), the ensuing revival of artistic activity provided an opportunity for the principalities to introduce Baroque architecture by welcoming French and Italian architects. Characterised by an irregularity of contour and a multiplicity of form, the Baroque style seeks, above all, the effect of movement and contrast. Taken to its extreme, it was soon saturated by Rococo decoration, which originated in the French *Rocaille* style; this style was originally secular and courtly but subsequently used in religious buildings.

From the mid-17C, Baroque influence was felt in southern Germany, encouraged by the Counter-Reformation's exaltation of dogmatic belief in Transubstantiation, the cult of the Virgin Mary and the saints, and in general all manifestations of popular piety. The aim was to achieve an emotional response from the spectator. This exuberance did not spread to Protestant Northern Germany.

THE MASTERS OF GERMAN AND DANUBIAN BAROQUE

There were exceptionally talented individuals in Bavaria who displayed equal skill across a variety of techniques, and who tended to prefer subtle ground plans, such as a round or elliptical focal shape. **Johann Michael Fischer** (Dießen, Zwiefalten and Ottobeuren), the **Asam brothers** (Weltenburg and the Asamkirche in Munich) and **Dominikus Zimmermann** (1685–1766, Steinhausen and Wies) were the virtuosi of this Bavarian School; their vibrant creations are covered by a profusion of Rococo decoration.

The Baroque movement in Franconia, patronised by the prince-bishops of the Schönborn family, who owned residences in Mainz, Würzburg, Speyer and Bamberg, was closely linked with the spread of similar ideas in Bohemia. The Dientzenhofer brothers decorated the palaces in Prague as well as the one in Bamberg. Perhaps the greatest of all Baroque architects was **Balthasar Neumann** (1687–1753), who worked for the same prelates, and whose breadth of cultural knowledge and creativity, enriched by his contact with French, Viennese and Italian masters, far surpassed that of his contemporaries. One of his finest creations was the Vierzehnheiligen Church near Bamberg, where he managed to combine the basilical plan with the ideal of the central plan. In Saxony, the Zwinger Palace in Dresden—joint masterpiece of the architect **Matthäus Daniel Pöppelmann** (1662–1736) and the sculptor Permoser – is a consummate example of German Baroque with Italian roots. The refinement of the Rococo décor in Schloss Sanssouci at Potsdam is even more astonishing given the reputed Prussian tendency towards austerity, but is explained by the periods of study undertaken in France and Italy by **Georg Wenzeslaus von Knobelsdorff**

(1699–1753), official architect and friend of Frederick the Great.

CHURCHES

A sinuous movement, generally convex in line, animates the façades, while the superposition of two pediments, different in design, adds vitality to the whole. They are additionally adorned with twin domed towers. Inside, huge galleries stand above the lateral chapels, at the height of pilaster capitals with jutting abaci. Chapels and galleries stop at the level of the transept, giving it a much greater depth. Clerestory windows at gallery level allow plenty of light to enter.

Bohemian and Franconian Baroque is typified by **complex vaulting**, round or oval bays being covered by complicated structures in which the transverse arches bow out in horseshoe shape, only to meet in their keystones.

Illusion is the keyword as regards the often **Rococo** decoration, using the effects of the white stucco, coloured marble and gilding. The numerous paintings and sculptures enhance this celebration of the sacred.

THE MONUMENTAL ALTARPIECE OR REREDOS

Reminiscent of a triumphal arch, in carved wood or stucco, the reredos became the focal point of the church, framing a large painting and/or statuary (Ottobeuren Abbey Church). Columns twisted into spiral form accentuate the sense of movement which characterises Baroque art, and back lighting from a hidden source, with its striking contrasts of brightness and shadow, is equally typical of the style.

PALACES

The one-story construction of these country residences was often lent additional importance by being built on a raised foundation. The focal point was a semi-circular central bloc with the curved façade facing the garden.

Monumental stairways with several flights and considerable theatrical effect are often the centrepieces of the larger German castles and palaces built in the 18C. The staircase, embellished with arcaded galleries and a painted ceiling, leads to the first floor state room which rises majestically to a height of two storeys.

Such elaborate arrangements characterise many of the great abbeys of this period, often complemented by that other ceremonial room, the library.

FROM NEOCLASSICISM TO NEO-GOTHIC
THE IDEAL OF AN ORIGINAL AUSTERITY

From 1750 on, Winckelmann's work on the art of Antiquity, and the excavations taking place at Pompeii, threw a new light on Greco-Roman architecture.

At the same time, the example of Versailles inspired in Germany a new style of court life, particularly in the Rhineland and the Berlin of Frederick II.

Many French architects were employed by the Electors of the Palatinate, of Mainz, of Trier and of Cologne; mainly, they produced plans for country mansions with names such as Monrepos ("my rest") or Solitude. Other German architects, such as **Carl Gotthard Langhans** (1732–1808), were instrumental in the transition from the Baroque to the Neoclassical style (Brandenburg Gate and the Charlottenburg Theatre in Berlin).

Features such as unadorned pediments, balustrades at the base of the roofs and columned porticoes at the main entrance all indicate a desire for unobtrusive elegance. A new fashion arose, in which architects favoured the Doric style coupled with a preference for the colossal – pilasters and columns of a single "order" no longer stood one-storey high but always two.

The interior decoration, carried out with a lighter touch, confined itself to cornucopias of flowers mingled with Rococo motifs that were now a little more discreet (garlands, urns, vases and friezes of pearls).

Architecture was now responding to a demand for rationality that had emerged in reaction to the Late Baroque and Rococo styles.

KARL-FRIEDRICH SCHINKEL (1781–1841)

Appointed state architect by Frederick William III in 1815, he designed many buildings, including the Neue Wache, Altes Museum and Schauspielhaus in Berlin. In a refined approach using elements inspired by Antiquity, this great exponent of Romantic Classicism constantly sought to blend his constructions in with their surroundings. The grandiose style of his buildings with their long Neoclassical colonnades, the dramatic contrasts of light and the use of Gothic elements are typical of the Romantic trend.

THE 19C AND THE NEO-GOTHIC

19C architecture was characterised by a great diversity of styles. By 1830, the Neoclassical movement had been superseded, except in Munich, by a renewed interest in the Gothic, emblematic for the Romantics of "the old Germany".

At the same time, the **Biedermeier** style – lightweight, cushioned furniture with flowing lines, glass-fronted cabinets for the display of knick-knacks – corresponding perhaps with the later Edwardian style in England, was popular in middle-class homes between 1815 and 1848.

1850 marks the beginning of the **Founders' Period** (*Gründerzeitstil*) with E Ludwig and A Koch pursuing an up-to-date style. But the wealthy industrialists fell for pretentious medieval or Renaissance reproductions, also to be found in public buildings such as the Reichstag in Berlin.

20C MOVEMENTS

In the late 19C, artists began exploring new avenues in a desire to move away from past styles and into the modern age. **Art Nouveau** or **Jugendstil**, a European movement, became the vogue in Germany. The architects' idea was to create a complete work of art accessible to all, combining structure, decoration and furniture.

This ideal, based on co-operation with industry, its methods of production and the use of its newest building materials (glass, iron, cement), resulted in the fundamental concept of an industrial aesthetic, brought to the fore by such pioneers as Peter Behrens, **Ludwig Mies van der Rohe** and **Walter Gropius**.

This style flourished mainly in Munich, Berlin and Darmstadt (with the Mathildenhöhe artists' colony).

The artists' commitment, expressed within the Secessions (Munich 1892, Berlin 1899), was coupled with a political demand for independence.

THE BAUHAUS AND BEYOND

In 1919, Walter Gropius founded the **Bauhaus** (Weimar: 1919–25, Dessau: 1926–32), a school of architecture and applied arts which radicalised the movement for modernisation, displaying an even greater interest in industrial production. The quest for unity between art and technique was a fundamental element (see DESSAU and WEIMAR). The movement instigated modern reflections on architecture and lent its vocabulary to modern design. The Nazis closed the Bauhaus in 1933 and adopted a pompous and monumental style of architecture intended to reflect their power.

At the end of the war, new concepts, characterised the construction of municipal and cultural enterprises such as Hans Scharoun's Philharmonie in Berlin and the Staatsgalerie in Stuttgart by British architect Sir James Stirling – buildings of an architectural audacity only made possible by the development of entirely new materials and construction techniques. These days, architectural innovation is especially prevalent in Berlin where the world's leading architects – including Daniel Libeskind, Lord Norman Foster and Helmut Jahn – have created such showcases of the avant-garde as the Potdamer Platz quarter or the Jewish Museum.

Cutting-edge buildings can also be seen in such places as Düsseldorf's Medienhafen (Frank Gehry, Renzo Piano) or in Munich, where the new stadium, the BMW Museum and the Museum Brandhorst made a recent splash.

RELIGIOUS ARCHITECTURE

Plan of a church

Cross section of a church

Hall Church

Unlike a basilica, a hall church has aisles the same height as the central nave and covered with one roof; their windows let light inside the edifice.

SPEYER – East End of the Cathedral (11C)

Cupola

Dwarf gallery

Blind arcading

Chevet: French term
for the east end of
a church (exterior)

Rhomboidal roof

Lombardy banding:
slightly projecting
decorative strips,
linked by a frieze of
small arcs

Lean-to roof on
east end of church

Base cornice

Base

FREIBURG – Cathedral Altar (14C-16C)

Network vaulting

Rib

Allège

Upper part of
the chancel

Chancel arches

High altar

Cell

Keystone

Engaged column

Mullioned window

Tracery: ornamental
stone ribwork in the
upper part of a
window

R. Corbel/MICHELIN

COLOGNE CATHEDRAL (1248 to 1880), South façade

The construction of the cathedral began in 1248 and took more than 600 years to complete. It was the first Gothic church in the Rhineland and the original design was based on those in Paris, Amiens and Reims. The twin-towered western façade marks the peak of achievement in the style known as Flamboyant Gothic. Stepped windows, embellished gables, slender buttresses, burst upwards, ever upwards, slimly in line with the tapering spires that reach a height of 157m/515ft.

Openwork spire

Crockets

Crossing tower

Gable: decorative, vertical triangular portion above windows or doorway

Flying buttresses

Pointed arch windows

Blind arcading

Buttress supporting the base of the wall

Pinnacle

Tympanum

Central doorway or **portal**

R. Corbel/MICHELIN

Schloß BRUCHSAL – Garden façade (18C)

Crowing piece

Agrafe: the voussoir or keystone of an arch, especially when carved as a cartouche

Triangular pediment

Mansard: a four-sided hipped roof

Œil-de-boeuf window

Painted trompe-l'œil

Pilaster or attached pier

Avant-corps, projecting from the rest of the façade, including the roof

Platform

Twin columns

R. Corbel/MICHELIN

POTSDAM – Sanssouci Palace and Park
(Georg Wenzelaus von Knobelsdorff and Friedrich II, 1745-47)

Spandrel: space between the arch and its frame

Urn

Œil-de-bœuf window

Entablature: comprises the architrave, the frieze and the cornice

Terminus or Herm: statue with lower part shaped like a square pillar

Central block projecting from the rest of the façade, including the roof

Step arrangement

M. Guillou/MICHELIN

73

OTTOBEUREN Abbey Church (18C)

Ottobeuren is characteristic of other Bavarian churches with its dazzling ornamentation and plays of light and symmetry.

Painted vaulting

Spandrel: triangular space between the curve of an arch and the frame in which it is set

Stuccowork

Cornice with projecting ornamental motifs

Retable or altarpiece

Tabernacle

Pulpit (or ambo): elevated stand from which sermons were preached

Sounding board

R. Corbel/MICHELIN

"Uncle Tom's Cabin" estate
(Bruno Taut, Hugo Häring, Otto Rudolf Salvisberg, 1926-32)

Designed to house 15 000 people, this estate built under the supervision of Martin Wagner, does not convey an impression of monotony. There is a U-Bahn Station in its centre as well as a shopping centre and a cinema.

All the buildings are of a moderate size

Terraced roof

The simplicity of the façades painted with bright colours, hence the nickname of "parrot estate", is due to a rational building plan and the use of standard, relatively cheap, materials.

The natural surroundings are in keeping with the concept of **garden cities** at the beginning of the century.

Individual houses have re-entrant angles and tall windows characteristic of the style of Salvisberg who designed the buildings along Riemeisterstraße.

Philharmonie (Hans Scharoun, 1960-63) and Chamber Music Hall
(Edgar Wisniewski, from a drawing by Scharoun, 1984-88)

In 1957, during a congress, H Scharoun expressed his wish to build "an adequately shaped hall for music making, where listening to music would be a common experience". The audience sits round the orchestra, which occupies the very heart of the arena.

Aluminium sheeting: perforated, it was only added in 1978-81. Before that time, the concrete roof was painted in an ochre colour.

The internal structure and the outside appearance are closely related. The place occupied by the orchestra determines the type of structure (three imbricated pentagons in the case of the Philharmonie, a hexagon in the case of the Chamber Music Hall): the tent-shaped roof provides good acoustics and adds a dynamic element to the visual aspect.

Philharmonie

Chamber music hall

Railing

Glass roof

Porch

M. Guillou/MICHELIN

GLOSSARY OF ARCHITECTURE

Absidiole or **apsidiole chapel**: Small apsidal chapel opening on the ambulatory of a Romanesque or Gothic church.

Aisles: Lateral divisions running parallel with the nave.

Ambulatory: Formed by an extension of the aisles around the chancel; in pilgrimage churches it allowed the faithful to file past the relics.

Apse: Rounded or polygonal end of a church; the outer section is known as the chevet.

Atlantes (or **Telamones**): Male figures used as supporting columns.

Atrium (or **four-sided portico**): Court enclosed by colonnades in front of the entrance to a early Christian or Romanesque church.

Basilica: Rectangular religious building, built on the Roman basilica plan with three or five aisles.

Bossage: Architectural motif or facing made of bosses, uniformly projecting blocks on the outer wall. They are surrounded by deep carving or separating lines. Bossage was in vogue during the Renaissance.

Buttress: External mass of masonry projecting from a wall to counterbalance the thrust of the vaults and arches.

Capital: Crowning feature of a column, consisting of a smooth part, connecting it to the shaft, and a decorated part. There are three orders in classical architecture: Doric, Ionic (with double volute), and Corinthian (decorated with acanthus leaves). The latter is often found in 16C–17C buildings.

Chancel: Part of the church behind the altar set aside for the choir, furnished with variously decorated wooden stalls.

Choir screen or **rood screen**: Partition separating the chancel from the nave.

Ciborium: Canopy over an altar.

Console (or **corbel** or **bracket**): Element of stone or wood projecting from a wall to support beams or cornices.

Corbelling: Projecting course of masonry.

Cornice: In Classical architecture, projecting ornamental moulding along the top of a building. Also designates any projecting decoration around a ceiling.

Cross (church plan): Churches are usually built either in the plan of a Greek cross, with arms of equal length, or a Latin cross, with shorter transept arms.

Crossing: Central area of a cruciform church, where the transept crosses the nave and choir. A tower is often set above this space.

Crypt: Underground chamber beneath a church, where holy relics were placed. Often a chapel or church in its own right.

Diagonal arch: Diagonal arch supporting a vault.

Drum: Circular or polygonal structure supporting a dome.

Embrasure: Recess for a window or door, splayed on the inside.

Entablature: In Classical architecture, the section above the columns consisting of architrave, frieze and cornice.

Gable: Decorative, triangular section above a portal.

Gallery: In early Christian churches, an upper storey opening on the nave. Later used in exterior decoration.

Grotesque: Fanciful ornamental decoration inspired by decorative motifs from Antiquity. The term comes from the old Italian word *grotte*, the name given to the Roman ruins of the *Domus Aurea*, uncovered in the Renaissance period.

Hall-church: Church in which the nave and aisles are of equal height and practically the same width, communicating right to the top.

High relief: Sculpture with very pronounced relief, although not standing out from the background (halfway between low relief and in-the-round figures).

Jamb or **pier**: Pillar flanking an opening (doorway, window, etc.) and supporting the lintel above.

Keystone: Wedge-shaped stone at the crown of an arch.

Lantern: Turret with windows on top of a dome.

Lintel: Horizontal beam connecting pilasters or columns and constituting the lower part of the entablature (in Classical buildings such as temples).

Lombard strips: Romanesque decoration consisting of vertical bands in slight relief or lesenes joined at the top by an arched frieze.

Low relief: Bas-relief, carved figures slightly projecting from their background.

Misericord or **miserere**: Bracket on the underside of a hinged choir stall used for support by canons or monks.

Moulding: ornamental shaped band which projects from the wall.

Mullion window: Window with two arches divided by a central post.

Narthex: Portico preceding the nave of a church.

Nave: Central main body of a church, flanked by aisles.

Oriel window: Window projecting from a wall on corbels.

Ovolo moulding: Egg-shaped ornamentation.

Pediment: Usually triangular ornament above buildings, doors, windows or recesses.

Pendentive: Triangular section of vaulting rising from the angle of two walls enabling the transition from a square space to an octagonal or circular dome.

Polyptych: Painted or carved work consisting of more than three folding leaves or panels.

Predella: Base of a polyptych or altarpiece.

Pulpit (or **ambo**): Elevated stand in various locations from which sermons were preached in a church.

Retable or **altarpiece**: Vertical structure, either painted or carved, above or set back from the altar, often found in Baroque churches.

Rib: Projecting band on the surface of a dome or vault that disperses the weight onto the structures below.

Rococo: Type of decoration in the late Baroque period typified by abstract combinations of shells and volutes.

Rose window: Circular window usually inserted into the front elevation of a church, decorated with delicate fan-shaped stone tracery (small columns, volutes, patterns).

Stalls: Wooden seats reserved for the clergy, grouped together in the chancel.

String course: Ornamental, horizontal band on an exterior wall marking the division between storeys.

Stucco: Form of plaster widely used from the Renaissance period for decoration in relief on walls and ceilings.

Transept: Transverse arms set at right angles to the nave and giving the church a cruciform shape.

Tribune: Upper platform in a church, overlooking the interior.

Triforium: In a Gothic church, a wall-passage above the aisles, opening on the nave, often via a blind arcade.

Triptych: Work comprising three painted or carved panels, whose outer sections can be folded over the central section.

Tympanum: In buildings, doors and windows, the triangular section between the horizontal entablature and the sloping sides of the pediment.

Vault: Arched structure forming a roof or ceiling.

Westwerk or **westwork**: The west end of a church containing a second chancel. A massive structure, often flanked by two stair turrets, typical of Carolingian and Ottonian architecture, sometimes reserved for the emperor.

Art

Germany has a long and illustrious arts pedigree and has produced masters in practically all fields of expression. Religious art dominated until the 19C when Romantic, Realist and Impressionist artists began depicting landscapes, people and scenes from daily life. A key modern movement in German art was Expressionism. After the Second World War, conceptual art and abstract expressionism became the main forms of expression. Since the 1990s, Neo-realism has emerged as a major style, especially as represented by members of the New Leipzig School such as Neo Rauch.

GERMANY'S GREAT PAINTERS AND SCULPTORS

15C

In the fields of painting and architecture, Germany remained for a long time attached to the Late Gothic tradition, which denied the realism so sought after in Italy. The country was divided into a large number of local schools under Dutch influence. Now came the time to seek an outlet for emotional expression and give vent to the religious concerns that marked the end of the Middle Ages.

Stefan Lochner (c. 1410–1451)
This leading master of the Cologne School perpetuated the tradition of international Gothic, giving it a lyrical and refined touch with his sweet expressions and an exquisitely delicate palette. The use of gold backgrounds afforded him a certain amount of leeway as regards the requirements of perspective (*Adoration of the Magi*, Cologne Cathedral; *Virgin and Rose Bush*, Wallraf-Richartz-Museum, Cologne).

Veit Stoß (c. 1445–1533)
Sculptor, painter and engraver with a distinctive, powerful style; one of the greatest woodcarvers of his age. His figures were generally of a pathetic nature (*Annunciation*, Lorenzkirche, Nuremberg; *Reredos of the Nativity*, Bamberg Cathedral).

Tilman Riemenschneider (c. 1460–1531)
Sculptor of alabaster and wood, he was master of an important studio where he created many altarpieces. His intricate works are executed with great finesse and richness of expression (*Tomb of Henry II the Saint*, Bamberg Cathedral; *Adam and Eve*, Mainfränkisches Museum, Würzburg; *Altarpiece to the Virgin*, Herrgottskirche, Creglingen).

The Master of St. Severinus (late 15C)
The intimacy and iridescent colours of his works reflect Netherlandish influence (*Christ before Pilate*, Wallraf-Richartz-Museum, Cologne).

The Master of the Life of the Virgin (late 15C)
Painter of original works, influenced by the Flemish artist Van der Weyden (*Scenes from the Life of the Virgin*, Alte Pinakothek, Munich; *Vision of St. Bernard*, Wallraf-Richartz-Museum, Cologne).

ENGRAVING

First emerging in Germany around 1400, engraving was espoused by the greatest German masters. One pioneer was the unidentified engraver **Master E.S.**, known by the monogram with which he signed his engravings, whose work dates from between 1450 and 1467. Copperplate engraving techniques were later perfected and best demonstrated by virtuosi such as **Martin Schongauer** (c. 1450–1491), whose designs were later followed by Albrecht Dürer.

16C

The German Renaissance did not emerge until the 16C with Dürer. The observation and idealism of nature resulted in works of increasing refinement. The Danube School showed a new interest in landscape, encouraging its development as a genre, while Holbein breathed new life into the art of portrait painting with his striking realism.

Matthias Grünewald (c. 1480–1528)

An inspired painter of the Late Gothic period, producing works of great emotional intensity capable of expressing the pain of humanity (*Crucifixion*, Staatliche Kunsthalle, Karlsruhe; *Virgin and Child*, Stuppach Parish Church).

Albrecht Dürer (1471–1528)

The greatest artist of the German Renaissance, he was fascinated by the art of Antiquity and the Italian Renaissance, with which he was able to lend Nordic gravity. Based in Nuremberg, Dürer produced woodcuts achieving some magnificent light effects and a broad range of greys *(The Apocalypse)*. His religious scenes and portraits are of an extraordinary intensity (*The Four Apostles*, *Self-Portrait with Cloak*, Alte Pinakothek, Munich; *Charlemagne*, Germanisches Nationalmuseum, Nuremberg).

Venus and Cupid Carrying the Honeycomb *(c. 1531)* *by Lucas Cranach, the Elder*

Self-portrait *(1498) by Albrecht Dürer*

Lucas Cranach the Elder (1472–1553)

Official painter to the prince-electors of Saxony and master of an important studio, he was the portraitist of the most eminent men of the Reformation, most notably of his friend Luther. His works reflect a strong sense of the wonders of nature, allying him with the painters of the Danube School. As court painter in Wittenberg, he produced Lutheran-inspired religious paintings. The more Expressionist works of his youth gave way to paintings full of grace and nobility, typical of the refinement towards which 16C German art was heading. (*The Electors of Saxony*, Kunsthalle, Hamburg; *The Holy Family*, Städel museum, Frankfurt; *Portrait of Martin Luther*, Germanisches Nationalmuseum, Nuremberg).

Albrecht Altdorfer (c. 1480–1538)

Leading member of the Danube School and one of the founders of landscape painting, his use of chiaroscuro creates dramatic and moving works, with the focus on landscapes shrouded in mystery (*Battle of Alexander*, Alte Pinakothek, Munich).

Hans Baldung Grien (c. 1485–1545)

His complex compositions feature dramatic lighting effects, unusual colours and tortured movement (Altarpiece: *The Coronation of the Virgin*, Freiburg Cathedral).

Hans Holbein the Younger (1497–1543)

Painter of German merchants and subjects from court circles and the high aristocracy, he breathed new life into the art of portrait painting. His subjects are depicted with incredible precision in skilfully composed settings that illustrate their office. His compositions, both solemn and realistic, mark a definitive departure from the Gothic tradition (*Portrait of the Merchant Georg Gisze*, Museum Dahlem, Berlin).

17C AND 18C

Italian influence remained evident during these two centuries. Court circles played host to many French and Italian artists who introduced an increasingly exuberant Baroque style.

Adam Elsheimer (1578–1610)

Elsheimer's often small-scale mythological and biblical paintings reflect a combination of Italian influence and a concept of landscapes peculiar to Flemish and German painting.

At the same time as Caravaggio, he experimented with the power of light in the evocation of nature, notably in his dramatic nocturnal landscapes (*The Flight into Egypt*, 1609, Alte Pinakothek, Munich).

Andreas Schlüter (c. 1660–1714)

This master of Baroque sculpture in northern Germany and talented architect produced some very powerful works (*Statue of the Great Elector*, Schloss Charlottenburg, Berlin; *Masks of Dying Warriors*, Zeughaus, Berlin).

Atlantes *on Wallpavillon by Balthasar Permoser, Zwinger, Dresden*

Balthasar Permoser (1651–1732)

Sculptor to the Court of Dresden, Permoser studied in Rome, Vienna and Venice. His masterful works reflect the exuberant style of the Italian Baroque, particularly at the Zwinger (*Wallpavillon* and *Nymphenbad*, Zwinger, Dresden).

Antoine Pesne (1683–1757)

This French-born painter in the service of the Prussian court became the portraitist of Frederick II, who admired his colouristic talent. He produced a great number of portraits and some mythological ceiling paintings and murals (*Portrait of Frederick II and his sister Wilhelmina,* apartments of Schloss Charlottenburg, Berlin).

Joseph Anton Feuchtmayer (1696–1770) and Johann Michael II Feichtmayr (1709–1772)

These members of a family of German painters and sculptors helped to perpetuate the Rococo style with their fanciful compositions (decoration of the abbey churches of Ottobeuren and St. Gall).

Matthäus Günther (1705–1788)

A pupil of CD Asam, master of Rococo painting in southern Germany, Günther is famous for his decoration of many churches in Swabia and Bavaria (Amorbach, Rott am Inn).

19C

The 19C was first of all dominated by the **Biedermeier style** (1815–48) which glorified middle-class values and way of life, as perfectly illustrated by the genre painting of GF Kersting. Then came the time for rebellion. Romanticism called Classical values into question, launching a dialogue between reason and feeling. Realism and Impressionism, which both originated in France, allowed German artists to express certain budding socialist ideas. These various forms of artistic expression came in response to the moral crisis of modern Europe.

Caspar David Friedrich (1774–1840)

German Romantic painter whose landscapes were represented as manifestations of the divine and places of wonderment ideal for meditation (*The Monk by the Sea, The Cross on the Mountain*, Alte Nationalgalerie, Berlin; *Wanderer above the Sea of Fog*, Kunsthalle, Hamburg).

Friedrich Overbeck (1789–1869)

Member of the Lucas Brotherhood, he was the most important member of the group of **Nazarenes** who occupied the abandoned monastery of San Isidoro in Rome in 1810. Advocating a form of painting that glorified moral values in a reaction against Neoclassicism, they revived medieval art and sought the purity of the early Italian and Flemish masters of the 15C (*Italia and Germania*, Neue Pinakothek, Munich).

Adolf von Menzel (1815–1905)

Representative of German Realism, initially illustrating anecdotal themes and later producing powerful portrayals of the industrial world, tempered by the influence of Impressionism (*Rolling Mill*, Nationalgalerie in Berlin).

Wilhelm Leibl (1844–1900)

Master of German Realism, he was influenced by Courbet and mostly painted scenes of village life (*Three Women in Church*, Kunsthalle, Hamburg; portrait of *Mina Gedon*, Neue Pinakothek, Munich).

Detail of The Wanderer above the Sea of Fog *(1818) by Caspar David Friedrich*

D.R.

Max Liebermann (1847–1935)

Greatly influenced by French Realism and Naturalism, he painted peasants and workers in all their harsh reality. Later, under the influence of Impressionism, he allowed light to suffuse his already rich palette. He led the Berlin "Sezession" movement in 1899, advocating freedom and realism as opposed to the patriotic insipidness of the court painters (*Jewish Street in Amsterdam*, Wallraf-Richartz-Museum, Cologne).

20C

The Expressionism which marked the beginning of the century gave way to a new form of revolt and glorification of subjective feeling. The shock of World War I and the ensuing social crisis plunged art into a period of darkness and disillusionment. Political and social dissent were embodied in a succession of new avant-garde movements. More than ever before, art was driven by a desire to change society and expose its failings.

Expressionism

German Expressionism introduced an emotionally charged, often violent or tragic vision of the world to modern painting. The movement owed much to Van Gogh and the Norwegian painter **Edvard Munch** (1863–1944). In Dresden and then in Berlin, the **Brücke (Bridge) Group** united from 1905 to 1913 such painters as Erich Heckel, Ernst Ludwig Kirchner and Karl Schmidt-Rottluff, whose work, with its use of pure colour, recalls that of the Fauves in France. See the works of **Emil Nolde** (1867–1956) at Seebüll and Berlin, and of Expressionism in general at the Brücke-Museum, also in Berlin.

Der Blaue Reiter (The Blue Rider Movement)

Association of artists founded in Munich in 1911 by **Wassily Kandinsky** and **Franz Marc**, later to be joined by **August Macke** and **Paul Klee**. Although the work of the artists involved differed widely, they were united by a general aim to free art from the constraints of reality, using bold colours and untraditional forms, thus opening the way to abstraction (*Deer in the Forest* by **Franz Marc**, Orangerie Staatliche Kunsthalle, Karlsruhe; *The Dress Shop* by **August Macke**, Folkwang-Museum, Essen). The movement broke up during the war.

The Bauhaus

This movement, which united all art forms, attracted a host of avant-garde painters and sculptors including Klee and Kandinsky, Oskar Schlemmer, Laszlo Moholy-Nagy, **Lyonel Feininger** and **Joseph Albers**.

Neue Sachlichkeit (New Objectivity)

This artistic early-1920s movement aimed to produce a realistic illustration of social facts and phenomena. It corresponds to the harshness of the postwar period. Pioneers of this movement were **Otto Dix** and **George Grosz** (*War* by **Otto Dix**, 1932, Albertinum in Dresden). The Dada movement, present in Cologne and Berlin, and in Hannover with **Kurt Schwitters**, used art for political ends. On the sidelines of these movements, **Max Beckmann** (1884–1950), who was also deeply affected by the war and its consequences, shared his very bleak view of humanity.

Second Half of the 20C

The Nazi regime brought an abrupt end to these artistic experiments labelled as "degenerate art", replacing them with a Neoclassical style glorifying race, war and family. This "Nazi art" died out at the end of the Reich in 1945.

Social Realism, an official art form which served the regime's ideology, was predominant in East German painting until the 1960s–70s. The painters of Leipzig in particular won international acclaim, among them Bernhard Heisig, Wolfgang Mattheuer, Willi Sitte and Werner Tübke. The 1960s saw a turning point in German artistic creativity. **Gruppe Zebra** took up the credo of New Objectivity against German Abstract art, while the members of **Gruppe Zero** (Heinz Mack, Otto Piene, Güntheb Uecker) concentrated on using kinetic art to transform thoughts into material objects. In the 1970s, **Joseph Beuys**, together with the artists of the school of **Constructivist Sculpture** in Düsseldorf, strove to create a direct relationship between the artist and the viewing public in his Happenings and Performances, and to redefine the role of art and the artist in contemporary society (**Neue Nationalgalerie** in Berlin; **Hessisches Landesmuseum** in Darmstadt; **Staatsgalerie** in Stuttgart).

From the 1980s, a new generation of German artists managed to break through onto the international scene with "new Fauves" *(Neue Wilde)* **Georg Baselitz** and **Markus Lüpertz** devel-oping a new form of Expressionism, **Sigmar Polke**, closer to pop art, and **Anselm Kiefer**, with his focus firmly on German history.

Since the 1990s German painting and photography have been enjoying international success under the label "Young German Artists". Many of the artists involved come from Leipzig, Berlin and Dresden. Neo Rauch is the best known representative of the "New Leipzig School". Katarina Sieverding and Andreas Gursky are the current stars of the photography world. Germany also hosts one of the most influential contemporary art fairs, the Documenta, held in Kassel every five years (next in 2012).

Literature

German literature, from the reign of Charlemagne up to the present day, has demonstrated an enduring vitality, constantly breaking with tradition and inventing new forms of expression. In the wake of Goethe's monumental influence in the 18C, the best authors have been guaranteed international renown.

FROM THE MIDDLE AGES TO THE 17C

German literature in the Middle Ages was written in a great variety of dialects. Largely drawing on the oral tradition, it was characterised by lyrical poetry and genres that can be described – not in any pejorative way – as popular: plays, ballads, songs and epics. One of the earliest works, dating back to Charlemagne's reign, is the **Lay of Hildebrand** (Das Hildebrandslied, 820), of which only a 68-line fragment has survived. The national folk saga of the **Nibelungen**, an anonymous work from the late 12C, draws on the sources of Germanic mythology and celebrates the heroic spirit that faces up to trials and tribulations without ever giving up. One of the big names in courtly epics was **Wolfram von Eschenbach**; his poem *Parzival* (c. 1200), which **recounts the** quest for the Holy Grail, revolves around religious and chivalrous themes. The 14C was an age of mystic literature, with writers such as **Meister Eckhart**. In a departure from the dryness of scholastic teaching, he sometimes forsakes Latin to discuss religious topics in powerful and eloquent German.

Satire took centre stage in the 16C (*The Ship of Fools* by **Sebastian Brant** appeared in 1494) along with folk songs and the poetry of the Meistersänger (master singers). **Hans Sachs** (1494–1576), a poet-cum-cobbler from Nuremberg, was a prominent figure in the latter genre, which provides the theme of Wagner's opera *Tannhäuser*.

Luther's contribution during this period also marked a turning point; his hymns and translation of the Bible (1534) paved the way for the writing of literary works in a common, modern German language. The late 16C witnessed the publication of the *Faust Book* (1587) by **Johann Spies**, a work of remarkable depth, which draws the captivating portrait of a man driven by an unquenchable thirst for knowledge which distances him from God.

The ravages of the Thirty Years' War (1618–48) profoundly marked the collective psyche; 17C literature bears echoes of this traumatic time.

Among the recurrent themes of these often edifying works is the vanity of human things and man's need to find God in order to ensure his salvation. *Adventurous Simplicissimus* (1669) by **Grimmelshausen** (1622–1676) is a picaresque novel whose hero, having experienced the suffering of war, finally chooses a life of retreat and meditation.

AUFKLÄRUNG (AGE OF ENLIGHTENMENT)

The 18C marked the beginning of the golden age of German literature, as its influence began to extend well beyond the German-speaking countries.

The spotlight was now on philosophical and moral themes, the flourishes of language belying a pursuit of the natural. The influence of **Leibniz** (1646–1716), whose *Theodicy* in French and Latin uses rational arguments to justify evil and show that we live in "the best of all possible worlds", still remains strong. **Rationalism**, apparent in the works of **Christian Wolff** (1679–1754), co-existed with the tenacious survival of Pietism, which highlights the emotional experience in any religious phenomenon.

This explains how **Lessing** (1729–1781), in his writings on religion (*The Education of the Human Race*, 1780), strives to combine a rationalist deism with a belief in revelation. In the purely literary field, Lessing also set the principles of new German theatre by creating middle-class drama *(Emilia Galotti)*.

His contemporary, **Immanuel Kant** (1724–1804), endeavoured to define the limits of what can be known; only that which is determined by pure forms of understanding can be the subject of rational knowledge. Whatever eludes such determination (the soul, God, etc.) can, of course, be "thought" and give rise to "belief", but cannot be "known". In the practical field, Kantianism defines the balance between liberty and the "moral law" that governs every rational being: man finds liberty by submitting to the "categorical imperative" and renouncing the influence of his "sensitivity".

STURM UND DRANG AND CLASSICISM

In reaction to the strict rationalism of the Aufklärung, the **Sturm und Drang** (storm and stress) movement, encompassing authors such as **Herder** (1744–1803) and **Hamann** (1730–1788), exalts freedom, emotion and nature. Poetry, "the mother tongue of the human race", takes pride of place and the past is revisited, with particular emphasis placed on folk songs.

The works of the young **Johann Wolfgang von Goethe** (1749–1832), such as *The Sorrows of Young Werther*, bear witness to the influence of *Sturm und Drang*. However, Goethe – poet and universal genius – soon tempered this fashionable enthusiasm with a move towards the **classical humanist** tradition.

As the leading light of German literature prior to the emergence of the Romantic trend, in which he never became involved, he penned a great number of works. Classical dramas (*Iphigenie auf Tauris*, *Egmont* and *Torquato Tasso*), novels (*Elective Affinities*, *Wilhelm Meister's Apprenticeship*) and *Faust* (Parts I and II, 1808 and 1832) contain the quintessence of Goethe's philosophy.

After settling in Weimar in 1775, Goethe was joined by Herder, **Wieland** and **Schiller** (1759–1805). The historical dramas of the latter, a poet and dramatist of genius, are undisguised hymns to liberty (*Don Carlos, Wallenstein, Wilhelm Tell*).

Two major literary figures emerged during the transitional period between Weimarian Classicism and actual Romanticism: **Friedrich Hölderlin** (1770–1843), a tragic, lyric author (*Hyperion, The Death of Empedocles*) with a passion for Ancient Greek civilisation, produced some powerful odes before sinking into madness at the age of 36.

The novelist Johann Paul Friedrich Richter (1763–1825), better known as **Jean Paul**, had a creative imagination, although a somewhat laboured style.

19C: BETWEEN ROMANTICISM AND REALISM

The **Romantic movement** charts the individual soul's quest for the infinite in all its forms. Besides literature, it incorporates the fine arts, philosophy, politics and religion. First Jena, then Heidelberg and Berlin were centres from which the movement blossomed. After initially being theorised by the **Schlegel brothers**, the Romantic doctrine was put into powerful poetic form by **Novalis** (1772–1801); a poet and mystic, Novalis exalts the art and religion of the Middle Ages and his "Blue Flower" symbol comes to represent the Absolute, or object of Romantic longing (*Heinrich von Ofterdingen*). While in the process of theoretical elaboration, budding Romanticism was exposed to the influence of post-Kantian idealist philosophers, in particular **Fichte** (1762–1814), **Schelling** (1775–1854) and **Hegel** (1770–1831). It also reflects a heightened interest in popular literature, often seeking inspiration in the sources of myths and legends, as can be seen in the tales of the **Brothers Grimm** (1812) or the more disturbing tales of **Hoffmann** (1776–1822). On the sidelines of the Romantic movement, the playwright **Heinrich von Kleist**, who tragically, committed suicide in 1811, wrote some remarkable plays, notably *The Prince of Homburg* (1810): A play about a man of action led away by his dreams.

The exuberant idealism of Romanticism was succeeded by a search for greater realism. An outstanding figure and "defrocked Romantic" poet of the *Loreley*, **Heinrich Heine** (1797–1856) treats the naivety of his age with bitter irony and enthuses about St. Simonian ideals. **Hebbel** (1813–1863), a fine psychologist, wrote plays often inspired by biblical or mythical subjects, focusing on conflict between the individual and the existing moral order (*Judith, Herodes und Mariamne, Agnes Bernauer*). Towards the mid-19C, a number of writers sought to bring literature closer to life and everyday experience; novelists such as **Stifter** (1805–1868) and **Keller** (1819–1890) were among the main exponents of this Realist trend. Some of them, such as **Fontane** (1819–1898) and **Raabe** (1831–1910), focus on the social and political conditions of human existence. Social drama is brilliantly illustrated by **Hauptmann** (1862–1946), a prolific author whose Naturalist writing is at times allegorical and symbolic, drawing inspiration from legend and mythology (*The Atrides Cycle*).

In the field of philosophy, **Schopenhauer** (1788–1860), pessimistic theorist of the will to live, describes the will as reality's true inner nature, and this will as suffering (*The World as Will and Idea*, 1819); he had a crucial influence on the thinking of authors such as Nietzsche, Freud and Wittgenstein. Political thought, moreover, took a new direction with **Karl Marx** (*The Communist Manifesto* was published in 1848); rejecting Hegelian idealism, Marx, who was both a philosopher and an economist, developed the theory of "historical materialism", a powerful conceptual tool enabling the analysis of human societies according to their historical development. Together with **Engels**, Marx co-founded "scientific socialism", in opposition to so-called "utopian" socialism, and launched the modern international workers' movement.

Jakob and Wilhelm Grimm

© World Pictures/Photoshot

THE MODERN PERIOD

Friedrich Nietzsche (1844–1900) belongs as much to the history of philosophy as to the history of literature. His tremendous influence over the history of literature and western thought is still in evidence today. His fundamentally life-affirming philosophy called, with great lyricism, for mankind to surpass itself (*Thus Spake Zarathustra*, 1886).

Focusing on the often irreconcilable duality of the mind and the senses, the irrational and the rational, the works of **Thomas Mann** *(Buddenbrooks, The Magic Mountain)* and **Hermann Hesse** *(Der Steppenwolf)* bear the stamp of Nietzscheism; the sanatorium in Davos in *The Magic Mountain* symbolises the "disease" that runs rife in decadent European societies. In this struggle between life and morbid instincts, the shadow of Thanatos hangs over our western civilisations. The Czech-born German-language writer **Franz Kafka** (1883–1924) differs from these authors in both style and thought; his nightmarish novels *(The Trial, The Castle, America)* contain a vision of a dehumanised world dominated by anxiety and the absurd. The works of Vienna-born **Stefan Zweig**, one of Kafka's contemporaries, were of a less tortured nature. This highly cultivated man, citizen of the world, traveller and translator proved in his best

Ernst Jünger
©UPPA/Photoshot

short stories *(Amok, Conflicts, The Royal Game)* to be a remarkable storyteller with humanist sympathies.

The early 20C also witnessed a revival in poetry. **Stefan George** (1868–1933) published poems which, in their formal perfection, ally him with the French Symbolists, while the Austrians **Rainer Maria Rilke** (1875–1926) and **Hugo von Hoffmannsthal** (1874–1929) reach the peak of lyrical impressionism.

The 1930s and 1940s were marked by an intensified search for the meaning of life; spurred on by Husserlian phenomenology, **Heidegger** and, to a lesser degree, **Jaspers**, put the question of being back at the heart of philosophy. Based on our essential finiteness, Heideggerian existentialism distinguishes between an existence marked by a sense of being and an "inauthentic" existence, led astray into the impersonal self.

The world of theatre was dominated by **Bertolt Brecht** *(The Threepenny Opera, Mother Courage, Galileo)*. A committed socialist, he rejected the "theatre of illusion", advocating *Verfremdungseffekt* ("the alienation effect"): the spectator must observe the action on stage with a critical eye and be able to decipher the methods by which the strong exploit the weak.

National Socialism forced numerous poets and writers into exile (Walter Benjamin, Alfred Döblin, Lion Feuchtwanger, Else Lasker-Schüler, Thomas and Heinrich Mann, Carl Zuckmayer, Stefan Zweig). **Gottfried Benn** (1886–1956) withdrew into silence, while **Ernst Jünger** (1895–1998) courageously published his novel *On the Marble Cliffs* in 1939: "...Such are the dungeons above which rise the proud castles of the tyrants... They are terrible noisome pits in which a God-forsaken crew revels to all eternity in the degradation of human dignity and human freedom."

POST-1945 LITERATURE

Twelve years under National Socialist rule had broken the flow of literary creativity in Germany, necessitating repair work in this domain too. The association of authors known as **Gruppe 47** (after the year of its founding), which centred upon **Hans Werner Richter** and **Alfred Andersch**, was instrumental in putting Germany back on the map as far as world literature was concerned. This loosely associated group of writers served as a forum for reading, discussion and criticism, until its last conference in 1967, exerting a lasting and formative influence on the contemporary German literary scene. Authors associated with Gruppe 47 included **Paul Celan**, **Heinrich Böll** (Nobel Prize winner in 1972), **Günter Grass** (Nobel Prize winner in 1999), **Siegfried Lenz**, **Peter Weiss** and **Hans Magnus Enzensberger**. By the end of the 1950s, works of international standing were being published: Günter Grass' masterpiece *The Tin Drum* is an extraordinary novel in the tradition of Celine; **Uwe Johnson**'s *Speculations about Jacob*, **Heinrich Böll**'s *Billiards at Half Past Nine* and **Martin Walser**'s novel *Marriages in Philippsburg*. Increasing politicisation was what finally put an end to Gruppe 47's activities. Authors not associated with Gruppe 47 were hard at work also; **Arno Schmidt** developed a very original and high-quality body of work, while **Wolfgang Koeppen** produced some wickedly satirical novels on contemporary society. The literature of the 1960s was characterised by a wave of criticism but, by the following decade, German literary concerns were withdrawing to a newly discovered "inner contemplation". A particularly prolific amount of good writing was produced by women during the 1970s and 1980s (**Gabriele Wohmann**, **Karin Struck**, **Verena Stefan**).

In the world of theatre, dominated initially by the dramatic theory of Bertolt Brecht, a new band of writers began to emerge, with works by **Tankred Dorst** (*Toller*, 1968), **Peter Weiss** (*Hölderlin*, 1971) and **Heinar Kipphardt**. **Rolf Hochhuth** was particularly successful with his "documentary dramas" in which he examines contemporary moral issues (*The Representative*, 1963), and **Botho Strauß**, the most widely performed modern German dramatist, has won international acclaim with plays such

as *The Hypochondriac* (1972), *The Park* (1983) and *Final Chorus* (1991).

The political division of Germany was also reflected in German literature. In the old East German Republic, the leadership viewed literature's *raison d'être* as the contribution it might make to the socialist programme for educating the masses. The Bitterfelder Weg, a combined propaganda exercise and literary experiment launched at the Bitterfeld chemical factory in 1959 as part of the East German Republic's cultural programme under Walter Ulbricht, was intended to unite art and everyday life and break down class barriers. Factory visits were organised for writers, so they could observe workers and then portray them glowingly in their novels, poems or plays, while the workers themselves were encouraged to write about their lives.

The results of the project were mixed, and although it gave authors a clearer idea of the primitive conditions that most East German workers were obliged to tolerate, those who wrote too honestly about what they saw found their works censored.

Poetry was the literary form least easily subject to Communist censorship, and poets such as **Peter Huchel**, **Johannes Bobrowski** and **Erich Arendt** produced some remarkable work. From the early 1960s the prose work of **Günter de Bruyn**, **Stefan Heym** and **Erwin Strittmatter** was widely appreciated. **Anna Seghers**, who returned from exile in America after the war, was considered the greatest East German writer of the older generation, while rising star **Christa Wolf** won acclaim in both Germanies. Important contributions to the theatre were made by playwrights **Ulrich Plenzdorf**, **Peter Hacks** and above all **Heiner Müller** (*The Hamlet Machine*, 1978).

Any overview of German-language literature since World War II must, of course, acknowledge the enormous contribution made by **Max Frisch** and **Friedrich Dürrenmatt**, of Switzerland, and **Ilse Aichinger**, **Ingeborg Bachmann** and **Thomas Bernhard** of Austria.

Music

Germany and the German-speaking world have made a considerable contribution to Western music. After reaching an initial high point in the 18C with the Baroque period, German music was propelled back into the limelight by the genius of composers such as Beethoven and Wagner. Modern experimentation since the emergence of the 12-tone system testifies to the continuing vitality of German music.

FROM MINNESÄNGER TO MEISTERSÄNGER

In the 12C and 13C, feudal courts constituted the main forum for musical expression. The **Minnesänger** (essentially troubadours – *minne* meaning "love" in Middle High German), who were often noble knights, such as **Wolfram von Eschenbach** and **Walther von der Vogelweide**, drew inspiration for their songs from French lyric poetry. They would perform their love songs before the nobility, accompanying themselves on the lute.

The *Meistersänger*, or mastersingers, of the 14C–16C preferred a more sedentary lifestyle and organised themselves into guilds. They introduced polyphony to German music and clearly set the musical forms of their art. Anyone wanting to become a *Meistersänger* had to prove

himself in a public contest. Among the prominent figures of the time was **Heinrich von Meißen** (1250–1318) who marked the transition from *Minnesang* (courtly love song/lyric) to the poetry of the *Meistersänger*. **Hans Sachs** (1494–1576), a cobbler by trade and an ardent supporter of Luther, was also a prolific poet; many of his compositions were turned into Protestant chorales. Sachs later became the subject of Wagner's opera *The Mastersingers of Nuremberg*.

FROM THE RENAISSANCE TO THE 17C

In the wake of the Reformation, German music began to develop an individual identity with the emergence of the chorale, the fruit of the collaboration between **Luther** and **Johann Walther** (1496–1570). *"Ein' feste Burg ist unser Gott"* (A Mighty Fortress is Our God) composed by the two men in 1529 was reworked by Bach. Originally a hymn with a simple melody, the chorale – sung in the vernacular – soon opened up to the secular repertoire, embracing popular genres of music. It subsequently gave rise to the German cantata and oratorio.

Religious music maestro, **Heinrich Schütz** (1585–1672) managed to produce a skilful combination of German and Italian elements. He composed the first German opera, *Dafne*, a work which was sadly lost. *The Seven Words*

Munich Philharmonic performing at Gasteig

of Christ (1645) shows the influence of Monteverdi who, along with Gabrieli, was one of Schütz's masters.

The second half of the 17C witnessed a proliferation of organ schools, one of the most famous of which was in Nuremberg. An inspiration for Bach, who is said to have walked hundreds of miles to hear him play in Lübeck, **Dietrich Buxtehude** (1637–1707) organised the first concerts of sacred music. **Johann Pachelbel** (1653–1706) was the great master of the organ school in southern Germany; the only surviving piece of his work is the *Canon in D Major*.

BACH AND BAROQUE MUSIC

His consummate skill as a composer, his genius for invention and his mastery of counterpoint enabled **Bach** (1685–1750) to excel in every kind of music he wrote. Based in Weimar until 1717, he spent several years at the court of Köthen, during which he composed *The Brandenburg Concertos*. In 1723, he was appointed "Cantor" at St. Thomas' School, Leipzig. Bach's duties included the composition of a cantata for every Sunday service, as well as the supervision of services at four other churches. He also taught Latin and voice and still found time to write his own instrumental and vocal works. His masterpieces include *The Well-Tempered Clavier* (1722 and 1744) and the *St. Matthew Passion* (1727).

A brilliant court composer, influenced by his travels in Italy, **Georg Friedrich Händel** (1665–1759) excelled in both opera and oratorio (*The Messiah*, 1742). Born in Halle, he was organist at the town's cathedral before pursuing his career at the Hamburg opera. Based in England from 1714, he spent most of the last 40 years of his life in London, and even obtained British nationality.

Händel's friend, **Georg Philipp Telemann**, (1681–1767) was influenced by French and Italian composers, and was himself a particularly prolific composer. He turned from counterpoint to harmony and composed chamber music and church music as well as operas. Telemann was godfather to Bach's second son, **Carl Philipp Emmanuel** (1714–

1788), who popularised the sonata in its classic form.

FROM THE MANNHEIM SCHOOL TO BEETHOVEN

In the mid 18C, the musicians of the **Mannheim School**, under the patronage of Elector Palatine Karl Theodor, helped establish the modern symphonic form, giving a more prominent role to wind instruments. Influenced by the innovations from Mannheim, **Christoph Willibald Gluck** (1714–1787) undertook a "reformation of opera", producing refined works where the lyrics took pride of place; he provoked the enthusiasm of the innovators – and the horror of fans of traditional, Italian-inspired opera – by staging, in Paris, his *Iphigenia in Aulis* and *Orpheus*. This period was also marked by the appearance in Germany of the **Singspiel**, a popular opera in which dialogue is interspersed with songs in the form of Lieder. Mozart's *Magic Flute* (1791) and Beethoven's *Fidelio* (1814) are excellent examples of this genre later identified with operetta.

The contribution of Viennese Classicism during the second half of the 18C proved to be crucial. **Joseph Haydn** (1732–1809) laid down the classical form of the symphony, the string quartet and the piano sonata. **Wolfgang Amadeus Mozart** (1756–1791) perfected these forms and created some truly immortal operas *(The Marriage of Figaro, Don Juan)*.

Born in Bonn, **Ludwig van Beethoven** (1770–1827) went to Vienna to study under Haydn and Antonio Salieri. With his innovative harmonisations, he developed a highly individual style and transformed existing forms of music, heralding the Romantic movement. The depth of his inspiration, ranging from pure introspection to a wider belief in the force and universality of his art, emanates from his work with extraordinary power, perhaps most particularly in his symphonies. It was in 1824, when he had already been suffering from total and incurable deafness for five years, that Beethoven's magnificent *Ninth Symphony* – inspired by one of Schiller's odes – was performed for the first time.

ROMANTIC MUSIC AND WAGNER

Franz Schubert (1797–1826) brought Romantic music to its first high point. He focused much creative energy on the *Lied* (song), blending folk and classical music in a unique style.

Carl Maria von Weber (1786–1826) created Germany's first Romantic opera, *Freischütz* (1821), paving the way for the characters of Wagnerian drama. It was a resounding success when first performed in Berlin, due in part to the use of folk songs. As for the lofty world of **Felix Mendelssohn-Bartholdy** (1809–1879), it was far removed from the forces of evil that inhabit the *Freischütz*. Although espousing classical music forms, Mendelssohn, who was a conductor, pianist and founder of the Leipzig Conservatory, also reveals a Romantic influence.

Robert Schumann (1810–1856), passionate and lyrical in turn, but brought up in the Germanic tradition, strives to reconcile a classical heritage with personal expression. A talented music critic (he founded the *Neue Zeitschrift für Musik* newspaper in 1834), he initially wrote for piano alone *(Carnival, Scenes from Childhood)*. Then, spurred on by his admiration for Schubert and the advice of his friend Mendelssohn, he began to compose *Lieder (Dichterliebe)*, subsequently turning his attention to symphonies and chamber music. A close friend of Schumann, whose wife Clara he loved with a passion, **Johannes Brahms** (1833–1897) exemplified a more introverted style of German Romanticism. After long being accused of formalism, he was rediscovered in the 20C, notably thanks to the influence of Schönberg *(Brahms the Progressive)*.

Crowning glory of the German Romantic movement, the work of **Wagner** (1813–1883) revolutionised opera. Wagner claimed that music should be subservient to drama, serving as "atmosphere" and a "backdrop of sound" without which the opera's message could not be fully conveyed. Orchestration thus becomes of paramount importance. Libretto and plot unfold continuously, preserving dramatic reality. Wagner introduces the use of "leitmotifs" – musical phrases used recurrently to denote specific characters, moods or situations – making them essential to the continuity of the action. *Lohengrin* was first performed in 1850 in Weimar, under the supervision of **Franz Liszt**.

Designed by Wagner himself as a stage for the performance of the entire work *(Gesamtkunstwerk)*, the Bayreuth Theater was inaugurated in 1876 with *The Ring of the Nibelung (Rheingold, Walküre, Siegfried* and *Götterdämmerung)*. The fruit of 22 years' work, the magnificent first public performance of *The Ring* lasted 18 hours. Although its artistic success was undeniable, the Bayreuth episode ended in financial ruin for the composer. *Parzival*, Wagner's last opera, revolves around the theme of redemption through sacrifice, and was first performed in Bayreuth in 1882.

At the end of the 19C, **Gustav Mahler** (1860–1911), Czech-Austrian composer and creator of the symphonic *Lied*, and **Hugo Wolf** (1850–1903) developed a new musical language which forms a bridge between Romanticism and dodecaphony.

Richard Strauss (1864–1949) excelled in orchestra music *(Thus Spake Zarathustra)*, uniting a certain harmonic audacity with a dazzling and multi-faceted style.

CONTEMPORARY MUSIC

Contemporary musical experimentation is derived principally from the Austrian school of atonal, or serial (especially 12-tone systems) music, represented by **Arnold Schönberg** and his two main disciples **Alban Berg** and **Anton von Webern**. Introducing a new method of composing music, the 12-tone system was first revealed to the public by Schönberg in 1928 in the *Variations for Orchestra*. Berg applied his master's innovation to lyrical drama *(Lulu)*, while Webern, turning his back on Romanticism, focused on the concision of form. The brilliant **Paul Hindemith** (1893–1963), initially influenced by Romanticism, remained untouched by Schönberg's innovations; in a break with German tradition, he forged a path of his own between atonality and dodecaphony.

Carl Orff (1895–1982), creator of the Orff Schulwerk, propounded innovative ideas about music education. His highly original theatrical compositions combine drama, speech and song in a fascinating rhythmic framework: his powerful collection of secular songs with infectious rhythms, *Carmina Burana* (1937), soon gained international renown. The compositions – mainly opera and ballet music – of **Werner Egk** (1901–1983), a student of Carl Orff, reveal the influence of Igor Stravinski and Richard Strauss. As for **Kurt Weill** (1900–1950), influenced at the beginning of his career by the atonal composers, he returned under the impact of jazz to tonal music, and composed *The Threepenny Opera* (1928) in collaboration with Brecht.

Although **Wolfgang Fortner** (1907–1987) was influenced initially by Hindemith, he nonetheless later turned to modal 12-tone serial music. His mature works introduce electronic elements into his musical compositions.

Bernd Alois Zimmermann (1918–1970) perceived past, present and future as one, and the multiple layers of reality are reflected in his composition technique. Quotations and collage were particularly important to him. His major work is the opera *The Soldiers*.

From 1950, a younger generation of musicians developed the potential of electronic music under the aegis of **Karlheinz Stockhausen** (1928–2007). **Hans Werner Henze** (b. 1926) created expressive operas, in which modernity and tradition, and atonality and tonality are combined. **Wolfgang Rihm** (b. 1952), a student of Fortner, like Henze, also mixes traditional stylistic elements with new techniques in his extremely complex musical language.

Cinema

After producing a number of masterpieces during the Expressionist period of the 1920s, German cinema fell into a decline from which it did not emerge until the 1960s. Although now struggling to make its mark in the face of the American productions, it has managed to produce some remarkable international award-winning works.

THE GOLDEN AGE OF EXPRESSIONISM

The creation in 1917 of UFA (Universum Film Aktiengesellschaft), a production company of considerable means which, from 1921, was directed by producer **Erich Pommer**, led to some lavish productions. The Expressionism that was apparent in literature, theatre and painting also seeped into film production in the troubled postwar political and social scene. Deliberately turning its back on Realism, it often revelled in angst-ridden

atmospheres, cultivating an exaggeration of forms and contrasts; it was typified by the use of chiaroscuro lighting effects and the geometric stylisation of the décor. Very few works could actually be classed as purely Expressionist, but among them is **Robert Wiene**'s masterpiece *The Cabinet of Dr Caligari* (1919), which was well received in the United States and France. Nevertheless, Expressionism was a great source of inspiration for German cinema in the 1920s; this period was dominated by the films of **FW Murnau** (*Nosferatu the Vampire*, 1922; *The Last Laugh*, 1924; *Faust*, 1926) and **Fritz Lang** (*Dr Mabuse*, 1922; *Metropolis*, 1925). Lang's German work reached its high point in 1931 with *M*, the director's first talking picture. Initially entitled *Murderers Among Us* (the title was changed under pressure from the Nazis), *M* paints the picture of a diseased society which, unable to cure its own ills, seeks scapegoat sinners on whom to place the blame. *The Last Will of Dr Mabuse* in 1932 attracted Nazi censure. Soon after being invited by Goebbels to supervise the Reich's film production, Lang went into exile, first moving to Paris and then to California, where he pursued his film-directing career.

The 1920s in Germany also witnessed a shift towards Realism and away from the dominant Expressionist trend. Examples of this new trend include the films of **GW Pabst** (*The Joyless Street*, 1925; *Diary of a Lost Girl,* 1926; *Lulu,* 1929) and **Josef von Sternberg**'s *The Blue Angel* (1930) starring **Marlene Dietrich** and **Emil Jannings**.

AN ABRUPT HALT

The promising surge of German cinema after World War I was sadly stopped in its tracks with the arrival of the Third Reich. Many actors and directors went into exile. The Nazis turned cinema into a tool to serve the regime's ideology. Filmmaker **Leni Riefenstahl** (1902–2003) stands out in the generally disappointing and inartistic genre of propaganda films, with her productions of amazing cinematic beauty, such as *The Gods of the Stadium*, a glorification of the 1936 Berlin Olympics.

The period immediately after World War II was a cultural desert. While "Socialist Realism" prevailed in East Germany, film production in the Federal Republic of the 1950s was of poor quality. Only a few films, such as *The Last Bridge* (1954) and *The Devil's General* (1955) by **Helmut Kaütner**, managed to escape the pervasive mediocrity. The 1962 **Oberhausen Manifesto**, signed by 26 young filmmakers, signalled the birth of a new cinematographic language; the long-awaited revival was here at last.

THE REVIVAL OF THE 1960s AND BEYOND

In the 1960s and 1970s makers of "New German cinema" rose up in the wake of the French *nouvelle vague*, seeking to distance themselves from old-style cinema with its run-of-the-mill commercial superficiality. Films made by **Werner Herzog**, **Volker Schlöndorff** (*Young Törless,* 1966) and **Alexander Kluge** (*Artists at the Top of the Big Top: Disorientated*, 1968) quickly met with success. It was not long – the mid 1970s – before this younger generation had re-established German cinema on an international scale. **Volker Schlöndorff** made *The Lost Honour of Katharina Blum* (in collaboration with **Margarethe von Trotta**, 1975), and *The Tin Drum* (1979). **Werner Herzog** went on to explore a fantastic, often quite exotic world in

---

Cinema in the Former East German Republic

East German cinema, like all other art forms, was compelled by the state to fulfil a didactic function. Thus a number of films used literary classics as a theme, since directors felt unable to confront issues relevant to contemporary East Germany. **Konrad Wolf** made his mark on three decades of East German filmmaking, with films such as *Sterne* (1958), which won him recognition worldwide. In *Solo Sunny* (1979) he put forward the case for individualism, thus paving the way for a breakthrough in the East German film industry. **Egon Güntheb** made the highly successful *Der Dritte* (1971), while the greatest hit was **Heiner Carow**'s *Die Legende von Paul und Paula* (1973).

1984 was a particularly fruitful year, with **Hermann Zschoche**'s *Hälfte des Lebens*, **Iris Gusner**'s *Kaskade Rückwärts*, and **Helmut Dzuiba**'s *Erscheinen Pflicht*. One of the leading East German filmmakers of the 1970s and 1980s was **Rainer Simon** (*Das Luftschiff,* 1982; *Die Frau und der Fremde,* 1985).

Finally, **Lothar Warneke** studied the problems of everyday life, and endeavoured to dismantle rigid ideological points of view (*Bear Ye One Another's Burdens (Einer trage des anderen Last)*, 1988).

The Berlinale

As one of the pioneers of celluloid history, it's only natural that Germany should be home to one of the world's most prestigious film festivals: The Berlinale (☀ see BERLIN), which brings hundreds of international stars to the German capital every February.

Founded in 1951 with the encouragement of the Western allies, the festival shows hundreds of flicks from around the world with some of them competing for the coveted Golden and Silver Bear trophies (www.berlinale.de). Munich and Hamburg also host major festivals and there quite literally dozens of other smaller ones, many specialising in particular genres such as documentaries, animated films, short films, children's cinema and gay and lesbian movies.

Aguirre, Wrath of God (1972), *Nosferatu the Vampyre* (1979) and *Fitzcarraldo* (1982). Prominent figures in the **Munich School** include **Rainer Werner Fassbinder** (1945–1982), who also worked in television, and who was responsible for a considerable number of excellent films (*Fear eats the Soul (Angst essen Seele auf)*, 1973; *The Marriage of Maria Braun*, 1978; *Berlin Alexanderplatz*, a 14-part television series, 1980), and **Wim Wenders** (*The American Friend*, 1977; *Paris, Texas*, 1984; *Wings of Desire*, 1987; *Buena Vista Social Club*, 1999).

Important and innovative women film directors include **Margarethe von Trotta** (*Rosa Luxemburg*, 1986; *Das Versprechen*, 1995). Wolfgang Peterson's fantasy world in *The Neverending Story* (1984) was a resounding commercial success.

Edgar Reitz won international acclaim with his film epic *Heimat* (1984) and its sequel *Heimat 2* (1993).

However, West German cinema has been characterised by a strongly individual narrative feel which perhaps makes it less approachable to outsiders. One refreshing filmmaker worthy of note is **Doris Dörrie** who, with *Men... (Männer)* (1985) and *Bin ich schön?* (1998), reduced the zeitgeist to a humorous point.

CONTEMPORARY CINEMA

Recent successful films include **Tom Tykwer**'s 1999 *Lola rennt (Run Lola Run)* and **Wolfgang Becker**'s *Goodbye Lenin!*, which won the Best European Film award at the 2003 Berlin Film Fes-

tival. Another critically acclaimed movie was **Oliver Hirschbiegel**'s *Downfall*, starring Bruno Ganz as Hitler holed up in his bunker during the last days of his life. More controversial was **Dani Levy**'s 2007 satire *Mein Führer*, which ridicules an allegedly depressed Hitler at the end of the war.

The most successful German film of late, however, was *The Lives of Others*, written and directed by **Florian Henckel von Donnersmarck**, which won the Academy Award for Best Foreign Language Film in 2007.

A year later, another German movie was nominated in Hollywood: the *Baader-Meinhof Complex*, by **Uli Edel** which tells the story of the early years of the Red Army Faction terrorist group and its impact on German society.

Goodbye Lenin! (2003) by Wolfgang Becker

© Archives du 7eme Art/Photos 12/Alamy

Nature

At the heart of Europe, bordered by the Alps to the south and by the Baltic Sea to the north, Germany is virtually without natural frontiers to the east and the west.
Such a lack of barriers, and the subsequent accessibility to outside influences, has had a profound effect on the country's history and civilisation.

GEOLOGY

In the **north** is the immense **Germano-Polish Plain**, formed by the glaciation of the Quaternary Era. The resistance of its crystalline bedrock meant that it was scarcely touched by the Hercynian and Alpine mountain-building movements. In the **centre**, during the Primary Era, the formidable Hercynian folding created a complex of minor massifs – now smoothed by erosion and for the most part wooded – separated by geographic depressions.

The most important of these Hercynian massifs are the Black Forest, the Rhenish schist massif and – encircling Bohemia in the Czech Republic – the Bavarian Forest, the Erzgebirge (Ore Mountains) and the Sudeten Mountains. On the edges of this Hercynian zone accumulated the coal-bearing deposits of the Ruhr and Silesia which led to the industrial expansion of the 19C.

The sedimentary basin of Swabia-Franconia, its vast area drained by the Main and the Neckar rivers, offers a less dramatic landscape. Abutting the Black Forest to the west and the Swabian Jura to the south, the limestone plateau is patterned with lines of hills sculpted according to the resistance of the varied strata.

In the **south**, the Alpine portion of Germany is delimited by the **Pre-Alps** (Voralpen) where the debris torn up and crushed during the final exertions of Quaternary glaciation formed the Bavarian plateau – a huge area stretching in a gentle slope as far as the Danube.

NORTHERN GERMANY
LOWER RHINE VALLEY AND WESTPHALIA

Lush, green and flat, protected from flooding, the plain of the Lower Rhine brings to mind the landscape of the neighbouring Netherlands. There is similar scenery around Münster, on the Westphalian plain, where farmlands patterned by hedges and trees offer the additional attraction of many moated castles (Wasserburgen).

GREAT NORTHERN PLAIN

Despite its apparent monotony, this enormous area (which extends eastwards into Poland) does offer a certain variety of landscapes.

In the south, below the Weser and Harz foothills, the Börde country lies between the Weser and the Elbe – a region covered by an alluvial topsoil whose fertility is legendary. Farms and market gardens flourish in this densely populated zone, which is favoured also with mineral deposits rich in iron and potassium.

Further north, on either side of the Elbe, is the Geest – a region of glacial deposits (sand, gravel, clay) with little to recommend it geographically, since it was covered by the Scandinavian glaciers right up to Paleolithic times. This has resulted in poor drainage and soils that are too sandy; between Berlin and the Baltic, the Mecklenburg plateau is scattered with shallow lakes interspersed with morainic deposits that bear witness to the prolonged glacial presence. The Spree and the Havel, meandering through the flatlands, supply the lakeland regions of the Spreewald and Potsdam. West of the Lower Weser, and in the Worpswede neighbourhood north of Bremen, peat bogs (Moore) alternate with very wet pastureland.

Most of the peat moors are now under cultivation, after having been drained using Dutch methods. The nature reserve south of Lüneburg, however, has preserved for all time a typical stretch of the original moorland.

THE BALTIC COAST

The German section of the Baltic Coast, which stretches from Flensburg all the way to the Stettin Haff, is a murrain landscape which, in addition to very flat parts also has a few elevations that rise above the 100m/320ft mark. Because of the relatively limited tidal differences of the shallow (on average 55m/180ft deep) Baltic Sea, the coastline has been subject to little change. That's why numerous cities with long traditions have evolved here. Between the bays of Lübeck and Kiel lies the Holsteinische Schweiz (Holstein Switzerland), the hilly and lake-dotted remainders of a ground and end moraine from the Ice Age.

The arms of the sea, which are the fjords and bays left over from the glaciers of the last Ice Age, cut deep into the land and form excellent natural harbours. Their banks are lined with beaches, forests and little fishing villages. Further to the east, the Baltic Coast is marked by shallow, water-filled inlets from the post-Ice Age period. Four islands lie offshore; the largest is the water-washed Rügen.

NORTH SEA COAST

Because of the winds and waves, the North Sea Coast between the Netherlands and Denmark is constantly undergoing change. The tides raise and lower the water level by 2m/6.4ft to 3m/9.6ft twice daily. Several island groups lie off shore in the Watt, a 5X30km/3X18mi strip of land that is washed by the sea when the tide is in, but is above sea level at ebb times. The Watt ecosystem is home to nearly 2 000 species, from sea lions to creatures a tenth of a millimetre in size. A strip of marshland created over centuries lies along the coast.

Once upon a time, the tides used to bring in animal and plant particles together with fine sand, which formed a fertile base for agriculture in the marshlands. Behind this is the less fertile, hilly "Geest". Broad moors have formed in the depressions, some of which have been turned over to farming. Germany's two largest seaports, Hamburg and Bremen, lie at the inner ends of the funnel-shaped Elbe and Weser estuaries.

CENTRAL GERMANY
THE RHENISH SCHIST MASSIF

This ancient geological mass, cut through by the Rhine – the only continuous natural channel of communication between the north and south of the country – the Lahn and the Moselle, comprises among others the highlands known as the Eifel, the Westerwald, the Taunus and the Hunsrück.

They share the same inhospitable climate and the same evidence of volcanic activity as the crater lakes, known as the *Maare*, of the Eifel plateau.

Red-sandstone cliffs of Helgoland, North Sea

© Rainer Jensen/Picture Alliance/Photoshot

95

The Eifel will be familiar to motoring enthusiasts as the home of the Nürburgring Grand Prix race circuit. The Upper Sauerland, a thickly wooded, mountainous region (alt 841m/2 760ft), with its many dams, acts as a water reserve for the Ruhr industrial area.

MOUNTAINS OF UPPER HESSEN AND THE WESER

Between the Rhenish schist massif and the Thuringian Forest (*Thüringer Wald*) lies an amalgam of heights, some of them volcanic (Vogelsberg, Rhön), and depressions which have been used as a highway, linking north and south, by German invaders throughout the ages. Between Westphalia and the north, the Weser Mountains – extended westwards by the Teutoburger Wald – form a barrier that is breached at the Porta Westfalica, near Minden. Further to the east, the Erzgebirge (Ore Mountains) form a natural frontier with the Czech Republic.

HARZ MOUNTAINS

This relatively high range (alt 1 142m/ 3 747ft at the Brocken) has a typical mountain climate, characterised by heavy snowfalls in winter.

SOUTHERN GERMANY
PLAIN OF THE UPPER RHINE

Between Basle and the Bingen Gap, a soil of exceptionally fertile loess – accompanied by a climate combining light rainfall, an early spring and a very hot summer – has produced a rich agricultural yield (hops, corn and tobacco) and a terrain highly suitable for the cultivation of vines. The whole of this low-lying, productive tract has become a crossroads for the rest of Europe, which is why certain towns – Frankfurt, for instance – have profited internationally from their development.

SCHWARZWALD (BLACK FOREST)

This crystalline massif (alt 1 493m/4 899ft at the Feldberg), which overlooks the Rhine Gap, is relatively well populated. The region's healthy climate and many thermal springs, with their attendant, highly reputed spa resorts, draw large numbers of tourists here every year.

SWABIAN-FRANCONIAN BASIN

Franconia, formed by vast, gently undulating plateaux, is bordered to the southeast by the small limestone massif of the Franconian Jura which produces Germany's building stone, and to the north and northeast by the wooded crystalline ranges flanking Bohemia and Thuringia. Swabia, once ruled by the kings of Württemberg, offers a variety of landscapes – barred to the south by the blue line of the Swabian Jura, which rises to 874m/2 867ft. Small valleys, enlivened by orchards and vineyards, alternate here with the gentle slopes of wooded hillsides.

THE ALPS AND THE BAVARIAN PLATEAU

The Bavarian Alps and the Allgäu Alps offer contrasts between the sombre green of their forests and the shades of grey of their rocks and escarpments, an impressive sight when seen against the backdrop of a blue sky. The Zugspitze, the highest point in Germany, reaches an altitude of 2 962m/9 720ft. Torrents such as Isar, Lech, Iller and Inn, have over time carved out corridors with broad, flat floors suitable for the cultivation of the land and the development of towns (Ulm, Augsburg and Munich).

UNSPOILT SCENERY AND PROTECTED SPACES

Although densely populated and highly industrialised, wide open natural spaces still characterise much of the German countryside. In fact, with 2 389km/1 484mi of coastline, several Alpine peaks approaching 3 000m/9 842ft, fertile river valleys where fine wines grow, pine and deciduous forests, sand dunes and wild-flower draped hillsides, nature has been as creative in Germany as Picasso in his prime. The most dramatic landscape is the Alpine region, where the Zugspitze forms the peak of the country with its summit at 2 064m/9 724ft. It juts out from a range of craggy peaks wrought

Lindau im Bodensee with a view to the Alps, Bavaria

H. Spiering/MICHELIN

by tectonic uplift and carved by glaciers and erosion since. The Black Forest is a so-called *Mittelgebirge*, or mid-size mountain range, with elevations topping out at 1 493m/4 898ft with the Feldberg. Patches of forest here alternate with rolling hills, bucolic valleys and cascading waterfalls all wrapped into one storied landscape. Other *Mittelgebirge* include the Bavarian Forest, the Harz Mountains and the Sauerland. Germany has 15 national parks protecting places of outstanding natural beauty and rare geographical features alongside many species of plants and wildlife, thus functioning as natural laboratories for researchers and scientists. Landscapes are hugely varied and include North Sea mudflats, the salt marshes and chalk cliffs on Rügen Island, the evocatively warped basalt and sandstone formations of Saxon Switzerland and the mighty peaks around Berchtesgaden, Germany's oldest national park. In addition there are over 90 nature parks, which enjoy a lower degree of environmental protection and are essentially outdoor playgrounds. But don't picture them as traditional "parks": these sprawling rural landscapes are crisscrossed by roads and wrapped around villages. Controlled logging and agricultural use is permitted.

Much of Germany's fauna is similar to what you might encounter in the rest of Europe, although there is a greater variety of bird life. Winged creatures roaming the skies includes osprey, grouse, owls, passerines and woodpeckers, as well as such protected birds as the black stork, the warbler and the great horned owl. Among the raptors, the rare and endangered sea eagle can still be observed with a little luck. The Bodden area in western Pomerania has the largest nesting site of cranes in Europe (nearly 30 000 each year).

Cranes in the Bodden area of Western Pomelania in autumn

© John Lens/Alamy

Schloss Neuschwanstein, Bavaria
© Giovanni Simeone/Sime/Photononstop

Dynamic, intriguing, individualistic, forward-looking – Berlin is Germany's most visited city and the third-most popular in Europe after London and Paris. And for good reason: the wealth and quality of its cultural life is peerless, with world-class museums, opera, theatre, music and a spirited art and gallery scene. Architectural gems also abound, some of them centuries old, others created only during the post-reunification construction maelstrom. By contrast, Brandenburg, the state surrounding it, is imbued with a soothing tranquillity and great natural splendour. This is a region shaped by water – rivers, lakes and canals – wending through a flat, windswept landscape, much of which is protected as a nature preserve. Culturally, Brandenburg's jewel is Potsdam, which packs more palaces and parks into its small frame than many a small nation.

Highlights

1. Get close-ups of the glass dome atop the **Reichstag** (p112)
2. Meet Nefertiti, Berlin's most beautiful woman, at the **Neues Museum** (p118)
3. Admiring the largest collection of 18C paintings outside of France at **Schloss Charlottenburg** (p123)
4. Enjoy a picnic in the lovely **Tiergarten** (p126)
5. Explore the "Wild East" on a **Trabi Safari** (p135)

Architecture

It may not feel right to put a positive spin on the destruction brought upon Berlin by war and division, but it did give the German capital the opportunity to re-define itself architecturally, especially since the fall of the Wall. Most of the world's leading architects – Frank Gehry, David Chipperfield, Daniel Libeskind and Lord Norman Foster among them – have created modern masterpieces fit for the 21C. Areas to check out closely are the new government quarter, Potsdamer Platz, Pariser Platz and the Embassy Quarter.

Shopping

The best shopping in Berlin is not done in shopping centres, but in small boutiques and shops lining the streets of its various neighbourhoods. Local designer boutiques cluster in the Scheunenviertel in Mitte, while Friedrichstraße offers upmarket brand names in the glamorous Friedrichstadtpassagen. In Kreuzberg you can pick up great vintage

Dome of Reichstag

M. Hertleir/MICHELIN

BERLIN AND BRANDENBURG

KOSZALIN

WISMAR

MECKLENBURG-
VORPOMMERN

Güstrow

MECKLENBURG LAKE DISTRICT

HAMBURG

Rheinsberg

Ravensbrück

POLAND

Kloster Chorin

Szczecin

Oranienburg

POZNAŃ

BERLIN

Francfurt
(Oder)

Dahlem

SAXONY-
ANHALT

Brandenburg

POTSDAM

Großer Müggelsee

Lehnin

HANNOVER

Magdeburg

BRANDENBURG

Spreewald

Lübbenau
Cottbus

WROCŁAW

Branitz

BERLIN	★★★	Highly recommended
Branitz	★★	Recommended
Rheinsberg	★	Interesting
Brandenburg		If you have time

SAXONY

DRESDEN

clothing and the latest in streetwear, while Charlottenburg has an entire street (Kantstraße) devoted to home decorations and furniture. Steps away is the famous Kurfürstendamm boulevard, which is dominated by department stores and chains.

Eating

From snack shacks to gourmet temples, Berlin offers a cornucopia of eating experiences. Traditional local fare includes *Eisbein* (boiled pork knuckle) and *Bouletten* (ground meat patties) but the most famous homegrown dish is the *Currywurst*, a slivered sausage drenched in a spicy tomato sauce and dusted with curry powder. Sophisticated foodies will

be happy to hear that Berlin now has a dozen restaurants boasting Michelin stars. And since Berlin is such an international city, you can also dine out on exotic dishes from Austria to Zambia.

Nightlife

When it comes to after-dark diversions, few cities can compete with Berlin. No matter whether your interests run to opera or clubbing, cabaret or comedy, theatre or art-house cinema, you'll be able to sate them in the German capital. Thanks to its legendary tolerance, Berlin also has a happening gay and lesbian scene. The area south of Nollendorf U-Bahn station in Schöneberg has been a traditional hub since the 1920s.

1

BERLIN CENTRE
map I

0 — 1km

N

Old position of the Berlin Wall

'Laubenkolonie' allotments

Sector under renovation

103

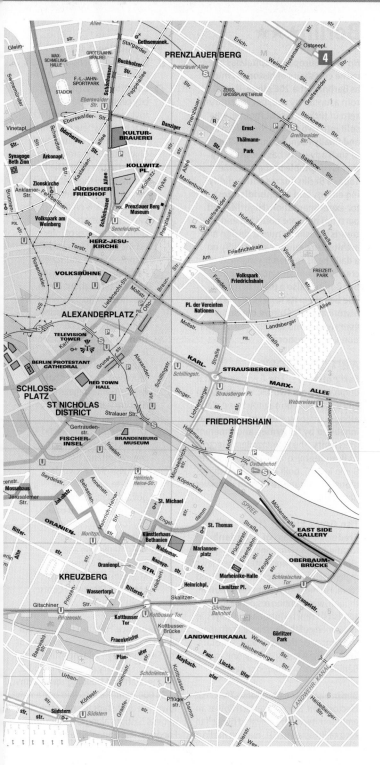

PRENZLAUER BERG

KULTUR-
BRAUEREI

KOLLWITZ-
PL.

ZEISS-
GROSSPLANETARIUM

Ernst-
Thälmann-
Park

JÜDISCHER
FRIEDHOF

Prenzlauer Berg
Museum

Synagoge
Beth Zion

Zionskirche

Volkspark am
Weinberg

HERZ-JESU-
KIRCHE

VOLKSBÜHNE

Volkspark
Friedrichshain

FREIZEIT-
PARK

ALEXANDERPLATZ

Pl. der Vereinten
Nationen

TELEVISION
TOWER

STRAUSBERGER PL.

BERLIN PROTESTANT
CATHEDRAL

RED TOWN
HALL

KARL-

MARX-

ALLEE

SCHLOSS-
PLATZ

ST NICHOLAS
DISTRICT

FRIEDRICHSHAIN

FISCHER-
INSEL

BRANDENBURG
MUSEUM

Mossehaus

Jerusalemer
Str.

ORANIEN-

St. Michael

Ostbahnhof

SPREE

St. Thomas

EAST SIDE
GALLERY

Künstlerhaus
Bethanien

Marianen-
platz

OBERBAUM-
BRÜCKE

KREUZBERG

Marheinike-Halle

STR.

Heinrichpl.

Lausitzer Pl.

Kottbusser
Tor

Kottbusser-
Brücke

LANDWEHRKANAL

Görlitzer
Park

LANDWEHR-KANAL

Südstern

105

Berlin★★★

No other European capital has been in the crosshairs of history as much as Berlin. In the 20C alone, it was torn asunder by war, became ground zero of Hitler's fascist regime, was split into two during the Cold War and finally reunited in 1989. Out of such adversity has grown a city that is adaptable in the extreme. Today's Berlin buzzes with a giddying energy and an unbridled zest for experimentation. Nightlife and partying here are non-stop and new trends in fashion, music, design and architecture emerge practically on a daily basis fuelled by an influx of creatives from around the planet. But Berlin is also a place of incredible beauty in its forests, rivers and historical sites. Culture blossoms everywhere and dining is an international smorgasbord.

A BIT OF HISTORY

Early history – The German capital originated from two 13C villages: Cölln and Berlin. Built on a sandy Spree island along a major trade route, each was inhabited by fishermen and itinerant merchants. The Hohenzollern Electors of Brandenburg became rulers over Berlin in 1417, built a palace and miraculously managed to remain in power until 1918.

The Great Elector (1640–1688) – **Frederick-William of Brandenburg** fortified the town, constructed quays along the Spree and established laws making Berlin a civilised, well-governed town. His most important contribution, though, was granting residence to thousands of French Huguenot refuges in 1685, many of them trained craftsmen, theologians, doctors and scholars. Within a few years, nearly one in five Berliners was of Huguenot descent.

Berlin becomes a kingdom – The Great Elector's son, Elector Friedrich III, was an ambitious type who elevated himself to king of Prussia in 1701, making Berlin a

▶ **Population:** 3 442 700
ℹ **Info:** ⟨ℓ⟩ *see Practical Information, opposite.*
◐ **Location:** Berlin has two city centres: the Mitte district around Alexanderplatz in the east, where most historic sights are located, and Charlottenburg around Zoo Station in the west. The two are linked by the vast Tiergarten Park. The Potsdamer Platz quarter is off the park's southeastern corner. Outlying districts of interest include Dahlem and Wannsee in the southwest.
🅿 **Parking:** Parking garages abound throughout Berlin. Visit http://wap.parkinfo.com for a complete listing of locations and charges.
⊘ **Don't Miss:** Museum Island (especially the Pergamon Museum and Neues Museum), Charlottenburg Palace, Gemäldegalerie (Picture Gallery), "Historic Centre" Walking Tour.
🕐 **Timing:** You could spend a week in Berlin and not see everything. Prioritise your visit. Allow two days for Mitte, including the government quarter and historic centre, and one day for Charlottenburg, including the palace.
👫 **Kids:** Berlin Zoo and Aquarium, German Museum of Technology, Legoland Discovery Centre.

royal residence. His son, **Frederick-William I** (1713–40) – otherwise known as the **Soldier King** – laid the foundations of Prussian military power by introducing the draft and building up an army of 80 000 men. He also laid out a new town, Friedrichstadt, beyond the city's original bastions along Leipziger Straße, Friedrichstraße and Wilhelmstraße.

PRACTICAL INFORMATION

TELEPHONE AREA CODE: *℘030*

TOURIST INFORMATION

Berlin Tourismus Marketing *(BTM; info hotline, room and ticket reservations ℘(030) 25 00 25; www.visitberlin.de; Mon–Fri 9am–8pm, Sat–Sun 10am–6pm.* **Tourist offices:** Brandenburg Gate, *Pariser Platz, South Wing, daily 10am–7pm*; Hauptbahnhof, *ground floor near Europaplatz entrance, daily 8am–10pm*; Alexa Shopping Centre, *Grunerstraße 20, near Alexanderplatz, Mon–Sat 10am–8pm*; Neues Kranzlereck, *Kurfürstendamm 21, Mon–Sat 10am–8pm, Sun 10am–6pm*; Humboldtbox, *Schloßplatz, Mon–Sat 10am–8pm, Sun 10am–6pm*. The Alexa, Brandenburg Gate and Nees Kranzlereck branches may offer extended hours April to October.

ENTERTAINMENT

Listings: The bi-weekly city magazines *Zitty* and *Tip* and the monthly *Berlin-Programm* (available at bookshops and kiosks) are the best sources of events listings. All are in German. The monthly English-language *Ex-Berliner* magazine also has some listings and reviews.

Tickets can be booked via www.visit berlin.de or call the BTM hotline *℘(030) 25 00 25*. The multilingual staff can also help with room reservations, a free service with a best-price guarantee.

POST OFFICES WITH LATE HOURS

The branch at Joachimstaler Straße 7 near Bahnhof Zoo is open Mon–Sat 9am–8pm and has a 24/7 self-service section; near Alexanderplatz, the branch at Rathausstraße 5 is open Mon–Fri 8am–7pm, Sat 9am–4pm. For additional branches, call *℘(01802) 33 33* or check www.deutschepost.de.

DAILY PAPERS

Berliner Morgenpost, Tagesspiegel, Berliner Zeitung, Die Tageszeitung.

INTERNET

www.berlin.de; www.visitberlin.de; www.museumsportal-berlin.de; www.meinberlin.de; www.exberliner.com

GETTING THERE AND AROUND

AIRPORT

For general information about any of Berlin's two airports, call *℘0180 500 0186*. From **Tegel (TXL)**, northwest of Berlin, bus nos. 109 and X9 travel through the western city centre to Zoo Station (Bahnhof Zoologischer Garten), while Jet Express Bus TXL serves Alexanderplatz in the eastern city centre. Jakob-Kaiser-Platz is the closest U-Bahn station. All three buses stop here as well. **Schönefeld (SFX)** is southeast of town and linked by Airport Express train to the city centre.

PUBLIC TRANSPORT

Berlin's public transport system consists of buses, trams, S-Bahn (light rail) and U-Bahn (underground, subway). For trip planning and general information, contact the 24hr hotline at *℘19449* or *www.bvg.de*. In-person information is available at the kiosk on Hardenbergplatz *(outside Bahnhof Zoo; open 6.30am–8.30pm)* and at many U-Bahn and S-Bahn stations. Berlin and its environs are divided into fare zones A, B and C. For rides within the city, a Zone AB ticket suffices. Potsdam and Schönefeld airport require an ABC ticket. Tickets are available from vending machines in all U-Bahn and S-Bahn stations, in trams and from bus drivers. They must be stamped prior to your journey. Single tickets cost 2.30€ for Zone AB, day passes (valid until 3am the next day) are 6.30€. The **Berlin Welcome Card** (www.visit berlin.de/welcomecard) is available for two, three and five days and costs 16.90€/22.90€/29.90€ respectively for fare zones AB and 18.90€/25.90€/34.90€ for ABC. Cards are sold at the tourist offices and at BVG ticket vending machines.

Useful Tip: Bus no. 100 shuttles between Bahnhof Zoo and Alexanderplatz, passing many of Berlin's major sights. Bus no. 200 follows a more southerly route via Potsdamer Platz and the Kulturforum museums.

Frederick II the Great (1740–1786), son of the Soldier King, sent his army to various battlefields but also embraced the ideals of the Age of Enlightenment, surrounding himself with the finest thinkers of the day, including Voltaire. His reign also saw the construction of the Forum Fridericianum (today Bebelplatz) and other buildings along Unter den Linden, many designed by Georg Wenzeslaus von Knobelsdorff (1699–1753). Major monuments completed were the Brandenburg Gate (1789) and the *Neue Wache* (1818).

19C Berlin – Napoleon's defeat of Prussia in 1806 and the three-year occupation by the French of Berlin was a humiliating moment for the fledgling kingdom. However, it also imbued Prussians with a greater sense of patriotism, led to a number of civic reforms and ultimately paved the way for the Industrial Revolution and the formation of the German Empire in 1871 with Berlin as its capital. As the city boomed economically, politically and culturally, its population rose to 1 million around 1870 and twice that by 1900.

Greater Berlin – In 1920 the city united six urban suburbs, seven towns, 59 villages and 27 demesnes under a single administration encompassing 4 million inhabitants. Despite the upheavals following World War I, the 1920s saw immense intellectual and artistic growth. A highlight was the 1928 premiere of Bertolt Brecht and Kurt Weill's *Threepenny Opera*.

The blossoming of this talent was violently interrupted by Hitler's regime, when, along with the persecution of the Jews, a wealth of German artistic and literary heritage was banned or destroyed in the campaign against "degenerate art".

The taking of Berlin – From 21 April to 3 May 1945 the German capital was a battlefield. The Red Army marched against the remnants of the German army, destroying everything above ground, including 120 of Berlin's 248 bridges. On 30 April 1945, the Reichstag was captured and Hitler committed suicide.

Berlin Divided – After the German surrender on 8 May, the four victorious allies – Great Britain, the United States, France and the Soviet Union – took over administration of greater Berlin. But political developments in the Soviet Sector hindered the municipal administration. The Berlin Blockade, triggered by Soviet opposition to currency reform in the western sectors, was undermined by an airlift of supplies from the west (26 June 1948 to 12 May 1949). Although this effort prevented Berlin's absorption into the Soviet state, it did

"Fall" of the Berlin Wall at the Brandenburg Gate in 1989

© Imagebroker/hemis.fr

Tiergarten in summer

© G. Giuglio/hemis.fr

not forestall the division of Germany. In 1949, Berlin's Soviet sector became the capital of the German Democratic Republic (GDR), while West Berlin remained under the control of the western Allies. At the height of the Cold War, in 1961, the city's division was completed with the construction of a concrete and barbed-wire wall by the East Germans. The goal? To prevent an exodus of its own people seeking freedom and opportunity in West Berlin and the Federal Republic of Germany (West Germany).

The "fall" of the Wall – In November 1989, the GDR government, bowing to increased public pressure, agreed to re-establish free passage between the two Germanies. A night of wild celebration, especially around the Brandenburg Gate, followed the official "opening" of the Berlin Wall on 9 November.
In June 1991, the Bundestag (German parliament) selected Berlin as the capital of a reunited Germany. Since then, Berlin has experienced an extraordinary building boom and the two city halves have physically grown back together.

An outdoor city – Berlin, the biggest city in Germany, covers an area eight times the size of Paris. Devastated by the war, the capital lost much of its historical heritage and is now essentially a modern city shaped by leading architects of the 20C and 21C, including Le Corbusier and Hans Scharoun and, more recently, Daniel Libeskind, Renzo Piano, Helmut Jahn and others. Berlin is also a very green city, with the vast Tiergarten Park at its heart, numerous neighbourhood parks and a greenbelt stretching along its periphery. Waterways, including the Spree River which cuts through the central city, the Havel River along its western edge and various lakes, including the Wannsee and Grunewaldsee, provide further open spaces and recreational opportunities.

A lively cultural scene – Berlin justly enjoys a reputation for the quality and diversity of its cultural scene. Fashion, art, design and music are all exploding, fuelled by artists and creative spirits from around the world. In February, a galaxy of stars descends for the Berlinale (*see INTRODUCTION: Cinema*), one of Europe's most prestigious film festivals.
There are venues everywhere, but much of the nightlife action centres on the **Scheunenviertel**, the old Jewish Quarter, in the Mitte district, just north of Alexanderplatz. The **Prenzlauer Berg** quarter just north of here also teems with bars, restaurants and clubs. Major hubs are Kollwitzplatz and Helmholtzplatz squares. The **Kreuzberg** district, south of Mitte, has a more alternative, multi-cultural flair, especially along

WHERE TO STAY

Am Wilden Eber..................⑦	Hotel Berlin-Plaza.................⑩
Grand Hotel Esplanade..........⑯	Hotel Hackescher Markt........⑲
Honigmond Garden Hotel......㉒	Hotel Künstlerheim Luise.......㉕
Hotel Adlon..........................①	The Circus...........................⑬
Hotel Am Anhalter Bahnhof....④	Transit-Loft Hotel.................㉘

WHERE TO EAT

Alt Luxemburg.....................①
Borchardt............................④
Diekmann............................⑦
Lutter und Wegner ....⑬

Bergmannstraße, Schlesische Straße and Oranienstraße. The **Potsdamer Platz** and Gendarmenmarkt areas have the most highbrow venues, including the Konzerthaus and the Philharmonie for classical music. Theatres also flank Kurfürstendamm in Charlottenburg and Friedrichstraße in Mitte.

The cosmopolitan sophistication evident throughout Berlin also extends to its cuisine. Restaurants serving traditional local dishes such as pigs' knuckles *(Eisbein)* with sauerkraut and pease-pudding have become a dying breed while gourmet restaurants catering to a sophisticated, international clientele are on the rise.

Of the points of interest shown on these maps, only those that are mentioned in the index at the back of this book are described in the text. For all others, refer to the Green Guide to Berlin.

WALKING TOUR
HISTORIC CENTRE★★

The itinerary starts at the Reichstag and follows the celebrated Unter den Linden ("Under the Lime Trees") boulevard from Pariser Platz to Schlossplatz.

Most of the great monuments of the former Prussian capital flank this grand avenue, which originated as a bridle path leading from the city palace to the Tiergarten hunting reserve. A veritable open book on the country's history, Mitte is a kaleidoscope of architecture mixing Baroque with Neoclassical buildings alongside Stalinist behemoths and contemporary designs. It's all best explored on foot.

Reichstag★★

This massive neo-Renaissance government building was inaugurated in 1894, damaged by fire in 1933 and heavily bombed in 1945. It was restored during the 1970s, but without the landmark dome that had been dynamited in 1954. After reunification the Reichstag was returned to its former glory thanks to British architect, **Lord Norman Foster**, who embarked on a top-to-bottom renovation in 1995. In 1999, the sparkling new glass dome became a shining beacon of the reunited city. Poignantly, it sits right above the Plenary Hall where the German parliament (Bundestag) has once more convened since 1999. Brave the inevitable queue for the free lift ride to the **viewing platform**★★ and take in the fantastic views of the historic centre and vast Tiergarten Park. And don't miss a stroll up the dome's ramp spiralling around its mirror-clad central funnel.

▷ *From the Reichstag head south on Ebertstraße towards the Brandenburg Gate.*

Brandenburger Tor (Brandenburg Gate)★★

This triumphal arch was for almost three decades the symbol of the city's division, trapped just behind the Berlin Wall. Inspired by the Propylaea of the Parthenon, the gate was built by Carl Gotthard Langhans in 1788–91 and is surmounted by Gottfried Schadow's famous Quadriga, a sculpture of the Goddess of Victory (1793). It was removed to Paris after one of Napoléon's campaigns and returned to Berlin in 1814. Today, the gate is the emblem of the reunited city.

▷ *Head south on Ebertstraße to Behrenstraße.*

Holocaust-Mahnmal (Holocaust Memorial)★★

Built to honour the memory of the millions of Jews killed by the Nazis, this powerful memorial was designed by Jewish German-American architect Peter Eisenman. Stretching over 2ha/5 acres just south of the Brandenburg Gate, it consists of over 2 700 concrete pillars of differing heights. The underground information centre (Ort der Information) provides historical context on the Holocaust and includes one room where the names of all known victims are read out aloud continuously. The memorial was inaugurated on 10 May 2005, exactly 60 years after the German capitulation.

▷ *Return to the Brandenburg Gate and turn right onto Unter den Linden.*

Unter den Linden★★

Berlin's most elegant boulevard was conceived by Great Elector Frederick William in 1647. It is lined by embassies, banks and expensive stores as well

---

The Huguenots, France's Contribution to Berlin

In 1685, in response to Louis XIV's Revocation of the **Edict of Nantes**, the Great Elector Frederick William of Brandenburg issued the **Edict of Potsdam** granting asylum to French Calvinists.

These Protestants, or Huguenots, came in droves. In fact, 100 000 passed through Frankfurt-am-Main alone in the space of 20 years. 15 000 Huguenots came to Brandenburg, including 6 000 to Berlin, representing one-quarter of the population. Most settled in the Friedrichstadt area around Gendarmenmarkt, developing trades, a textile industry and fruit and vegetable husbandry. They also introduced several popular new dances: the cotillon, the gavotte and the minuet. Until the 19C, Berlin's French community had its own ecclesiastical and legal organisation.

as by a parade of beautifully restored monuments and buildings dating back to the 17C.

▷ *Head south on Friedrichstraße.*

Friedrichstadtpassagen★
Friedrichstraße 67–76.

Chic shops, fancy restaurants, high-end galleries… Over the past 20 years, Friedrichstraße, which until World War II used to be one of Berlin's ritziest boulevards, has definitely returned to its old glamorous self. Some 2.6 billion euros have been invested here, about half of them in three block-size *Quartiere*, a trio of buildings linked by an underground walkway between Mohrenstraße and Französischer Straße.

Quartier 207, at the corner of Französische Straße, was designed by architect Jean Nouvel and houses the Berlin branch of the luxurious French department store Galeries Lafayette. Immensely popular with both Berliners and visitors, its most spectacular feature is the giant central glass cone that playfully catches and reflects light. Next door, Quartier 206 is the brainchild of the American architectural firm Pei Cobb Freed & Partners and is particularly lovely when illuminated at night. The bi-level interior is an Art-Deco inspired kaleidoscope of inlaid coloured marble tented by a glass roof. By comparison, Quartier 205, designed by the late Oswald Mathias Ungers, is more austere. Its most eye-catching element is the *Tower of Clythe*, a three-storey tall sculpture made from crushed cars by the American artist John Chamberlain.

Gendarmenmarkt★★
Berlin's most beautiful square was named after the "Gens d'Armes", a Prussian regiment made up entirely of Huguenots who had settled here after having being forced out of their native France in 1685. The square is bookended by the **Deutscher Dom**★ (German cathedral) and the **Französischer Dom**★ (French cathedral), both of which contain exhibits. The tower of the latter can be climbed.

Konzerthaus★★ (Concert Hall)
Linking the two Gendarmenmarkt churches is the Konzerthaus, built by Karl Friedrich Schinkel in 1821. Originally a theatre called the Schauspielhaus, it is now a classical concert hall. Schinkel found inspiration in Greek antiquity: note the grand staircase leading to a portico supported by six pillars.

▷ *Take Markgrafenstraße north, turn right on Behrensstraße and follow it to Bebelplatz.*

Bebelplatz★
This wide open square was once the heart of the **Forum Fridericianum**, a Neoclassical arts and cultural complex conceived by Frederick the Great and designed by Knobelsdorff. Since the king's military exploits diminished his cashflow, only some structures were completed. The most magnificent is the **Staatsoper Unter den Linden** (national opera house) on the east side. The ensemble also encompasses the Baroque Old Royal Library on the western side, the Hotel de Rome in a 19C bank building on the south side and St. Hedwig Cathedral in the southeastern corner.

In 1994, Micha Ullman created the below-ground **Versunkene Bibliothek** (sunken library), a glass-fronted, empty-shelved room in the square's centre. It commemorates the first official book-burning held by the Nazis on Bebelplatz on 10 May 1933.

St. Hedwigs-Kathedrale
Knobelsdorff drafted the plans for this copper-domed Catholic church (1773), which was inspired by the Pantheon in Rome. Since Frederick the Great had been victorious in capturing Silesia, the church was dedicated to St. Hedwig, the patron saint of Silesia. It was badly damaged during World War II and rebuilt with a modern interior.

Staatsoper Unter den Linden★
Built by Knobelsdorff between 1740 and 1743, the national opera house burned down in 1843; Langhans' reconstruction

fashion it zeroes in on various aspects that characterised this now extinct society: price controls, product shortages and the Stasi secret service and its ubiquitous surveillance cameras. The exhibit of holiday photos is especially hilarious. Don't miss climbing aboard the Trabi, the legendary GDR-made car, or to step inside the living room where you can watch some of the most popular shows of the era on a black and white television.

▶ *Climb back up the stairs and take a left on Karl-Liebknecht-Straße.*

Alexanderplatz★

Named for Tsar Alexander, who visited Berlin in 1805, this square – known as "Alex" – is the commercial and traffic hub of the eastern city centre. It was completely destroyed in World War II and rebuilt in an austere socialist style that is still in evidence today, despite improvements.

On your way to Alex, you will pass by the 13C **Marienkirche** (St. Mary's Church) with its macabre Dance of Death fresco that recalls the ravages of the Black Plague. The red-brick pile just south of here is the **Rotes Rathaus** (red town hall), where the Berlin mayor makes his home. Above it all looms the 368m/1 207ft-high **Fernsehturm**★ (TV tower) with a viewing platform and revolving restaurant at 203m/667ft.

Nikolaiviertel★
(St. Nicholas Quarter)

With its narrow cobbled streets and old taverns, this quarter teems with restored period houses like the **Knoblauch House**★ *(Knoblauchhaus – Poststraße 23; free; open year-round, Tue & Thu–Sun 10am–6pm, Wed noon–8pm; closed Dec 24 & 31; ℘(030) 24 00 21 62; www.stadtmuseum.de)* and the **Ephraim Palace**★ *(Ephraim-Palais – Poststraße 16; open: see Knoblauchhaus; 5€; ℘(030) 24 00 21 62; www.stadtmuseum. de).* The Nikolaiviertel is dominated by the bell-towers of the Late Gothic 1230 **Nikolaikirche**★, Berlin's oldest church, which is now a history museum.

ADDITIONAL SIGHTS IN THE HISTORIC CENTRE
Hamburger Bahnhof – Museum für Gegenwart Berlin★★
(Hamburg Station – Museum of Contemporary Art)

Invalidenstraße 50–51. Open year-round, Tue–Fri 10am–6pm, Sat 11am–8pm, Sun 11am–6pm. 8€. ℘(030)39 78 34 11. www.hamburger-bahnhof.de.

Berlin's key contemporary art museum occupies a former railway station built in the 1840s, closed in 1884 and converted into a transport museum in 1906.

Today the main building and an extension in a 300m/984ft-long warehouse present artworks from 1960 to the present. The collection includes such top artists as Anselm Kiefer, Richard Long, Bruce Naumann and Cindy Sherman along with Cy Twombly, Robert Rauschenberg and Andy Warhol. An entire wing is devoted to Joseph Beuys.

Märkisches Museum★
(Berlin Regional History Museum)

Am Köllnischen Park 5. Open year-round, Tue & Thu–Sun 10am-6pm, Wed noon–8pm). Closed Dec 24 & 31. 5€. ℘(030) 24 00 21 62. www.stadtmuseum.de.

This rambling red-brick building (1908) tells the history of Berlin and the surrounding region (called the March of Brandenburg) from the Middle Ages onwards.

A copy of a 1474 Roland figure – a symbol of civic liberties and privileges – guards the museum entrance.

Emil Nolde Museum★

Jagerstraße 55. Open year-round, daily 10am–7pm. 8€. ℘(030) 40 00 21 62. www.nolde-stiftung.de.

Emil Nolde (1867–1956) was one of the most important German Expressionist artists and a member of the artist group Die Brücke. He is best known for his intensely colourful, sometimes melancholic and often lyrically captivating canvasses, a selection of which can be seen in this bright and airy former bank building near Gendarmenmarkt.

Madame Tussauds★

Under den Linden 74. ◷Open year-round, daily 10am–7pm. ≈20€. ℘*(01805) 54 58 00. www.madame tussauds.com/berlin.*

Meet Elvis, Obama, the Pope, Albert Einstein, George Clooney and dozens of other personalities from entertainment, politics, sports and religion at the Berlin branch of London's famous waxworks. All can be photographed and even touched. The most controversial figure is that of Adolf Hitler which made headlines when its head was torn off by a local man on opening day. It has since been restored.

Sammlung Boros★★ (Boros Collection)

Reinhardstraße 20. ◷Open year-round, Sat & Sun 10am–5.40pm. ≈10€. ℘*(030) 27 59 40 65. www.sammlung-boros.de.*

One of the most spectacular contemporary art collections in Germany, the private Sammlung Boros showcases such major players as Olafur Eliasson, Elmgreen & Dragsted, Sarah Lucas, Henrik Olesen and Daniel Pflumm in a spectacularly converted bunker from World War II. It can only be seen on hugely popular guided tours which should be booked online several weeks in advance.

MUSEUMSINSEL★★★ (MUSEUM ISLAND)

The brainchild of Frederick William III, this vast museum complex occupies the northern end of the Spree island where Berlin's settlement first began in the 13C. Its five museums deliver a survey of 6 000 years of the art and cultural history of Europe. Since 1999, they have also been included on UNESCO's list of World Heritage Sites. Under a master plan conceived by British architect David Chipperfield, the compound is undergoing a complete overhaul expected to last until 2025. Restoration of the Bode-Museum and the Alte Nationalgalerie

have already been completed. Next up are the Altes Museum and the Pergamon Museum – expect sections to be closed during the process. Open since late 2009 is the spectacular Neues Museum, a complete reconstruction of the original which was destroyed in World War II. It houses the famous Egyptian Collection and the Museum of Pre- and Early History. Chipperfield will also design a modern new entrance building, called the James Simon Gallery. Eventually a walkway called the "Archaeological Promenade" will link all but the Alte Nationalgalerie with each other.

Pergamonmuseum★★★ (Pergamon Museum)

Entry on Kupfergraben. ◷Open year-round, daily 10am–6pm (Thu 10pm). ≈10€. ♿. ℘(030) 20 90 55 77. www.smb.spk-berlin.de.

The most popular museum on Museum Island on was also the last to be completed, in 1930. It harbours three world-class collections. The **Collection of Classical Antiquities**★★★ *(Antikensammlung)* features the **Pergamon Altar**★★★, a masterpiece of Hellenistic art (2C BC); the **market gate of Miletus**★★ (2C AD); and Greek and Roman sculptures. The **Museum of the Ancient Near East**★★ *(Vorderasiatisches Museum)* includes the **Processional Way and Ishtar Gate**★★ from ancient Babylon, 580 BC; the plinth of Asachadon, 7C BC; and the façade of the Temple of Irmin at Uruk. Highlights of the **Museum of Islamic Art**★★ *(Museum für Islamische Kunst)* include the façade of Mshatta Palace (8C) from Jordan; the painted Aleppo room (early 17C); and miniatures (15C–17C).

Alte Nationalgalerie★★ (Old National Gallery)

Entry on Bodestraße. ◷Open year-round, Tue–Sun 10am–6pm, Thu 10pm. ≈8€. ♿. ℘(030) 20 90 55 77. www.smb.spk-berlin.de.

This museum exhibits 19C European paintings and sculptures. Romantic artists take centre stage on the top floor, with outstanding works by **Caspar**

The Museums of Berlin

The Altes Museum, the first museum in Berlin, was built in 1830 by Karl Friedrich Schinkel on what would become Museumsinsel (Museum Island). It was followed in 1855 by the Neuesmuseum, in 1876 by the Alte Nationalgalerie, in 1904 by the Bode-Museum and in 1930 by the Pergamonmuseum. Wilhelm von Bode, director of the Berlin museums after 1906, painstakingly organised the city's collections, bringing them to the attention of connoisseurs worldwide.

Reconstruction began after World War II – no small task considering collections had to be gathered from storage or re-acquired from victorious pillagers. Postwar Germany further divided the collections between East and West. The Stiftung Preußischer Kulturbesitz (Foundation for Prussian Cultural Property) preserved those in the West while in the East artefacts gathered at the Museumsinsel. In 1992 Berlin's museums rejoined under the umbrella of the Stiftung Preußischer Kulturbesitz – Staatliche Museen zu Berlin.

David Friedrich and Karl Friedrich Schinkel. Galleries on the middle floor are dedicated to French Impressionists, Realists including Max Liebermann and Wilhelm Leibl, and German and Flemish historical scenes. On the ground floor are works by Berlin artists (**Adolph Menzel**, Krüger, Schadow) along with Realist landscapes (Constable, Courbet).

Bode-Museum★★

Entry via Monbijoubrücke.
🕐*Open year-round, daily 10am–6pm (Thu 10pm).* 8€. ♿. ℘*(030) 20 90 55 77. www.smb.spk-berlin.de.*
Housed in a splendid 1904 Neo-Baroque edifice at the northern tip of Museumsinsel, this museum emerged from a thorough renovation in 2006 and once again delights visitors with its stunning **Sculpture Collection**.

Particular strengths lie in medieval Italian sculpture (e.g. *Man of Sorrows* by Giovanni Pisano), Late Gothic German works by such masters as Tilman Riemenschneider and Hans Leinberger, and Rococo sculpture by Ignaz Günther and Jean Antoine Houdon.

The museum also features a sprinkling of objects from the **Museum of Byzantine Art** such as the "Great Berlin Pyx" (around AD 400), a small vessel carved of ivory. Another highlight is the four rooms crammed with the rare and precious coins of the **Numismatic Collection**.

Bode-Museum

© Stefan Merker/Fotolia.com

Altes Museum★★
(Old Museum)

Enter from Lustgarten. ◷*Open year-round, daily 10am–6pm (Thu 10pm).* ◉*8€.* ♿. ℘*(030) 20 90 55 77.* *www.smb.spk-berlin.de.*

Designed by Schinkel and open since 1830, Berlin's first public museum is a Neoclassical architectural masterpiece fronted by 18 Ionic columns. On display is the prestigious **Antikensammlung** (Collection of Antiquities – the monumental pieces are in the Pergamon museum), composed of Greek sculpture on the ground floor and Roman and Etruscan works upstairs. One of the most famous pieces of Hellenic art is the **Praying Boy sculpture** from around 3000 BC on Rhodes. The famous Etruscan collection is one of the largest outside Italy and on display for the first time since 1939. It includes complete tomb finds and magnificent objects of Etruscan art and such objects from everyday life as amphorae, jewellery and coins. Late Hellenistic cremation urns and sarcophagi lead to a section on Roman tomb art, which includes the **Medea sarcophagus**. Other rooms feature Roman mummy portraits, silverware and cosmetic utensils made of glass and jewellery. A portrait gallery of marble busts featuring famous Roman leaders, including Caesar and Caracalla, rounds off the upstairs galleries.

Neues Museum
(New Museum)

Enter from Bodestraße. ◷*Open year-round, daily 10am–6pm (Thu 10pm).* ◉*10€.* ♿. *Admission by timed ticket only.* ℘*(030) 266 42 42 42.* *www.neues-museum.de.*

Shortly after the opening of the Old Museum, **Friedrich August Stüler** (1800–1865) was entrusted with the construction of another building: the New Museum, created in an elegant classical style between 1841 and 1859. Badly damaged during World War II, it remained in a state of ruin during GDR times but was reconstructed as part of the Museum Island masterplan and re-opened in late 2009. The museum houses Berlin's renowned **Egyptian Museum and Papyrus Collection**, including the famous bust of Queen Nefertiti, as well as the **Museum of Pre- and Early History**.

The building – The building itself is as interesting as the exhibits inside. Architect David Chipperfield sifted through the rubble of the original structure and integrated every useable shard, brick, stone, piece of marble or whatever he could find into the new structure. As a result, it's a harmonious blend of old and new that instantly won several design awards, including the prestigious "European Award" from the Royal Institute of British Architects (RIBA). The central hall with its grand staircase is the magnificent centrepiece of the museum and gives access to three of the exhibition floors.

Basement – Furniture, utensils, funerary masks and sarcophagi depict life and death in the Nile Valley. Note the unrolled papyrus of the Book of the Dead.

Ground floor – Among Egyptian sculpture, the **"Green Head of Berlin"**★★ (c. 300 BC) is regarded as one of the masterpieces of the late period. Other galleries are devoted to the treasure of King Priam discovered in the late 19C by Heinrich Schliemann in Troy. However, what you see here are all copies: the originals were confiscated by the Red Army in 1945 and are partly on display in the Pushkin Museum in Moscow.

First floor – This floor gets the most visitors thanks largely to one exhibit: the 3 300-year-old, yet timelessly beautiful, **bust of Egyptian Queen Nefertiti**★★★. It is part of the stunning **collection**★★★ of sculptures, figurines and objects dating back to the time of King Akhenaten (Nefertiti's husband, 1353–36 BC) and unearthed between 1911 and 1914 in Tell el-Armana by a team of German archaeologists. The bust was discovered in the workshop of the sculptor Thutmose and served as a model for future effigies of the queen (which explains why only one eye was embedded). Other masterpieces include the representation of Akhenaten's father Amenhotep III wearing a crown; the portrait of his wife Tiye carved from yew that was originally bright orange; reliefs of Akhenaten and other royal family members and an impressive collection of papyri.

Other rooms on this floor are devoted to the Museum of Pre- and Early History. Key items include the exquisite bronze statue of the **Xantener Knabe** (Boy of Xanten; 1C AD), colossal statues of gods from the 2C AD and a coin from the time of Charlemagne (8C).

Upper floor – The Museum of Pre- and Early History continues on this floor. Don't miss the preserved **Neanderthal skull** and the 3 000-year-old **Berliner Goldhut**★ (golden hat), a gilded conical ceremonial hat that also functions as a combined lunar and solar calendar. It is the best preserved of four known copies.

KULTURFORUM★★★

A clutch of museums and cultural venues, the Kulturforum was designed, in the late 1950s, to become the West Berlin counterpart to the Museumsinsel in the eastern part of the city.

Gemäldegalerie★★★ (Picture Gallery)

Matthäikirchplatz. Open year-round, *Tue–Sun 10am–6pm (Thu 10pm).* 8€. (030) 266 423 040. www.smp. spk-berlin.de.

This collection was born of the passion of the Great Elector (1620–1688) and Frederick the Great (1712–1786). But it was **Wilhelm von Bode**, director of the Gemäldegalerie who, beginning in 1890, tirelessly acquired European paintings from the 13C to the 18C. Despite war losses (400 paintings were destroyed), the collection is still considered one of the finest in the world.

The modern building's 53 rooms are arranged in a horseshoe around a foyer and provide space for over 1 100 paintings. Works are presented in chronological order and arranged by school:

Rooms I–III, Galleries 1–4: German School, 13C–16C (Late Gothic/Renaissance). Notably illustrated by Martin

Gemäldegalerie
© René Mattes/hemis.fr

Schongauer *(The Birth of Christ)*, Lucas Cranach the Elder *(Venus und Amor, Adam and Eve)*, Hans Holbein the Younger *(The Merchant Georg Gisze)* and Albrecht Dürer *(Portrait of Hieronymus Holzschuher)*.

Rooms IV–VI, Galleries 5–7: Dutch School, 15C–16C (Late Gothic/Renaissance). Features works by Gérard David, Hans Memling, Hugo Van der Goes, Jan Gossaert, Jan Van Eyck, Quentin Metsys and Pieter Bruegel the Elder (including his famous painting *Dutch Proverbs*).

The 5-7-9 Series

The three-naved foyer of the Gemäldegalerie, a wonderfully designed space, boasts a single work of art: a sculpture by the American conceptual sculptor Walter De Maria entitled *The 5-7-9 Series*. It consists of 27 polygonal, highly polished steel staffs ordered in three rows in a granite water basin. The geometric staffs are assembled according to various mathematical combinations. This artwork is a good conclusion to a visit to the Gemäldegalerie: it brings the viewer back to earth, tests his or her imagination and simply permits a rest.

Rooms VII–XI, Galleries 8–19: Flemish and Dutch Schools, 17C (Baroque). Extensive section including Peter Paul Rubens *(Child with a Bird, Virgin and Child)*, his pupil Anthony van Dyck *(Portrait of a Wealthy Genoan Couple)*, Matthias Stomer *(Esau Sells his Birth Right)*, Rembrandt *(Self-portrait, Moses Shatters the Decalogue, Susanna and the Two Old Men, The Man with the Golden Helmet)*, Jacob van Ruisdael *(Oaks by the Lake with Water Lilies)*, Jan Bruegel the Elder *(Flower Bouquet)*, Frans Hals *(Singing Child with Flute)* and Jan Vermeer van Delft *(The Glass of Wine)*.

Galleries 20–22: English, French and German Schools, 18C (Rococo/Neoclassical). Artists include Thomas Gainsborough *(The Marsham Children)*, Antoine Watteau *(The Dance)*, Jean-Baptiste-Siméon Chardin *(The Painter)* and Antoine Pesne *(Frederick the Great as Crown Prince)*.

Rooms XII–XIV, Galleries 23–26, 28: Italian School, 17C–18C (Baroque/Mannerism); **French School, 17C; Spanish School, 16C–17C** (Mannerism/Baroque). Exhibits here include Francesco Guardi *(Canal Grande in Venice)*, Canaletto *(Canal Grande with View of the Rialto Bridge)*, Velázquez *(Portrait of a Lady)*, Caravaggio *(Amor as Victor)*, Claude Lorrain *(Ideal Roman Landscape)*, Nicolas Poussin *(Self-portrait)* and Georges de La Tour *(Peasant Couple Eating Peas)*.

Rooms XV–XVII, Galleries 29–32: Italian School, late 15C–16C (late Renaissance/Mannerism). This part of the museum contains works by Correggio *(Leda with the Swan)*, Parmigianino *(Christ's Baptism)*, Titian *(Venus with the Organist, Portrait of a Bearded Young Man)*, Tintoretto *(Virgin and Child)* and several paintings by Raphael (including the *Madonna Terranuova)*.

Gallery 34: miniatures, 16C–18C, including *Katharine of Bora* (Martin Luther's wife) by Lucas Cranach the Elder.

Room XVIII, Galleries 35–41: Italian School, 13C–late 15C (Gothic/Early Renaissance). Includes Botticelli *(Saint Sebastian, Virgin Enthroned)*, Giovanni Bellini, Andrea Mantegna *(Representation of Christ in the Temple)*, Fra Angelico *(The Day of Judgement)* and Lorenzo Monaco *(The Last Supper)*.

Kunstgewerbemuseum★★ (Museum of Decorative Arts)

Matthäikirchplatz. ⏱*Open year-round, Tue–Fri 10am–6pm, Sat–Sun 11am–6pm.* 🎟*8€.* ♿ ✆*(030) 266 423 040.* *www.smb.spk-berlin.de.*

The vast treasures of the Museum of Decorative Arts are displayed in two locations. The Kulturforum branch presents a broad overview of European applied arts and design from the Middle Ages to the present. The second part of the collection is at Schloß Köpenick.

At the Kulturforum branch, Gallery I *(ground floor)* is devoted to the Middle Ages. Inside the entrance is the Enger-Herford (Westphalia) **Treasure of Dionysius**★, with a remarkable reliquary purse decorated with precious stones (late 8C).

In the centre of the gallery, the **Guelph Treasure**★★★ includes a reliquary resembling a Byzantine church (Cologne c. 1175). Gallery II *(ground floor)*: Italian furniture and majolica from the 14C to the 16C, Venetian glassware from the 16C to the 17C. Gallery III *(ground floor)*: **Lüneburg's municipal silver**★★★ (late Gothic and Renaissance) and jewellery from Nuremberg. Gallery IV *(first floor)*: the splendid **Pommern Cabinet**★ and its contents. Gallery V *(first floor)*: 17C–18C porcelain from China and Germany. Gallery VI *(first floor)*: Biedermeier and Jugendstil objets d'art, a panelled glass cabinet from Schloss Wiesentheid in Franconia (1724). Gallery VII *(first floor)*: porcelain, glazed earthenware and Art Nouveau and Art Deco period glass.

Galleries IX and X *(basement):* modern international design by such practitioners as Charles Eames and Philippe Starck.

Kupferstichkabinett★ (Museum of Prints and Drawings)

Matthäikirchplatz. Exhibition: ○*Open year-round, Tue–Fri 10am–6pm, Sat–Sun 11am–6pm. Study room:* ○*Open Tue–Fri 9am–4pm.* ◉*8€.* &. ℘*(030) 266 29 51. www.kupferstichkabinett.de.*

In 1652 the Great Elector laid the foundation for this internationally renowned **collection** of 500 000 prints and 110 000 watercolours, oil sketches, drawings and pastels from the 14C to the 20C.

Many famous Italian, Old German and Old Dutch masters are represented, including Rembrandt, Botticelli and Dürer, along with 20C Pop Art, Conceptual Art and Minimal Art.

Neue Nationalgalerie★★ (New National Gallery)

Potsdamer Straße 50. ○*Open year-round, Tue, Wed & Fri 10am–6pm, Thu 10am-10pm, Sat–Sun 11am–6pm.* ◉*8€.* &. ℘*(030) 266 29 51. www. neue-nationalgalerie.de.*

This steel and glass "temple of the arts", designed in 1968 by Ludwig Mies van der Rohe, houses paintings and sculptures from the early 20C to the 1960s. Particularly impressive is the collection of **German Expressionists** which includes a smattering of works by members of the artist group *Die Brücke* (🔎 *see INTRODUCTION: Art*), including Kirchner, Schmidt-Rottluff and Heckel. The **Bauhaus** is represented by such artists as Klee and Kandinsky, **Surrealism** by Max Ernst and Dalí, and **Cubism** by Picasso and Gris. The collection ends with **American paintings** from the 1960s featuring works by Frank Stella, Ellsworth Kelly and others.

Philharmonie★★★

Herbert-von-Karajanstraße 1. ☜*Guided tour (1hr) at 1pm. Meeting point: stage door.* ○*Closed Jan 1, Dec 24–26 & 31.* ◉*3€.* &. ℘*(030) 25 48 80. www.berliner-philharmoniker.de.*

The roof of this asymmetrical building designed by **Hans Scharoun** (1963) resembles a giant wave. It is the home base of the Berlin Philharmonic Orches-tra, directed by **Sir Simon Rattle**, and surrounded by terraced seats accommodating up to 2 200 people. The **Chamber Music Hall** (1988) next door seats up to 1 150 under a tent-shaped roof.

In an adjacent building *(Tiergartenstraße 1, enter via Ben-Gurion-Straße)*, the **Musikinstrumenten-Museum**★ (Musical Instruments Museum) displays keyboards, strings and percussion instruments from the 16C to today, including a mammoth 1929 Wurlitzer theatre organ and flutes played by Frederick the Great. *(*○*Open year-round, Tue, Wed, Fri 9am–5pm, Thu 9am-10pm, Sat–Sun 10am–5pm;* ◉*4€;* &. ℘*(030) 25 48 11 78; www.mim-berlin.de.)*

Staatsbibliothek Preußischer Kulturbesitz★ (State Library of the Prussian Cultural Heritage Foundation)

Potsdamer Straße 33. ○*Open year-round, Mon–Fri 9am–9pm, 9am–7pm Sat.* ☜*Guided tour (1hr 30min) at 10.30am, 3rd Sat of month.* ◉*Free.* &. ℘*(030) 26 00. http://staatsbibliothek-berlin.de.*

This huge library, designed by Hans Scharoun and wedged between Potsdamer Platz and the Kulturforum, harbours 3.7 million volumes. Scenes from the Wim Wenders movie *Wings of Desire* were filmed in the reading room.

POTSDAMER PLATZ★★

East of the Kulturforum, this quarter stands as the biggest of Berlin's post-reunification developments. Before World War II, the area was a busy traffic hub and entertainment zone. Completely destroyed, it was bifurcated by the Berlin Wall during the Cold War. After reunification some of the world's top architects collaborated on its reincarnation. Today, Potsdamer Platz is again a lively quarter teeming with hotels, theatres, restaurants, a casino, museums and shops.

Sony Centre★★★

The Sony Centre is dominated by the BahnTower, a glass tower housing the headquarters of the railway company

Deutsche Bahn. Designed by Helmut Jahn, the massive steel and glass complex centres on a plaza encircled by restaurants, cinemas and beer gardens. Integrated into this postmodern setting is the historic Kaisersaal, one of the few original remnants from the pre-war Potsdamer Platz. In 1996, during construction of the Sony Centre, it had to be moved a few dozen metres in an astonishing technological feat. Another historic section is the façade of the Hotel Esplanade which can be seen from Bellevuestraße.

Overlooking the central square, the Filmhaus hosts film-related institutions, including the Museum of Film and Television. Also part of the Sony Centre is the **Legoland Discovery Centre** (Ⓞopen year-round, daily 10am–7pm; ⊜16€; ♿ ℘(030) 301 04 00; www.legolanddiscoverycentre.de/berlin), an indoor theme park that will keep kids under 10 entertained for hours.

Museum für Film und Fernsehen★★ (Museum of Film and Television)

In the Sony Centre. Potsdamer Straße 2. Ⓞ Open year-round, Tue, Thu–Sun 10am–6pm, 10am–8pm Thu. ⊜6€. ♿ ℘(030) 300 90 30. www.filmmuseum-berlin.de.

Germany's film history goes back to the earliest days of the medium. This multimedia museum includes exhibits on such silent-era blockbusters as Fritz Lang's *Metropolis* or *The Cabinet of Dr Caligari* by expressionist filmmaker Robert Wiene. Leni Riefenstahl's genial but controversial Nazi-era documentary *Olympia* gets examined closely, while the great Marlene Dietrich takes centre stage in one of the largest galleries, complete with lots of personal artefacts such as gowns, luggage, cosmetics and jewellery. The upper floors house the Fernsehmuseum, which takes you on a journey through 50 years of TV history in both East and West Germany. On the top floor you can catch up on your favourite old-time programmes at private viewing consoles.

Martin-Gropius-Bau★★ (Martin Gropius Building)

Niederkirchner Straße 7. Ⓞ Open year-round, Wed–Mon 10am–8pm. ⊜Varies with exhibition. ♿ ℘(030) 25 48 60. www.gropiusbau.de.

A stately Italian Renaissance-style building by Martin Gropius (great-uncle of Walter Gropius) and Heino Schmieden originally served as a museum of decorative arts and now houses travelling exhibitions of international rank.

Topographie des Terrors (Topography of Terror)

Niederkirchner Straße 8. Ⓞ Open 10am –8pm. Ⓞ Closed Jan 1, Dec 24 & 31. ⊜Free. ♿ ℘(030) 25 4 09 50. www.topographie.de.

Next to the Gropius-bau is a short stretch of the **Berlin Wall**★ and beyond it a largely empty field where once stood the key institutions of oppression and persecution in Nazi Germany: the Gestapo headquarters, the SS central command, the SS Security Service and, after 1939, the Reich Security Headquarters. The compound was completed destroyed in World War II, but since 1997 an outdoor memorial exhibit has commemorated the site's fearsome legacy. In 2010, the enlarged exhibit moved into a permanent **Documentation Centre** inside an austere charcoal-grey cube in the middle of the grounds.

Museum für Kommunikation Berlin★ (Museum of Communication)

Leipziger Straße 16. Ⓞ Open year-round, Tue 9am–8pm, Wed–Fri 9am–5pm, Sat–Sun 10am–6pm. ⊜3€. ♿ ℘(030) 20 29 40. www.mfk-berlin.de.

Considered the world's oldest postal museum, this exhibit counts an ultra-rare **Blue Mauritius** stamp, entertaining robots and decades' worth of communication devices among its treasures.

👥 Museum Haus am Checkpoint Charlie★ (Berlin Wall Museum)

Friedrichstraße 43–45. 🕐*Open year-round, daily 9am–10pm.* 💶*12.50€.* 📞*(030) 253 72 50. www.mauer museum.de.*

The Berlin Wall Museum houses Wall-related artefacts and illustrates the often hair-raising escapes attempted by East Germans trying cross over into the West through tunnels, in a hot-air balloon, hidden in the boot of a car, in a suitcase; even via a chairlift. Many attempts, of course, ended unsuccessfully, usually resulting in the incarceration of the brave souls. A separate section spotlights human and civil rights movements.

SCHLOSS CHARLOTTENBURG★★★ (CHARLOTTENBURG PALACE)

Schloss Charlottenburg is a summer residence commissioned by King Friedrich I for his wife Sophie-Charlotte. Designed by Arnold Nering and later expanded by Johann Friedrich Eosander, it is Berlin's most exquisite Baroque palace.

An equestrian statue of the Great Elector by Andreas Schlüter greets visitors arriving in the front courtyard. Allow a full day to see all of Schloss Charlottenburg's buildings and the park and consider an evening visit for a classical music concert or meal at the Orangery *(www.concerts-berlin.com).*

Altes Schloss★★ (Old Palace)

Spandauer Damm, ground floor of central block. 📷*Visit by guided tour or audioguide, Apr–Oct Tue–Sun 10am–6pm, 10am–6pm (Nov–Mar 5pm).* 🕐*Closed 24 Dec.* 💶*10€.* ♿*.* 📞*(030) 32 09 11. www.spsg.de.*

After viewing models of the 18C palace and gardens, visitors approach three small rooms in the **Mecklenburg Apartment**. The official function rooms span 140m/460ft overlooking the gardens. They house family portraits of the Houses of Hohenzollern and Hanover, finely lacquered furniture and Sophie-Charlotte's harpsichord. The famous **Porcelain Room**★★ features a magnificent collection of Asian porcelain, while the **Palace Chapel**★ *(Schloss Kapelle)* is occasionally used as a concert venue. Above the royal pew an enormous crown carried by two allegorical figures bears the Prussian eagle. The fine freestanding **staircase** by Eosander (1702) was the first of its kind in Germany.

Passing through the upper rooms overlooking the courtyard and gardens, you then continue to the **apartments of Frederick William IV**, the last king to live at the palace. The painting *Parade along Unter den Linden in 1837* by Franz Krüger features some of this avenue's most important buildings, still recognisable today. Adjoining rooms exhibit part of the East Prussian noble Schlobitten Collection, including paintings, tapestries, porcelain and metalwork. The **Crown Prince's silverware**★★ is particularly interesting *(♿see below).*

The Crown Prince's Silverware

This masterpiece of 20C German craftsmanship was a gift from 414 Prussian cities at the marriage of Crown Prince William to Duchess Cecilia of Mecklenburg-Schwerin in 1904. Completed in 1914, the dinner service never belonged to the couple. Following the Hohenzollerns' abdication, it became property of the Berlin Senate and is now on long-standing loan to Schloss Charlottenburg. The service originally contained 2 600 pieces for 50 at a 16m/53ft-long table. Tureens, plates and salad bowls are displayed on a magnificent sideboard. Architects, sculptors and the director of the Museum of Decorative Arts supervised the creation of the dinner service, which is in classical and *Jugendstil* style. The statuettes include elephants surmounted by an obelisk, equestrian statues and candelabras, all part of a long tradition of royal dinner services.

Schloss Charlottenburg – Schlossgarten and Altes Schloss

© Wolfgang Scholvien/Berlin Tourismus Marketing GmbH

Neuer Flügel★★ (New Wing)

East of the central block. ⏱*Open year-round, Wed–Mon 10am–6pm (Nov–Mar 5pm).* ◎6€. ♿. ℘*(030) 32 09 11. www.spsg.de.*

Also known as the Knobeldorff Wing after its architect, the New Wing was commissioned by Frederick the Great and completed in 1746. This is the most beautiful part of the palace and the one section to see if you're short on time. Stairs lead up to the **White Room** *(Weisser Saal)* used by Frederick II as a dining and throne room. The ceiling painting is a modern work by Hann Trier which replaced the original by Antoine Pesne destroyed in 1943. The 42m/138ft-long **Golden Gallery**★★ is a Rococo music room and dance hall restored to its original pastel green, pink and gold hues. Frederick II's apartments, which follow, feature white and gold Rococo décor and important 18C French paintings: **Gersaint's Signboard**★★★ (1720) in the concert hall and **Embarkation for Cythera**★★★ by Watteau in particular.

Winter Apartments★

Frederick the Great's successor, Frederick William II, lived in these apartments in the late 18C and early 19C. These south-facing rooms display the disciplined elegance of early Prussian Neoclassicism. **Queen Louise's Bedchamber**★ is decorated in harmonious mauve tones and draped in white net. The final room contains a fine collection of **portraits**★ by court painter Antoine Pesne.

On the ground floor a model shows the **Berlin City Palace** *(Berliner Stadt Schloss),* blown up in 1950 on the orders of the East German government. In the adjoining room are Baroque tapestries and portions of Frederick the Great's **antique collection**. The **Chinese Gallery and Chinese Room**, part of Frederick William II's summer apartments, overlook the gardens.

Schlossgarten★★

This English-style park is an oasis of tranquillity and great for strolling, picnicking, sunning by the pond or lounging beneath shady trees. To the west, at the end of a yew and cypress walk, a small **mausoleum** *(*⏱*open Mar–Oct, Tue–Sun 10am–6pm, Nov–Mar, noon–4pm;* ◎*2€)* contains the marble sarcophagi of Frederick William III and his wife Queen Louise carved by Christian Daniel Rauch, as well as those of Emperor Wilhelm I and Queen Augusta. More royal family members are buried in the crypt, which is not accessible to the public.

The **New Pavilion**★ **(Schinkel Pavilion)** *(east of the New Wing)* was built in 1824 as a summer residence for Frederick William III and is under restoration until 2012.

North of the lake, toward the Spree, is the **Belvedere**★ *(*⏱*open Apr–Oct, Tue–Sun 10am–6pm, Nov–Mar noon–4pm;* ◎*3€)*, a gleaming white miniature palace overlooking a shaggy meadow. It houses an exhibit of precious historic porcelain made by the *Königliche Porzel-*

lan Manufaktur (KPM), the Prussian royal factory established in 1763.

Museum Berggruen★★

Schloßstraße 1. ◔*Open year-round, Tue–Sun 10am–6pm.* ◎*8€.* ♿*(partly).* ℘*(030) 32 69 58 15. www.smb.spk-berlin.de.*

Art dealer Heinz Berggruen was an avid collector of **Pablo Picasso** and his contemporaries and donated a sizeable portion of his private collection to this intimate museum in a former royal guard barracks built by Friedrich August Stüler in 1859. On display are about 100 Picassos from all his creative periods, including the famous *Horses on a Hill* (1909). These are cleverly juxtaposed with works by Cézanne, Van Gogh, Matisse, Giacometti and others, as well as African tribal art. The second floor features over 60 works by **Paul Klee**: *Stadtartiger Aufbau (Urban Structure)* (1917), *Betrachtung beim Frühstück* (1925, watercolour) and *Klassische Küste* (1931).

Bröhan Museum★

Schloßstraße 1a. ◔*Open year-round, Tue–Sun 10am–6pm.* ◔*Closed Dec 24 & 31.* ◎*6€.* ♿. ℘*(030) 32 69 06 00. www.broehan-museum.de.*

Fine art, furniture and decorative objects from the **Art Nouveau**, **Art Deco** and **Functionalism** periods (1889–1939) get the star treatment at this museum. Downstairs are period rooms by Hector Guimard and Peter Behrens, while the upper floor is dedicated to paintings by artists from the **Berlin Secession** movement, including Willy Jaeckel and Hans Baluschek.

A special exhibition on the third floor shines the spotlight on Belgian multi-talent **Henry van de Velde**.

KREUZBERG DISTRICT★

Kreuzberg has been the hub of counter-cultural Berlin since long before reunification. These days, it is one of the city's liveliest neighbourhoods with a buzzing nightlife; a wide range of restaurants, often in unusual locations; and plenty of galleries, theatres, dance clubs and cultural centres. The eastern section around the Kottbusser Tor U-Bahn station has a large Turkish population and is sometimes nicknamed "Little Istanbul". At the other end, the area around Viktoria Park is considerably more sedate and upmarket.

Jüdisches Museum Berlin★★ (Jewish Museum)

Lindenstraße 9–14. ◔*Open year-round, Mon 10am–10pm, Tue–Sun 10am–8pm.* ◔*Closed Rosh Hashanah, Yom Kippur, Dec 24.* ◎*5€.* ♿. ℘*(030) 2599 33 00. www.juedisches-museum-berlin.de.*

American architect Daniel Libeskind designed this spectacular lightning-bolt-shaped museum, which opened in 2001. A veritable labyrinth, with hall-

The Wall

Masterminded by the East German government in 1961, the Berlin Wall divided the city's western districts from East Berlin and the surrounding Brandenburg region for 28 years. Since 1989, the bricks, watchtowers, barbed wire and machine guns have been replaced by new construction or parks, but a few sections of the Wall still commemorate this unique period in history.

The longest stretch, and the most rewarding for visitors, is the **East Side Gallery**, which runs for 1.3km/0.8mi along Mühlenstraße, parallel to the Spree river, just south of Ostbahnhof train station. After reunification, artists from around the world were asked to turn it into an outdoor art gallery. The picture of a Trabi car bursting through the Wall is one of the most iconic images. There are also shorter Wall remnants on Niederkirchner Straße near the Topography of Terror exhibition, on Potsdamer Platz and at the **Berlin Wall Memorial Site** (*Gedenkstätte Berliner Mauer*) on Bernauer Straße, a documentary centre that combines an exhibition, an outdoor installation and a memorial chapel.

*Voids with Shalechet (Fallen leaves)
by Menashe Kadisman,
Jüdisches Museum Berlin*

© Dieter and Si Rosenkranz, Berlin
(long-termn loan). Photo: Jens Ziehe/Jüdisches Museum Berlin

ways leading into empty spaces called "voids", the building is an architectural metaphor for the torturous experiences of German Jews. The exhibition traces 2 000 years of their history, with special emphasis given to the cultural and artistic contributions made by prominent Jewish Berliners – such as the philosopher Moses Mendelssohn – between the 18C and the 20C.

A special section examines the post-reunification renaissance of the local Jewish community.

⚐ Deutsches Technikmuseum Berlin★★ (German Museum of Technology)

Trebbiner Straße 9. ⏱*Open year-round, Tue–Fri 9am–5.30pm, Sat–Sun 10am–6pm.* ⏱*Closed May 1, Dec 24–26.* ♿*4.50€ (child 2.50€).* ✆ *(030) 90 25 40. www.dtmb.de.*

This temple of technology takes you on an eye-opening journey past the milestones of transport, energy, communication and production. It features outstanding exhibits on **aviation and nagivation**★★, an early computer designed by pioneer Konrad Zuse, a historical brewery and an entire hall of **historic locomotives**★★.

Interactive displays, live demonstrations and experiments further enliven visits. Kids gravitate to the **Science Centre Spectrum** (*Möckernstraße 26*) where they can playfully learn about scientific phenomena at 250 interactive stations.

Viktoriapark★

Kreuzberg hill, the highest natural elevation in central Berlin (66m/216ft), is entirely covered by the Viktoriapark. The top is crowned by Karl Friedrich Schinkel's monument to the "Wars of Liberation" and delivers nice city views. There is also a children's playground and a leafy beer garden.

TIERGARTEN AND THE CHARLOTTENBURG DISTRICT★

Berlin's oldest public park stretches almost 3km/1.8mi from Charlottenburg Gate to Brandenburg Gate. Originally a royal hunting reserve, it was transformed into a delightful English-style park by landscape architect Peter Joseph Lenné (1789–1866) in the 19C. Further west is the vast district of Charlottenburg, which was the centre of West Berlin during the years of division. Its main spine, the Kurfürstendamm, is a popular shopping strip. Outer area sights include the Olympic Stadium and the Funkturm (radio tower).

Siegessäule (Victory Column)

⏱*Open Apr–Oct, Mon–Fri 9.30am–6.30pm, Sat–Sun 9.30am–7pm; Nov–Mar, Mon–Fri 10am–5.30pm, Sat–Sun 10am–5pm.* ♿*2.20€. www.monument-tal.*

All of 67m/220ft high, this landmark monument, surmounted by a gilded sculpture of the Goddess of Victory (nicknamed Gold Else), commemorates the successful Prussian campaigns of 1864, 1866 and 1870 against Denmark, Austria and France. From the top *(285 steps)*, **views**★ extend across Tiergarten Park to the Spree, the Hansa residential quarter and the Brandenburg Gate.

Schloss Bellevue

Built in the Neoclassical style by Philipp Boumann in 1785, this was the summer palace of Frederick the Great's younger brother, Prince Augustus-Ferdinand.

Olympic Games of 1936

When Germany beat Barcelona in 1931 to become the host of the 1936 Olympic Games, no one could have predicted that the country would by then have fallen under the rule of Adolf Hitler and his totalitarian National Socialist Party. The United States almost boycotted the Games, largely because of the regime's anti-Semitic policies, but was assuaged when Hitler declared that athletes of all races and confessions would be allowed to participate. Ironically, it was African-American runner Jesse Owens who became the star of the show as the winner of four gold medals in the sprint and long jump events. On 1 August 1936 Hitler opened the Games at Berlin's new Olympic Stadium in front of 100 000 people. It marked the second time that the Olympic Flame was used but the first time that it was carried from Olympia, Greece, in a torch relay by thousands of runners.

Today it is the official residence of the German president and is backed by a lush park that is closed to the public.

Bauhaus-Archiv/Museum für Gestaltung★ (Bauhaus Archives/Museum for Design)

Klingelhöferstraße 14. Open year-round, Wed–Mon 10am–5pm. Closed Dec 24. 6€ (Wed–Fri), 7€ (Sun–Mon). & (030) 254 00 20. www.bauhaus.de.
In a building designed by Bauhaus founder **Walter Gropius**, this museum and archive highlights the concepts and philosophy of this early 20C aesthetic movement that greatly influenced modern design and architecture. Exhibits include sculptures, blueprints, models and paintings by Schlemmer, Moholy-Nagy, Feininger, Kandinsky, Klee and other Bauhaus School members.

≛≛ Zoologischer Garten★★★ (Berlin Zoo and Aquarium)

Hardenbergplatz 8. Open Apr–mid-Sept, daily 9am–7.30pm; mid-Sept–Oct, 9am–7pm; Nov–Mar, 9am–5pm. 12€. & (030) 25 40 10. www.zoo-berlin.de.
Some 16 000 creatures make their home in Berlin's venerable zoo, including Knut, the world's most famous polar bear. Next door is the aquarium *(entry Budapester Straße;* open year-round, daily 9am–6pm; & 12€; (030) 25 40 10; www.aquarium-berlin.de) which has some 650 different species, including some fearsome crocodiles on the first floor. Combination tickets with the zoo are 18€.

Kurfürstendamm★★

This busy 3.5km/2mi-long boulevard started life as a riding path to the royal hunting lodge in the Grunewald forest. In the 1880s, Bismarck transformed it into the prestigious thoroughfare known as the "Ku'damm". With its many department stores and boutiques, it is still Berlin's major shopping street and also lined by cafés, restaurants, theatres and galleries.

Kaiser-Wilhelm-Gedächtniskirche★ (Kaiser Wilhelm Memorial Church)

Open year-round, daily 9am–7pm. & (030) 218 50 23.
www.gedaechtniskirche-berlin.de.
This neo-Romanesque church was consecrated in 1895 in honour of Emperor Wilhelm I. After World War II its ruined tower was left standing as a reminder of the horrors of war. A much-photo-

Knautschke the Survivor

The end of the war was a difficult time for the animals at the zoo; the locals used them for food, just as they used trees from the Tiergarten for heat. One writer, Stefan Reisner (*Stadtfront, Berlin West Berlin*, 1982), recalls his father melting a camel's hump in a frying pan. However, the hippopotamus Knautschke was more fortunate. He stayed underwater during the conflict, re-emerging a true hero once the bombardments were over.

graphed Berlin landmark, it sits next to a modernistic octagonal house of worship (1961) famous for its deep blue glass walls made by artists from Chartres. The original church entrance beneath the tower is now a **Memorial Hall**. The entire complex is under restoration that's expected to last until at least 2012. It will remain open during that time.

Tauentzienstraße

South of the Gedächtniskirche, this fashionable shopping street is home to Europe's second-largest department store, the **"KaDeWe"**. The abbreviation stands for Kaufhaus des Westens: Department Store of the West.

Käthe-Kollwitz-Museum★

Fasanenstraße 24. ⊙Open year-round, daily 11am–6pm. ⊙Closed Dec 24 & 31. ⊛6€. ℘(030) 882 52 10. www.kaethe-kollwitz.de.
In a lovely villa, this small museum presents a broad survey of one of the most important German women artists, the Berlin-born Käthe Kollwitz (1867–1945). Highlights include engravings *The Weavers' Revolt* (1893–98) and *The Peasants' War* (1903–08), woodcuts titled *War* (1920–24) and *The Proletariat* (1925), and self-portraits and lithographs labelled *Death*. 1920s-era posters such as *Nie Wieder Krieg (No More War)* underline Kollwitz's pacifist ideals; sculptures on the upper floor include *Muttergruppe (Mother Group)* (1924–37).

Funkturm (Radio Tower)

Masurenallee. ⊙Open year-round, Mon 10am-8pm, Tue–Sun 10am–11pm. ⊙Closed Jan 1 & Dec 24.⊛4.50€. ℘(030) 30 38 19 05.
Known to Berliners as *Langer Lulatsch* ("lanky laddie"), this 150m/492ft tower looms above the trade show grounds and looks like a smaller brother of Paris' Eiffel Tower. Designed in the 1920s by Heinrich Straumer, it features a viewing platform at 126m/413ft and a restaurant about halfway up.

GREATER BERLIN

Sprawling across nearly 900sq km/350sq mi, the city state of Berlin boasts a surprising diversity of landscapes. Lakes and vast forests form a greenbelt around the city, which is also dotted with villages exuding provincial charm.

DAHLEM★★★

The leafy residential suburb of Dahlem is home to the Freie Universität (Free University), which was founded in 1948 and has nearly 40 000 students. The main visitor attraction, though, is the **Museen Dahlem** (⊙*open year-round, Tue–Fri 10am–6pm, Sat–Sun 11am–6pm; ⊛6€; ℘(030) 830 14 38; www.smb.spk-berlin.de)*, a vast museum complex that, aside from collections detailed below, also harbours the child-oriented ♟♟ **Junior Museum**.

Ethnologisches Museum★★★ (Museum of Ethnology)

Enter on Lansstraße 8.
This museum is home to 400 000 outstanding ethnographic objects divided into several permanent collections.

American Archaeology★★★

This stunning exhibition presents a survey of pre-Hispanic cultures from 2 000 BC to the early 16C. It reveals such treasures as **carved stelae** from Guatemala, painted **stone vessels** of the Maya, Aztec **stone figures** of gods and **gold objects** from Central America, Colombia and Peru.

North American Indians★

Showcases the cultural and artistic diversity that developed among Indian cultures throughout North America and also seeks to debunk myths created by western fiction and modern media (films in particular). Items include moccasins, medicine pouches, tomahawks and peace pipes but also contemporary Native American art.

South Seas★★

Among the items gathered during sea voyages since the 18C, some by Captain James Cook, note the painted **masks** and **wooden sculptures** from New Guinea, the spectacular boats from **Oceania** and the **feathered cloak** of the king of Hawaii.

Africa★★

The most interesting objects in this collection include **terracotta heads from Ife** (Nigeria), **bronzes** from the ancient kingdom of Benin, and Berber jewellery, along with wooden sculptures from Cameroon. It was recently expanded to include art created by Africans living in Berlin. A standout here is the *ijele* mask created by a Nigerian artist for the local Igbo community.

Music Ethnology

This section documents global music culture and encompasses more than 150 000 **sound recordings**. One of the earliest is from 1900, when the psychologist Carl Stumpf used an Edison phonograph to record a group of Thai musicians performing in Berlin.

Museum für Asiatische Kunst★★ (Museum of Asian Art)

Enter on Lansstraße 8.
The East Asian collections cover art and artefacts from China, Japan and Korea and were recently combined with collections from the Museum of Indian Art. Galleries display objects from the fourth millennium BC to today, including stone sculpture, ceramics, cult objects,

Japanese woodcuts and lacquer arts, most notably a **17C imperial throne**★★ made of palisander wood with mother-of-pearl inlaid into lacquer and gold. Another highlight is the **Japanese tea room**★, which is occasionally used for tea ceremonies, and a **video installation**★ by the late Korean artist Naim June Paik. Folk art from Japan is another focus of the museum.

Museum Europäischer Kulturen★ (Museum of European Cultures)

Focused on everyday European culture from the 18C to the present, this museum is undergoing major renovations and is expected to remain closed until at least mid-2011.

Botanischer Garten und Museum★★ (Botanical Gardens and Museum)

Königin-Luise-Straße 6–8. ◐*Open year-round, daily 9am–dusk, latest 9pm.* ◐*Closed Dec 24.* ⊜*6€, incl. museum.* ♿ *℘(030) 83 85 01 00. www.bgbm.org.*
At 43ha/106 acres, Berlin's botanical garden is one of the world's largest and most diverse with more than 22 000 plant species. Vegetation is arranged geographically from mountains to plains. Rare species of trees and shrubs are in the **Arboretum**, while 15 **greenhouses** shelter a wealth of tropical and sub-tropical plants.

Botanischer Garten

The **Botanical Museum**★ *(Botanisches Museum;* ⏱*open year-round, daily 10am–6pm;* ⮕*2.50€, museum only)* chronicles the evolution of flora and documents common plant uses.

NEAR DAHLEM
Brücke-Museum★

Bussardsteig 9. ⏱*Open year-round, Wed–Mon 11am–5pm.* ⏱*Closed Dec 24 & 31.* ⮕*5€.* ♿. ✆*(030) 831 20 29. www.bruecke-museum.de.*

This museum contains works by members of the **Die Brücke** (The Bridge), an artist group of German Expressionists. It was founded in Dresden in 1905 by architecture students Erich Heckel, Ernst Ludwig Kirchner, Fritz Bleyl and Karl Schmidt-Rottluff. Rejecting traditional painting styles taught at the art academies, they sought to explore new forms of expression, especially by employing bold colour and working with distorted compositions. In 1911, the group moved to Berlin where it disbanded two years later. The small museum, which was founded by Schmidt-Rottluff himself and opened in 1967, presents works by all major Brücke members, including Max Pechstein, Otto Mueller and Emil Nolde in addition to those by its founders.

Grunewald★★

A hunting reserve of the Prince-Electors in the 16C, this mixed forest covers 3 100ha/745 acres and is bounded by a chain of small lakes. Near one of them, the Grunewaldsee, is **Jagdschloss Grunewald**★ *(*⏱*open Apr–Oct, Tue–Sat 10am–6pm; guided tours only Nov–Mar, Sat & Sun 11am, 1pm & 3pm;* ⮕*4/5€ without/with tour;* ✆*(030) 813 35 97; www.spsg.de),* an elegant hunting lodge built in 1542.

Originally a Renaissance palace, it was converted into the Baroque style for King Frederick I some 160 years later. There's documentation about its most recent overhaul on the ground floor. Since its completion visitors can again admire paintings by Dutch and German masters from the 15C–18C. Highlights include the famous portraits of the royal

family by Lucas Cranach the Elder and his son. There's also an exhibit on the royal hunt in the storehouse.

Grunewald forest is bordered by **Lake Havel**★★, whose eastern shore is parallelled by the picturesque Havelchaussee road. It leads south to the beaches of the **Wannsee**★★, a hugely popular recreational area in summer.

Pfaueninsel★★
(Peacock Island)

Ferries leave from the landing at the end of Nikolskoer Weg, May–Aug daily 8am–9pm, Apr & Sept 9am–7pm, Mar & Oct 9am–6pm, Nov–Feb 10am–4pm. ⮕*2€.*

There's a dreamy quality about this island in the Havel River, which was turned into a romantic retreat by King Frederick William II in the 18C.

It is still a popular escape from the city bustle with gardens landscaped by Peter Joseph Lenné inviting extensive strolling. Paths lead to a snowy-white fairytale **castle**★ *(1794–97) (*⮕*visit by guided tour (30min) only, May–Sept, Tue–Sun 10am–6pm, Oct 10am–5pm;* ⮕*3€;* ✆*(030) 805 86 75 13; www.spsg.de)* that displays souvenirs of Queen Louise in salons panelled with exotic woods.

SOUTHEAST OF THE CITY
Kunstgewerbemuseum★
(Museum of Decorative Arts)

In Schloss Köpenick (Schloßinsel). ⏱*Open year-round, Tue–Sun 10am–6pm.* ⮕*4€.* ♿. ✆*(030) 266 36 66. www.smb.museum/kgm.*

The second branch of the Museum of Decorative Arts (the main one is at the Kulturforum) occupies a restored 17C Baroque palace on a little peninsula in the southeastern Berlin suburb of Köpenick.

The 16C–19C furniture is especially interesting, as are the **panelled room**★ from Haldenstein castle (Switzerland, 16C), the **Treasury**★, with jewellery and 16C Baroque gold- and silverware, the silver **sideboard**★★ from the Knights' Room in the old Berlin city palace and the **coats of arms hall**★.

Großer Müggelsee★★

Berlin's largest lake is 4km/2.5mi long and 2.5km/1.5mi wide and among the city's most majestic. It's fringed by the Köpenick city forest, which is criss-crossed by trails where you could easily walk for hours.

EXCURSIONS
Gedenkstätte und Museum Sachsenhausen (Sachsenhausen Memorial and Museum)

▷ *31km/19.2mi north of Berlin.*
◷*Open mid-Mar–mid-Oct, daily 8.30am–6pm (rest of year 4.30pm).*
◷*Closed Jan 1, Dec 24, 25 & 31.* ♿
℘(033 01) 20 02 00. www.stiftung-bg.de.
The Nazi-era concentration camp of **Sachsenhausen** near the town of Oranienburg north of Berlin opened in 1936. Tens of thousands of the 220 000 prisoners that passed through its gates until 1945 perished. Exhibits occupy such sites as the camp commander's house, the kitchen, the hospital wing and Baracke 38 where Jewish prisoners were kept. You'll also learn about the organisation of the Nazi concentration camp system, whose cynicism is epitomised by the slogan above the entrance gates: *"Arbeit macht frei"* (work sets you free).

Schloss Rheinsberg★

▷ *87km/54mi northwest of Berlin.*
◷*Open year-round, Tue–Sun 10am–6pm (Nov–Mar 5pm).* ⊙*6€ (Nov–Mar 4€).* ◷*Closed 24–25 Dec.* ⊶*Guided tour of park 2.50€.* ℘*(033931) 72 60. www.spsg.de.*
Frederick the Great spent four years living in this palace, calling them the happiest of his life. Purchased by Frederick's father in 1734 it was remodelled in Rococo style by the architect Knobelsdorff, the painter Pesne and the sculptor Glume. Until German reunification, the palace was used as a sanatorium. Highlights include the Spiegelsaal (Hall of Mirrors), decorated with a ceiling fresco by Antoine Pesne, and the Muschelsaal (Shell Room). Tickets are also valid at the **Tucholsky Literaturmuseum** on the ground floor which portrays the life of journalist, satirist, poet and social critic Kurt Tucholsky (1890–1935).

Ravensbrück

▷ *24km/15mi south of Neustrelitz on the E 251, 1km/0.6mi from Fürstenberg.*
◷*Open year-round, May–Sept, Tue–Sun 9am–6pm (to 5pm Oct–Apr).*
◷*Closed Dec 24–26 & 31.* ℘*(033093) 603 85. www.ravensbrueck.de.*
Construction of Ravensbrück concentration camp on the shores of Schwedtsee lake began in 1938. It was the only major camp for women and by 1945 had seen 132 000 prisoners from over 40 nations. Tens of thousands died. The camp is now a memorial site with a permanent exhibition in the old SS camp commander's headquarters that documents the history of the camp and the lives and deaths of its victims. There are also additional smaller exhibits.

Kloster Chorin★★ (Chorin Abbey)

▷ *71km/44mi north of Berlin. Amt Chorin 11a.*
◷*Open year-round, daily 9am–6pm (Nov–Mar 4pm).* ⊙*4€.* ℘*(033366) 703 77. www.kloster-chorin.com.*
Romantically ruined Chorin Abbey, near a small lake and surrounded by a park, was originally constructed in the 13C by Cistercian monks. The abbey was dissolved in 1542 and, after centuries of neglect, was saved by the architect Karl Friedrich Schinkel and the king of Prussia. Now partially restored, it is one of the finest Gothic red-brick structures in northern Germany and hosts a popular summer festival of classical music.

SPREEWALD★★

▷ *The Spreewald region is about 100km/62mi southeast of Berlin and covers about 260sq km/100sq mi. Lindenstraße 1, 03226 Vetschau. ℘(035433) 722 99. www.spreewald.de.*
☺*Don't miss a barge trip from Lübbenau.*
A network of hundreds of waterways crisscrosses this lush countryside, painstakingly drained to give it the appear-

ance of a "Venice in the Woods". Another regional interest is its Sorbian minority, western Slavs who settled in Germany's Lausitz area in the 6C and who have managed to retain their language and culture to this day (&see BRANITZ).

Lübbenau

The 18C Parish Church of **St. Nikolai**★ (◷open May–Oct, Tue–Sun 2pm–4pm; ◷closed public holidays; ✏donation requested; &; ✆(03542) 36 68) is an important example of the Dresden Baroque architectural style. Inside are impressive tombs and epitaphs, most notably the high **tomb** (c. 1765) of Prince Moritz Carl, count of Lynaer. To learn more about the region's cultural history, heritage and traditions, take a spin around the **Spreewald Museum** (◷open Tue–Sun 10am–6pm (Oct–Mar 5pm; ✏3€; ✆(03542) 24 72).

≗≗Barge Trips

Boat trips launch from throughout the Spreewald, but **Lübbenau** has established itself as the centre. Boats leave from Grosser Hafen or Kleiner Hafen, Mar–Oct (weather permitting; limited service in Nov–Feb); 2–9hrs, with stopovers. ✏9.50€–21€. ✆(03542) 22 25. www.spreewaldexpress.de.
A favourite destination is **Lehde**★, a tiny lagoon village of 150 people. The **Freilandmuseum** (Open-air Museum) consists of three 19C farms, complete with living quarters and outbuildings, furniture, folk art, costumes and agricultural tools. The walk from Lübbenau to Lehde takes about 30 minutes.

ADDRESSES

🏠 STAY

🛏**Circus Hostel** – Weinbergsweg 1a, Mitte. ✆(030) 20 00 39 39. www.circus-berlin.de. 35 rooms. Only a few minutes' walk from Hackescher Markt, this is a lovely hostel with modern furnishings. Rooms are clean and colourful, but most have shared bathrooms. If you want private facilities, book one of the spacious apartments. Services include

internet, bike rental and in-house café and pub.

🛏**Hotel Am Anhalter Bahnhof** – Stresemannstraße 36, Kreuzberg. ✆(030) 258 00 70. www.hotel-anhalter-bahnhof.de. 35 rooms. The best things about this no-frills property are its convenient location near Potsdamer Platz and a bus stop on its doorstep. Basic rooms are clean and cheap, but only some have private facilities; others must share bathrooms down the hall.

🛏**Transit Loft Hotel** – Greifswalder Straße 219, Prenzlauer Berg. ✆(030) 48 49 37 73. www.transit-loft.de. This former factory building in the hip quarter of Prenzlauer Berg started out in 2001 as a hostel for young people. Rooms are simple but well-maintained.

🛏🛏**Arte Luise Kunsthotel** – Luisenstraße 19, Mitte. ✆(030) 28 44 80. www.luise-berlin.com. 50 rooms. This beautifully restored listed building from 1825 houses a unique boutique hotel where the rooms have been designed by different artists who receive a small stipend every time their room is rented. There are also smaller rooms with shared bathrooms.

🛏🛏**Hotel Berlin-Plaza** – Knesebeck straße 63, Charlottenburg. ✆(030) 88 41 30. www.plazahotel.de. 131 rooms. Restaurant🍽. This dog-friendly hotel puts you close to Ku'damm shopping and has modern, clean and plain rooms.

🛏🛏**Honigmond Garden Hotel** – Invalidenstraße 122, Mitte. ✆(030) 28 44 55 77. www.honigmond-berlin.de. 16 rooms, 4 apts. Rooms here exude plenty of character with their polished parquet floors and antique furniture. The hotel is in a quiet area close to the historic centre. In summer, breakfast is served in the garden.

🛏🛏**Am Wilden Eber** – Warnemünder Straße 19, Wilmersdorf. ✆(030) 89 77 79 90. www.hotel-am-wilden-eber.de. 15 rooms. This simple hotel in a leafy suburb has well-kept and quiet rooms, and a small pool and sauna in the basement.

🛏🛏🛏**Hotel Hackescher Markt** – Große Präsidentenstraße 8, Mitte. ✆(030) 28 00 30. www.loock-hotels.com. 31 rooms. Charmingly decorated in English country style, this intimate boutique hotel occupies a modern building concealed by a historic façade. It is right in the heart of the happening Scheunenviertel nightlife district, so get a room facing the small inner courtyard for extra quiet.

Hotel Adlon – *Unter den Linden 77, Mitte.* ℰ*(030) 226 10. www.hote-adlon.de. 336 rooms. Restaurant* . Truly a living legend! Since 1997 it is once again possible to stay in this sumptuous building next to the Brandenburg Gate. It is a very close copy of the 1907 original and oozes luxury from every nook and cranny.

Grand Hotel Esplanade – *Lützowufer 15, Tiergarten.* ℰ*(030) 254 788 255. www.esplanade.de. 386 rooms. Restaurant* . This updated urban designer hotel features elegant rooms dressed in natural hues and accented with wood and chrome. The generous pool and sauna are welcome relaxation zones while four restaurants feed tummy and soul.

⏚/EAT

Vapiano – *Postdamer Platz 5, Tiergarten.* ℰ*(030) 23 00 50 05. www.vapiano.de.* At this self-service restaurant you can order mix-and-match pasta, salad or pizza, which is then prepared in front of you in the open kitchen. Each table features a basket with fresh basil, rosemary and mint which you can use to add a little spice to your dish.

Marjellchen – *Mommsenstraße 9, Charlottenburg.* ℰ*(030) 883 26 76. www.marjellchen-berlin.de. Closed Sun.* This homey Berlin restaurant serves substantial dishes from eastern Prussia and Silesia that taste just like in the old days.

Mutter Hoppe – *Rathausstraße 21, Mitte.* ℰ*(030) 241 56 25. www.prost mahlzeit.de/mutterhoppe.* A rustic restaurant in the Nikolaiviertel, Mutter Hoppe celebrates Old Berlin nostalgia in its warren of rooms filled with faded photographs and yesteryear's memorabilia. On Friday and Saturday nights, live bands play music from the 1920s and 1930s.

Diekmann – *Meinekestraße 7, Charlottenburg.* ℰ*(030) 883 33 21. www.j-diekmann.de. Closed Sun lunch-*

time. Reservation necessary. Josef Diekmann's original restaurant serves upmarket Franco-German fare prepared with locally sourced game, fish and other produce. The space itself is beautifully old-fashioned with plank flooring and the quaint charm of an early 20C grocers'.

Lutter und Wegner – *Charlottenstraße 56, Mitte.* ℰ *(030) 202 95 40. www.l-w-berlin.de.* Behind a sandstone facade, this popular restaurant is close to Gendarmenmarkt. The cuisine shows a distinct Austrian influence while the wine menu features 700 choices in all price categories.

Borchardt – *Französische Straße 47, Mitte.* ℰ*(030) 81 88 62 62.* With impressive gilded columns, stuccoed ceilings and refined furniture, this chic restaurant attracts celebrities, politicians and the merely monied. The *Wiener schnitzel* is reportedly the best in town.

Zander – *Kollwitzstraße 50, Prenzlauer Berg.* ℰ*(030) 44 05 76 78. www.zander-restaurant.de. Closed Mon. Reservations recommended.* This bi-level bistro serves freshly prepared regional and international dishes with a creative, modern touch. The signature dish is the namesake pike perch *(Zander)* which is served as carpaccio, in soup or fried.

Parc Fermé – *Wiebestraße 36–37, Moabit close to Charlottenburg.* ℰ*(030) 20 61 30 30. www.kaiser stuben.de. Closed Sun–Mon. Reservation recommended.* This charming restaurant occupies a small section of a 1901 tram depot that also houses a huge collection of antique cars. The classic and refined cuisine pairs well with an impressive wine selection.

Alt Luxemburg – *Windscheidstraße 31, Charlottenburg.* ℰ*(030) 323 87 30. www.altluxemburg.de. Closed Mon.* The family Wannmacher has been serving high-level classic cuisine in their colourfully decorated restaurant since 1982.

Uma – *Behrenstraße 72, Mitte.* ℰ*(030) 301 117 333. www.ma-restaurants.de.* At this stunning restaurant behind the Adlon, you can enjoy contemporary interpretations of classic Japanese cuisine. Put together a meal from a selection of exquisitely crafted plates while surrounded by original art from around Asia.

⚲ CAFÉS

Café Einstein Stammhaus – *Kurfürstenstraße 58, Schöneberg.* ℘*(030) 261 50 96. www.cafeeinstein.de.* This Vienna-style coffeehouse in the former villa of silent-movie star Henny Porten is popular with artists, intellectual types and politicians. Enjoy breakfast, a light lunch, afternoon coffee and cake or Austrian dishes at dinnertime.

Ephraim's – *Spreeufer 1, Mitte.* ℘*(030) 24 72 59 47. www.ephraims.de.* Nostalgia rules at this café-restaurant in the Nikolaiviertel serving Berlin specialities, homemade cakes and a warm atmosphere. In fine weather, sit outside with views of the Spree River.

Telecafé – *Panoramastraße 1a, Mitte.* ℘*(030) 242 33 33. http://tv-turm.de.* Pinpoint Berlin landmarks from this TV tower café at a lofty 207m/680ft height. It completes a full revolution in 30 minutes.

☺ NIGHTLIFE

Useful tips – Berlin's nightlife is decentralised and constantly evolving. Current hotspots cluster in the Scheunenviertel and around Gendarmenmarkt in Mitte; Kollwitzplatz, Kastanienallee and Helmholtzplatz in Prenzlauer Berg; Bergmannstraße, Oranienstraße, Schlesische Straße and Paul-Lincke-Ufer in Kreuzberg; Winterfeldtplatz in Schöneberg; and Savignyplatz in Charlottenburg.

Clärchen's Ballhaus – *Auguststraße 24, Mitte.* ℘*(030) 282 92 95. www.ballhaus.de.* This 19C dance hall draws young and old with tango, swing, ballroom, disco and more. Live bands perform on Friday and Saturday nights and dance lessons are offered, too. German and Italian food (pizza) is served from 12.30pm.

Die Tagung – *Wühlischstraße 29, Friedrichshain, east of Warschauer Straße.* ℘*(030) 29 77 37 88.* This funky been-here-forever bar is a tongue-in-cheek nostalgic celebration with a hodgepodge of retro busts, signs, posters and other memorabilia.

Universum Lounge – *Kurfürsten-damm 153, Charlottenburg.* ℘*(030) 89 06 49 95. www.universumlounge.de.* A cool crowd of cashed-up locals, theatre-goers and hipsters convenes for cocktails and conversation in this sleek, space-age themed lounge. It's right in the Schaubühne theatre, designed by Expressionist architect Erich Mendelssohn in the 1920s.

Zillemarkt – *Bleibtreustraße 48a, Charlottenburg.* ℘*(030) 881 70 40. www.zillemarkt.de.* This Old Berlin hangout with its cobbled courtyard, bric-a-brac décor and earthy cooking is much beloved by tourists and locals alike.

Prater Garten Berlin – *Kastanienallee 7–9, Prenzlauer Berg.* ℘*(030) 448 56 88. www.pratergarten.de.* Dating back to 1873, this is Berlin's oldest, largest and most beautiful beer garden. Quaff a cold one sitting at long blond-wood tables beneath mature chestnut trees.

Philharmonie – *Herbert-von-Karajan-Straße, Tiergarten.* ℘*(030) 25 48 81 32. www.berliner-philharmoniker.de.* Enjoy supreme acoustics, a top-notch orchestra led by Sir Simon Rattle and renowned soloists in one of Germany's finest concert halls, built by Hans Scharoun in the 1960s.

Staatsoper Unter den Linden – *Unter den Linden 7, Mitte.* ℘*(030) 20 35 45 55. www.staatsoper-berlin.org.* The most prestigious among Berlin's three opera houses, the Staatsoper is helmed by Daniel Barenboim. Until at least 2013, performances take place in the Schillertheater in Charlottenburg *(Bismarckstraße 110)* while the historic 18C opera house is under renovation.

⛏ SHOPPING

Useful tips – Berlin's main shopping streets are Kurfürstendamm and Tauentzienstraße in Charlottenburg and Friedrichstraße in Mitte. The biggest shopping centres are the Potsdamer Platz Arkaden and the Alexa mall near Alexanderplatz. Independent boutiques cluster in the Scheunenviertel in Mitte, along Bergmannstraße in Kreuzberg; on Bleibtreustraße and Fasanenstraße in Charlottenburg; and on Kastanienallee in Prenzlauer Berg.

DEPARTMENT STORES

Berlin's most famous department store is **KaDeWe** on Tauentzienstraße in Schoeneberg with a wonderful food hall on the 6th floor. **Galeries Lafayette** brings Parisian style and fashion to Friedrichstraße in Mitte.
On Alexanderplatz, the Galeria Kaufhof has been redesigned by architect Josef Paul Kleihues and is now an elegant place to max out those credit cards.

Art galleries – Galleries abound around Savignyplatz and along Fasanenstraße in Charlottenburg, on Zimmerstraße and Markgrafenstraße near Checkpoint Charlie and along Auguststraße, Linienstraße and Brunnenstraße in Mitte. An emerging quarter is along Potsdamer Straße and Kurfuerstenstraße in Schöneberg.

Flea markets – Flohmarkt am Tiergarten, Straße des 17. Juni, Charlottenburg, *Sat–Sun 10am–5pm*; Flohmarkt am Mauerpark, Bernauer Straße 63–64, Prenzlauer Berg, *Sun 10am–5pm*; Flohmarkt am Arkonaplatz, Prenzlauer Berg, *Sun 10am–5pm*; Flohmarkt am Boxhagener Platz, Friedrichshain, *Sun 9am–4pm*.

Farmers' markets – Winterfeldtplatz, Schöneberg, *Wed 8am–2pm, Sat 8am–4pm*; Turkish market Maybachufer, Kreuzberg, *Tue and Fri noon–6.30pm*; Kollwitzplatz, Prenzlauer Berg, *Thu noon–7pm, Sat 9am–4pm*.

SIGHTSEEING

BUS TOURS

Severin & Kühn (℘880 4190; www.severin-kuehn.de); Berolina Sightseeing (℘88 56 80 30); BBS (℘35 19 52 70; www.bbsberlin.de); Tempelhofer Reisen (℘752 40 57; www.tempelhofer.de) all provide hop-on, hop-off bus tours with taped commentary taking in all major city attractions. Buses run at 15 or 30min intervals between 10am and 5pm and leave from Kurfürstendamm and outside the Park Inn Hotel on Alexanderplatz.

WALKING AND BIKING TOURS

The following companies all provide excellent English-language walking and biking tours: *New Berlin Tours (℘51 05 00 30; www.newberlintours.com), Original Berlin Walking Tours (℘301 91 94; www.berlinwalks.de), Brewer's Berlin Tours (℘22 48 74 35; www.brewersberlin), Insider Tours (℘692 31 49; www.insider tour.com).* Look for their flyers in hotel lobbies and the tourist offices.

BOAT TOURS

Stern und Kreisschiffahrt (℘536 36 00; www.sternundkreis.de) offers 1hr cruises along the Spree River through the historic city centre from various landing docks, including in the Nikolaiviertel and at Friedrichstraße. Longer tours go out to Charlottenburg Palace, along the Landwehrkanal or to Berlin's green suburbs.

SPECIALITY TOURS

Trabi Safari (℘2759 2273; www.trabi-safari.de). Imagine yourself behind the steering wheel of a tinny GDR-era Trabi car exploring Berlin's Wild East following your guide in another vehicle. The ultimate "ostalgia" tour (i.e. nostalgia for the East).

Berliner Unterwelten Bunker Tour (℘030 4991 0518; www.berliner-unterwelten.de). See what Berlin looks like beneath the surface by joining an eye-opening tour of an underground bunker built during World War II.

Fritz Music Tours (℘ 030 3087 5633; www.musictours-berlin.com). Delve deep into Berlin's popular music history and find out where David Bowie lived, where Depeche Mode and U2 produced some records or where Rammstein keeps their offices. Both walking and driving tours are available.

Berlinagenten (℘030-4372 0701; www.berlinagenten.com). Find out what makes Berlin tick, visit locals in their homes, visit secret corners and the newest hotspots on lifestyle tours led by clued-in guides. Or for a primer on the culinary scene, book a **Gastro-Rallye**, where you'll enjoy one course each at four restaurant stops while being peppered with insider scoops on the city.

Potsdam★★★

Just west of Berlin, Potsdam was chosen in the 17C as the residence of the Electors of Brandenburg because of its lovely setting in a natural woodland dotted with lakes and crisscrossed by canals and the River Havel. It is to Frederick the Great that Potsdam owes its renown as "rococo jewel". In 1990, the city's palaces and parks garnered a spot on the list of UNESCO World Heritage Sites.

A BIT OF HISTORY

A Prussian Versailles – Under Frederick William (1713–40) Potsdam became an administrative centre and a garrison town. By contrast, the king's son, **Frederick the Great** (Frederick II) was a great patron of the arts.

Most of the sights for which Potsdam is famous were built on his watch, notably Sanssouci Palace and the Neues Palais. Frederick, as fluent in French as in German, welcomed many eminent Frenchmen to his court, among them **Voltaire**.

The Potsdam Conference – The treaty defining the occupation and the future of Germany after World War II was signed at Cecilienhof Palace on 2 August 1945 by the leaders of the Allied powers (Atlee, Truman and Stalin).

SANSSOUCI PALACE AND PARK★★★

This huge complex is a harmonious marriage of architecture and landscape. Wandering around, it is easy to understand why Frederick the Great took such delight in staying here.

Friedenskirche (Peace Church)

Modelled on Rome's basilica of San Clemente, the church contains a fine 18 C Murano **mosaic**★. The mausoleum harbours statues of Emperor Friedrich III and his wife and the sarcophagus of Friedrich Wilhelm I (1678–1740), which was hidden during World War II and only brought here in 1991.

▶ **Population:** 148 700

Info: Am Neuen Markt 1, 14467 Potsdam. (0331) 27 55 80. www.potsdam.de.

Location: Potsdam, the capital of the state of Brandenburg, is just west of Berlin, in the heart of the Havelland, an area of canals and lakes.

Parking: Garages are located throughout the city, including one near Sanssouci Palace.

Don't Miss: Sanssouci Palace.

Timing: Allow at least half a day for a tour of Sanssouci.

Bildergalerie★ (Picture Gallery)

Open May–Oct, Tue–Sun 10am–5pm. 3€. (0331) 969 41 81.

Amid the rich 18C Rococo of the great rooms visitors can admire works mainly from the Italian (Bassano, Tintoretto and Caravaggio), Flemish (Van Dyck, Rubens and Terbrugghen) and French (Simon Vouet and Van Loo) schools, all acquired by Friedrich II.

Schloss Sanssouci★★★

Tours are limited to 2 000 visitors a day and often sell out before noon. Admission is by timed ticket.
Open Tue–Sun 10am–6pm (until 5pm Nov–Mar). Closed Dec 24, 25 & 31. 12€ Apr–Oct, 8€ Nov–Mar. (0331) 969 42 00. www.spsg.de.

It is impossible to remain unmoved by the majestic façade as one climbs the great staircase leading to the palace from the park side. Architect Knobelsdorff originally planned for the façade, adorned with 36 atlantes, to encompass the entire terrace area. But Frederick the Great preferred a generous proportion of the space which indeed became one of his favourite places for relaxing. In fact he so loved Sanssouci he gave specific instructions to be buried

Schloss Sanssouci

© Jean-Baptiste Rabouan/hemis.fr

next to his beloved dogs on the highest terrace of the vineyards in front of the palace.

A self-guided tour with commentary provided by an audioguide takes in a dozen beautifully decorated rooms. Highlights include the Concert Room, the domed Marble Hall, the king's study and bedchamber and the Music Room, his personal favourite.

Neue Kammern★ (New Chambers)

🕐 Open May–Oct, Tue–Sun 10am–6pm. 🚭4€. ♿. 𝒫(0331) 969 42 06.
Designed in 1747 by Knobelsdorff, this former orangery was soon transformed into the palace guesthouse. A highlight of the captivating Rococo interior is the **Ovidsaal★**, decorated with scenes from Ovid's *Metamorphoses*.

Orangerie (Orangery)

🐾 Visit by guided tour (30min) only, Apr, Sat–Sun 10am–6pm, May–Oct, Tue–Sun 10am–6pm. 🚭4€. ♿
𝒫(0331) 969 42 80.
The orangery was built in the style of an Italian Renaissance palace between 1851 and 1860, after plans by Friedrich Wilhelm IV, and served as a guesthouse for visiting royalty. The magnificent apartments where Czar Nicolas I and his wife stayed and the **Raphael Hall★**, which houses 47 copies of paintings by Raphael are highlights of the tour. The tower can be climbed *(🚭2€)*.

Neues Palais★★ (New Palace)

🐾 Visit by audioguide or tour (1hr), Wed–Mon 10am–6pm (Nov–Mar until 5pm). 🕐 Closed Dec 24, 25 & 31. 🚭6€.
𝒫(0331) 969 42 00.
This imposing building was commissioned by Frederick the Great to demonstrate Prussia's economic power after the Seven Years' War. Some 400 rooms, with excessively lavish decorations and a superabundance of sculpture, testify to the ambitious nature of the project – which was nevertheless completed in only six years.

Only a small section of rooms can be visiting, including the Grotto Hall, decorated with shells and fossils; the elegant Marble Hall with its stunning ceiling fresco, and the theatre in the south wing. Separate admission *(🚭5€)* gives you access to a tour of Frederick the Great's **private apartments**. Also here is the **Pesne-Galerie** *(🚭2€)* with a broad survey of works by this French painter. The latter two are only open April to October.

Schloss Charlottenhof★

🐾 Visit by guided tour (45min) only, May–Oct, Tue–Sun 10am–6pm. 🚭4€.
𝒫(0331) 969 42 28.
Karl-Friedrich Schinkel and his pupil, Ludwig Persius, drew up the plans for this palace, built in the Classical Italian style between 1826 and 1829. Tours include a stop in the bedchamber and in the office of Alexander von Humboldt.

Römische Bäder (Roman Baths)

⏱ *Open May–Oct, Tue–Sun 10am–6pm.* 🎫*3€.* ☏ *(0331) 969 42 25.*

Schinkel, Perseus and landscaper Lenné made these baths look like an Italian country estate. The **interior décor★** of the baths is tastefully done. A pergola leads to the Tea Pavilion, not unlike a temple, with a single room decorated all in blue, which has a good view of the lake and gardens.

Chinesisches Haus★★ (Chinese House)

⏱ *Open May–Oct, Tue–Sun 10am–6pm.* 🎫*2€.* ☏ *(0331) 969 4225.*

A circular pavilion decorated with gilded statues, this structure arose from the "Sino-mania" so popular in 18C Germany. Inside is an exhibition of Chinese and Meissen porcelain.

TOWN CENTRE

Alter Markt (Old Market)

The Church of St. Nicholas (Nikolaikirche) dominates the square. Designed by Schinkel (1837) it is one of the finest examples of Neoclassical architecture in Germany. The dome, completed in 1850 by students of the master, was inspired by the Basilica of St. Peter's and St. Paul's Cathedral in London.

Before World War II the "Great Bridge" (Lange Brücke) led directly to the city palace (Stadtschloss), the first built in Potsdam in 1660 by the Great Elector. Severely damaged by bombing in 1945, this symbol of the Prussian monarchy was demolished in 1960 by the East German government. It is currently being reconstructed; completion is scheduled for 2013. Its entrance gate is topped by a steeple, in place since 2003.

Neuer Markt★★ (New Market)

This tiny square is framed by beautiful buildings from the 18C–19C, making it one of the oldest and most beautiful in the city. The most impressive is the Kutschenstall, where the royal carriages used to be stored. Built between 1787 and 1790 according to plans designed

by Andreas Ludwig Krüger, it is an early example of Neoclassical architecture and now houses the House of Brandenburg and Prussian History (Haus der Brandenburgisch-Preussischen Geschichte).

Brandenburger Tor★

Luisenplatz.

This monumental gateway was built in the Baroque fashion in 1770 but takes the form of a Roman triumphal arch.

Filmmuseum★

Breite Straße 1a. ⏱*Open year-round, daily 10am–6pm.* 🎫*5€.* ☏ *(0331) 271 81 12. www.filmmuseum-potsdam.de.*

Dating from 1685 and modified by Knobelsdorff in 1746, the former royal stables now house this small museum. Exhibits focus on German Expressionist films, émigré film directors and the history of the local Babelsberg film studios. Founded in 1912 as the UFA Studios, it produced such silent-era classics as Fritz Lang's *Metropolis* and *The Blue Angel* starring Marlene Dietrich. Recent productions include Roman Polanski's *The Pianist* and Tarantino's *Inglorious Basterds*.

Holländisches Viertel★ (Dutch Quarter)

The pretty Dutch Quarter is a small grid of lanes lined by gabled red-brick houses. It was built for Dutch artisans who were invited to come to Potsdam by King Frederick William I. Mittelstraße is the main artery.

Dampfmaschinenhaus★★ (Pump House)

Breite Straße 28. 🚶*Visit by guided tour (30min) only, May–Oct, Sat–Sun 10am–6pm.* 🎫*2€.* ☏ *(0331) 969 42 25.*

Frederick the Great built the lovely fountains at Park Sanssouci but it would take another century before they would actually spout water. Under Frederick William IV this steam-powered pump began operating. It allowed jets of water from the great fountain in front of Sanssouci Palace to shoot an impressive 38m/125ft high. Designed by Ludwig Persius, it is nicknamed the "Mosque" and is Potsdam's most exotic building.

NORTH OF THE CITY
Neuer Garten★★ (New Garden)

This park was laid out in the late 18C by Peter Lenné on the shore of the Heiliger See for Frederick the Great, who was a great fan of English-style landscaped gardens. Interesting features in the park include the orangery and a pyramid.

Marmorpalais (Marble Palace)

Visit by guided tour, May–Oct Tue–Sun 10am–6pm, Nov–Mar Sat–Sun 10am–4pm. Closed Dec 24, 25 & 31. 5€. (0331) 969 45 50. www.spsg.de.

This Neoclassical palace was built by Karl von Gontard and converted into a summer residence for Frederick William II by Carl Gottard Langhans (1744–1797). The king's beautiful private and state apartments are open to visitors. The concert hall and the Oriental Room, which resembles a Turkish tent, are particularly delightful.

Schloss Cecilienhof★

Open Apr–Oct, Tue–Sun 10am–6pm (Nov–Mar to 5pm). 6€. (0331) 969 42 00. www.spsg.de.

This English-style country residence built during World War I for Crown Prince Wilhelm (1882–1951) and his wife Cecilia of Mecklenburg-Schwerin (1886–1954) is worth seeing for its own sake. But it is the historic **meeting rooms of the Potsdam Conference** of 1945 that draw the most attention. Members of the Allied delegations signed the Potsdam Agreements here on 2 August 1945, outlining Germany's occupation and future development.

The luxury hotel **Relexa Schlosshotel Cecilienhof** also occupies space in this palace *(www.relaxa-hotel.de)*.

Russische Kolonie Alexandrowka★★ (Russian Colony)

About 1.5km/1mi north of the town centre. Bus 90 or 92 leaves from Hauptbahnhof, Alter Markt and Nauener Tor. Get off at Puschkinallee.

This Russian-style village was commissioned by Frederick William III in honour of his friend Czar Alexander I (1777–1825) and built between 1826 and 1827. It consists of 13 wooden houses arranged in the form of St. Andrew's Cross and surrounded by gardens. The original inhabitants were Russian singers of a Prussian military regiment. Ownership could be passed down through the generations. Descendants of two original inhabitants still live here today. The **Alexandrowka Museum** recounts the history of this curious colony (*open May–Oct Tue–Sun 10am–6pm, Nov–Apr Tue–Sun 11am–5pm; 4.50€; (0331) 817 02 03; www.alexandrowka.de*).

EXCURSIONS
Brandenburg

38km/23.6mi west.

It was in the 14C that this small town in the heart of the Havelland (an area of scattered lakes fed by the River Havel) began to prosper, mainly through the cloth trade. The **Dom St. Peter und St. Paul★**, founded in 1165 and remodelled in the 14C, is furnished with several Gothic altarpieces. In the two-aisle crypt is a mausoleum memorialising the clergy murdered during the Nazi regime. Rich exterior decoration distinguishes the 15C **St. Katharinenkirche★**, which boasts a hall chancel with an ambulatory typical of red-brick Gothic churches.

Kloster Lehnin★ (Lehnin Abbey)

28km/17.4m southwest.

Open Mon–Fri, 10am–4.15pm, Sat–Sun, 12.30pm–5.30pm. Closed Jan 1, Dec 24–26 & 31. (03382) 76 88 55. www.klosterkirche-lehnin.de.

This three-aisle brick basilica, commissioned by Margrave Otto I of Brandenburg and occupied in 1192 by the Cistercian Order, combines Romanesque and Early Gothic elements. Worth seeing on the inside are a Triumphal Cross dating from 1225 and the funerary stone of the Margrave Otto IV.

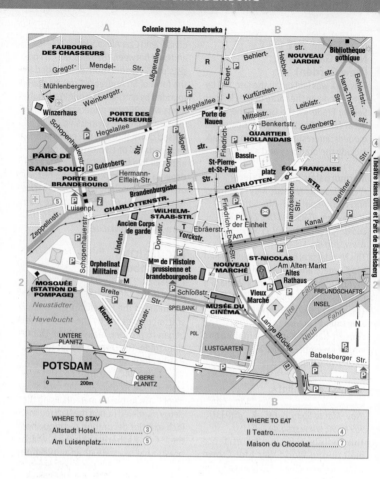

WHERE TO STAY

Altstadt Hotel.....................③
Am Luisenplatz....................⑤

WHERE TO EAT

Il Teatro...........................④
Maison du Chocolat.............⑦

ADDRESSES

🛏 STAY

🍴 Bed and Breakfast am Luisenplatz – *Zimmerstraße 1.*
☎(0331) 971 90 20. www.bed-breakfast-potsdam.de. 15 rooms. 🚇. The relatively central location and reasonable prices make this little hotel a real find. The welcoming guestrooms are modern and furnished in light wood; breakfast is served on the Luisenplatz.

🍴🍴 Altstadt Hotel – *Dortustraße 9.*
☎0331 284 990. www.altstadt-hotel-potsdam.de. 29 rooms. 🚇.
This charming hotel has rooms that are comfortably furnished but don't have much elbow room. Some of them are in the attic. If you need more space, get one of the studios or the apartment.

🍴 EAT

🍴🍴 Il Teatro – *Schiffbauergasse 12.*
☎0331 200 97 291. www.ilteatro-potsdam.de. Right next to the Hans-Otto Theatre, this pleasant restaurant is run by an Italian family. In fine weather, the Havel-facing terrace is the perfect spot for enjoying the seasonal cuisine or perhaps just a cup of excellent espresso.

🍴🍴🍴 Maison du Chocolat – *Benkertstraße 20. ☎(0331) 237 07 30.*
At this restaurant you can enjoy a French country-style meal and then stock up on all manner of succulent cakes and chocolate truffles in the attached store. A little corner of France in the Dutch quarter of Potsdam.

Schloss Branitz★★

The gardens at Branitz Palace were the crowning achievement of Hermann Fürst von Pückler-Muskau (1785–1871), a nobleman, travel writer and one of the most distinguished landscape architects of the 19C. Branitz had been in his family's possession since 1696 but it wasn't until the prince moved here in 1845 that it was transformed into the glorious park and garden you see today.

VISIT

Gardens

Hermann Prince of Pückler-Muskau was born at Muskau Palace but sold the estate in 1845 and moved to Schloss Branitz, about 37km/23mi to the north-west. He used the proceeds from the sale to transform the surroundings into an exquisite **landscaped park**.

Covering 90ha/222 acres, it is divided into several zones, including a sculpture-studded flower garden adjacent to the Schloss itself. Soil from the excavation of lakes was used to shape hills and pyramids. Pückler placed particular emphasis on the alternation between open spaces, tree groupings, sculpture and pools. He and his wife, Lucie, are buried in the 11m/36ft high pyramid – called **Tumulus** – that rises from one of the lakes.

Approaching the compound, the first building you get to is the **Gutshof** (🕐 *open Apr–Oct daily 10am–6pm, Nov–Mar Tue–Sun 11am–5pm;* ⚏*4.50€*), which served as Pückler's office and now harbours the visitor centre with an interactive, **multimedia exhibit** on the man, his peers, his life and achievements.

Palace

🕐*Open Apr–Oct daily 10am–6pm, Nov–Mar Tue–Sun 11am–5pm.* ⚏*4.50€.*

At the park's centre, **Branitz Palace** was completed in 1772 by Gottfried Semper. Inside is an exhibit about

Info: Kastanienallee 11. 03042 Cottbus. ✆(0355) 751 52 21. www.pueckler-museum.de.

Location: Branitz is less than 5km/3mi east of Cottbus.

Parking: Parking is available near the gardens.

Timing: Schloss Branitz and its gardens can be seen in half a day.

Pückler's life and work alongside many original furnishings, especially in the dining room and the library. There's also a gallery featuring the paintings of Carl Blechen (1798–1840), the Romantic painter who was born in nearby Cottbus.

Opposite the palace, the Tudor-style **royal stables** (Marstall) are used for temporary exhibitions (🕐*open Mar–Oct daily 10am–6pm;* ⚏*3.50€*). The adjacent **Cavalier's House** (Cavalierhaus) is now a restaurant. Between the two buildings lies the **"Pergola"** with reliefs by the Danish sculptor Berthel Thorwaldsen, zinc copies of antique sculpture and a bronze casting of the Venus Italica by Canova. On the garden side is a terrace featuring two bronze griffins.

A combination ticket to the Gutshof, the palace and the Marstall costs 9€.

Schloss Branitz

© Udo Kruse/Fotolia.com

THE BALTIC COAST AND INLAND

Germany's Baltic coast stretches for 2 247km/1 396mi between Denmark and Poland across the *Länder* (states) of Schleswig-Holstein and Mecklenburg-Vorpommern. Thinly populated, its seaside resorts have been a favourite with German holidaymakers since the 19C, although the region is rarely overrun with tourists. Families especially value the shallow and calm waters, wide sandy beaches and relaxing ambience. Hanseatic towns like Lübeck, Stralsund and Wismar are not only picturesque reminders of the region's former power but are also UNESCO World Heritage Sites. Fans of the offbeat can delve into Viking history in Schleswig, climb aboard a World War II submarine near Kiel or ride a historic train in Bad Doberan.

The Lure of Nature

Much of the appeal of Germany's northeast lies in its pristine and diverse landscapes. This is a region where you can truly connect with nature in places where birds and other wildlife outnumber people and where the flora is similar to what it was centuries ago.

The seaside itself is a pastiche of narrow fjords with steep banks, flat and sandy beaches, sweeping bays and dramatic cliffs plunging into calm waters. Unspoiled Poel and Hiddensee islands provide quiet retreats, while away from the coast the Mecklenburg lake district offers wide expanses of forest, moorland and an endless string of rivers and lakes, making it a paradise for boaters, birdwatchers, cyclists and nature lovers.

The Legacy of the Hanse

Numerous cities on the Baltic Coast once belonged to the powerful medieval trade alliance called the Hanseatic League (☾ see sidebar p175). Its birthplace was Lübeck, whose old quarter, dramatically accessed via the picturesque Holstentor gate, is a must-see (also try delicious local marzipan made from almonds and sugar!).

Other Hanseatic cities line up like pearls on a string east of here, most notably Wismar, Rostock, Stralsund and Greifswald. All of them have beautifully restored old towns and blend maritime

Highlights

1 Exploring the medieval town of **Lübeck** (p144)

2 Gazing the horizon from the chalk cliffs on **Rügen Island** (p162)

3 Recharging your batteries on car-free **Hiddensee Island** (p164)

4 The beautiful palace at **Schwerin** (p170)

5 Boating on **Lake Müritz** (p172)

levity with sturdy Gothic red-brick architectural gems so typical of the Baltic region.

Lübeck★★★

The "queen" of the Hanseatic League, Lübeck is a vivacious town that still retains much of its medieval character despite being badly damaged in World War II. In 1987, its entire Old Town was placed on the UNESCO World Heritage list. Its port, 20km/13mi north in Travemünde, is one of the busiest on the Baltic Sea. Don't miss the marzipan here: it is a local culinary speciality.

▶ **Population:** 210 900

Info: Holstentorplatz 1, 23552 Lübeck. ℘(0451) 889 97 00. www.luebeck-tourism.de.

Location: Lübeck is 60km/37mi northeast of Hamburg via the A1 autobahn.

Parking: Garages are plentiful in the Old Town.

Don't Miss: Strolling the Old Town, a taste of marzipan.

Timing: Allow a day to do this lovely town justice.

A BIT OF HISTORY

At the head of the League – The 14C marked the peak of Lübeck's power as capital of the Hanseatic League. In the 16C, merchants and shipowners joined forces to revitalise the port by establishing relations with Holland and France. For a long time, Dutch architecture was the preferred style for the rich burghers on the banks of the Trave.

WALKING TOUR
OLD TOWN★★★

Girdled by canals, crowned by belfries and towers, the old town of Lübeck is on a largely pedestrianised island. The nicest way to enter is through the **Holstentor**, a national symbol in Germany.

Holstentor★★ (Holsten Gate)

This fortified gate was built between 1466 and 1478, before the construction of the city fortification, more as a matter of prestige than protection. Today it houses the city history museum know as **Museum Holstentor** (◐open Apr–Dec, daily 10am–6pm; Jan–Mar, Tue–Sun 11am–5pm; ◐closed Jan 1, Easter Mon, Dec 24–25 & 31; ▰5€; ℘(0451) 122 41 29).

♟♟Theater Figuren Museum Lübeck★★ (Lübeck Puppet Theatre Museum)

Kolk 14. ◐Open Tue–Sun 11am–6pm (Nov–Mar 5pm). ▰5€. ℘(0451) 786 26. www.tfm-luebeck.com.
Hidden in a gabled 16C building in one of old Lübeck's most picturesque lanes, the puppet museum has one of the richest collections of puppets in the world, assembled by Fritz Frey. Displayed on four floors are puppets from the 18C to the 20C centuries with origins in Europe, Africa and Asia. Don't miss the Indonesian shadow puppets, the tall puppets from Nigeria or the great characters of Japanese Bunraku. A few steps from the museum, a puppet theatre offers regular performances.

▷ *Continue on, then follow Große Petersgrube to the Petrikirche.*

Petrikirche (Church of St. Peter)

Tower ◐Open Apr–Sept, daily 9am–9pm; Oct–Mar, Tue–Sun 10am–7pm. ▰3€. ℘(0451) 39 77 30.
This handsome Gothic church was destroyed in World War II and reconstructed in the late 1950s. Views from the 50m/164ft-high viewing platform in the tower extend over all of old Lübeck.

▷ *Take Schmiedestraße to the Dom (cathedral).*

Dom (Cathedral)

The 14C Gothic expansion transformed this Romanesque church. Note the monumental late-Gothic **Crucifix**★ by Bernt Notke and the stone screen (early 14C) with a wooden tracery balustrade.

Holstentor

M. Hertlein/MICHELIN

○ *Take Fegefeuer to St. Annen-Straße. Alternatively, extend the walk to the river bank for lovely views of the cathedral.*

St. Annen-Museum★

St. Annen-Straße 15. ○*Open Apr–Dec, Tue–Sun 10am–5pm; Jan–Mar, 11am–5pm.* ○*Closed Jan 1, Easter Mon, Whit Mon, Dec 24–25 & 31.* ✆5€. ✆(0451) 122 41 37. www.die-luebecker-museen.de.

Paintings and sculpture from Lübeck's churches are displayed in this museum alongside German modern art.

○ *Resume on St. Annen-Straße and continue straight until Glockengießerstraße (left turn).*

Höfe und Gänge (Courtyards and alleyways)

These open courtyards *(Höfe)* set back from the street are typical for Lübeck. Note the delightful **Füchtingshof** *(no 25)* with its Baroque doorway; the **Glandorps-Gang**, a narrow alleyway, at no 41 and, from nos 49 to 51, the **Glandorps-Hof**. The building at no 21 is now the **Günter Grass Haus**.

Günter Grass Haus

Glockengießerstraße 21. ○*Open Jan–Mar, Tue–Sun 11am–5pm; Apr–Dec, daily 10am–5pm.* ○*Closed Jan 1, Dec 24–25 & 31.* ✆5€. ✆(0451) 122 42 30. www.die-luebecker-museen.de.

Born in Lübeck, Günter Grass is one of Germany's most famous contemporary writers, author of *The Tin Drum* (1961) and winner of the Nobel Prize for Literature.

This exhibit set up in his office and workshop displays manuscripts as well as examples of his work as a sculptor and graphic designer.

○ *At the end of Glockengießerstraße, turn left towards the church.*

Katharinenkirche★ (Church of St. Catherine)

○*Open Apr–Sept, Tue–Sun 10am–5pm.* ✆1€. ✆✆(0451)122 4137. www.die-luebecker-museen.de.

Converted into a museum, the lower niches of the façade of this 14C church contain modern **statues**★, the first three on the left being by Ernst Barlach. As you enter, note on the right *The Resurrection of Lazarus* by Tintoretto.

Willy-Brandt-Haus

○*Open Apr–Dec, daily 10am–5pm; Jan–Mar, Tue–Sun 11am–5pm.* ✆(0451) 122 42 50. www.willy-brandt-luebeck.de.

This exhibit is dedicated to Willy Brandt, a native of Lübeck and winner of the Nobel Peace Prize in 1971 for his policy of rapprochement with East Germany. Photos, audio and video tell his life story, with a particular focus on his work for human rights. Video screens feature TV news coverage in East and West Germany about such events as John F. Kennedy's visit to Berlin in 1963.

▷ *Upon exiting turn right.*

Museum Behnhaus und Drägerhaus

🕐*Open Apr–Dec, Tue–Sun 10am–5pm; Jan–Mar, Tue–Sun 11am–4pm.* ♿*5€. (0451) 122 41 48. www.luebecker-museen.de.*

This 18C former mansion of a wine merchant houses primarily furniture and paintings from the 18C and 19C Romantic era as well as works by Friedrich Overbeck (1789–1869), head of the Nazarene School. Other artists represented include Max Liebermann, Ernst Ludwig Kirchner and the Lübeck artist A Aereboe. There is also a smattering of paintings by Edvard Munch created during his time in Lübeck.

▷ *Upon exiting, continue straight up Königstraße.*

Heiligen-Geist-Hospital★ (Hospice of the Holy Spirit)

Since the late 13C, the three turreted gables of this almshouse have stood above the Koberg. The chapel, a large Gothic hall embellished with 13C and 14C paintings, is just outside the even bigger Great Hall of the hospice.

▷ *Follow Königstraße, which turns into Große Burgstraße.*

Burgtor★ (Castle Gate)

This fortified gateway defended the narrow isthmus, once the only land approach to Lübeck. The structure is a fine example of 13C–15C military architecture.

▷ *Retrace your steps, then take your first right.*

Haus der Schiffergesellschaft★ (Sailor's Guildhall)

Breite Straße 2.
Behind the stepped Renaissance gable awaits a handsomely decorated ancient seaman's tavern with rough wooden tables, copper lamps and model ships dangling from the beams. It is now a restaurant (♿*see Addresses*).

Jakobikirche★ (Church of St. Jacob)

Opposite the Haus der Schiffergesellschaft. The magnificent woodwork of the two organ **lofts**★★ (16C–17C) in this small Gothic hall-church is noteworthy. Larger than life-size representations of apostles and saints adorn the pillars of the central nave.

The chapel north of the tower is now a memorial to shipwrecked sailors and displays a lifeboat from the *Pamir*, the full-rigged Lübeck ship lost with all hands aboard in 1957.

▷ *Continue south along Breite Straße, then hook a right on Mengstraße.*

Buddenbrookhaus

Mengstraße 4. 🕐*Open Apr–Dec, daily 10am–6pm; Jan–Mar, 11am–5pm.* 🕐*Closed Jan 1, Dec 24–25 & 31.* ♿*5€.* ♿ ℱ*(0451) 122 4240. www.buddenbrookhaus.de.*

The name derives from Thomas Mann's 1901 novel *Buddenbrooks*, which chronicles the decline of a patrician Lübeck family. No matter how attractive the concept, Heinrich and Thomas Mann were not born in the Buddenbrookhaus. However, it is true that in 1841 their grandfather Johann Siegmund Mann bought the 18C Baroque house, and the brothers were frequently guests there during their childhood and adolescence.

Marienkirche★★ (Church of St. Mary)

The north side of Marktplatz is dominated by one of the finest red-brick Gothic churches in Germany. In the 17C, composer Dietrich Buxtehude was church organist here. The interior is audacious in design and grandiose in proportion. A fire in 1942 exposed the original 13C and 14C decoration.

LÜBECK

KIEL | TRAVEMÜNDE

Gustav-Radbruch-Platz
Roeckstr.

WALLHAFEN
Hubbrücke

HANSAHAFEN

Drehbrücke
Untertrave
Engelswisch
Engelsgrube
der
An Fischer-
grube

BURGTOR

OLD TOWN

HOSPITAL OF THE HOLY SPIRIT

SAILORS' GUILDHALL
ST JACOB

Behnhaus und Drägerhaus
Willy Brandt House
Günther Grass House

FÜCHTINGSHOF

ST CATHERINE
Glockengießerstr.
Tünkenhagen

Langer Lohberg

Beckergrube

SCHABBELHAUS
POL.
Mengstr.

Buddenbrook House

Rosengarten
Hundestr.

ST MARY
Julius-
Leber-
Straße

Fischstr.

HOLSTENTOR
Holstenstr.
Marktpl.

TOWN HALL
Fleischhauerstr.

Hüxstraße

St Peter
Kohlmarkt

Schlumacherstr.

Wahmstr.

Hüxterdamm

MUSEUM OF THEATRE PUPPETS

Schmiedestr.

Große Petersgrube
Marlesgrube
Klingenberg

Balauerfohr

Krähenstr.

Rehderbrücke

Dankwartsgrube

Mühlenstraße

ST ANNE'S MUSEUM

der

Krähenteich

Hüxtertor

Hartengrube

Cathedral

Domkirchhof

An

STADTHALLE

Bismarckstr.

Mühlendamm

Wallstraße

Mühlenteich

Mühlentorbrücke

Möhlentorpl.

STADION

FREILICHTBÜHNE

HAMBURG | HAMBURG | LAUENBURG, RATZEBURG

WHERE TO STAY

Am Dom	①
Atlantic Hotel	③
Hotel an der Marienkirche	⑥
Hotel zu alten Stadtmauer	⑨
Jensen	④
Kaiserhof	⑦

WHERE TO EAT

Alte Mühle	③
Jazz Café	⑥
Kartofell Keller	⑨
La Piazzetta, Pizzeria da Gianni	⑪
Lübecker Hanse	⑬
Paulaner's	①
Remise	⑭
Remix	⑰
Roberto Rossi	④
Schiffergesellschaft	⑦

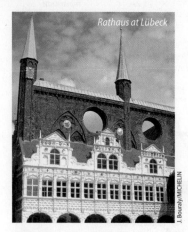

Rathaus at Lübeck

J. Bouraly/MICHELIN

Rathaus★ (Town Hall)

Visit by guided tour only, year-round, Mon–Fri 11am, noon and 3pm; Sat–Sun 1.30pm (provided there are no public events). ℘(0451) 122 10 05.
One of the most beautiful town halls in Germany, Lübeck's Rathaus flanks two sides of the Marktplatz.

Construction began in 1250 and resulted in an elegant edifice in dark glazed brick and supported by a gallery of arcades. Note the high protective walls pierced with blind arcades.

Pass beneath the arcades to see, on the Breite Straße, a stone staircase (1594) in Dutch Renaissance style.

EXCURSION
Travemünde★

▷ *20km/12.4mi northeast.*

This smart Baltic spa resort boasts a fine sandy beach, a 2.5km/1.5mi-long promenade and a casino. Ferries leave to Scandinavia and Estonia. Explore the charming old town, with its half-timbered houses and the fishermen's Church of St. Lorenz. The waterfront is lined with gabled houses from the 18C and 19C.
In summer, it hosts **Travemünde Week**, an international yachting event.

ADDRESSES

🛏 STAY

🍽 **Hotel Am Dom** – *Dankwartsgrube 43. ℘(0451) 399 94 10. www.cvjm-luebeck. de. 17 rooms.* Located in a quiet street in the old centre, near the dock, this small hotel has simple but well-kept rooms.

🍽 **Hotel zur Alten Stadtmauer** – *An der Mauer 57. ℘(0451) 737 02. www. hotelstadtmauer.de. 10 rooms.* ⌧.
This quiet townhouse has renovated rooms exuding warm family flair.
It sits just steps from the bustling Mühlenstraße.

🍽🍽 **Hotel an der Marienkirche** – *Schüsselbuden 4. ℘ (0451) 79 94 10. www.hotel-an-der-marienkirche.de. 18 rooms.* ⌧. Some rooms in this charming brick building have views of the Church of St. Mary. Guests receive a warm welcome and a hearty breakfast.

🍽🍽 **Ringhotel Jensen** – *An der Obertrave 4. ℘(0451) 70 24 90. www.ringhotel-jensen.de. 42 rooms. Restaurant* 🍽🍽. Located within the historic triangle formed by the Trave,

the Holstentor and the Salzspeicher, this comfortably appointed gabled house was built in 1307. It has modernised rooms and a dining room with nautical flourishes.

🍽🍽 **Hotel Kaiserhof** – *Kronsforder Allee 11. ℘(0451) 70 33 01. www.kaiserhof-luebeck.de. 60 rooms. Restaurant* 🍽🍽.
Two fine patrician houses were united to form this pleasantly decorated hotel only a few minutes walk from the town centre. High-ceilinged rooms and chandeliers create an elegant ambience here and in the classic restaurant. Also of note: the Roman steam bath.

🍽🍽🍽 **Atlantic Hotel** – *Schmiedestraße 9–15. ℘(0451) 38 47 90. www.atlantic-hotel.de. 135 rooms.* ⌧. Open since early 2010, this stylish hotel offers modern comforts in the heart of the historic old town. The sauna and fitness area boast remarkable views across Lübeck.

♥/EAT

🍽 **Remix Café** – *Königstraße 26. ℘(0451) 709 88 73. www.remix-cafe.de.* Opposite the church of St. Catherine, this bistro serves simple dishes in a cosy atmosphere and has courtyard seating on sunny days.

Alte Mühle – *Mühlendamm 24. (0451) 707 25 92. www.altemühle-lübeck.de.* In a historic mill, this place offers a large choice of *Flammkuche* (French pizza), seasonal dishes and a good wine selection.

Jazz Café – *Mühlenstraße 62. (0451) 707 37 34. www.jazzcafe-hl.de.* You will be spoilt for choice among the many cocktails, cognacs, brandies and whiskeys available in this jazzy bar-restaurant. There is also hearty and cleverly prepared food as well as live music on the second Thursday of the month. Heated smoking terrace and lounge upstairs.

La Piazzetta (Pizzeria da Gianni) – *Pferdemarkt 19. (0451) 709 89 98.* Enjoy pizza in a charming garden setting with a view of the cathedral. There is a small, tree-shaded playground for children.

Kartoffel Keller – *Koberg 8. (0451) 762 34. www.historischer-weinkeller-hl.de.* Enjoy creative regional dishes built around the humble potato. Sit at long tables in the vaulted former wine cellar of the Hospital of the Holy Spirit.

Lübecker Hanse – *Kolk 3–7. (0451) 780 54. www.luebecker-hanse.de.* You will feel warmly welcomed in this beautiful restaurant in the historic district, which specialises in regional fish dishes.

Remise – *Wahmstraße 43–45. (0451) 777 73. www.remise-luebeck.de.* The courtyard of this restaurant is ideal for brunch or a light lunch. The kitchen serves mostly Italian-inspired cuisine prepared with seasonal ingredients. Wonderful atmosphere and live music some nights.

Paulaner's – *Breite Straße 1–5 (0451) 707 94 50. www.paulaners.de. Reservation recommended.* Munich beer and Bavarian specialities in northern Germany? It works, although local specialities are also served, if you prefer. Pleasant beer garden.

Schabbelhaus / Roberto Rossi – *Mengstraße 48–52. (0451) 720 11. www.schabbelhaus.de. Closed Sun.* This early 20C building is the legacy of

local master baker Schabbel. Built as a foundation after his death, it is now an Italian restaurant but retains its original charm. Budget-priced weekday lunches.

Schiffergesellschaft – *Breite Straße 2. (0451) 767 76. www.schiffergesellschaft.de. Reservations recommended.* This charming tavern, built as a sailors' meeting-house, guildhouse and almshouse back in 1535, is decorated with a maritime-style. Seating is on solid wood benches at long rustic tables.

TRAVEMÜNDE

Weinwirtschaft – *Außenallee 10 (04502) 307 07 47. www.a-rosa.de.* This bistro and wine shop serves tapas and international cuisine.

🍴 TAKING A BREAK

Café Niederegger – *Breite Straße 89. (0451) 530 11 26. www.niederegger.de.* This café-shop is *the* place to buy and sample marzipan, although the famous hazelnut-cream cake is just as delicious. Also check out the marzipan museum on the 2nd floor.

Café Utspann – *Wahmstraße. 35–37 (in the Hansehof court). (0451) 707 06 77. www.cafe-utspann.de. Closed Sun.* Frisian-style décor distinguishes this inviting cafe specialised in homemade cakes served inside or on the old Hansehof court.

🍷 NIGHTLIFE

Brauberger – *Alfstraße. 36. (0451) 714 44. www.brauberger.de. Closed Sun, 1st week in Jan.* This split-level brew-pub opened in 1988 but sits atop cellars dating from 1225. Light snacks and regional fare are available along with daily changing specials. On the 1st floor is a small terrace.

Im Alten Zolln – *Mühlenstraße 93–95. (0451) 723 95. www.alter-zolln.de.* A young and young-at-heart crowd gravitates to this lively pub in a 16C customs post. Pick from several draught beers served in three drinking areas, all with wooden panels and benches.

Kiel★

A key German naval base since 1860, Kiel was obliterated in World War II and postwar reconstruction was largely in a functional, modern style. Today it has recaptured its role as gateway to Scandinavia and celebrates its maritime tradition with the world's largest sailing event, the annual Kiel Week.

A BIT OF HISTORY

A maritime city – Kiel, founded in the 13C, was always a seafaring town, even if it never achieved more than regional importance as a Hanseatic city. For centuries Kiel led a tranquil existence, until 1871 when it became Germany's main naval base. Within a few years, the little harbour town grew into an industrial metropolis. Today, the capital of Schleswig-Holstein is a quiet, leafy city where you feel the ocean breeze on a walk along the docks and observe the giant container ships passing through its port.

SIGHTS

Harbour★★

A string of resort towns line up along the harbour: Stein, Strande, Schilksee, Schönberger Strand, Laboe and Heikendorf. Kiel has hosted regattas for more than a century and draws as many as 5 000 sailors from around the world to its annual "Kiel Week".

▶ **Population:** 233 000
- **Info:** Andreas-Gayk-Straße 31, 24103 Kiel. ℘(0431) 67 91 00. www.kiel-tourist.de.
- **Location:** Kiel is at the end of a 17km/10.5mi deep inlet in the Baltic Sea at the eastern end of the North Sea-Baltic Sea canal (Kiel Canal).
- **Don't Miss:** A leisurely stroll along the picturesque Hindenburgufer.
- **Timing:** Allow a day for Kiel and environs.
- **Kids:** The U-Boat at Laboe, Schleswig-Holstein Open-air Museum (€see Excursions).

Hindenburgufer★★

This promenade extends for almost 4km/2.5mi along the shore, with shady parks on one side and extended **views**★ on the other.

Rathaus (Town Hall)

Fleethörn 18–24. ℘(0431) 90 10. Completed in 1911, the Rathaus is dominated by its 106m/347.7ft tower inspired by the Campanile in Venice. A lift takes you to the top for splendid **views**★ and a carillon chimes hourly.

Parade of sailing ships during Kiel Week

©imagebroker.net/Photoshot

EXCURSIONS

👥 Schleswig-Holsteinisches Freilichtmuseum★★ (Schleswig-Holstein Open-air Museum)

▶ *Hamburger Landstraße 97. 6km/3.7mi south in Molfsee.*

🕐 *Open Apr–Oct, daily 9am–6pm; Nov–Mar, Sun 11am–4pm (only some houses open).* 💶*7€ (child 2€) Apr–Oct; 3€ (child 1.50€) Nov–Mar.* ♿. *℘(0431) 65 96 60. www.freilicht museum-sh.de.*

Sixty traditional buildings typical of the north Elbe countryside have been relocated to this charming open-air museum. Watch craftspeople operate the forge, the potter's workshop, the old-fashioned bakehouse and the traditional weavers' looms.

👥 Laboe★

▶ *20km/12.4mi north.*

This pretty Baltic resort is popular with families for its sandy dunes and calm waters. Overlooking the mouth of the Kiel Firth is the **Marine-Ehrenmal** *(German naval war memorial;* 🕐*open Apr–Oct, daily 9.30am–6pm; Nov–Mar, daily 9.30am–4pm;* 💶*5€;* ♿*;* *℘(04343) 42 70 30; www.deutscher-marinebund. de/ehrenmal),* which was built in honour of the 35 000 German navymen who died in World War I, but now serves as a memorial for all naval war casualties. **Views**★★ from the 85m/279ft-high tower extends as far Denmark on clear days. Next door, you can explore an original World War II submarine, the **U 995** *(*🕐*same hours as Marine-Ehrenmal;* 💶*3.50€; combination tickets 7.50€).*

ADDRESSES

🏨STAY

💶💶💶 **Consul** – *Walkerdamm 11.* *℘(0431) 53 53 70. www.hotel-consul-kiel.de. 40 rooms. Restaurant*💶💶💶. Close to the harbour and railway station, this hotel has been family-run for three generations. Rooms are individually decorated, clean and well equipped.

💶💶💶 **Parkhotel Kieler Kaufmann** – *Niemannsweg 102.* *℘(0431) 881 10. www.kieler-kaufmann.de. 43 rooms. Restaurant*💶💶💶. This historic, ivy-draped hotel sits in a small park upstream from the harbour. Rooms in the main building, a former banker's villa, are particularly elegant and spacious. Bright and cheerful, the restaurant serves upscale international cuisine and has lovely views of the firth.

🍴EAT

💶💶 **Alte Mühle** – *An der Holsatiamühle 8 (east bank of the Kieler Förde, follow signs for "Schwentinetal"). ℘(0431) 205 90 01. www.altemuehle-kiel. de.* In a former 19C mill on the River Schwentine, this lovely restaurant-café serves modern German cuisine and good-value weekday lunches.

💶💶💶 **Lüneburg-Haus – Zum Hirschen** – *Dänische Straße 22. ℘(0431) 982 60 00. www.lueneburghaus.com. Closed 4 weeks Jul–Aug, Sun, holidays.* In an old town house, above a delicatessen, modern regional fare is served in a relaxed bistro ambience. Hand-selected wine list, attentive staff.

☕ TAKING A BREAK

Werkstatt-Café – *Falckstraße 16 (in the town centre). ℘(0431) 918 65. Closed Sun. www.werkstattcafe-kiel.de.* Try the delicious homemade cakes or daily specials at this congenial garden café.

🌙 NIGHTLIFE

Café-Restaurant Schöne Aussichten – *Düsternbrooker Weg 16 (north of the town centre, west bank of the Kieler Förde). ℘(0431) 210 85 85. www.schoene-aussichten-kiel.de.* This restaurant lives up to its name (beautiful views), especially on the summer terrace. Mediterranean-inspired food (mainly fish) dominates the menu, but it is also fine to drop in for cake or a beer.

Kieler Brauerei – *Alter Markt 9 (town centre). ℘(0431) 90 62 90. www.kieler-brauerei.de.* This sociable micro-brewery has a salad bar, lunch specials and an all-you-can-eat buffet on Sunday.

Schleswig★

Schleswig-Holstein's oldest town has origins as a Viking village first mentioned in 804. Today, it is a pleasant town on the Schlei, an inlet of the Baltic Sea, with interesting sights and a relaxing, easy-going atmosphere.

A BIT OF HISTORY

The Vikings – Viking traders settled on the south bank of the Schlei by the 9C. Set on major crossroads, the settlement became an important northern European trade centre.

The area, Haithabu, was encircled by a vast defence system of which a portion remains beside the Haddebyer Noor. In the 11C, Haithabu's residents, seeking better defences, crossed to the north bank of the Schlei to found Schleswig.

SIGHTS

Schloss Gottorf (Gottdorf Palace)

🕐 *Open Apr–Oct, daily 10am–6pm; Nov–Mar, Tue–Fri 10am–4pm, Sat–Sun 10am–5pm.* 🎟8€. ♿. 📞*(04621) 81 32 22. www.schloss-gottorf.de.*

Two large museums devoted to Schleswig-Holstein's cultural history are housed in this 16C–18C palace, once the seat of the Holstein-Gottorf ducal family. In 1762, some members married into the Imperial House of the Russian czars.

Landesmuseum für Kunst und Kulturgeschichte★★ (State Museum of Art and Cultural History)

This museum contains extensive cultural and historical collections (arts, crafts and traditions). Note the collection of paintings by **Lucas Cranach the Elder** and the **Renaissance chapel★★** with its ducal loggia and oratory. Another memorable section contains exquisite **Jugendstil★** pieces.

An adjacent building houses Rolf Horn's collection of 20C paintings – Expressionism to the present. Particularly striking are paintings by Emil Nolde and Alexei von Jawlensky and sculptures by Ernst

▶ **Population:** 24 000

ℹ **Info:** Wall 55. 📞(01805) 60 06 04. www.sh-tourismus.de.

▶ **Location:** Schleswig was built on low-lying banks at the inner end of a Baltic fjord, the Schlei, which extends for 43km/26.7mi from the coast.

◉ **Don't Miss:** The Viking Museum, the Nydam Boat and the Globushaus.

🕐 **Timing:** Allow at least half a day to explore Schleswig.

👫 **Kids:** The Viking Museum.

Barlach. Another highlight is the extensive collection of works by members of the Brücke artist group. It is the largest outside the Brücke Museum in Berlin. On the second floor, you can admire arts and crafts from throughout northern Germany.

Archäologisches Landesmuseum★ (National Museum of Archaeology)

This museum offers a systematic presentation of Schleswig-Holstein's pre- and early history from the Paleolithic Age to the time of the Vikings.

There are spectacular finds from the 4C (bodies found perfectly preserved, fragments of clothing, shoes, weapons) rescued from the peatbogs.

Housed in its own hall is the **Nydam Boot★★**, an oak-hulled longship from around 320 AD that is 23m/75.4ft long by 3m/9.8ft wide and was powered by 36 oarsmen. It is the oldest surviving Germanic longship, and was probably sunk in the peatbogs as a sacrifice c. AD 350.

Globushaus★★

In a separate building, about a five-minute walk from the palace through a Baroque garden, is the reconstructed **Gottorfer Globus** (globe; 🕐 *open Apr–Oct, 10am–6pm;* 🎟*10€*). At over 3m/9.8ft high, it can be entered. The

Globushaus

© Wolfgang Diederich/imagebroker/Alamy

original was created in the 17C and is now in the Lomonosov Museum in St. Petersburg.

Dom St. Peter★

Thanks to its graceful spire, this brick Gothic hall-church can be easily spotted from far away. The most remarkable work of art is the 1521 **Bordesholm altarpiece**★★ in the chancel.

Holm★

This picturesque sailors' and fishermen's quarter with its 18C–19C houses is centred around a small cemetery and chapel.

👥 Wikinger Museum Haithabu (Viking Museum)★

Follow B76 towards Kiel. ⏱**Open Apr–Oct, daily 9am–5pm; May–Sept, 9am–7pm; Nov–Mar, Tue–Sun 10am–4pm (museums only, houses closed).** ⏱**Closed Dec 24 & 31.** ⬤**6€.** ♿ ℘*(04621) 81 32 22. www.haithabu.de.*
Near the Haddebyer Noor lagoon, next to the original Viking settlement, this engaging museum sheds light on the daily lives of the Haithabu residents. It features recreated huts and displays jewels, weapons and domestic imple-

ments along with models of the Viking village. A highlight of the boat hall *(Schiffshalle)* is a Viking longship, reconstructed from fragments dredged from the ancient port.

ADDRESSES

🛏 STAY

🍽 **Zollhaus** – *Lollfuß 110.* ℘*(04621) 29 03 40. www.zollhaus-schleswig.de. Closed mid-Jan–mid-Feb and 15–30 Oct.* **10 rooms.** In a bustling side street near the Schlei, this small hotel has bright rooms with functional beechwood furniture. The bistro presents changing art exhibitions.

🍴 EAT

🍽🍽 **Hotel and Restaurant Olschewski's** – *Hafenstraße 40.* ℘*(04621) 255 77. www.hotelolschewski. de.vu. Closed Mon, Tue and Jan–Feb.* This restaurant is in the heart of Schleswig's historic centre, close to the palace and Holm and with a view of the harbour. It serves international cuisine, including plenty of fish dishes. Lovely terrace. It is attached to a hotel with nicely decorated, comfortable rooms.

Wismar★

Midway between Rostock and Lübeck, Wismar is known for its fisheries and naval dockyards. Evidence of the Swedish reign in the 17C and 18C remains throughout the town today. In 2002, the historic town centre with its characteristic step-gabled red-brick houses and cobblestoned streets was included on the UNESCO World Heritage List.

▶ **Population:** 45 700

Info: Am Markt 11, 23966 Wismar. ℘(03841) 251 30 25. www.wismar.de.

Location: Wismar hugs a bay in the Baltic Sea opposite the island of Poel. The A20 links the town to Lübeck.

Don't Miss: Meandering through the Old Town.

Timing: Allow three hours to explore the Old Town.

Kids: A visit to Poel Island.

A BIT OF HISTORY

A trading town – Wismar dates back to 1229 and enjoyed a heyday as a member of the Hanseatic League. Breweries and wool-weaving were further sources of wealth. Wismar's downfall came at the end of the Thirty Years' War, when it fell under Swedish rule, which lasted until 1803.

SIGHTS
Marktplatz★ (Market Square)
Situated in the old town, Wismar's Marktplatz – one of the largest town squares in Germany – is dominated by the white Neoclassical **Rathaus** (town hall), built between 1817–19. A permanent **exhibit** (⏰ *open year-round, daily 10am–6pm;* ⊜*1.50€*) on town history is to be found in the beautifully vaulted cellars.

Other gabled houses from various eras frame the rest of the square. The most eye-catching is the **Alter Schwede** (Old Swede) on the east side, which dates back to 1380. On the right is the **Reuterhaus**, a now-UNESCO building where the works of the Mecklenburg writer Fritz Reuter were published. Destroyed during the GDR-era, the building was fully reconstructed in the late 1980s and now houses a hotel/restaurant; the house on its left sports charming Jugendstil ornamentation.

On the southeast side of the market stands an artistic pavilion, the **Wasserkunst★** (waterworks). It was built in 1580–1602 in the Dutch Renaissance style and supplied the town with water for centuries.

Marienkirchturm (Church of St. Mary's Tower)
⏰*Open May–Sept, daily 8am–8pm, Apr & Oct, 10am–6pm, Nov–Mar 11am–4pm.*
Only the 80m/262ft-high **tower** remains of the early 13C Marienkirche, which was destroyed during World War II. A carillon comes to life at noon, 3pm and 7pm.

Fürstenhof (Palace)
Originally the seat of the dukes of Mecklenburg, this large building was erected in two phases. The older, western, wing dates to 1512–13 and is Late Gothic in style, while the longer "New House" from 1553–55 shows off elements of the Italian Renaissance, including impressive pilasters and terracotta friezes. Those facing the road represent the Trojan Wars; those facing the courtyard, the parable of the Prodigal Son.

Grube (Ditch)
The "Grube" is one of Germany's oldest artificial watercourses running through a town (1255). It served as a source of water for drinking and domestic use right up into the 20C.

Schabbellhaus★
Schweinsbrücke 8. ⏰*Open May–Oct, Tue–Sun 10am–8pm, Nov–Apr to 5pm.* ⊜*2€.* ℘*(03841) 224 31 10. www.schabbellhaus.de.*
This sumptuously decorated red-brick building was built 1569–71 as the brew-

Wismar harbour

D. Scherf/MICHELIN

ery and home of the later mayor, Hinrich Schabbell, and is one of the oldest Renaissance buildings in the Baltic area. The house is now home to a local history museum with a special section on medical history.

St. Nikolaikirche★

⊙*Open May-Sept, Mon-Sat 8am–8pm, Sun 11.15am–8pm; Apr & Oct, Mon-Sat 10am–6pm, Sun 11.15am–6pm; Nov–Mar, daily 11am–4pm.* ⊛*1€.* ℘*(03841) 21 36 24.*
Built between 1381 and 1487, this brick church's central nave soars skyward for 37m/121.4ft, making it the fourth highest in Germany.
The **Altar der Krämergilde**★ (Grocers' Guild Altarpiece), a 15C hinged, panelled altarpiece, is worth a closer look.
The 1335 bronze font originally stood in the Marienkirche; it depicts the Life of Christ, the Last Judgement and the Wise and Foolish Virgins.

Alter Hafen (Old Harbour)

From the Grube and the idyllic street Am Lohberg, just a few steps lead to the harbour, at the end of which stands an unadorned Baroque building, the **Baumhaus** (tree house). In former times a massive tree was lowered from here into the water at night in order to prevent access to the harbour.

EXCURSION
♣♣ Insel Poel (Poel Island)

This little Baltic island north of Wismar can be reached by car, or in the summer, by boat from the old harbour.
Poel makes a pleasant day trip; its charming seaside villages and wild coastal stretches invite exploration. The flat relief makes a perfect cycling destination; the local tourist office has bikes for hire.

ADDRESSES

⌂STAY

⊜⊜ **Willert** – *Schweriner Straße 9.* ℘*(03841) 261 20. www.hotel-willert. m-vp.de. 17 rooms.* ⊒. This Jugendstil villa was built in 1910 and meticulously restored in the 1990s. Rooms are modern and elegant; some of the stucco-ornamented ceilings are original.

⊜⊜ **Reuterhaus** – *Am Markt 19.* ℘*(03841) 222 30. www.hotel-reuter haus.de. 10 rooms. Restaurant* ⊜⊜⊜. This small hotel in a nicely renovated building on the market square has fairly large, comfortable rooms tastefully outfitted with Italian furniture. The elaborately carved wainscoting lends traditional charm to the restaurant.

Rostock★

Rostock, once a member of the Hanseatic League, is the biggest city in the northern German state of Mecklenburg-Vorpommern. Its strategic location on the wide Warnow estuary has always favoured its development. Rostock's port continues to play an important role in international maritime commerce. Though postwar reconstruction was not always pleasing, Rostock still has its charms, especially in its seaside suburb of Warnemünde.

A·BIT OF HISTORY

Object of Desire – By the 13C, Rostock was already a member of the Hanseatic League, minting its own money and asserting independence from the princes of Mecklenburg. The first Baltic university was founded here in 1419. Such an exalted position drew the envy of powerful neighbours and the town suffered substantial damage during the Thirty Years' War (1618–48), the Nordic struggle for supremacy (1700–21) and the Napoleonic Wars (1803–15). In more modern times, until German reunification, Rostock was East Germany's only significant outlet to the Baltic.

WALKING TOUR

OLD TOWN★

Rostock's historic centre forms an oval outline south of the Warnow River. At its centre is the Church of Notre Dame. To the west it is bounded by the Kröpelin Gate, to the south by the Steintor Gate.

Kröpeliner Tor★ (Kröpelin Gate)

At the western end of Kröpeliner Straße, this 14C red-brick gate is six storeys high and houses the local history museum.

Kröpeliner Straße

This pedestrian zone is Rostock's shopping and commercial centre. It is bordered by gabled houses with façades from Baroque and Renaissance times. At no 82, the brick façade of the 15C

▶ **Population:** 201 100

Info: Neuer Markt 3, 18055 Rostock. ℘(0381) 381 22 22 www.rostock.de.

Location: A key Baltic port, Rostock is served by the A19 and A24 autobahn from Berlin (allow 2hrs 30min); the A 20 links the town to Lübeck. The area west of the Kröpeliner Tor is a lively student zone.

Parking: Garages are situated throughout Rostock, also near the train station.

Don't Miss: The Baltic resorts of Warnemünde, Fischland, Darß and Zingst.

Timing: Allow half a day to see all the sights.

Kids: Navigational Museum, beach at Warnemünde.

Heilig-Geist-Spital has an unusual stepped gable.

Kulturhistorisches Museum (Cultural History Museum)

Klosterhof 7. ⏱ *Open year-round, Tue–Sun 10am–6pm.* ⏱ *Closed Jan 1, Good Fri, Dec 24–25 & 31.* ℘(0381) 381 94 51. www.kulturhistorisches-museum-rostock.de.

This former 13C Cistercian convent, founded by Danish Queen Margarethe, is the region's only completely preserved abbey complex. It houses medieval art, including the **Altarpiece of the Three Kings★** (late 15C), crafts, toys, coins and Dutch paintings from the 16C to 19C.

Marienkirche★★

Am Ziegenmarkt.

The imposing 13C cross-shaped basilica is one of the biggest churches in northern Germany. The massive tower was not completed until the 18C. From the top is a **panorama★** of the city and the docks. Inside the church, note the 1472 **astronomical clock★★** (its face was remodelled in 1643), which comprises a calendar valid until 2017.

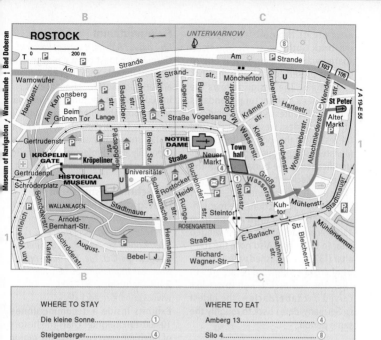

WHERE TO STAY

Die kleine Sonne.............................①

Steigenberger.................................④

WHERE TO EAT

Amberg 13......................................④

Silo 4...⑧

Stilbruch...①

Rathaus (Town Hall)

Neuer Markt.

Rostock's town hall is a jumble of three 13C–14C gabled houses topped by a brick gallery supporting seven towers. The Baroque façade was added in 1727.

Petrikirche (Church of St. Peter)

Am Alter Markt. ○*Open Jun–Aug, Mon–Fri 10am–7pm; Sept–Oct, Apr–May 10am–5pm; Nov–Mar 10am–4pm, Sat–Sun year-round 10am–5pm. Tower* ☞*2€.* ✆*(0381) 49 23 739. www.petrikirche-rostock.de*

Rostock's oldest church (14C) is dedicated to St. Peter, the patron saint of fishermen. Its 117m/384ft-high tower long served as a landmark for seafarers. The church was destroyed in World War II and took several decades to restore. The crowning glory is the historic bell tower, which was only completed in 1994.

EXCURSIONS

Bad Doberan

▶ *A short drive west via the B105. Severinstraße 6, 18209 Bad Doberan.* ✆*(038203) 621 54. www.bad-doberan.de.*

Doberan was put on the map in 1793 as the summer residence of Grand Duke Friedrich Franz I, who also founded Germany's first seaside resort in nearby Heiligendamm. Today, the town's principal sight is its superb Gothic brick cathedral. It is also the terminus of a historic narrow gauge train that has delighted young and old since 1886 and hosts international thoroughbred horse races in July and August.

Münster★★

○*Open May–Sept, Mon–Sat 9am–6pm, Sun 11am–6pm; Mar, Apr and Oct to 5pm; Nov–Feb to 4pm.* ○*Closed Good Fri and Dec 24.* ☞*2€.* ⚐*Guided tours available.* ⚐ ✆*(038203) 627 16. www.muenster-doberan.de.*

Consecrated in 1368, this former Cistercian monastery church is a prime example of the northern German red-brick Gothic style. Having been spared wartime ravages, it is one of the best-preserved Cistercian churches in Germany. The design follows the strict order's architectural mandates with such features as mighty windows on the towerless western façade and friezes below the roof line. Inside, the Münster's sumptuous décor reflects its significance as the burial place of the dukes of Mecklenburg.

The church is filled with 13C–14C art worth closer inspection. The magnificent wood-carved **high altar**★ from 1300 is considered the oldest winged altar in existence. Also note the rood altar (1370), embellished with a **triumphal cross**★ (depicted as the Tree of Life). The 11.6m/38ft-high tower-like carved oak **tabernacle**★, the oldest in Germany, dates back to roughly the same period.

Molli-Bahn★★

Departs from Bad Doberan Bahnhof (train station) Apr–Oct, daily 8.30am–6.45pm (hourly); Nov–Mar, daily 8.30am–4.45pm (every 2hrs). 11.40€ round trip. (038203) 41 50. www.molli-bahn.de.

Kids and nostalgia buffs love this 1886 steam-powered narrow-gauge railway affectionately known as "**Molli**". It chugs for 15.4km/9.5mi from Bad Doberan to Heiligendamm *(20min)* and on to Kühlungsborn *(35min)*.

Heiligendamm

▶ *22km/13.5mi northwest of Rostock.*
Germany's oldest coastal playground was fashionable with the rich, famous and aristocratic throughout the 19C. In 2007 it again captured the international spotlight when hosting the G8 summit. The architecture is typical of 19C spa resorts with elegant villas, especially along Professor-Vogel-Straße, attesting to the town's illustrious past.

🏛️ Schiffahrtsmuseum★★ (Navigational Museum)

▶ *About 10km/6mi north of Rostock's centre towards Warnemünde's international garden exhibit grounds.*
Open Apr–Oct, Tue–Sun 9am–6pm; Nov–Mar 10am–4pm. 4€ (child 2.50€). (0381) 12 83 13 00. www.iga-park-rostock.de.

Exhibits inside a decommissioned 10 000-ton freighter chart the history of maritime travel in the Baltic region from its earliest days to the present. Models of ships, paintings, navigational instruments and photographs document maritime life and work.

Warnemünde★

▶ *11km/6.8mi north of Rostock.*
This former fishing village, bought by its citizens from the Prince of Mecklenburg in 1323, has become Rostock's most popular seaside resort, with charming little streets and a wide beach. The

Old Port of Warnemünde

estuary and beach are lined with cafés, restaurants and bars.

Fischland, Darß and Zingst

▶ *Northeast of Rostock.*

The peninsular chain of Fischland–Darß–Zingst is an attractive coastal area alternating with woods, salt-marshes and moorland. The narrow tongue of land extends north and east, parallel to the mainland and separated from it by a lagoon of brackish Baltic sea water and fresh river water. The artists' village of **Ahrenshoop** in the slightly hilly **Fischland** is a popular vacation resort. **Darß** and **Zingst** form part of the Vorpommern Boddenlandschaft National Park. The little villages and seaside resorts feature attractive reed-covered houses and cottages.

Güstrow

▶ *50km/31mi south of Rostock.*

Güstrow became the residence of the dukes of Mecklenburg-Güstrow in the 16C and grew increasingly wealthy over the next centuries. The elegant burghers' houses around the **cathedral** and **market squares** and along surrounding streets are evidence of this period.

A highlight is the **Schloss**★(○*open mid-Apr–mid-Oct, daily 10am–6pm; mid-Oct–mid-Apr, Tue–Sun 10am–5pm; ○closed Dec 24;* ◎*5€;* ℘*(03843) 75 20; www.schloss-geustrow.de)*, a superb 16C Renaissance palace that blends Italian, French and German elements. The **Dom**★, a 14C Gothic brick basilica, is richly endowed with artworks, having been the court church of the dukes of Mecklenburg.

Note the **Güstrow Apostles**★, 12 almost life-size oak figures by Claus Berg of Lübeck from c. 1530. A stark contrast to these is Ernst Barlach's modernist sculpture *Der Schwebende*.

Ernst-Barlach Stiftung★ (Barlach Museum)

Heidberg 15 & Gertrudenplatz 1.
○*Open Apr–Oct, Tue–Sun 10am–5pm; Nov–Mar, Tue–Sun 11am–4pm, also Mon Jul–Aug. Atelierhaus & Ausstellungsforum.* ◎*5€; Gertudenkapelle 4€,*

combination ticket 7€. ♿ ℘*(03843) 84 40 00. www.ernst-barlach-stiftung.de.*
This museum honouring Ernst Barlach (1870–1938) has two locations: his religious works are in the Late Gothic **Gertrudenkapelle**.

Further works are presented at the artist's studio, the **Atelierhaus**, on the shores of the Inselsee.

A new building from 1998, the **Ausstellungsforum** (exhibition forum) with an attached annex displaying Barlach's graphic work (mostly drawings and prints), is just a few yards from the studio. It presents largely temporary exhibitions.

ADDRESSES

🛏 STAY

⊖ **Die Kleine Sonne** –
Steinstraße 7. ℘*(0381) 461 20. www.die-kleine-sonne.de. 48 rooms.* ⊡*12€.* This central hotel is welcoming and well maintained. Rooms are enlivened by paintings and engravings created by Egyptian artists.

⊖⊜ **Steigenberger Hotel Sonne** –
Neuer Markt 2. ℘*(0381) 497 30. www.rostock.steigenberger.de. 111 rooms.* ⊡*17€.* Ideally located opposite the town hall, this hotel delivers modern and very comfortable rooms.

🍴/ EAT

⊖⊜ **Stilbruch** –
Eselföterstraße 27. ℘ *(0381) 452 822.* This nicely decorated restaurant has an upper level overlooking the garden. Excellent schnitzel.

⊖⊜⊜ **Amberg 13** – *Amberg 13.* ℘*(0381) 490 62 62. www.altstadt restaurant.de.* At this bistro-style restaurant in the old town the chefs themselves bring out the dishes to the tables. Sunday brunch.

⊖⊜⊜ **Silo 4** – *Am Strande 3d.* ℘*(0381) 458 58 00. www.silo4.de.* Elegant and modern restaurant with superb views of the harbour. The Asian-influenced international cuisine is prepared in a large open kitchen.

Stralsund★

Stralsund, one of the most agreeable cities on the German Baltic, looks back on a long maritime tradition in fishing and ship building. Tourism is also a backbone of the local economy, thanks in large part to the beautifully restored and UNESCO-protected medieval city centre.

A BIT OF HISTORY

A coveted city – Stralsund was founded in the early 13C and quickly found itself competing with Lübeck. After being razed by Lübeck in 1249, Stralsund was fortified with a city wall and became a member of the Hanseatic League in 1293. Besieged by Wallenstein during the Thirty Years' War, it was liberated by Swedish and Danish troops. In 1815, it became part of Prussia.

SIGHTS
Altstadt (Old Town)★

Stralsund's UNESCO-listed old town is anchored by the **Rathaus** (*Town Hall*), a splendid 13C and 14C edifice whose magnificent **north façade★★** was added c. 1450. Arcades open onto a covered market hall leading to the 13C **Nikolaikirche★** (*Church of St. Nicholas*) whose magnificent altar has sculptures by Baroque artist Andreas Schlüter.

Deutsches Meeresmuseum★ (German Oceanographic Museum)

Katharinenberg 14. Open daily 10am –6pm (Oct–May 5pm). Closed Dec 24 & 31. 7.50€, 8.50€ with Nautineum (child 5.50€, 5€ with Nautineum). (03831) 265 02 10. www.meeresmuseum.de.

In a former abbey, this museum zeroes in on the flora and fauna of the Baltic Sea. Crowd-pleasers include a massive shark tank and a 15m/49.2ft long finback whale skeleton. The museum also operates the **Nautineum** (3€) on an islet off Stralsund, where you can learn about the local fishing industry, ocean research and boat construction.

▶ **Population:** 57 870

▦ **Info:** Alter Markt 9, 18409 Stralsund. (03831) 246 90. www.stralsund tourismus.de.

▶ **Location:** Stralsund is at the far northeasterly point of Germany. A causeway and a bridge link the town to the island of Rügen.

☺ **Don't Miss:** The Old Town or the Ozeaneum.

🕐 **Timing:** Allow two hours.

Kids: The Oceanographic Museum and Ozeaneum.

Ozeaneum★★

Hafenstraße 11. Open daily 9.30am– 9pm (Oct–May to 7pm). 14€, 18€ with Meeresmuseum. (03831) 265 06 01. www.ozeaneum.de.

This state-of-the-art aquarium takes visitors on an exciting underwater journey from Stralsund to the frigid Polar Sea. Highlights include a giant tank where 2 500 herring swim their merry rounds and a huge hall with life-size whale models.

Marienkirche★

Neuer Markt.
A Gothic high altar featuring the Coronation of the Virgin Mary (15C) and an original organ (c. 1659) by Lübeck builder Friedrich Stellwagen are what warrant attention in St. Mary's.

Kulturhistorisches Museum (History Museum)

Mönchstraße 25/27. (03831) 287 90. Open year-round, daily 10am–5pm (closed Mon Nov–Jan). 4€.

Displays on Stralsund's history, Hiddensee island in prehistoric times and sacred medieval art in beautiful netvaulted rooms.

Ramparts

The best-preserved section of the city wall is west of the centre on Knieperteich pond, between Kniepertor and Kütertor.

STRALSUND

S T R E L A S U N D

WHERE TO STAY

An den Bleichen..............①

Steigenberger
 Hotel Baltic.................④

WHERE TO EAT

Tafelfreuden
 im Sommerhaus...........②

ADDRESSES

🛏️ STAY

An den Bleichen – *An den Bleichen 45.* ℰ*(03831) 39 06 75. www.hotelanden bleichen.de. 23 rooms.* ☕. In a residential area, this family-run place has pretty gardens. Close to the old town, port and beach.

Steigenberger Hotel Baltic – *Frankendamm 22.* ℰ*(03831) 20 40. www.stralsund.steigenberger.de. 134 rooms.* ☕. *Restaurant*. This hotel is located in a former barracks renovated in an elegantly modern style. Even the standard rooms are pretty spacious, even if the décor

is rather generic. The contemporary bistro-restaurant serves Baltic fish dishes as well as Spanish tapas.

🍽️ EAT

Tafelfreuden im Sommerhaus – *Jungfernstieg 5a.* ℰ*(03831) 29 92 60. Closed Mon. www.tafelfreuden-stralsund.de.* Bright colours, wooden floors and a winter garden give this small Swedish country-style house Mediterranean flair. It is also a good-value spot for lunch, with a three-course menu costing 15€. If you feel like spending the night here, there are also three charming guest rooms, each individually decorated.

Rügen Island★

Insel Rügen

The Baltic island of Rügen, Germany's largest, offers a surprising variety of scenery. In the west, the straits widen towards the open sea. Fabled chalk cliffs and sandy beaches in the east attract summer crowds. The southern shores are wooded; and to the north is the deep, jagged Jasmunder Bodden (Gulf).

Info: Bahnhofstraße 15. 18528 Bergen auf Rügen. ℰ(03838) 80 77 80. www.ruegen.de.

Location: Rügen can be reached by train or car via a long bridge (2.5km/1.5mi) that straddles the straits at Stralsund. Ferries to Scandinavia leave from the port of Saßnitz.

Don't Miss: Chalk cliffs of the Stubbenkammer, Hiddensee Island.

Timing: Allow one or two days to explore Rügen and another half-day to visit Hiddensee (⟲see Excursion).

Kids: Rügen's seaside resorts, Hiddensee Island.

🚗 DRIVING TOUR

FROM PUTBUS TO KAP ARKONA

75km/46.5mi – Allow half a day.

Putbus★

The "white town" in the southeast of the island was founded in 1810 by Prince William Malte of Putbus as a royal seat and bathing resort. The princely castle no longer remains, but the Neoclassical town does, centred around a circular square – the **circus**★. It is anchored by a 21m/69ft-high obelisk from 1845 and surrounded by 16 mansions that are finished in dazzling white and stand out from the green of the oaks. Nearby, the 19C **theatre**★ *(Alleestraße)* bears a portico of four Tuscan columns and is endowed with fabulous acoustics. One frieze represents Apollo and the muses. The 75ha/185-acre **Schlosspark**★ with its orangery (modified in 1853 by Friedrich August Stüler), royal stables and parish church, is laid out in the style of an English garden.

Störtebeker

Klaus Störtebeker was a notorious pirate said to have been born in Ruschwitz on Rügen in 1370. As a young man, he drank from his master's tankard at work and, having been seen by his boss, was promptly chained and beaten. But Störtebeker's strength was such that he broke free and thrashed his tormentor. Then he took off in a fishing boat as far as the Cape of Arkona. There he joined Michael Gödecke and his band of brigands whose reputation struck terror into all who sailed the coast. Störtebeker became one of the most feared buccaneers of his age, scouring the seas until eventually being captured in Hamburg and condemned to the guillotine. As a mark of the respect, his last wish was granted: mercy for the companions arrested with him.

Legend has it that Störtebeker hid his booty beneath the cliffs of the Stubbenkammer, and once a year a ship steered by phantom buccaneers is said to haunt this coast. Every summer, at Ralswiek, islanders put on a play commemorating the adventures of this anti-hero, scourge of the rich and benefactor of the poor.

Jagdschloss Granitz (Granitz Hunting Palace)

12km/7.4mi east of Putbus, south of Binz. ○*Open May–Sept, daily 9am–6pm; Oct–Apr, Tue–Sun 10am–4pm.* ○*Closed Dec 25.* ∞*3€.* ☏*(038393) 22 63. www.mv-schloesser.de.*

In 1837 Prince William Malte I of Putbus built a neo-Gothic Tudor hunting lodge atop the Tempelberg, the highest point in eastern Rügen.

The four crenellated corner towers of the "castle" rise up in the middle of Granitz Forest. A 19C viewing tower and platform are reached via a cast-iron **spiral staircase**. From the top, the **view**★★ of Rügen Island is breathtaking. The rooms inside the house are open to the public.

👥 Beach Resorts★

Binz, **Sellin**, **Baabe** and **Göhren** are in the southwest of the island, luring visitors with sandy beaches, beautiful 19C spa architecture and a wooded backdrop. They can be reached via the **"Rasender Roland"** (Racing Roland), a nostalgic steam train shuttling between Putbus and Göhren.

Saßnitz

Ferries bound for Scandinavia embark from this port city that is backed by beautiful beech woods.

Jasmund National Park★★

Germany's northernmost national park is famous for its stunning chalk cliffs that border the deep blue sea. This postcard idyll greatly inspired Romantic painter Caspar David Friedrich, especially a spot called the **Stubbenkammer**★★.

The most famous cliff is the 117m/384ft-high **Königsstuhl** *(King's chair;* ∞*1€)*. For background and information, visit the **National Park Visitor Centre** *(*○*open Easter–Oct, daily 9am–7pm; Nov–Easter 10am–5pm;* ∞*6€;* ☏*(038392) 66 17 66; www.koenigsstuhl.com)*, where you can watch a film and peruse exhibits on the park's flora, fauna and geology.

Kap Arkona★

Kap Arkona, with its 50m/164ft-high chalk cliffs, is the northernmost point of the island. The **old lighthouse** *(*☏*(038391) 41 90; www.kap-arkona.de)*, a square, three-storey brick building, was built in 1826–29 according to plans by Karl Friedrich Schinkel. There is a wonderful **view**★★ from here to the neighbouring island of Hiddensee. The walls located not far from the lighthouse are the remains of the fortress of Jaromarsburg built by the Slavs and destroyed by the Danes in 1168. Near the ramparts stands the watchtower of the Navy, built in 1927; it houses an exhibition on the Baltic Coast.

Chalk cliffs of Jasmund National Park

© C. Doerr/Sime/Photononstop

EXCURSION

≗ Hiddensee Island★

▶ *Ferries depart from Wiek and Schaprode on Rügen (14.50–16.90€; one-way trip duration 25–45min) and from Stralsund (18.10–18.90€; one-way trip duration 90min–2hrs 30min). Reederei Hiddensee, Fährstraße 16, Stralsund. ℘(0180) 321 21 50. www.reederei-hiddensee.de.*
No cars allowed on the island; bicycle rental recommended.

Hiddensee Island is 17km/10mi off the west coast of Rügen and almost entirely within the Nationalpark Vorpommersche Boddenlandschaft. Its gorgeous landscape features towering cliffs, land spits, lagoons and coastal inlets. The highest point is the **Dornbusch peak** (72m/236ft) in the north, site of the island's trademark **lighthouse** (1888). Hiddensee is crisscrossed by trails and bicycle paths.

The village of **Grieben** is famous for its thatched houses. **Kloster** has developed into a bathing resort. The playwright **Gerhart Hauptmann** (1862–1946), best known for his Naturalist dramas, is buried in the churchyard. Hauptmann's summer residence, Haus Seedorn on Kirchweg, is open to the public. The island's administrative centre is at **Vitte**, a fishing village turned tourist resort. South of Vitte are vast dunes interspersed with marshland (*Dünenheide*). **Neuendorf**, the island's most southerly village, has fishermen's houses built so that living quarters face the sun.

ADDRESSES

STAY

Strandhotel Lissek – *Strandpromenade 33, 18609 Binz. ℘(038393) 38 10. www.strandhotel-lissek.de. 40 rooms.* Carefully restored spa architecture with great attention to detail, along with all major mod cons. Some rooms have fine views of the Baltic Sea. The restaurant specialises in fish and is often packed to the gills.

Wreecher Hof – *Kastanienallee, 18581 Putbus-Wreechen. ℘(038301) 850. www.wreecher-hof.de. 43 rooms. Restaurant.* This off-the-beaten track resort consists of seven reed-thatched buildings in an idyllic location. It is a good place for those needing plenty of elbow room since most are suites with separate bed and sitting quarters. The international restaurant has a winter garden and beautiful terrace.

Greifswald★

There is evidence that Greifswald was granted municipal rights as early as 1250. Once it joined the Hanseatic League in 1281, the town flourished and continued to prosper for the next four centuries. Greifswald boasts a decidedly Scandinavian flavour and a number of historic buildings largely spared destruction during World War II.

A BIT OF HISTORY

Swedish tule – After the Thirty Years' War, Greifswald became part of the Kingdom of Sweden in 1648. The Swedes granted the town an unusual degree of autonomy. After being absorbed by Prussia in 1815, a busy period of construction began, to which the numerous well-preserved burghers' houses testify.

The greatest German romantic painter – Highly influential landscape painter **Caspar David Friedrich** was born in Greifswald in 1774 and although he left the town at the age of 20, he remained deeply attached to and inspired by it.

SIGHTS
Marktplatz★ (Market Square)

Greifswald's central square is dominated by the arcaded **Rathaus** (1738) and framed by several architecturally distinguished houses. Standouts include the one at **no 11**★ from the 15C.

Marienkirche★

⊙Open Jun–Oct, Mon–Fri 10am–6pm, Sat 10am–4pm Sat, Sun 11am–1pm; shorter hours the rest of the year. ⸝ 𝒫 (038 34) 22 63.

This red-brick hall-church has a 14C east gable whose ornate tracery contrasts with the 13C stocky tower. Inside, the 1587 **pulpit**★, richly carved and adorned with inlaid wood, merits a closer look, as do the faded 15C frescoes in the southern tower.

- ▸ **Population:** 53 000
- ▪ **Info:** Rathaus am Markt, 17489 Greifswald. 𝒫 (03834) 52 13 80. www.greifswald.de.
- ▶ **Location:** This Baltic Sea town is about 30km/18.6mi east of Stralsund and bisected by the little Ryck River.
- ⊛ **Don't Miss:** The Marktplatz, Marienkirche, Museum of Pomerania.
- ⊙ **Timing:** About half a day to take in the main sights.

Dom St. Nikolai★

⊙Open year-round Mon–Sat 10am–6pm, Sun 11.30am–3pm. 𝒫 (03834) 26 27. www.dom-greifswald.de.

Caspar David Friedrich was baptised in this 13C Gothic hall church with its landmark onion-domed spire. The interior is rather plain thanks to a 19C remodel, although some Late Gothic frescoes remain in chapels 19 and 20.

Klosterruine Eldena (Eldena Abbey)

Wolgaster Landstraße.

The picturesque ruins of this medieval Cistercian abbey (1199) were a favourite subject of Caspar David Friedrich.

Wieck★

The thatched fishermen's cottages, idyllic harbour and 19C **wooden swing bridge**★ (Zugbrücke) of this historic fishing village at the mouth of the River Ryck present a delightful scene.

Pommersches Landesmuseum★ (Museum of Pomerania)

Rakower Straße 9. ⊙Open Tue–Sun 10am–6pm (Nov–Mar 5pm). ⸜4.50€. ⸝ 𝒫 (03834) 31 20. www.pommersches-landesmuseum.de.

In a converted Franciscan friary, this museum has local history exhibits but is more notable for its picture gallery starring paintings by Friedrich, Runge and Liebermann.

Usedom Island★

Insel Usedom

Usedom's wonderfully unspoilt natural landscape is a pastiche of moors, estuaries, forests, dunes, sandy beaches and steep cliffs. The island is part of the Usedom-Oderhaff Nature Reserve and is dotted with elegant bathing resorts. For some time the island was known as "Berlin's bathtub" because of the large number of Berliners who came here to relax and recuperate.

SIGHTS

Wolgast

On the mainland.

One point of access to Usedom is in the south at Zecherin; the other lies in the northwest, from Wolgast over the River Peene. The 14C **Pfarrkirche St. Petri** *(parish church;* ◷ *open May–Sept, Mon–Sat 10am–5pm, Oct–Mar Mon–Fri 10am–12.30pm and 1.30–4pm;* ♿ *;* ✆ *(03836) 25 12 15)* merits a peek. Its formidable octagonal tower and austere exterior contrast sharply with the sumptuous interior. Highlights include 15C–16C frescoes and a 1700 *danse macabre* cycle painted by Caspar Sigmund Köppe based on a woodcut by Hans Holbein the Younger.

Krummin

East of Wolgast.

The most beautiful avenue of **lime trees★** *(Lindenallee)* in Usedom leads to the right off B111 and extends to the little fishing village on the Krummin cove. The surfaced road is just 2km/1.2mi long but is marvellous; the arched canopy of leaves overhead gives the impression of being in a Gothic cathedral formed by Nature.

Peenemünde

In 1936, the German army located its V2 rocket-testing centre to the northeastern tip of Usedom. A rocket museum, the **Historisch-Technisches Infor-** mationszentrum (◷ *open Apr–Sept, 10am–6pm; Oct–Mar to 4pm;* ◷ *closed 24–26 Dec, Nov–Mar, Mon;* ⛖*6€;* ♿ *;* ✆ *(038371) 50 50; www.peenemuende. de)* in the old power station, retraces the history of rocket development and its associated perils. It was where Werner von Braun developed the V2 rocket unveiled in October 1942. It killed thousands of people during World War II but also signalled the beginning of space exploration.

👪 Usedoms "Taille" (Isthmus)

At the island's narrowest point, the white sandy beaches of the resorts of **Zinnowitz**, **Koserow**, **Kölpinsee** and **Ückeritz** lie side by side, protected by steep cliffs. At Koserow, the island is barely 200m/656ft wide.

Bansin, Heringsdorf, Ahlbeck

These "three sisters" in the island's southeast are linked by a 10km/6.2mi-long beach promenade. In the 19C, aristocrats and the merely moneyed convened in these fashionable resorts that were also known as "Kaiserbäder"

- 🛈 **Info:** Waldstraße 1, 17429 Seebad Bansin. ✆ (038372) 477 110. www.usedom.de.
- ▶ **Location:** Usedom is Germany's easternmost island, although its far eastern portion, with the town of Swinoujscie, belongs to Poland. The flat northwest contrasts with the hilly southeast, sometimes called "Usedom's Switzerland".
- 👁 **Don't Miss:** The 19C beach resort of Heringsdorf.
- 🕐 **Timing:** Allow one day to soak up the ambience of Usedom.
- 👪 **Kids:** Outdoor recreation on sandy beaches and dunes.

USEDOM ISLAND

BALTIC SEA

Peenemünde
Zinnowitz
Koserow
Wolgast
Kölpinsee
Krummin
Naturpark
Ückeritz
Bansin
Achterwasser
Heringsdorf ★
Usedom-
Oderhaff
Ahlbeck
Lassan
Gothensee
ŚWINOUJŚCIE
Mellenthin
peene
Usedom
Zirchow
Kleines
Haff
ANKLAM
POLAND
BERLIN
GREIFSWALD
SZCZECIN

(imperial spas). Numerous imposing and attractive late 19C beach villas and hotels with frilly white wrought-iron decorations remain to this day.

Heringsdorf was especially trendy and often visited by Emperor Wilhelm II who resided in the still extant Villa Staudt (*Delbrückstraße 6*). At 508m/1 666ft long, Heringsdorf's pier is the longest on mainland Europe.

Ahlbeck is also proud of its **historical pier★**, built in 1898. A restaurant was added in 1902. With its white walls, red roof and four green-roofed corner towers, it is one of the most photographed subjects on the island. **Bansin** is the westernmost resort and maintains a more relaxed and family-friendly air.

Mellenthin
Northeast of the town of Usedom, 2km/1.2mi north of the B110.

This seldom-visited village and its Renaissance castle create a rural idyll. Although relatively plain, the three-winged castle surrounded by a moat boasts a colourfully mounted 17C Renaissance fireplace in the entrance hall. The 14C village church in the town cemetery remains a little pearl with its 17C interior **decoration★**.

ADDRESSES

STAY

⊟⊟⊟ **Zur Post** – *Seestraße 5, 17429 Usedom-Bansin. ℰ(038378) 560. 159 rooms. Restaurant*⊟⊟⊟. A fine example of coastal architecture, this 1901 villa was enlarged with modern guesthouses and an elegant spa centre. There are two restaurants, a casual one serving rib-sticking traditional cuisine, and an elegant dining room specialising in well-prepared international fare.

⊟⊟⊟ **Romantik Seehotel Ahlbecker Hof** – *Dünenstraße 47, 17419 Usedom-Ahlbeck. ℰ(038378) 620. www.ahlbeckerhof.de. 70 rooms. Restaurant*⊟⊟⊟. Set in a beautifully modernised Neoclassical mansion, this hotel satisfies even the most demanding patrons with its elegant and sumptuously outfitted rooms and spa complex. The crystal chandeliers and timeless ambience of the restaurant make this an unforgettable place to stay.

Neubrandenburg

This town, founded in 1248 at the behest of Margrave Johann von Brandenburg, is built on an almost circular ground plan, crisscrossed by a gridlike network of streets. Although 80 percent of the old town was destroyed in 1945, the fortifications with their four unique gates were miraculously spared and are now a principal tourist attraction.

SIGHTS

Fortifications★★

Some 50 years after Neubrandenburg was founded in 1248, construction began on the town's defensive fortifications. In the end, the formidable wall was 2.3km/1.4mi long, over 7m/23ft high and 1.4m/4ft 6in thick at the base. It was built using boulders from the vicinity and capped by several rows of bricks. The wall's four gates were closed every evening and only opened in return for payment. They remained the only access to the town right up to the mid-19C.

The gates are all of the same design, each an individual fortification. So that the town could be safely defended, three- to four-floor sentry posts were built into the wall every 30m/98ft. There were 56 of them in the 16C, 25 of which have been reconstructed. All able-bodied citizens were expected to

▶ **Population:** 68 600
▯ **Info:** Marktplatz 1, 17033 Neubrandenburg, ✆(0395) 194 33. www.neubrandenburg.de.
◖ **Location:** Midway between Berlin and the Baltic Coast, Neubrandenburg is to the northeast of the pretty lake of Tollensesee.
▣ **Parking:** Garages are in the heart of the old city, on Neutorstraße and on Stargarder Straße.
◉ **Don't Miss:** Neubrandenburg's medieval wall.
◷ **Timing:** Plan at least an hour to explore the town wall.
👥 **Kids:** Climbing the old wall and towers, and outdoor recreation in the Feldberger Seenlandschaft.

maintain the posts, while defence of the gates was the duty of the four principal guilds: Bakers, Wool Weavers, Shoemakers and Blacksmiths.

The oldest gate, the **Friedländer Tor**, was built just after 1300. It is 19m/62.3ft high. On the outside it is possible to see the transition from the Romanesque to the Gothic period. The **Stargarder Tor**, built during the early 14C, is embel-

Friedländer Tor

© Neppomuk/Fotolia.com

lished with nine terracotta figures in long pleated robes, known as "Die Jungfrauen" *(the maids)*. The outer gate is especially sumptuously decorated. The **Treptower Tor**, built around 1400, stands 32m/105ft tall and is the highest of the gate towers. Both the main gate and the outer gate are richly decorated with brick tracery. The **Neues Tor** (New Gate), built after 1550 in the Late Gothic style, combines decorative elements of the other three gates.

Of the two towers that further reinforced the fortifications, only the 19m/62ft-high **Fangelturm** remains. It was used as a prison. The spire was added in 1845.

Konzertkirche (Concert Church)

Formerly the Church of St. Mary, this brick church was completed late in the 13C and was partly rebuilt in Neo-Gothic style in the mid-19C. In the 1990s, Finish architect Pekka Salminen converted the church into a state-of-the-art concert hall. Endowed with supreme acoustics, it is one of the main performance venues of the Neubrandenburg Philharmonic Orchestra *(www.theater-und-orchester.de)*.

St. Johanniskirche (Church of St. John)

Stargarder Straße 2. ⏱*Open year-round, Tue–Sat 10am–noon, 1pm–6pm, Sat 10am–4pm.* ⏱*Closed public holidays.* ♿ ✆*(0395) 582 22 88.*

The 13C–14C church of the former Franciscan monastery features a Renaissance **pulpit**★ supported by a figure of Moses (1598). It is made of limestone and displays alabaster reliefs of Christ and the Evangelists.

👥 Tollensesee

This lovely lake, which is 10.4km/6.5mi in length and almost 3km/1.8mi wide, lies to the south of the town, in the middle of an attractive landscape. The western bank slopes steeply up to Brodaer Woods. In summer, locals and visitors flock to its shores for swimming, boating, tanning and picnicking. Boat rentals are available, or explore the lake on a leisurely **boat cruise** (⏱*May–Oct;* 🚢*10.50€; Fahrgastschiff Mudder Schulten;* ✆*(0395) 584 12 18; www.fahrgastschiff-mudderschulten.de).*

EXCURSIONS
Burg Stargard

▶ *11km/6.8mi south of Neubrandenburg, via the E251 and L33.*

The castle ruins dominate their surroundings here.

Woldegk

▶ *20km/12.4mi further on via the B104.*

This town, with its five windmills, borders the Feldburger Seenlandscaft (👣*see below).*

Seenlandschaft

Southwest of Woldegk, in the Mecklenburg-Strelit district, lies this lovely hilly lake region. It is home to the rare European otter as well as to the sea eagle, osprey and lesser spotted eagle. Woods, meadows, moors and lakes alternate between **Fürstenwerder** and **Feldberg**. The lakes offer plenty of diving opportunities, such as Tauchcenter-Feldberg (✆*(039831) 223 39; www.tauchcenter-feldberg.de).*

Carwitz

▶ *29.5km/18.3mi southwest of Woldegk along the B198.*

In an idyllic lakeside location, the 1848 half-timbered home of the writer **Hans Fallada** (author of *Alone in Berlin,* among many others) contains a museum about the man and his life.

Neustrelitz

▶ *39km/24.2mi northeast of Carwitz.*

The former residence of the dukes of Mecklenburg-Strelitz still bears witness to their proud past.

Admire the **Schlossgarten**★ with its graceful buildings and monuments and the orangerie with its remarkable Pompeii-style **paintings**★.

The Baroque town **church** (1768–78), the classical **Rathaus** (1841) and the neo-Gothic **Schloßkirche** (1855–59) are all worth closer inspection.

Schwerin★

The state capital of Mecklenburg-Vorpommern, Schwerin is one of the most pleasant towns in northern Germany. Defined by the numerous lakes surrounding it, the city is endowed with plenty of fine architecture, most famously the lordly castle on an island opposite the old town.

A BIT OF HISTORY

The oldest town in Mecklenburg – The origins of Schwerin date to the 11C, when the Slavs built a fortress on what is now Schloßinsel. They were soon expelled by Henry the Lion, who colonised Schwerin in 1160 as the first German town east of the Elbe. In 1358 Schwerin was absorbed into the Duchy of Mecklenburg and became the seat of the local dukes from that time onwards.

SCHLOSSINSEL★★
Schloss★ (Palace)

Lennéstraße 1. ○Open mid-Apr–mid-Oct, daily 10am–6pm; mid-Oct–mid-Apr, Tue–Sun, 10am–5pm. ≈6€. ℘(0385) 525 29 20. www.schloss-schwerin.de.

Built as the residence of the Grand Dukes of Mecklenburg-Schwerin, the castle is today the home of the state parliament of Mecklenburg-Vorpommern and a

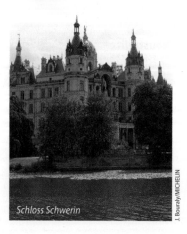

Schloss Schwerin

J. Bouraly/MICHELIN

- ▶ **Population:** 95 560
- **Info:** Am Markt 14, 19055 Schwerin. ℘(0385) 592 52 12. www.schwerin.de.
- ◑ **Location:** Schwerin is surrounded by lakes and forests. The A24 autobahn (Hamburg–Berlin) passes by about 20km/12.4mi to the south.
- P **Parking:** Near the Old Town you'll find garages at Reiferbahn and Wittenburger Straße and on Geschwister-Scholl-Straße.
- **Don't Miss:** Schloßinsel and Ludwigslust (○see Excursion).
- ◑ **Timing:** Allow two hours to visit the Schloßinsel.

harmonious hodgepodge of architectural styles ranging from Gothic to neo-Renaissance. The oldest wing (15C–17C) harbours the **Schlossmuseum**, which takes in a series of rooms richly decked out with 18C and 19C art, furniture and Meissen porcelain. The most impressive are the **Thronzimmer★** (Throne Room) and the **Ahnengalerie** (Ancestors' Gallery), whose paintings are an uninterrupted roll call of all Mecklenburg dukes from the 14C to the 18C.

Schlosskirche★ (Palace Church)

This 16C Renaissance chapel was commissioned in 1560 by Duke Albrecht I. It was the first Protestant church in Mecklenburg and was originally a simple, rectangular, galleried space. The Neo-Gothic choir with splendid stained-glass windows was added in the 19C. A triumphal arch links the choir and the original chapel.

Schlossgarten★ (Palace Garden)

Created in the 19C, this formal Baroque garden is organised around canals, lime trees and ornamental flowerbeds. Lining the canals are statues by Balthazar Permoser.

OLD TOWN
Markt
Four 17C half-timbered houses are preserved beside the town hall. The 18C Neoclassical **Neues Gebäude** (new building) is fronted by a monument of Henry the Lion.

Dom★ (Cathedral)
This Gothic red-brick cathedral was built in the 14C and 15C on the site of an ancient Roman building. It is filled with wonderful treasures, most notably a **Gothic high altar** (workshop Lübeck, 1480), **tombstones** (14C), a **triumphal cross** of the Church of St. Mary of Wismar (1420) and **frescoes** in the Chapel of the Assumption (14C).

Staatliches Museum Schwerin★ (State Museum)
Alter Garten 3. ○*Open mid-Apr–mid-Oct 10am–6pm (Thu 8pm); mid-Oct–mid-Apr Tue–Sun 10am–5pm (Thu 1 –8pm).* ○*Closed Dec 24 & 31.* ⬤*5€.* ♿*(0385) 595 80. www.museum-schwerin.de.*
This museum houses 17C Flemish and Dutch paintings (Brueghel, Rembrandt, Rubens), European painting from the 16C to the 20C (Cranach, Gainsborough) and contemporary art (Cage, Polke).

EXCURSION
Schloss Ludwigslust★
40km/24.8mi south. ○*Open mid-Apr–mid-Oct, daily 10am–6pm; mid-Oct–mid-Apr, Tue–Sun 10am–5pm.* ⬤*5€.* ♪*(03874) 571 90. www.schloss-ludwigslust.de.*
This ducal palace has early 18C origins as a hunting lodge but was significantly enlarged after Duke Friedrich made Ludwigslust the capital of his duchy in 1764. It is an E-shaped, 18C late-Baroque building with some early Neoclassical elements. The 18 vases and 40 statues adorning the attic parapet represent the arts, sciences and virtues.

The **interior** is dominated by white and gold ornamentation. Paintings, furniture, miniatures and gilded decorations made from papier mâché reflect the life-

Ludwigslust Cardboard Décor
Duke Friedrich's intensive building activity exhausted his funds but he was determined to decorate his palace in a manner befitting his social standing. Expensive material was replaced by Ludwigsluster Karton, a type of papier mâché that could be polished and painted and was even weather resistant. The Ludwigslust workshop achieved such mastery that its products were exported as far as Russia. Production ceased in 1835 due to lack of demand. The original formula was closely guarded and remains a secret to this day.

styles of the ducal family. A particular highlight is the **Golden Room**. The sprawling **Schlosspark★** got its naturalistic English landscape design in the 19C under Peter Joseph Lenné. Take a stroll to view streams, monuments, mausoleums and a grotto.

ADDRESSES

🛏STAY
⊜⊜**Niederländischer Hof** – *Alexandrinenstraße 12–13.* ♪*(0385) 59 11 00. www.niederlaendischer-hof.de. 32 rooms. Restaurant* ⊜⊜. In an old building with a listed façade, this hotel fits perfectly into the surrounding urban landscape. The tasteful interior is elegantly furnished.

🍽 EAT
⊜⊜**Weinhaus Uhle** – *Schusterstraße 15.* ♪*(0385) 56 29 56. www.weinhaus-uhle.de.* Located near the market place, this neat town house is home to a well-run, elegant restaurant with an 18C vaulted ceiling and pretty arched windows. Extensive wine list.

Mecklenburg Lake District★★★
Mecklenburger Seenplatte

Sprinkled with more than 1 000 lakes, the intensely rural Mecklenburg lake district is also known as Land der Tausend Seen (Land of the Thousand Lakes). Formed during the last Ice Age, it is a peaceful region, untouched by mass tourism. Time seems to move a little slower here, so plan on savouring the area's considerable charms slowly. Since only a few lakes have roads along their shores, you will need to get out of the car and onto a trail or the water to truly enjoy this area.

 DRIVING TOUR

FROM SCHWERIN TO MÜRITZ LAKE
150km/94mi – Allow one day.

The **Schweriner See** forms an idyllic backdrop to the provincial capital **Schwerin**★ and its castle (*see p170*). The novelist Fritz Reuter (1810–1874), who was born in this region, found inspiration and solace on the peaceful wooded shores of **Krakower See**. Today, the lake is a paradise for birdwatchers. The **Plauer See**, the third-largest lake

- **Info:** Turnplatz 2, 17207 Röbel/Müritz. (039931) 53 80. www.mecklenburgische-seenplatte.de.
- **Location:** The lake district is about 80km/49.7mi north of Berlin and centres on the Müritz National Park.
- **Don't Miss:** Müritz National Park.
- **Timing:** Allow one full day for the Driving Tour.
- **Kids:** Outdoor activities at Müritz National Park.

in Mecklenburg-Vorpommern, offers flat shores to the north and thick forest to the south. Together with the **Müritz**, it forms the heart of the Mecklenburg Lake District.

Northeast of the lakes, **Mecklenburg's "Switzerland"** is a stretch of hills. The road leads through the town of **Malchin**, with its fine brick basilica, to the **Kummerower See**. To the west of the **Malchiner See** *(on the B108)* **Schlitz Castle** is set in a wonderful park.

The pearl of the district is **Lake Müritz** with **Waren** on its north shore being the main tourist centre. In addition to the two parish churches of St. Georg and St. Maria, the old and new town halls and the Löwenapotheke (pharmacy) draw the eye. **Röbel** has a pretty marina with attractive boathouses.

Lake Müritz with boathouses

Canoeing in Müritz National Park

© Wolfram Steinberg/Picture Alliance/Photoshot

MÜRITZ NATIONAL PARK★

This nature reserve sprawls across 310sq km/120sq mi east of Lake Müritz. Two-thirds of the area are covered in forest, 12 percent is taken up by the lake and 8 percent are wetlands. In East German times, a section was reserved for hunting, but today it is entirely given over to walkers, cyclists and other nature-lovers.

The birdlife here is astonishingly diverse. Bring binoculars to keep an eye out for the rare osprey, which seems to take pleasure in preparing its nest on high-voltage pylons. Chances of encountering osprey, whose territory reaches up to 50sq km/19sq mi, are greatest near the fish pools of Boek. White storks have been seen nesting near Kargowa, and black storks and cranes may also be sighted. When it comes to fauna, pine and beech trees predominate, but the marshes and sloughs of the eastern Müritz bank are also dappled with alder, birch and ash.

All in all, an estimated 150 bird and 700 plant species call this national park home. Take a guided tour in order to gain a more thorough appreciation for this extraordinary natural wealth.

ADDRESSES

🍽 STAY

🛏 **Hotel Seestern** – *Müritzpromenade 12, 17207 Röbel. ✆(039931) 580 30. Closed Jan, Feb and Nov. 29 rooms. Restaurant🍽.* This hotel sits on a small tongue of land jutting into the lake. Ask for one of the bi-level rooms with superb views. The restaurant is in a welcoming annex and has a winter garden and a terrace.

🛏 **Insel-Hotel** – *An der Drehbrücke, 17213 Malchow. ✆(039932) 86 00. www.inselhotel-malchow.de. 16 rooms.* This property in the old town, on the edge of a swinging bridge, has good-sized rooms with crisp, no-nonsense style; some have views of Malchow Lake.

🛏🛏 **Hotel Kleines Meer** – *Alter Markt 7, 17192 Waren. ✆(03991) 64 80. www.kleinesmeer.com. 30 rooms. Restaurant🛏🍽🛏.* A central location near the harbour and friendly, modern rooms with a good range of communication devices are among the assets of this hotel. The restaurant exudes contemporary flair and serves ambitious international cuisine.

🛏🛏 **Hotel Paulshöhe** – *Falkenhäger Weg, 17192 Waren. ✆(03991) 171 40. www.hotel-paulshoehe.de. 14 rooms, 7 bungalows. Restaurant🛏🍽.* In a pleasant location 200m/220yd from the Tiefwarensee lake you'll find lodging with all the mod-cons and a warm and well presented restaurant.

This vast region forms a triangle between the windswept beaches of the North Sea, the dense forests of the Harz Mountains and the cycle-friendly expanses of the Münsterland with its moated castles. Aside from natural splendours galore, historical towns abound. Germany's second-largest city, Hamburg, lures visitors with its cosmopolitan flair, maritime spirit and some of the country's best nightlife. The red-brick architecture that dominates the north gives way to half-timbered gems in such pretty towns as Celle, Hameln and Goslar. Goslar is also a gateway to the Harz Mountains, a paradise for outdoorsy types. Hiking, cycling and even skiing are all popular activities. If water is your element, head to the Frisian Islands for great surfing, swimming and sailing.

Highlights

1 HafenCity and Speicherstadt in **Hamburg** (p186 and p182)

2 Exploring Germany's largest surviving medieval town hall in **Lüneburg** (p192)

3 The wind-swept beaches and dunes of **Insel Sylt** (p198)

4 Half-timbered towns of **Celle** and **Goslar** (p217 and p221)

5 Celebrate the annual Libori Festival at **Paderborn** (p236)

Hanseatic Cities

Northwestern Germany's Hanseatic legacy is still evident in several cities, most famously of course its birthplace, Lübeck, the "Queen of the Hanseatic League"

(*see BALTIC COAST AND INLAND, p142*). A short drive south, Hamburg on the Elbe River is still a major trading town that is home to Europe's second-largest port. There is also an entire quarter of warehouses called the historic Speicherstadt as well as imposing merchants' houses, such as the eccentric Chilehaus. Finally, there is Bremen, sitting pretty on the Weser River. Shaped both by history and high-tech, its port section of Bremerhaven was the launch pad for millions of emigrants bound for the New World.

Historic Heritage

UNESCO World Heritage Sites in northern Germany captivate visitors with religious art treasures, mining monuments and Hanseatic history. Hildesheim for example is blessed with beautiful churches, while fascinating

Old Town, Celle

© Bildagentur RM/Tips Images

The Hanseatic League

Long before the European Union, there was the Hanseatic League, a federation of trading cities that dominated commercial activity in northern Europe from the 13C to the 15C. The League's actual origins are hard to determine, although scholars generally agree that its history began in 1159 in Lübeck as a loose alliance of guilds and individual merchants. At its peak, though, it counted as many as 200 member cities and stretched from the Baltic to the North Sea and inland to Münster, Goslar, Hildesheim and beyond. Most towns were located along international trade routes; many were free imperial cities, meaning they reported directly to the Holy Roman Emperor. The member towns had their own system of laws and furnished their own protection, allowing them to influence imperial policy and to prosper economically. Many of the grand medieval homes and public buildings have survived over the centuries and still attest to this phase of great prosperity.

mining and industrial heritage awaits in Goslar. The Hanseatic city of Bremen makes an enthralling destination with its historic old quarters, fine monuments, religious art and traditional brick buildings. Further south, Münster and Osnabrück catapulted to historic fame as the sites where the treaty ending the bloody Thirty Years' War was signed.

Unique and Offbeat

Germany's northwest has plenty in store for those with a penchant for the unusual. How about a walk on the ocean floor at low tide in the Wadden Sea or communing with witches and warlocks in the Harz Mountains? You can pay your respects to Anne Frank at Bergen-Belsen and worship at the altar of the auto in the Volkswagen theme park in nearby Wolfsburg. Delving deep into German folklore comes easy in Hameln, of Pied Piper fame, and in Bremen, whose "Town Musicians" were immortalised in the Brothers Grimm fairytale. Bremen is also home to the bizarre "lead-cellar" where you can gawp at grisly mummified bodies.

Coastal Delights

If you need to rid yourself of the stresses nibbling at your psyche, Germany's North Sea Coast may just be what the doctor ordered. Remote and tranquil, its sandy, dune-fringed beaches are tailor-made for long walks in the breeze. Flocks of sheep graze on green man-made dikes that protect the coast from the power of the sea.

The offshore Frisian Islands are hugely popular with holidaymakers, especially families, although the glamorous isle of Sylt is still the darling of the international jet-set. Watch in awe as the water retreats dramatically during low tide, exposing the bottom of the sea and inviting barefoot explorations of the mudflats, which are protected as a national park and as a UNESCO Natural Heritage Site. The windswept landscape dotted with Frisian thatched houses has also inspired many artists, including the Expressionist painter Emil Nolde and the poet Theodor Storm.

Sign on Rattenfängerhaus, Hamelin

© M. Berg/Fotolia.com

THE NORTHWEST

HAMBURG
Münster
Hameln
Hannover

0   30 km

★★★ Highly recommended
★★ Recommended
★ Interesting
Driving Tour showing point of departure

N

North Sea
East Frisian Islands — Borkum, Juist, Norderney, Baltrum, Langeoog, Spiekeroog, Wangerooge

Helgoland

North Frisian Islands — Sylt, List, Kampen, Westerland, Keitum, Dunsum, Amrum, Nebel, Wyk, Föhr, Langeneß, Oland, Hooge, Hallige, Pellworm, Süden, Nordstrand

Husum, Eider, Flensburg, Schleswig

Baltic Sea — Lolland, Langeland, Ærø

COPENHAGEN, ÅRHUS, ESBJERG, DENMARK

ROSTOCK, BERLIN

Wismar, Schweriner See, Schwerin, MECKLENBURG-VORPOMMERN, ELBE

LÜBECK, Kiel, SCHLESWIG-HOLSTEIN

HAMBURG, Altona, +Lüne, Lüneburg, Stade, Cuxhaven, Bremerhaven, Wilhelmshaven, Emden

A1, A14, A20, A24, A25, A250, A7, A23, A21, A210, A215, A27, A28, A29, A31, A210, A24, 104, 105, 207, 202, 76, 199, 5, 73, 74, Fehmarn

Hamburg★★★

Germany's second-largest city after Berlin, Hamburg is one of the most important ports in Europe. Its historic title of "Free and Hanseatic Town" and its status as a "city state" *(Stadtstaat)* testify to its eminence and influence through the centuries. Germany's publishing capital, renowned for its commercial dynamism and cosmopolitan atmosphere, is a city of contrasts. Not far from the lively – and sometimes rowdy – St. Pauli district, upscale residential areas such as Harvestehude and Blankenese serve as reminders that Hamburg is home to more millionaires than any other city in Germany. Take time to explore the city and you will soon fall under its spell.

A BIT OF HISTORY

The Hanseatic town (13C–15C) – Originally a modest settlement on the banks of the Alster, a small tributary of the Elbe, Hamburg enjoyed its first taste of prosperity when it became a member of the Hanseatic League, headed at that time by Lübeck. It was then that merchants started to build warehouses and docks along the banks of the Elbe.

Liberty and neutrality – The geographic discoveries of the 16C and the sea routes they opened up destroyed the Hanseatic monopoly, so Hamburg traders set their sights on warehousing and distribution. The foundation of the first German stock exchange *(Börse)* in 1558 reflected the intense business activity in Hamburg, a situation helped by the city's policy of strict neutrality, which kept it out of the Thirty Years' War. North- and Latin-American development helped greatly to expand the city. By 1913, the Hamburg-Amerika steamship line was the largest in the world and ship building became the city's key industry.

Business and leisure – Like many big ports, Hamburg has a reputation for

▶ **Population:** 1 777 000

ℹ **Info:** Hauptbahnhof, exit Kirchenallee. ℰ(040) 30 05 13 00. www.hamburg-tourismus.de.

◐ **Location:** Hamburg is at the confluence of the Bille and the Alster, on the estuary of the Elbe River, which flows into the North Sea about 100km/62mi to the northwest. The A1 autobahn links it to Bremen, the A7 to Hannover and the A24 to Berlin.

🅿 **Parking:** Garages are located throughout the city. Visit http://wap.park info.com for specific locations and fees.

👁 **Don't Miss:** Port, Speicherstadt, HafenCity, Hamburger Kunsthalle, Alster Lake.

🕐 **Timing:** Allow one day for exploring the city centre; half a day for a tour of the port (including a boat cruise); and half a day for the Altona Excursion.

👪 **Kids:** A cruise of Hamburg's port, Miniatur Wunderland; Tierpark Hagenbeck Zoo.

unbridled nightlife. The St. Pauli quarter, west of the city centre, sees the most action in side streets flanking the **Reeperbahn** and the Große Freiheit. Its bars, dance clubs, restaurants and erotic establishments go strong and lurid 24/7. But there is much more to Hamburg leisure pursuits than the Reeperbahn district. The Alster Lake lies like a sparkling jewel in the heart of the city. Between the Staatsoper (opera house) and the Rathaus (town hall), pedestrian precincts and covered shopping arcades form an almost uninterrupted labyrinth of galleries, boutiques and restaurants. The Mönckebergstraße, which links the Rathaus with the railway station,

Port of Hamburg

www.mediaserver.hamburg.de, C. Spahrbier

is another major commercial artery. Antique shops around the Gänsemarkt specialise in Asian art. Between the Rathaus and the station, an impressive variety of old maps, prints and travel works can be found in booksellers' shops, while philatelists and tobacco fiends frequent the small shops in the printing and counting-house quarter. The people of Hamburg are said to be very "British" Germans: they tend to be more reserved and serious than their lively southern compatriots. For visitors, Hamburg is among the most welcoming of German cities, and English is spoken in many of the restaurants, stores and wine cellars.

Culinary specialities – Local dishes often mix local produce with Asian spices, sometimes combining meat, fruit and sweet-and-sour sauces all in one dish. Typical are *Aalsuppe* – eel soup – and *Labskaus*, a seaman's dish of minced meat, herring, chopped gherkins, beetroot and mashed potato, topped with fried eggs.

SIGHTS
THE PORT★★
St. Pauli landing pier. ○*Open Sun–Mon, Wed 8am–6pm (Nov–Mar 10am–6pm), Tue, Thu–Sat 8am–7pm (Nov–Mar 10am–7pm).*
Exploring the port of Hamburg is one of the highlights of any trip to the city.

Apart from the tower of the St. Michaelis Kirche, the best **viewpoint**★ from which to see the port is the Stintfang – a raised terrace below the youth hostel *(U/S-Bahn St. Pauli Landungsbrücken).*

♣♣ Boat Trip Around the Port
Boats depart from the dock near the Baumwall U-Bahn station. Duration 1hr. Commentary. ⊜*10€.* ℘*(040) 37 31 68. www.barkassen-centrale.de.*
Visitors will be astonished by the sheer size of the dockyards and by the extraordinary activity in the shipyards on either side of the Elbe, where every type of vessel is constructed. Motorised ferries ply back and forth all day long, transporting south bank workers back to the city during the rush hour.

The Port of Hamburg

The Hamburg docks comprise 60 basins and more than 68km/42.3mi of quays. The overall surface area is more than 75sq km/29sq mi. Thanks to a relatively small tidefall (3m/9.8ft average), no locks are necessary in the basins accessible to ocean-going traffic able to navigate the Elbe. Some 320 shipping lines call regularly (about 650 departures a month) to transport goods to a thousand ports all over the world.

PRACTICAL INFORMATION

TELEPHONE PREFIX: ☎040
VISITOR INFORMATION: For general information or room and ticket reservations: *Tourismus-Zentrale Hamburg GmbH, ☎(040) 30 05 13 00, www.hamburg-tourism.de. Open Mon–Sat 9am–7pm.* **Information offices:** Main train station (Hauptbahnhof), Kirchenallee main exit, *Mon–Sat 9am–7pm, Sun 10am–6pm*; Harbour, St. Pauli Landungsbrücken between piers 4 and 5, *Sun–Wed 9am–6pm, Thu–Sat 9am–7pm*; Airport, at new Airport Plaza between terminals 1 and 2, *daily 6am–11pm*.

All branches distribute the free monthly cultural listings magazine *Vorschau…* (followed by the month), which can also be picked up in many hotels. Newsstands sell the magazines *Prinz* (bi-weekly) or *Szene Hamburg* (monthly).

Internet – www.hamburg.de; www. hamburg-web.de (in German); www. hamburg-information.de (in German).

Daily papers – *Hamburger Morgenpost, Hamburger Abendblatt*.

Post offices with late hours – The post office at Hachmannplatz at the main train station is open Mon–Fri 8am–8pm, Sat 8am–6pm and Sun 10am–4pm.

PUBLIC TRANSPORT

Hamburg is best explored using the buses and underground trains (U-Bahn) of the **HVV** (*Hamburger Verkehrsverbund; ☎194 49; www.hvv.de*). There are information offices at the Hauptbahnhof and in many U- and S-Bahn stations. Tickets are available from orange vending machines and bus drivers. Single tickets for rides in the city centre start at 1.30€. Day tickets valid after 9am cost 5.40€ for one person and 9.20€ for groups of up to five people

The one-day **Hamburg Card** costs 8.50€ and is valid for one adult and up to three children under 15; the group version (13.50€) is good for up to five people of any age on the issue date and after 6pm the day before. Three- and five-day versions are also available. Benefits include unlimited public transport, free or discounted museum admissions and discounts to sightseeing tours, restaurants and shops. The Hamburg Card is available at tourist offices, in many hotels, at vending machines, in the HVV customer offices and online at www.hamburg-tourism.de.

St. Pauli District

North of the port and west of the new town.

St. Pauli had its golden age in the 1960s when the Beatles played the Star Club and Kaiserkeller in **Große Freiheit**. Its image was later considerably tarnished by prostitution and drug trafficking, but over the last few years this district, which has the city's biggest police station (**Davidwache**), has undergone a renaissance. Although the sex industry is still in full swing, the area is also teeming with trendy bars, cafés and restaurants, many with a genuinely warm atmosphere and popular with locals and non-locals alike. St. Pauli spreads out around the **Reeperbahn**, the main thoroughfare, which runs parallel to the port.

🐾 WALKING TOURS

CITY CENTRE

This walk begins at the Jungfernstieg landing dock of the Inner Alster. It explores different aspects of the Alster lakes in the historic city centre and continues to the warehouse district (Speicherstadt), whose stately brick buildings harbour a clutch of interesting museums. Allow an entire day for this tour if you want to build in a boat trip and explore some of the museums.

👥 Binnenalster and Außenalster★★★ (Inner and Outer Alster Lakes)

Departures from the Jungfernstieg pier. Alster–Rundfahrt (50min): Apr–Sept daily 10am–6pm, half-hourly; Oct 10am,

*11am–4pm half-hourly, 5pm; Nov–Mar
10.30am, noon, 1.30pm & 3pm (Nov–
Dec also 4pm, 4.30pm, 5.30pm, 6pm).*
🎫*11€ (child 5.50€). Alster–Kreuz–Fahrt
(hop-on-hop-off at 9 stops): Apr–Oct,
daily 10.15am–5.15pm.* 🎫*1.50€ (child
0.75€) per dock or 9.50€ (child 4.75€)
round trip.* 🕾*(040) 357 42 40.
www.alstertouristik.de.*

The Alster Lake, north of the old town,
is a beautiful stretch of water. It consists
of two basins, the Binnenalster and the
Außenalster, the latter (the larger of
the two) offering sailing and canoeing.
A fleet of motorboats ferries passengers
regularly between nine landing docks.
It is also possible to sail on the Alster
canals (past beautifully kept parks and
villas interspersed with undeveloped
areas) and on the canals in the old town
and port (two locks allow access to the
port area from the Binnenalster).

Those with transportation can drive
clockwise around the Alster, bordered
by luxury apartments on one side and
immaculate parks on the other.

Jungfernstieg★

Bordering the southern end of the
Inner Alster, the Jungfernstieg is among
Hamburg's most cosmopolitan thoroughfares. The crowded terraces of the
waterfront Alsterpavillon café-restaurant, the boats crossing the basin, the
presence nearby of one of the world's
most famous hotels (Vier Jahreszeiten),
and the imposing new office blocks lining the Ballindamm all contribute to the
spirited ambience.

▷ *Leave Jungfernstieg and walk along
the Alsterfleet to the Town Hall.*

Rathausmarkt

Hamburg's majestic **town hall** (👁*visit
by guided tour (in English) only, year-
round, Mon–Fri 10.15am–3.15pm, Sat
10.15am–5.15pm, Sun 10.15am–4.15pm;*
🎫*3€;* ♿*;* 🕾*(040) 428 31 20 63) with its
112m/367ft-high clock-tower dominates
this central square. Rebuilt after the fire
of 1842 in neo-Renaissance style and
completed in 1887, it is a maze of 647
rooms and boasts a façade adorned

with statues of 20 German emperors.
The bridge *(Schleusenbrücke)*, which
forms part of the Alster's lock system,
crosses the Alsterfleet, a relic of the city's
former canal system. On the far bank the
colonnade of the Alsterarkaden shelters
elegant shops and cafés.

▷ *Turn into Mönckebergstraße.*

St. Petri Kirche
(Church of St. Peter)

Mönckebergstraße. 🕐*Open year-round,
Mon–Fri 10am–6.30pm, Sat 10am–5pm,
Sun 9am–8pm.* 🕾*(040) 325 74 00.
www.sankt-petri.de.*

This 12C church was rebuilt in neo-
Gothic style after the great fire of 1842.
The **lion's head door handles**★ (1342)
on the left west portal are regarded as
Hamburg's oldest surviving work of art.
The tower can be climbed (🕐*Mon–Sat
10am–5pm, Sun 11.30am–5pm).*

St. Jakobi-Kirche
(Church of St. Jacob)

Jacobikirchhof 22. 🕐*Open Apr–Oct,
Mon–Sat 10am–5pm, Sun 11.30am–
5pm (Nov–Mar from 11am).* 🕾*(040)
303 73 70. www.jacobus.de.*

Among the treasures of this 14C–15C
hall church are the **reredos**★ of St. Luke
and the Fishers' Guild; a triptych of the
Coopers' Guild on the high altar; Georg
Bauman's alabaster and marble pulpit
(1610); and the famous 1693 **organ by
Arp Schnitger**★.

▷ *Cross Steinstraße heading south
to Burchardplatz.*

Kontorhäuser
(Counting House Buildings)

These imposing brick buildings dominate the printing, press and business
quarter around Burchardplatz square.
Of particular interest is the **Chilehaus**
(between Burgstraße and Meßberg).
Designed by Expressionist architect
Fritz Höger, this 1924 building looms
against the sky like the prow of a ship.
It was built for a rich local merchant who
made his fortune mainly through trade
relations with Chile, hence the name.

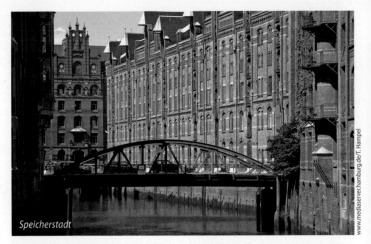

Speicherstadt

www.mediaserver.hamburg.de/T. Hampel

The **Sprinkenhof** (1931) is a town within the town, an office complex complete with roadways open to vehicles.

▶ *Continue southwards and cross the canal to explore Speicherstadt.*

Speicherstadt★ (Warehouse Quarter)

Guided tours from Baumwall U-Bahn station (exit Speicherstadt) Feb–Dec, Wed 3pm and Sun 2pm; www.speicherstadt-erleben.de)

After Hamburg joined the German Customs Federation in 1871, it became necessary to create a free trade zone. An entire district along the Zoll Canal and its side channels was flattened to make room for the Speicherstadt warehouses, set up between 1885 and 1927. Still the world's largest continuous warehouse complex, they store coffee, tobacco, spices, raw silk, oriental carpets and other goods. With its rows of gabled brick buildings topped with green copper roofs, Speicherstadt is an appealing quarter for a stroll or a **boat cruise**.

For a birds-eye view, catch a flight aboard the **High Flyer hot-air balloon** *(Deichtorstraße 1; ⏰ open year-round, daily 10am–10pm, weather permitting; 15min; every 15min; 15€; ✆(040) 30 08 69 68; www.highflyer-hamburg.de).*

Dialog im Dunkeln (Dialogue in the Dark)

Alter Wandrahm 4. Guided tours (90min) year-round Tue–Fri 9am–5pm, Sat 10am–8pm, Sun and holidays 11am–7pm. 15€, reservation required. ✆(0700) 44 33 20 00. www.dialog-im-dunkeln.de. English tours on request.

There is really nothing to look at in this unusual museum but there is certainly plenty to explore. Blind guides lead small groups of people through a world of total darkness. Scents, temperatures, winds and sounds create non-visual experiences, which are discovered by passing through various scenarios such as a park, a city centre or a bar. It is also possible to dine in the dark, but you must book well in advance.

The Fish Market

The Hamburg fish market originated in the early 18C and has become a veritable institution. It is held every Sunday morning in the south of the St. Pauli district along the Elbe from 5.30am–9.30am (from 7am Oct–Mar). The cheerful fishmongers, crowds of people of all ages who come to buy or browse and musical entertainment in the *Fischauktionshalle* have made it part of living Hamburg folklore.

Speicherstadt Museum

St. Annenufer 2. ◷Open Tue–Sun 10am –5pm (Apr–Oct Sat–Sun until 6pm). ☞3€. ✆(040) 32 11 91. www.speicherstadtmuseum.de.

In an old red-brick warehouse, this museum chronicles the history of the district and its businesses for more than a century. Measuring instruments and storage tools, bags of coffee and other goods, photos and maps illustrate the various stages of development.

▷ *Continue within the Speicherstadt via Zollcanal, where you will find two small museums, or cross the second bridge on your right to get back into the old town.*

Hamburg Dungeon

Kehrwieder 2. ◷Open Jul–Aug, daily 10am–7pm; Mar–Jun and Sept–Dec 10am–6pm; Jan–Feb 11am–6pm. ◷Closed Dec 24. ☞18.95€. ♿. Not suitable for children under 10. Advance reservation recommended to avoid the ticket queue. ✆(040) 36 00 55 00. www.hamburgdungeon.com.

Allow at least 90 minutes for this indoor horror theme park where you encounter graphic scenes related to the history of Hamburg such as the great fire of 1842, the blood-thirsty Thirty Years' War and the execution of the 14C pirate Störtebeker. The visit concludes with a free-fall (Drop Ride) and a boat ride illustrating the deadly flood of 1717.

⚇ Miniatur Wunderland★

Kehrwieder 2–4. ◷Open Mon, Wed– Fri 9.30am–6pm, Tue 9.30am–9pm, Sat 8am–9pm, Sun 8.30am–8pm. ◷Closed Dec 24. ☞10€. ♿. Reservation recommended to avoid the queue. ✆(040) 300 6 800. www.miniatur-wunderland.de.

At over 4000sq m/43 055sq ft, this is one of the world's largest model railways. Some 700 trains travel through miniature versions of Hamburg, the Alps, the USA, Scandinavia, Switzerland, the Harz Mountains and a town called Knuffingen. Visits include a stop in the control room where you can watch staff put in motion this ballet of miniatures. Additional sets (France, Italy) will be added in the coming years.

Altstadt (Old Town)

Hamburg's old town is bounded by the Nikolaifleet, the Binnenhafen (docks reserved for river craft and tugboats) and the Zoll Canal.

Highlights of the old town include the **St. Katharinen Kirche**, a 14C–15C Gothic brick church featuring a bulbous openwork tower. It was on **Deichstraße** that the great fire of 1842 erupted.

Many of the 17C–18C merchants' houses have today been converted into bars and taverns. The restored façades of warehouses opposite, lining the curve of the Nikolaifleet canal, recall the Hamburg of yesteryear.

The best view is from the **Hohe Brücke**, which crosses the Nikolaifleet and parallels the Binnenhafen.

▷ *Cross the bridge, turn right on Admiralitätstraße, then left on Martin-Luther-Straße.*

St. Michaelis Kirche★ (Church of St. Michael)

◷Open May–Oct, daily 9am–7.30pm, Nov–Apr 10am–5.30pm. ☞3.50€ tower, 3€ crypt and HamburgHiStory, all three 5€. ✆(040) 37 67 81 00. www.st-michaelis.de.

Designed in 1762 by Ernst Georg Sonnin, this church is one of the finest examples of the Baroque tradition in northern Germany. Its landmark tower (1786) rises high above the Elbe and offers sweeping **views**★ from the platform at 132m/433ft.

Another level features **HamburgHiStory** *(every 30min, 12.30pm–3.30pm)*, a multimedia show explaining high and low points of the city's past 1 000 years.

Near the east end of the church, a blind alley off Am Krayenkamp 10 is lined with 17C brick and timber houses, built as **almshouses** *(Krameramtswohnungen)*; today they are mostly art galleries.

WHERE TO STAY

HAFENCITY

*HafenCity Information Centre,
Kesselhaus, Sandtorkai 30. ◐Open year
-round, Tue–Sun 10am–6pm (May–Sept,
Thu 10am–8pm). ℘(040) 36 90 17 99.
www.hafencity.com.*

Just beyond the Speicherstadt, Europe's
largest urban construction project is
taking shape on 155ha/383 acres: HafenCity. A 20-year project, the city-centre
extension will include a mix of shops,
offices, leisure and cultural facilities and
residences.

A few thousand people have already
moved into the completed western
section (Am Sandtorkai/Dalmannkai),
which has become a popular area for
strolling. To help you visualise this
enormous project, visit the HafenCity
Information Centre. For an overview of
the vast construction site, visit the bright
orange **viewpoint** tower.

Pavillon Elbphilharmonie

*Viewing point at Magellan Terraces (bet-
ween Am Kaiserkai and Am Sandtorkai).
◐Open daily 9am–8pm (Nov–Mar to
6pm). ☞Free guided tours (90min) of
the pavilion and the Elbphilharmonie
site 11am, 1pm and 3pm. Register 30
minutes prior on the ground floor of
the pavilion.*

The shining beacon west of the Hafen-
City will be the Elbphilharmonie (Elbe
Philharmonic Hall), designed by the
Swiss firm of Herzog & de Meuron. Set
to be completed in 2011, the impressive
concert hall combines the classical brick
architecture of the historic warehouses
with a boldly modernist sweep of glass
façades and a wavelike roof line.

The pavilion illustrates this mammoth
project using digital animations. On
the ground floor, you can enter a scale
model of the main concert hall (◐open
Apr–Oct, Tue–Sun 10am–5pm; Nov–Mar
Thu–Sun 10am–5pm).

Internationales Maritimes Museum (International Maritime Museum)

*Koreastraße 1 (formerly Magdeburger
Straße). ◐Open Tue–Sun 10am–6pm
(Thu 8pm). ∞10€. ♿ ℘(040) 30 09*

Internationales Maritimes Museum

www.mediaserver.hamburg.de/C. Spahrbier GmbH

*23 00. www.internationales-maritimes-
museum.de.*

Ensconced in Hamburg's oldest warehouse (from 1879 and classified as a
historical monument), this is one of
the newest museums to open near
the Speicherstadt and HafenCity. Its 10
"bridges" explore the close relationship
between man and the sea through the
ages and civilisations. Standouts among
the many exhibits include the nearly
7m/23ft-long Lego model of the *Queen
Mary 2*, a reconstructed "France" ocean
liner passenger cabin, a scale model of
a boat from Lake Titicaca, the "Nautilus"
cup and a model of the commercial port
of Bremerhaven.

ADDITIONAL SIGHTS
Beatlemania

*Nobistor 10. ◐Open daily 10am–7pm.
∞12€. ♿ ℘(01805) 85 37 53.
www.beatlemania-hamburg.com.*

This "shrine" to the four boys from Liv-
erpool charts their odyssey from their
humble Hamburg debut to international
stardom. The engaging exhibit features
family interviews, photographs, posters,
original documents, videos, recreations
of scenes and even a room dedicated to
Beatles fans. You can record a song in
the Abbey Road studio, visit the famous
"Yellow Submarine" and join the cast of

characters of Sergeant Pepper's Lonely Hearts Club Band.

Hamburger Kunsthalle★★ (Fine Arts Museum)

Glockengiesserwall. ○*Open year-round, Tue–Sun 10am–6pm (Thu 9pm).* ○*Closed Dec 24.* ∞*10€.* ♿ *(040) 428 13 12 00. www.hamburger-kunsthalle.de.*

Consisting of three buildings, the Kunsthalle is one of Germany's largest art museums. Among Dutch 17C masters is an early work by Rembrandt *(Simeon in the Temple)*, land- and seascapes by Avercamp, Van Goyen, Ruisdael, Van de Velde, and genre paintings by Jan Steen and Pieter de Hooch.

The museum is especially proud of its collection of 19C German painting. Look for works by Caspar David Friedrich *(The Sea of Ice, The Wanderer above the Sea of Fog)*, Philipp Otto Runge, Anselm Feuerbach and Arnold Böcklin. There is also an entire room devoted to Adolph Menzel as well as a key work by Wilhelm Leibl *(Three Women at the Church)*. Also look for a dazzling range of works by Max Liebermann, Lovis Corinth and Edvard Munch as well as ground-breaking canvases by Max Beckmann, Oskar Kokoschka, Paul Klee and other members of the early 20C *Brücke* and *Blaue Reiter* artist groups.

The **Galerie der Gegenwart** is devoted to post-1960 art. Look for works by Richard Serra, Claes Oldenburg, Jenny Holzer, Bruce Naumann and Andy Warhol. German art is also well represented by artists like Sigmar Polke, Georg Baselitz, Markus Lüpertz, Mario Merz, Gerhard Richter, Rosemarie Trockel and Joseph Beuys.

Museum für Kunst und Gewerbe★ (Museum of Decorative Arts)

Steintorplatz 1, opposite the train station. ○*Open year-round, Tue, Fri–Sun 10am–6pm, Wed–Thu 10am–9pm.* ○*Closed Jan, May 1, Dec 24 & 31.* ∞*8€.* ♿ *(040) 428 134 27 32. www.mkg-hamburg.de.*

In a 19C neo-Renaissance palace, this vast museum houses collections of sculptures, ceramics, furniture, jewellery and musical instruments from antiquity to the present. The Jugendstil gallery is a knock-out.

Museum für Hamburgische Geschichte★ (Museum of Hamburg History)

Holstenwall 24. ○*Open year-round, Tue–Sat 10am–5pm, Sun 6pm.* ○*Closed Jan 1, May 1, Dec 24 & 31.* ∞*7.50€.* ♿. *(040) 428 132 23 80. www.hamburgmuseum.de.*

Hamburg's fascinating history gets the full treatment at this engaging museum through city models and numerous themed sections (emigration, Jewish Hamburg, the Hanseatic period, etc.).

♟ Tierpark Hagenbeck★★ (Hagenbeck Zoo)

Via Grindelallee. ○*Open Mar–Jun and Sept–Oct, daily 9am–6pm; Jul–Aug 7pm; Nov–Mar 4.30pm.* ∞*16€.* ♿. *(040) 530 03 30. www.hagenbeck.de.*

This delightful animal park (1907) boasts ancient trees, artificial lakes and some 2 500 creatures representing 360 species from five continents. Next door, the vast **Tropen-Aquarium** *(tropical aquarium;* ○*open 9am–6pm;* ∞*13€, combination with Tierpark 25€)* takes visitors on an undersea encounter with 14 000 creatures.

BallinStadt Emigration Museum★★

Veddeler Bogen 2. ○*Open Apr–Sept 10am–6pm, Oct–Mar 10am–4.30pm.* ∞*12€.* *(040) 31 97 91 60. www.ballinstadt.de.* *You can visit by train, car, or boat (which includes a trip around Hamburg Harbour). See the website for details.*

On the Elbe island of Veddel, BallinStadt was the embarkation centre for 5 million Europeans headed for America between 1850 and 1938. Multi-media exhibits in three recreated structures vividly portray all phases of emigration – from packing to settling – and bring to life people's hopes and hardships, dreams and realities. You can even trace your own roots in the Family Research Centre.

EXCURSIONS

Altona

▶ *3.2km/2mi southwest.*

**Altonaer Museum★★
(Altona Cultural History Museum)**

Museumstraße 23. ◷*Open year-round, Tue–Sun 10am–5pm.* ◷*Closed Jan 1, May 1, Dec 24 & 31.* ⬠*6€.* ♿. ℘*(040) 428 135 82. www.altonaer-museum.de.* Art, culture and day-to-day life in the lower Elbe valley and Schleswig-Holstein are illustrated here. Exceptional displays are 18C–19C ships' figureheads, models of North Sea boats, ceramics, fine Frisian embroidery, old toys and north German landscape paintings.

Altonaer Balkon (Altona Balcony)

The terrace south of Altona's Town Hall affords a **view**★ of the Köhlbrandbrücke and confluence of the two branches of the Elbe. Follow the **Elbchaussee★**, a spacious avenue bordered by fabulous mansions since the early 19C.

Stade★

▶ *60km/37mi west.*

In the Middle Ages, 1 000-year-old Stade boasted a port the size of Hamburg's. Most buildings in the beautiful **old town**★★ were built after the great fire of 1659. Note especially: Hökerhaus *(Hökerstraße 27)*, Doppelhaus *(Bäckerstraße 1–3)*, Haus Knechthausen *(Bungenstraße 20)* and **Bürgermeister-Hintze-Haus** *(Wasser West)*.

The **Schwedenspeicher Museum★** *(Wasser West 43;* ◷*open year-round, Tue–Fri 10am–5pm, Sat–Sun 10am–6pm;* ⬠*3€;* ℘*(041 41) 32 22; www.schwedenspeicher.de)* in a late 17C brick granary now houses local history exhibits, including prehistoric **bronze wheels★** (c. 700 BC), antique jewellery, weapons and pots.

ADDRESSES

🏠 STAY

🛏 Pension Am Rathaus –
Rathausstraße 14. ℘*(040) 33 74 89. www.pension-am-rathaus.de. 15 rooms.* This small guest house has just a few simple and clean rooms. The cheaper ones must share a bathroom in the hallway.

🛏 Hotel Schwanenwik –
Schwanenwik 29. ℘*(040) 220 09 18. www.hotel-schwanenwik.de. 18 rooms.* This charming boarding house (completely non-smoking) occupies a magnificent 18C white townhouse on the Alster. The simple, modern rooms face the lake or the back garden.

🛏 My Place – *Lippmanstraße 5.* ℘*(040) 28 57 18 74. www.myplace-hamburg.de. 14 rooms.* ⬡*10€.* This pint-sized hotel has lovely, individually decorated rooms named for Hamburg city quarters as well as a few apartments.

🛏 Michaelis Hof – *Herrengraben 4, in the Catholic Academy.* ℘*(040) 35 90 69 12. www.michaelishof-hamburg.de. 22 rooms.* ⬡*10€ at Baseler Hof.*

There are a few well-kept and quiet rooms for rent on the 4th floor of the Catholic Academy. Check-in 7am to 11am.

🛏🛏 Fritz Hotel – *Schanzenstraße 101–103.* ℘*(040) 82 22 28 30. www.fritzhotel.de. 17 rooms.* This small hotel is ideally located in the heart of the bustling Schanzenviertel neighbourhood and within stumbling distance of cafés, restaurants, bars and designer boutiques.

🛏🛏 Commodore Hotel – *Budapester Straße 20.* ℘*(040) 31 99 96 03. www.hotel-commodore.de. 107 rooms.* ⬡. This hotel near St. Pauli station provides classic rooms and warm hospitality.

🛏🛏 Hotel Imperial – *Millerntorplatz 3–5.* ℘*(040) 31 17 20. www.hotel-imperial-hamburg.de. 50 rooms.* ⬡. In the heart of St. Pauli, this hotel offers functional rooms with double-glazed windows, although the noise-sensitive should still request one facing away from the Reeperbahn. Comfortable lounge.

Hotel St. Annen – *Annenstraße 5.* (040) 31 77 130. www.hotelstannen.de. *36 rooms.* Close to St. Pauli and the Reeperbahn, this hotel enjoys a quiet location on a leafy square. Rooms are small but comfortable and service is friendly. In summer, days start with breakfast on a beautiful garden terrace. Great value for money.

Aussen Alster Hotel – *Schmilinskystraße 11–15.* (040) 24 15 57. www.aussenalster.eu. *27 rooms.* In a beautiful garden property, this hotel is just 50m/164ft from the Aussenalster. Guest services include a solarium and free bicycle and rowing-boat rentals.

Hotel Hafen Hamburg – *Seewartenstraße 9.* (040) 31 11 30. www.hotel-hafen-hamburg. de. *353 rooms.* Overlooking the Landungsbrücken pier, this hotel offers comfortable rooms, some with stunning views over the harbour. The restaurant too has panoramic windows and a spacious terrace.

Europäischer Hof – *Kirchenallee 45.* (040) 24 82 48. www.europaeischer-hof.de. *353 rooms.* Especially convenient because of its location opposite the train station, this hotel has a wellness centre that spans over four levels and includes a pool and even an indoor slide.

EAST – *Simon-von-Utrecht-Straße 31.* (040) 30 99 32 04. www. east-hamburg.de. *128 rooms.* Just off the Reeperbahn, this beautiful boutique hotel was converted from a former foundry. Every detail speaks of refinement and fits harmoniously into the overall design. Gorgeous dining room, plus several cocktail lounges.

SIDE – *Drehbahn 49.* (040) 30 99 90. www.side-hamburg. de. *178 rooms.* Located in a business district, everything is carefully calibrated for maximum comfort at Side. An atrium with choreographed lighting effects gives way to clean, stylish rooms. Beautiful design, a chic bar and a beautiful terrace overlooking the city.

Hotel Vier Jahreszeiten – *Neuer Jungfernstieg 9.* (040) 349 40. www.hvj.de. *157 rooms.* 25€. *Restaurant* . Unpretentious luxury

characterises this lakeside grand hotel with luxurious Gründerzeit décor and charming, modern and supremely comfortable rooms. Upscale cuisine is served in three separate restaurants.

EAT

Bok Restaurant – *Schulterblatt 2.* (040) 431 900 70. www.bokrestaurant. de. This small local chain offers Thai and Japanese dishes in a lively atmosphere and at reasonable prices. Food service until 11.30pm.

Trattoria Remo's – *Hein-Hoyer Straße 75.* (040) 31 29 03. www.trattoria-remos.de. Thumbs up for this friendly trattoria where you can enjoy a varied menu of delicious authentic Italian fare served in a warm, vaulted room.

Das Feuerschiff – *City Sporthafen Vorsetzen, station Baumwall.* (040) 36 25 53. www.das-feuerschiff.de. For something unusual, book a table on the deck of this bright-red lightship, which used to double as a helicopter landing pad. Views of the harbour and the Elbphilharmonie concert hall are truly breathtaking. The onsite bar is a great spot for sunset drinks and has live jazz and blues on Sundays and Mondays.

Rialto – *Michaelisbrücke 3.* (040) 36 43 42. www.rialto-hamburg.de. This elegant dining room overlooks the canal from the Alster port. On sunny days, tables spill out onto the deck and there is live music some nights. If Rialto is full, try one of the other terrace restaurants surrounding the square.

Atlas – *Schützenstraße 9a.* (040) 851 78 10. www.atlas.at. Closed Sat lunch. A former fish smokehouse has been re-cast as an upbeat bistro/restaurant/cocktail bar with an ivy-covered terrace. It is somewhat hidden away in Phönixhof.

Café Paris – *Rathausstraße 4.* (040) 32 52 77 77. www.cafeparis.net. This classic brasserie feels so fantastically French, you half expect to see the Eiffel Tower through the window. Mirrors and framed prints line the walls, the servers wear crisp white shirts and the menu features *salad Niçoise* and *Côte de boeuf. Très* Gallic, *très* charming.

Gröninger Haus – *Ost-West-Straße 47. ☏(040) 33 13 83. www.groeninger-hamburg.de. Closed Sat lunchtime and Sun. Reservation recommended.* This private brewery inside the city's oldest hotel (first documented in 1260) is a lovely spot for winding down the day. Meals are hearty and come in belt-loosening portions. Wash them down with the in-house brew.

Warsteiner Elbspeicher – *Große Elbstraße 39. ☏(040) 38 22 42. www.warsteiner-elbspeicher.de.* Ingeniously converted from an old riverside warehouse, this friendly bi-level establishment is divided into a casual downstairs bistro and a rustic restaurant upstairs where meals come with splendid harbour views. Overall, a fine place for fresh fish and typical Hanseatic dishes.

Restaurant Eisenstein – *Friedensallee 9. ☏(040) 390 46 06. www.restaurant-eisenstein.de.* In a converted warehouse in Altona, this restaurant attracts a trendy clientele. In the same building are an art-house cinema, a café and a nice tapas bar (flamenco some nights).

VLET – *Am Sandtorkai 23/24. ☏(040) 334 75 37 50. www.vlet.de.* This brick warehouse in the Speicherstadt has been nicely renovated and provides a suitable setting for expertly prepared regional cuisine. To get there, cross Kibbelstegbrücke bridge.

Old Commercial Room – *Englische Planke 10. ☏(040) 36 63 19. www.oldcommercialroom.de. Reservation recommended.* A Hamburg institution since 1795, the Old Commercial Room was founded by an English shipowner, which might explain the pub décor with mahogany, copper and maritime pictures. Traditional sailors' dishes dominate the menu (*Labskaus*), which also features lobster, sole and pork knuckle.

Louis C. Jacob – *Elbchaussee 401, Hamburg-Nienstedten. ☏(040) 82 25 50. www.hotel-jacob.de. Reservation recommended.* Fine dining does not get much more refined than at this elegant hotel-restaurant overlooking the Elbe. The delicious French cuisine is a delight. In fine weather, the most coveted tables are on the terrace with its lime trees; the scene was immortalised in a painting by Max Liebermann in 1902.

Le Canard Nouveau – *Elbchaussee 139, Hamburg-Altona. ☏(040) 880 50 57. www.lecanard-hamburg.de. Closed Sun. Reservation required.* New culinary heights are reached in this French restaurant in an elegant white building overlooking the Elbe. Sit in the modern and bright dining room or grab a seat on the plank terrace for sweeping views of the port's container terminal. Gourmets on a budget should come for the affordable lunches.

TAKING A BREAK

Destille – *Steintorplatz 1 (enter from Brockesstraße). ☏(040) 280 33 54. Open 11am-5pm, closed Mon, Dec 24–Jan 1. Free admission if visiting the museum, otherwise 1€.* On the first floor of the Museum of Arts and Crafts, this little self-service café is an excellent lunch stop, and not only for museum goers. Restful views of the leafy courtyard are gratis.

NIGHTLIFE
USEFUL TIPS
Hamburg's nightlife has been synonymous with St. Pauli since time immemorial. In addition to its established temples of eroticism, the area around the Reeperbahn and Große Freiheit has become a rather trendy spot of late with more than 400 restaurants squeezing into these quarters. The inner centre, too, between the Gänsemarkt and Millerntor (especially around Großneumarkt) offers plenty of opportunities to eat and drink. The young and alternative crowd congregates in the Schanzenviertel, especially around Susannenstraße and Schulterblatt, and in the Altona district around Spritzenplatz.

Alex im Alsterpavillon – *Jungfernstieg 54. ☏(040) 35 01 87 15. www.alexgastro.de.* People of all ages gather throughout the day for a drink or a light meal on this great waterfront terrace.

Amphore – *Hafenstraße 140 (follows the Elbe towards the west from Landungsbrücken).* ℰ*(040) 31 79 38 80. www.cafe-amphore.de.* Friendly little café with a lovely harbour view from the terrace above old blockhouses. Breakfast served until 3pm.

Christiansen's Fine Drinks & Cocktails – *Pinnasberg 60 (in St. Pauli, near the Fischmarkt).* ℰ*(040) 317 28 63. www.christiansens.de. Closed Sun.* Dedicated drinkers flock to this bar with 250 cocktails, 160 brands of rum and 150 varieties of whisky on offer.

Cotton Club – *Alter Steinweg 10.* ℰ*(040) 34 38 78. www.cotton-club.org.* Hamburg's jazz institution was founded 1959, renamed the "Cotton Club" in 1963 and moved to this location in 1971. Performances during most nights.

Grosse Freiheit 36 & Kaiserkeller – *Grosse Freiheit 36.* ℰ*(040) 31 77 78 11. www.grossefreiheit36.de.* The Beatles rocked the Kaiserkeller back in 1960 and this venue is still going strong.

Laeiszhalle – *Johannes-Brahms-Platz 1.* ℰ*(040) 34 69 20. www.elbphilharmonie.de.* Until the Elbphilharmonie in HafenCity opens (set for 2011), the neo-Baroque Laeiszhalle (1908) is Hamburg's premier classical music venue.

Staatsoper Hamburg – *Grosse Theaterstraße 25.* ℰ*(040) 35 68 68. www.hamburgische-staatsoper.de.* One of the world's most renowned opera houses.

🛍 SHOPPING

USEFUL TIPS

Department stores and mainstream chain stores line Mönckebergstraße and Spitalerstraße west of the main train station. Deeper pockets are required in the 9 exclusive shopping arcades around Jungfernstieg and Neuer Wall, which are the haunts of international designer boutiques and specialist shops. Steer toward the suburb of Eppendorf (Klosterstern to Eppendorfer Markt) to browse through independent boutiques selling trendy fashions, home accessories and gift items.

Harry's Hamburger Hafenbasar – *Balduinstraße 18 (corner of Erichstraße, in St. Pauli).* ℰ*(040) 31 24 82. www.hafenbasar.de. Open Tue–Sun noon–6pm. Admission 2.50€ (refunded with purchase).* A jumble of objects brought back by sailors from the four corners of the world, labyrinthine Harry's has been around for half a century and is really more a museum than a shop. Great for browsing for unique gifts.

Antique dealers – Mainly in the *Quartier Satin* on ABC-Straße and the *Antik-Centre* of the covered arcade at Klosterwall 9–21; the latter has more than 60 stalls selling the best of yesteryear's collectibles.

Flea markets – The best regular flea markets is the Flohschanze Markt in an old slaughterhouse in St. Pauli (every Sat 8am–4pm).

Markets – Hamburg's most famous market, the Fish Market (*www.fischmarkt-hamburg.de*) draws crowds early on Sunday (summer 5.30am–9.30am, winter 7am–10am). A particularly nice farmers' market is held on Monday and Friday around the Eppendorf U-Bahn bridge.

SIGHTSEEING

CITY TOURS

All tours described below depart from the Hauptbahnhof/Kirchenallee exit.

Hop-on-hop-off tours (15€) stopping at eight major landmarks, including St. Michaelskirche and St. Pauli Landungsbrücken, operate Apr–Oct, daily every 30min, 9.30am–5pm; Nov–Mar, Fri–Sun half-hourly 10am–4pm, Mon–Thu hourly 10am–4pm. Narrated 2hr 30min city tours depart daily at 10.10am and 2.10pm (20€). Details from **Top Tour Hamburg** (ℰ*(040) 641 37 31; www.top-tour-hamburg.de*) or **Hamburger Stadtrundfahrt** (ℰ*(040) 792 89 79; www.hummelbahn.de*).

The Hamburg tourist office organises a variety of themed **walking tours** Apr–Oct, for instance of the red light district or in the footsteps of the Beatles. See website for dates and times.

Lüneburg★★

Lüneburg was quite literally built on salt, a coveted mineral and source of its prosperity since the 10C. The last salt mine closed in 1980, ending a 1 000-year tradition. Lüneburg was spared during World War II and today is a colourful university town and gateway to the Lüneburg Heath.

SIGHTS
Historisches Rathaus★★ (Historic Town Hall)
Am Markt 1. ☞*Guided tours (1hr, in German) year-round, Tue–Sat 10am, 2pm, 3.30pm Sun 11am and 2pm.* ⏰*Closed Jan 1, Dec 24–26 & 31.* ☜*4.50€.* ☏*(0800) 220 50 05.*
Consisting of a cluster of eight buildings, Lüneburg's municipal headquarters is the largest surviving medieval town hall in northern Germany.
The **Great Council Chamber**★★ (*Große Ratsstube*), to the right of the entrance hall, is a Renaissance masterpiece (1566–84). Panelled throughout, it is adorned with intricate wood sculptures carved by Albert von Soest.
The **Fürstensaal** (*Princes' Apartment*) is equally striking. Gothic in style, it has lamps fashioned from stags' antlers and a superbly beamed and painted ceiling.

Marktplatz (Market Square)
Aside from the town hall, other noteworthy buildings framing the market square include the Court of Justice, the former Ducal Palace and the **Heinrich-Heine-Haus**, where the parents of the famous 19C poet lived on the second floor.

Altstadt★ (Old Town)
The houses of the old town are characterised by traditional red-brick architecture and boast steeply stepped gables prevalent throughout northern Germany. The nicest ones line a long, narrow square known as **Am Sande**★. Note especially no 1, the 16C **Shwarze Haus** (black house), which was once a brewery and now houses an international chamber of commerce.

▶ **Population:** 71 000
ℹ **Info:** Am Markt, 21335 Lüneburg. ☏(04131) 207 66 20. www.lueneburg.de.
▶ **Location:** Lüneburg is about 56.5km/35mi southeast of Hamburg, east of the A7 autobahn (Hannover–Hamburg). Coming from Hamburg, though, the quickest route is via the A255 and A250. The Ilmenau river, a tributary of the Elbe, flows through town.
🅿 **Parking:** Garages are located near the main train station and the Rathaus on Graalwall.
⌾ **Don't Miss:** The Rathaus and the rest of the old town.
🕐 **Timing:** Exploring Lüneburg's charms takes about half a day.

At Große Bäckerstraße 10 you'll find the 1598 **Rathsapotheke** (pharmacy), with its fine twisted brick gables.
The Reitende-Diener-Straße is another attractive lane with a double row of identical low houses, each embellished with medallions and curled brick cornices.

St. Johanniskirche (Church of St. John)
⏰*Open Mar–Dec, Mon–Wed 10am–5pm, Thu 5pm, Fri 8pm, Sat 6pm, Sun 4pm.* ⏰*Closed Jan–mid-Mar, Mon–Thu.* ☏*(04131) 445 42.* *www.st-johanniskirche.de.*
Am Sande culminates in this hulking 15C church, easily recognised by its leaning steeple. Inside all eyes are on the high altar with precious sculpted reredos by Heinrich Furnhoff. Its painted panels depict scenes from the lives of St. John the Baptist, St. Cecilia, St. Ursula and St. George (late 15C).

Nikolaikirche (Church of St. Nicholas)

Lüner Straße 15. ◐*Open Jan–Mar, daily 10am–5pm; Apr–Dec, 9am–5pm.* ℘*(04131) 243 0770.*

The central nave of this triple-aisled 15C Gothic church soars an impressive 30/90ft high and ends in an intricate star-vaulted ceiling. Have a closer look at the gilded high altar by Hans Bornemann, which depicts 20 carved scenes from the life of Jesus. There is also a bronze baptismal font dating back to 1325. The jaunty church steeple was not added until the 19C.

Wasserviertel★ (Old Port Quarter)

Enjoy a particularly fine view of this district from the bridge across the Ilmenau. On the left you will spot the *Alter Kran*, a crane dating from the 14C and in use until the 19C. Looking upstream, there is a good view of the Lüner Mühle, a grand 16C half-timbered mill.

Deutsches Salzmuseum (German Salt Museum)

◐*Open May–Sept, Mon–Fri 9am–5pm, Sun 10am–5pm; Oct–Apr, daily 10am–5pm.* ◉*6€.* ℘*(04131) 450 65.* *www.salzmuseum.de.*

Salt has shaped the history of Lüneburg for thousands of years. In the Middle Ages, it supplied a large part of Scandinavia with the precious mineral. Shipments followed the old Salt Road, via Lauenburg, Ratzeburg and Lübeck. Lüneburg's Salt Museum occupies the city's historic salt production plant and was the first in Germany to be installed in a converted industrial site. It traces the history of salt mining in the region and touches on aspects such as extraction technology, the economic importance of salt and the various salt routes.

EXCURSIONS
Kloster Lüne (Lüne Abbey)

◗ *2km/1.2mi northeast via Willy-Brandt-Straße. Am Domänenhof.*
◗◗*Abbey visits by guided tour only (1hr), Apr–mid-Oct, Tue–Sun 10.30am (Sun 11.30am), 2.30pm and 3.30pm.*

◐*Closed Good Fri.* ◉*5€ (8€ with museum).* ℘*(04131) 523 18.* *www.kloster-luene.de.*

Founded in the 12C as a Benedictine convent, the complex welcomes you with a murmuring fountain surrounded by Gothic buildings on three sides and a late-Baroque guesthouse on the fourth. Particularly fine features include the stained glass windows from the 14C–17C, the frescoed refectory and the muralled nuns' cells. The church boasts a Baroque organ, a Gothic baptismal font and the nuns' choir with a *Lamentation* from the workshop of Lucas Cranach the Elder. There is also an interesting little **tapestry museum**★ (◐*open Apr–mid-Oct, Tue–Sun 10.30am–12.30pm, 2.30pm–5pm;* ◉*4€*) with Gothic tapestries and finely worked embroidery.

Bergen-Belsen Memorial Site

◗ *72km/48mi southwest of Lüneburg. Anne-Frank-Platz, 29303 Lohheide.*
◐*Open Apr–Sept, daily 10am–6pm; Oct–Mar, 10am–5pm.* ◐*Closed Jan 1, Dec 24–26 & 31.* ℘*(05051) 475 92 00.* *www.bergenbelsen.de.*

The **memorial** *(Gedenkstätte)* to the victims of Bergen-Belsen concentration camp was erected in 1946. A recently revamped and award-winning exhibit in a building near the entrance chronicles the history of the camp. Bergen-Belsen started out in 1939 as a POW camp but was turned into a concentration camp in 1943. Among those incarcerated here was **Anne Frank** whose famous diary is a heart-wrenching personal account of the horrors of the Nazi period. Along with her sister, she died at the camp in 1945 at the age of 15. There is a tombstone erected in their honour.

A **monument** *(◗◗45min from the car park)* is beyond the tumulus marking the site of the mass graves. It is a simple obelisk with inscriptions in 13 languages honouring the memory of the murdered. From 1945–50, the Allies used the camp to provide shelter and assistance to "displaced persons" (former concentration camp prisoners and slave labourers who had been deported to Germany from all over Europe).

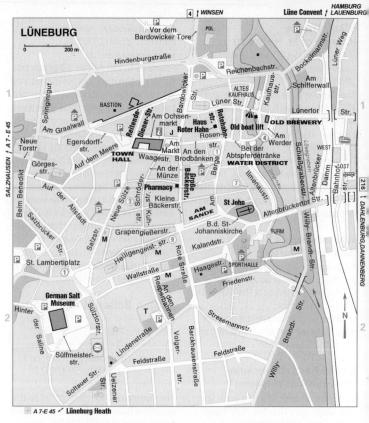

LÜNEBURG

0 200 m

WHERE TO STAY

Bargenturm.....................................①
Bergström.......................................④

WHERE TO EAT

Café Mäxx......................................③
Lanzelot...⑦
Mälzer..⑨
Zum Heidkrug.................................①

Another section of the exhibition details what happened to the Nazi officers and guards who ran the camp. Arrested by the British Army immediately after its liberation, they were tried before a British military tribunal in Lüneburg in late 1945. Eleven defendants were sentenced to death and 19 received prison sentences.

Kloster Ebstorf (Ebstorf Abbey)

◉ 26km/16mi south of Lüneburg.
 Visit by guided tour (90min) only, Apr–mid-Oct, Tue–Sat 10am–11am, 2pm–5pm, Sun 11.15am, 2pm–5pm;

mid-Oct–end Oct, Tue–Sun 2pm.
Closed Nov–Mar and holidays.
4€. (05822) 23 04.

Do not miss the former Benedictine abbey in the village of Ebstorf, where impressive features include the 14C and 15C cloister and the nuns' gallery with its life-size wooden statue of St. Maurice (1300) and several Virgins from the Romanesque and Gothic periods. A unique exhibit is the replica of the **Ebstorfer Weltkarte**★, a circular medieval map of the world with a diametre of 3.57m/11ft. The original was destroyed in 1943.

The Heath

In the Middle Ages, the name "Heide" signified the boundary of a village; only later did it come to mean the common heather (Calluna vulgaris), which carpets the ground in August and September. The bell-heather (Erica tetralix) blooms in July, if rarely, preferring marshy areas.

The heath is actually a man-made shrubland. 5 000 years ago Lüneburg Heath was covered in forest which was eventually uprooted by farmers. To keep the forest at bay, farmers utilised controlled burning, grazed cattle and sheep or lifted the turf with hoes. Only then was the light-hungry heath able to spread.

Moorland sheep

© WoodyStock/Alamy

Flora and Fauna – Juniper (Juniperus communis) thrives on the Lüneburg Heath, as well as birch, mountain ash, pine and oak, gorse, broom, silver grass, crowberries, bilberries and cranberries.

Moorland sheep serve as living mowers. They maintain the heather at a height of 20cm/7.8in. Both genders have horns; those of the male are spectacularly coiled. There were 1 million moorland sheep on Lüneburg Heath at the turn of the 19C, when it was much larger, but only a few thousand are left today.

Bees are also an intrinsic feature of the heath. They frequently come with travelling beekeepers who carry their swarms in baskets called Lüneburg Bogenstülpern.

The largest bird on the heath is the nearly extinct blackcock or capercaillie. There are plenty of buzzards, red kites, hobbies and kestrels, with herons and snipes in the lowlands and high moors. Autumn sees flocks of fieldfares.

Boulders – Large and small granite boulders are scattered over Lüneburg Heath. They came from Scandinavia as boulder clay and were left behind when the glaciers of the last Ice Age retreated over 18 000 years ago.

Lüneburg Heide

© Gerhard Köhler/Fotolia.com

ADDRESSES

🛏 STAY

😑😑 **Bargenturm** – *Vor der Sülze 2.* ℘*(04131) 72 90. 40 rooms. Restaurant*😑😑. Close to the pedestrian zone, this property exudes contemporary flair from the lobby to the rooms. The restaurant has a friendly, modern ambience and a small inner courtyard.

😑😑😑 **Bergström** – *Bei der Lüner Mühle.* ℘*(04131) 30 80. www.bergstroem.de. 125 rooms.* 🚭*. Restaurant*😑😑😑. Hugging a particularly scenic stretch of the Ilmenau river, this hotel has tastefully appointed rooms and is well equipped with modern communication devices. Rooms in the ancient water tower are particularly appealing. The brasserie-style restaurant extends to a winter garden, and there is a wine bar as well.

🍴 EAT

😑 **Mälzer Brauhaus** – *Heiligengeiststraße 43.* ℘*(04131) 477 77. www.maelzerbrauhaus.de.* Match your mood to the differently decorated floors of this traditional pub. House specialities on the extensive menu include *Flammkuche* (French pizza), and baked potatoes, best washed down with the tasty home-made brew.

😑 **Cafe Mäxx** – *Schröderstraße 6.* ℘*(04131) 73 25 05. www.cafe-maexx.com.* Take a trip back to the 1970s in this cafe decorated with psychedelic wallpaper. Small and big appetites should find something to suit their taste on the varied menu. Good choice of cocktails, shakes and homemade pastries. Terrace with blankets to ward off the chill.

😑 **Lanzelot** – *Wandfärberstraße 7.* ℘*(04131) 40 48 13. www.lanzelot-lueneburg.de.* This cosy, dark-wood-panelled restaurant-bar is the place to stop for pasta, pizza, fish and meat dishes. Vegetarians will also feel well catered for, while the cash-strapped invade for the budget-priced tapas buffet on Mondays and Tuesdays. In summer, the shaded beer garden beckons.

😑😑😑😑 **Zum Heidkrug** – *Am Berge 5.* ℘*(04131) 241 60. www.zumheidkrug.de. Closed 1 week Jan, 1 week around Easter, 2 weeks in Jun–Jul and 1 week in mid-Oct, Sun, Mon, Tue lunch.* This brick Gothic building was built in the 15C and has been a restaurant since the 19C. The current incarnation is a rustic yet elegant place whose classic dishes show off the chef's considerable talent. The less expensive lunch specials are very popular. A few country-style rooms are available too.

👨‍👧 FOR KIDS

Vogelpark Walsrode – *Am Rieselbach, 29664 Walsrode. Open mid-Mar–Oct, daily 9am–7pm; Nov–Feb, 9am–6pm. 16€.* ℘*(05161) 604 40. www.vogelpark-walsrode.de.* Almost 4 000 feathered creatures live in this fun and family-friendly **bird park**, most of them in their natural habitat and at semi-liberty. You can help feed playful penguins, walk through an exotic tropical jungle, visit owls in an abandoned castle and watch a bird show.

Wildpark Lüneburger Heide – *Am Wildpark, 21271 Nindorf-Hanstedt. Open Mar–Oct, daily 8am–7pm (ticket office closes 5.30pm); Nov–Feb, 9am–4.30pm (ticket office closes 3.30pm). 9€ (child 6.50€).* ℘*(04184) 893 9 0. www.wild-park.de.* The whole family can enjoy a day at this wildlife park with animals including otters, buffalo, bears and birds of prey. Kids can also let off steam on the adventure and water playgrounds and get close to their favourite animals in the petting zoo. From April to October big crowds turn out for the bird of prey shows.

Heidepark Soltau – *Heidenhof, 29614 Soltau. Open late Mar–Oct, daily 9am–6pm (Jul–Aug 8pm). 36€ (ages 12 and up), 29€ (4–11yrs), under-4s free.* ℘*(05191) 91 91 and (01805) 91 91 01. www.heide-park.de* This small amusement park keeps kids entertained with dozens of rides and attractions centred around themes such as Little America. Thrills include rollercoasters, bird and dolphin shows and water log rides. Online tickets are about 25 percent cheaper.

Husum

The birthplace of writer Theodor Storm (1817–1888) has survived the battering of the North Sea since time immemorial. Today this "grey city on the sea", as Storm described it, is the commercial hub of North Friesland as well as a modern holiday region with abundant cultural offerings.

SIGHTS
▲▲ Nordseemuseum Husum★ (North Sea Museum)

Herzog-Adolf-Straße 25. ◷*Open Apr–Oct, daily 10am–5pm; Nov–Mar, Tue–Sun 11am–5pm.* ◷*Closed Jan 1, Dec 24 –25 & 31.* ◌5€ *(child 2€).* ♿ ✆*(04841) 25 45. www.museumsverbund-nord-friesland.de/nordseemuseum.*

This family-friendly museum illuminates various aspects of the North Sea region's cultural history. The exhibits explore the variety of Germany's coastal landscapes as well as the flow of daily life among its inhabitants. The catastrophic consequences of floods are addressed, as are the construction of dikes and the reclamation of land by polders.

Storm-Haus

Wasserreihe 31. ◷*Open Apr–Oct, Tue–Fri 10am–5pm, Sat 11am–5pm, Sun & Mon 2pm–5pm; Nov–Mar, Tue, Thu & Sat 2pm–5pm.* ◷*Closed Dec 24–25 & 31* ◌3€. ✆*(04841) 803 86 30. www.storm-gesellschaft.de.*

Novelist and poet Theodor Storm (1817–1888) lived in this typical 1730 merchant's house from 1866 to 1880. Its rooms provide a look at life during the Biedermeier age and include the writer's living room and the study where he penned more than 20 of his novellas. Paintings and documents from the writer's estate are also on view.

Schloss vor Husum (Castle at Husum)

König-Friedrich V.-Allee. ◷*Open Mar–Oct, Tue–Sun 11am–5pm; Nov–Feb, Sat–Sun 11am–5pm.* ◷*Closed Jan 1, Dec 24–25.* ◌3.50€. ✆*(04841) 897 31 30.*

▶ **Population:** 21 000
ℹ **Info:** Großstraße 27, 25813 Husum. ✆(04841) 898 70. www.tourismus-husum.de.
◉ **Location:** In the far northwestern corner of Germany, close to the Danish border, Husum is linked to the A7 autobahn via the B201 and B202.
✥ **Don't Miss:** The port and the North Frisian Museum.
◷ **Timing:** Husum can be easily covered in a day.

www.museumsverbund-nordfriesland.de.

This 16C castle of Duke Adolf von Schleswig-Holstein-Gottdorf was renovated in the Baroque style in the 18C and now hosts concerts, readings, lectures and contemporary art exhibits. The central tract is a museum where you can explore the palace's chapel, banquet hall and residential quarters.

EXCURSIONS
Eidersperrwerk★ (Eider Dam)

▶ *35km/21.7mi south.*

Skirting a bird sanctuary, the road arrives at the mouth of the River Eider, closed off by a **dam** built between 1967 and 1972. The five colossal steel sluice gates close when the coast is threatened by high seas.

Nolde-Museum★ at Seebüll

▶ *56km/34.7mi north.*

◷*Open year-round, daily 10am–6pm (Jun–Sept Thu 8pm).* ◌8€. ♿. (04664) 98 39 30. www.nolde-museum.de.

In 1927, Expressionist painter **Emil Nolde** (born Emil Nansen, 1867–1956), built his private residence in the solitude of the Seebüll marshes based on his own designs. The stark, angular Bauhaus-style structure presents annually changing exhibits showing off all of Nolde's major creative phases. Works with a religious theme are displayed in his former studio and you can also catch glimpses of his living quarters.

North Frisian Islands★

Nordfriesische Inseln

This group of beautiful and windswept islands forms part of the Schleswig-Holsteinisches Wattenmeer (Wadden Sea) National Park, which was created in 1985. The islands' fragile environment, including tall dunes, is protected from the ravages of the North Sea by dykes and artificial banks.

INSEL SYLT★★

Stephanstraße 6, 25980 Westerland. ℘(04651) 820 20. www.sylt.de.

The largest of the Northern Frisian Islands (100sq km/39sq mi), this long, narrow island is a patchwork of varied landscapes: sandy beaches and dunes, marshes and mudflats, fields and meadows and open heathland. Its spas, North Sea swimming and largely unspoilt nature make it popular with holidaymakers. An historic attraction is the primeval burial mounds.

Westerland★

Sylt's largest resort is also one of the most popular on the North Sea Coast and is often flooded with visitors. It has the best infrastructure on the island and

Info: Zingel 5, 25813 Husum. ℘(0180) 506 60 77. www.nordseetourismus.de.

Location: The North Frisian Islands are off the west coast of Schleswig-Holstein, in the North Sea, close to Denmark.

Don't Miss: Amrum, mudflat hikes, the megalithic graves of Denghoog near Keitum.

Timing: Spend at least a day relaxing on these islands.

Kids: Island cruising and exploration.

offers everything from window-shopping (Strandstraße and Friedrichstraße) and gallery hopping to challenging Lady Luck in the Art Nouveau casino. In foul weather, the boat-shaped water park and health spa called **Sylter Welle** beckons. On sunny days, though, the main attraction is of course the 7km/4.3mi-long sandy beach. It is hemmed in by a paved beachfront promenade, where people come to see and be seen or to listen to a concert in the domed shell. On and off the beach there is plenty of action in bars, bistros and nightclubs.

Beach near Ratum, Sylt Island

© Sabine Lubenow/Look/Photononstop

GETTING THERE

Since 1927 **Sylt** has been connected to the mainland via rail across the Hindenburgdamm causeway. Cars must be loaded onto the Sylt Shuttle in Niebüll *(35min; car with passengers 86€ round trip; ℘(04661) 93 45 67; www.syltshuttle.de)*.

Car ferries leave from Havneby on the Danish island of Rømø – accessible by road *(5–7 ferries a day, up to 12 daily in Jul and Aug; 50min; ⊜53€ round-trip per vehicle including passengers, ⊜6.20€ round trip for pedestrians; ℘(0180) 310 30 30; www.sylt-faehre.de)*.

Ferries *(℘(0180)508 01 40; www.faehre. de)* for **Föhr** and **Amrum** depart from Dagebüll, a small village and harbour on the northwesternmost point of Schleswig-Holstein. Dagebüll–Föhr 9–12 times daily *(⊜12.70€; 45min)*; Dagebüll–Amrum 6–10 times daily *(⊜18.60€; 60min, 90min via Föhr)*. For **Amrum**, ferries also leave from Schlüttsiel (7km/4.3mi south of Dagebüll) 1–2 times daily *(⊜18.60€; 2hrs 30min)*.

For **Pellworm**, embark from Nordstrand (17km/10.5mi west of Husum).

For the **Halligen**, catch a ferry from Husum or Nordstrand.

Keitum

This idyllic village and its craft shops presents the most relaxed, unpretentious face of Sylt. Keitum's traditional thatched Frisian houses hidden among trees and lilacs, the embankments of dog roses, and cliffs overlooking the sea and mudflats earn it the nickname "the green heart".

Kampen

This resort is popular with the German jet-set (models, football players, aristocrats, etc.) and international VIPs. It brims with fancy international boutiques, while impeccably shiny BMWs and Mercedes patrol the streets.

The main "catwalk" is the Stroenwai, also known as Whiskey Alley. South of town, the **Rotes Kliff** towers above the sea. Embracing it is the **Uwe Dune**, at 52.5m/172ft the highest on Sylt. There are great **views**★ over Sylt and neighbouring islands from the top.

Wenningstedt

In Wenningstedt-Braderup, the **Denghoog**★ is a 4 000-year-old megalithic grave open to the public. **Morsum-Kliff**, featuring 10 million years of geological history, is an interesting geological feature.

List

Around the port of **List**, where ferries from Rømø drop off Danish daytrippers, the **Wanderdünen** are moving dunes extending 1 000m/3 280ft long and 30m/98.4ft-high.

FÖHR

Föhr is a peaceful island blessed with a mild climate. The landscape is largely marshland, dotted with pretty villages (including Nieblum, Süderende and Oldsum). The beaches lie in the south; on the northern end is a windswept forest rich with birdlife.

The port of **Wyk** in the southeast is crisscrossed by well-tended lanes perfect for exploring at leisure. Those interested in local nature, history and culture should drop by the **Friesen-Museum** *(◐open Jul–Aug, daily 10am–5pm; mid-Mar–Oct, Tue–Sun, 10am–5pm; mid-Oct–Feb, Tue–Sun 2pm–5pm; ◐closed Dec 24 & 31; ⊜4.80€; ℘(04681) 25 71; www.friesen-museum.de)*.

Dunsum is the departure point for a walk across the mudflats to Amrum.

AMRUM

The smallest of the North Frisian islands, Amrum's west coast is home to sand dunes, heaths, woods, farmland and mudflats that provide a rich habitat for seabirds, making them a paradise for birdwatchers. Its biggest natural asset is the **Kniepsand**, a gloriously white, fine 12km/7.4mi-long beach. From the **lighthouse** in **Wittdün**, enjoy sweeping views as far as **Sylt** (*see INSEL SYLT*). The village of **Nebel** grew up around the medieval Church of **St. Clemens** in the 16C. The town also features the **Öömrang-Hüs**, a 19C sea captain's house. The far north of the island is a bird sanctuary and departure point for guided walks across the mudflats to Föhr.

HALLIGEN★

These tiny islands are all that remain of mainland marshes once part of the coastal region. In 1600 there were more than 25 recorded islets, but all but 10 of them have since been swallowed up by the fierce sea. Most of the Halligen are unprotected by sea dikes, resulting in temporary island submersions up to 50 times a year. At these times only a few reed-thatched houses perched on artificial mounds (*terps*) stay above the water. The prettiest Hallig is **Hooge**, but **Langeneß**, the largest with 18 mounds, is popular also, and Gröde also gets a fair number of visitors, most of them day-trippers. Various shipping companies offer boat trips to the Halligen.

PELLWORM

Pellworm lie below sea level and would be inundated were it not protected by a 25km/15.5mi-long and 8m/26.2ft-high dike. Its main feature is the ruined tower of the 11C–12C **Alte Kirche St. Salvator** church.

Nearby lies the **Friedhof der Heimatlosen**, a cemetery where the bodies of strangers washed up on the island's shores are buried.

NORDSTRAND

Marshy Nordstrand is linked to the mainland by a 4km/2.5mi causeway and is formed of reclaimed farmland (polders) and villages sitting on *terps*. The main town is charming Süden, where artisans have settled. The north island is a bird refuge.

ADDRESSES

⊟ STAY

⊜⊟ **Ekke Nekkepenn** – *Waasterstigh 19, Nebel, Amrum.* ℘*(04682) 945 60.* *www.ekkenekkepenn.de. 8 rooms.* Charming, petite hotel welcomes you with prettily decorated rooms. Mornings start with an ample breakfast featuring freshly baked bread and served in a cheerful room.

⊜⊟ **Duus-Hotel** – *Hafenstraße 40, Wyk, Föhr.* ℘*(04681) 598 10. www.duus-hotel.de. Jan 8–Feb 18, mid-Nov–Dec 24. 22 rooms. Restaurant*⊜⊟. A convenient location and well-kept, contemporary rooms (some with harbour views) are among the assets of this family-run hotel. The restaurant serves regional and international meals.

⊜⊟ **Weiße Düne** – *Achtern Strand 6, Wittdün, Amrum.* ℘*(04682) 94 00 00. www.weisse-duene.de. 12 rooms. Restaurant*⊜⊟. Handsomely decorated rooms and self-catering apartments with modern amenities await at this delightful family-run hotel. Enjoy local feel-good food with a rustic bent in the traditional restaurant.

⍾/EAT

⊜⊟ **Friesenstube** – *Süderstraße 8, Wyk, Föhr.* ℘*(04681) 24 04. Closed mid-Jan–mid-Feb, Mon.* The Frisian décor, complete with cheerful wall tiles, gives this casual inn a winning ambience. The kitchen is known for its excellent fish dishes.

⊜⊟⊟ **Land- und Golfhotel Villa Witt** – *Alkersumstieg 4, Nieblum, Föhr.* ℘*(04681) 587 70. www.hotel-witt.de. Closed Jan 10–mid-Feb.* Handpicked antiques contribute to the stylishly elegant setting at this restaurant where imaginatively prepared regional dishes dominate the menu. Rooms are just as pleasant and a 18-hole golf course is close by as well.

Helgoland★★

Only 1sq km/0.38sq mi in size, the island of Helgoland is a mere blip in the North Sea, but its stark red-sandstone cliff silhouette exudes a timeless mystique. Home to unique flora and fauna, it draws thousands of tourists each year who come in pursuit of solitude, natural beauty and duty-free shopping bargains.

A BIT OF HISTORY

Helgoland was originally part of Denmark but ceded by the Danes to Britain in 1814 as part of the post-Napoleonic settlements. In 1890, it changed hands again as a result of the Zanzibar Treaty. This time Germany took possession in exchange for commercial rights in the East African island of Zanzibar. Helgoland was subsequently annexed to Schleswig-Holstein (at that time part of Prussia).

SIGHTS

Battered by the sea since time immemorial, tiny Helgoland is home to an aquarium, an ornithological observatory and a marine biology station. Blessed with natural beauty, it attracts leisure travellers eager to engage in **outdoor pursuits★★**: cliff walks, hiking, swimming, birding, biking and more. Shoppers can look forward to bargains on chocolates, cigarettes and spirits because neither duty nor VAT (currently 19 percent) are charged.

Lange Anna★ (Long Anna)

Helgoland's most famous natural landmark, this 80m/262.4ft-high bright-red rock column stands guard off its northwestern shore like some petrified sentinel.

Nearby is the **Lummenfelsen**, Germany's smallest nature reserve (1.1ha/2.7 acres), which draws countless breeding bird species, most notably Helgoland's signature bird, the *Trottellumme* (common murre).

Düne

About 1km/0.6mi from the main island.

▸ **Population:** 1 300
▸ **Info:** Rathaus, Lung Wal 28, 27498 Helgoland. ☎(04725) 813 70. www.helgoland.de.
▸ **Location:** Helgoland is about 70km/43mi off the coast of Schleswig-Holstein. It is served by ferry from Cuxhaven, Hamburg and the Frisian Islands.
▸ **Don't Miss:** Hiking, swimming and other outdoor pursuits.
▸ **Timing:** Helgoland can be visited on a day trip.
▸ **Kids:** The sea voyage to the island, beaches.

GETTING THERE

Ferries leave from Hamburg, Wedel and Cuxhaven to Helgoland. *Katamaran "Halunder Jet"* departs Hamburg late Mar–Oct, daily at 9am, calling at Wedel 9.40am and Cuxhaven 11.30am; return trip 4.30pm, arriving at Cuxhaven around 5.45pm, Wedel around 7.40pm, Hamburg around 8.15pm. ☎(0180) 320 20 25. www.helgoline.de. Reederei Cassen Eils also offers a ferry service from Cuxhaven to Helgoland: www.helgolandreisen.de.

Turquoise water lapping at white sandy beaches – no, this is not the Caribbean but a small islet that got separated from the main island during a stormy night on New Year's Eve 1720. Today, it is a swimmers' and nature-lovers' paradise. The southern beaches are particularly family-friendly, while sealions can be observed lazing in the sand on the northern shore. Düne is also one of the few places in the world where you can find the carmine-red firestone. Stone Age people used them as tools but today they are turned into precious jewellery.

A ferry from Helgoland serves the islet year-round.

Bremen★★

Bremen, Germany's oldest maritime city, is famous for Beck's beer and the Town Musicians of the eponymous Brothers Grimm' fairytale, *The Town Musicians of Bremen*. Enjoying trade rights from 965, it has a long and proud history of civic independence, joining the Hanseatic League in 1358 and beginning trading directly with America in 1783. Today, Bremen is a lively, compact, congenial city with a charming old town and bustling nightlife districts.

A BIT OF HISTORY

Bremen ports – The twin ports in Bremen and Bremerhaven directly or indirectly employ about a third of the city-state's population and are Germany's second busiest after Hamburg. Each year more than 5 million containers and 1.4 million vehicles pass through the port's terminals.

River and port tours (75min) leave from the quay by the St. Martinikirche. Up to five departures daily from Mar–Oct. 9.80€. ℘(0421) 33 89 89. www.hal-oever.de.

⚓WALKING TOUR
OLD BREMEN
Allow two hours.

Marktplatz★★ (Market Square)

Bremen's market square is one of the most beautiful in Germany. At its centre is the 5.5m/18ft-high canopied statue of the knight **Roland** (1404), a symbol for freedom and civic autonomy.

Together with the **Rathaus** (town hall), the statue is on UNESCO's list of World Heritage Sites. Perhaps even more beloved is Gerhard Marcks' bronze sculpture (1951) on the Town Hall's west side. This pyramid formed by a donkey, dog, cat and cockerel represents the characters from the popular Grimm fairytale, **The Town Musicians of Bremen** (*Bremer Stadtmusikanten*). The **Schütting**, an elegant 16C build-

▶ **Population:** 547 500

ℹ **Info:** Am Bahnhofsplatz, 28195 Bremen. ℘(0421) 308 00 10. www.bremen-tourismus.de.

▷ **Location:** Bremen is at the southern end of the Weser estuary, while its sea port Bremerhaven is 59km/37mi downstream.

🅿 **Parking:** Look for garages near the Hauptbahnhof and throughout the inner city, including a large 24hr one on Pelzerstraße (enter on Knochenhauerstraße).

⊘ **Don't Miss:** Marktplatz, Böttcherstraße, German Emigration Centre.

👪 **Kids:** Universum Bremen, German Emigration Centre, German Maritime Museum.

🕐 **Timing:** Allow at least one full day to see Bremen and another half day for Bremerhaven.

ing, used to house Bremen's Guild of Merchants.

Rathaus★ (Town Hall)

Am Markt 21. ⚓Visits by guided tour (1hr) only, Mon–Sat 11am, noon, 3pm and 4pm, Sun 11am and noon. No tours during official receptions. 5€. ℘(01805) 10 10 30. www.bremen-tourism.de.

The original town hall was built in Gothic style in the 15C, shortly after Bremen joined the Hanseatic League. A renovation in Weser Renaissance style in the 17C added its decorative gables and a three-story façade rising above an arcaded gallery.

Above this, tall windows alternate with statues of Charlemagne and the seven Electors (note that these are copies; the Gothic originals are in the Focke-Museum).

Inside, a splendid spiral **staircase**★★ (*Wendeltreppe*) in carved wood (1620) is worth taking a closer look at. The

Bremer Rathauskeller *(entrance on the west side)* serves 650 different German wines.

Pfarrkirche Unser Lieben Frauen (Church of Our Lady)

The interior of this 13C hall-church, bare of decoration except for the 1709 chancel, is relieved by rounded ogive vaulting dating to its construction. The four main stained-glass windows, on biblical themes, were executed between 1966 and 1979.

The church's simple **crypt** dates from the preceding church (St. Veit), whose origins have been traced to 1020.

St. Petri-Dom★
(St. Peter's Cathedral)

Sandstraße 10–12. ⏰*Open year-round, Mon–Fri 10am–5pm, Sat 10am–2pm, Sun 12pm–5pm.* ⛪*Tower 1€, Bleikeller 1.40€.* ☏*(0421) 36 50 40. www.stpetridom.de.*

St. Peter's Cathedral (Lutheran) was constructed in the 11C, and updated in the 16C and 19C. Notable religious artworks include a 16C **Virgin and Child**★ and, along the organ balustrade, 16C carvings of Charlemagne and Willehad, the first Bishop of Bremen. Beneath the organ loft, the 11C western crypt houses Romanesque capitals and a magnificent bronze **baptismal font**★★ (*Taufbecken*, c. 1220).

A separate entrance just south of the main portal leads to the hugely popular – if macabre – **lead cellar** (*Bleikeller;* ⏰*open Easter–Oct, same hours as church;* ⛪*1.40€)*, which contains eight perfectly preserved, centuries-old mummified corpses in open coffins. The church tower can be climbed for birds-eye views of the city.

Böttcherstraße★

Running only 110m/360ft from the Marktplatz to the Weser, this narrow street is an architectural gem commissioned in the 1920s by coffee mogul Ludwig Roselius and designed primarily by architect Bernhard Hoetger. Expressionist in style, with Art Nouveau and Art Deco overtones, buildings feature whimsical design elements, such as façades buttressed by stone sculptures, a spiral staircase and a golden entrance relief. A carillon made of Meissen porcelain chimes hourly between noon and 6pm (*Jan–Mar at noon, 3pm and 6pm*). The buildings house galleries and shops as well as the **Paula-Modersohn-Becker-Museum**★ (*Böttcherstraße 6–10;* ⏰*open year-round, Tue–Sun 11am–6pm;* ⏰*closed Dec 24 & 31;* ⛪*5€;* ☏*(0421) 336 50 66; www.pmbm.de)*. It features paintings, drawings and graphic works by the eponymous modern-art pioneer and member of the Worpswede art colony. Tickets are also good for the **Museum im Roseliushaus** (*same hours*) in the

same building. Here you can tour nine period rooms brimming with precious furniture, carpets, porcelain, paintings by Lucas Cranach the Elder and sculpture by Tilman Riemenschneider.

Schnoorviertel★

The cottages in this quarter, once the homes of fishermen and their families, are all that remains of Old Bremen. Built between the 15C and the 19C, they have all been restored and are used as art galleries, antique shops, restaurants and boutiques and are popular with tourists. After dark, night-owls descend on the quarter's bars and restaurants.

ADDITIONAL SIGHTS
Kunsthalle★
(Art Gallery)

⚬*Closed for renovation until at least spring 2011. Am Wall 207.* ♿ ☏*(0421) 32 90 80. www.kunsthalle-bremen.de.*

This museum features an outstanding collection of several centuries-worth of European art. Key names include Courbet, Delacroix, Monet, Menzel, Leibl, Beckmann, Rubens, Rembrandt and Tiepolo, to name just a few.

Focke-Museum★★

Schwachhauser Heerstraße 240. ⏰*Open year-round, Tue 10am–9pm, Wed–Sun 10am–5pm.* ⏰*Closed Jan 1, Oct 3, Dec 24–25 & 31.* ⛪*5€.* ♿ ☏*(0421) 699 60 00. www.focke-museum.de.*

This regional museum presents 1 200 years of Bremen's history. The **Main House** (*Haupthaus*) covers major milestones in themed exhibits, then follows a chronological trail culminating with displays about modern Bremen. The prehistoric collections are displayed in a thatched annex, the Eichenhof.

Haus Mittelsbüren, a 16C farmhouse spotlights Bremen's agricultural and industrial development, while exhibits in the 1803 **Tarnstedt Barn** (*Tarnstedter Scheune*) zero in on various agricultural activities, such as animal husbandry, haymaking and dairy farming.

Also part of the complex is the 18C **Haus Riensberg**, a one-time summer residence for wealthy Bremen families

Marktplatz with Rathaus

Titus Czerski/BTZ Bremer Touristik-Zentrale

where decorative arts, Fürstenberg porcelain and European glass art are now on display. Kids gravitate to the 👥 **Children's Museum** *(Kindermuseum)* with its big toy collection as well as to **Studio Focke**, where they can engage in hands-on experiments and activities.

Neues Museum Weserburg (New Museum Weserburg)

Teerhof 20. 🕐*Open Tue–Fri 10am–6pm (Thu 9pm), Sat–Sun 11am–6pm.* 🕐*Closed May 1, Oct 3, Dec 24–25 & 31.* 💶*8€.* ♿ ✆*(0421) 598 39 70.* *www.nmwb.de.*

This is one of the largest museums in Germany dedicated to contemporary art. Housed in old red-brick warehouses on an island in the Weser, it boasts several private collections and provides a global overview of the past 40 years in contemporary art.

Universum Bremen★★

Wiener Straße 1a, enter via Schaubox. 🕐*Open year-round, Mon–Fri 9am–6pm, Sat–Sun 10am–7pm; last admission 90min before closing.* 💶*16€ (5€ during last 90 minutes before closing).* ♿ ✆*(0421) 364 60.* *www.universum-bremen.de.*

Science gets a fun and entertaining twist at this state-of-the-art park. Visits start at the **SchauBox**, a rust-coloured cube containing special exhibits, a restaurant and a multimedia theatre.

A bridge leads to the **Science Centre**, housed in a silvery building shaped like a closed clam. Inside are 250 experiment and interactive stations divided into three themes: Earth, Humanity and the Cosmos. You can take a virtual journey into space, experience an earthquake or dive 2km/1.2mi below the sea.

The outdoor **EntdeckerPark** (Explorer Park) counts a climbing wall and a water playground among its attractions. Skip mornings when school groups invade.

Überseemuseum Bremen★★ (Overseas Museum)

Bahnhofsplatz 13. 🕐*Open year-round, Tue–Fri 9am–6pm, Sat–Sun 10am–6pm.* 🕐*Closed Jan 1, May 1, Dec 24–25 & 31.* 💶*6.50€.* ♿ ✆*(0421)16 03 81 01.* *www.uebersee-museum.de.*

History, ethnology, culture and trade combine into an exciting journey of discovery back in time and around the world. Learn about colonial trading, admire exotic artefacts from the South Seas or inspect shiny Samurai armour.

EXCURSION

Bremerhaven

▶ *58km/36mi north.*

The town's maritime history is given its due at the 🏛 **German Maritime Museum**★ *(Deutsches Schifffahrtsmuseum; Hans-Scharoun-Platz 1;* ⏱*open Mar–Oct, daily 10am–6pm,* ⏱*closed Mon Nov–Feb, Dec 24–25 & 31;* ∞*6€;* ♿*;* 𝄞 *(0471) 48 20 70; www.dsm.national. museum)*, whose 500 historic boats could keep salty types busy for hours. Bremerhaven's main draw is the **German Emigration Cente**★★★ *(Deutsches Auswandererhaus; Columbusstraße 65;* ⏱*open Mar–Oct, daily 10am–6pm, Nov–Feb 10am–5pm;* ∞*10.50€;* ♿*;* 𝄞*(0421) 90 22 00; www.dah-bremerhaven.de)*.

This vast centre tells the story of the European emigrants who traded poverty and persecution for hopes of a better life in the New World. Around 7 million embarked from this very spot in Bremerhaven between 1830 and 1974.

A tour recreates every phase of the emigration process, from the quayside farewell to conditions aboard the vessel to the arrival at Ellis Island. Especially moving is the **Gallery of the 7 Millions** that lets you explore the biographies of individuals and learn what prompted them to leave their homelands.

ADDRESSES

🛏 STAY

🍽 **Bölts am Park** – *Slevogtstraße 23.* 𝄞*(0421) 34 61 10. www.hotel-boelts.de. 16 rooms.* Quiet and family-run, this classic Bremen townhouse offers well-tended rooms and a breakfast nook overlooking the small garden.

🍽 **Hotel Buthmann** – *Löningstraße 29.* 𝄞*(0421) 32 63 97. www.hotel-buthmann.de. 9 rooms.* This little inn within walking distance of the train station and the old town has clean and spacious, if fairly nondescript, rooms.

🍽 **Hotel Classico** – *Am Markt 17.* 𝄞*(0421) 24 40 08 67. www.hotel-classico-bremen.de. 4 rooms.* ⌨. This mini-boutique hotel overlooks the market. The charming rooms have evocative names such as "Moulin Rouge" and "Alexander the Great". The café on the ground floor serves homemade pastries.

🍽 **Hotel Hanseat** –*Löningstraße 29* 𝄞*(0421)146 88. www.hotel-hanseat.com. 33 rooms.* ⌨. Opposite the train station, this hotel has clean and functional rooms. Those facing the courtyard are quieter. Friendly service and hearty breakfast.

🍽🍽 **Hilton Bremen** – *Böttcherstraße 2.* 𝄞*(0421) 369 60. www.hilton.com. 235 rooms.* ⌨. This high-end hotel wraps around a central atrium linked to the Atlantis House on Böttcherstraße.

🍽🍽 **Hotel-Bateau Perle** – *Schlachteanleger 7.* 𝄞*(0421) 790 300. www.hotelschiff-perle-bremen.de. 2 rooms.* ⌨. For a unique lodging option, book a room aboard this charming little boat moored on the Weser River. Reservations essential. Or contact Hotel Stadt Bremen *(Heinkenstrasse 3–5;* 𝄞*(0421) 790 300)*.

🍽🍽🍽 **ÜberFluss Hotel** – *Langenstraße 72.* 𝄞*(0421) 32 28 60. www.hotel-ueberfluss.de. 50 rooms.* ⌨. This designer hotel overlooking the Weser River welcomes guests with sophisticated décor, precious woods, beautiful lighting and plenty of attention to detail.

🍽🍽🍽 **Park Hotel** – *Im Bürgerpark.* 𝄞*(0421) 340 80. www.park-hotel-bremen.de. 177 rooms. Restaurant*🍽🍽🍽. A sense of luxury embraces you the moment you enter the domed lobby of this elegant manor house right by a little lake within the park. Facilities include a vast spa area and two restaurants.

🍴 EAT

🍽 **Paulaner's** – *Schlachte 30.* 𝄞*(0421) 169 06 91. www.paulaners.de.* At this pleasant, riverside Bavarian-style beer hall and beer garden you will find efficient, friendly service and a long menu that mixes northern and southern German specialities.

⊝**Ständige Vertretung** – *Böttcherstraße 3–5. ℰ(0421) 32 09 95. www.staev.de.* The walls of this popular brewery are lined with photographs depicting the history of Germany before reunification. The place to come for traditional German cuisine and seafood at reasonable prices.

⊝**Weser Haus** – *Hinter der Mauer 5. ℰ(0421) 246 390 00. www.weserhaus-bremen.de.* Since this café doubles as a TV studio you may well find yourself included in a programme while sipping your cappuccino. In summer, the large shaded riverside terrace beckons.

⊝**Aioli** – *Schnoor 3. ℰ(0421) 32 38 39. www.aioli-bremen.de.* Warm and welcoming, this tapas bar in the Schnoor district also serves more substantial fish and meat dishes.

⊝**Kaffee Mühle** – *Am Wall 212. ℰ(0421) 144 66. www.muehle-bremen.de.* This charming restaurant in Bremen's only remaining mill is the place to steer towards for budget lunches, hot drinks and a big Sunday brunch buffet. The staff is generous with the smiles.

⊝**Katzen-Café** – *Schnoor 38. ℰ(0421) 32 66 21. www.katzen-cafe.de.* For warm and attentive service point the compass to this terraced restaurant with cheerful red gingham tablecloths and a menu that hopscotches from schnitzel to spaghetti, steak to coq au vin.

⊝**Ristorante da Francesco** – *Martinistraße 12. ℰ(0421) 244 26 03.* On sunny days it's hard to land a table on the lovely riverside terrace of this popular pizza restaurant.

⊝⊝**Comturei** – *Ostertorstraße 30. ℰ(0421) 32 50 50. www.restaurant-comturei-bremen.de.* Traditional cuisine and fresh fish and crab are on the menu at this rustic and cosy restaurant in a 13C vaulted cellar.

⊝⊝**John Benton Restaurant** – *Am Markt 1. ℰ(0421) 32 30 33.* Delicious cuts of aged steak are the main draw at this bi-level restaurant whose terrace offers beautiful cathedral views.

⊝⊝⊝**Bremer Ratskeller** – *Am Markt. ℰ(0421) 32 16 76 . www.ratskeller-bremen.de.* This excellent restaurant is right below the city hall. For extra privacy, snag a comfortable booth

Coffee Bean City

Bremen's close links with coffee date back over three centuries. The first-ever coffee house in German-speaking countries was built here in 1673, before those in Vienna and Hamburg. Half of all the cups of coffee drunk in Germany are brewed from beans imported via the port at Bremen.

lining the main hall. The excellent wine list includes only German wines (about 600 different bottles).

🚲 TAKING A BREAK

F. L. Bodes – *Bischofsnadel 1–2 (alleyway leading from Wallanlagen to Domshof). ℰ(0421) 32 41 44. www.bodes.de. Closed Sun, Mon.* This fish shop and snack bar is a mere stone's throw from the town centre. Try seafood and fish à la carte, choose from the blackboard menus or make your selection directly from the stalls. Queues are longest at lunchtime.

Konditorei Knigge – *Sögestraße 42–44. ℰ(0421) 137 13. www.knigge-shop.de.* Bremen's classic café is the place to try such local specialities as the "Bremer Klaben", a hearty fruitcake.

🍸 NIGHTLIFE

Useful tip – Cafés, bars, restaurants and shops cluster in the historic Schnoor district, south of the cathedral. The riverside Schlachte promenade, on the right river bank, is chock-full of trendy restaurants and bars, many with river terraces.

Pannekoekschip Admiral Nelson – *Schlachte Anleger 1. ℰ(0421) 3 64 99 84. www.admiral-nelson.de.* Ahoy there! Friendly "pirates" serve sweet or savoury pancakes on this three-masted ship.

🛍 SHOPPING

The elegant shopping arcades of **Lloydpassage**, **Domshof Passage** and **Katharinen-Viertel** in the heart of town make for a fun browse. Independent boutiques are located in the historic **Schnoor district** and along **Böttcherstraße**.

Oldenburg

Steeped in tradition, this lively university city is the cultural and economic hub of the region. Seat of government for the Weser-Ems region, Oldenburg is becoming an increasingly popular commercial centre.

SIGHTS
OLD TOWN

The old city embraces Germany's first pedestrian zone and buildings from five centuries, generous parkland and the ancient ramparts.

Landesmuseum für Kunst und Kulturgeschichte (State Museum of Art and Cultural History)

⏱Open year-round, Tue, Wed and Fri 9am–5pm, Thu 9am–8pm, Sat–Sun 10am–5pm. ⏱Closed Jan 1, Good Fri, Easter Sun, May 1, Pentecost, Dec 24–25 & 31. ⊜3€. ♿. ℘(0441) 220 73 00. www.landesmuseum-oldenburg. niedersachsen.de.

The collections of the State Museum of Art and Cultural History are spread across three buildings: the Oldenburg Palace, the Augusteum and the Prince's Palace.

▶ **Population:** 158 000
ℹ **Info:** Kleine Kirchenstraße, 26122 Oldenburg. ℘(0441) 36 16 13 66. www.oldenburg-tourist.de.
▶ **Location:** Oldenburg is about 70km/43.5mi west of the Dutch border. Its river port is linked to the Weser and the North Sea by the Hunte, and to the Benelux countries by a coastal canal (Küstenkanal).
🅿 **Parking:** You'll find parking on the Schlossplatz and near the main train station on Willy Brandt-Platz.
👁 **Don't Miss:**
The landscaped castle park.
🕐 **Timing:** Allow half a day to see the main sights of Oldenburg.

Oldenburger Schloss (Oldenburg Palace)
Schlossplatz 1.

Oldenburg's palace was originally built in Renaissance style for Count Anton Günther (1583–1667) but embellished with Baroque flourishes in the 17C. It

Oldenburger Schloss

© fotobeam/Fotolia.com

served as the residence of the grand dukes of Oldenburg until the end of World War I.

Today, it is an extraordinary museum whose permanent exhibition "The Cultural History of an Historical Landscape" shows the variety and cultural heritage of the former grand duchy from the Middle Ages to the 20C. Exhibits are displayed on three floors in lavish rooms that reflect the tastes and wealth of the grand dukes.

Highlights include the "Homer Room" and the cycle of 40 miniature idyllic scenes created by court painter Johann Heinrich Tischbein (1751–1829), who is also known as "Goethe-Tischbein" because of his special friendship with the famous poet.

Augusteum
Elisabethstraße 1.
The grand ducal collection of paintings makes a perfect fit for this 19C Italian Renaissance-style edifice. The emphasis is on Italian and Dutch masters from the 16C to the 18C and on 18C–19C paintings by other Europeans. On the ground floor are changing exhibitions about the history of painting and contemporary art.

Prinzenpalais (Prince's Palace)
Damm 1.
This townhouse is filled with two floors of art from the 19C and 20C, starting with the Romantic period. Of particular interest are works by German Impressionists as well as by members of *Die Brücke* (The Bridge) artists' group. There is also a fine selection of canvasses by Franz Radziwill (1895–1955), a leading member of the Magic Realists (a style related to Surrealism) that developed in the 1920s.

Stadtmuseum★
Am Stadtmuseum 4–8. Open year-round, Tue–Sun 10am–6pm. 1.50€. &(0441) 235 28 81. http://stadt museum.oldenburg.de.
Of interest are rooms from the villas of Francksen (1877), Jürgens and Ballin, with paintings, furnishings and décor

dating from the 17C to the early 20C. There are also departments on local history and an antiques collection.

Next door is the **Horst-Janssen-Museum** (open year-round, Tue–Sun 10am–6pm; closed May 1, Dec 24–25 & 31; 5€; &(0441) 235 28 91) dedicated to the illustrator and graphic artist (1929–1995) who was born and buried in Oldenburg.

Schlossgarten★ (Castle Park)
A mild coastal climate favours the growth of magnificent trees and shrubs in this landscaped garden. A nice view of the Lambertikirche unfolds from the weeping willows on the lakeshore.

Landesmuseum Natur und Mensch Oldenburg (State Museum of Natural and Human History)
Damm 38–44. Open year-round, Tue–Fri 9am–5pm, Sat–Sun 10am–5pm. Closed Jan 1, May, Pentecost, Dec 24–25 & 31. 3€. &(0441) 924 43 00. www.naturundmensch.de.
These nature exhibits are focused on the northwest region of Germany with its varied landscapes and traces of pre- and early historic settlements. Natural, archaeological and cultural aspects are presented. A huge block of peat, in which ancient bodies were found buried, always attracts attention.

EXCURSION
Museumsdorf Cloppenburg★
31km/19mi south.
Open Mar–Oct, daily 9am–6pm; Nov–Feb, 9am–4.30pm. Closed Dec 24 & 31. 6€. &(04471) 948 40. www.museumsdorf.de.
In an area of about 20ha/49 acres, 53 historic rural buildings from the 15C to the 19C have been moved and rebuilt here around a lake and a church. Most of the buildings come from the region between the rivers Weser and Ems. Large farmsteads, mills and peasants' and tenants' houses illustrate various aspects of the history of Lower Saxony.

East Frisian Islands ★

Ostfriesische Inseln

The East Frisian Islands are part of the Wattenmeer (Wadden Sea) National Park, created in 1986. Due to the prevailing northwesterly tides and winds, the East Frisians are drifting ever further southeast. The northern and eastern coasts of these islands are fringed by sandy beaches dotted with wicker-hooded deck chairs and windbreaks in summer. For visitors the main appeal lies in the island's remoteness, tranquillity and natural splendour conducive to outdoor explorations.

BORKUM

*Ferries depart from Emden. 2hrs.
27.80€ round trip. AG EMS: (01805) 18 01 82, www.ag-ems.de.*
The largest of the Eastern Frisians boasts an impressive beach promenade and good views of the mainland and a seal bank from the 60m/196.8ft **Neuer Leuchtturm**, a lighthouse from 1879 *(315 steps)*.

JUIST

Ferries depart from Norddeich. 1hr 30min. 17.80€ same-day return. Reederei Frisia: (04931) 98 70, www.reederei-frisia.de.
This (17km/10.5mi long) island is home to an interesting **Küstenmuseum**

- **Info:** Ledastraße 10, 26789 Leer. (0491) 91 96 96 60. www.ostfriesland.de.
- **Location:** The seven inhabited Eastern Frisian islands lie between the Ems and the Weser deltas off the North Sea Coast of Germany. They are served by ferries whose timetables depend on the tides.
- **Don't Miss:** Quiet exploration of these islands. Take your time.
- **Timing:** Allow 30mins–2hrs for the ferry service, depending on the island.
- **Kids:** North Sea cruises and island exploration.

Ferry Routes

Emden–Borkum

Norddeich–Juist

Norddeich–Norderney

Neßmersiel–Baltrum

Bensersiel–Langoog

Neuharlingersiel–Spiekeroog

Harlesiel–Wangerooge

(Coastal Museum) in the attractive village of Loog. It documents local coastal living, the history of lifeboat service and the importance of dyke building. Beyond the village is the **Bill** nature reserve.

The Local Brew

Tea-drinking is a way of life in the East Frisian Islands, whose inhabitants consume 14 times more tea per capita than people in the rest of Germany. The beverage was introduced to the region by the Dutch c. 1670 and soon caught on. Frederick the Great attempted to ban tea in 1777 but was forced to reconsider when so many disgruntled people left the region. Even during World War II the East Frisians were allocated a more generous tea ration than others.

East Frisian "tea ceremonies" are full of ritual. First warm the teapot. Then pour boiling water onto the tea leaves in the pot and leave to brew for five minutes. Place a piece of white sugar crystal into a porcelain cup and pour on the strong, hot tea, which crackles pleasantly as it hits the sugar. Finally, add a splash of cream over the back of a special curved spoon made for this purpose. Stirring the tea, however, is a complete no-no – doing so is a grave breach of local etiquette!

Juist Island

©Martin Sach/istockphoto.com

NORDERNEY

Ferries depart from Norddeich. 1hr.
15€ same-day return. Reederei Frisia:
(04931) 98 70, www.reederei-frisia.de.
The most urbanised of the East Frisian
islands, Norderney is nicknamed "Queen
of the Frisian Islands" and was once the
summer residence of the royal House of
Hanover. Its main town still has much of
its old charm with its well-tended spa
gardens and 19C houses. Spa A state-of-
the-art thalassotherapy centre called
Bade:haus occupies the historic ambience of the Art Nouveau sea-water baths.

BALTRUM

Ferries depart from Neßmersiel. 30min.
16€. Reederei Baltrum: (04933) 99
16 06, www.baltrum-linie.de.
Around the smallest of the Eastern Frisians, the sea is usually calm. The main
sight here is the **old church** in Westdorf,
built one year after the great floods of
1826. The church bell was originally a
ship's bell, washed up as jetsam. On the
island's east side are impressive **sand
dunes** *(Großes Dünental).*

LANGEOOG

Ferries depart from Bensersiel.
1hr. Up to 7 ferries daily. 18.50€
same-day return. Schiffahrt Langeoog,
(04972) 69 30, www.langeoog.de.
The **Schifffahrtsmuseum** (Museum
of Seafaring) on this island features

Langeoog's first rescue ship, in service from 1945 to 1980. From the raised
promenade along the chain of sand
dunes, near Ebbe, there is a fine view of
14km/9mi of beach and sand banks.

SPIEKEROOG

Ferries depart from Neuharlingersiel.
45min. 17€ same-day return.
(04976) 919 31 01.
www.spiekeroog.de.
This car-free island combines state-of-
the-art spa facilities with traditional
village infrastructure. The **Alte Insel-
kirche** of 1696 is the oldest surviving
church in the Eastern Frisians. A pietà
made of wood and fragments of a pulpit
are said to have come from a ship in the
Spanish Armada that sank in 1588.
One of the island's more unusual sights is
the **Muschelmuseum** (Mussel Museum)
in the basement of the seaside hall.

WANGEROOGE

Ferries depart from Harlesiel. 80min.
*Up to 5 ferries daily. 19.20€ round-
trip. (04464) 94 94 11.*
Over the course of history, this easternmost island has belonged to Holland,
France, Russia (twice) and the Grand
Duchy of Oldenburg. It is now a peaceful family vacation destination. The colourful island train runs from the isolated
southwest point past lagoons rich in bird
life straight to the village centre.

211

ON THE MAINLAND
Emden
Bahnhofsplatz 11, 26721 Emden.
☎(04921) 974 00.
www.emden-touristik.de.

Sitting on the mouth of the Ems River across from the Dutch border, Emden is an easygoing and pleasant town with remarkable museums, most notably the Kunsthalle gallery of contemporary art. Thanks to the Dortmund-Ems canals, the town has regained its position as Lower Saxony's chief maritime port.

It traces its history back to the 8C and was an important trading place until the 16C. Completely flattened during World War II, Emden was rebuilt in modern but aesthetic fashion with a picturesque harbour, little canals and red-brick houses. Today, the driving force behind its economy is the huge Volkswagen factory.

Kunsthalle Emden★★
(Art Museum Emden)
Hinter dem Rahmen 13; northwest of town. ◷*Open year-round, Tue–Fri 10am–5pm, Sat–Sun 11am–6pm.* ◷*Closed Dec 24–25.* ⊜*8€.* ♿
☎(04921) 97 50 50.
www.kunsthalle-emden.de.

This Postmodern red-brick museum houses the sizeable private collection of *Stern* magazine founder and local boy Henri Nannen. A major emphasis

Kunsthalle Emden

Gaby Ahnert/Kunsthall Emden

is on **German Expressionist** art, with works by *Brücke* (Bridge) artists Kirchner, Heckel and Schmidt-Rottluff along with *Blue Rider* members Marc, Macke, Münter and Jawlensky brightening the walls. More recent creativity is represented by the **Neue Wilde** group (New Wild Ones) that included Hödicke, Zimmer, Richter and Damisch – less familiar names, perhaps, but all seminal post-1980 artists.

Ostfriesisches Landesmuseum★
(East Frisian Regional Museum)
Rathaus am Delft, Neutorstraße 7–9.
◷*Open year-round, Tue–Sat 10am–6pm.* ⊜*6€.* ☎*(04921) 87 20 58.*
www.landesmuseum-emden.de.

This modernised museum is a comprehensive treasure trove of all things East Frisian going back to the Stone Age.

Pride of place goes to the **Rüstkammer**★★ (armoury), one of Germany's largest collections of 16C and 17C weapons.

The **mummified body**★ of a young man who lived during the early Middle Ages and who was unearthed in a local peat bog always gets good crowds as well. A fine sampling of Dutch paintings, mostly from the 17C, and graphic arts, including works by Alfred Rethel and Max Liebermann, shows off Emden's artistic heritage.

Port
Ratsdelft.

The oldest section is the **harbour gateway** *(Hafentor)* built in 1635 and bearing the Latin inscription *"God is Emden's bridge, harbour and sailing wind"*. In the historical harbour basin are several **museum ships** *(Museumsschiffe)*.

Pelzerhäuser
◷*Open year-round, Tue–Wed and Fri–Sun 11am–6pm.* ☎*(04921) 253 35.*

The steeply gabled, red-brick town houses at Pelzerstraße 11 and 12 are the only surviving examples of the 16C Dutch-Flemish Renaissance style that once dominated Emden. One contains period rooms that shed light on upper middle-class lifestyles in the 17C and 18C.

Hannover

Hannover is one of northern Germany's main economic hubs and a host of important trade shows such as the annual Cebit computer fair. But the city is not all buttoned-down business: visitors will find a wealth of pleasant pastimes to choose from, most notably exploring its glorious gardens.

SIGHTS
Herrenhäuser Gärten★★ (Herrenhausen Gardens)

Begun in the 17C, one of Europe's most beautiful public parks comprises four separate and varied gardens linked by the Herrenhäuser Allee.

Großer Garten★★

⏱Open May–Aug 9am–8pm; Sept–Apr, 9am–sunset. ⌨5€, includes Berggarten.

Creation of this splendid Baroque garden started in 1666 but it didn't get its finishing touches until Electress Sophie turned her attention to it between 1696 and 1714. The oldest section, a French pleasure garden, features statues of allegorical figures and Roman gods.

The first thing you will likely see is the huge **fountain** with its 80m/262.4ft-high plume. An exciting modern highlight is the whimsical **grotto** (⏱open

Info: Ernst-August-Platz 8, 30159 Hannover. 📞(0511) 12 34 51 11. www.hannover.de.

Location: Set on a plain on the banks of the Leine and the Mittelandkanal, Hannover is halfway between the Baltic Sea and the North Sea. The A2 (Dortmund–Berlin) and A7 (Kassel–Hamburg) autobahns intersect here.

Parking: Garages are located throughout Hannover. The ones around the Hauptbahnhof are easiest to find.

Don't Miss: Hannover's terrific gardens.

Timing: Allow at least two hours to see the Herrenhäuser Gardens.

Kids: Hannover Zoo.

May–Aug, 9am–7.30pm; Mar and Sept 6.30pm, Oct 5.30pm, Oct–Mar, Sat–Sun 9am–4pm) decorated by the late French artist Niki de Saint Phalle. Illustrating the theme of human life, the octagonal foyer and two adjacent rooms sparkle with coloured glass mosaics, mirrors, pebbles and painted fibreglass figurines.

Southern façade of Neues Rathaus

© Norbert Speicher /istockphoto.com

WHERE TO STAY

CVJM City Hotel	①	da Vinci Restaurant	⑨
Kastens Hotel Luisenhof	④	Der Gartensaal	④
WHERE TO EAT		Le Monde	⑫
Basil	③	Neue Zeiten	⑮
Broyhan-Haus	①	Röhrbein Restaurant	⑰

Berggarten★

🕑 *Open, see Grosser Garten.* 🎫*3.50€.*
One of the oldest botanical gardens in Germany, the Berggarten is a charming and colourful riot of 11 000 plant species, including cacti, orchids and flora native to the Canary Islands. There are some great greenhouses as well as the **Sealife Hannover** (🕑 *open year-round, daily 10am–6pm;* 🎫*14.50€, combination ticket with Grosser Garten/Berggarten 15.50€; www.sealifehannover.com*), which takes you on a virtual journey from the local Leine River to the Caribbean and the Amazon rainforest.
Along the way, visitors are introduced to 5 000 creatures residing in these aquatic habitats. A highlight is the 8m/26.2ft-long glass tunnel "through" the ocean. At the far end of the garden's principal walk is the mausoleum of the Royal House of Hanover.

Georgengarten

🕑 *Open 24hrs.*
Inspired by English landscape gardens, this romantic patch was laid out between 1835 and 1841 and is distinguished by great expanses of lawn.
Enjoy fabulous views from the **Leibniztempel**, a memorial dedicated to the philosopher and scientist, Wilhelm Gottfried Leibniz (1646–1716), on a raised peninsula.

The Wallmodenschlösschen is a pavilion housing the **Wilhelm-Busch-Museum** (○ *open year-round, Tue–Sun 11am– 6pm;* ○ *closed Dec 24 & 31;* ☞*4.50€;* ♿*;* ✆*(0511) 16 99 99 11; www.wilhelm-busch- museum.de)* dedicated to the famous poet, illustrator and humourist (1832– 1908) who launched the advent of comic strips with such stories as "Max und Moritz".

Welfengarten

The Welfenschloss (now part of the university) stands in the Welfengarten and is fronted by the trademark of the state of Niedersachsen, the Saxon Steed, created in 1876 by Friedrich Wolff.

Marktkirche (Market Church)

A four-gabled tower crowned by a sharp pinnacle presides over this Gothic brick church, rebuilt after 1945 to mimic the 14C original. The modern 1957 bronze doors by Gerhard Marcks contrast sharply with the overall style of the church. Inside, note the superb 15C sculpted polychrome **reredos**★★ representing the Passion.

Niedersächsisches Landesmuseum Hannover★ (Lower Saxony State Museum)

Willy-Brandt-Allee 5. ○ *Open year- round, Tue–Sun 10am–5pm (Thu 7pm).* ○ *Closed Jan 1, Good Fri, May 1, Dec 24 –25 & 31.* ☞*4€.* ♿*.* ✆*(0511) 980 76 86. www.nlmh.de.*

This museum is divided into four depart- ments. The **archaeological depart- ment**★ *(Archäologie-Abteilung)* travels back in time half a million years and sheds light on the daily lives of our ancestors. One of the most memorable exhibits is a mummified male from AD 300, whose curly red hair has garnered him the nick- name "Roter Franz" (Red Francis).

Fossils, dinosaurs and exhibits on tectonic plates and earthquakes are among the highlights of the **nature department** *(Naturkunde-Abteilung).*

Living fish, amphibians, lizards, spiders and insects from around the world can be observed in recreated habitats in the attached vivarium.

😊 A Bit of Advice 😊

The red line painted on the side- walk throughout central Hannover is the **Roter Faden** *(Red Thread; www.roterfaden-hannover.de),* a 4.2km/2.6mi self-guided city tour. It kicks off at the tourist office and ticks off 36 sights, including the Neues Rathaus and the Nanas. Pick up the *Red Thread Guide (2€)* at the tourist office.

The **picture gallery** *(Landesgalerie)* is particularly proud of its extensive collec- tion of German Impressionism and early Expressionism, with a healthy smattering of works by Liebermann, Slevogt, Corinth and Modersohn-Becker.

Names associated with the Middle Ages and the Renaissance include Meister Bertram, Lucas Cranach and Tilman Rie- menschneider. Rubens, Rembrandt and Ruisdael represent the Rococo.

Finally, there is the **ethnography department** *(Völkerkunde-Abteilung),* which features exotic exhibits from New Guinea, Mexico, Indonesia and other non-European cultures.

Sprengel-Museum Hannover★

Kurt-Schwitters-Platz. ○ *Open year- round, Tue 10am–8pm, Wed–Sun 10am –6pm.* ○ *Closed Good Fri, Dec 24–25 & 31.* ☞*7€.* ♿*.* ✆*(0511) 16 84 38 75. www.sprengel-museum.de.*

A stabile by Calder, the *Hellebardier,* welcomes you to this first-rate museum of 20C and 21C art. Key names include Picasso, Klee, Nolde, Beckmann, Han- nover-born Kurt Schwitters and Georg Baselitz as well Brücke (Schmidt- Rottluff) and Blaue Reiter (Kandinsky, Jawlensky, Macke) members. Fans of Niki de St. Phalle will get their fill as well.

👫 Erlebnis-Zoo Hannover★ (Hannover Zoo)

Adenauerallee 3. ○ *Open Mar–Oct, daily 9am–6pm; Nov–Feb, 10am–4pm.* ☞*23€ (child 16€).* ✆*(0511) 28 07 41 63. www.zoo-hannover.de.*

The Hannover Zoo is divided into five themed areas: the gorilla mountain with its waterfall; a jungle palace for elephants, tigers and leopards; a Zambezi landscape with lions, giraffes and okapis; Meyer's Hof, where farm animals make their home, and Mullewapp, a fantasy land based on a children's book.

Neues Rathaus (New Town Hall)

Open Mar–Nov, daily 9.30am–6.30pm Nov–Dec 11am–4.30pm. Closed Jan 1, Dec 24–26 & 31. 2.50€. (0511) 16 80.

Anchored in the marshy soil by 6 026 beech poles, Hannover's new town hall was completed in 1913. Ride the unique slanted elevator to the dome to enjoy sweeping city views.

The Nanas
Leibnitzufer.
Niki de St. Phalle's colourful if grotesque female doll sculptures caused quite an uproar when first installed along the Leine banks in 1974, but they have since become a beloved landmark.

ADDRESSES

STAY

CVJM City Hotel – *Limburgstraße 3. (0511) 360 70. www.cityhotelhannover.de. 47 rooms.* Rooms are functional at this impeccably run hotel in the pedestrian zone. The breakfast room exudes a cheerful Mediterranean mood.

Kastens Hotel Luisenhof – *Luisenstraße 1. (0511) 304 40. www.kastens-luisenhof.de. 145 rooms. Restaurant.* Comfort reigns supreme in Hannover's oldest hotel (1856), centrally located near the main train station. Rooms are elegantly furnished and the rooftop spa and leisure area are wonderful relaxation stations with a view.

EAT

Der Gartensaal – *Trammplatz 2. (0511) 16 84 88 88. www.gartensaal-hannover.de.* This bistro has an unusual location in the south entrance of the Neues Rathaus. Enjoy superb views of the Maschsee lake from the terrace or through the floor-to-ceiling windows.

Röhrbein – *Joachimstraße 6. (0511) 93 66 17 12 00. www.clichy.de. Closed Sun.* This bistro-style restaurant in the Luisenpassage arcade serves regional dishes in a friendly ambience.

Le Monde – *Friedrichswall 21. (0511) 856 51 71.* This classic French bistro delivers meals prepared with quality ingredients.

Basil – *Dragonerstraße 30. (0511) 62 26 36. www.basil.de. Closed Sun dinner.* The charismatic restaurant specialises in tasty fusion cuisine and is house in a beautiful 1867 brick building with vaulted ceilings.

Neue Zeiten – *Jakobistraße 24. (0511) 39 24 47. www.restaurant neuezeiten.de.* This restaurant gets plenty of return guests hooked on its Mediterranean-style contemporary cuisine. The walls double as a changing modern art gallery.

Broyhan-Haus – *Kramerstraße 24 (0511) 32 39 19. www.broyhanhaus.de. Reservation necessary.* This 14C building, one of the city's oldest town houses, was bought in 1537 by master brewer Cord Broyhan. Today it offers three floors of timeless cosiness along with hearty German cuisine (schnitzel, roast lamb) best washed down with a cold house brew.

Da Vinci – *Hildesheimer Straße 228. (0511) 843 65 56. www.rist-da-vinci.de.* From antipasti buffet to meat and fish dishes and pizza and pasta, this place offers the gamut of Italian fare.

TAKING A BREAK

Holländische Kakao-Stube – *Ständehausstraße 2–3 (Luisenstraße to the southwest). (0511) 30 41 00. www.hollaendische-kakao-stube.de. Closed Sun and public holidays.* If you lust for thick and steamy hot chocolate, check out this charming café decorated with Dutch ceramics. Homemade pastries also figure prominently on the menu.

Celle★★

The former residence of the dukes of Brunswick-Lüneburg, Celle retains the vaunted air of an aristocratic retreat. Its carefully preserved centre of half-timbered houses miraculously escaped war damage and is a joy to explore along with the restored ducal castle and the folklore museum.

SIGHTS
OLD TOWN★★
Celle's largely car-free old town boasts some of Germany's most elaborate half-timbered houses, especially along Neue Straße, Zöllnerstraße, Poststraße (note the richly carved Hoppener Haus, dating from 1532) and romantic Kalandgasse, near the church.

Altes Rathaus (Old Town Hall)
The heavily scrolled and pinnacled north gable (1579) of Celle's imposing Town Hall is a masterpiece of the Weser Renaissance. The *Ratskeller* (council cellar) has original Gothic vaulting.

Residenzmuseum im Celler Schloss★
Schlossplatz 1. Visit by guided tour (50min, in German) only, Apr–Oct, Tue–Fri 11am, 1pm, 3pm, Sat 11am–3pm hourly; Nov–Mar, Tue–Fri 11am and 3pm, Sat–Sun 11am, 1pm and 3pm. Closed Dec 24–25. 6€. (05141) 123 73. www.region-celle.de.
Begun in 1292, Celle's castle is flanked by massive corner towers and features dormer windows topped by rounded pediments, as is characteristic of the Weser Renaissance style.
Tour highlights include the private rooms of exiled Queen Caroline-Matilde of Denmark (1751–1775), the last royal to live at the palace, and the Renaissance-style **chapel**★ *(Hofkapelle)*.
The 17C Baroque *Schlosstheater* (theatre) is still in use. An exhibition from the Bomann Museum in the eastern wing documents the history of the House of Hanover.

- **Population:** 71 300
- **Info:** Markt 14, 29221 Celle. (05141) 12 12. www.region-celle.com.
- **Location:** Celle is part of the Lüneburg Heath, a region filled with charming villages and lots of opportunities to immerse yourself in nature.
- **Don't Miss:** Celle's old town and its 13C castle.
- **Timing:** Allow half a day to wander.

Bomann-Museum★
Schlossplatz 7. Open year-round, Tue–Sun 10am–5pm. 5€. (05141) 123 72. www.bomann-museum.de.
Come here for an in-depth study of the cultural history of Lower Saxony and Celle. Pride of place goes to heavily detailed period rooms, including the kitchen and a farmhouse.

Stadtkirche★ (City Church)
Open year-round, Apr–Dec, Tue–Sat 10am–6pm, Nov–Mar 11am–5pm. www.stadtkirche-celle.de.
Originally Gothic, this church got a 17C Baroque makeover and is noteworthy for its 1613 altar, the 16C *Fürstenstuhl* (Prince's Seat) and the 1610 baptismal font. The tower can be climbed.

EXCURSION
Kloster Wienhausen★
10km/6.2mi south. An der Kirche 1. Visit by guided tour (75min) only, Apr–Oct, Tue–Sun 10am, 11am, then hourly 2pm–5pm (Oct 4pm), Sun hourly noon–5pm. Closed mid-Oct–Mar, Good Fri, Tue after Pentecost, Sept 29. 4€. (05149) 186 60. www.kloster-wienhausen.de.
Run by Protestant cannonesses since the Reformation, this 13C abbey counts wooden sculptures of the Virgin and Christ Resurrected among its treasures. The Nuns' Choir is embellished with early 14C **frescoes**★.

Wolfenbüttel★★

For three centuries, until the court transferred to Brunswick in 1753, Wolfenbüttel was the seat of the dukes of Brunswick and Lüneburg. The precise, spacious plan, with perfectly straight streets linking large symmetrical squares, makes it one of the most successful examples of Renaissance town planning in Germany.

SIGHTS
Fachwerkhäuser★★ (Half-timbered Houses)

The homes of high court officials lining Kanzleistraße, Reichstraße and western Harzstraße, built c. 1600, are distinguished by majestic façades with overhangs flanking the main entrance. At Harzstraße 12 note the grimacing heads above cornices carved with

▸ **Population:** 53 800

▪ **Info:** Stadtmarkt 7, 38300 Wolfenbüttel. ℘(05331) 862 80. www.wolfenbuettel.com.

◐ **Location:** Straddling the banks of the Oker, Wolfenbüttel is the ideal base for exploring the Harz Mountains.

◉ **Don't Miss:** The city's half-timbered houses.

◐ **Timing:** Allow at least three hours to see everything.

biblical inscriptions. The decoration of smaller houses owned by lesser dignitaries and merchants is, surprisingly, more elaborate. A single gable normally tops their wide, flat façades (Lange Herzogstraße, Brauergildenstraße, Holz-

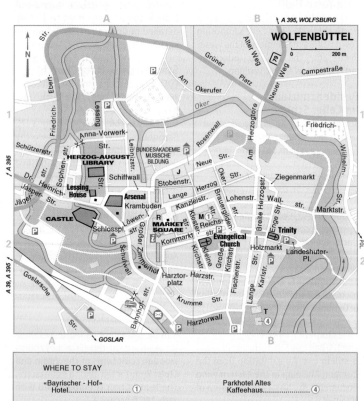

WHERE TO STAY

«Bayrischer - Hof» Hotel..............................① Parkhotel Altes Kaffeehaus......................④

Fachwerkhäuser

markt, Krambuden). Even the simpler, two-storey houses of the less well-to-do (Krumme Straße, Stobenstraße) are ornamented with coloured fan designs. Corner houses with slightly projecting oriels are a particular characteristic of Wolfenbüttel and are prevalent around the Stadtmarkt (main town square).

Stadtmarkt★ (Town Market Square)

The **Rathaus** (town hall) occupies a number of 16C and 17C buildings on the north and west of the square. The Weights and Measures Office has a distinctive arched doorway surmounted by King Solomon's Edict and the Wolfenbüttel coat of arms.

Schloss★ (Palace)

Open year-round, Tue–Sun, 10am–5pm. Closed Jan 1, Good Fri, May 1, Dec 24–25 & 31. 3.50€. (05331) www.wolfenbuettel.de/fmis.
The palace is reached via an attractive narrow street bordered by arcades known as *Krambuden*. Originally a 12C stronghold conquered by Henry the Lion, the building experienced many transformations before it evolved into Lower Saxony's second-largest palace (after the *Leineschloss* in Hannover).
The **Schlossmuseum** (palace museum) consists of the **Ducal Apartments** as they were in 1690–1750. Rare furniture, tapestries, porcelain and paintings illus-trate Baroque court life. Note the ivory scenes adorning the walls of the small study. *Access via the central courtyard and main stairway.*

Herzog August Bibliothek★ (Library)

Lessingplatz 2. Open year-round, Tue–Sun 10am–5pm. Closed Jan 1, Good Fri, Dec 24–25 & 31. 3€, also good for Lessinghaus. (05331) 80 80. www.hab.de.
Founded in 1572 by Augustus the Young, this was the largest, most important library in Europe in the 17C. Still a treasure for researchers and scholars, it today houses some 860 000 volumes. Among the priceless manuscripts and illuminated documents from the Middle Ages are a rare example of the 14C *Saxon Mirror*, and a gospel book from 1188 that once belonged to Henry the Lion *(shown periodically in the first-floor Vault Room).*
In the Globe Room are terrestrial and celestial globes from the 16C and 17C, as well as ancient maps. The Malerbuchkabinett hall contains books illustrated by great artists of the 20C.

Lessinghaus

Lessingplatz 2. Open year-round, Sat–Sun 10am–5pm. Closed Jan 1, Good Fri, Dec 24–25 & 31. 3€, also good for Herzog August Library. (05331) 80 80. www.hab.de.

Jägermeister Town

Jägermeister (literally, master of the hunt) first appeared in Wolfenbüttel in 1935. This uniquely-flavoured alcoholic drink is made from 56 plants, roots and extracts ripened for a year. The stag on the label refers to St. Hubert, patron saint of hunters. Legend has it that 7C King Hubert rejected his wealth when his wife Floribana died, devoting himself to hunting. During one of his solitary outings a stag with a cross floating between its antlers appeared to him. The vision gave him his calling; he immediately forsook his wealth and title and founded several monasteries.

Gotthold Ephraim Lessing, the great innovator of German drama, spent 11 years working as official ducal librarian in Wolfenbüttel (1770–81) and penning, among other works, *Emilia Galotti* and *Nathan the Wise*. His former home is now a museum with exhibits providing insight into his life, times and work. Beside the Lessing house is the **Zeughaus** (Arsenal, 1613), a distinctive Renaissance building with projecting gables, obelisks and scrolls.

Hauptkirche (Main Church)

⏰*Open year-round, Tue–Sun 10am–noon, 2pm–4pm.* ✆*(05331) 311 72.*
Built on Kornmarkt in 1608, this Protestant church was influenced by the Late Gothic hall-church tradition. The massive tower with its Baroque roof resembles the shape of the castle tower. The altar, pulpit and organ case date from the late Renaissance.

Trinitatiskirche (Trinity Church)

Holzmarkt. ⏰*Open year-round, Tue 11am–1pm, Wed 11am–1pm and 2pm–4pm, Thu 3pm–5pm, Sat 11am–4pm.* ✆*(05331) 311 72.*
This Baroque church was built in 1719 on top of an existing, twin-towered structure, thus explaining its strangely flat silhouette. Near the church is a **park**, formed from the old city walls.

EXCURSION
👤👤 Autostadt★★

▶ *40km/25mi northeast, in Wolfsburg.*
⏰*Open year-round, daily 9am–6pm.*
⏰*Closed Dec 24 & 31.* 🎫*15€.* ♿.
✆*(05361) 400. www.autostadt.de.*
This vast and hugely popular **Volkswagen theme park** sits next to the VW factory where landscaped parkland forms a pleasant backdrop to modernist pavilions. Sections include the **AutoLab**, which explain car manufacturing and vehicle technology. The **ZeitHaus** tells the history of the automobile and features famous cars such as John Lennon's Beetle. Elsewhere ride a lift to the top of the 48m/157ft **Autotürme** (car towers) where the new cars are stored. Combination tickets with the interactive science centre **Phaeno** (🎫*23€;* ✆*(0180) 106 06 00; www.phaeno.de*), opposite Autostadt, are available as well.

ADDRESSES

🏨 STAY

🍽🍽 **Bayrischer Hof** – *Brauergildenstraße 5.* ✆*(05331) 50 78. www.bayrischer-hof-wf.de. 17 rooms.* 🛏. *Restaurant*🍽. The individually designed rooms occupy a beautiful half-timbered house from the 16C. Some of the rooms overlook the square and the church of Santa Maria.

🍽🍽 **Parkhotel Altes Kaffeehaus** – *Harztorwall 18.* ✆*(05331) 88 80. www.parkhotel-wolfenbuettel.de. 75 rooms. Restaurant*🍽🍽. Converted from a Turkish coffeehouse, this modern hotel has attractive, comfortable rooms Dine in the bright restaurant or in the vaulted wine cellar *(Weingrotte)*.

Goslar★★

Goslar is often deluged by daytrippers and for good reason: its historic centre is a wonderful maze of narrow cobbled lanes lined with some of the most richly decorated half-timbered houses in Germany. In 1992, the old town, along with the 1 000-year-old Rammelsberg Mines, became a UNESCO World Heritage Site. In 2010, the 800-year-old Upper Harz mining water management system nearby was also added.

THE OLD TOWN★★★ (ALTSTADT)

The old town of Goslar is largely a pedestrian zone, making it a pleasant place to wander round.

Marktplatz★ (Market Square)

The market square is surrounded by slate-clad houses.
Two Gothic buildings, the Kaiserworth and the Rathaus, stand before the spires of the 12C **Marktkirche**. In the centre of the square is a **fountain** (*Marktbrunnen*) with two bronze basins (1230). The square also features a chiming **animated clock** with four different scenes (*at 9am, noon, 3pm and 6pm*) represent-

Restaurant opposite Marktkirche
J. Bouraly/MICHELIN

- ▶ **Population:** 43 750
- **Info:** Markt 7, 38640 Goslar. ℘(05321) 780 60. www.goslar.de.
- **Location:** Goslar lies on the northern edge of the Harz National Park and makes a good base of operations for exploring this mountainous forest region.
- **Don't Miss:** The Old Town.
- **Timing:** Allow three hours for a walking tour of the Old City and another half-day if visiting the Rammelsberg Mines.
- **Kids:** Rammelsberg Mines.

ing the history of mining in the Harz Mountains.

Rathaus★ (Town Hall)

Following the medieval custom, this 15C building was designed with an arcaded gallery opening onto the Marktplatz. On the south side, an exterior staircase leads to the first floor **State Room** (*Diele*).

Huldigungssaal★★ (Hall of Homage)

Open Apr–Oct and Dec Mon–Fri 11am–3pm, Sat–Sun 11am–4pm. Jan–Mar Tue–Sun tour only 10am. Closed Dec 24. 3.50€. ℘(053 21) 780 60. www.goslar.de.
This room, transformed into the **city council assembly hall** in 1490, was magnificently decorated c. 1520. The wall decorations feature Roman emperors alternating with sibyls in Renaissance costume, while the ceiling depicts biblical figures, including Christ, the prophets and the Evangelists. A tiny side chapel contains an arm-bone reliquary (c. 1300) of St. Margaret.

Hotel Kaiserworth

Opposite the Rathaus, this Gothic edifice (1494) is decorated with statues of eight German emperors along with the irreverent **Ducat Man** (Dukatenmännchen). He is depicted as excreting a gold coin – an allusion to Goslar's ancient right to mint coins.

Fachwerkhäuser★★ (Half-timbered Houses)

The Schuhhof, a small square northwest of the Rathaus, is entirely surrounded by half-timbered buildings. Further on, a passageway on the left leads to the narrow Münzstraße, which in turn passes an old inn, **Am Weißen Schwan**, and then the **Alte Münze** (old mint). Now a restaurant, this timbered building dates from 1500. The fine house on the corner of the Münzstraße and the Marktstraße was constructed in 1526.

Facing the Marktkirche is the **Brusttuch** (1521), built for a rich mine owner and decorated with biblical, mythological and legendary characters. It is now a hotel and restaurant. Not far away looms the tall gable of the **Bäckergildehaus** (bakers' guild hall, 1501–1557).

The **Renaissance houses** at the Marktstraße-Bäckerstraße intersection are adorned with friezes of the fan motif, typical of Lower Saxony (e.g., Bäckerstraße 2).

Siemenshaus★★

Schreiberstraße 12. ⏱Open year-round, Tue 9am–noon, Thu 10am–noon. ♿ ℰ(05321) 238 37.
One of Goslar's most spectacular houses is the ancestral home of the industrial Siemens family, built in 1693. Note the tiled entrance (Däle) and picturesque inner courtyard.

ADDITIONAL SIGHTS
Neuwerkkirche★ (Neuwerk Church)

⏱Open Mar–Oct, Mon–Sat 10am–noon, 2.30pm–4.30pm, Sun 2.30pm–4.30pm. ℰ(05321) 228 39.
www.neuwerkkirche-goslar.de.
This former Cistercian collegiate church (12C) is a three-aisled basilica whose tall polygonal towers are exceptionally elegant for a Romanesque church. Heavily ribbed, pointed vaulting characterises the interior. Of particular artistic merit is the former 13C **choir screen★** festooned with sculptures of Christ, the Virgin Mary, the apostles Peter and Paul and two saints; it now serves as the organ loft.

The frescoes in the choir date back to the early 13C and depict Mary on the throne and Old Testament scenes.

Pfarrkirche Peter und Paul★ (St. Peter and St. Paul Church)

Enter on Frankenberger Plan.
⏱Open Apr–Oct, daily 9am–6pm. ℰ(05321) 224 64.
Also known as Frankenberger Kirche (1108), this was once the principal church of the local miners. The three-nave basilica beautifully preserves its Romanesque features despite Gothic alterations in the choir and southern transept and a lavish Baroque altarpiece. Pillars and vaults are richly decorated with stone carvings, while the frescoes above the choir and upper loft were painted in the early 13C.

The 12C altar bears a splendid Baroque retable dating to 1675, which, like the 1698 chancel, originated in the Goslar woodcarving workshop of Heinrich and Jobst Lessen.

Kaiserpfalz (Imperial Palace)

⏱Open Apr–Oct, daily 10am–5pm; Nov–Mar, 10am–4pm. ⏱Closed Dec 24 & 31. ✦4.50€. ♿ ℰ(05321) 311 96 93. www.goslar.de.
One of best-preserved Romanesque palaces in Germany, the Kaiserpfalz was built in the 11C under Emperor Henry III and for two centuries hosted several imperial diets. It was heavily restored in a Historicist style in the late 19C.

At that time, the gigantic **Reichssaal** (on the first floor) was swathed in romanticised paintings depicting significant moments from Goslar's medieval glory days. Beyond the Reichssaal is the early 12C **Palatine Chapel of St. Ulrich**, where the floorplan transitions from a Greek cross into an octagon.

Inside is a tomb holding the heart of Heinrich III (the body is buried in the cathedral at Speyer).

Le Rammelsberg

WHERE TO STAY	WHERE TO EAT	
Der Achterman...............⑥	Die Butterhanne...............③	Kaiserworth .... S
Die Forest Lodge.............⑨	Restaurant Aubergine........⑥	Maison de la Guilde des Boulangers ... Y
Die Tanne......................①	Worthmühle.....................①	
Goldene Krone................⑫		
Hotel Kaiserworth............④		

Mönche Haus Museum für Moderne Kunst★ (Monks' House Modern Art Museum)

Mönchestraße 1. ⏺*Open year-round, Tue–Sun 10am–5pm.* ⏺*5€.* ♿ *℘(05321) 295 70. www.moenchehaus.de.*

A roll-call of such top 20C artists as Beuys, Hundertwasser, Serra, Baselitz, Chilida and de Kooning is the bread and butter of this museum set up in a stately 1528 patrician mansion, adjacent half-timbered buildings and vaulted cellars.

👥 Rammelsberg Mines★

Bergtal 19, southwest of town via Clausthaler Straße and Rammelsberger Straße. ⏺*Guided tours (60–75min) year-round, daily 9am–6pm (last tour 4.30pm).* ⏺*Closed Dec 24 & 31.* ⏺*12€, incl. museum and one guided tour.* ℘*(05321) 75 01 22. www.rammelsberg.de.*

The source of Goslar's prosperity, the 1 000-year-old Rammelsberg mines are now a major tourist attraction. Spend a little time above ground at the **museum** to gain a better appreciation of their importance before descending deep into the bowels of the earth on a guided tour.

Two types of tours are available. During the "Fire and Water: The Roeder Gallery" you enter an impressive network of galleries, water wheels and shafts and come face to face with the amazing blaze of colour of its minerals.

Kids usually prefer the other tour because it involves a ride on an under-

The Mines

Goslar's fortunes have always been pegged to the abundance of silver in the nearby Rammelsberg Mines. They were the main reason Emperor Heinrich II made the town an imperial residence in the 11C. Goslar remained a home of the German kings and emperors until 1253 when it became a Free Imperial City and member of the Hanseatic League. Its prosperity peaked during the 15C and 16C, as is reflected in the abundance of the lavish half-timbered town houses still gracing the town centre.

ground railway and noisy demonstrations of old and modern equipment.

Grauhof★

3 km/2mi. Exit via Okerstraße.

This church was commissioned by the Augustinians of the Grauhof monastery (1527) and built between 1701–1717 by an Italian architect. Noteworthy features include a boat-shaped chancel (1721), the splendid organ (1737) and the carved choir stalls where the life of St. Augustine is depicted in 56 scenes.

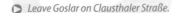

🚗 DRIVING TOURS

1 THE UPPER HARZ

81km/50mi – Allow half a day.

▶ *Leave Goslar on Clausthaler Straße.*

This itinerary passes through vast tracts of rolling hills draped in pine.

Clausthal-Zellerfeld

This twin town is the former mining capital of the Harz. At Zellerfeld, the **Upper Harz Mine Museum** (*Oberharzer Bergwerksmuseum; Bornhardtstraße 16;* 🕐 *open year-round, daily 9am–5pm;* 🕐 *closed Dec 24;* ◉ *5€;* 🖋 *(05323) 989 50; www.bergwerksmuseum.de*) illustrates mining techniques used until 1930 and documents the history of the region.

At Clausthal the **Pfarrkirche zum Heiligen Geist** (*Hindenburgplatz*) was built in the 17C and is one of the largest wooden churches in Europe.

From the top of the **Oker Dam** (*Okertalsperre*) there is a fine **view**★ over the widely dispersed waters of the reservoir.

St. Andreasberg

🎫 *Visit by guided tour (1hr), year-round, daily 11am and 2.30pm. Museum: 8.30am–4pm.* 🕐 *Closed Jan 1 and Dec 24* ◉ *4.50€.* 🖋 *(055 82) 12 49. www.sankt-andreasberg.de.*

The road leads first to an **old silver mine**★ (*Silberbergwerk Samson,* at the bottom of the valley), closed in 1910 but since reopened for tourists. The *Fahrkunst,* a machine of ingenious simplicity, which sent down and brought back the miners, still functions.

Braunlage

Served by the Brocken railway, this spa resort, prized for its climate and ski slopes, lies high up on a plateau overlooked by the wooded **Wurmberg** (971m/3185.6ft).

Schierke

If you want to climb the summit of the **Brocken** – or at least have a go at it – the Schierke station on the **Brockenbahn** (Brocken narrow-gauge railway) is the place to start. Schierke is a lovely place in its own right and a gateway to the Harz National Park.

Wernigerode★

Wernigerode is one of the most delightful small towns in this region.

Its **Rathaus**★★ (*town hall, on Marktplatz*) was first mentioned in 1277 and originally served as a courthouse and dance hall. The current model is mostly from the 16C and is considered one of the finest half-timbered buildings in Germany.

Breite Straße, as it leaves Marktplatz, is lined with more residential half-timbered beauties.

The most admired building, though, is the **Krummelsches Haus** (1674) at no 74 whose timbered front has been covered up with a wooden façade so

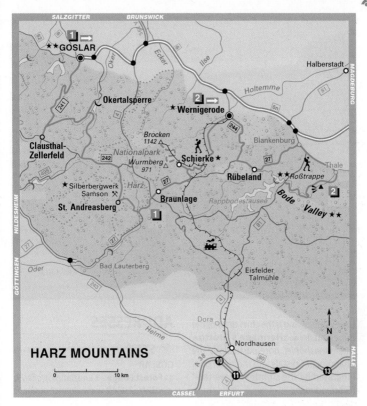

HARZ MOUNTAINS

0   10 km

intricately carved that it resembles a copper-etching.

Schloss Wernigerode

🕐 *Open May–Oct, daily 10am–6pm; Nov–Apr, Tue–Fri 10am–4pm, Sat–Sun 10am–6pm.* ⊛*5€.* 🖉*(03943) 55 30 30. www.schloss-wernigerode.de.*
Originally a medieval fortress built to protect the emperors while on hunting expeditions, this castle was repeatedly altered and given a romantic makeover in the 19C. Rooms are filled with original paintings and furniture and illustrate the exalted lifestyle once enjoyed by the German aristocracy.

2 THE EASTERN HARZ

89km/55mi – Allow half a day.

In the eastern stretches of the Harz mountains, pine forests dominate. Although not quite as dramatic, the landscape still offers great natural beauty.

Wernigerode★
(👟See above)

Rübeland

🚂*Visit by guided tour (1hr) only, Jul–Aug, daily 9am–5.30pm; Feb–Jun and Sept–Oct, 9am–4.30pm; Nov–Jan, 9am–3.30pm.* ⊛*7€.* 🖉*(039454) 491 32. www.harzer-hoehlen.de.*

😊 A Bit of Advice 😊

Nostalgia fans will love riding the narrow-gauge trains powered by steam locomotives that crisscross the eastern Harz. The Harzquerbahn runs for 60km/37mi from Wernigerode to Nordhausen. The Brockenbahn chugs up Brocken mountain from Drei Annen Hohne. And the Selketalbahn runs from Quedlinburg to Hasselfelde.

Bodetal near Thale in Spring

© hsvrs/iStockphoto.com

Limestone caving is the chief draw of the Rübeland. In **Hermann's Grotto**★ *(Hermannshöhle)*, note particularly the Chamber of Crystals and the small pool inhabited by the sightless "cave fish" *(Grottenolmen)*.

▶ *Continue via Blankenburg and Thale to reach the Bode Valley.*

Bodetal★★ (Bode Valley)

The river here has gouged a passage through a maze of rock masses and now flows along the foot of craggy cliffs. The most spectacular site is the **Roßtrappe**★★ (charger's hoofmark), a 10-minute walk from the car park. From the look-out point, which juts out dizzyingly above the river far below, there is an incredible **view**★★★ of the cliffs, the tumbling stream, a steep gorge and the distant woods.

The place owes its name to the legend of a horse which, ridden by a princess and chased by a giant, leapt with such force across the chasm that it left an imprint in the rock.

Following the course of the river, the scenic stretch of road twists and turns through the rugged forest landscape as far as the junction with the B81.

ADDRESSES

⌂ STAY

GOSLAR

➤ **Forest Lodge** – *Clausthaler Straße 19.* ℰ *(0394) 57 97 60. www.zimmer-goslar.de 4 rooms.* ⊡ *6.50€.* A bit outside of town, this charming wooden chalet has a just few rooms but is surrounded by lush greenery. The breakfast is organic and is best enjoyed on the terrace in fine weather.

➤ **Goldene Krone** – *Breite Straße 46.* ℰ *(05321) 344 90. www.goldene-krone-goslar.de. 16 rooms.* ⊡. This small family-hotel occupies a half-timbered house (1733) and makes for an excellent launch pad for explorations around the region.

➤ **Hotel Die Tanne** – *Bäringer Straße 10.* ℰ *(05321) 343 90. www.die-tanne.de. 22 rooms.* Behind the shale façade of this cosy hotel in a listed building await bright, modern rooms fitted with all major comforts. The Finnish sauna and hotel bar make good spots to unwind.

➤ **Hotel der Achtermann** – *Rosentorstraße 20.* ℰ *(05321) 700 00. www.der-achtermann.de. 154 rooms.* ⊡. Near the pedestrian zone and railway station, this elegant hotel has nicely decked out rooms with a good range of mod cons. Relaxation spots include an indoor pool and a spa. The restaurant served traditional German fare.

🍴🍷🛏 **Hotel Kaiserworth** – *Markt 3.* 📞*(05321) 70 90. www.kaiserworth.de. 66 rooms.* 🚗. This richly decorated building from 1494 used to belong to the Guild of Clothmakers and Traders. It is right on the market square and boasts a superb restaurant ensconced in a series of arcades.

HARZ MOUNTAINS
🍴 **Hotel Zum Brockenbäcker** – *Lindenwarte 20, 38875 Tanne.* 📞*(0394) 57 97 60. www.brockenbaecker.de. Closed 1 week in Nov. 16 rooms.* 🚗. This half-timbered property was converted into a hotel in 1912. Rooms are comfortable in a rustic sort of way. The restaurant serves freshly baked breads for breakfast.

🍴 EAT
GOSLAR
🍴 **Die Butterhanne** – *Marktkirchhof 3.* 📞*(05321) 228 86. www.butterhanne.de.* In this brasserie you sit at large tables and fortify yourself with meaty dishes, including some game specialities (e.g. venison, wild boar sausage and steak).

🍴🍷🛏 **Aubergine** – *Marktstraße 4.* 📞*(05321) 421 36. www.aubergine-goslar.de.* Modern and sophisticated, yet warm and welcoming, this restaurant will charm you with candlelight, fresh flowers and a trickling fountain and tempt you with cleverly composed Mediterranean cuisine. Great wines and romantic summer terrace, too.

🍴🍷🛏 **Worthmühle** – *Worthstraße 4,* 📞*(05321) 434 02. www.worthmuehle.de. Closed 1–7 Jan, Tue, Sat lunch.* This restaurant in a riverbank mill feels as welcoming as a hug from an old friend. In summer, the beer garden is the best place for enjoying the regional dishes and locally brewed beers.

Hildesheim★

Founded as a bishopric in 815, Hildesheim managed to preserve its beautiful medieval buildings until an Allied air-raid laid waste to most of the city in 1945. In the 1980s, part of the old town was faithfully reconstructed, especially around the market square. The cathedral and the Church of St. Michael are both UNESCO World Heritage Sites.

SIGHTS
Marktplatz★
The historical market square has been beautifully restored and is framed by buildings reflecting eight centuries of architectural styles. The east side is flanked by Gothic buildings from the 13C, including the **Rathaus** (town hall), where a carillon plays its merry tune daily at noon, 1pm and 5pm.

Medieval Architectural Gems
Housing the tourist office, the unusual early 14C **Tempelhaus** dominates the

▶ **Population:** 103 000
ℹ **Info:** Rathausstraße 18–20, 31134 Hildesheim. 📞*(05121) 179 80. www.hildesheim.de.*
▶ **Location:** Hildesheim is 34km/21mi south of Hannover, just off the A7 autobahn.
▶ **Don't Miss:** The Marktplatz and the Cathedral.
▶ **Timing:** Allow at least half a day to do Hildesheim justice.

south side of the Marktplatz. Its most distinctive feature is the ornate 16C Renaissance **oriel★**, which depicts the parable of the Prodigal Son. The nearby 16C half-timbered **Wedekindhaus** has bay windows spanning from ground level up to the roof, a typical feature of the Weser Renaissance style. Not far off is the **Lüntzelhaus** (1755), now a local bank, and the 14C Gothic **Rolandstift** with a Baroque porch (c. 1730).

Marktplatz with butchers' guild hall and Stadtschänke

© Urs Schweitzer/imagebroker/Alamy

The **bakers' guild hall** (*Bäckeramtshaus, 1451*) and **butchers' guild hall**★ (*Knochenhauer Amtshaus, 1529*) occupy the square's west side. The five upper floors house the **Stadtmuseum** (*local history museum;* ⏱*open year-round, Tue–Sun 10am–6pm;* ⏱*closed Dec 24 & 31;* ⏺*2.50€;* ☎*(05121) 936 90; www.stadtmuseum-hildesheim.de*).

The **Rokokohaus** on the north side of the square is wedged between the **Stadtschänke**, a local restaurant, and the **weavers' guild hall** (*Wollenwebergildehaus*).

Dom★ (Cathedral)

⏱*Open mid-Mar–Oct, Mon–Sat 9.30am–5pm, Sun 9am–5pm; Nov–mid-Mar, Mon–Sat 10am–4.30pm, Sun noon–5pm.* ⏱*Closed Good Fri & Dec 24.* ♿☎*(05121) 179 17 60. www.bistum-hildesheim.de.*

Hildesheim's reconstructed 11C Romanesque cathedral is endowed with rare and precious artworks. Two bronze casts commissioned by Bishop Bernard in the early 11C are worth closer inspection: the **Christussäule**★ (*Christ Column*) and the **Bernwardstüren**★★ (*Bernward*

doors), both depicting biblical scenes. The doors stand almost 5m/16.4ft tall and are 1m/3.28ft wide and were cast as a single piece, an amazing achievement for the time and one of the reasons they are today a UNESCO World Heritage Site. Also note the massive 11C chandelier and the 13C baptismal font supported by figures representing the rivers of Paradise.

The **legendary rosebush** is in the Romanesque **cloister**★ (⏱*open 10am–4pm Mon–Sat, noon–5pm Sun;* ⏺*0.50€*).

Roemer- und Pelizaeus-Museum★

Am Steine 1–2. ⏱*Open year-round, Tue–Sun 10am–6pm.* ⏺*8€.* ♿☎*(05121) 936 90. www.rpmuseum.de.*

Named for its 19C benefactors, the lawyer Hermann Roemer and the merchant Wilhelm Pelizaeus, this museum houses one of Germany's richest collections of Egyptian antiquities.

Highlights include the life-size figure of Heimunu and the statue of the scribe Heti from excavations near Giza. Rare items from ancient Peru form another focal point.

Medieval Churches

Dating from the 11C, the UNESCO-protected **St. Michaelis-Kirche**★ exemplifies Ottonian architecture. Note the 13C painted ceiling depicting the Tree of Jesse. The 12C **St. Godehardikirche**★ sports an elegant silhouette marked by three slender spires. **St. Andreaskirche**, (14C–15C), is a massive Gothic church whose tower can be climbed. Fronted by a Baroque façade, the **Heiligkreuzkirche** is built on an 11C Early Romanesque church but now has Ottonian, Gothic and Baroque elements jostling for attention.

Einbeck★

In the Middle Ages, no fewer than 600 small breweries in this former Hanseatic town supplied the whole of Germany with "Einpöckisches Bier" (forerunner of Bock beer). Einbeck retains part of its medieval fortifications as well as hundreds of half-timbered houses, richly decorated with multi-coloured carvings.

▶ **Population:** 28 200

▪ **Info:** Marktstraße 13, 37574 Einbeck. ℘(05561) 313 19 10. www.einbeck-online.de.

▶ **Location:** Einbeck is on the B3, about halfway between Göttingen and Hildesheim.

▸ **Don't Miss:** The old town.

▲ **Timing:** Allow at least one hour to see Einbeck's old town.

WALKING TOUR
OLD TOWN★

The most distinctive building on Einbeck's historic **Marktplatz**★★ (market square) is the **Rathaus** (old town hall), dating from 1606 and fronted by a trio of miniature towers reminiscent of witches' hats.

Also looming over the square is the 14C **Marktkirche** (market church) whose off-kilter tower accounts for its nickname "Leaning Tower of Einbeck". Church treasures include a 12C Romanesque baptismal font and a 14C Gothic altar.

On the corner of Münsterstraße, the **Brodhaus** (1552) with its jutting upper story was once owned by the baker's guild. Like most of the old houses, the impressive **Ratsapotheke** (1590) has ventilated attics that served as storage lofts for hops and barley.

▶ *Follow Tiedexerstraße, west of the square.*

Tiedexerstraße★★

This lane is lined with especially ornate half-timbered houses. The one at no 31 abuts the old town fortifications.

▶ *Turn left on Maschenstraße and follow it to Marktstraße.*

Marktstraße

The tourist office is housed in the fabulous **Eickesches Haus**★★ (1612–14) at the corner of Knochenhauer Straße. See if you can spot the female figures representing the five senses, the four Evangelists and four of the apostles in the ornate facade.

EXCURSION
Bad Gandersheim

▶ *20km/12.4mi northeast.*

The birthplace of Roswitha von Gandersheim, Germany's first (10C) poetess, is best known as a hot spring and saltwater spa. The twin octagonal towers of the **cathedral**★ overlook the town centre. Inside are two altars, one 15C and the other 16C. The well-preserved half-timbered houses around the market square date from the 16C.

Hann. Münden★★

The famous traveller and naturalist, Alexander von Humboldt, described Hann. Münden as one of Germany's seven most beautifully-sited cities. Built at the confluence of the rivers Fulda, Werra and Weser, this charming town boasts a remarkable historic centre lined with carefully restored half-timbered houses.

SIGHTS
The Old Town★
This medieval jewel comprises over 700 **half-timbered houses**★★ that reflect six centuries of local architecture. The most interesting line the streets between the Rathaus (town hall) and the River Werra. The castle ruins add a picturesque finishing touch to the charming ancient streetscape.

Rathaus (Town Hall)★
The main façade of the town hall is typical of the Weser-Renaissance style (see HAMELN), decorated with scrolls, pyramids and statues on its gables.

SchlossGuelph municipal museum
Schlossplatz 5. Open Wed–Thu 10am–noon, 2.30pm–5pm; Sat 10.30am–noon, 2.30pm–4pm; Sun 10am–12.30pm. *Guided visits May–Sept Fri afternoon and Heritage Day (in German only, book in advance for English).* 1.70€. 05541 75 202.
The highlight of a visit to the small city history museum is the opportunity to take a tour of the town hall and castle, including its Renaissance and White Horse rooms. Occasional classical music concerts are held inside the castle.

St-Blasiikirche (St. Blaise Church)
The hexagonal church tower rises proudly from the steep roof. Once inside this converted late-15C Gothic hall church, note in the right aisle, the tomb of Duke

▶ **Population:** 24 505

ℹ **Info:** Lotzestraße 2 (in the town hall). 055 41 753 13. www.hann. muenden-tourismus. de. Open Mon–Fri May–Oct 9.30am–6pm, (Sat 10am–3pm, Sun 11am–2pm); Nov–Apr Mon–Thu 9.30am–4pm, Fri 9.30am–1pm. Cyclists should ask about special bike maps of the region.

▷ **Location:** Hann. Munden is set at the crossroads of the A7, linking Cassel and Göttingen. The B80 runs through the town along the River Weser.

William of Brunswick (d. 1503), and, to the left of the choir, the epitaph of his son, and a 14C baptismal font.

🚗 DRIVING TOUR

THE UPPER WESER VALLEY★
67km/42mi – Allow 2hrs.

(see the region map on pp176–177)

Between Münden and Bad Karlshafen, the Weser winds through a wooded valley. It was settled in the 18C by French Huguenots, under the jurisdiction of the Landgrave (count) of Hesse.
The villages bear symbolic names such as Gottstreu (true to God) and Gewissenruh (clear conscience).

Wahlsburg-Lippoldsberg
The ancient abbey church of Lippoldsberg is one of the earliest Romanesque vaulted shrines in Northern Germany. Take the ferry across the river to the left bank.

Gewissenruh
Note the tiny temple (1779) and the French inscriptions on the houses.

Where Rivers Meet

Hann. Münden is built deep in a wooded valley where the rivers Fulda and Werra unite to form the Weser ("where the Werra and Fulda kiss, and leave their names behind"). Excavations have revealed that a colony existed here at the time of Charlemagne. The foundation of the city dates back to the late 12C from the time of Henry the Lion. It enjoyed special trading privileges from 1247 to 1823, and this age of prosperity is still reflected today in the many beautiful half-timbered houses in the old town.

Originally, the town was called Münden, though by the 18C, it was referred to as Hannoversch Münden, to avoid confusion with the Prussian town of Minden (Minden Preussisch) which is similarly pronounced. With the advent of the railways, in 1870, the name was abbreviated to Hann. Münden, though inhabitants still refer to their town as Münden.

Bad Karlshafen

This small town was founded in 1699 by the Landgrave Charles of Hesse, to shelter his French religious refugees; its geometric plan and its uniform buildings lend it a monumental character.

Deutsches Hugenotten-Museum (German Huguenots Museum)

Hafenplatz 9. ⏰*Open mid-Mar–end Dec Tue–Fri 10am–5pm, Sat–Sun 2–5pm.* ✱*4€.* ♿ ☏*056 72 14 10. www.hugenottenmuseum.de.*

This small museum is housed in a former tobacco factory. On the first floor, the history of the Huguenots in France is related, with particular emphasis on the story of the famous potter, Bernard Palissy, and his tragic fate. The second floor is devoted to the reception that the Huguenots received in Germany, and their influence on crafts, science and the arts.

Fürstenberg

The famous Fürstenberg porcelain has been manufactured here since 1747. Adjacent to the "factory", in the castle, the **Schlossmuseum** (⏰*open Apr–Oct Tue–Sun 10am–5pm; Nov–Mar Sat–Sun 10am–5pm;* ⏰*closed Jan 1–11, Dec 24–26 & 31;* ⬤*guided tours Sun 3pm (1hr, min 5 people);* ✱*5€; guided tour additional 4€;* ♿*;* ☏*05271 40 11 61; www.fuerstenberg -porzellan.com)* tells the history of porcelain and has hundreds of beautiful pieces on show. You can also learn about the local production techniques with films and actual demonstrations.

Höxter★

The town's half-timbered houses are decorated in Renaissance and Baroque styles, topped by ancient pink-sandstone roofs. The most picturesque of these line Westerbachstraße.

St. Kilian's Church has a beautiful decorated **choir**★★ with precious alabaster Renaissance motifs (1597).

Corvey Abbey

⏰*Open Apr–Oct. www.schloss-corvey.de.*

During the early Middle Ages the Benedictine Abbey of Corvey, founded by Ludwig the Pious in 822, was one of the most significant abbeys in Germany. Even today, the 9C west end, the only one of its kind in Europe, still reflects the power and splendour of its era. Highlights include the oldest frescoes in Westphalia, the magnificent Baroque Imperial Hall, the picture gallery, the imposing cloister with its Romanesque triumphal crucifix, the oldest post-Reformation reliquary shrine (of St. Vitus) in Germany, and the former abbey buildings themselves.

⊙*Don't miss the private library of the Dukes of Ratibor (who still own the property) which includes over 74 000 extremely rare volumes. The Höxter-Corve Museum relates the rich story of the abbey.*

Hameln★

Occupying a special spot in German folklore, Hameln is best known as the home of the Pied Piper, the legendary rat charmer who was immortalised in a fairytale by the Brothers Grimm. Hameln glories in fine old houses, most of them in ornate Weser Renaissance style. It is also the starting point for explorations into the surrounding Weserbergland, a charming region of rolling hills, golden fields and rivers, all protected as a nature park.

A BIT OF HISTORY

A jewel of the Weser Renaissance – The Weser Renaissance style (late 16C– early 17C) so well displayed in Hameln is distinguished architecturally by ram's-horn scrollwork and pinnacled gables. Other characteristics include delicately worked stone bands encircling the building, jutting bay windows *(Utluchten)* and large, well-developed dormers *(Zwerch-häuser)* with decorated gables.

The Pied Piper of Hameln – In 1284, a mysterious man in multi-coloured clothes promised the townspeople that, for a substantial reward, he would free Hameln from a plague of rats and mice. He played his pipe, and all the rodents emerged to follow him to the banks of the Weser, where they drowned.

When the townspeople didn't pay him, the piper returned and played again in revenge. This time it was the children who emerged from their houses. There were 130 of them, and they too followed him, never to be seen again. Only two escaped; one was mute, the other blind. The rather less romantic but more accurate version of this tale is that 13C overpopulation led to a troop of young people being sent by the authorities to colonise territories to the east.

But it is the former 👫 **Grimm fairytale** that is acted out every Sunday at midday on the terrace of the Hochzeitshaus.

▶ **Population:** 58 500

📑 **Info:** Deisterallee 1, 31785 Hameln. ✆(05151) 95 78 23. www.hameln.de.

🧭 **Location:** Hameln hugs the banks of the Weser and is located just south of the A2, about halfway between Bielefeld and Hannover. It extends into the Weserbergland, a hilly expanse that becomes a nature park.

👁 **Don't Miss:** The unique Weser-Renaissance architecture, best seen on foot.

🕐 **Timing:** Allow a couple of hours to see the Altstadt.

👫 **Kids:** Weekly fairytale re-enactments.

🚶 WALKING TOUR
OLD TOWN★

Rattenfängerhaus★ (The Rat Catcher's House)

This large 1603 building has little to do with rats but it combines all the major elements of the Weser Renaissance architectural style. The symmetrical façade features sculpted bands of stonework, adorned with carved busts and masks. The two-storey projecting oriel used to feature a crown.

▷ *Take the Osterstraße, one of the most well-known streets in Hameln. It was here on 26 July 1284 that the children followed the Pied Piper. Stop at the top of the Kleine Straße to look at the splendid Renaissance houses (Haus Osterstraße 12, Leisthaus and Stiftsherrenhaus).*

Stiftsherrenhaus (Canons' House)

Osterstraße 8. 🕐*Closed for renovation until at least spring 2011.* ✆*(05151) 202 12 16.*

Another remarkable house, this one half-timbered and built in 1558, is the only one in Hameln featuring figurative decorations. Represented are Greek and Roman as well as numerous biblical characters, including Christ, the apostles, David, and Cain and Abel.

The Stiftsherrenhaus is joined with the adjacent **Leisthaus** via a bridge on the first floor. Rooms in both rambling buildings now harbour the **local history museum**, which counts the world's largest collection of Pied Piper memorabilia among its exhibits.

Dempterhaus
In the market square.
An outstanding building from 1607; note its fine Weser Renaissance projecting oriel.

Hochzeitshaus (Marriage House)★
The Weser Renaissance-style building, constructed between 1610 and 1617, was used as a reception hall for burghers' weddings. Three elegant gables break the horizontals of the façade.

A **carillon** from 1964 plays the *Rattenfängerlied* (rat catcher song) at 9.35am, the *Weserlied* (by Gustav Pressel) at 11.35am and the *Rattenfängerlied* again at 1.05pm, 3.35pm and 5.35pm.

▷ *Take Fischpfortenstraße and pass in front of Wilhelm-Busch-Haus, then continue to the Weser.*
Retrace your steps until you reach Wendenstraße.

Haus Lücking
Wendenstraße 8.
This rich, half-timbered house of 1638 features a rounded doorway and is lavishly adorned with inscriptions and ornamentation.

▷ *At the end of the road, turn right into Bäckerstraße.*

Rattenkrug
Bäckerstraße 16.
A projecting bay window and a five-floor-tall gable distinguish this 1568 building.

▷ *Continue until the Münsterkirchhof.*

Münsterkirchhof (Collegiate Church)
From the gardens to the south, the church appears to cower beneath its massive polygonal tower, once part of a 12C Romanesque basilica. Inside, the columns and their capitals draw attention to the raised transept.

▷ *Finish the tour by coming back along Alte Markt-Straße, noticing the Kürie Jerusalem passageway.*

EXCURSION
Hämelschenburg★
▷ *11km/6.8mi south in Emmertal.*
☞*Visit by guided tour (50min) May–Sept, Tue–Sun 11am–5pm, Apr and Oct 4pm.* ☞*6€.* ℘ *(05155) 95 16 90. www.schloss-haemelschenburg.de.*
This horseshoe-shaped Schloss (palace), surrounded by a moat and built between 1588 and 1618, is considered a masterpiece of the Weser Renaissance. The wing facing the street is the most ornate, with alternating bands, bay windows and four decorative gables. The interior is filled with furniture, weapons, trophies and paintings.

ADDRESSES

⌂STAY
⊜⊜**An der Altstadt** –
Deisterallee 16. ℘*(05151) 402 40. www.hotel-an-der-altstadt.de. Closed late Dec–mid-Jan. 19 rooms.* This small *Jugendstil* hotel in the heart of town is a nice place to unpack your suitcase in comfortably appointed guestrooms furnished in cherrywood.

☌/EAT
⊜**Grüner Reiter** – *Kastanienwall 62.* ℘*(05151) 92 62 00. www.gruenerreiter.de.* This building was built in 1713 as a chapel for the soldiers of the Hameln Fortress. The bistro-style restaurant in a glass extension in the courtyard serves breakfast, light lunches, afternoon cakes and Italian dinners.

Lemgo★

Lemgo was founded in the late 12C at the crossroads of two trading routes and surrounded in 1365 by a still-extant town wall. Its late Gothic and Renaissance townhouses still testify to the prosperity of this former Hanseatic town.

▶ **Population:** 43 000

▪ **Info:** Kramerstraße 1, 32657 Lemgo. ℘(05261) 988 70. www.lemgo.net.

◐ **Location:** Lemgo is in rural eastern North Rhine-Westphalia, a short distance from the A2 (Hannover–Dortmund).

◔ **Timing:** Allow two hours for the Walking Tour.

SIGHTS
Junkerhaus★

Hamelner Straße 36. ◔*Open Apr–Oct, Tue–Sun 10am–5pm; Nov–Mar, Fri–Sun, 11am–5pm.* ℘*(05261) 21 32 76. www.junkerhaus.de.*

Karl Junker (1850–1912) was a painter, sculptor and architect with an eccentric streak, which explains the unusual look of his 1891 half-timbered home that he personally designed and crafted. Organised around a spiral, it offers changing views from every perspective and is adorned with whimsical sculptures, carvings, imaginative furniture and other touches.

Schloss Brake (Brake Palace)

Schlossstraße 18. ◔*Open year-round, Tue–Sun 10am–6pm.* ◔*Closed Jan 1, Dec 24–25 & 31.* ◉*3€.* 🔆 ℘*(05261) 945 00. www.wrm.lemgo.de.*

This mighty palace dates back to the 12C but was repeatedly tinkered with until the 19C, although its predominant style is Weser Renaissance. Inside is the **Weserrenaissance-Museum**, which is dedicated to art and culture between the Reformation and the Thirty Years' War. Also stop by the palace chapel and climb up the seven-storey tower to take in sweeping views over Lemgo.

⟿WALKING TOUR
OLD TOWN★

▷ *Head east from the Ostertor gate towards Mittelstraße with its grand half-timbered houses. Note the fine façades of no 17 and no 36, the House of Planets (Planetenhaus).*

Rathaus★★
(Town Hall)

The town hall is a hodgepodge of eight joined buildings overlooking the market square. The elegant façade of the old apothecary's shop displays sculpted portraits of ten famous philosopher-physicians, from Aristotle to Paracelsus. Beneath the central arcades, witchcraft trials were held around 1670.

▷ *Bear left into Breite Straße.*

Hexenbürgermeisterhaus
(Witch Hunter's House)

Breite Straße 19. ◔*Open year-round, Tue–Sun 10am–5pm.* ◉*3€.* ℘*(05261) 21 32 76. www.hexenbuergermeister-haus.de.*

This splendid 16C Weser Renaissance building houses the **city museum** with exhibits on everyday culture, trade and witch-hunting. A creepy highlight is the collection of torture and execution instruments from the estate of an actual family of executioners.

Marienkirche
(Church of St. Mary's)

A Renaissance 16C organ, among the oldest in German, adorns this triple-aisle Gothic church. Admire, too, the baptismal font (1592), the pulpit (1644) and the Triumphal Cross (c. 1500).

▷ *Backtrack to Papenstraße, then turn right.*

St. Nicolaikirche (Church of St. Nicholas)

Lemgo's oldest church (13C) is dedicated to the patron saint of merchants and combines Romanesque (three-figure tympanum), Gothic (frescoes) and Renaissance (pulpit) elements; it is often used as a concert venue.

▷ *Papenstraße leads back to the starting point.*

EXCURSIONS

Herford

▷ *20km/12.4mi west.*

This former Hanseatic town between Teutoburger Wald and the Weser River sprouted around an 8C convent and has beautifully preserved half-timbered houses. The convent's Romanesque church, the **Münster** (1220–1280), is one of the oldest in Westphalia and sports a 16C late Gothic baptismal font and Romanesque capitals. Nearby, the 14C **Johanniskirche** bears fine 17C **carvings★**, both sculpted and painted.

Paderborn★

▷ *71km/44mi north via the A33.*

Founded by Charlemagne in the 8C and situated in eastern Westphalia, modern Paderborn is a commercial hub and university town with about 15 000 students. Though badly pummelled during World War II, it boasts a good range of artistic, historical and architectural sights, plus one of the world's largest computer museums.

Birthplace of the Holy Roman Empire – Paderborn's beginnings are tied to Charlemagne who, in 776, established a power base here from which to defeat the Saxons and to oversee their Christianisation. In 799, a deposed Pope Leo III fled to Paderborn to ask for Charlemagne's help in restoring him to the papal throne. In exchange, he was to be crowned emperor, thus laying the foundation for the Holy Roman Empire that lasted until 1806. The coronation took place in Rome on Christmas Day 800.

Dom★ (Cathedral)

Marktplatz. ⏱*Open year-round, daily 10am–6.30pm. www.erzbistum-paderborn.de.*

Paderborn's cathedral was built between 1225 and 1270 as a three-aisled Gothic hall-church attached to a Romanesque west tower. The main entrance is through the south portal known as "Paradies". It dates to 1250 and is richly festooned with sculptures of St. Mary, Christ, the apostles and other biblical figures. Inside, the elaborate **tomb of Prince-Bishop Dietrich von Fürstenberg★** and the late-Gothic high altar are artistic highlights.

The crypt is the largest in Germany and shelters the relics of Paderborn's patron saint, St. Liborius (348–398), which were transferred to the city in 836.

Be sure to follow the signs to the cloister to have a look at the endearing **Drei-Hasen-Fenster★** *(Three Hares' Window)*. It shows three hares chasing each other in a circle with each of the ears shared by two animals so that only three ears are shown in all.

Diözesanmuseum (Cathedral Treasury)

Markt 17. ⏱*Open year-round, Tue–Sun 10am–6pm.* ◉*2.50€.* ♿ ✆*(05251) 125 14 00. www.erzbistum-paderborn.de/museum.*

Clocktower of Dom, Paderborn
©Paul Rüsing/istockphoto.com

Libori Festival

Every year in late July, the people of Paderborn mix up religious tradition and worldly entertainment for one week of fun in honour of the city's patron, St. Liborius. The largely pedestrianised town centre is transformed into a veritable drinking and partying zone where up to a million visitors let their hair down during live concerts, exhibitions, shows and even impromptu singalongs with local nuns!

Thrill-seekers can enjoy carousels and rollercoasters, shopaholics can indulge their addiction at the Pottmarkt arts and crafts market, while night-owls keep the city's dance floors hopping until dawn. See www.libori.de for the full run-down (click on the British flag for the English-language version).

A modern building next to the cathedral houses religious treasures from 20 centuries, including such celebrated items as a Madonna from 1058 and the gilded silver Shrine of Liborius from 1627.

Kaiserpfalzen★★
(Imperial Palaces)

In 1964 archaeologists made a sensational find: just north of the cathedral they discovered the foundations of Charlemagne's 8C palace.

Continued excavations also unearthed the adjacent remnants of Heinrich II's palace from the early 11C. The latter has been meticulously reconstructed and now houses a modern **museum** (©*open year-round, Tue–Sun 10am–6pm;* ©*closed Dec 24–25 & 31;* ∞*2.50€;* ℘*(05251) 10 51 10; www.kaiserpfalz-pad erborn.de)*. Its displays shed light on daily life in the early Middle Ages.

Bartholomäuskapelle
(Chapel of St. Bartholomew)

©*Open year-round, daily 10am–6pm.* This tiny chapel next to the imperial palaces is the oldest hall-church north of the Alps (1017). It has splendid acoustics and elaborate capitals.

▲▲Heinz Nixdorf
Museumsforum★★

Fürstenallee 7. ©*Open year-round, Tue–Fri 9am–6pm, Sat–Sun 10am–6pm.* ©*Closed Jan 1, Nov 1, Dec 24–25 & 31.* ∞*7€.* ♿. ℘*(05251) 30 66 00. www.hnf.de.*

The evolution of communication technology gets the spotlight at this engag-

ing and interactive museum. In one section you can travel back 5 000 years to the beginnings of writing in Mesopotamia, then fast-forward into cyberspace in another. In between you come face to face with all sorts of historic calculating machines, typewriters, telephone exchanges and even a full-scale replica of Eniac, a 1940s US Army computer that is the size of an entire room.

Museum für Stadtgeschichte
(City History Museum)

Hathumarstraße 7–9. ©*Open year-round, Tue–Sun 10am–6pm.* ℘*(05251) 882 35 01. www.paderborn.de/stadt-museum.*

City history is chronicled in one of the oldest and prettiest half-timbered buildings in town, the 16C **Adam-und-Eva-Haus**. It is so named because sculptures on the façade depict the expulsion of Adam and Eve from the Garden of Eden.

Rathaus (Town Hall)

This splendid example of Weser Renaissance architecture is one of the most beautiful town halls in the region. Completed in 1616, it sports a triple gable and arcades supported by Doric pillars. In front stands a Baroque fountain decorated with the city's coat of arms.

Paderquellen (Pader Springs)

Paderborn derives its name from the Pader, Germany's shortest river. It originates from 200 springs in a park just north of the cathedral and flows into the Lippe River after a mere 4km/2.5mi.

Münster★★

Münster, the historical capital of Westphalia, lies at the centre of a wooded plain studded with moated castles and manor houses. Thanks to a busy post-World War II restoration programme, it is an attractive city whose streets are flanked by Renaissance, Gothic and Baroque facades. Münster's key moment in world history came in 1648 with the signing of the treaty that ended the Thirty Years' War. Cycling enthusiasts will love this pancake-flat university town: its roads are lined with hundreds of kilometres of bike trails. Bicycles, by the way, are called *"Leeze"* in the local dialect.

A BIT OF HISTORY

The Peace of Westphalia – This twin treaty ended the Thirty Years' War and was signed in two towns: in Protestant Osnabrück on 15 May 1648, and in Catholic Münster on 24 October 1648. The treaties involved Emperor Ferdinand III, the kingdoms of Spain, France and Sweden, the Dutch Republic and their respective allies among the princes of the Holy Roman Empire.

It recognised and confirmed the cession to France of Alsace, guaranteed the independence of Switzerland and the Netherlands, and favoured the development of Prussia. Protestants

- ▶ **Population:** 271 000
- **Info:** Heinrich-Brüning-Straße 9, 48127 Münster. ℰ(0251) 492 27 10. www.tourismus.muenster.de.
- **Location:** Münster can be reached via the A1 (Dortmund–Bremen), and is one hour by car from the big towns of the Ruhr.
- **Parking:** Garages are located throughout the old city, near the main train station, near the Residenzschloss and near the theatre on Wasserstraße.
- **Don't Miss:** The cathedral and the Prinzipalmarkt with the Peace Hall.
- **Timing:** Allow one full day to see the sights of Münster.

and Catholics were redefined as equal before the law, and Calvinism was given legal recognition.

SIGHTS
St. Paulus-Dom★★ (Cathedral)

Domplatz 28. Open year-round, daily 6.30am–7pm (Sun 7.30pm). ℰ(0251) 49 53 22. www.paulusdom.de.
Münster's squat twin-towered cathedral reflects the transitional style from

Prinzipalmarkt in the evening

© Frankonius/Fotolia.com

237

The Anabaptists

Believed to have originated in Zurich, this radical religious reform movement endorsed adult baptism, polygamy and community of goods. In 1534, its followers attempted to establish a theocracy in Münster, deposing the magistrates and introducing its tenets. The era was brought to an end after a 16-month siege ending with the torture and execution of its leaders in the market square. The Anabaptists, or Rebaptists, were spiritual forerunners of the Mennonites and the Amish.

Romanesque to Gothic prevalent in the 13C. The entrance is via the 16C south porch decorated with statues of the apostles and overlooked by Christ in Judgement. Inside, don't miss the 1540 **astronomical clock**★ in the southern ambulatory whose hours are struck by metal figurines wielding hammers. A carillon kicks into gear at noon Mon–Sat and 12.30pm Sun, and there is also a calendar that goes up to 2071 and a display of the moon phases and planet constellations. The **Chapel of the Holy Sacrament**★ is richly furnished (note especially the 18C silver tabernacle). The cathedral's modern **treasury**★★ (Domkammer; ⓒopen year-round, Tue–Sun 11am–4pm; ⓒclosed Jan 1, Good Fri–Easter Sun, May 1, Whitsun, Dec 24–26 & 31; ⊕3€; ⚹; ℘(0251) 49 53 33; www.domkammer-muenster.de) is reached via the cloister. On the ground floor, 15C reliquary busts in copper and silver, the 11C head-reliquary of St. Paul and a 13C Virgin surround a 13C **processional cross.**

Westfälisches Landesmuseum für Kunst und Kulturgeschichte★ (Regional Art and History Museum)

Domplatz 10. ⓒOpen year-round, Tue–Sun 10am–6pm (Thu 9pm). ⓒClosed Dec 24–25 & 31. ⊕5€. ⚹. ℘(0251) 59 07 01. www.landesmuseum-muenster.de.

This museum's collections span the artistic arc from the Middle Ages to today. Particularly noteworthy are **altarpieces**★★ by Conrad von Soest, Koerbecke and the Masters of Liesborn and Schöppingen.

Prinzipalmarkt★ (Principal Market)

The Prinzipalmarkt is Münster's busiest and most historic street with elegant houses that were once the homes of rich burghers. Under the arcades, attractive shops jostle for attention with restaurants and cosy pubs.

Rathaus (Town Hall)

The dominant building on Prinzipalmarkt is the late 14C town hall, an impressive example of Gothic civic architecture. The diplomatic negotiations between 1644 and 1648 that brought an end to the Thirty Years' War were held in the **Friedensaal**★ (Peace Hall; ⓒopen year-round, Tue–Fri 10am–5pm, Sat–Sun 10am–4pm; ⊕1.50€; ⚹; ℘(0251) 492 27 24), a wood-panelled council chamber.

Lambertikirche (St. Lambert's Church)

Groined vaulting lidding the centre nave and star vaults above the side aisles are the striking features of this Gothic hall-church. Dangling from the tower are the iron cages that once held the dead bodies of the Anabaptist rebel leaders displayed to the public following the defeat of their uprising in 1535.

Residenzschloss (Palace)

This Baroque palace was once the residence of the prince-bishops and is now part of the university. The red-brick of the elegant three-part façade designed by Johann Conrad Schlaun is variegated with sandstone facings. The park in the back segues into a botanical garden.

EXCURSIONS
Telgte

▶ 12km/8mi east on B51.

In the centre of Telgte, next to the Baroque pilgrimage chapel with a pietà from 1370, is the local museum, the Heimathaus Münsterland. One of its prize exhibits is a folk-art textile, the **Lenten Veil**★ (1623), which measures 32sq m/344.4sq ft.

Freckenhorst

◐ *26km/16mi east on B51.*
Freckenhorst's **Collegiate Church**★ *(Stiftskirche)* is a fine example of pre-Romanesque German architecture.

Ostenfelde

◐ *36km/22.3mi east on B51.*
The graceful, privately owned **Schloss Vornholz**★ (Vornholz Castle, 1666) stands in a rolling landscape forested with ancient oaks. Built on two islets, it is a typical Münsterland "water castle".

Osnabrück

◐ *Osnabrück is at the northern end of the Teutoburg Forest, about 46km/28.5mi northeast of Münster.*
Bierstraße 22, 49074 Osnabrück.
℘*(0541) 323 21 52. www.osnabrueck-tourism.de.*
The birthplace of writer Erich Maria Remarque *(All Quiet on the Western Front)*, Osnabrück made world history in 1648 with the co-signing of the treaty ending the Thirty Years' War (it was also signed in Münster).
Its other famous native son is the painter Felix Nussbaum whose work is showcased in a dramatic Libeskind-designed museum.

Rathaus (Town Hall)

◷*Open year-round, Mon–Fri 8am–6pm, Sat 9am–4pm, Sun 10am–4pm.*
◷*Closed Jan 1, Dec 24 & 31.* ♿
℘*(0541) 323 21 52.*
This early 16C building had to be restored after World War II but still retains its Gothic look. The Peace of Westphalia treaty of 1648 was announced from its steps. A statue of Charlemagne stands above the entrance.

Friedensaal (Peace Hall)

The hall in which the peace negotiations took place is adorned with portraits of the heads of state and their delegates. The floor and ceiling have been rebuilt; the 16C wooden seats and chandelier

are original. In the **treasury** is the priceless 14C *Kaiserpokal* (Imperial goblet).

Felix-Nussbaum-Haus★★

Lotter Straße 2.
☛*Closed for renovation until at least April 2011.* ♿ ℘*(0541) 323 22 07. www.osnabrueck.de/fnh.*
This Deconstructivist museum building (1998) was designed by **Daniel Libeskind** to house 160 works by native son Felix Nussbaum (1904–44). Its broken architectural lines and eccentric details are meant to be deliberately disorienting and are intended to reflect the emotional turmoil experienced by Nussbaum. His work places him under *Neue Sachlichkeit* (New Objectivity).

MOATED CASTLES

The rural, sparsely populated area surrounding the historic town of Münster is an attractive patchwork of flat fields, pastures and meadows dotted with some 100 moated fairytale castles. Most are privately owned and can only be viewed from the outside, but some are open to visitors.

Vornholz★

◐ *36km/22.3mi southeast.*
The graceful, privately owned **Schloss Vornholz**★ (Vornholz Castle, 1666) stands in a rolling landscape forested with ancient oaks. Built on two islets, it is a typical Münsterland moated castle.

Burg Hülshoff★

◐ *20km/12.5mi west. Schonebeck 6, Havixbeck.* ◷*Open Apr–Nov, daily 11am–6.30pm.* ⊜*5€.* ℘*(02534) 10 52. www.burg-huelshoff.de.*
One of Germany's finest female poets, **Annette von Droste-Hülshoff** (1797–1848) was born in this red-brick Renaissance villa embedded in a lovely park *(admission free)*. Some fully furnished period rooms are open to the public, and there are also exhibits recalling her life and work.

Burg Vischering

© Heinz Schiffer/Fotolia.com

Vischering★

◐ *30km/18.5mi south. Berenbrock 1, Lüdinghausen.* ◐*Open Apr–Oct, Tue–Sun 10am–5.30pm; Nov–Mar, 10am–4.30pm.* ◐*Closed Jan 1, Dec 24–26 & 31.* ◉*2.50€.* ℘*(02591) 799 00. http://burg vischering.luedinghausen.de.*

Built on two islands and protected by a double fortified wall, Vischering is the oldest and still one of the most formidable fortresses in the Münster region. It is essentially a Renaissance building constructed atop the foundations of a medieval castle. The fortress houses a museum displaying furniture through the ages. The wall and ceiling paintings and splendid sandstone fireplaces are particularly impressive.

The Vorburg, on a separate island, once housed farm outbuildings. There is also a richly decorated carriage house.

Lembeck Castle★

◐ *50km/31mi southwest, in Lembeck.* ☛*Visit to the castle museum by guided tour (40min, in German) only, Mon–Fri 1pm–5pm, Sat–Sun 11am–5pm. Park open 11am–6pm.* ◉*5€.* ℘*(02369) 71 67. www.schlosslembeck.de.*

The impressive approach to this castle follows a driveway punctuated by Baroque gateways and flanked by arched entrances. The monumental 17C palace features massive towers with onion-domed Baroque steeples protecting each corner. Guided tours take in splendidly furnished rooms reflecting

the styles of the 17C and 18C. **Großer Saal**, the biggest one, is embellished with fine panelling and stuccowork.

Raesfeld Castle

◐ *74km/45mi southwest, in Raesfeld.* ☛*Visit by guided tour (1hr) only.* ℘*(02865) 609 10. www.raesfeld.de.*

Raesfeld Castle, built between 1643 and 1658 by Alexander von Velen, now consists only of a building with two wings, the Vorburg and the castle chapel. It is used as a training centre for various crafts and trades. Visible from afar is the 52.5m/172ft-high **onion-domed tower** the highest one of the region's moated castles.

Gemen Castle

◐ *63km/39mi west. Schlossplatz 1, Borken.*

This castle is a church-owned youth centre (Jugendburg) and can only be visited by prior arrangement. ℘*(028 61) 93 92 52. www.borken.de.*

The towers, battlements and buildings of this castle (15C, remodelled in the 17C) are grouped on a fortified islet arising from beautiful, shaded stretches of water.

Anholt Castle★

◐ *100km/62mi west. Schlossplatz 1, Isselburg-Anholt.* ☛*Visit by guided tour (1hr) only, May–Sept, Tue–Sun 11am–5pm; Oct–Apr, Sun 1pm–5pm.* ◐*Closed Dec 24–Jan 1.* ◉*6€, com-*

Remains of Medieval Wars

The charming **Wasserburgen** – literally "water castles" – are found all over the Münster region. Witness to the incessant defensive battles between rival nobles, they are built on the sites of temporary encampments set up by the Teutonic tribes. The castles first appeared in the 12C in the form of wooden strongholds erected on artificial hills *(Motten)* protected at the base by a surrounding defensive wall and a moat. The invention of firearms in the early 16C made this system of defence precarious, and it was replaced over time with proper fortifications isolated still more by moats or lagoons.

Many of these compounds are spread over two islands, joined by a bridge. The first isle, or "Vorburg", was used for outbuildings; the second, or "Hauptburg" for the main residence. Their defensive character became less distinct over the centuries, especially after the Thirty Years' War (1618–48). After that, palaces set in formal gardens began to appear.

bined ticket for guided tour and park, 8€.
(02874) 453 53. www.fuerst-salm.de.
Surrounded by a landscaped park and restored Baroque garden, this moated castle (*Hauptburg* and *Vorburg* 12C–17C, converted into a Baroque palace c. 1700) frames a square inner courtyard. The museum contains evidence of three centuries of royal home décor. There are paintings (Rembrandt, Brueghel, Murillo), tapestries, furniture, porcelain and weapons.

Nordkirchen Castle

▶ *36km/23mi south. Schloss 1, Nordkirchen.*

Visit by guided tour (1hr) only, May–Sept, Sun 11am–5pm; Oct–Apr, Sun 2pm–4pm; otherwise by prior arrangement daily 9am–6pm. 2€. Park free anytime, year-round. (02596) 93 30. www.schloss.nordkirchen.net.
This 18C moated castle is the region's largest and is known as "Westphalia's Versailles". The surrounding gardens are sprinkled with splendid sculptures.

ADDRESSES

STAY

Hotel Hiltruper Hof – *Westfalenstraße 148, 48165 Münster-Hiltrup (0251) 278 80. www.hiltruper-hof.de. 17 rooms.* For 150 years this little family-run hotel has welcomed guests into well-cared-for rooms. Sports and leisure equipment are available locally.

Hotel Central – *Aegidiistraße 1. (0251) 51 01 50. www.central-hotel-muenster.de. 20 rooms. Closed second half of Aug, Dec 22–31.* Run by an art-loving couple, this small city hotel has works from Beuys to Warhol decorating the public areas and the modern and good-sized rooms.

EAT

Pinkus Müller – *Kreuzstraße 4. (0251) 451 51. www.pinkus-mueller.de. Closed Sun.* This classic Westphalian brew-pub exudes rustic flair, makes its own beer and serves hearty meals to mixed crowds sitting around polished wooden tables. The same street has several other restaurants and cafés.

Kleines Restaurant im Oer'schen Hof – *Königsstraße 42. (0251) 484 10 83. www.kleines-restaurant-im-oerschen-hof.de. Closed Sun–Mon.* This three-floor establishment in an old glazed-brick house boasts a tasteful mix of rustic furniture and modern paintings. The chef ingeniously infuses Westphalian fare with Mediterranean accents.

THE WEST

Germany's western regions deliver a cornucopia of diverse and awe-inspiring sightseeing opportunities. Soak up cosmopolitan flair and stunning art and architecture in cities such as Düsseldorf, Cologne and Frankfurt or escape to historic villages in the hilly Sauerland or the gentle Eifel. Follow the mighty Rhine or the meandering Moselle Rivers past a fairytale setting of medieval castles, steep vineyards and little towns that are veritable symphonies in half-timber. Walk in the footsteps of the Romans in Trier, check out Charlemagne's legacy in Aachen and see for yourself why beautiful Heidelberg has inspired so many great poets and artists.

Highlights

1 The mighty **Cologne Cathedral** (p249)

2 Fine Art at **Museum Folkwang** in the Ruhr Region (p266)

3 Roman ruins in **Trier** (p283)

4 Wine tasting at Kloster Ebebach in the **Rhine Valley** (p304)

5 Views of **Heidelberg** and its castle from Philosopher's Walk (p326)

Milestones in History

Two millennia of German history unfold before you as you travel through Germany's western region. The legacy of the Romans survives in Cologne, Bonn and Koblenz, but nowhere more so than in Trier, where you can wander among some of the best-preserved Roman ruins north of the Alps. Aachen also has Roman origins but was most lastingly put on the map by Charlemagne, the "father of modern Europe" who made the town the capital of his enormous Frankish Empire in the 8C. More than 30 German kings were crowned in the chapel he built (now part of Aachen Cathedral) before the ceremony was moved to Frankfurt, where Germany's greatest poet, Johann Wolfgang von Goethe, was born in 1749. A few centuries earlier, nearby Mainz had already given the world Johannes Gutenberg, whose invention of the modern printing press turned the world on its head. Cities that shaped Germany during the Industrial Age can be found in the Ruhr Region and in the Saarland. The former colliery Zollverein in Essen and the Völklinger Ironworks near Saarbrücken are both UNESCO-protected World Heritage Sites.

Great Cathedrals

This region boasts many churches and cathedrals originally built in the Middle Ages. One of the oldest on German soil is the palace chapel in Aachen, a superb

In Vino Veritas

The region described in this chapter comprises seven of 13 wine-growing regions in Germany. The smallest and northernmost is the **Ahr Valley** along the Ahr River south of Bonn, which is especially famous for its velvety red Spätburgunder. South of here, Koblenz marks the beginning of the **Moselle** region, where Riesling and Müller-Thurgau grow on some of the steepest slopes in the world, and the **Mittelrhein**, which cuts through the scenic Rhine Gorge. Its slate soil and terraced vineyards are also particularly conducive to growing Riesling. The most refined Rieslings, though, hail from the famous **Rheingau** around Rüdesheim. West of the Rhine, the **Nahe** produces diverse wines from relatively few grape varieties, including the earthy Silvaner. Further south, **Rheinhessen** is Germany's largest growing region with soft, fragrant and medium-bodied wines. Wedged between the Rheinhessen region and France is the **Palatinate**, where smooth Rieslings and mild yet full-bodied Müller-Thurgau dominate.

Museum Folkwang, Essen

example of Carolingian architecture. It was completed in 800, making it the oldest section of Aachen's otherwise largely Gothic cathedral. Driving east, you will soon spot the twin spires of Cologne's magnificent cathedral looming in the distance. The grandeur and loftiness of this French Gothic pile attracts more visitors than any other tourist sight in Germany. For fabulous views, it's worth braving the dizzying climb up the tower. Cologne also boasts a dozen Romanesque churches from the 12C and 13C. Most were destroyed in World War II and have been carefully rebuilt. To see the finest examples of this architectural style in Germany, though, point the compass south and follow the Rhine to Mainz, Speyer and Worms. Each of these cities boasts an awe-inspiring cathedral that exudes solemn ambience and is packed with artistic treasures.

Hubs of Fine Art
Art-ficionados could design an entire itinerary hopping from one museum to the next while exploring Germany's western regions. Düsseldorf especially has a long and distinguished tradition in the art world, ever since Elector Carl Theodor founded the Academy for Painting, Sculpture and Architecture in 1773. Still going strong today as the Düsseldorfer Kunstakademie, it has produced such hotshots as Joseph Beuys, Gerhard Richter, Jörg Immendorf and Andreas Gur-

sky. Their work graces the walls of the Kunstsammlung Nordrhein-Westfalen in Düsseldorf as well as the Museum Ludwig in neighbouring Cologne. Cologne itself also enjoys a stellar reputation in the art world, not only for its museums but also for hosting Art Cologne, one of Europe's most important contemporary art fairs. Cutting-edge exhibits can also be viewed down the Rhine in Bonn's Kunst- und Ausstellungshalle and in Aachen's Ludwig Forum für Internationale Kunst. Away from the Rhineland, the Städel Museum in Frankfurt will soon be opening a new wing showcasing postwar works by German artists, with Anselm Kiefer, Georg Baselitz and Markus Lüpertz among them.

Reliquary bust of Charlemagne in Dom, Aachen

THE WEST

0   30 km

★★★ Highly recommended
★★ Recommended
★ Interesting

Driving Tour showing point of departure

HEIDELBERG
Monschau
Düsseldorf
Dortmund

ERFURT
FULDA
FULDA

HESSE

HANNOVER

Marburg

Kahler Asten 841
Bad Berleburg
Grafschaft
480
Oberkirchen 236
Nordenau
Ruhr
Möhnesee
Hohe Bracht 584
Lenne
Siegen
Sauerland
Arnsberg
229
Soest
475
Attahöhle
Attendorn
Biggetalsperre
Schnellenberg
55

MÜNSTER

LINGEN

ARNHEM

Recklinghausen
Dortmund
Bochum
RUHR BASIN
Essen
Hagen
Wuppertal
Solingen
Altenberg

NORTH RHINE-WESTPHALIA

Bottrop
Oberhausen
Duisburg
Neandertal
Zons
Düsseldorf

Siebengebirge
Ahrweiler
Bonn
Altenberg
Altenahr
RHIN

Cologne

Augustusburg
Phantasialand
Nideggen
Bad Münstereifel
Rur

Korneliminster
Eifel Lake District
258
Aachen

Monschau

NETHERLANDS

EINDHOVEN
MAASTRICHT
LIÈGE

Edersee
Eder
Gießen
Lahn

244

WURTZBOURG WURTZBOURG NUREMBERG

BAVARIA

Aschaffenburg

Saalburg
Bad Homburg
Frankfurt ob der Tauber

HEIDELBERG
Fürstenlager
Heppenheim
Weinheim
Königstuhl
Schwetzingen

BADEN-
WÜRTTEMBERG

Bad Wimpfen

Maulbronn

Lorsch
Bensheim
Bruchsal
BADEN-BADEN

Limburg an der Lahn
Taunus
Großer Feldberg
Königstein
Wiesbaden
Mayence
Worms
Spire
Deidesheim
Hambacher Schloss
Ludwigshöhe
Karlsruhe

STUTTGART

Diez
Nassau
Arnstein
Ehrenbreitstein
Eberbach
Rüdesheim
Pfalz
Freinsheim
Bad Dürkheim
Neustadt
Kalmit
Trifels
Bad Bergzabern

STRASBOURG

Lahn Valley
Bad Ems
Marksburg
RHINE VALLEY
Lorelei
Bingen
Ravengiersburg
Palatinat
Pfälzer Wald
Dahn
Wasgau
Berwartstein

Koblenz
Thurant
Burg Rheinfels
Oberwesel
Bacharach
Simmern
Kirchberg
Dhaun
Idar-Oberstein
Dahner Felsenland

Eltz
Beilstein

RHINELAND-
PALATINATE

Kaiserslautern

Maria Laach
Nürburgring
Ulmen
Hunsrück
Hunsrückhöhen-
strasse
Erbeskopf

SAARLAND

Sarrebruck
Sarreguemines

Hohe Acht
Eifel Mountains
Maare
Niederburg
Manderscheid
Bernkastel-Kues
MOSELLE VALLEY

Trèves
Saarburg
Mettlach
Lower
Saar Valley
Usine de Völklingen

FRANCE

SAVERNE

Cloef

Römische
Villa Nennig

Thionville

Metz

BELGIUM

LUXEMBURG

Luxembourg

NANCY

VERDUN

NAMUR

245

Cologne★★★

Köln

The city of Cologne likes to have a good time. Case in point: Kölsch – a word synonymous for the local dialect and the local beer. Although this pleasant Rhineland city went through a bleak period after nearly being levelled during World War II, it has managed to rebuild itself with remarkable vigour. Visitors will enjoy the city's imposing churches, colourful riverside houses and top-notch museums.

A BIT OF HISTORY

Cologne in Roman Times – Once the Roman legions extended the Empire as far as the Rhine, General Agrippa, coloniser of the region, named the local settlement Oppidum Ubiorum, after the Germanic Ubii who lived there. By AD 50, the town had adopted the name which would stick, at least in part: *Colonia Claudia Ara Agrippinensium*. Roman ruins still exist in the Zeughausstraße, outside the cathedral, and at the Praetorium, beneath the present Town Hall. From its official recognition onwards, the town flourished: it was the start of an era, rich in craftwork, trade and architecture, which did not end until the time of the Great Invasions, in the 5C.

The Holy City beside the Rhine – Cologne's political power in the Middle

▶ **Population:** 996 000

Info: Kardinal-Höffner-Platz 1 (opposite the cathedral). ℘(0221) 22 13 04 00. www.koelntourismus.de.

▶ **Location:** Cologne is surrounded by a ring road linking up with ten autobahns, the A3 (Frankfurt–Essen), A4 (Aachen), the A59 (Düsseldorf) and the A555 (Bonn) chief among them.

▶ **Don't Miss:** Cologne's Cathedral, the Roman-Germanic Museum, Museum Ludwig, Schnütgen-Museum.

▶ **Timing:** Cologne warrants a couple of days of exploration. Allow at least a minimum of one hour for the cathedral and lots of time for the museums, boat cruises and beer halls.

▲▲ **Kids:** Chocolate Museum.

Ages derived from the Church. Until 1288, the archbishops of Cologne exercised powers both spiritual and temporal. In the 13C and early 14C, the city became the religious, intellectual and artistic centre of the Rhine Valley.

Eminent men came to preach: the Dominican **Albertus Magnus** (teacher of Thomas Aquinas) and **Master Eckhart**, as well as the Scottish Franciscan **Duns Scotus**.

Cologne at night with the cathedral in the background

© www.koelntourismus.de

© Bruno Morandi/hemis.fr

Carnival

In Cologne, Carnival is considered the 'fifth season', which officially begins at 11 minutes past 11 on the 11th day of the 11th month. The main celebrations, though, don't actually take place until months later, during the week preceding the beginning of Lent. Normal business essentially shuts down between Fat Thursday and Ash Wednesday when costumed locals are joined by revellers from around the world in a raucous party taking over streets and pubs. The typical greeting during the festival is *Kölle Alaaf!*, a phrase in local dialect that roughly translates as "Cologne alive!"

Carnival has been celebrated for centuries but since 1823 a number of customs and traditions have emerged. Women rule on Fat Thursday *(Weiberfastnacht)* when they demonstrate their cheekiness by indiscriminately cutting off men's neckties. Celebrations on the weekend are more family-oriented and held in the individual districts, leading up to the big School and City Quarter Procession *(Schull- un Veedelszöch)* on Sunday. The biggest parade, though, and the culmination of Carnival, snakes through the city on Rose Monday *(Rosenmontag)*. Organised by the local Carnival associations, it features marching bands, costumed dancers and elaborately decorated floats, often with a political or satirical theme. Hundreds of thousands of merrymakers line the streets cheering them on. It is a huge event that is even shown on German television. Celebrations end on Shrove Tuesday *(Veilchendienstag)* with the burning of straw dolls (called *Nubbel*) at midnight. The traditional way to combat hangovers on Ash Wednesday is with a meal of fish in one of the old-timey brewpubs.

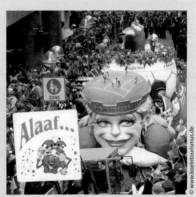

© www.koelntourismus.de

To learn more about this fascinating festival, visit www.koelnerkarneval.de or, if already in town, the Cologne Carnival Museum (www.kk-museum.de).

It was the work of such religious scholars that led in 1388 to the creation of Cologne University by local citizens.

Trade and commerce – Because of its strategic location on the Rhine and along important trade routes, Cologne soon became a power in the commercial world, imposing its own system of weights and measures over the whole of northern Germany. It held its first major fair in 1360. Its elevation to the status of Free Imperial City in 1475 did no more than set an official seal on the dominant role Cologne had in fact been playing since the 13C.

COLOGNE TODAY

The modern city – Industrialisation in the late 19C quickly expanded Cologne. After World War II, **Konrad Adenauer** continued the process of modernisation begun while he served as the city's mayor from 1917 to 1933. It was on the watch of the man destined to become the Federal Republic's first chancellor that the university (shut down under French occupation in 1798) was reopened in 1919; that the Deutz exhibition halls (Messehallen) were built; and that greenbelts were added throughout the city.

Art and culture – Diversity, above all, marks cultural life in Cologne today. Apart from music and drama, the fine arts hold pride of place: more than 100 galleries are devoted to contemporary art exhibitions alone. Art Cologne is a highly regarded annual international art fair. The Wallraf-Richartz Museum and the Museum Ludwig are among venues mounting important temporary exhibitions.

Heinrich Böll (1917–85), one of the pre-eminent German postwar writers and winner of the Nobel Prize for Literature in 1972, was born in Cologne. His work, sparing neither the Church nor society, is inseparable from his birthplace.

Publishing houses and printers have been based in Cologne for centuries. Building on this history has been the postwar push into electronic media.

Although it's been losing some of its influence to Berlin and Hamburg, Cologne still has a number of broadcasting companies, including several television stations along with recording studios and an Academy of Media Arts.

Town life – There is a strong sense of neighbourhood in Cologne. Each locality centres on its individual parish church, each of which preserves its own traditions. St. Severin is the oldest and most typical. But all Cologne citizens appreciate the old town bordering the Rhine. Remodelled in the 1980s, it is one of the liveliest parts of the city, especially at night. Since the riverside highway has been diverted underground between the Hohenzollern and Deutzer bridges, land has been transformed into attractive gardens (Rheingarten) perfect for walking, relaxing or embarking on a leisurely boat cruise.

DOM★★★
(COLOGNE CATHEDRAL)

Self-guided tour pamphlets available in the foyer. ⏱Open May–Oct daily 6am–9pm, Nov–Apr daily 6am–7.30pm. Guided tours available. ♿. ℘(0221) 17 94 01 00. www.koelnerdom.de.

Stained glass window of the cathedral

This monumental cathedral was built over the course of 600 years. In 1164, when Frederick I Barbarossa donated the relics of the Three Magi to the city, an influx of pilgrims created the need for a larger church. Thus began construction of the first Gothic church in the Rhineland whose design was inspired by the cathedrals at Paris, Amiens and Reims. Builders first set to work in 1248 and by 1320 the chancel was completed. The south tower followed by 1410 but soon after building was suspended because of lack of funds and political turmoil. When it resumed in the 19C, the original plans were used, and in 1880 the cathedral was finally consecrated before Emperor Wilhelm I. Miraculously, it survived World War II almost intact and was declared a UNESCO World Heritage Site in 1996.

Inside the cathedral

© Vivalapenler/Dreamstime.com

Exterior

The twin-towered western façade marks a high point in the Flamboyant Gothic style. Embellished gables and slender buttresses burst ever upward, in line with tapering spires 157m/515ft high. The bronze doors **(1)** in the south transept entrance (1948–54) are by Ewald Mataré.

Interior

The building's colossal proportions are fully appreciated from the nave, 144m/472.4ft long, 45m/147.6ft wide and 43.5m/142.7ft high. The five late- Gothic **stained-glass windows**★ in the north aisle (1507–08) depict the lives of the Virgin and St. Peter. In the south transept is a new window by German artist Gerard Richter composed of 11 500 glass squares in 72 colours, which creates a kaleidoscopic effect when hit by the sun. The same transept houses a Flemish polyptych of 1521 with double side panels known as the **Altarpiece of the Five Moors (2)** *(Agilolphusaltar)*. The Cross Chapel *(Kreuzkapelle)*

COLOGNE CATHEDRAL

0   20m

← N —

Windows★

4

Shrine of the Three Kings ★★★

CHANCEL

3

Altar of the city's patron saints ★★★

Treasury★

Stalls★

2

1

TRANSEPT

Roncalli-

NAVE

platz

South tower

13C

14C

15C and 16C

19C and 20C

COLOGNE
plan I

0   200 m

A   B   Zons ↑   LEVERKUSEN

Neusser Str.
Krefelder Str.
Riehler Str.
Theodor-Heuss-Ring
Ebertpl.
Ebertpl.   BASTEI

Rheinpark, Tanzbrunnen
Botanischer Garten Flora

MEDIA-PARK
HANSAHOCHHAUS
Hansaring
EIGELSTEINTOR
Theodor-Heuss-Ring
WECKSNAPP

Maybach-
Hansaring
Turiner Str.
straße
Adenauer
Köln Triangle Panorama

Erftstr.
Dom-
St.Kunibert

Gladbacher Str.
Hansaring
Eintrachtstr.
Machabäerstr.
Konrad-

ALTE STADTMAUER
St.Ursula
Victoria-
Konrad-

Christophstr./
Mediapark
Kyotostr.   str.
Ursulastr.
① see map II
Goldgasse

Christophstr.
Kardinal-
Frings-Str.
Gereonstr.
RHINE

St-Gereon
Kattenbug
Tunisstr.
CATHEDRAL
Hohenzollern
Bridge

ring
Appellhofpl.
L
Zeughaus-
str.
Cologne Municipal
Museum
LUDWIG
MUSEUM

Friesenpl.
RÖMER TURM
J
National Socialist
Documentation
Centre
MUSEUM OF
DECORATIVE ARTS

Hohenzollern
Albertusstr.
Auf dem Berlich
OLD
TOWN HALL

Ehrenstr.
Aposteln-
str.
Richmod-
str.
Breite
Zeppelin-
str.
Str.
KOLUMBA
Hohe Str.

AACHEN ↓
Rudolfpl.
Mittelstr.
M
T
Wallraf-Richartz
Museum
KÖLN-
DÜSSELDORFER

HAHNENTOR
St. Aposteln
Neumarkt
Neumarkt
Cäcilien-   straße
Deutzer Br.
OLPE

Hahnen-   straße
Habsburgerring
M
Nord-
Pipinstr.
An der
Malzmühle
M
St. Maria
in Lyskirchen

Museum of East
Asian Art
Hohenstaufen
Mauritius-
SCHNÜTGEN
MUSEUM
Süd-
Fahrt
Blaubach
Pforte
CHOCOLATE
MUSEUM

Rautenstrauch-Joest
Museum of Ethnography
Poststr.
Hohe
Mühlenbach
Mathiasstr.
MALAKOFFTURM

Jahnstraße
steinweg
Poststr.
Blaubach
Tel-Aviv-Str.
Severinstr.
POL.
St. George
Follerstr.
Olympic Games
Museum

ring
Neue Weyerstr.
Rothgerberbach
gasse
Perlengraben
An   St.
Kleine
Witschgasse
Severinsbr.

Roonstr.
St-Pantaleon
Katharinen
Severinstr.
markt
RHEINAUHAFEN

Pfälzer Str.
Barbarossaplatz
Waisenhaus-
An   St.
Mechtildis-
str.
Bayenstraße
BONN

Trierer
Saliring
Str.
ALTE
STADTMAUER
Ulrichgasse
Severinstr.
Am
Bayenturm
Annostr.

Luxemburger Str.
Eifelstraße
Sachsenring
Ulrepforte
Severinswall
Severinstraße
BONN

Eifelstraße
Volksgartenstraße
Sachsenring
St. Severin
Severinstor
Chlodwigplatz

VOLKSGARTEN
Vorgebirgstraße
Karolingerring
Ubierring
Bonner Str.

A   B   BONN, BRÜHL
Phantasialand   Augustburg Castle,
Falkenlust Castle

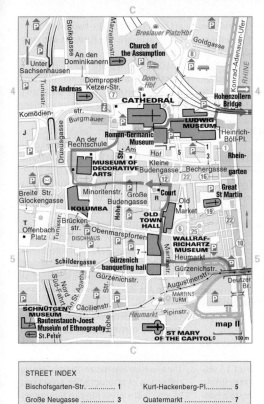

off the north ambulatory features the **Gero★ Crucifix** (Gerokreuz) **(3)**, an early example of 10C Ottonian art. In the axial chapel (Dreikönigskapelle) the stained-glass window, the Älteres Bibelfenster **(4)**, was installed in 1265. The shrine behind the high altar contains the relics of the Three Magi. Called **Schrein der Heiligen Drei Könige★★★**, it is a 12C masterpiece in gold. The last chapel in the south ambulatory (Marienkapelle) contains the altar of the city's patrons, the **Altar der Stadtpatrone★★★**. Painted c. 1440 by **Stefan Lochner**, it illustrates The Adoration of the Magi, St. Ursula and St. Gereon. Finally, the finely carved **choir stalls★** (14C) (Chorgestühl), the most extensive in Germany, contain 104 seats.

For panoramic views, climb the 509 steps of the **south tower** (Südturm; ∞2.50€) to a platform at 97m/318ft. The belfry (Glockenstube) houses the world's largest swinging church bell: the 24t **St. Peter's Bell** (Petersglocke), which was cast in 1923.

The **cathedral treasury★** (Domschatz-kammer; ⏰open year-round, daily 10am –6pm; ∞4€; ♿; ✆(0221) 17 94 05 55) contains a wealth of religious art. Gold and silver liturgical plates, the shrine to St. Engelbert and a reliquary monstrance with St. Peter's chain are among the highlights.

WALKING TOUR
OLD TOWN

The cultural heart of Cologne extends south of the central station and the super-busy Hohenzollernbrücke.
Several outstanding museums sit in the shadow of the cathedral. The Römisch-Germanisches Museum and Diöz-esanmuseum rub shoulders with the Museum Ludwig, a 1986 edifice whose distinctive saw-tooth roof contrasts with

the Gothic spires of the cathedral. The complex also includes, at basement level, a concert hall, the **Kölner Philharmonie**. From Heinrich-Böll-Platz, behind the museums, a series of terraces leads down to the Rheingarten riverside promenade.

Römisch-Germanisches Museum★★ (Roman-Germanic Museum)

Roncalliplatz 4. Visit afternoons or weekends to avoid school groups. Open year-round, Tue–Sun 10am–5pm. Closed Jan 1, Carnival week, Dec 24–25 & 31. 8€. (0221) 244 38. www.museenkoeln.de.

As capital of the Roman province of Lower Germania, Cologne enjoyed immense prosperity between the 1C and the 4C, due largely to trade between the Roman colonisers and the Germanic Ubii tribe. Evidence of these exchanges is displayed in this stellar museum.

In the basement is the **Dionysius Mosaic**★, an exceptionally well-preserved Roman mosaic made of 1.5 million fragments of stone (measuring 14.5x7m/48x23ft). Belonging to a banqueting hall of a 3C Roman villa, it was uncovered during the construction of an air-raid bunker in 1941 and preserved on its original site.

Adjacent rooms evoke funerary rites and the daily lives of the ancient Romans. Exhibits also include the enormous **Poblicius Tomb**★★ (AD 40), created for an officer of the Roman Legion; the **Philosophers' Mosaic**; and an array of Roman **glassware**★★.

Museum Ludwig★★

Heinrich-Böll-Platz. Open year-round, Tue–Sun 10am–6pm. Closed Jan 1, Carnival week, Dec 24–25 & 31. www.museen-koeln.de. 10€. (0221) 22 12 61 65. www.museenkoeln.de.

This spacious museum with its unusual roof houses an important collection of 20C art, with particular emphasis on the Expressionist movement and works by the Brücke and Blaue Reiter groups. There is also a good display of

art from between the two world wars: Constructivism, the Bauhaus and New Objectivity.

Another strong point is a collection of **Russian Avant-Garde** art. The Surrealist department reveals Dadaism's birth in Cologne and includes a variety of works by **Max Ernst** (he was born nearby in Brühl), Miró, Dalí and Magritte. **Cubism** is represented by Gris, Léger and Delaunay, and **Nouveau Réalisme** by Klein, Tàpies, Burri and Dubuffet. Curators are especially proud of their **Picasso** collection, which encompasses several hundred works.

German postwar and contemporary art includes works by the **Gruppe Zero**, mainly by **Beuys**, Baselitz, Richter, Penck and Kiefer. American abstract painting is represented (Rothko, de Kooning), as is **Pop Art** (Rauschenberg, Warhol and Segal).

Canvasses, video, installations and other media by contemporary artists from Europe, America and Asia illustrate the most recent artistic trends.

The museum also has an comprehensive collection of photography, selections of which are presented in temporary shows.

▶ *Cross the bridge going east.*

The Hohenzollern Bridge (Hohenzollernbrücke) is the world's busiest railway bridge with one train every two minutes, day and night.

Köln Triangle Panorama

Ottoplatz 1. Open May–Sept, Mon–Fri 11am–10pm, Sat & Sun 10am–6pm. 3€. (0221) 82 73 30 38. www.koelntriangle.de.

From the panoramic platform of this tower you can discover Cologne from above and identify its main monuments, churches and other important landmarks.

▶ *Walk south along the Rhine and cross the Deutzer Bridge to arrive at Heumarkt Square.*

The School of Cologne

Manuscript illumination and altar ornamentation were blossoming arts in Cologne in the early 14C. Painting reached its peak in the early 15C with the works of **The Master of St. Veronica** and **Stefan Lochner**, a native of Meersburg (on Lake Constance). From 1450 onward, under the influence of the Dutch schools, the artists of Cologne abandoned the idealistic mysticism of the Gothic period for the gracious realism of the Renaissance.

This later work is characterised by delicate colours and an emotional depiction of subjects. Religious sculpture in Cologne peaked between the 14C and 15C. Many **Madonnas** display this style of tenderness sweeping Europe around 1400: the hinted smile, draping fabrics and a relaxed stance.

Heumarkt (Hay Market Area)

Heumarkt is dominated by an equestrian statue of Prussian King Frederick William III (1770–1840). South of here, across Cäcilienstraße, is the Church of St. Maria-im-Kapitol. From here, continue on south to the Rheinauhafen peninsula, where you'll find the Chocolate Museum and the German Sports & Olympic Museum (see description below). The Church of St. Maria in Lyskirchen, opposite the island, has beautiful arches and a painted Madonna and Child from approximately 1420.

▶ *Follow Bolzenstraße west and note the amusing window displays of the costume shop Dieters.*

Gürzenich Dance Hall

This was one of the first secular Gothic buildings (1441–44) and served as a model for many townhouses. The "council's dance hall" was used for banquets in the Middle Ages and then again since the 19C when the modern carnival was born.

▶ *Pick up Martinstraße and head north.*

Wallraf-Richartz-Museum and Fondation Corboud★★

Obermarspforten. ◷*Open year-round, Tue, Wed & Fri 10am–6pm, Thu 10am–10pm, Sat–Sun 11am–6pm.* ⊜*5.80€.* ☎*(0221) 22 12 11 19. www.wallraf.museum/.*
Housed in an angular Postmodern building designed by the late OM Ungers, this museum specialises in fine art from the 13C to the 19C, with a particular emphasis on local artists. The Medieval Painters of Cologne collection culminates with the late-Gothic work of Stefan Lochner. Also of note are the **Master of St. Veronica** and the **Master of Life of the Virgin**. Among the **German Old Masters** on view are **Dürer** and **Lucas Cranach the Elder** *(Virgin and Child).* Baroque art is represented by Rubens, Ruisdael, Hals and **Rembrandt**, including a famous late self-portrait. Spanish, Italian and French artists include Murillo, Tiepolo and Boucher. There are also canvasses by 18C–19C German artists Caspar David Friedrich and Cologne-born **Wilhelm Leibl**. French Impressionists Renoir, Monet, Sisley, Cézanne, Van Gogh and Gauguin rank among the perennial crowd-pleasers.

Altes Rathaus★ (Old Town Hall)

This building with its reconstructed 15C Gothic tower (carillon at noon and 5pm) and the Flemish Renaissance pavilion (1569–73) lies at the heart of the old Jewish quarter. In 1349, the ghetto was stormed, its inhabitants killed and their homes torched.

Praetorium

Kleine Budengasse 2. ◷*Open year-round, Tue–Sun 10am–5pm.* ⊜*2.50€.* ☎*(0221)221 23 04.*
Below the town hall are the foundations of the Roman governor's palace (1C–4C), called the Praetorium. In the antechamber are small sculptures, bricks

Eau de Cologne

The people of Cologne were familiar with Cologne's "aqua mirabile" as early as the 16C, although it did not become widely known until the 18C. Its success is due to the enterprising spirit of an Italian immigrant family, the Farinas, of whom the most famous is **Johann Maria Farina**. "Cologne water" (*Kölnisch Wasser)* was thought to have medicinal properties and to cure a number of ills. In the wake of the Farina family's success, other producers of the miracle water sprang up, making "Eau de Cologne" famous. The new wave of producers included **Wilhelm Mühlens**, who founded a company in Glockengasse in 1792.

Under Napoleon, the use of Eau de Cologne as medicine was banned, so manufacturers began marketing their cure-all as toilet water. Mühlens' business was located at no. 4711 Glockengasse, and in 1875 this number was registered as a trade mark for authentic Eau de Cologne *(Echt Kölnisch Wasser). The carillon in the gable of no 4711 Glockengasse plays the Marseillaise every hour from 9am to 9pm.*

and receptacles from Roman times. Visitors can also view the old sewer, used as an air-raid shelter in World War II. Excavations beneath the town hall square will soon result in a much larger archaeological exhibition. When all is finished, perhaps as early as 2011, visitors will be able to get close-ups of original remnants, ruins and foundations of both Roman Cologne and the Jewish quarter. A 3D model in the Praetorium illustrates the project.

○ *Follow Kleine Budengasse, then Grosse Budengasse west to Minoritenstrasse, then left on Kolumbastrasse.*

Kolumba★

Kolumbastraße 4. ○*Open year-round, Wed–Mon noon–5pm.* ○*Closed Carnival Mon, Dec 24 & 25.* & *℘(0221) 933 19 30. www.kolumba.de.* The Archdiocese of Cologne possesses a stunning collection of 2 000 years of religious art, which is displayed in this evocative modernist space into which Swiss architect Peter Zumthor has integrated the remains of the late-Gothic church of St. Kolumba. Among the most famous works is Stephan Lochner's **Virgin with Violets**.

○ *Consider making a brief detour to House 4711, where eau de cologne was invented, or continue north on Drususgasse and turn right at An der Rechtschule.*

Museum für Angewandte Kunst★ (Museum of Applied Arts)

An der Rechtschule. ○*Open year-round, Tue–Sun 11am–5pm.* ○*Closed Jan 1, Carnival week, Dec 24, 25 & 31.* ⊜*4.20€.* & *℘(0221) 22 12 67 35. www.museenkoeln.de.* This museum contains an extensive collection of furniture, ceramics, glassware, metalwork, jewellery and textiles from the Middle Ages through to the present. Of particular interest are tapestries from Basel, a Venetian wedding goblet from the 15C, two life-size animal figures made from Meissen porcelain, and Baroque and *Jugendstil* glassware.

ADDITIONAL SIGHTS
Museum Schnütgen★★

Cäcilienstraße 29. ○*Open year-round, Tue–Fri 10am–5pm, Sat–Sun 11am–5pm.* ○*Closed Jan 1, Carnival, Dec 24–25 & 31.* ⊜*3.20€.* *℘(0221) 22 12 36 20. www.museenkoeln.de.* The 12C Cäcilienkirche makes a suitable site for this museum of sacred art from the 6C to the 19C. Since late 2010, some works are also housed in a modern extension. Numerous **Madonnas in wood** illustrate the local "tender" style in statuary. A collection of medieval items in ivory, most of them from Byzantium, France or other parts of Germany, displays particularly fine workmanship. Also note the works in gold, silver and bronze and medieval textiles.

PRACTICAL INFORMATION

Public Transport – The main local transport network in Cologne is the **Kölner Verkehrsbetriebe** *(KVB; 24hr hotline ℘(01803) 50 40 30)*, which operates buses, subways *(U-Bahn)* and trams *(Straßenbahn)*. The KVB is linked with the regional Rhein-Sieg transport authority (VRS), which extends as far as Bonn.

The city is divided into price zones. Short trips costs 1.90€, longer ones are 2.30€. A *Tageskarte* (day pass) costs 5.20€ or 6.70€ respectively, for one person and 7.60€ and 9.80€ for up to five people travelling together. Both are valid for unlimited trips between 9am and 3am the following day. A one-week pass is 14.70€ or 18.90€. The most central service centre is in the Neumarkt U-Bahn station, open Mon–Fri 8am–8pm, Sat 8.30am–5pm. *www.kvb-koeln.de.*

The **Köln Welcome Card**, available at the tourist office and in hotels, entitles you to unlimited public transport and discounts at museums, attractions, entertainment venues, tours, restaurants, bars and other places. Single cards cost 9€ for 24hrs, 14€ for 48hrs and 19€ for 72hrs. Group cards are good for three adults or families (two adults, up to three children) and costs 18€, 28€ and 38€, respectively.

Museum für Ostasiatische Kunst★★ (Museum of East Asian Art)

Universitätsstraße 100. ⏱*Open year-round, Tue–Sun 11am–5pm (Thu 8pm).* ⏱*Closed 1 Jan, Carnival week, 24, 25 & 31 Dec.* ⌷*4.20€.* ♿℘*(0221) 22 12 86 08. www.museenkoeln.de.*
Germany's oldest museum of Asian art (founded in 1909) is surrounded by a Japanese garden laid out by Masayuki Nagare (b. 1923). The permanent exhibition displays works from China, Japan and Korea and covers all periods of artistic endeavour from the Neolithic Age to the present. Among the oldest items are Chinese vessels (16C–12C BC). Other highlights include Buddhist art from China and Japan; Chinese ceramics from all phases; 17C Chinese furniture and writing equipment, as well as Japanese screens.

Rautenstrauch-Joest-Museum (Ethnographic Museum)

Cäcilienstraße 29–33. ⏱*Open year-round Tue–Sun 10am–6pm (Thu 8pm).* ⏱*Closed Dec 24–25 & 31, Jan 1 and Mon.* ℘*(0221) 22 13 13 01. www.museenkoeln.de.*
Now in a new location, this well-respected museum is a treasure-trove of non-European art and culture. High-lights include Thai and Khmer ceramics from the 8C to the 16C, ancient Egyptian art and Native American art.

👥 Schokoladenmuseum★ (Chocolate Museum)

Rheinauhafen. ⏱*Open year-round, Tue–Fri 10am–6pm, Sat–Sun 11am–7pm.* ⏱*Closed Jan 1, Carnival week, Dec 24–25 & 31.* ⌷*7.50€.* ♿℘*(0221) 931 88 80. www.schokoladenmuseum.de.*
This sweet museum in a late 19C customs warehouse and a modern glass annex takes as its subject the tastiest of foodstuffs, chocolate. Inside are dis-

Japanese Garden, Museum für Ostasiatische Kunst

© Photo: Rheinisches Bildarchiv Köln/Marion Mennicken

plays about the 3 000-year history and production of chocolate, a miniature chocolate factory and a chronology of the local Stollwerck company. A delicious treat from a chocolate fountain completes the visit.

German Sports and Olympic Museum★

Im Zollhafen 1. ⏰*Open year-round, Tue–Fri 10am–6pm, Sat–Sun 11am–7pm.* ⏰*Closed Jan 1, Carnival week, Dec 24–25 & 31.* ⬤*6€.* ♿. ✆*(0221) 33 60 90 www.sportmuseum-koeln.de.*

This museum traces the history of the Olympics, especially the Berlin Games of 1936 and the Munich Games of 1972. Alongside a collection of photos, videos and sound recordings, there are some interactive stations where you can step into a boxing ring or onto a racing bike. Other sections address the changing role of sport in society and the impact of women, who entered the realm of professional sports relatively late.

NS-Dokumentationszentrum (Nazi Documentation Centre)

Appellhofplatz 23–25. ⏰*Open year-round, Tue–Fri 10am–4pm, Sat–Sun 11am–4pm.* ⏰*Closed Jan 1, Carnival week, Dec 24–25 & 31.* ⬤*3.60€.* ♿ ✆*(0221) 22 12 63 32. www.museenkoeln.de.*

Between 1935 and 1945, this building served as the headquarters of the local Gestapo. It was used as a prison for regime opponents, who were often subjected to interrogation under torture. The harrowing scribbling on the walls of the narrow cells bear witness to this dark chapter of German history.

ROMANESQUE CHURCHES

The High Middle Ages (1150–1250) saw the construction of numerous churches built in the Romanesque style. Certain design elements, like the clover-leaf chancel, originated in Cologne (⬤*see INTRODUCTION: Art*).

Most were destroyed in World War II, but a dozen were subsequently rebuilt.

St. Maria-im-Kapitol★

Marienplatz 19. ✆*(0211) 21 46 15. www.maria-im-kapitol.de.*

This late Ottonian church (11C) features the oldest **cloverleaf chancel★** in Cologne. The crypt extends beneath almost the entire body of the chancel, the second-largest in Germany after Speyer Cathedral. To the left is an altarpiece of the Madonna of St. Hermann-Joseph (c. 1180). The **Renaissance choir screen** is richly decorated with sculpture (c. 1525). At the west end of the south side aisle are the original wooden **church doors★** from 1065.

St. Severin

Im Ferkulum 29. ✆*(0221) 931 84 20. www.sankt-severin.de.*

St. Severin is the oldest Christian foundation in Cologne, dating to the 4C and built on a Roman-Frankish burial ground. The present building dates from the 13C (chancel) and 15C (west tower and nave).

The chancel in the fine Gothic nave features paintings by the Master of St. Severinus. The tomb of St. Severinus, bishop of Cologne around 400 AD and one of the city's patron saints, is buried in the crypt.

St. Pantaleon★

Am Pantaleonsberg 2. ✆*(0221) 31 66 55. www.sankt-pantaleon.de.*

The nave and impressive Westwerk are examples of Ottonian architecture (10C). The **rood screen★** at the chancel is late Gothic.

St. Gereon★

Gereonsdriesch 2. ✆*(0221) 13 49 22. www.stgereon.de.*

The originality of this church lies in its elliptical floor plan and the addition, in 1220, of a **decagon★** between its towers. The crypt with its 11C mosaic floor contains the tomb of St. Gereon. The frescoes date from the 13C.

St. Andreas

*Komödienstraße 4–8. ℘(0221) 160 66
18. www.sankt-andreas.de.*
Built in the early 13C with a clover-leaf
apse, this church teems with remarkable
architectural details. At the beginning of
the 15C, the Romanesque chancel was
replaced with a Gothic one modelled on
that in Aachen.

St. Ursula

Ursulaplatz 24. ℘(0221) 13 34 00.
In the north aisle are 30 plates (1456)
by Stefan Lochner depicting the martyrdom of St. Ursula. The daughter of a
British king, the saint was murdered by
Huns along with ten of her companions
in the 5C. In the south transept is the
Goldene Kammer★ *(Golden Chamber;
1€)*, which contains 120 reliquary
busts.

EXCURSIONS
Schloss Augustusburg★★ (Augustusburg Palace)

▶ *13km/8mi south, in Brühl.*
*Visit by guided tour (1hr) only;
year-round, Tue–Fri 9am–noon,
1.30pm–4pm, Sat–Sun 10am–5pm.
5€. ℘(02232) 440 00.
www.schlossbruehl.de.*
The town of Brühl developed around a
fortress, whose foundations, in the 18C,
were used to build this fantastic Rococo
extravaganza commissioned by Cologne
archbishop and Prince Elector Clemens
August. Together with his hunting
lodge, **Jagdschloss Falkenschloss**★,
it was entered on UNESCO's World Heritage List in 1984.
Clemens August, a member of the Bavarian Wittelsbach ruling family, hired
François de Cuvilliés as chief architect
of his palatial residence. Cuvilliés in turn
drew some of the era's finest artists and
craftmen from throughout Europe. Chief
among them was **Balthasar Neumann**,
the mastermind behind the magnificent
staircase★★, a riot in greyish-green
and yellowish-orange faux marble and
elaborate stuccowork throughout. Crane
your neck to study the **ceiling fresco**★,
a work of Carlo Carlone that celebrates

the prince and the House of Wittelsbach.
Tours take in about two dozen rooms,
each one seemingly more lavish than
the last. Highlights include the **large
new suite**, comprising a garden room
with more Carlone frescoes; the **summer suite**, with floors covered in blue
and white tiles from Rotterdam; and
the **yellow suite**, used principally by
Clemens August as his private quarter.
The **Schlosspark** (palace gardens) starts
out as a French Baroque **garden**★. It was
designed by Lenôtre student Dominique
Girard in 1728 and is sprinkled with
reflective ponds and elaborate flowerbeds. It gives way to an English-style
park masterminded by Peter Joseph
Lenné after 1840.

Phantasialand★

▶ *Berggeiststraße 31–41, 50321
Brühl (shuttles available from Brühl
train station, see website).*
*Open Apr–Oct, daily 9am–6pm,
Dec–mid-Jan daily 11am–8pm.
34.50€ (children 1m/3.28ft–1.45m/
4.7ft 29.50€; smaller children free).
℘(018 05) 36 66 00.
www.phantasialand.de.*
The sprawling amusement park offers
thrill rides and attractions within six
themed areas. You can take a watery
log flume ride, watch a Wild West stunt
show or embark on a simulated space
flight. Many adventures are geared
towards small children, but there are
also hair-raising thrill rides, including
the Black Mamba rollercoaster and the
Talocan suspended top spin.

Altenberger Dom★

▶ *20km/12.4mi northeast.*
This former Cistercian abbey church
(known locally as the Bergischer Dom),
lies in a lush green valley. The pure
Gothic building (1255–1379) has celebrated Roman Catholic and Protestant
services alternately since 1857. Its huge
(18x8m/59x26ft) coloured canopy (c.
1400) above the west entrance is considered the largest stained-glass window
in Germany.

ADDRESSES

🏠 STAY

Rhein Hotel – *Frankenwerft 31–33. ℘(0221) 257 79 5. www.koeln-altstadt. de/rheinhotel. 45 rooms.* All rooms at this central budget hotel have showers but the cheapest ones share toilets down the hall.

Pension Otto – *Richard Wagner Straße 18. ℘(0221) 252 977. www. pensionotto.de. 5 rooms.* You really feel like family in this small, 1st-floor guesthouse where each room is decorated individually. Those facing the courtyard are quieter.

Hotel Hayk – *Frankenwerft 9. ℘(0221) 925 74 40. www.haykhotel.com. 6 rooms.* You'll get great value for money at this riverside hotel. Expect lots of charm and a warm welcome.

Hotel Im Kupferkessel – *Probsteigasse 6 (north of Christophstraße near St. Gereon's Church). ℘(0221) 270 79 60. www.im-kupferkessel.de. 13 rooms.* This well-kept hotel on the edge of the old town is a fine budget pick even if rooms are small and some must share the bathroom down the hall. The sunny breakfast room is anchored by a wooden spiral staircase.

Hotel Kunibert der Fiese – *Am Bollwerk 1–5. ℘(0221) 92 54 680. www. kunibertderfiese.de. 22 rooms.* A good compromise between comfort, price and location (near the centre). Other hotels in this category are nearby, all overlooking the Rhine.

Hotel Allegro – *Thurnmarkt 1. ℘(0221) 240 82 60 70. www.hotel-allegro.de. 40 rooms.* Choose from modern rooms or traditional ones Bavarian-style (four-poster beds!) at this charmer near the Chocolate Museum.

Günnewig Kommerz Hotel – *Johannisstraße 30–34. ℘(0221) 161 00. www.guennewig.de. 77 rooms.* Just outside the main train station north exit (opposite the cathedral), this bright orange 1970s building quickly catches the eye. Completely renovated, it has and comfortable rooms as well as a sauna.

Hotel Krone – *Kleine Budengasse 15 ℘(0221) 92 59 310. www.hotel-krone-koeln.de. 28 rooms.* Behind a brown façade, this central hotel has friendly service and clean and functional rooms easily reached by lift.

Hotel Brandenburger Hof – *Brandenburger Straße 2 ℘(0221) 12 28 89. www.brandenburgerhof.de. 31 rooms.* North of the old town, this reasonably priced hotel has small but functional rooms and a petite garden for relaxing. It is close to the main train station and cathedral.

Lint Hotel – *Lintgasse 7. ℘ (0221) 92 05 50, (0800) 545 84 58. www.lint-hotel.de. 18 rooms.* This contemporary hotel is equipped with all mod-cons and is right in the heart of the historic centre.

Hotel Im Wasserturm – *Kaygasse 2. ℘(0221) 200 80. 88 rooms ⌑22€. Restaurant.* A listed 19C brick water tower has been ingeniously converted into a chic designer hotel with a soaring lobby and rooms boasting the full complement of creature comforts. Enjoy magnificent views from the 11th-floor restaurant.

Excelsior Hotel Ernst – *Domplatz. ℘(0221) 27 01. www.excelsior hotelernst.de. 122 rooms. ⌑25€.* Cologne's most illustrious defender of the grand tradition sits directly opposite the towering cathedral. A sumptuous marble lobby leads to refined rooms and grand suites, along with a sauna and fitness facilities.

🍴 EAT

Paprica – *Zülpicher Straße 46. ℘(0221) 271 628 44.* In the heart of the lively student quarter, this cosy restaurant is decorated in its namesake colour and serves hearty schnitzel, salads, pastas and pizzas at very reasonable prices.

Gilden im Zims – *Heumarkt 77. ℘(0221) 16 86 61 10. www.gilden-im-zims.de.* While waiting (briefly) for a snack, schnitzel or traditional regional dish, you can read stories about some of the heroes in Cologne history. The décor seamlessly melds contemporary design and old bricks. In the basement, a nightclub comes alive on weekends.

🍴 **Delix Food & Wine** – *Friesenstraße 72–74.* 📞*(0221) 126 02 00. www.delix wineshop.de.* This trendy wine bar and restaurant has a daily-changing menu featuring whatever's fresh that day. A good place to start the evening, it is located at the corner of Friesenwall and Friesenstraße, which teem with other bars and restaurants.

🍴 **Belgischer Hof** – *Brüsseler Straße 54.* 📞 *(0221) 54 81 70 17. www.belgischer-hof.de.* The little table lights lend Mediterranean flair to this place where you'll be tempted by tarte flambee and other French-inspired dishes.

🍴 **Hase** – *St. Apern-Straße 17.* 📞*(0221) 25 43 75. Closed Sun.* Quality ingredients are woven into dishes that are creative without getting too tricky. The chic dining room with its pale wooden tables is great for kicking back at the end of the day.

🍴 **Pfaffen Brauerei** – *Heumarkt 62.* 📞*(0221) 257 77 65. www.max-paeffgen.de.* One of the few breweries in Cologne where the beer is brewed on site, Pfaffen has retained its traditional, rustic flair and is especially conducive to trying the local *Kölsch* beer alongside regional dishes. In summer you can enjoy the pleasant beer garden.

🍴 **Peters Brauhaus** – *Mühlengasse 1.* 📞*(0221) 257 39 50. www.peters-brauhaus.de.* This classic Cologne brewery has woodsy décor that adds warmth and friendliness to the rustic and comfortable place. There are multiple rooms, each one uniquely decorated.

🍴 **Heising und Adelmann** – *Friesenstraße 58.* 📞*(0221) 130 94 24. www.heising-und-adelmann.de. Closed Sun and public holidays.* This lively restaurant in fashionable bistro style delivers relaxed flair and modern, international cuisine. Choose from 50 cocktails at the bar or relax on the lovely terrace out back.

🍴 **Em Krützche** – *Am Frankenturm 1* 📞*(0221) 258 08 39. www.em-kruetzche.de. Closed Mon.* This traditional brew-pub has fed tummies and souls for over 400 years with hearty regional specialities.

🍴 **Osman 30 Restaurant** – *Im Mediapark 8.* 📞*(0221) 50 05 20 80. www.osman-cologne.de. Dinner only.* This trendy and modern restaurant serves upmarket Mediterranean fare amid fabulous views from the 30th floor of the KölnTurm in the Media Park. There's also a wine bar, weekend brunch and afternoon tea.

🍴 **Le Moissonnier** – *Krefelder Straße 25.* 📞*(0221) 72 94 79. www.lemoissonnier.de. Closed Mon, around Christmas, Easter and in August. Reservation advised.* You will feel like the king of the world at this Art Nouveau bistro in a historic building in the heart of town, especially after indulging in the creative French gourmet cuisine.

SIGHTSEEING
CITY TOURS
A hop-on, hop off tour bus with recorded commentary operates Wed–Sun 10.30am–3.30pm (*15€*). Buses depart nine times daily from outside the tourist office and stop at 13 major attractions. Without getting off, the loop takes 90 minutes. For self-guided walking tours (in English), the staff here rent out i-guides (*8€ for 4hrs*), small hand-held devices that takes you to 47 sights in 100 minutes.

BOAT TOURS
Boat tours run Apr–Oct and start at 7.50€ for one hour. For all options, tickets and directions to the landing docks, stop by KölnTourimus. Alternatively, just look for operators along the western river bank near Hohenzollernbrücke Bridge.

🎭 EVENTS
Carnival starts on the Thursday before Ash Wednesday (when Lent begins). A highlight is the parade on Rose Monday (🔖*see Carnival, p247*). April brings art connoisseurs from around the world to town for **Art Cologne**.

PUBLICATIONS
Cultural calendars of events can be found in the monthly publication *Köln im...* (followed by the month) at tourist information offices. Other monthly listings magazines like *StadtRevue* and *Prinz* are sold at news kiosks.

Aachen★

Aachen snuggles up against the border with Holland and Belgium and has a special place in German history. Its natural hot springs were already popular with Celtic tribes, but it was the Romans who built the first thermal baths. Charlemagne (747–814) made Aachen capital of his Frankish Empire in 794 and, after being crowned emperor in 800, unleashed his military campaigns on Saxony and Bavaria from here. He's buried in the spectacular cathedral that also saw the coronation of 30 German kings between 936 and 1531.

CATHEDRAL DISTRICT
Dom★★★ (Cathedral)

Open daily 7am–7pm (Jan–Mar 6pm). *Guided tours daily (2pm tour in English).* *4€.* *(0241) 47 70 90. www.aachendom.de.*

The first German entry on UNESCO's list of World Heritage Sites, Aachen's cathedral soars above the historic district. The oldest part, Charlemagne's palace chapel *(Pfalzkapelle)* was completed around 800 and is a superb example of Carolingian architecture.

The Gothic chancel was added in 1414 to accommodate the growing number of pilgrims wishing to see relics (including Jesus' loin cloth) that Charlemagne had brought to Aachen. They're still displayed every seven years (next in 2014).

Interior

Aachen's cathedral is remarkable for the harmonious design of the domed Carolingian palace chapel, an octagonal structure surrounded by a 16-sided gallery awash with mosaics. Its other main decorative element is the magnificent 12C wheel-shaped **chandelier** ★★, donated by Emperor Frederick I Barbarossa.

The nave is also a treasure trove of supreme artworks, most notably the 11C **ambo**★★★, a copper pulpit decorated with precious stones and

- **Population:** 265 208
- **Info:** Elisenbrunnen, Friedrich-Wilhelm-Platz, 52062 Aachen. *(0241) 180 29 60 and 180 29 61. www.aachen-tourist.de.*
- **Location:** Among the northern foothills of the Ardennes (Hohes Venn), near the Belgian and Dutch borders, Aachen is Germany's most westerly town, easily accessible by road from Cologne, Düsseldorf and Liège, Belgium.
- **Parking:** Public parking is available in garages and car parks near the main train station, the market, the cathedral and Kaiserplatz. Computerised signs throughout town indicate space availability.
- **Don't Miss:** The cathedral and its treasury.
- **Timing:** Allow half day for the cathedral district.

donated by Henry II. Other highlights are the 13C **Shrine of Mary**★; the 14C Virgin of Aachen statue; and the high altar adorned with a **Pala d'Oro**★★★, a gilded panel relief depicting the Passion of Christ (c. 1020).

Behind the altar rests the **Shrine of Charlemagne**★★★ (Karlsschrein: 1200–15), a hand-worked gold and silver reliquary containing the emperor's bones. His **marble throne** in the upper gallery was also used as the coronation throne of 30 German kings (*must be seen on guided tours; meet in the treasury*).

Domschatzkammer (Cathedral Treasury)★★★

Access via Klostergasse. *Open year-round, Mon 10am–1pm; Jan–Mar, Tue–Sat 10am–5pm; Apr–Dec, Tue–Sat 10am–6pm.* *Closed Jan 1, Carnival, Good Friday, Dec 24–25 & 31.* *5€.* *Guided tours daily, 5€.* *(0241) 47 70 90.*

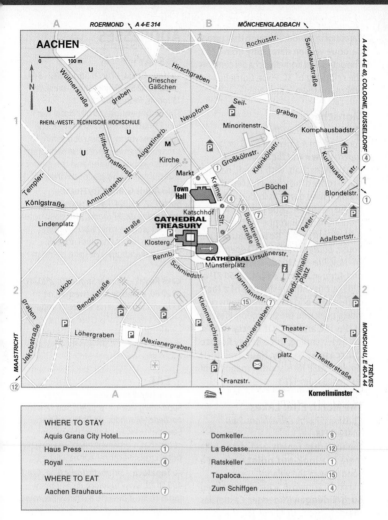

WHERE TO STAY

Aquis Grana City Hotel	⑦
Haus Press	①
Royal	④

WHERE TO EAT

Aachen Brauhaus	⑦
Domkeller	⑨
La Bécasse	⑫
Ratskeller	①
Tapaloca	⑮
Zum Schiffgen	④

The treasury is one of the most important north of the Alps, with over 100 outstanding artworks arranged in five thematic sections. Highlights include several major silver and gold reliquaries including the bust of Charlemagne (1349) and the Lothar Cross (c. 1100).

Rathaus (Town Hall)

Markt. ⏰*Open year-round, daily 10am–16pm.* ⏰*Closed major holidays and during special events.* 💶*5€.* ♿ 📞*(0241) 432 73 10. www.aachen.de.*
The Gothic 14C town hall has sprouted from the foundations of Charlemagne's palace of which only the Granus Tower remains. The palatial building overlooks the market square with its **fountain** and **emperor's statue**. The most important room is the **Reichssaal** decorated in the 19C by Alfred Rethel with romanticised scenes from Charlemagne's life.

The same room also contains replicas of the imperial insignia, including the crown, the orb and several swords (originals in Vienna).

EXCURSION
Kornelimünster

▶ *10km/6.2mi southeast.*
This is an enchanting village with slate-roofed, blue and grey stone houses typical of the Eifel region. Its key sight is the **abbey church**★ with origins in the

Carolingian period, although the current Baroque version dates only from 1728. The octagonal Kornelius chapel contains the reliquary of 3C Pope Cornelius for whom the town is named.

Monschau

▶ *33km/20.5mi southeast.*
Coming from Aachen via B258, enjoy a superb **view**★★ *of the town.*

Pretty Monschau, with its tall, narrow, slate-roofed houses clustered in a winding river gorge, is lorded over by a ruined medieval castle but is otherwise predominantly Baroque in style.

A highlight is the **Rotes Haus**★ *(red house; Laufenstraße 10; ⏱open Good Fri–Nov, Tue–Sun 10am, 11am, 2pm, 3pm and 4pm; ⌂2.50€; ℘(024 72) 50 71)* of 1765, a one-time residence of a local cloth-maker and merchant. Rooms provide a peek into the bourgeois lifestyle of the 18C and 19C. Of special note is the free-standing, three-storey **Rococo staircase**★. Nearby Haus Troistorff *(Laufenstraße 18)* is another magnificent residence from 1783.

The North Eifel Lakes

▶ *85km/52.8mi. Leave Monschau on the B258.*

The road rises rapidly, and after a mile there is a **look-out point**★ giving a good view of the village.

Leaving the town of Schmidt, the ruined **Burg Nideggen** (Nideggen Castle) lies straight ahead. Until the 15C the rose-coloured sandstone castle was the residence of the counts and dukes of Jülich. The restored 12C church has a Romanesque chancel with frescoes.

Rurtalsperre★ (Rur Dam)

In a wild stretch of countryside, this reservoir forms, with the Urft reservoir to the south, the largest stretch of water in the Eifel. Motorboat services operate on both.

ADDRESSES

🏠STAY

⬭ **Haus Press** – *Trierer Straße 842–844.* ℘*(0241) 92 80 20. www.haus-press.de. 15 rooms. Restaurant⬭.*
This unpretentious family hotel has functional rooms furnished in rustic country-style, including some family rooms with three beds. The restaurant serves regional cuisine and the garden and pub are good places to unwind.

⬭⬭ **Aquis Grana City Hotel** – *Büchel 32.* ℘*(0241) 44 30. www.hotel-aquisgrana.de. 97 rooms.* This cosy hotel is decorated warmly with woodsy elements. Rooms are individually furnished and quiet despite being in the heart of town.

⬭⬭ **Royal** – *Jülicher Straße 10.* ℘*(0241) 18 22 80. www.royal.bestwestern.de. 35 rooms. ⌂15€.* This modern and comfortable hotel is close to the town centre. Rooms are nicely furnished; those at the back are especially quiet.

🍴EAT

⬭ **Aachen Brauhaus** – *Kapuzinergraben 4.* ℘*(0241) 360 17. www. aachener-brauhaus.de.* This traditional German brewery-pub in the town centre has a great variety of reasonably priced regional and national dishes.

⬭ **Tapaloca** – *Elisabethstraße 6.* ℘*(0241) 400 50 78. www.tapaloca.de.* For tasty tapas make a beeline to this welcoming place with sunny décor and palm trees. There's also a menu for larger appetites.

⬭⬭ **Zum Schiffgen** – *Hühnermarkt 23.* ℘*(0241) 335 29. www.zum-schiffgen.de.* Enjoy traditional regional specialities at this long-running favourite. The terrace offers delightful views of the town hall.

⬭⬭⬭ **Ratskeller** – *Markt 40.* ℘*(0241) 350 01. www.ratskeller-aachen.de.* This traditional restaurant in the vaulted cellars of the town hall offers traditional German fare updated for the 21C.

⬭⬭⬭⬭ **La Bécasse** – *Hanbrucher Straße 1.* ℘*(0241) 744 44. www.labecasse.de.* The kitchen of this modern restaurant sources quality products from Belgium. Everything is prepared with expertise and creativity.

Ruhr Region
Ruhrgebiet

Historically, the Ruhr Region is best known as one of the world's largest industrial areas, a conglomeration of 53 cities joined together by sweat, coal and steel. No more. The Ruhr has been reinventing itself at a steady clip, embracing its industrial past but focusing on a future filled with culture and the arts. Aspiring to undergo a model transformation from industrial to creative powerhouse, it could become a model for other urban areas worldwide. No wonder then that Essen (on behalf of the whole Ruhr Region) was selected as the European Capital of Culture 2010.

A BIT OF HISTORY
Important industrial centre – Although most of the furnaces and mines are no longer in operation, the Ruhr Region remains one of the world's most important industrial centres. Much of German steel is manufactured here; Duisburg is the largest inland port in Europe and the largest river port in the world. The landscape in the region's north is shaped by the chemical industry and modern mining operations. Former industrial plants have been turned into cultural venues, shopping centres and adventure playgrounds. Old pits and factories have been converted into industrial museums, offering insight into the production methods and social history of the region.

BOCHUM
Kunstmuseum Bochum (Fine Arts Museum)
Kortumstraße 147, opposite the Stadtpark. ○*Open year-round, Tue–Sun 10am–5pm (Wed 8pm).* ⊜*3€.* ○*Closed Jan 1, Good Fri, May 1, Dec 24–25 & 31.* ♿ ✆*(0234) 910 42 30. www.bochum. de/kunstmuseum.*
The collections in this spacious, airy building concentrate mainly on contemporary international art.

Info: Königswall 21, 44137 Dortmund. ✆(0231) 18 16 186. www.ruhrgebiettouristik.de.

Location: The Ruhr Basin (4 400sq km/1 700sq mi) lies along the Ruhr, Rhine and Lippe rivers and encompasses the cities of Duisburg, Essen and Dortmund plus scores of mid-size and smaller towns.

Don't Miss: Religious art lovers will be impressed by Essen's cathedral and its artworks. About two dozen of the biggest attractions (covering 150 years of cultural heritage) are linked by a 400km/248mi-long **Industrial Heritage Trail**.

Timing: Allow two days to get a flavour of the Ruhr region.

Kids: Warner Bros. Movie World, the Open Air Technical Museum and the Schwebebahn.

Exhibits are drawn from the collection which ranges from Josef Albers to Ossip Zadkine.

Deutsches Bergbau-Museum★★ (German Mining Museum)
Am Bergbaumuseum 28. ○*Open year-round, Tue–Fri 8.30am–5pm, Sat–Sun 10am–5pm.* ○*Closed Jan 1, May 1, Dec 24–26 & 31.* ⊜*6.50€.* ♿ ✆*(0234) 587 70. www.bergbaumuseum.de.*
Founded in 1930, this museum examines the evolution of mining from antiquity to the present. A miners' lift descends 20m/65.6ft underground, where the 2.5km/1.5mi of abandoned workings in the **Schaubergwerk** illustrate methods of coal extraction and transport. The tour ends with a trip up the 71m/233ft-high mining tower.

Eisenbahnmuseum★ (Railway Museum)

Dr-C-Otto-Straße 191, in northern Bochum-Dahlhausen surburb. ◷*Open Mar–mid-Nov, Tue–Fri & Sun 10am–5pm.* ⌷*6€.* ☎*(0234) 49 25 16. www.eisenbahnmuseumbochum.de.*
Founded by railway enthusiasts, this museum is installed in an abandoned station and repair shop on the north bank of the Ruhr. Equipment from as long ago as 1914 is for the most part still in working condition. More than 180 steam and electric locomotives trace the evolution of the railway as a form of transportation.

BOTTROP
Josef Albers Museum

Im Stadtgarten 20 (near town centre). ◷*Open year-round, Tue–Sat 11am–5pm, Sun 10am–5pm.* ◷*Closed Jan 1, Dec 24–25 & 31.* ⌷. ☎*(02041) 297 16. www.quadrat-bottrop.de.*
Bottrop-born Constructivist painter and Bauhaus theorist Josef Albers referred to his work as *Hommage an das Quadrat* (Homage to the Square). This ultramodern museum displays a survey of his work and other Constructivists'. The adjoining sculpture park contains works by Max Bill, Donald Judd, Norbert Kricke etc. The same complex also harbours a **Museum of Pre- and Local History**. The **Ice Age Hall**★ houses Germany's largest Quaternary Era collection.

👤👤Movie Park Germany★

Warner Allee 1, in Bottrop-Kirchhellen, via A31, exit Kirchhellen. ◷*Open late Mar–Oct, daily 10am–6pm, 8pm or 10pm, depending on the day. Call for specific opening times.* ⌷*31€.* ☎*(02 045) 89 90. www.movieparkgermany.com.*
This film and amusement park features more than 35 attractions, thrill rides and live shows spread across such themed sections as Old West, Streets of New York and Santa Monica Pier. Scream your head off on the MP Xpress rollercoaster, join SpongeBob on a Back Splash water ride or take in the scene from the Ferris wheel. If you need a little peace and quiet, head for the **Museum of Ger-**man Film History★, examining over 100 years of celluloid history.

DORTMUND★

Königswall 18a, 44137 Dortmund. ☎*(0231) 189 99 20. www.dortmund-tourismus.de.*
Bye-bye collieries and steel mills, hello high-tech and culture! On the eastern edge of the Ruhrgebiet (and its largest city), Dortmund has successfully mastered the transition from powerhouse of the Industrial Revolution to future-oriented metropolis. Today, innovation and research, along with trade, insurance and the service sector support the local economy. Also famous for its beer and football team, the city boasts extensive parks and hosts major trade shows. A ring road following the course of the medieval town wall encircles the centre where most of the museums and churches are located. The Westfalenpark, football stadium and trade fair grounds are south of the city centre.

Westfalenpark★

An der Buschmühle, enter from Florianstraße. ◷*Open year-round, daily 9am–11pm.* ⌷*3€ until 6pm, 1.50€ after.* ☎*(0231) 502 61 00. www.westfalenpark.dortmund.de.*
Dortmund's "green heart", this huge park was created for the 1959 *Bundesgartenschau* (federal horticultural show), which the city hosted twice more, in 1969 and 1991. Its most prominent feature is the Florianturm television tower but the vast park is also home to an open-air stage, a puppet theatre, a gallery, a planetarium and the Mondo Mio! interactive children's museum. Another highlight is the **rose garden** (*Rosarium*), a fragrant oasis with 3 200 varieties of the noble blossom from all over the world.

Florianturm

◷*Open year-round, Tue noon–8pm, Wed–Sun noon–11pm.* ⌷*2.50€.* ☎*(0231) 138 49 75. www.westfalenpark.dortmund.de.*
Dortmund's television tower stands 220m/722ft tall and was named for the

patron saint of gardeners. At 141m/462ft, it features a restaurant and a terrace with superb **panoramas**★ extending as far as the Sauerland on clear days.

Reinoldikirche★

Ostenhellweg 2. ⏲*Open year-round, Mon–Sat 10am–6pm, Sun 1pm–6pm.* ℘*(0231) 59 43 51. www.sanktreinoldi.de.* Right in the heart of town, this three-nave basilica was first consecrated in 1280 and was repeatedly damaged and rebuilt in subsequent centuries, the last time after World War II.

It houses some outstanding 14C and 15C religious works: a sculpted reredos, probably Burgundian work; the bronze eagle pulpit *(Adlerpult)*; a wooden statue of St. Reinold, patron saint of the town; and a statue of Charlemagne.

The church tower can be climbed for great city views (⏲*Sat noon–3pm;* ⬤*1.50€).*

Museum für Kunst und Kulturgeschichte (Museum of Art and Cultural History)

Hansastraße 3. ⏲*Open year-round, Tue –Sun 10am–5pm, Thu 8pm, Sat noon– 5pm.* ⏲*Closed Jan 1, Dec 24–25 & 31.* ⬤*5€.* ♿. ℘*(0231) 502 55 22. www.mkk.dortmund.de.*

Delve into Dortmund history by perusing the paintings, sculptures, furnishings and crafts engagingly displayed inside a converted Art Deco bank building. Keep an eye out for the **Dortmund Treasure**★ *(Dortmunder Goldschatz),* consisting of 444 Roman gold coins, most from the 4C.

The emotive quality of Conrad von Soest's Madonna sculptures is striking, as is the craftsmanship of the Romanesque triumphal cross. Other rooms feature paintings by Spitzweg, Liebermann, Slevogt, Corinth and other 18C and 19C masters.

Museum am Ostwall

Ostwall 7. ⏲*Open year-round, Tue–Sun 10am–5pm, Thu 8pm, Sat noon–5pm.* ⏲*Closed Jan 1, Dec 24–25 & 31.* ⬤*3€.* ♿. ℘*(0231) 502 32 47. www.museumostwall.dortmund.de.*

Fans of 20C and 21C art will be drawn to this fine museum where works by German Expressionists, most notably members of the Blue Rider and Bridge artist groups (Schmidt-Rottluff, Marc, Macke), form the core of the collection. Since late 2010 the museum occupies three floors of the so-called "Dortmund U", a landmark tower that was once part of the local Union Brewery and has reinvented itself as a centre for arts and culture.

DUISBURG
Wilhelm-Lehmbruck-Museum★★

Friedrich-Wilhelm-Straße 40, in Duisburg town centre. ⏲*Open year -round, Tue–Sat 11am–5pm, Sun 10am– 6pm.* ⏲*Closed Jan 1, Dec 24–25 & 31.* ⬤*8€.* ♿ ℘*(0231) 283 26 30. www.lehmbruckmuseum.de.*

This museum is home to a prestigious collection of over 700 20C sculptures and objets d'art. Look for emotional works by Barlach and Kollwitz, Cubist and Constructivist sculpture by Archipenko, Duchamp and Brancusi and otherworldly Surrealist contributions by Arp and Dalí.

One museum wing showcases works by Duisberg sculptor **Wilhelm Lehmbruck** (1881–1919). The surrounding park contains outdoor sculptures by international artists against a wooded backdrop.

Museum der Deutschen Binnenschiffahrt★

Apostelstraße 84, in Duisburg-Ruhrort. ⏲*Open Tue–Sun 10am–5pm.* ⏲*Closed Jan 1, Dec 24–26 & 31.* ⬤*3€.* ♿ ℘*(0203) 8088 940. www.binnenschiffahrts museum.de.*

The former Art Nouveau swimming pool is one of the country's largest museums about the economic, technological and social aspects of inland shipping. Visitors examine developments from dug-outs to modern tug boats.

Two museum ships (⬤*2€, accessible May–Sept only)* from 1882 and 1922 are a 10-minute stroll through the port, near the maritime stock exchange.

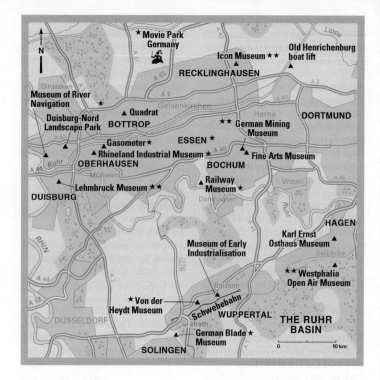

Landschaftspark Duisburg Nord

Emscherstraße 71, in Duisburg-Meidrich. *(0203) 429 19 19. www.landschaft-spark.de.*

This enormous retired iron- and steel-works has been ingeniously recycled into a adventure playground and cultural events venue. You can learn scuba diving in the old gas tank, go rock climbing on its ore bunkers, brave a high-wire parcours suspended between buildings or ascend to the top of the blast furnace for fine views. The cultural programme includes movie screenings, theatre productions and dance parties.

ESSEN★

Am Hauptbahnhof 2, 45127 Essen. *(0201) 194 33. www.essen.de.*

Essen is one of the largest cities in the Ruhr region, wedged between Bochum and Duisburg along the A40 autobahn. The city traces its pedigree back to the 8C but made its biggest mark on history during the Industrial Age. Closely asso-ciated with the Krupp family dynasty, its steelworks and collieries were the engines driving the German economy until well into the 1960s. Since then, Essen has been a city in transition, replacing its smokestacks with "clean-air" industries such as finance, administration, a university and plenty of business, commerce and culture. Along with the rest of the Ruhr region it was European Cultural Capital in 2010.

Museum Folkwang★★★

Museumsplatz 1. Open year-round, Tue–Sun 10am–6pm, Fri 10.30pm. Closed Jan 1, May 1, Easter Mon, Pentecost Mon, Dec 24 & 31. 5€. (0201) 884 54 44. www.museum-folkwang.de.

An Aladdin's cave of paintings, sculpture, graphic art and photography stretching across the 19C and 20C, this museum is one of Germany's premier repositories of fine art with particular emphasis on German and French artists. Galleries are filled with a veritable who's who of famous names, from Romantic artist Caspar David Friedrich and modern trailblazers Cézanne, Gauguin and van Gogh to German Expressionists Heckel, Kirchner, Schmidt-Rottluff and postwar bigshots like Baselitz, Kiefer and Pollock.

Since spring 2010, exhibits are showcased in a fabulous new building designed by British architect David Chipperfield. It features galleries (some naturally lit) radiating out from inner courtyards and gardens of the glass-fronted building.

Ruhr Museum★★

Gelsenkirchner Straße 181. ○*Open year-round, daily 10am–7pm.* ○*Closed Dec 24 & 31.* ●6€. ♿ *(0201) 884 52 00 www.ruhrmuseum.de.*

The history of the Ruhr is engagingly and creatively chronicled in the dramatically adapted former coal-washing plant of the colliery Zollverein, a UNESCO-protected Bauhaus-style complex that's been rebooted as a cultural and arts complex. Descend several floors into the depth of the building to explore all facets of Ruhrgebiet culture, from its medieval beginnings on a major trading route to its Industrial Age heyday and the recent metamorphosis into a place of culture, high-tech and logistics.

Münster (Cathedral)★★

Burgplatz 2. ○*Open year-round, Mon–Fri 6.30am–6.30pm, Sat 9am–7.30pm, Sun 9am–8pm.* ○*Closed Mon, Fri 8am–10am.* ♿ *(0201) 220 42 06. www.dom-essen.de.*

Just off the main pedestrian shopping strip, Essen's medieval cathedral offers peaceful respite and a bonanza of art treasures, including some from the Ottonian period. The undisputed highlights are the **Golden Madonna**★★★ (AD 980), one of the oldest surviving sculptures from the early Middle Ages, and a massive **seven-branch candelabrum**★ (c. 1000). The **cathedral treasury**★★ *(Domschatzkammer;* ○*open year-round, Tue–Sat 10am–5pm, Sun 11.30am–5pm;* ○*closed major religious and public holidays;* ●4€; *(0201) 220*

42 06; www.domschatz-essen.de) holds, among other items, four splendid **processional crosses**★★★ (10C and 11C) and a reliquary said to contain a nail from Jesus' cross.

Villa Hügel★

Haraldstraße. ○*Open year-round, Tue–Sun 10am–6pm, park daily 8am–8pm.* ●3€. ♿ *(0201) 61 62 90. www.villahuegel.de.*

This imposing Gründerzeit mansion stands in an attractive park on the north shore of **Lake Baldeney**. Three generations of the industrialist Krupp family lived here from 1873 to 1945. You can tour their private quarters, study company history and stroll around the lovely park. The biggest crowds turn out for the periodic special art exhibits.

HAGEN
Kulturquartier Hagen

Hochstraße 73. ○*Open year-round, Tue–Fri 10am–5pm, Sat & Sun 11am–6pm.* ○*Closed Jan 1, Easter Mon, Whit Monday, Dec 24–25 & 31.* ●6€. *(02331) 207 31 38. www.kunstquartier-hagen.de.*

Hagen's new cultural quarter encompasses two museums. First up is the renovated and expanded Osthaus Museum, which displays early Modernist works (German Expressionm, New Objectivity) in a beautiful Art Nouveau space designed by Belgian artist Henry van de Velde. Next door is the brand-new Emil Schumacher Museum, which is dedicated to the Hagen-born artist who was a founder of the German Abstract Art movement after World War II. The exhibit encompasses oil paintings, watercolours, graphic works, ceramics and porcelain. Tickets are good for admission to both museums.

👤👤 Westfälisches Freilichtmuseum★★ (Westphalian Open-Air Museum)

At Hagen-Selbecke, in the valley of Mäckingerbachtal. Leave Hagen heading south towards Frankfurt, then take the Eilpe road. At Eilpe, turn right towards Breckerfeld-Halver and continue for just over 1.5km/1mi to Selbecke. 10min walk from the parking lot. ⏲Open mid-Mar–Oct, Tue–Sun 9am–6pm. ⬤5€. ☎(02331) 780 70. www.freilichtmuseum-hagen.de.

Along 2.5km/1.5mi of the Mäcking valley, more than 60 workshops and buildings illustrate the evolution of crafts and trades from the late 18C through the 19C. Exhibits include a working forge, examples of James Nasmyth's steam hammer (c. 1840) and the zinc rolling mill of Hoesch (1841), a printing museum and a traditional craft village, where saddlers, smiths, rope makers, bakers and brewers demonstrate their skills and sell their products.

OBERHAUSEN
Gasometer★
Arenastraße 11, next to CentrO shopping centre. ⏲Viewing platform: year-round, Tue–Sun 10am–5pm (Wed to 3pm). Special exhibits: Tue–Sun 10am–6pm. Tours ⬤2€; exhibition prices vary. ♿ ☎(0208) 850 37 30. www.gasometer.de.

Europe's largest blast furnace gas storage tank (68m/220ft in diameter, built in 1928–29) has a new life as an exhibition hall. It is an impressive space and worth visiting even when no exhibitions are on. A lift whisks you to a viewing platform at 117m/350ft for sweeping views across the entire Ruhr region. You can also rent an audioguide (⬤3€) for a self-guided tour. Next door is the CentrO, one of the largest shopping centres in Germany.

Rheinisches Industriemuseum★ (Rhenish Industrial Museum)
Hansastraße 20, Oberhausen (behind the main train station). ⏲Open year-round, Tue–Fri 10am–5pm, Sat & Sun 11am–6pm. ⏲Closed Jan 1, Good Fri, May 1, Dec 24–25 & 31. ⬤4€. ☎(02234) 992 15 55. www.rim.lvr.de.

The Altenberg zinc works was in operation until 1981 and is a rare completely preserved factory site from the early days of industrialisation. The "Heavy

Industry" exhibit shows the 150-year history of the iron and steel industry in the Ruhr region and displays such objects as ingot moulds, mill rollers, a steam hammer and a steam locomotive.

RECKLINGHAUSEN
Ikonen-Museum★★ (Icon Museum)
⛔Closed until at least early 2012. Kirchplatz 2a. ☎(02361) 50 19 41. www.ikonen-museum.com.

Considered the most important museum of icons outside the orthodox world, this museum boasts more than 1 000 works from Russia, Greece and the Balkan countries. Aside from icons, the collection includes embroideries, miniatures and wood and metal sculptures.

Altes Schiffshebewerk Henrichenburg (Historic Ship Lift)
Am Hebewerk 2, Waltrop. ⏲Open year-round, Tue–Sun 10am–6pm. ⏲Closed Dec 24–Jan 1. ⬤3.50€. ♿ ☎(02363) 970 70. www.schiffshebewerk-henrichenburg.de.

In 1899 Emperor Wilhelm II inaugurated this amazing construction, which lifted river barges travelling on the Dortmund–Ems Canal 14m/46ft high, thereby opening up a direct waterway to the North Sea. It was in operation until being replaced with a larger, more modern ship lift in 1962. An exhibition illustrates the construction process and technical, political and economic aspects of canal building and river shipping.

SOLINGEN
Deutsches Klingenmuseum★ (German Blade Museum)
Klosterhof 4, Solingen-Gräfrath. ⏲Open year-round, Tue–Sun 10am–5pm (Fri from 2pm). ⏲Closed Jan 1, 24–25 & 31 Dec. ⬤3.50€. ♿ ☎(0212) 25 83 60. www.klingenmuseum.de.

Solingen is known the world over for its quality knives and other cutting instruments. In the former Gräfrath Abbey, an elegant Baroque building, this museum traces the cultural history of cutting and eating utensils, showcasing silverware

Solingen – The Art of Steel

"Cutting edge" is a term that has defined Solingen for centuries, as it is here that steel has been turned into legendary cutting instruments. The town's first mention in history was in 1067 and by the 1600s local craftsmen were creating knives, swords and instruments that were unequalled in quality. Being close to large forests that provided charcoal and being positioned atop rich deposits of iron guaranteed the prosperity of its skilled townspeople. Of course it did not hurt that the key trading centre of Cologne was pretty close by too. Such tradition of excellence continues to this day, through firms such as Henkels and Wüsthof. About 90 percent of all blades made in Germany still hail from this small town.

from the Bronze Age to today. Another focal point is on weapons from around the world with a collection that includes bronze swords from Iran as well as ceremonial rapiers from France.

WUPPERTAL
Von der Heydt-Museum★

Turmhof 8, Wuppertal-Elberfeld.
🕐*Open year-round, Tue–Sun 11am–6pm (Thu to 8pm.* 🕐*Closed Easter Mon, May 1, Whit Mon, Dec 24–25 & 31.* 9€.
&. ℘(0202) 563 62 31. www.von-der-heydt-museum.de.
This museum, housed in a 19C town hall, displays 16C and 17C Flemish and Dutch painting; French and German painting from the 19C to Impressionism, Expressionism (Kirchner, Beckmann), Fauvism, Cubism (Braque) all the way to the present. Sculptures from the 19C and 20C are also on display (Rodin, Maillol).

Museum für Frühindustrialisierung (Museum of Early Industrialisation)

Engelsstraße 10–18, Wuppertal-Barmen. 🕐*Open year-round, Tue–Sun 10am–6pm.* 🕐*Closed Jan 1, Dec 24–26.* 4€. & ℘(0202) 563 43 75. www.historisches-zentrum-wuppertal.de.
Housed in a former factory, this museum is devoted to the economic and social history of the Wupper valley since the mid-18C.

♟♙ Schwebebahn (Suspended Railway)

A unique mode of transport for getting around Wuppertal is the world's oldest suspended passenger railway (1898–

1903). Completely non-polluting, the electric cars travel 12m/36ft above the Wupper River for just over 13km/8mi.

ADDRESSES

🛏STAY

🍴🛏 **Ferrohotel** – *Düsseldorfer Straße 122, 47051 Duisburg.* ℘(0203) 28 70 85. www.ferrotel.de, www.sorat-hotels.com. 30 rooms. This modern boutique hotel scores points with the lifestyle crowd thanks to its streamlined design and stylishly integrated industrial decorations, including historic fire extinguishers. Rooms are comfortable and lack none of the expected mod-cons. Some rooms and public areas have free Wi-Fi.

♟EAT

🍴 **Livingroom** – *Luisenstraße 9, 44787 Bochum.* ℘(0234) 953 56 85. www.livingroom-bochum.de. Closed Sun. The menu at this trendy lifestyle bistro is wide enough to cater to every taste and diet. Walls are decorated with paintings and photographs.

🍴🛏 **Bahnhof Nord** – *Am Vorthbach 10, 46240 Bottrop.* ℘(02041) 98 89 44. www.bahnhofnord.de. Reservation recommended. Dinner only. At this converted railway station, market-fresh ingredients find their destiny in light and tasty dishes with modern flair. Tables on the terrace and in the winter garden are particularly coveted.

Düsseldorf★

Finance, fashion and fun are the hallmarks of this modern Rhineland city and capital of the German state of North Rhine-Westphalia. Shopping is a major pastime here and the old town is nicknamed the "world's longest bar" for good reason, while a long tradition in the arts is reflected in a multitude of first-rate museums and cultural institutions.

A BIT OF HISTORY

City of the arts – Düsseldorf has been an artistic mecca since the reign of Elector **Johann Wilhelm** (1679–1716, also known as Jan Wellem) who surrounded himself with brilliant musicians, painters and architects. Elector Carl Theodor provided additional artistic impetus when he founded a prestigious art academy in 1773. Its faculty has included Paul Klee and Joseph Beuys; since 2009, British artist Tony Cragg serves as its director. Düsseldorf also has a few contemporary architectural gems by Frank Gehry and others, most notably in the revamped old harbour known as the Mediahafen (Media Harbour)

The world of fashion – Exhibitions, fairs and collections of haute couture secure Düsseldorf's reputation as one

- ▶ **Population:** 573 000
- ℹ **Info:** Immermannstraße 65b. 40210 Düsseldorf. ✆(0211) 17 20 20. www.duesseldorf-tourismus.de.
- ◖ **Location:** Düsseldorf straddles the River Rhine and is served by an international airport, long-distance trains and several autobahns. Most of the sights and action concentrate along the river, especially in the Altstadt (old town).
- 🅿 **Parking:** Garages are plentiful, notably around the Hauptbahnhof and near the Königsallee.
- 🕹 **Don't Miss:** Quaff local *Altbier* in a traditional brew-pub; K20 art museum.
- 🕐 **Timing:** You'll want to devote an entire day to seeing the city.

of Germany's fashion capitals. The city hosts several fashion trade shows throughout the year. Everything elegant centres on the graceful **Königsallee★**, with boutiques and arcades on either side of the old royal moat.

Medienhafen

© Mauritius/Photononstop

DÜSSELDORF

ESSEN

N
0   200 m

Oberkasseler Brücke

Victoriapl.

FINE ART MUSEUM

EHRENHOF

TONHALLE

Hofgartenrampe · Tonhalle

Heine-Denkmal

COURT GARDENS

GOETHE MUSEUM

RATINGER TOR

Max.-Weyhe-Allee

K20 CONTEMPORARY ART MUSEUM

Heinr.-Heine-Allee

SCHAUSPIEL HAUS

COURT GARDENS

Am Wehrhahn

Grabbepl.

Schlossturm

STADTHAUS

Burgpl.

Market square

H. Heine Allee

Old town hall

Old Town

Schneider-Wibbel-Gasse

ALTER HAFEN

KUNSTHALLE

OPERNHAUS

Elberfelder Str.

Jan-Wellem-Pl.

Schadow-platz

Dreischeibenhaus

Tonhallen-str.

Flingerstr.

Heinr.-Heine-Allee

W-MARX-HAUS

Martin-Luther-Platz

Carlsplatz

Benrather

Steinstr./Königsallee

Steinstr.

Friedrich-Ebert-Str.

Bastion-

straße

Bismarckstr.

Schwanen-markt

Graf-Adolf-Platz

Haroldstr.

Graf-

Adolf-

Ernst-Reuter-Pl.

Luisenstr.

Cornelius-str.

Luisenstr.

RHEIN

Rheinufertunnel

Mannesmannufer

Berger Allee

KÖNIGSALLEE

RATINGER TOR

Mühlenstr.

Bolkerstr.

RHEIN

Rhine Tower, Medienhafen

Hubertus Str.

Kavalleriestr.

K21 Contemporary Art Museum   A 46

A 59 COLOGNE

NEANDERTAL   WUPPERTAL

WHERE TO STAY		WHERE TO EAT	
Doria	(1)	Berens am Kai	(1)
Flora	(7)	Bistro im Victorian	(6)
Jugendherberge Düsseldorf	(4)	Brauerei zum Schiffchen	(9)
Orangerie	(9)	Fischhaus	(12)
Windsor Hotel	(12)	La Piazzetta di Positano	(15)
		Monkey's West	(18)
		Rheinturm Top 180	(4)

Poetry and Music in the 19C

Heinrich Heine (1797–1856), son of a Bolkerstraße merchant, spent his youth in Düsseldorf, deeply impressed with the French and Napoleon. A poet, pamphleteer, traveller, defender of liberalism and a Francophile, Heine described himself as "a German nightingale which would have liked to make its nest in Voltaire's wig". Among the musicians who have given Düsseldorf its reputation as an artistic centre are Robert Schumann and Felix Mendelssohn-Bartholdy. **Robert Schumann** (1810–1856) was appointed conductor of the municipal orchestra in 1850 and lived on Bilkerstraße for four years. In 1854, he suffered a nervous breakdown and attempted to drown himself in the Rhine. His friend **Felix Mendelssohn** (1809–1847) brilliantly directed the city's Rhine Festival. He made his first journey to England in 1829, conducting his own *Symphony in C Minor* at the London Philharmonic Society.

East Asian connection– Düsseldorf has long played an important role in economic relations linking Germany with East Asia, Japan in particular. More than 500 Japanese firms are based here, including banks, insurance companies, and transport firms.

SIGHTS
Altstadt (Old Town)
This largely car-free riverside quarter is jam-packed with pubs, bars and shops. One of the busiest thoroughfares is **Bolkerstraße**, where the poet Heinrich Heine was born in the house at no 53. The area is also linked with the story of the tailor Wibbel, who attended his own funeral after switching identities to escape a prison sentence. This legend is recalled by the figures of the Schneider-Wibbel-Gasse carillon clock, which operates at 11am, 1pm, 3pm, 6pm and 9pm. The Altstadt is parallelled by a pleasant **riverside promenade** (*Rheinuferprom-enade*). Stroll from Burgplatz square, where the medieval castle tower houses a shipping museum, all the way to the 234m/767ft-high **Rheinturm**, a TV tower with a revolving restaurant.

Marktplatz (Market Square)
Separated from the Rhine by the 16C Renaissance **Altes Rathaus** (old town hall), this square is embellished by the bronze equestrian statue (18C) of Elector Jan Wellem. He is buried in the Baroque **Andreaskirche** (Church of St. Andrew) a short walk north of here.

Hofgarten and Schloss Jägerhof★ (Court Garden and Jägerhof Palace)
Hofgarten park is a shady continuation of the Königsallee. Its Napoleon Hill is crowned with a small bronze titled *Harmony*, a modest monument to native son Heinrich Heine.
At the nearby pink Jägerhof Palace, the **Goethe-Museum**★ (*Jacobistraße 2; ◷open year-round, Tue–Sun 11am–5pm, Sat 1pm–5pm; ⌾3€; ☏(0211) 899 62 62; www.goethe-museum-kippenberg-stif-tung.de*) takes you on a journey through the life, times and work of this much-revered poet and playwright.

Museum Kunst Palast★ (Fine Arts Museum)
Ehrenhof 4–5. ◷Open year-round, Tue–Sun 11am–6pm, Thu to 9pm. ⌾10€. ♿. ☏(0211) 899 02 00. www.museum-kunst-palast.de.
This encyclopedic art gallery touches on all genres from the Middle Ages to the present.
Works by the Düsseldorf School dominate but you'll also find large-scale paintings by Rubens, moody landscapes by Caspar David Friedrich and warped Expressionism by Max Beckmann.
The museum also houses a collection of medieval sculpture, and the **Glasmuseum Hentrich**★★, an outstanding collection of vessels from Roman times via *Jugendstil* to the present day.

K20 building, Kunstsammlung Nordrhein-Westfalen

© Walter Klein/ Kunstsammlung NRW

Kunstsammlung Nordrhein-Westfalen★★ (Art Collection of North Rhine-Westphalia)

🕐 *Open year-round, Tue–Fri 10am–6pm, Sat–Sun 11am–6pm.* ✆*6.50€ or 10€ for both K20 and K21.* 🚻 ✆*(0211) 838 16 00; www.kunstsammlung.de.*

This top-rated art collection spans a century of art history with an emphasis on western European and American works. Top paintings by Picasso, Chagall, Ernst and Beuys are complemented by nearly 100 works by Paul Klee, who taught at the Düsseldorf Arts Academy from 1930 to 1933. The collection extends all the way into the 21C with works by such stellar artists as Andreas Gursky, Nam June Paik, Candida Höfer, Thomas Ruff and Thomas Schütte.

Exhibits are distributed across three locations: the recently renovated and enlarged **K20 building** *(Grabbeplatz 5)* in the old town; a converted 19C state parliament building known as **K21** *(Ständehausstraße 1)* south of here; and the newly acquired **Schmela Haus**

(Mutter-Ey-Straße 3), a puristic 1970s building by the Dutch architect Aldo van Eyck opposite K20. A free shuttle bus operates between K20 and K21 every 15 minutes during museum opening hours.

Medienhafen★ (Media Harbour)

South of the Altstadt, an old-time river port has been reborn as a high-tech, office and entertainment complex that doubles as a showcase for Postmodern architecture. The overall design cleverly integrates the old with the new, the industrial with the edgy. Red-brick silos and warehouses have been converted, while new buildings have sprung up, most notably the **Neuer Zollhof** (new customs court).

Designed by Frank Gehry, this three-part complex is a classic example of his undulating, organic style. Claude Vasconi's nautically-inspired **Grand Bateau** (big ship) is another highlight. The tallest building is the **Colorium** by London-based Will Alsop with its random colour-patterned façade.

EXCURSION
Neandertal

▶ *14km/8.7mi east, via A46 autobahn, exit Haan-West, follow signs.*

In this deep valley carved by the little Düssel creek the 60 000-year-old skeletal remains of Neanderthal Man were first discovered in 1856.

The bones are the star exhibit of the multimedia **Neanderthal Museum** *(Talstraße 300;* 🕐 *open year-round, Tue–Sun 10am–6pm;* 🕐*closed Dec 24–25 & 31;* ✆*7€;* 🚻*;* ✆*(02104) 7 97 97; www.neanderthal.de).* Take a virtual journey through the stages of human evolution broken down into such themes as "daily life and survival", "tools and knowledge" and "myth and religion".

🙂 A Bit of Advice 🙂

Local Gastronomy: The Altstadt taverns ooze Rhenish earthiness and are perfect for sampling such regional culinary specialties as *Himmel und Erde* (literally "heaven and earth", it is black pudding with onions) and *Halve Hahn* (rye roll with cheese). On Friday evenings, there is a tradition of eating *Reibekuchen* (potato cake). Indigenous to Düsseldorf is the *Altbier*, a copper-coloured, heavily hopped ale served in cylindrical 0.2l/0.4 pint-size glasses.

ADDRESSES

STAY

Jugendherberge Düsseldorf – *Düsseldorfer Straße 1. ℰ(0211) 55 73 10. www.duesseldorf.jugendherberge.de. 184 beds.* ⌧*5.50€.* Newly renovated, this youth hostel offers fine river views and comfortable beds in clean, secure rooms, each with its own shower and toilet. It is located opposite the Altstadt and easily reached on foot via the Oberkasseler Bridge.

Doria – *Duisburger Straße 1a. ℰ(0211) 49 91 92. www.doria.de. 41 rooms.* A 10-minute walk from the Altstadt, this mid-range hotel has soundproof rooms with modern facilities. It is in a commercial area teeming with cafés and restaurants.

Flora – *Auf'm Hennekamp 37. ℰ(0211) 93 49 80. www.hotel-flora.info. 40 rooms.* Close to an S-Bahn station, this well-kept hotel has modern and functional rooms, some with a pleasant, courtyard-facing balcony.

Windsor – *Grafenberger Allee 36. ℰ(0211) 91 46 80. www.windsorhotel.de. 18 rooms.* Expect a warm welcome and high-quality rooms in this small hotel furnished with attention to detail.

Hotel Orangerie – *Bäckergasse 1. ℰ(0211) 86 68 00. www.hotel-orangerie.de. 27 rooms.* This pretty hotel in a 19C town palace sits in a quiet corner of the Altstadt. The bright rooms are minimalist but comfortable and each is named after a different artist.

EAT

Fischhaus – *Bergerstraße 3–7. ℰ(0211) 854 98 64. www.fischhaus-duesseldorf.de.* Fresh fish is the name of the game at this jolly bistro where you can watch the goings-on through large bay windows or, in fine weather, while perched on the terrace.

Zum Schiffchen – *Hafenstraße 5. ℰ(0211) 13 24 21. www.brauerei-zum-schiffchen.de.* This classic Rhenish brew-pub has had a loyal following for more than 350 years. Grab a seat at a polished wooden table, order a hearty meal and wash it down with the *Altbier* house brew. Nice beer garden, too.

Top 180 – *Stromstraße 20. ℰ(0211) 863 20 00. www.guennewig.de.* A lift whisks you up Düsseldorf's television tower where you can enjoy superb views of the city from this slowly rotating restaurant at a lofty 172m/564ft.

Bistro im Victorian – *Königstraße 3a. ℰ(0211) 865 50 20. www.restaurant-victorian.de.* At this restaurant near the popular pedestrian zone, Volker Drkosch is known for well-prepared innovative cuisine served in a Victorian setting. The bistro is more modern but just as good.

La Piazzetta di Positano – *Kaiserstraße 5. ℰ(0211) 130 04 16. www.rossini-gruppe.de.* This friendly restaurant not only serves fine Italian cuisine and a delicious antipasti buffet but also offers cooking classes in an adjacent space.

Berens am Kai – *Kaistraße 16. ℰ(0211) 300 67 50. www.berensamkai.de.* Catering to business folks and discerning hipsters, this Medienhafen restaurant affords splendid views of the Rhine through the panoramic glass front. The décor – concrete walls, chrome chairs, black cushions – is as contemporary as the international cuisine.

Monkey's West – *Graf-Adolf-Platz 5. ℰ(0211) 64 96 37 26. www.monkeyswest.de.* This vibrant blend of trendy bar and restaurant has some stunning design elements, such as chandeliers and sculptures by the late artist Jörg Immendorf.

TAKING A BREAK

Eis-Café Pia – *Kasernenstraße 1. ℰ(0211) 326 233. Closed mid-Oct–mid-Feb.* Expect queues to snake out of the door at this hugely popular Italian ice cream parlour. The café also serves hot and cold drinks.

NIGHTLIFE

A warren of car-free lanes wedged between the River Rhine and the Königsallee boulevard, the Altstadt is known as "the longest bar in the world". With all sorts of drinking dens – from historic brew-pubs to sleek bars – it can get packed at weekends.

Sauerland★

The meandering Lenne and Ruhr rivers cut through the forest-draped medium-range mountains of the Sauerland – a popular getaway for residents of the heavily urbanised Ruhr Region. In winter, skiers converge on the town of Winterberg while in summer walkers, cyclists and water-sports enthusiasts enjoy the area's many lakes, trails, limestone caverns and cute little hamlets.

A BIT OF GEOLOGY

Mountains, lakes and forests – The Sauerland is the most mountainous area of the Rhineland Schist Massif. It is crowned by the **Kahler Asten** (843m/2 766ft), near Winterberg. Lake reservoirs supply water and hydro-electric energy to the Ruhr towns and serve as water-sports centres. The Upper Sauerland, especially the forested Rothaargebirge, is popular with Nordic walkers, hikers and mountain bikers.

🚗 DRIVING TOUR

FROM SOEST TO BAD BERLEBURG

181km/112.4mi – Allow one day.

Soest★

A northern gateway to the Sauerland, the historic town of Soest is still amost entirely encircled by its 16C town wall and is famous as the birthplace of German **Pumpernickel**, a dense black rye bread. The pious and fans of church architecture and religious art will find plenty to like about the town. Dominating its silhouette is the massive 11C–12C Romanesque **Patrokli Dom** (Propst-Nübel-Straße 2; ⏱ *open year-round, daily 10am–6pm),* noted for its elaborate **western façade**★★ and perfectly balanced square **tower**★★.
The Romanesque frescoes (c. 1165) in the choir are the originals, while those found elsewhere were restored in 1950. The 14C Gothic hall-church, **St. Maria**

Info: Johannes-Hummel-Weg 1, 57392 Schmallenberg. ℰ(02974) 969 80. www.sauerland.com.

Location: The Sauerland stretches from the southeastern Rhineland to eastern Westphalia. It is bisected north-south by the A45 autobahn (Hagen–Frankfurt) and is also served by the A4 from Cologne.

Don't Miss: The historic town of Soest and the outdoor pursuits at the Möhnesee.

Timing: Allow one day for the suggested driving tour.

Kids: The Attahöhle caves and water sports throughout the region.

zur Wiese★ *(Wiesenstraße;* ⏱*open year-round, Mon–Sat 11am–4pm, Sun noon–4pm),* better known as Wiesenkirche, sports two filigree spires that were added in the 19C. Inside, note especially the 1520 **stained-glass window** depicting a "Westphalian Last Supper" showing Jesus and disciples sitting down for a meal of local food specialities (boar's head, ham, jugs of beer and rye bread loaves).
Finally, there is **St. Maria zur Höhe** *(Hohe Gasse;* ⏱ *open Mon–Fri 10am–5.30pm, Sat 10am–5pm, Sun noon–5pm; closes 4pm Oct–Mar),* also known as Hohnekirche. It contains Romanesque wall paintings, a high altar with paintings of the Passion, and a circular Scandinavian-style cross, called a *Scheibenkreuz.*

▷ *Follow the B229 south for about 13km/8mi.*

Möhnesee★

This lake reservoir on the northern edge of the Sauerland is 10km/6.2mi long. The northern lakeshore is open to visitors and water-sports enthusiasts. The south bank is a well-forested nature reserve known for its birdlife.

▷ *Follow the B229 south for about 20km/12.4mi towards Arnsberg.*

Arnsberg

The old town is built on a spur of the Ruhr. To the north, a clock-tower commands the approach to the Schlossberg ruins; to the south is a hunting-themed Rococo gate.

▷ *Beyond Arnsberg, the B229 skirts the right bank of the Sorpesee reservoir before crossing the Lennegebirge massif. There are many scenic viewpoints.*

Attahöhle★
(Grotto)

Finnentroper Straße, Attendorn. Look for signposts just before reaching Attendorn. Visit by guided tour (40min) only; May–Aug 10am–4.30pm; mid-Apr to late Apr and Sept 10am–4pm; Oct 10.30am–4pm; Nov–mid-Apr 10am–3.30pm. Closed Dec 24–25, Mon mid-Jan–Feb and Nov. 7.50€ (child 4.50€). (02722) 937 50. www.atta-hoehle.de.

Near the north shore of the Biggesee lake, this is one of Germany's largest and most impressive limestone caverns with a subterranean network of trails extending for 3km/1.8mi. There are dozens of beautiful stalactite and stalagmite formations, as well as translucent stone "draperies" and an underwater lake.

Attendorn

This typical old Sauerland town boasts a 14C Rathaus (town hall) with stepped gable, an arcaded covered market (Alter Markt), and the **"Sauerland Cathedral"** (Sauerländer Dom). Southeast of Attendorn, high above town, is the 13C **Burg Schnellenberg**, which is now a hotel and a formal restaurant.

Biggetalsperre

This dam, dating from 1964, forms with the **Lister Barrage** the largest reservoir in Westphalia. It is popular for swimming, sailing and windsurfing.

▷ *About 2km/1.2mi before Olpe, fork left on the B55. Soon after Bilstein, on a small mountain road, turn right turn toward the Hohe Bracht.*

Hohe Bracht
Alt 584m/1 916ft.

From the viewing tower (620m/2 034ft above sea level) is a fine panorama that includes the Rothaargebirge massif as far as the Kahler Asten.

▷ *After crossing the rural Lenne Valley, the route passes **Grafschaft** and **Oberkirchen**, with charming half-timbered houses, before the landscape becomes wilder and hillier. Beyond **Nordenau**, a typical slate-roofed Upper Sauerland village, is the ski station of Altastenberg. On the far side of a plateau, the road nears Kahler Asten.*

Kahler Asten

At 843m/2 765ft above sea level, this is the highest point of the Sauerland region. Views from the look-out tower are superb. To the northeast is the spa and winter-sports centre of Winterberg where diversions include skiing, snowboarding and tobogganning as well as an indoor skating rink and a 1 600m/5 249.3ft-long bobsled run. In summer, the 5km/3mi trek up the Kahler Asten get visitors' hearts pumping.

▷ *Slate quarries flank the road back down. There are many attractive views towards the south.*

Bad Berleburg

This Kneipp spa resort is dominated by **Schloss Berleburg** (Berleburg Palace; visit by guided tour (1hr) only; May–Oct, daily 10.30am and 2.30pm, Oct–Apr, Tue, Thu, Sat–Sun 2.30pm; 4€; (02751) 93 60 10 ; www.castlewelt.cm/schloss-berleburg), which dominates the historic town centre. Although it has origins in the 13C, the current Baroque structure was built in 1733 and is still owned by the ancestral local rulers, the family of Sayn-Wittgenstein.

Bonn★

In 1949, Bonn beat Frankfurt am Main to become the capital of the newly created Federal Republic of Germany. The decision surprised many people given the town's modest size and provincial character. Bonn, however, rose to the occasion and has maintained an international, cosmopolitan flair even since the capital was moved back to Berlin in 1991. There's plenty to see and do for visitors in the birth town of Ludwig van Beethoven, which has a lovely river location and a wealth of first-rate museums.

A BIT OF HISTORY

Origins – Bonn has been inhabited since Roman times but only achieved importance in the 16C as a residence of the electors and archbishops of Cologne.

Capital of the Federal Republic of Germany – Bonn served as West Germany's capital for 50 years and became in the process a well-respected seat of government. Since reunification and the transfer of government offices to Berlin in 1999, huge sums of money have been spent redefining the nature of the city. Several United Nations offices have opened here, along with the headquarters of international corporations and it is now more vibrant than ever.

WALKING TOUR

HISTORIC CENTRE★★
Beethoven-Haus
(Beethoven's Birthplace)

Bonngasse 24–26. ⏱Open Apr–Oct, Mon–Sat 10am–6pm, Sun 11am–6pm (Nov–Mar 5pm). ⏱Closed Jan 1, Thu & Mon before Shrove Tue, Good Fri, Easter Sun, Dec 24–26 & 31. ✎5€. ☎(0228) 98 17 50. www.beethoven-haus-bonn.de. Visit the room where Beethoven was born in 1770 in this modest townhouse that now chronicles the life and achievements of this great composer. You get to peruse portraits, original documents, musical instruments, listening horns and

- ▶ **Population:** 312 000
- **Info:** Windeck-straße 1, 53103 Bonn. ☎(0228) 77 50 00. www.bonn.de.
- **Location:** Bonn is on the left bank of the River Rhine and easily accessible from Cologne by the A555 or A59 autobahns. Historic sights cluster in the old town while Museum Row is along the Adenauerallee south of here.
- **P Parking:** Garages are located throughout the city: near the train station, near Beethoven's birth house, and near the old cemetery on Oxfordstraße.
- **Don't Miss:** Beethoven's birth house, House of History, Bonn Museum of Art and the Rhenish Regional Museum.
- **Timing:** Allow one day for Bonn and another half day for the Siebengebirge.
- **Kids:** House of History, and the Siebengebirge (*see Excursions*), especially the funicular.

Beethoven's Formative Years

Precursor of the Romantic music movement, **Ludwig van Beethoven** (1770–1827) was born in Bonn and grew up near the Church of St. Remigius. At 13, Beethoven was already an accomplished musician, playing violin, viola and harpsichord in the court of the Elector. At 22 the fervent admirer of Mozart and Haydn left Bonn for Vienna to follow in their footsteps.
The **Beethovenhalle** hosts the annual international Beethoven Festival.

Beethoven-Haus

Beethoven-Haus Bonn

his life and death masks. Tickets also include admission to the **Digitales Beethoven-Haus**, a multimedia 3D experience next door.

▷ *Go south on Bonngasse towards the Markt.*

Altes Rathaus (Old Town Hall)

This charming Rococo building (1738) with its frilly pink and silver façade dominates the triangular market square.

▷ *Head east on Stockenstraße.*

Kurfürstliche Residenz (Electoral Princes' Castle)

The lawns of the Hofgarten make a fine backdrop for this imposing Baroque building, built by Enrico Zucalli between 1697 and 1702 as a residence for the Prince-Electors. Since 1818 the palace has been part of the university.

▷ *From the south end of the Kurfürstliche Residenz, take a right on Am Neutor and walk towards Münsterplatz.*

Münster★ (Cathedral)

The former Stiftskirche Sts. Cassius and Florentius beautifully melds 11C–13C Romanesque and Gothic architectural features.

The Romanesque baptismal font and stone carvings are noteworthy, as are the drawings (c. 1200), and fresco (c. 1200) depicting Mary. The quiet **cloister**★

(c. 1150) is one of the best preserved from the Romanesque period.

▷ *Backtrack to the electoral palace, then head south on tree-lined Poppelsdorfer Allee.*

Poppelsdorfer Schloss (Poppelsdorf Palace)

Meckenheimer Allee 171.
About 1km/0.6mi south of the Altstadt, this palace was designed in the early 18C by Enrico Zucalli for the Prince-Electors of Cologne and completed by Balthasar Neumann in 1756. In 1818, it became part of the university; the extensive park was turned into a **botanical garden**.

ADDITIONAL SIGHTS

Rheinisches Landesmuseum★★ (Rhenish Regional Museum)

Colmanstraße 14–18. ◷*Open year-round, Tue–Sun 10am–6pm (Wed 9pm).* ◷*Closed Jan 1, Thu before Shrove Tue, Dec 24 & 31.* ⌷*7€.* ⌷ *℘(0228) 207 00. www.rlmb.lvr.de.*
This museum offers an overview of the history, culture and art of the region from prehistory to the present. Pride of place in the **Neanderthal** section goes to the skull and partial skeleton of a 42 000-year-old locally-found hominid. Other treasures include the *Pietà Roettgen*, a heart-wrenching wooden Madonna sculpture (c. 1360) and stag masks used in prehistoric rituals around 7 700 BC. There are also some impressive

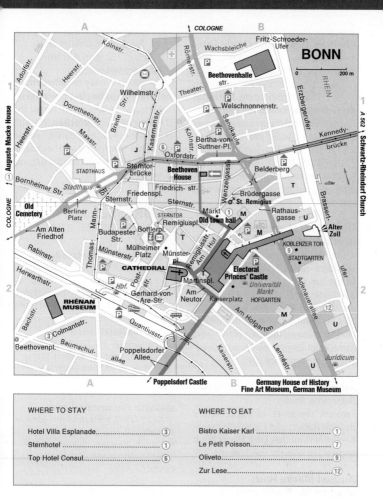

Celtic items, including gold jewellery and a bronze helmet.

Alter Zoll

The panorama of Bonn, the Rhine and the surrounding area as far as the Siebengebirge (see nearby) from this bastion is particularly attractive in the late afternoon and early evening.

Haus der Geschichte ★★ (House of History)

Willy-Brandt-Allee 14. ○Open year-round, Tue–Sun 9am–7pm. 🚻 ℘(0228) 916 50. www.hdg.de.
Germany's first museum of post-World War II history is an intriguing display of original objects, multimedia screens and interactive stations. Highlights include a

1951 Mercedes that belonged to Konrad Adenauer, Germany's first chancellor, an original 1950s ice cream shop and a section of a *Rosinenbomber* (candy bomber) plane used during the 1948–49 Berlin Airlift. A large section of the exhibits trace the history of the former East Germany.

Kunstmuseum Bonn★★ (Bonn Museum of Art)

Friedrich-Ebert-Allee 2. ○Open year-round, Tue–Sun 11am–6pm (Wed 9pm). ○Closed Thu and Mon before Shrove Tue, Dec, 24–25 & 31. ◉7€. 🚻 ℘(0228) 77 62 60. www.bonn.de/kunstmuseum.
Expressionism forms the core collection of this excellent art museum which is especially famous for its works by one-

time Bonn resident August Macke. Other rooms emphasise German art since 1945, with works by Richter, Kiefer, Baselitz, Penck, Lüpertz, Beuys and other top artists. The neighbouring **National Art Gallery and Exhibition Hall** *(Kunst- und Ausstellungshalle der Bundesrepublik Deutschland;* ◐*open year-round, Tue– Wed 10am–9pm, Thu–Sun 10am–7pm;* ◐*closed Dec 24 & 31;* ⊕*8€;* ♿*;* ☏*917 12 00; www.bundeskunsthalle.de)* houses temporary exhibitions of international calibre.

Deutsches Museum Bonn (German Museum Bonn)

Ahrstraße 45. ◐*Open year-round, Tue– Sun 10am–6pm.* ◐*Closed Thu before Shrove Tue , Good Fri, May 1, Dec 24–25 & 31.* ⊕*4€.* ♿ ☏*(0228) 30 22 55. www.deutsches-museum-bonn.de.*
This museum, which is an offshoot of Munich's famous museum of the same name, emphasises research and technology in Germany since 1945.

Alter Friedhof (Old Cemetery)

Bornheimer Straße.
Famous "residents" of this cemetery include Robert and Clara Schumann, Beethoven's mother, Ernst Moritz Arndt and August Wilhelm von Schlegel.

August Macke Haus (August Macke House)

Bornheimer Straße 96. ◐*Open year- round, Tue–Fri 2.30pm–6pm, Sat–Sun 11am–5pm.* ⊕*4€.* ☏*(0228) 65 55 31. www.august-macke-haus.de.*
Expressionist painter August Macke (1887–1914) lived in this Neoclassical villa from 1910 until 1914. See his re-cre- ated studio, examples of his work and a survey of Rhenish Expressionism.

EXCURSION
Siebengebirge★

▶ *15km/9.3mi south on the right bank of the Rhine.*
Cogwheel train: ◐*operates May–Sept, daily 9am–7pm (every 30min); Jan, Feb & early Nov, Mon–Fri noon–5pm, Sat–Sun 11am–6pm (hourly); Mar & Oct 10am– 6pm (every 30min); Apr 10am–7pm*

(every 30min). ⊕*9€ (children 5€).* ☏*(02223) 920 90. www.drachen- felsbahn-koenigswinter.de.*
Since 1883, a creaky cogwheel train, the **Drachenbahn**, has chugged up these forested hills to the top of the 321m/1 050ft-high **Drachenfels** with its romantically ruined castle. Legend has it that Siegfried slew the dragon here and bathed in its blood to become invincible.

ADDRESSES

🛏 STAY

⊖⊜🛏 **Hotel Villa Esplanade** – *Colmanstraße 47.* ☏*(0228) 98 38 00. www.hotel-villa-esplanade.de. 17 rooms.* This 19C villa has preserved its historic charm, especially in the breakfast room with its high ceilings.

⊖⊜🛏 **Top Hotel Consul** – *Oxfordstraße 12.* ☏*(0228) 729 20. www.consul-bonn.de. 95 rooms.* ☐. Centrally located, this hotel offers functional but individually decorated rooms.

⊖⊜⊜🛏 **Sternhotel** – *Markt 8.* ☏*(0228) 726 70. www.sternhotel-bonn.de. 80 rooms.* ☐. Near the former town hall, this hotel is part of Bonn's history. Expect every convenience in a quiet, central location.

🍴 EAT

⊖⊜🛏 **Bistro Kaiser Karl** – *Vorgebirgsstraße 50.* ☏*(0228) 69 69 67. Closed Sat lunchtime and Sun.* This bistro has a nice terrace and lovely *Jugendstil* décor, including ornamented ceilings, chandeliers and mirrored walls.

⊖⊜🛏 **Zur Lese** – *Adenauerallee 37.* ☏*(0228) 22 33 22. www.zurlese.de.*
This restaurant serves international cuisine and has lovely river views from its summer terrace.

⊖⊜🛏 **Oliveto** – *Adenauerallee 9.* ☏*(0228) 260 10. www.hotel-koenigshof- bonn.de.* Mediterranean flair and upmarket Italian cuisine, best enjoyed on the riverside terrace.

⊖⊜⊜🛏 **Le Petit Poisson** – *Wilhemstraße 23.* ☏*(0228) 63 38 83.*
Decorated in warm colours, this intimate restaurant serves classic cuisine.

Eifel★

This volcanic central highland region near the Belgian border has lots in store for travellers wishing to get off the beaten track. Roman ruins, a world-class race track, sparkling blue crater lakes, medieval castles and large swaths of quiet and unspoiled countryside await. Take your time: the Eifel's charms need to be sipped and savoured like the fine red wine it produces, not gulped in haste.

🚗 DRIVING TOUR

FROM BAD MÜNSTEREIFEL TO MANDERSCHEID

145km/90mi – Allow one day.

This leisurely drive follows the valley of the Ahr with its popular resorts, climbs to the forested Upper Eifel, and then meanders between the volcanic lakes of the Maare.

Bad Münstereifel

Hemmed in by massive **ramparts**★, this quaint town is littered with historic houses and monuments. The **Stift-skirche St. Chrysanthus und Daria** is an outstanding twin-towered abbey church with an 11C Romanesque front. A few miles east of Münstereifel, the road passes a giant **radio-telescope**, rejoins the Ahr at Kreuzberg and continues along the winding valley. The telescope is 100m/328ft in diameter and its parabolic depth is 21m/69ft.

Altenahr

In a rocky valley between two bends in the river, charming Altenahr is dominated by the scattered ruins of the 12C hilltop Burg Are Castle. Catch the chairlift up the Ditschardhöhe hill for sweeping views.

Following the valley, with steep vineyards wedged in among rocky outcrops, takes you to a string of pretty, wine-producing villages: Rech with its Roman bridge, Dernau and its "wine fountain" and Marienthal and its ruined convent.

🛈 **Info:** Kavalrienbergstraße 1, 54595 Prüm. ✆ (06551) 965 60. www.eifel.info.

▶ **Location:** The Eifel is near the border with Belgium and straddles the German states of Rhineland-Palatinate and North Rhine-Westphalia. It is roughly bounded by Aachen, Koblenz, Trier and Cologne.

🏵 **Don't Miss:** The volcanic lakes called *Maare*.

🕐 **Timing:** Allow one day for the driving tour from Bad Münstereifel to Manderscheid.

Bad Neuenahr-Ahrweiler

This twin town has a delightfully split personality. At **Ahrweiler**★, which is still encircled by medieval fortifications, half-timbered houses line narrow, pedestrian-only streets. Study its Roman roots at the **Museum Römervilla**. By contrast, Bad Neuenahr is a bubbly spa town with celebrated mineral springs, a casino and elegant 19C architecture.

▶ *Leaving Ahrweiler, the road climbs towards the forest before reaching the highlands.*

Hohe Acht★

Take in sweeping views of deep valleys, rolling hills and the ruined Nürburg Castle from the tower atop the Eifel's highest mountain (747m/2 451ft).

Nürburgring★

✆ (02691) 30 20. www.nuerburgring.de.
This legendary **Formula 1 racetrack** is home to the feared North Loop (*Nordschleife*), nicknamed "Green Hell" by Jackie Stewart. On certain days, you can take your own car along the track or hop aboard a BMW or Viper and let a professional do the driving. Car and motorcycle races take place during the warmer months.

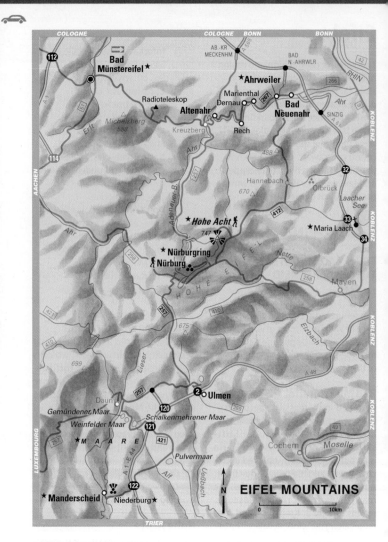

EIFEL MOUNTAINS

N

0   10km

Maare★
(Crater Lakes)

Aeons ago, volcanic activity engulfed the upper reaches of the Eifel, resulting in a series of bright-blue crater lakes. To learn more about this phenomenon, visit the **Eifel Vulkanmuseum** (Leopoldstraße 9; ◷open Mar–mid-Nov, Tue–Fri 1pm–4.30pm, Sat–Sun 11am–4.30pm; ◉3€; ℘(06592) 98 53 53) in Daun and the lakes themselves: the **Gemündener Maar**, the **Weinfelder Maar** (also known as Totenmaar), the **Schalkenmehrener Maar** and the almost perfectly circular **Pulvermaar**★.

◯ Follow the brown "Maare" route signs.

Manderscheid★

From atop the castle keep of the ruined Niederburg, **views**★ extend to the Oberburg ruins and the Lieser Valley.

In the car park at Pension Burgenblick, you can catch a trail leading up to another great **viewpoint**★★, the so-called Kaisertempelchen (little imperial temple) overlooking the Oberburg and Niederburg ruins.

ADDRESSES

🛏 STAY

🛏 **Pension Oos** – *Lieserstraße 16, 54550 Daun-Gemünden.* ☎*(06592) 29 09. www.pension-oos.de. Closed Nov–mid-Mar. 6 rooms.* This simple little B&B near the volcanic lakes has well-kept rooms sleeping two or three as well as a guest kitchen with fridge and coffeemaker.

🛏🛏 **Hotel Seemöwe** – *Am Obersee 10, 52152 Simmerath-Einruhr.* ☎*(02485) 271. www.hotel-seemoewe.de. Closed Jan –Feb. 50 rooms. Restaurant🍴.* Good hotel on the edge of the Rursee lake, with clean, well-cared for rooms (many with balcony) and a lakeview terrace. The country-style restaurant offers traditional cuisine.

🛏🛏🛏 **Burg Adenbach** – *Adenbachhutstraße 1, 53474 Bad Neuenahr-Ahrweiler.* ☎*(02641) 389 20. www.burghotel-adenbach.com. Restaurant closed Wed. 7 rooms. Restaurant🛏🛏🛏.* Romance rules at this medieval castle in Ahrweiler. Beautiful, comfortable rooms come with four-poster beds, pleasing colour schemes and large bathrooms. The hearty yet creative home-cooking served in the restaurant pairs well with the red wines from the property's own vineyard.

🍴 EAT

🍴🍴🍴 **Landgasthaus Steinsmühle** – *Kölner Straße 122, 53902 Bad Münstereifel.* ☎*(02253) 45 87. www.landgasthaus-steinsmuehle.de. Closed Thu.* Feast on international cuisine amid the romantic, brick-walled ambience of this 12C watermill. One room is only lit by candle-light.

Trier★★

Capital of the Western Roman Empire in the 3C, Trier is one of the oldest cities in Germany, along with Worms. Its remarkable collection of Roman ruins earned it a place on UNESCO's World Heritage list in 1986. The city is an ideal starting point to explore the nearby Moselle Valley or Luxembourg.

A BIT OF HISTORY

The oldest city in Germany – After the conquest of the Treveri, a Celtic tribe from eastern Gaul, the Roman Emperor Augustus founded on their territory the town of **Augusta Treverorum** (c. 16BC). It evolved into a centre of economic, cultural and intellectual activity until the invasion of Germanic tribes in AD 274. When Diocletian reorganised the Roman Empire, Trier was retaken and became capital of the western territories (Gaul, Spain, Germania and Britain). As the town regained its former eminence, the Emperor Constantine (306–37) surrounded it with a defensive wall within which magnificent buildings were erected.

▶ **Population:** 100 800
ℹ **Info:** An der Porta Nigra, 54290 Trier. ☎(0651) 97 80 80. www.trier.de.
📍 **Location:** Trier straddles the Moselle River, near the Luxembourg border. The Eifel Mountains lie to the north and the Hunsrück massif to the southeast.
🅿 **Parking:** Parking is found in garages throughout town. The Hauptmarkt is convenient for visiting the old city.
🚫 **Don't Miss:** The Porta Nigra, the cathedral, the Roman Baths and the Library Treasury.
🕐 **Timing:** Allow one day for a tour of the old town.

SIGHTS
OLD TOWN
Porta Nigra★★

🕐*Open Apr–Sept, 9am–6pm; Oct and Mar, 9am–5pm; Nov–Feb, 9am–4pm.* 👁3€. ☎*(0651) 460 89 65.*

The **Porta Nigra** (black gate) is Trier's most famous landmark and the largest Roman edifice on German soil. This monumental gateway (2C), built to defend the northern town wall, is made of stones fitted together without mortar, held together only by iron crampons. The double arcade of the central block leads to an inner court with pierced upper arcades. Assailants that had broken through the outer gates would find themselves exposed to attack from all sides.

In the 11C, the fortified gateway was transformed into a church dedicated to St. Simeon. The Romanesque apse and Rococo decoration are still discernible. Napoleon ordered the monument restored to its original form in 1804.

Stadtmuseum Simeonstift (City Museum)

🕐 *Open year-round, Tue–Sun 10am–6pm.* 🕐 *Closed Jan 1, Dec 24–25 & 31.* ✆5€. ♿ *(0651) 718 14 59. www.museum-trier.de.*

This municipal museum occupies a Romanesque convent, the Simeonstift, built beside the Porta Nigra in the 11C. Galleries creatively illustrate the history of Trier with models, paintings, engravings, maps and sculptures. The museum also encompasses a two-storey Romanesque **cloister**.

Dreikönigenhaus★ (House of the Three Kings)

This early-Gothic townhouse (c. 1230) with arched windows, recalls the Italianate towers of the patricians of Regensburg.

Hauptmarkt★ (Main Square)

This is one of the finest old squares in Germany, anchored by a **Marktkreuz**★ (market cross) from 958 and a 16C **Brunnen** (fountain) surrounded by figures representing the cardinal virtues.

Standing next to the cross, you are surrounded by 15 centuries of architectural history: to the north is the Porta Nigra; to the east the Romanesque cathedral; to the south the Gothic **Gangolfkirche**, its 16C tower once used as a look-out post; and half-timbered houses to the west. The **Steipe**, a 15C municipal building, is elegantly built over an open gallery. It now houses a café and the privately-owned **toy museum** with an abundance of stuffed animals, dolls' houses and other childhood delights. Beside it, the 17C **Rotes Haus** (red house) bears the proud inscription: "There was life in Trier for 1 300 years before Rome even existed."

Frankenturm

This sturdy Romanesque tower (c. 1100) is named after one of its early owners, Franco of Senheim (14C).

Porta Nigra

M. Herlein/MICHELIN

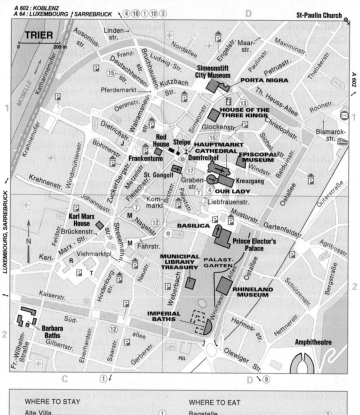

Dom★ (Cathedral)

🕐 *Open Apr–Oct, daily 6.30am–6pm, Nov–Mar until 5.30pm. www.dominformation.de.*

With its six towers, Trier's cathedral looks more like a fortress than a church. A rounded apse projects from a massive, austere façade, which is a fine example of Early Romanesque architecture.

A flattened gable and rectangular plan, visible from the north side, point to the 4C Roman core of the building. West of this central block is the 11C Romanesque section; east of it the 12C polygonal chancel. A Baroque axial chapel crowned by a dome was added in the 18C.

The interior is primarily Baroque. Near the main door, note the fallen Roman **Domstein** (column) that supported part of the former church. A splendid **tympanum★** in the south aisle depicts Christ flanked by the Virgin Mary and St. Peter.

Silver and gold plate, valuable ivories, and magnificently illuminated Gospels are on view in the **Domschatzkammer★** *(cathedral treasury, 🕐 open Apr–Oct, Mon–Sat 10am–5pm, Sun 12.30pm–5pm; Nov–Mar, Mon–Sat 11am–4pm, Sun 2pm–4pm; 🕐 closed Jan 1, Easter Sun, Dec 25; ☞1.50€; ✆ (0651) 979 07 90; www. dominformation.de).*

Liebfrauenkirche★ (Church of Our Lady)

☛ *Closed until at least late 2011.*
One of the earliest Gothic sanctuaries in Germany (1235–60), this church was inspired by one in the French Champagne region and has a ground plan in the form of a Greek cross. Four apsidal chapels are flanked by two smaller, three-sided chapels, giving the entire church the layout of a rose with 12 petals. The elegant interior is enhanced by rings of foliage around each column and the lofty central vault.

Bischöfliches Dom und Diözesanmuseum★ (Episcopal Museum)

◷*Open Mon–Sat 9am–5pm, Sun 1pm–5pm.* ◷*Closed Mon Nov–Mar, Jan 1, Dec 24–26 & 31.* ⌨*3.50€.* ♿
℘(0651) 710 52 55. www.museum.bistum-trier.de.
Dedicated to sacred art, a key feature of this museum is the 4C ceiling frescoes from a residential palace that was replaced by an early Christian church. The central picture is believed to represent Constantine's wife, Fausta.

Basilika★

This large rectangular building was once the **Aula Palatina** (main hall) of the Imperial palace, built by Constantine c. 310 AD. Modified many times over the centuries, it was rebuilt in 1954 and is used today as a Protestant church.

Ehemaliges Kurfürstliches Schloss (Palace of the Electors)

Only the north and east wings remain of the 17C Renaissance electoral palace. The 18C Rococo wings were designed by Johannes Seitz, a student of Balthasar Neumann whose virtuosity finds expression in a magnificent staircase.

Rheinisches Landesmuseum★★ (Rhineland Museum)

Weimarer Allee 1. ◷*Open year-round, Tue–Sun 9.30am–5.30pm.* ◷*Closed Carnival, Dec 24.* ⌨*6€.* ♿ *℘(0651) 977 40. www.landesmuseum-trier.de.*

This museum of archaeology has exceptional items from as far back as the **Paleolithic**, featuring Stone Age implements and ceramics; objects from the Bronze Age; and jewels set in gold from Iron Age sepulchres. A major highlight is the **Roman** section, featuring mosaics, bronzes and bas-reliefs as well as the famous Neumagen ship stone carving, a representation of a ship sailing down the Moselle loaded with wine.

Kaiserthermen★★ (Imperial Roman Baths)

◷*Open Apr–Sept, daily 9am–6pm, Oct–Mar to 5pm, Nov–Feb to 4pm.* ⌨*3€.* *℘(0651) 460 89 65.*
Among the largest in the Roman Empire, these baths date from the time of Constantine. These days, it is used for theatre performances.

Schatzkammer der Stadtbibliothek★★ (Municipal Library Treasury)

◷*Open year-round Mon–Thu 9am–5pm, Fri 9am–1pm.* ♿ *℘(0651) 718 14 29. www.stadtbibliothek-trier.de.*
The library counts ancient manuscripts and illuminations, illustrated books and old documents among its treasures.

Karl-Marx-Haus

Brückenstraße 10. ◷*Open mid-Mar–Oct, daily 10am–6pm; Nov–mid-Mar, Mon 2pm–6pm, Tue–Sun 10am–1pm, 2pm–5pm.* ◷*Closed Jan 1, Mon before Shrove Tue, Dec 24–26 & 31.* ⌨*3€.* *℘(0651) 97 06 80. www.museum-karl-marx-haus.de.*
The birthplace of the socialist theoretician Karl Marx has been turned into a museum, displaying letters, manuscripts and a first edition of the *Communist Manifesto*.

NORTH OF PORTA NIGRA
Basilika St. Paulin★ (St. Paulin Church)

Access via Thebäerstraße.
◷*Open Apr–Sept, Mon, Wed–Sat 9am–6pm, Tue 11am–6pm, Sun 10am–7.30pm; Oct–Mar to 5pm.*
Tall windows illuminate the single nave of this 18C church whose interior was

designed by Balthasar Neumann. The martyrdom of St. Paul, citizens of Trier, and of the Theban Legion (AD 286) are illustrated in ceiling paintings by Christoph Thomas Scheffler of Augsburg. The high altar was based on Neumann's designs with woodcarving by Trier artist Ferdinand Tietz.

SOUTH OF THE OLD TOWN
Amphitheater★ (Amphitheatre)

🕐Open Apr–Sept, daily 9am–6pm, Oct–Mar to 5pm, Nov–Feb to 4pm. 🖾2.10€. ✆(0651) 730 10.

Once seating 20 000 spectators, this hillside arena was used as a quarry in the Middle Ages. The cellars housed theatrical equipment and machinery. Every summer, the amphitheatre hosts the **Antikenfestspiele** (Festival of Ancient Drama).

🚗 DRIVING TOUR

LOWER SAAR VALLEY

57km/35.4mi – Allow two hours.
🌿See region map pp244–245.

South of the Moselle, the Lower Saar Valley parallels the Belgian and French borders. Far from the mainstream tourist routes, this lovely region remains largely unspoiled. The B51 road links the Saar to Saarburg and Trier. Between Mettlach and Konz, where it flows into the Moselle, the Saar River cuts its way through the Hunsrück massif. Grapes, predominantly Riesling, have been cultivated here since the 18C.

▷ *Leave Trier and drive 25km/ 15.5mi south.*

Saarburg

This picturesque town on the banks of the Saar is dominated by a mighty ruined fortress. Dating from at least 964 and later property of the Prince-Electors of Trier, it was blown up by the French in 1705. There is a good view of the town and the Saar Valley from the site.

The **old town**, with its charming medieval alleyways, half-timbered houses and a 20m/65ft **waterfall** in the town centre, makes a delightful scene.
The local museum, **Müseum am Wasserfall** (Am Markt 29; 🕐open Sun–Fri 11am–4pm; 🖾3€; ✆065 81/99 46 42; www.saarburg.eu) shines the spotlight on historic arts and crafts in the area.
🖾Ask at the museum for details of the **Hackenberger Mühle** (watermill).

▷ *21km/13mi south of Saarburg, then a 15min round-trip walk.*

Cloef★★

From a viewpoint high above the river is a breathtaking view of the Montclair loop, a hairpin curve of the Saar River enclosing a wide, densely wooded promontory.

▷ *From Cloef or Orscholz, a detour (about 30km/18.6mi round-trip via L177 and B406) takes you towards the Moselle Valley and the town of Nennig.*

Römische Villa Nennig★★ (Roman Villa)

🕐Open Apr–Sept, Tue–Sun 8.30am–noon and 1pm–6pm; Mar, Oct & Nov, 9am–noon, 1pm–4.30pm. 🖾1.50€. ♿✆(06866) 13 29. www.saarland museum.de.

In 1852, a farmer accidentally discovered the remains of an enormous Roman villa thought to date from the 2C or 3C AD. A superb **floor mosaic** (16x10m/52x33ft) survives, consisting of eight medallions framed by intricate geometric designs and gladiator scenes.

Mettlach

The red sandstone Baroque façade of the abbey, now headquarters of Villeroy & Boch ceramics, rises above the road to Merzig. In the abbey gardens stands the 10C "Alter Turm", a ruined octagonal funerary chapel for the Merovingian duke Lutwinus, the abbey's founder.

ADDRESSES

🏨STAY

Berghotel Kockelsberg – *Kockelsberg 1, 54293 Trier-Trier-Kockelsberg. ℘(0651) 824 80 00. www.kockelsberg.de. 32 rooms. Restaurant ⊖, closed Nov–Mar Sun dinner.* Enjoy lovely views of Trier from this early 20C hotel with its white façade and turrets. Rooms are charming and comfortable and the country-style restaurant has perfect pitch as well.

Hotel Alte Villa – *Saarstraße 133. ℘(0651) 93 81 20. www.hotelaltevilla.de. 20 rooms.* This hotel on the outskirts of the city occupies a charmingly restored Baroque villa from 1743. Rooms are well-proportioned and modern.

Hotel Deutschherrenhof – *Deutschherrenstraße 32. ℘(0651) 875 42. www.hotel-deutschherrenhof-trier.de. 30 rooms.* Close to the pedestrian zone, this hotel has simple but well-kept rooms.

Hotel Deutscher Hof – *Südallee 25 ℘(0651) 977 80. www.hotel-deutscher-hof.de. 102 rooms.* South of the town centre, this professionally managed hotel has spacious rooms as well as a sauna and jacuzzi.

Römischer Kaiser Hotel – *Porta Nigra Platz. ℘(0651) 977 01 00. www.friedrich-hotels.de. 43 rooms.* A pleasant option in a century-old building close to the Porta Nigra.

Hotel Petrisberg – *Sickingenstraße 11. ℘(0651) 46 40. www.hotel-petrisberg.de. 33 rooms.* Rooms are charming, balconied and well equipped, but it's the idyllic nature-preserve location and trails leading into town that set this property apart.

Becker's Weinhaus – *Olewiger Straße 206. ℘(0651) 93 80 80. www.beckers-trier.de. 30 rooms.* Rooms at this sophisticated hotel a few minutes' drive southeast of town are spread over a rustic old building and a more modern one. The latter houses a gourmet restaurant.

Hotel Aulmann – *Fleischstraße 47. ℘(0651) 976 70. www.hotel-aulmann.de. 36 rooms.* This modern hotel close to the city offers comfortable accommodation at a reasonable price.

🍴EAT

Restaurant Krim – *Glockenstraße 7. ℘(0651) 739 43. www.restokrim.de.* Perfect for a nibble or full meal, this popular restaurant serves tapas, pasta, salads and grilled meats alongside some vegetarian options. Sit inside or on the terrace facing the lively pedestrian street.

Kartoffel Restaurant Kiste – *Fahrstraße 13–14. ℘(0651) 979 00 66. www.kistetrier.de.* Everything revolves around the humble potato *(Kartoffel)* which here is served fried, mashed, baked and in soups, salads and casseroles or paired with meat or local specialities.

Weinstube Kesselstatt – *Liebfrauenstraße 10. ℘(0651) 411 78. www.kesselstatt.com.* The nicest tables at this wine tavern are those on the terrace facing the cathedral.

Zum Domstein – *Hauptmarkt 5. ℘(0651) 744 90. www.domstein.de.* Enjoy a meal prepared with authentic Roman recipes at this original restaurant on the market square.

Gasthaus Mosellied – *Zurlaubener Ufer 86. ℘(0651) 265 88. Closed Jan and Feb.* Half a dozen eateries, from snack stand to gourmet restaurant, cluster on the riverbank. All have a terrace. Gasthaus Mosellied is particularly popular with locals.

Schlemmereule – *Domfreihof 1b ℘(0651) 736 16. www.schlemmereule.de. Closed 8–18 Feb and Sun.* Modern and elegant, this restaurant in an 18C courthouse delivers a daily-changing menu. In fine weather, the courtyard terrace beckons.

Weisshaus Restaurant – *Weisshaus 1. ℘(0651) 834 33. www.weisshaus.de. Closed Jan and Feb, Mon and Tue.* This chic restaurant on the opposite riverbank offers beautiful views over the city. Foodwise, the focus is on delicious meaty fare.

Bagatelle – *Zurlaubener Ufer 78. ℘(0651) 297 22. www.bagatelle-trier.com.* Casual bistro flair characterises this converted fisherman's house on the banks of the Moselle. The cuisine is classic infused with French elements.

Moselle Valley★★★

Moseltal

Scattered with picturesque villages and renowned for its wines, the Moselle Valley is an enchanting region best explored on a leisurely drive or boat cruise. Castles, vineyards and romantic villages line both sides of the river.

 DRIVING TOUR

FROM TRIER TO KOBLENZ

195km/121mi – Allow one day.

Trier★★ – 🕐*See TRIER.*

Neumagen-Dhron

This town is known for its Roman discoveries, which can be admired at the Rhineland Museum in Trier. A copy of the famous stone-carved **wine ship** sits next to the chapel, opposite the Am Römerweinschiff café.

Bernkastel-Kues★

This double town straddles the Moselle about 50km/31mi east of Trier. Bernkastel is the prettier of the two with higgledy-piggledy half-timbered houses lining a warren of narrow, cobbled lanes. The nicest surround the **Markt★**, a small, sloping square centred on the 17C **Michaelsbrunnen** (St. Michael's fountain).

South of town, Burg Landshut (Landshut Castle) squats atop a rocky promontory. It was built in the 13C by the archbishops of Trier but has been in ruins since the 17C War of the Orléans Succession.

> **Info:** Kordelweg 1, 54470 Bernkastel-Kues. 𝒫(06531) 973 30. www.moselland touristik.de.
> **Location:** The peaceful Moselle River enters Germany near Trier and meanders to Koblenz where it flows into the Rhine.
> **Don't Miss:** Sampling the famous white wines, Bernkastel-Kues, Burg Eltz.
> **Timing:** Allow at least one day for the suggested driving tour.

From up here panoramic **views★★** take in a bend in the Moselle where even the steepest slopes are planted with vines. The main draw of Kues across the river is the **St. Nikolaus-Hospital** *(chapel and cloisters 🕐 open year-round, Sun–Fri 9am–6pm, Sat 9am–3pm; ↰guided library tours Apr–Oct, Tue 10.30am, Fri 3pm; ◌5€; 𝒫(06531) 22 60; www.cusanus.de),* a hospice founded in 1447 by humanist and theologian Nikolaus Cusanus. The number of lodgers was restricted to a symbolic 33 – the age of Christ at his death – a tradition that is still respected to this day.

Admire the late-Gothic cloister, the chapel with its fine 15C reredos, and the bronze copy of the cardinal's tombstone (the original is in Rome, at San Pietro in Víncoli). Note the fresco depicting the Last Judgement *(to the left of the entrance)* and the **tombstone of Clara Cryftz**, the prelate's sister.

The **library** houses almost 400 manuscripts as well as astronomical instruments once used by Cusanus himself.

Wines Full of Character

The slopes of the Moselle Valley are draped in vineyards producing dry and semi-dry white wines, including the main varietal, Riesling. The ground shale plays an important role in the maturation of the grapes as it absorbs the sun's power during the day and continue to radiate the heat back to the grape vines throughout the night. The harvest can be as late as 6 December. Light and with a delicate bouquet, the Moselle vines get dryer the further north one goes.

MOSELLE VALLEY

Finish your sightseeing with a wine tasting in the atmospheric cellars of the **Vinothek**.

▶ *The road passes through typical wine-growing villages: Ürzig, Kröv, Enkirch (make a 5km/3mi detour to Starkenburg for fabulous valley views) and Pünderich among them. One magnificent vineyard follows another. Some 3.5km/2mi after the bridge at Zell, take the left turn towards Marienburg.*

Marienburg

The old convent here enjoyed an exceptional **setting**★★. From the restaurant terrace and the wooden "Prinzenkopf" look-out tower *(follow the trail; 45min round trip)* there are impressive **views**★★ of the river and its environs.

Beilstein

This tiny fortified village is nicknamed "Sleeping Beauty of the Moselle" because of its compact shape and

fairytale setting amid steeply sloping vineyards. A cluster of half-timbered houses huddles around a picturesque Marktplatz.

Note especially the Zehnthaus, the church of St. Christopher and the 18C wine cellars. The village is lorded over by an enormous Baroque hall-church (1635) and a romantically ruined castle. The latter is reached via a steep staircase *(30min round trip)* and will treat you to sweeping views across the town and the meandering river valley.

Cochem

Cochem is presided over by the playfully turreted and pinnacled **Reichsburg**★★ (✆📷*guided tours (40min) mid-Mar–Oct, daily 9am–5pm, restricted hours in winter, call ahead; ⌖4.50€; ℘(02671) 255; www.reichsburg-cochem.de).*

The 11C original was badly destroyed by French troops in the 17C, but the castle was elaborately restored in the 19C. It is one of the most celebrated sites in the

Cochem with Reichsburg

©Anja Frost/istockphoto.com

region thanks to its spectacular setting atop a vine-clad hill.

Views are great from up here but even better from the **Pinner-Kreuz**★ hill, comfortably reached by **chairlift** (🕐*open mid-Mar–Nov; 🚠4.30€ one-way, 5.80€ round-trip; 𝒫(02671) 98 90 65; www.cochemer-sesselbahn.de).*

Treis-Karden

The Church of St. Castor in the village of Karden represents the transitional stage between the Rhenish Roman-esque ("gallery dwarf" in the apse) and Gothic (ribbed vaults). Inside, note the high altar, the altar of the Magi (1420) and, in the chapel of the choir (left), the small Gothic wooden shrine of St. Castor (1490).

Burg Eltz★★

10km/6.2mi from Hatzenport, plus 15min walk or 5min by bus. 🔦*Guided tours (40min), Apr–Oct, daily 9.30am–5.30pm. 🚠8€. 𝒫(02672) 95 05 00. www.burg-eltz.de.* This romantic 1 000-year-old **castle**★★ bristles with towers and turrets rising majestically from the thick forest at the far end of the Eltz Valley. It has been owned by the same family for more than 30 generations. Tours take you into fab-ulously decorated rooms with wooden and netvaulted ceilings, a bedroom with 15C frescoes, the splendid Knights Hall and the still-intact medieval kitchen.

Another highlight is the painting *Madonna with Child and Grapes* by Lucas Cranach the Elder complemented by other works from the Cranach School. Tickets also give access to the **treasury**★, a feast of gold, silver, porcelain and fancy knick-knacks.

Burg Thurant★

🕐*Open May–Oct, daily 10am–6pm, Nov–Feb to 4pm, Mar & Apr to 5pm. 🚠3.50€. 𝒫(02605) 20 04. www.thurant.de.* Stroll through the gardens of this small, romantic 12C castle, then soak up medi-eval flair as you explore its ramparts, chapel and wine cellar, and even sneak a peek inside the dungeon. Don't miss climbing up the Kölner Turm (Cologne tower) to snap panoramic pictures of the hilly countryside and charming river valley.

Koblenz★ – 🕭*See KOBLENZ.*

EXCURSIONS
IDAR-OBERSTEIN

▶ *37km/23mi south of Bernkastel-Kues. Hauptstraße 419, 55743 Idar-Oberstein.* ✆*(06781) 563 90. www.idar-oberstein.de.*

Twin towns form this municipality: picturesque Oberstein at the foot of a gorge carved by the River Nahe, and Idar on the river's tributary.

Since the Middle Ages, the history of Idar-Oberstein has been linked to the production and sale of gemstones. The abundance of agate, jasper, amethyst and other deposits here has made the town a centre for cutting and polishing of the precious stones. The many jewellery museums and shops bear witness to this trade.

Deutsches Edelsteinmuseum ★★ (German Precious Stone Museum)

In the Idar-Zentrum (Diamond Exchange), Hauptstraße 118. ◷*Open mid-Feb–Apr, daily 10am–5pm; May–Oct, daily 9.30am–5.30pm; Nov–Jan 7 10am–5pm.* ◷*Closed Dec 24–25 & 31, Jan 8–mid-Apr.* ✆*5€.* ✆*(06781) 90 09 80. www.edelsteinmuseum.de.*

The museum houses precious stones from around the world – agates to diamonds. Its collection has grown to 10 000 glittering objects and includes raw rocks, crystals and cut stones.

Some of the treasures are presented in darkened rooms under black light, making them phosphorescent. Elsewhere you can admire replicas of famous gems, including the legendary Hope diamond.

Felsenkirche★

30min round-trip walk. Access via stairs (214 steps) from Oberstein Marktplatz. ◷*Open mid-Mar–Oct, daily 10am–6pm; Nov 1–15, daily 11am–4pm.* ✆*2€. www.felsenkirche-oberstein.de.*

Framed by a rock overhang above the river, this church, restored several times, is worth a visit for the 15C winged altarpiece alone. The scenes of the Passion depict the event with a ferocious realism. According to legend, the church was built in atonement for a fratricide by the surviving brother.

Museum Idar-Oberstein

Hauptstraße 426 at Oberstein Marktplatz (below the Felsenkirche stairway). ◷*Open Apr–Oct, daily 9am–5.30pm; Nov–Mar, daily 11am–4.30pm.* ◷*Closed Jan 1, Dec 24–25 & 31.* ✆*4.70€.* ✆*(06781) 246 19. www.museum-idar-oberstein.de.*

This museum emphasises the region's minerals and precious stones. Aside from gemstones, you can get a close-up look at an old agate watermill as well as a 19C workshop of a goldsmith. A darkened room features fluorescent minerals sparkling in a rainbow of colours beneath ultraviolet light.

♒ Edelsteinminen Steinkaulenberg

Tiefensteiner Straße 87. ✦*Visit by guided tour (30min) only, mid-Mar–mid-Nov, daily 9am–5pm.* ✆*4.50€.* ✆*(06781) 90 19 61. www.edelstein-minen-idar-oberstein.de.*

At the only gemstone mine in Europe open to the public, you can see first-hand how the precious minerals are harvested. If you want to dig up your own, head to the **Edelsteincamp** *(gemstone camp;* ◷*sessions by prior arrangement: Mon–Fri 9am–11am, noon–2pm, 3pm–5pm;* ✆*10€ (child 7€);* ☂*sturdy footwear and comfortable clothes required).* You get to keep whatever you dig up during the two-hour session.

Industriedenkmal Jakob Bengel★★ (Industrial Monument Jakob Bengel)

Wilhelmstraße 42a. ✆*(067 81) 27 030. www.jakob-bengel.de.* ✦*Visit by guided tour. Make arrangements one day in advance.* ✆*4.50€.*

This workshop had its heyday between 1910 and 1920 when Art Deco and Bauhaus jewellery were all the rage. At that time, the house worked for Coco Chanel and Parisian department stores. Today, production is virtually zero, but all the machines (including a 120t press, chain-making machines and polishing stations) are activated during guided visits.

THE HUNSRÜCK

▶ *37km/23mi east of Bernkastel-Kues.*
The Hunsrück, a low mountain range, forms the southern rim of the Rhine schist massif, a region of low mountains and game-stocked forests slashed by steep valleys.

Erbeskopf

At 818m/2 683.7ft, this is the highest peak in the Hunsrück. Enjoy fine views from the wooden tower as well as the **Hunsrückhöhenstraße★**. The road passes the Stumpfer Turm, an old Roman watchtower.

Kirchberg

Clinging to a hillside, this village is filled with half-timbered houses, especially around the Marktplatz. Also note the pre-Romanesque St. Michaelskirche.

Simmern

The farming centre of the Hunsrück, Simmern is home to the parish church of St. Stephan (15C). The church's **tombs★** of the Dukes of Pfalz-Simmern feature some of the finest Renaissance sculptures in the middle Rhineland.

Ravengiersburg

Tucked into the bottom of a valley, this village boasts a Romanesque church with an imposing west front. Above the porch: Christ in Majesty.

Dhaun

The partly ruined medieval castle perches dramatically atop a steep promontory and is considered the largest in the region. The complex includes the St. George's Chapel (1661) and the kitchen as well as two bastions and defensive towers.

ADDRESSES

🛏 STAY

🍴 **Wein- und Gästehaus Port** – *Weingartenstraße 57, 54470 Bernkastel-Kues.* ✆*(06531) 911 73. www.ferienweingut-port.de. 5 rooms, 4 apartments.* At this peaceful wine estate days start with a hearty breakfast in the winter garden and wrap up with a wine tasting, perhaps paired with a robust steak from the grill.

🍴 **Reichsschenke "Zum Ritter Götz"** – *Robert-Schuman-Straße 57, 54536 Kröv.* ✆*(06541) 816 60. www.reichsschenke.de. Closed 2 weeks in Feb and 3 weeks in Nov. 16 rooms. Restaurant.* This historic inn has smart, uncluttered rooms and a woodsy low-ceilinged restaurant. The menu caters to all tastes with classic German fare, regional dishes and upscale French cuisine.

🍴 **InterCity Hotel Hahn** – *At Hahn airport, Bldg 1380, 55483 Hahn.* ✆*(06543) 50 98 00. www.hahn.intercityhotel.com. 35 rooms. ⊡9€.* This hotel next to Hahn airport is convenient for travellers. Rooms are simple but well-equipped.

🍴 **Hotel Bären** – *Schanzstraße 9, 54470 Bernkastel-Kues.* ✆*(06531) 95 04 40. www.hotel-baeren.de. Closed Nov–Mar Sun–Tue. 33 rooms. Restaurant.* It's well worth spending a little extra for modern rooms with river-facing balconies at this family-owned hotel. The adjacent restaurant serves everything from snacks to rib-sticking meals.

🍴 **Römischer Kaiser** – *Markt 2, Bernkastel-Kues.* ✆*(06531) 91 90 04. www.roemischer-kaiser-bernkastel.de. 22 rooms. ⊡.* Behind its pale pink façade, this centrally located traditional hotel has modern rooms with a good range of amenities.

Koblenz★

In a strategic location at the confluence of the Rhine and the Moselle rivers, Koblenz was established in 9 BC as a Roman camp and has grown into a mid-size, modern town dotted with historic buildings and charming wine taverns. The departure point for river excursions, Koblenz is also one of the towns hosting the "Rhine in Flames" summer festival, a celebration of music, fireworks and illuminated boats.

A BIT OF HISTORY

A refuge for French aristocracy – Koblenz came under French influence after the 1789 French Revolution when it welcomed scores of refugees. Over the coming decades France and Prussia fought repeatedly over this region, alternating control until 1815 when the defeat of Napoleon returned the land to Prussia. The impressive **Rheinanlagen**, a splendid riverside promenade, dates from the 19C French occupation.

SIGHTS

Deutsches Eck★
(German Corner)

A monumental equestrian statue of Wilhelm I presides over this tongue of land marking the confluence of the Rhine and

▶ **Population:** 107 500

Info: Bahnhofplatz 17, 56068 Koblenz. ℘(0261) 313 04. Or at the Rathaus, Jesuitenplatz 2. ℘(0261) 13 09 20. www.touristik-koblenz.de.

Location: At the confluence of the Rhine and the Moselle rivers, Koblenz is also at the junction of the Hunsrück, Eifel and Westerwald mountain ranges.

Don't Miss: Deutsches Eck, wine taverns, Ehrenbreitstein Fortress.

Timing: It takes half a day to explore the town and the fortress.

the Moselle. Enjoy fine views from the base of the statue *(107 steps)*.

Museum Ludwig

Ballei Building, right next to the Deutsches Eck. ℘*(0261) 30 40 40. www.ludwigmuseum.org.* ⦿*Open year-round, Mon–Sat, 10.30am–5pm, Sun and holidays 11am–6pm.* ⊛*2.50€.* Designed to support the city's relationship with France in the arts, this museum is dedicated to contemporary art. The collection includes works by Pablo

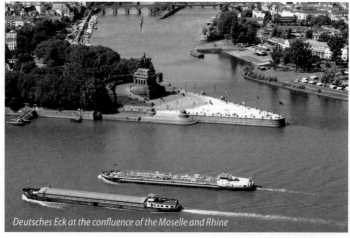
Deutsches Eck at the confluence of the Moselle and Rhine

© Paul Wander/Fotolia.com

WHERE TO STAY		WHERE TO EAT	
Continental-Pfälzer Hof	①	Einstein	③
Hotel Gülser Weinstube	③	Havana	⑤
Hotel Kornpforte	④	Historischer Weinkeller	①
Rhein Hotel Merkelbach	⑥	Weinhaus Hubertus	⑦
Trierer Hof	⑧	Wirtshaus Alt Coblenz	⑨

295

Picasso and Jean Dubuffet as well as big names from North America such as Jasper Johns, Willem de Kooning and Robert Rauschenberg and German artist KO Götz. Also shown are the New Realists (Arman, César, Tinguely, Martial Raysse) and the famous "Thumb" of Caesar in the garden.

Stiftskirche St. Kastor (Collegiate Church of St. Castor)

The south transept of this Romanesque church features 16 painted wood panels that were once part of a rood screen. St. Castor is depicted on the bottom left.

Liebfrauenkirche

This Romanesque church got its late-Gothic chancel in the 15C and Baroque belfries in the 17C. The modern windows are by HG Stockhausen (1992).

Jesuitenplatz

In the courtyard of a 17C Jesuit College (now the town hall), the *Schängelbrunnen* (fountain) evokes the mischief perpetrated by the city's street urchins.

Mittelrheinmuseum

Florinsmarkt 15–17. ⏱*Open year-round, Tue–Sat 10.30am–5pm, Sun 11am–6pm.* ⏱*Closed Jan 1, Shrove Tue, Good Fri, Easter Mon, Dec 24–25 & 31.* ⬌*2.50€.* ☎*(0261) 129 25 20. www.mittelrhein-museum.de.*
This museum retraces the history of the town and environs through paintings, religious artefacts and everyday items dating as far back as the Middle Ages.

EXCURSIONS
Festung Ehrenbreitstein★ (Ehrenbreitstein Fortress)

▶ *4.5km/3mi. Cross the Rhine on Pfaffendorfer Brücke then turn left.* ☎*(0261) 66 75 40 00. www.festunge-hrenbreitstein.de.*
This strategic hilltop fortress was destroyed by French troops in 1801 but rebuilt and expanded by the Prussians

between 1817 and 1828. **Views**★★ from the top are great and the compound also harbours a youth hostel and a restaurant. A chairlift operates during the warmer months (⏱*Easter–May & Sept–Oct 10am–5pm, Jun–Sept 9am–6pm;* ⬌*8€ round trip).*

Kloster Maria Laach★ (Maria Laach Abbey)

▶ *20km/12.4mi west.*
Near a volcanic lake, this well-preserved 12C Romanesque basilica is part of a Benedictine abbey. The cloister-style **entrance portico**★ has intricately worked capitals and the hexagonal baldaquin over the altar suggests a possible Moorish influence.

THE LAHN VALLEY AND LIMBURG

☺*The tourist offices of Nassau and Diez offer many activities: hiking, bike and boat rides, kayaking and wine tasting.*

The Lahn Valley cuts through the Taunus-Rhine massif and meanders through the forests of the Nassau Natural Park east of Koblenz. The winding course of the lower Lahn is characterised by wild scenery and steeply wooded banks. The valley makes a charming setting for excursions to a number of castles and the delightful historic town of Limburg.

The following towns, all located east of Koblenz, may be explored on a 60km/37mi-long loop.

Bad Ems

▶ *17km/10.5mi from Koblenz.*
The Lahn Valley, separating the Westerwald and the Taunus-Rhine schist massif, is rich in mineral springs. A flagstone bearing the date 13 July 1870, commemorates the Bad Ems meeting of Prussian King Wilhelm I and the French Ambassador to Prussia, Count Vincent de Benedetti, which precipitated the outbreak of the Franco-Prussian War of 1870–71.

Nassau

▶ *25.9km/16mi from Koblenz.*
🛈 *℘0260 495 250.*
www.nassau-touristik.de.
This health resort in the Lahn Valley was
the cradle of the counts of Laurenburg,
from whom Dutch royalty, including William of Orange, William III of England
and the current Dutch royal family, are
descended. Points of interest include
the Adelsheimer Hof (town hall), the
Stammburg (ancestral castle) and the
Steinisches Schloss.

Kloster Arnstein

▶ *1km/0.6mi by a steep uphill road*
from the Obernhof Bridge.
The Premonstratensian church bears
one Romanesque chancel (west) and
one Gothic (the east).

Diez

▶ *56.8km/35.3mi from Koblenz.*
🛈 *℘06 432 501 275.*
www.urlaubsregion-diez.info.
Dominating this small town, the 17C
Schloss Oranienstein is an early-
Baroque edifice that was the ancestral
seat of the House of Nassau-Orange. It
boasts stucco ornamentation by Castelli
and Genone and ceiling frescoes by Jan
van Dyck. In the 19C the palace served as
barracks for Prussian cadets; today sections are used by the German army.
Some rooms are taken up by the **Oran-
ien-Nassau-Museum** (👁visit by
guided tour (1hr) only, Apr–Oct, Tue–Fri
9am, 10.30am, 2pm, Sat 10.30am and
2pm, Sun also 3.30pm; Nov–Mar, Tue–Fri
9am, 10.30am, 2pm and 3.30pm; ⊚3€;
℘(06432) 940 16 66). Tours take you
inside the **Blue-Golden Hall** with its
copper etchings and paintings. The
Calvinist chapel is decorated with rich
stucco ornamentation and frescoes.

Burg Runkel★

▶ *62.5km/38.8mi from Koblenz.*
The picturesque **setting**★★ of the
castle, built into the rock face, and the
ancient village below it can best be
appreciated from the 15C bridge over
the river.

LIMBURG AN DER LAHN★

▶ *Bordering Hessen and Rheinland-*
Pfalz, Limburg is south of Koblenz
via the A3.
Hospitalstraße 2, 65549 Limburg.
℘(06431) 61 66. www.limburg.de.
The powerful yet elegant silhouette of
the cathedral dominates the Limburg
skyline. The town centre consists
largely of half-timbered houses dating
from the 13C to the 18C.

Dom★
(Cathedral)

Limburg's St. Georgsdom enjoys a picturesque **setting**★★ on a rocky spur
and is especially noted for its striking
architecture, which is a classic example
of the Romanesque-Gothic transitional
style. The exterior remains Romanesque
and closely resembles the Rhineland
Romanesque-style cathedrals (👁see
INTRODUCTION: Architecture), but its
interior is already Gothic. Look for Gothic
hallmarks: galleries, arcades, a triforium
and clerestory windows. Artistic highlights include the 13C stone rood screen
and the frescoes in the nave. From the
cemetery terrace is a good **view**★ of the
Lahn River.

Staurothek
Diözesanmuseum★

Domstraße 12.
⊶*Closed until further notice.*
℘(06431) 29 54 82. www.staurothek.de.
The 10C Byzantine reliquary cross
known as the Limburger Staurothek is
the jewel of the religious art collection
displayed in this museum. The most precious exhibit, though, is the so-called
15C "Dernbacher Beweinung", a group
of sculptures representing the lamentation over Christ's Passion and Death.

Old Town★ (Altstadt)

Take time to discover the beautiful old
houses along Limburg's winding alleys
and pretty squares, most notably
Domplatz, Fischmarkt, Brückengasse,
Römer, Rütsche and Bischofsplatz. Wal-
derdorffer Hof (Fahrgasse) is an impressive Renaissance construction.

ADDRESSES

🏠 STAY

KOBLENZ

Continental-Pfälzer Hof – *Bahnhofsplatz 1. ℘(0261) 301 60. www.tagungshotel.com. 35 rooms.* ☐. This modern hotel is close to the train station. Double-glazed windows ensure a good night's sleep. There are several other hotels close by, although all are a fair distance from the town centre.

Rhein Hotel Merkelbach – *Emserstraße 87. ℘(0261) 974 41 33. www.hotel-merkelbach.de. 15 rooms.* ☐. On the bank of the Rhine, this hotel has functional and well-maintained rooms, some of them with river views.

Hotel Gülser Weinstube – *Moselweinstraße 3. ℘(0261) 98 86 40. www.hotelguelserweinstube.de. 14 rooms.* ☐. This small family hotel in a beautiful half-timbered house sits right on the banks of the Moselle and has a restaurant/wine bar where you can taste the local wines.

Trierer Hof – *Clemensstraße 1. ℘(0261) 100 60. 35 rooms.* ☐. Beautiful house close to the city centre and the River Rhine.

Hotel Kornpforte – *Kornpfort-straße 11. ℘(0261) 311 74. www.hotel-kornpforte.de. 19 rooms.* ☐. Pleasant and affordable accommodation in the city centre. Expect a friendly welcome and pleasantly furnished, high-ceilinged rooms.

LIMBURG AN DER LAHN

Martin – *Holzheimer Straße 2. ℘(06431) 948 40. www.hotel-martin. de. 25 rooms. Restaurant ☐, closed Sun.* This family-run hotel opposite the train station welcomes guests with handsome rooms sporting wooden floors and soothing hues.

Romantik Hotel Zimmermann – *Blumenröder Straße 1. ℘(06431) 46 11. www.romantik-hotel-zimmermann.de. 19 rooms.* With English-inspired furnishings, rooms exude an air of luxury at this centrally located hotel near the train station. Huge breakfasts are served in a lovely room.

🍴 EAT

KOBLENZ

Havana – *Kornpfortstraße 6. ℘(0261) 100 46 84.* This restaurant serves snacks and Mexican cuisine in a relaxed atmosphere. Happy hour is from 6pm to 8pm.

Einstein – *Firmungstraße 30. ℘(0261) 914 49 99. www.einstein-koblenz.de.* This busy restaurant in the pedestrian zone serves international fare. The Sunday brunch is worth a linger. Some terrace tables available.

Wirtshaus Alt Coblenz – *Am Plan 13. ℘(0261) 16 06 56. www.alt-coblenz.de.* The rustic setting is perfect for enjoying a traditional German meal or tasting the local wines.

Weinhaus Hubertus – *Florinsmarkt 6. ℘(0261) 311 77. www. weinhaus-hubertus.de.* The dining room in this beautiful half-timbered house is panelled in dark wood and decorated with hunting trophies. One of the best addresses in the old town to enjoy the regional cuisine. Attentive and friendly service.

Historischer Weinkeller – *Mehlgasse 14. ℘(0261) 973 89 87. www. weinkeller-koblenz.de. Open noon–2pm and 6–10pm, closed Mon lunch and Tue.* In an alley in the old town, not far from the Liebfrauenkirche church, is this 13C wine cellar where you can sample traditional cuisine beneath rustic vaulted ceilings.

LIMBURG AN DER LAHN

Bella Città Vecchia – *Fischmarkt 8. ℘(06431) 210 608. www.bella-citta-vecchia.de.* In the heart of the old town, this charming restaurant serves authentic Italian cuisine, including pastas, pizzas, meat and fish dishes. Some rooms available, too *(85€)*.

Himmel und Erde – *Joseph-Heppel-Str. 1a. ℘(06431) 584 7208. www.kapelle-himmelunderde.de.* This restaurant in an ancient chapel has maintained its rustic character.

CRUISES

Cruises run between Koblenz and Cochem May–Sept. 🚢25€ one way.
KD Deutsche Rheinschiffahrt
℘(0221) 208 83 18; www.k-d.com.

Rhine Valley★★★

Few rivers have captured the imagination of artists and travellers as much as the Rhine, a 1 320km/820mi ribbon rushing northwards from the Swiss Alps to the North Sea. Along the nicest stretch between Mainz and Koblenz, dreamy wine villages with dainty half-timbered houses are lorded over by legend-shrouded medieval castles. In 2002, the region became a UNESCO World Heritage Site.

A BIT OF HISTORY

The Rhine legends – There is not, along the whole length of the Rhine, a castle, an island, even a rock without its tale of chivalry or legend. **Lohengrin**, the Knight of the Swan, appeared at the foot of the Castle of Kleve (Cleves); at the **Loreley**, a beautiful enchantress bewitched boatmen with her song, leading their vessels to disaster.

But the single outstanding Rhine legend is the story of the Nibelungen *(⬖see INTRODUCTION: Literature)*, which provided Richard Wagner with inspiration for his *Ring* cycle. The epic **Nibelungenlied** (Song of the Nibelungen) was probably composed late in the 12C and tells of murder, the splendours of the 5C Burgundian court at Worms, and of the passions inflaming the hearts of its

- 🛈 **Info:** Loreley Besucherzentrum, 6346 St. Goarshausen. ℘(06771) 959 91 11. www.romantischer-rhein.de.
- ◗ **Location:** Roads parallel both river banks, but there are no bridges – only ferries – between Koblenz and Mainz. A more leisurely way to experience the region is by tour boat with service from nearly all the nearby villages.
- ◉ **Don't Miss:** A boat tour or drive along the river, Loreley Rock, Marksburg, Burg Rheinfels, Bacharach.
- ◕ **Timing:** Allow four hours for suggested driving tour ① and one day for driving tour ②.
- 👫 **Kids:** Marksburg, Burg Rheinfels.

heroes. The tribal treasure is rumoured to be buried in the Rhine near Worms.

From the Alps to the North Sea – The Rhine rises in the Swiss Alps. Gushing down the mountains, it quickly reaches the Bodensee (Lake Constance). After exiting the lake, rock outcrops and the foothills of the Jura produce the famous Rhine Falls at Schaffhausen *(⬖see Green*

Burg Gutenfels and the fortified island of Pfalz on the Rhine

D. Scherf/MICHELIN

Guide Switzerland). Further downstream, limestone strata cause *Laufen* (rapids). At Basel, the Rhine abruptly changes direction, veering north towards the Vosges Mountains and the Black Forest.

From Bingen to Neuwied, north of Koblenz, the Rhine cuts its way through the Rhineland schist massif, where the rock can foment dangerous whirlpools. This "romantic" stretch of river valley, with its pastiche of steeply terraced vineyards, woods, escarpments and castle ruins, is the most picturesque part of the River Rhine.

Later, having passed through the industrial region around Duisburg, the river turns west and curls slowly across the plain towards the sea.

An exceptional shipping lane – The Rhine is navigable over almost 1 000km/620mi between Rotterdam and Rheinfelden and has always been an important European waterway. The world's largest river port is in Duisburg.

🚗 DRIVING TOURS

1 THE LORELEY★★

From Rüdesheim to Koblenz.
75km/47mi – Allow 4hrs.

This route, following the Rhine's east bank, passes through the wildest and steepest part of the Rhine Gorge, with splendid views of the castles and fortresses lining the river.

Rüdesheim★

Geisenheimerstraße 22, 65385 Rüdesheim. ℰ(06722) 194 33. www.ruedesheim.de/tourist.
The wine town of Rüdesheim am Rhine lies at the gateway to the "Romantic Rhine" and is a key tourist centre in the valley. Its narrow streets, most famously the Drosselgasse, are crammed with traditional wine taverns where you can sample the celebrated local Riesling and other varietals.

Rheingauer Weinmuseum Brömserburg (Wine Museum)

Rheinstraße 2. ◷Open Mar–Oct, daily 10am–6pm. ⬤5€. ℰ(06722) 23 48. www.rheingauer-weinmuseum.de.
This museum is housed in a medieval castle that has seen stints as a 13C residence of the Mainz bishops, as a stronghold of the knights of Rüdesheim, and as a meeting place for brigands. Exhibits include old winepresses and Roman *amphorae* (vases and jars for storing or transporting wine).

Niederwalddenkmal (Niederwald Memorial)

Access on foot, by road (2km/1.2mi) or by cable-car (terminal on Oberstraße: 20min round trip; ⬤6.50€ round trip). www.niederwalddenkmal.de.
Built in 1883 to commemorate the 1871 founding of the German Empire, this memorial comprises a massive statue of Germania sitting on a bronze plinth featuring Bismarck, Emperor Wilhelm I, German princes and their armies.

After Rüdesheim the road runs beneath terraced vineyards overlooked by the ruins of **Burg Ehrenfels**. This fortress was built by the archbishops of Mainz at the same time as the Mäuseturm on the opposite bank, which served as a tollbooth.

After Aßmannshausen, silhouetted high up on the oposite bank, the crenellated towers of Rheinstein, Reichenstein and Sooneck appear one after the other. The tower of Fürstenberg, on the wooded slopes facing Lorch, marks the start of an open stretch of vineyards and the towers of **Bacharach**, followed by the fortified isle of Pfalz.

The Pfalz at Kaub

The village of Kaub is dominated by the ruins of Gutenfels castle and has a picturesque main street called Metzgerstraße. More interesting, though, is the fortress that sits on a spit of land in the middle of the Rhine. This medieval toll castle is called the **Pfalz**★ *(◷open Apr–Oct, daily 10am–6pm, Nov and Jan–Feb Sat–Sun 10am–5pm, Mar daily 10am–*

5pm; ⏱ *closed Dec;* ✆ *(0172) 262 28 00;* *www.burgen-rlp.de;* 🎫 *4.10€)* and also known as Pfalzgrafenstein. Its main tower is surrounded by a wall evoking the shape of a ship. Its location and the thickness of its walls kept it out of reach of attackers.

Before arriving at a right bend in the river, note the castle of Schönburg above Oberwesel on the opposite river bank. This is the starting point of the valley's most romantic section.

The Loreley★★

This legendary spur, 132m/433ft high, symbolises the Romantic Rhine and enjoys a special place in German literature. The outcropping reduces the river's width by one quarter. According to legend, the Loreley was a water sprite who bewitched boatmen with her beauty and melodious songs at the river's narrowest and thus most dangerous spot.

St. Goarshausen

The town, strung out along the riverbank, is dominated by **Burg Katz** (Cat Castle), said to have been built to neutralise **Burg Maus** (Mouse Castle), a little further downstream.

Loreley Viewpoint★★

From St. Goarshausen take the road signposted "Loreley-Burgenstraße".
From April to October, shuttle buses leave from St. Goarshausen boat landing.
There are impressive **views**★★ of the romantic gorge from several accessible spurs here. On the plateau a landscape garden with marked trails is laid out and a **visitor centre** (⏱ *open Mar–mid-Nov, daily 10am–6pm;* 🎫 *2.50€;* ♿ *;* ✆ *(06771) 59 90 93; www.loreley-touristik.de*) has interactive displays covering the Loreley legend and local geology, flora and fauna.

Wellmich

Dolkstraße 6. ✆ *(06 771) 940 00.* *www.kath-kirche-loreley.de.*
Have a peek inside the parish church with its nicely restored 15C frescoes depicting the Crucifixion, the Last Judgement and the martyrdom of the apostles.

▶ *Continue to Kamp-Bornhofen, turn right towards Dahlheim, then right again at the sign "Zu den Burgen".*

The Rival Brothers

The hill slopes become wild again. Beyond Kestert there is a fine **panorama**★★; from the ruins of **Liebenstein Fortress**, the castle of **Sterrenberg** and the valley below come into view. The two castles are traditionally linked to a legend concerning two rival brothers. From Boppard on, where the Rhine swings into a huge double loop, the landscape becomes densely cultivated with vines. Soon the fortress of Marksburg emerges on its promontory above the town of Braubach.

▶ *At Braubach, take the road to Nastätten.*

🏠🚶 Marksburg★

🎧 *Visit by guided tour (50min) only, Apr–Oct, daily 10am–5pm; Nov–Mar, 11am–4pm.* ⏱ *Closed Dec 24 & 25.* 🎫 *5€.* ✆ *(02627) 206.* *www.marksburg.de.*
The **castle**, the only one in the whole Rhine Valley never to have been destroyed, is spectacularly sited on a craggy hilltop. Tours take you inside a Gothic assembly hall, the medieval kitchen and the torture chamber. Also note the medieval garden and a collection of armour from 600 BC to the 15C.

Burg Lahneck

3km/1.8mi from Lahnstein, near the confluence of the Rhine and the Lahn.
🎧 *Visit by guided tour (40min) only; Apr–Oct, daily 10am–5pm.* 🎫 *3.50€.* ✆ *(02621) 91 41 71.*
www.burg-lahneck.de.
The ruins of this fortress, originally built in the 13C to protect neighbouring silver mines, were reconstructed in neo-Gothic style in the 19C. From the keep is a **view** of the junction of the two rivers and the turreted fairytale castle of Stolzenfels, across the Rhine.

2 THE RHINE CASTLES★★★

From Koblenz to Bingen. 63km/39mi –
Allow one day.

This itinerary retraces the previous one, in the opposite direction, on the west bank of the river. Soon after leaving Koblenz, Lahneck comes into view again, its tower overlooking the river confluence. Above, on the right, is Stolzenfels.

Schloss Stolzenfels (Palace)

⚲ *Closed indefinitely for renovation.*
This enormous **castle** was reconstructed in 1842 in neo-Gothic style.

From the terrace you can enjoy a love-ley view of Koblenz and the citadel of Ehrenbreitstein.

Rhens

This town is known for its many painted half-timbered houses.

Gedeonseck

1hr round trip, including 20min on a chairlift. ⏱ *1–10 Apr & mid–end Oct, daily 10am–5pm; Apr 11–30 & Oct 1–15 to 5.30pm; May–Jun & Sept to 6pm; Jul & Aug 9.30am–6.30pm.* ✆6.50€ *roundtrip.* 📞*(06742) 25 10. www.sesselbahn-boppard.de.*

In fine weather, a trip up this 240m/787ft-high rock outcrop will treat you to superb **views**★ of the Rhine's hair-pin curve near Boppard. The **Four Lake View**★ gives you the illusion of looking at four separate lakes rather than a con-tinuous river.

Boppard

Originally a Roman camp, Boppard became a Free Imperial City in the Mid-dle Ages. Sights include the late-Roman-esque Severuskirche and the Gothic Car-melite Church with its 15C choir stalls and Renaissance tombs. The **museum** in the 14C fortress displays, among other things, bentwood furniture by native son Michael Thonet. There is also a pleasant riverside walk and the Römer-kastell where you can see a section of the 4C Roman town wall and graves from the Frankish period in the 7C.

The beginning of the "romantic" Rhine Gorge is marked by the two Rival Broth-ers fortresses (🔂 *see above*) on the opposite slopes. After Hirzenach, the Cat and Mouse castles loom above St. Goarshausen.

St. Goar

The village, clinging to the hillside at the foot of the impressive **Burg Rheinfels**★★ (⏱*open mid–Mar–Oct, daily 9am–6pm; Nov–mid–Mar, Sat–Sun 11am–5pm, if weather permits;* ✆4€; 📞*(06741) 7753)* stands guard over the Loreley passage along with St. Goarshausen across the river. Rheinfels was, until it fell to the

The Rhine Valley Castles

The Rhine Valley boasts an impressive number of castles. Stately residences, defensive forts, toll gates, travellers' refuges; each served a purpose. While many were severely damaged in fighting during the 17C and 18C, many castles were rebuilt in following the creation of the German Confederation in 1815.

French in 1797, the valley's most pow-erful fortress. Climb the clock-tower for panoramic views of the river and the Cat and Mouse castles. Kids love exploring Rheinfels Castle's maze of towers, gates and courts. Bring or bor-row a torch to go inside the under-ground defensive tunnel network. Beyond St. Goar, the river banks are steep and heavily wooded until Ober-wesel.

Oberwesel

Sixteen towers survive of the original town wall hemming in this appealing wine-growing village. It is possible to walk along sections of it, from where there is a good view of the Rhine.

South of the town, the Gothic **Liebfrau-enkirche**★ has a fine 14C altarpiece, one of the oldest in Germany, a Gothic rood screen and an unusual 1510 triptych illustrating the 15 cataclysms presag-ing the end of the world.

From the terrace of **Schönburg Castle**★, you can spot Kaub and the fortified Isle of Pfalz in the distance. The castle itself consists of three forts with a common defensive wall.

Bacharach★

Surrounded by vineyards, protected by an ancient town wall, Bacharach is one of the prettiest – and thus most popular – towns in the Rhine Valley. The row of half-timbered houses on Marktplatz and along Oberstraße are a delight, espe-cially when decked out with flowers during the warmer seasons. The Peter-skirche has one of the last Romanesque naves built in Germany. From here, a trail leads up to the romantically ruined Gothic Wernerkapelle (chapel) and the medieval Burg Stahleck, now a youth hostel.

The ruined towers of Nollig and Fürstenberg mark the end of the valley's most grandiose stretch. The road runs past a trio of audaciously perched castles.

Burg Sooneck

At Niederheimbach. ♦*Open Apr–Sept, daily 9am–6pm; Oct–Mar daily 9am–5pm.* ♦*Closed Dec.* ⌷*2.60€.* ℘*(06743) 60 64.*

This restored **fortress** clings to a steep slope of the Soonwald outcrop and is tiered to suit the terrain with a maze of staircases, platforms and terraced gardens beneath the turrets.

Burg Reichenstein

♦*Open Mar–mid-Nov, daily 9am–6pm, mid-Nov–Mar daily 9am–5pm.* ♦*Closed Dec.* ⌷*4€.* ℘ *(06721) 61 17. www.burg-reichenstein.de.*

Strategically situated at the mouth of a valley, this 10C **castle** has a collection of arms and hunting trophies. After serving as an imperial tollhouse,

it was converted into a summer residence in the 19C. Inside is a hotel and restaurant.

Burg Rheinstein

♦*Open Apr–Oct, daily 9.30am–5.30pm; Nov–Mar, Sat–Sun 10am–5pm.* ♦*Closed Dec 20–Jan 10.* ⌷*4.30€.* ℘*(06721) 63 77. www.burg-rheinstein.de.*

This **castle** is perched on a rock spur, in a commanding position above the Rhine. From the foremost watchtower there is a birds-eye **view**★★ of the valley. Rheinstein was the first of the Rhine castles to be rebuilt by the Hohenzollerns (after 1823).

Once past the **Mäuseturm**, balanced on its tiny islet in the middle of the river, the valley widens and the east bank becomes covered with terraced vines.

Bingen

Bingen started out as a strategic Roman camp set up at the confluence of the Rhine and the Nahe *(Castellum Bingium)*. Nowadays, tourism and wine-growing are the town's main sources of income. Sights include the landmark **Burg Klopp** and the **Historisches Museum am Strom** (♦*open Feb 20–Jan 5, Tue–Sun 10am–5pm, Jan 6–Feb 19 Sat–Sun 10am–5pm;* ♦*closed Jan 1, Dec 24–25;* ⌷*3€;* ⌷; ℘*(06721) 991 531)* with exhibits on local history and on the 12C abbess, artist and author Hildegard von Bingen.

EXCURSION
Kloster Eberbach★★

▶ *20km/12mi northeast of Rüdesheim am Rhein.*

♦*Open Apr–Oct, daily 10am–6pm; Nov–Mar, daily 11am–5pm.* ♦*Closed Mon before Shrove Tue, Dec 24–25 & 31.* ⌷*3.50€.* ⌷*Audio-guides.* ⌷*3.50€.* ⌷ ℘*(06723) 917 81 00. www.klostereberbach.de.*

Founded by Bernard of Clairvaux in 1136, this former Cistercian abbey existed for nearly 700 years before its secularisation in 1803. During the Middle Ages, it evolved into one of the region's finest wine estates and at one time even had its own fleet of ships plying the Rhine. It is still a famous wine producer today.

The Name of the Rose

The cameras began rolling at Eberbach in 1986 for the filming of the monastic whodunnit *The Name of the Rose*. Director Jean-Jacques Annaud allegedly chose the Cistercian abbey of Eberbach from a list of 300 abbeys as the primary setting for Umberto Eco's novel. The dispute between the papal envoy and the Franciscan monk William of Baskerville, played by Sean Connery, was filmed in the chapter-house, where monastic law was once laid down.

The scriptorium was reconstructed in the monks' dormitory. In the film, sentences were passed by the Holy Inquisition where people now gather to taste wine, in the monastery cellar. The abbey church and hospice also feature in the film.

Abbey Church

Built in two stages, in 1145–60 and in 1170–86, this three-nave Romanesque basilica reflects the understated and elegant austerity typical of Cistercian architecture. Gothic side chapels with tracery windows were added in the 14C, and there are remarkably elaborate **tombs**★ dating from the 14C to the 18C.

Abbey Buildings

Outlying 13C–14C buildings wrap around the **cloister**★ which, on the north side, gives access to the **monk's refectory**★★. Only the Romanesque portal remains of the original dining room; the rest was rebuilt in Baroque style and lidded by a magnificent stucco ceiling by Daniel Schenk, a court artist from Mainz.

The refectory is flanked by the **abbey museum** (Abteimuseum) on the left and the **monks' dormitory**★ to the right. Dating to c. 1250–70, the double-naved, rib-vaulted room has a slightly rising floor and shortened pillars to create the illusion of length.

Monks usually gathered in the adjacent **chapterhouse**★ (Kapitelsaal), which got its beautiful star-ribbed vaulting in the middle of the 14C and stylised plant ornamentation around 1500.

The lay brothers slept and ate in the area west of the cloister. Their old refectory now contains a collection of mighty **winepresses**★, documenting the abbey's 800-year-old history of wine-producing. The oldest press dates from 1668. Wine tastings, food and lodging are also available in the complex.

ADDRESSES

🏨 STAY

😊😊 **Altkölnischer Hof** – Blücherstraße 2, 55422 Bacharach. ☎(06743) 13 39. www.altkoelnischer-hof.de. Closed Nov–Mar. 20 rooms. Restaurant 😊😊.
Rooms at this family-run hotel in a half-timbered building ooze plenty of charm and history. Rhenish specialities are served in a panelled dining room.

😊😊😊 **Flairhotel Landsknecht** – Aussiedlung Landsknecht 4–6 (B9), 56329 St. Goar-Fellen. ☎(06741) 20 11. www.hotel-landsknecht.de. Closed Jan and Feb. 15 rooms. Restaurant 😊😊 closed Nov–mid-Mar, Tue and Wed.
This pleasant, modern family-run property with attached wine estate has comfortable rooms facing the Rhine or a lovely garden. The restaurant serves modern, regionally sourced cuisine and also has a terrace with river views.

😊😊😊 **Park-Hotel** – Marktstraße 8, 55422 Bacharach. ☎(06743) 14 22. www.park-hotel-bacharach.de. Open mid-Mar–mid-Nov. 25 rooms. Restaurant 😊😊😊. This family-run establishment offers comfortable rooms, some with Rhine views, and regional dishes in the Pfalzgrafen room.

😊😊😊😊 **Schloss Rheinfels** – Schlossberg 47, 56329 St. Goar. ☎(06741) 80 20. www.schloss-rheinfels.de. 56 rooms. Restaurant 😊😊😊. Across from the Loreley Rock, next to Rheinfels Castle, this hotel and villa offer an elegant ambience in comfortable rooms, as well as an extended spa centre. There is a fine dining restaurant as well as a castle tavern with a panoramic river terrace.

🍴 EAT

😊😊 **Gasthaus Hirsch** – Rheinstraße 17, 56154 Boppard-Hirzenach. ☎(06741) 26 01. www.gasthaus-hirsch.net. Closed Mon and Tue. A tasteful, rustic establishment with a panelled dining room adorned with paintings. The kitchen uses market-fresh regional ingredients whenever possible.

😊😊😊 **Zum Turm** – Zollstraße 50, 56349 Kaub. ☎(06774) 922 00. www.rhein-hotel-turm.com. Closed 1 week in early Jan, 1 week late July, 2 weeks late Nov and Tue. This establishment near the old tower was founded over 300 years ago and has housed an upscale family-run restaurant for over a century. The menu includes treats such as sage-laced roast pork, trout mousse and dove pot au feu.

Frankfurt am Main★★

Germany's financial and commercial capital, Frankfurt's centre is a forest of skyscrapers filled with international companies, government organisations and banks. Some of the world's biggest trade shows, including the famous Frankfurt Book Fair, take place in high-tech halls near the airport, the largest and busiest on the continent. But Frankfurt isn't all business. Join the locals in the traditional cider taverns, visit Goethe's birth house or take in the stellar exhibits in the string of museums hugging the south bank of the Main River.

A BIT OF HISTORY

The second coronation city – Built in the 8C on the site of a Roman military camp, Frankfurt rose to prominence in 1152 with the election of Frederick I Barbarossa as German king. All subsequent royal elections until 1796 took place here, a status officially confirmed in 1362 by the Golden Bull issued by Emperor Charles IV. In 1562 Frankfurt even replaced Aachen as the **coronation place** of the Holy Roman emperors – a privilege it retained until the dissolution of the Reich in 1806.

The young Goethe – Johann Wolfgang von Goethe was born in Frankfurt in 1749. Between 1772 and 1775, he penned many of his classics here, including *The Sorrows of Young Werther*, which allegedly took him only four weeks.

Capital of finance and economy – In the 16C Frankfurt was granted the right to mint money. The money market flourished and the **stock exchange** followed. German banks dominated the economy in the 18C; in the 19C they acquired a worldwide reputation thanks to financiers such as **Bethmann** and above all, **Rothschild**, whose sons, "the Five Frankfurters", established branches throughout Europe. Industry quickly

- ▶ **Population:** 643 000
- ℹ **Info:** Lobby of Hauptbahnhof (main train station). ℘(069) 21 23 88 49. www. frankfurt.de.
- ◖ **Location:** Two major autobahns join near Frankfurt: The A3 (Köln–Nuremburg) and the A5 (Karlsruhe). The city is 2hrs from Köln and 2hrs 30min from Nuremburg.
- Ⓟ **Parking:** Garages are located throughout the city. Visit http://wap.park info.com for specific locations and fees.
- ◉ **Don't Miss:** Städel Museum, Römerberg, the cathedral and a glass of apple cider in a traditional Sachsenhausen tavern.
- ◷ **Timing:** Allow a day to take in the major sights.
- ▲▲ **Kids:** Zoo; Senckenberg Natural History Museum.

followed in the wake of such a favourable climate. Frankfurt has always been a trade show city, starting in 1240 with the first Autumn Fair. Since the 20C, the Fur Fair *(Pelzmesse)*, the Motor Show *(Automobilausstellung)* and the famous Book Fair *(Buchmesse)* have underscored Frankfurt's role as Germany's capital of commerce and finance as did the EU's decision to base the European Central Bank here.

City life – Despite its cosmopolitan character, this metropolis on the Main has preserved an easygoing flair. The **Hauptwache** is a lively square dating from 1729, while the adjacent **Zeil** is said to be Germany's busiest shopping strip. To the north, the Westend quarter is losing the fight to stave off office blocks encroaching from the commercial centre. Cafés, cabarets, bars and restaurants are grouped around the central station, while the taverns of the olde-worlde Sachsenhausen quarter, on

View of Frankfurt from the roof top of Zeil Galerie

© Lubenow Sabine/Sime/Photononstop

BASIC INFORMATION
TELEPHONE PREFIX: ✆069
VISITOR INFORMATION
The Frankfurt tourist office can help
with room reservations (✆21 23 88 00;
*www.frankfurt-tourismus.de; open Mon–
Fri 8am–9pm, Sat–Sun 9am–6pm).*
There are two walk-in branches:
Hauptbahnhof, central station foyer,
*open Mon–Fri 8am–9pm, Sat–Sun
9am–6pm*; and Römer, Römerberg 27,
*open Mon–Fri 9.30am–5.30pm, Sat–Sun
9.30am–4pm. Both offices are closed
Jan 1 and Dec 25–26.*
Post Offices with late Hours –
Zeil 90 branch *(Mon–Wed 9.30am–8pm,
Thu–Sat 9.30am–9pm)*; main train station
– Hauptbahnhof, 1st floor *(Mon–Fri
7am–7.30pm, Sat 8am–4pm)*; airport
branch *(daily 7am–10pm).*
Daily Papers – *Frankfurter Allgemeine
Zeitung; Frankfurter Rundschau;
Frankfurter Neue Presse.*
Internet – *www.frankfurt.de; www.
rhein-main.net; www.frankfurt-online.
net; www.frankfurt-tourismus.de.*

GETTING AROUND
The largely pedestrianised city centre
is a pedestrian zone, meaning the
best way to get around is on foot.
PUBLIC TRANSPORT
Regional services are offered by **RMV**
(✆(01805) 768 46 36 (0.14€/min);
www.rmv.de; daily, 6am–midnight).
Local public transport is provided
by **VGF** (✆*(069) 194 49; www.vgf-
ffm.de; Mon–Thu 8am–5pm, Fri 8am
–1pm).* Information kiosks are at
Hauptwache (Mon–Fri 7am–8pm)
and at Konstablerwache, Passage B
level (Mon–Fri 9am–4pm) as well as
in many other U-Bahn and S-Bahn
stations. The tariff rate 3 is valid for all
rides within Frankfurt. Single tickets
are 2.40€; day tickets costs 6€ and
are also valid for travel to the airport.
Tickets are sold at vending machines
and from bus drivers but not aboard
trams and U-Bahn and S-Bahn trains.

The **Frankfurt Card** costs 8.90€ (valid
for 24hrs) and 12.90€ (valid for 48hrs)
for travel within the VGF network
(Tariff rate 3, plus to the airport). It also
entitles you to a 50 percent discount
on admission to 15 museums and
other attractions, such as the zoo and
the airport visitor terraces, and 20–25
percent off selected boat and coach
tours. The Frankfurt Card is available at
www.frankfurt-tourismus.de, selected
hotels, Hauptbahnhof and Römerberg
tourist information offices and
Frankfurt airport.

Useful Tip: For S-Bahn rides to the
airport you need a ticket at tariff rate 4.

the south bank of the Main, specialise in the celebrated **Äppelwoi** or **Ebbelwei** (slightly bitter cider), and *Handkäse mit Musik* (a small yellow cheese served with onions and vinegar sauce).

A general view – Frankfurt suffered tremendous destruction in World War II and was rebuilt as a modern city. Its distinctive skyline of skyscrapers has even garnered it the nickname "Mainhattan". The silhouette is most striking from the **Untermainbrücke** bridge.

For the best birds-eye view, take the lift up the **Main Tower** *(Neue Mainzer Straße)*, which has an open-air platform at 200m/656ft.

SIGHTS
Römer and Römerberg

The Römerberg is Frankfurt's historical central square and is ringed by a collection of step-gabled, half-timbered houses, built in the 15C by rich merchants. What you see today, however, are faithful postwar reconstructions.

The most imposing building is the Römer itself, on the western side of the square, which is a jumble of three joined buildings. The block has served as town hall since 1405. After 1562, its banquet hall was used to celebrate the election and coronation of the emperors. The hall where the coronation itself took place – the **Kaisersaal** *(○open year-round, daily 10am–1pm, 2pm–5pm; ○closed Jan 1, 24–25 & 31 Dec and during official functions; ◎2€; &; ℘(069) 21 23 40 64)* – doubles as a gallery of oil portraits depicting all 52 emperors, from Charlemagne to Franz II (1806).

Other reconstructed buildings ringing the Römerberg include the 13C **Alte Nikolaikirche**, the half-timbered **Haus Wertheim**, the 1464 Italianate **Steinernes Haus** and a row of half-timbered 15C–18C mansions.

In the centre of the square is the **Gerechtigkeitsbrunnen** (Fountain of Justice, 1543). Contrasting with the historical architecture is the Postmodern starkness of the **Schirn Kunsthalle**, a contemporary art gallery on the south side of Römerberg.

Kaiserdom St. Bartholomäus★ (Cathedral St. Bartholomew)

○*Open year-round, daily 8am–noon, 2.30pm–6pm.* ○*Closed Fri morning.* *www.dommuseum-frankfurt.de.*

Though technically not a cathedral (it is not a bishop's seat), Frankfurt's Dom played a key role in German history. The elections of all German kings from 1356 onwards took place in what is called the *Wahlkapelle*, an austere chapel attached at the south end of the choir. Between 1562 and 1792, the church also hosted 10 imperial coronations.

The Dom's outstanding feature is the tall **west tower★★** *(Westturm)*, ornamented with a gabled polygonal crown and lantern. Inside are several artworks worth noting: the 16C sandstone **Crucifixion** by Mainz artist Hans Backoffen; the 14C finely worked **choir stalls★** crafted in the Upper Rhine; and **mural paintings** from 1427, of the Cologne School, illustrating the legend of St. Bartholomew. In the north chancel is the **Altar of Mary Sleeping** *(Maria-Schlaf Altar)*, from 1434, also of the Cologne School, and the sole surviving altar from the original church. The large **Descent from the Cross** on the west wall was painted by Anthony van Dyck in 1627.

Dommuseum★ (Cathedral Museum)

○*Open year-round, Tue–Fri 10am–5pm, Sat–Sun 11am–5pm.* ○*Closed Jan 1, Dec 24–25 & 31.* ◎3€. &. ℘(069) 13 37 61 86. *www.dommuseum-frankfurt.de.*

This small museum is accessed from the cathedral cloister. Besides the treasury *(Domschatz)*, preserving precious gold works and vestments from the high Middle Ages, the late-Merovingian tomb of a young girl merits special attention. West of the cathedral is an **Archaeological Garden** *(Historischer Garten)*, with remains of Roman, Carolingian and Baroque fortifications.

Museum für Moderne Kunst★ (Modern Art Museum)

Domstraße 10.

🕐*Open year-round, Tue–Sun 10am–6pm (Wed 8pm).* 🕐*Closed Ascension Day, Pentecost, Corpus Christi Day.* 🎫*8€, free admission last Sat of month.* ♿ ✆*(069) 21 23 04 47.* *www.mmk-frankfurt.de.*

Viennese architect Hans Hollein designed this triangle-shaped museum dubbed "a slice of cake" by locals. It is a suitably edgy setting for an impressive collection of 20C art with particular emphasis on the New York School (Claes Oldenburg, Andy Warhol) and German contemporary artists (Joseph Beuys, Mario Merz, Katharina Fritsch and Gerhard Richter). Displays from the permanent collection rotate every few months.

Leonhardskirche

The exterior of this 15C Gothic church conceals its Romanesque origins. Two octagonal towers remain at the east end, along with a doorway embellished with fine carvings by **Master Engelbert**. The central nave is surrounded on three sides by a gallery. Fine stained-glass windows illuminate the chancel. To the left of the chancel are a superbly carved reredos representing scenes from the life of the Virgin and a painting by Holbein the Elder depicting the Last Supper. The baptismal chapel is in the north aisle.

Paulskirche

It was in this circular building that the German National Assembly, elected after the revolution of March, met from 1848 to 1849. Originally a church, it now houses an exhibition devoted to the history of the German democratic movement.

Goethe-Haus★ and Goethe-Museum

Grosser Hirschgraben 23–25. 🕐*Open year-round, daily 10am–6pm (Sun 5.30pm).* 🕐*Closed Jan 1, Good Fri, Dec 24–25 & 31.* 🎫*5€.* ✆*(069) 13 88 00.* *www.goethehaus-frankfurt.de.*

Fans of the poet, playwright, diplomat and scientist Johann Wolfgang von Goethe (1749–1832) flock to this large townhouse where the great man first saw the light of day. You can see the study on the top floor where he penned many of his early works – usually standing at a high desk. It has been recreated as it was in his lifetime. Right by the door hangs a silhouette portrait of Charlotte Buff, the object of his youthful passion and the inspiration for the character of Lotte in *The Sorrows of Young Werther*. A separate exhibition examines the lives of the Goethe family in 18C Frankfurt.

The adjoining **museum** is in fact a picture gallery dedicated to works by Goethe's contemporaries, including Tischbein, Graff, Hackert and Friedrich.

Jüdisches Museum and Museum Judengasse

Untermainkai 14–15. 🕐*Open Tue–Sun 10am–5pm (Wed 8pm).* 🎫*4€ for Jüdisches Museum, 2€ for Museum Judengasse, 5€ combination ticket.* ♿ ✆*(069) 21 23 50 00 (* ✆*(069) 297 74 19 for Judengasse branch).* *www.juedischesmuseum.de.*

The Jewish Museum occupies the 1821 Palais Rothschild (1821) and traces the history of the Jewish community of Frankfurt – one of Germany's most important – from the Middle Ages to today. At the Judengasse branch, you can see the foundations of five houses and two baths that once formed part of the ghetto where Jews lived from 1462 to 1796.

MUSEUMSUFER (MUSEUM BANK)

Frankfurt's delightful "Museum Row" extends along the Schaumainkai between the Eiserner Steg and Friedensbrücke bridges.

Städel Museum★★

Holbeinstraße 1. 🕐*Open year-round, Tue–Sun 10am–6pm (Wed–Thu 9pm).* 🕐*Closed May 1, Dec 24 & 31.* 🎫*12€.* ♿ ✆*(069) 605 09 80.* *www.staedelmuseum.de.*

This stronghold of art houses 700 years' worth of European masters, making it one of the biggest and most important such collections in Germany. All the heavy hitters are there, from Old Masters such as

Holbein the Elder, Grünewald, Altdorfer, Dürer, Vermeer, Rembrandt, Rubens and Tiepolo to French and German Impressionism, German Expressionism, Fauvism, Cubism, Surrealism, the Bauhaus and contemporary art. Part of the collection is in a stately 19C neo-Renaissance building; the rest in more modern wing. Yet another annex (expected to open in 2011) will house art after 1945 by such German artists as Anselm Kiefer, Georg Baselitz, Markus Lüpertz und Gerhard Richter.

Museum für Angewandte Kunst★ (Museum of Applied Arts)

Schaumainkai 17. ◷*Open year-round, Tue–Sun 10am–5pm (Wed 9pm).* ◉*8€.* ♿ ℘*(069) 21 23 40 37. www.angewandtekunst-frankfurt.de.*
The museum (1985) was designed by New York architect Richard Meier and consists of a modern building wrapped around a Neoclassical villa from 1803. Artefacts include furniture from the Middle Ages, Renaissance, Baroque and *Jugendstil* periods; 15C and 16C glassware; Islamic porcelain and carpets; and a book and calligraphy section.

Liebieghaus Skulpturen-Sammlung★ (Liebieg Sculpture Collection)

Schaumainkai 71. ◷*Open year-round, Tue & Fri–Sun 10am–5pm, Wed–Thu 8pm.* ◉*9€.* ℘*(069) 650 04 90. www.liebieghaus.de.*
This museum is a fine place to trace the evolution of sculpture through the ages. The oldest works are from ancient Egypt, Greece and Rome, but there are also fine examples from the Middle Ages (*Tilmann Riemenschneider*), the Renaissance (*Giambologna*) and Rococo and Neoclassical (*Thorvaldsen*) periods. A sprinkling of Asian works provides an interesting contrast.

Deutsches Filmmuseum★ (German Film Museum)

Schaumainkai 41. ⊶*Closed until spring 2011 for renovation.* ♿ ℘*(069) 961 220 220. www.deutschesfilmmuseum.de.*

The permanent exhibition of this museum is divided into two sections: one illustrates the origins of the cinema and displays such early inventions as a *laterna magica* and Edison's Kinetoscope (1889). The other zeroes in on the magic of film-making and the many steps involved in the production of both silent movies and "talkies". This is supplemented by special exhibits and daily screenings of rare films in the on site cinema.

Museum für Kommunikation★

◷*Open Tue–Fri 9am–6pm, Sat–Sun 11am–7pm.* ◉*2.50€.* ♿ ℘*(069) 606 00. www.mfk-frankfurt.de.*
Tracing the history of communications from clay tablets to computers and the telegraph to MP3 players, this museum is a great place to come with kids and teens. Treasures include one of the world's first telephones by Philip Reis and a VCR the size of a suitcase.

GREATER FRANKFURT

♿♟ Zoo★★

◷*Open year-round, Apr–Oct, daily 9am–7pm, Nov–Mar, 9am–5pm.* ◉*8€ (6€ during the last 2hrs).* ♿ ℘*(069) 21 23 37 35. www.zoo-frankfurt.de.*
Germany's second-oldest animal park (since 1858) is home to 4 800 denizens representing 565 species, including such endangered species as black rhinos and okapis. The bird section with its huge free-flight aviary is also quite impressive. Penguins, reptiles, fish and insects inhabit the Exotarium, while nocturnal animals such as koalas and the desert fox can be observed In the artificially darkened Grzimek-Haus. Kids especially love the simulated tropical storm in the crocodile enclosure.

♿♟ Senckenberg Naturmuseum★ (Senckenberg Natural History Museum)

Senckenberganlage 25, via Bockenheimer Landstraße. ◷*Open Tue, Thu–Fri 9am–5pm, Wed 8pm, Sat–Sun 6pm.* ◉*6€ (children 6–15yrs 3€).* ♿ ℘*(069) 754 20. www.senckenberg.de.*
Germany's largest natural history museum takes visitors on an eye-

opening trip back in time and around the world. It is especially famous for its extensive **dinosaur collection**★★ (nearly 20 specimens) that includes a triceratops skull and a complete Edmontosaurus skeleton with preserved sections of scaled skin. Other highlights you will stumble upon include the 50-million-year-old fossils of a **primitive horse**★★ and other prehistoric animals dug up in the UNESCO-recognised pit mine of Messel.

The shrunken head from the Ecuadorean Shuar Indian culture and the mummified bodies of two boys from Ancient Egypt are among the more macabre (and memorable!) objects on display.

Palmengarten★

Siesmayerstraße 61, via Bockenheimer Landstraße. ◯*Open Feb–Oct, daily 9am–6pm, Nov–Jan 4pm.* ⊕*5€.* ♿ ✆*(069) 21 23 39 39. www.palmengarten-frankfurt.de.*

If you need a break from the city bustle, make a beeline to these lovely gardens that put on a dazzling display of plants and flowers throughout the year. The eponymous subtropical palms are housed in the 1869 **Palmenhaus**, one of the oldest greenhouses in Germany. The gardens are part of the Westend greenbelt and segue into the city's botanical garden and the vast Grüneburgpark, which is immensely popular with joggers.

 DRIVING TOUR

TAUNUS

62km/39mi – Allow 4hrs. ◔*See region map pp244–245.*

These slate Rhenisch mountains are covered by beautiful forests and dotted with numerous mineral springs; the tallest peak in the range is the Großer Feldberg, reaching a modest 880m/2 887ft.

▶ *The first stop is 24km/15mi northwest of Frankfurt.*

Königstein★

This attractive spa town boasts a number of historic buildings, including the old 13C town hall and the *Burgruine* (castle ruins). All that remains of the town's 16C feudal castle is its original round bastions and 17C Vauban fortifications, set on massive foundations (◯*open Apr–Sept 9am–7pm; Feb–Mar and Oct 9.30am–4.30pm, Nov–Jan Fri noon–4pm, weekends 9am–4pm; last entry 30min before closing;* ◯*closed Jan 1 & Dec 25;* ⊕*2€;* ✆*061 74 20 22 51; www. koenigstein.de).* Climb the 166 steps of the tower for views over the town and the slopes of the Taunus.

Großer Feldberg★

◯*Open 9am (Sun 8am) until dusk.* ◯*Closed Nov.* ⊕*1.60€.* ✆*061 74 93 35 84.*

The Aussichtsturm (lookout tower; 163 steps) of this important telecommunications hub offers a wide-ranging **panorama**★★ taking in the Westerwald plateau to the northwest, the Wetterau depression to the northeast, and the plains of the Lower Main, including the encroaching Frankfurt, to the southeast. On a clear day you can see the spires of the cathedrals of Cologne and Strasbourg.

Römerkastell Saalburg (Saalburg Roman Fort)

◯*Open Mar–Oct Tue–Sun 9am–6pm, (Nov–Feb 4pm).* ◯*Closed hols, Dec 24 & 31. Last admission 30min before closing.* ✆*06175 93740. www.saalburgmuseum.de.*

This is claimed to be the world's only fully reconstructed Roman fort, complete with all the buildings, fixtures and fittings used in that period. It is adjacent to the Limes Straße, once the ancient frontier between the Roman Empire and the Germanic tribal territories, now a UNESCO World Heritage Site. Once beyond its striking exterior, the buildings in the central courtyard house an archaeological museum.

Bad Homburg★

This small spa town was transformed into one of Europe's elite gambling centres by the Blanc brothers, when they opened a casino here in 1840. Today Bad Homburg is a modern city but retains its exclusive character. Visitor activity revolves around the Kurpark (hydrotherapy spa), designed by Peter Joseph Lenne, which, with its fountains, Kaiser-Wilhelm Spa, casino, Russian church and Siamese temple, lends the town a somewhat exotic air.

Bad Homburg Schloss (ℰ 06172 926218, www.schloesser-hessen.de), dominated by the tall tower that survives from the previous White Castle, was originally the palace of the Landgrave (count) of Hesse-Homburg. It then became the summer residence of the Prussian kings, who, from William I (1871) onwards, ruled as Emperors of Germany. The castle possesses the only surviving furnished apartment of the last German Imperial couple, and was also the home of Landgrave Frederick II (1633–1708), immortalised as the hero of Kleist's drama, "Prince Friedrich of Homburg". The count's wooden leg is still here, on show to visitors.

EXCURSIONS
Offenbach

◗ 7km/4.3mi east. Leave from the Deutschherrn-Ufer.

This town on the south bank of the Main is the centre of the German leather industry and hosts an International Leather Fair twice yearly.

DLM Ledermuseum★★ (DLM Leather Museum)

Frankfurter Straße 86. ⊶ Partly closed for renovation until spring 2011. ◷Open year-round, Tue–Sun 10am–5pm. ◷Closed Jan 1, Dec 24–25 & 31. ⊜4€. ℰ (069) 829 79 80. www.ledermuseum.de.

This museum unites three collections under a single roof: the **Shoe Museum** featuring four millennia of foot fashion from around the world; the **Museum of Applied Arts** with crafts and design from the Middle Ages onwards, leather in particular; and the **Ethnological Museum** with objects from Africa, America and Asia.

Friedberg★

◗ 28km/17.4mi north via Friedberger Landstraße.

Friedberg is an attractive example of a medieval community with two distinct centres: the town enclosed within the Imperial castle and the bourgeois town grouped at the foot of the church, at either end of the main street (Kaiserstraße). The **castle** (Stauferburg) erected by Frederick Barbarossa in 1180 together with its outbuildings follows the pattern of a Roman camp and still has the air of a small, self-sufficient town. The ramparts, now a promenade, have been made even more attractive with the addition of bays of greenery and lookout points. The 54m/177ft-high **Adolf's Tower**★ (Adolphsturm, 1347) with its four watchtowers overlooks the assembled buildings and contains a local history museum. The **Jewish Baths**★ (Judenbad, 13C) at Judengasse 20 in the bourgeois sector, consist of a 26m/85ft-deep domed well used by Jewish women for ritual ablutions required by Jewish law. The **church** (Stadtkirche) is a 13C–14C building with a typically Hessian exterior: transverse attics with separate gables jutting from the roof above the aisles. Inside, an unusually tall **ciborium**★ (a chalice-like vessel that contains the sacrament) from 1462 looms in the chancel. On the left of the late-Gothic rood screen is the **Friedberg Madonna** (c. 1280), expressively carved from sandstone.

Darmstadt

◗ 30km/18.6mi south of Frankfurt on the A5.

Luisen-Centre, Luisenplatz 5, 64283 Darmstadt. ℰ (06151) 13 45 13. www.darmstadt.de.

The former capital of the grand duchy of Hesse-Darmstadt, Darmstadt has a pedigree as an intellectual and cultural centre thanks to a succession of art-loving princes but was practically obliterated by Allied bombs during World War II.

During reconstruction, function often won out over aesthetics, although the former artists' colony of Mathildenhöhe continues to delight fans of Art Nouveau design and architecture.

Mathildenhöhe★★
*Olbrichweg 13. ℘(06151) 13 33 85.
www.mathildenhoehe.info.*
In 1899 Grand Duke Ernst Ludwig invited seven artists, including Peter Behrens and Joseph Maria Olbrich, to build an **artists' colony** *(Künstlerkolonie)* on the eastern edge of the city. The result: one of the world's finest *Jugendstil* (Art Nouveau) architectural ensembles. Studios and villas were grouped around a Russian Orthodox Chapel built between 1897 and 1899 at the behest of the last Russian czar Nicholas II, whose wife Alexandra was a member of the ducal family.

Olbrich's Ernst-Ludwig-Haus, which opened in 1901, today houses the **Museum Künstlerkolonie** *(⏱open year-round, Tue–Sun 10am–6pm; ⊜5€).* Fronted by monumental sculptures of Adam and Eve, it showcases products designed by colony artists – silverware, furniture, jewellery – along with temporary exhibits. There are also changing displays in the **Ausstellungsgebäude** *(exhibition hall; ⏱open year-round, Tue–Sun 10am–6pm, Thu 9pm; ⊜8€),* completed in 1908 and renovated in 2008. Next to this spacious hall looms the 48m/157ft-high **Hochzeitsturm** *(⏱open March–Oct, Tue–Sun 10am–6pm; ⊜1.50€).* Its distinctive roofline resembles the outline of a hand and has become the city's emblem. There's a viewing platform on top.

ADDRESSES

🛏STAY

⊜ **A Casa Bed & Breakfast** – *Varrentrappstraße 49. ℘(069) 97 98 88 21. www.hotel-acasa.de. Closed end of Dec to beginning of Jan. 6 rooms.* This small B&B in an old villa has tasteful, individually decorated rooms, each reflecting a theme: Miami, Goethe, Rose Garden, Montparnasse, Bahama and Piccolo.

⊜⊜ **Hotel-Pension Gölz** – *Beethovenstraße 44. ℘(069) 74 67 35. www.hotel-goelz.de. Closed Dec. 12 rooms.* A stone's throw from the city centre and trade fair grounds, this family-run hotel in a 19C villa has spacious doubles and basic singles.

⊜⊜ **Hotel Hamburger Hof** – *Poststraße 10. ℘(069) 27 13 96 90. www.hamburgerhof.com. 66 rooms.* ⊒. Light and airy rooms with stylish contemporary touches make this business hotel opposite the Hauptbahnhof north exit a good base.

⊜⊜⊜ **Liebig-Hotel** – *Liebigstraße 45. ℘(069) 24 18 29 90. www.hotelliebig.de. Closed Dec 22–Jan 2. 20 rooms. ⊒15€.* Small hotel in a villa in the bank district with charming and luxurious rooms sporting Italian- and English-style furniture and beautiful fabrics.

⊜⊜ **Hotel Miramar** – *Berliner Straße 31. ℘(069) 920 39 70. www.miramar-frankfurt.de. 39 rooms.* ⊒. Modern and comfortable and close to the historic centre.

⊜⊜⊜ **Hilton** – *Hochstraße 4. ℘(069) 133 80 00. www.hilton.com. 342 rooms. ⊒29€. Restaurant⊜⊜.* A spacious, open atrium-style lobby provides access to rooms with all mod-cons, reached via a glass lift. The fitness club boasts a 25m/82ft-long swimming pool. The restaurant serves American and international fare.

⊜⊜⊜ **Steigenberger Frankfurter Hof** – *Am Kaiserplatz. ℘(069) 215 02. www.frankfurter-hof.steigenberger.de. 332 rooms. ⊒23€. Restaurants⊜⊜⊜, closed Sun.* This 1876 grand hotel has been perfectly renovated. Luxury reigns throughout, from the elegant lobby to the rooms. Dining options are the bistro-style Oscar, the pan-Asian Iroha and gourmet restaurant Français.

♟/EAT
⊜ **Fichte Kränzi** – *Wallstraße 5. ℘(069) 61 27 78. www.fichtekraenzi.de.* This café has served cider since 1849 along with local fare, all at reasonable prices. The shaded beer garden is lovely on a hot summer day.

⊜ **Lorsbacher Thal** – *Große Rittergasse 49–51 (descends south-east from Deutschherrnufer near Alte Brücke).* ✆*(069) 61 64 59. www.lorsbacher-thal.de.* This is a particularly charming cider restaurant that serves traditional, hearty food and has a beautiful garden tucked away at the back.

⊜ **Koh Samui** – *Grosse Friedberger Straße 32.* ✆*(069) 39 28 28. www.kohsamui24.net.* Find your favourite from among the huge selection of Thai dishes amid décor that is both cosy and exotic and accented with orchids and lilies.

⊜⊜ **Steinernes Haus** – *Braubachstraße 35.* ✆*(069) 28 34 91. www.steinernes-haus.de. Reservation necessary.* This pleasant, rustic establishment is over 500 years old. Typical Frankfurt cuisine and specialities grilled on lava stone can be sampled here.

⊜⊜ **Toan** – *Friedberger Anlage 14.* ✆*(069) 44 98 44.* By the zoo and Frankfurt's greenbelt, this modern restaurant serves excellent Vietnamese food and also has a garden terrace.

⊜⊜⊜ **Meyer's Restaurant** – *Grosse Bockenheimer Straße 54.* ✆*(069) 91 39 70 70. www.meyer-frankfurt.de. Closed Sun.* At this small bistro-restaurant near the old opera house, you can see the chefs at work in the open kitchen.

⊜⊜⊜ **Restaurant-Café Zum Schwarzen Stern** – *Römerberg 6.* ✆*(069) 29 19 79. www.schwarzerstern.de Reservation recommended.* This half-timbered house was painstakingly rebuilt after the war and sports pleasant, rustic décor. Upscale seasonal German cuisine dominates the menu.

⊜⊜⊜ **Estragon** – *Jahnstraße 49.* ✆*(069 597 80 38). www.estragon-ffm.de.* This pretty restaurant is decorated in warm colours and serves international cuisine infused with the Mediterranean.

⊜⊜⊜ **Heimat** – *Berliner Straße 70.* ✆*(069) 29 72 59 94. www.heimat-frankfurt.com.* The menu at this simple and relaxed place is small but changes with the seasons. The bar overlooks the open kitchen. Good choice of wines.

⊜⊜⊜ **Medici** – *Weißadlerwasse 2.* ✆*(069) 21 99 07 94. www.restaurant medici.de.* A family business in the city centre, near the Zeil. Serves international cuisine.

⊜⊜⊜ **Gargantua** – *Liebigstraße 47.* ✆*(069) 72 07 18. www.gargantua.de.* This small villa in the business district is home to a charming restaurant where walls are adorned with contemporary paintings.

⊜⊜⊜⊜ **Ernos Bistro** – *Liebigstraße 15.* ✆*(069) 72 19 97. www.ernosbistro.de. Closed Sat, Sun and holidays (except during fair days), Jan 4, Jul 26–Aug 17.* A comfortable ambience reigns at this West End restaurant that delivers classic cuisine injected with a creative, personal touch. The list of French wines is superb.

⊜⊜⊜⊜ **Tiger-Restaurant** – *Heiligkreuzgasse 20.* ✆*(069) 92 00 22 25. www.tigerpalast.com. Closed Jul 14–Aug 26, Sun.* This modern restaurant shares space with the Tigerpalast variety theatre and serves classic cuisine with a Mediterranean inflection. Candlelight and brick vaulting create a relaxed atmosphere.

🚒 TAKING A BREAK

The section of Grosse Bockenheimer Straße between Opernplatz and Börsenstraße (nicknamed the *Fressgasse* or "eating alley") is lined with casual eateries and is a good place to grab a quick bite to eat.

🍸 NIGHTLIFE

After dark, Frankfurt's liveliest quarter is Sachsenhausen on the left bank of the Main. It is laced with olde-world cobble-stoned streets lined with traditional taverns serving *Äppelwoi*, the dry cider that is a local speciality. To keep it cool, it is usually served in grey-blue earthenware jugs called *Bembel*. Look for taverns along Grosse Rittergasse (one block south of Deutschherrnufer) and along Schweizer Straße.

🛒 SHOPPING

Frankfurt's **main shopping street** (department stores, mainstream chains) is the Zeil. More exclusive boutiques have set up along Große Bockenheimer Straße and Goethestraße, while indie stores line the streets of Sachsenhausen, Schweizer Straße in particular. A fun **flea market** is held along Museumsufer on Saturdays.

Wiesbaden★

Lying at the foot of the Taunus mountains and favoured by the mild climate of the Rhine Valley, the capital city of Hessen has the refined atmosphere of a spa town and the flair of an elegant city.

OLD TOWN

The largely pedestrianised town centre wraps around the Schlossplatz. Shop-lined Landgasse and Neugasse are two particularly lively streets.

Schlossplatz (Palace Square)

This elegant and well-proportioned square is the heart of the town. It is lined with beautiful buildings and hosts a market twice weekly.

The former residence of the dukes of Nassau, the 19C **Schloss** was built in the unadorned Neoclassical style and today is the seat of the Hessen Parliament.

Altes Rathaus (Old Town Hall)

Built in 1609–10 and the city's oldest surviving building, the old town hall retains its late-Renaissance features on the ground floor. The upper storey dates from 1828 and bears the Romantic Historicist style.

Neues Rathaus (New Town Hall)

Georg Hauberisser, architect of the Munich town hall, erected this building in the German Renaissance style in 1886–87. It was destroyed in World War II and has been rebuilt since.

Marktkirche (Market Church)

This first brick-built church in the Nassau region was erected in the mid-19C. Its architect, Carl Boos, copied the Schinkel-designed Friedrichwerder Church in Berlin. A carillon chimes daily at 9am, noon and 5pm.

▶ **Population:** 276 750

Info: Marktplatz 1, 65183 Wiesbaden. ✆(0611) 172 99 30. www.wiesbaden.de.

Location: Some 40km/ 24.8mi west of Frankfurt and across the Rhine from Mainz. Take the A66 if you are coming from Frankfurt.

Parking: Old City parking garages can be found near the market on Bahnhof-straße and at Neugasse and Friedrichstraße.

Don't Miss: A peak at the Kurhaus.

Timing: Allow one hour each for the old town and the Spa Quarter.

SPA QUARTER

The spa quarter has developed west of the old town.

Kaiser-Friedrich-Therme (Emperor Friedrich Baths)

Langgasse 38–42. ⏱*Open year-round, Sun–Thu 10am–10pm, Fri–Sat 10am–midnight.* ⬤*3.50€ per hr May–Aug, 5€ per hour Sept–Apr.* ✆*(0611) 172 96 60.* This *Jugendstil* building boasts impressive frescoes in the entrance hall and a Roman-Irish steam bath festooned in glazed tiles. It is a fantastic place for visitors to enjoy Wiesbaden's famous thermal springs.

Kochbrunnen

This fountain is made up of 15 springs. Its hot salty water contains iron, evident from the reddish deposit on the granite basin. The octangular Kochbrunnen Temple dates from 1854.

Kurhaus★ (Casino and Conference Centre)

A lawn as flat as a bowling green, flanked by colonnades and lofty plane trees, leads up to what Emperor Wilhelm II called "the most beautiful *Kurhaus* in the world". Built in 1907, the sumptuous interior has always been a social gathering spot for spa visitors. Today is it used as a conference centre, but to enjoy its special ambience, you need to visit the casino, where Dostoyevsky allegedly found inspiration for his novel *The Gambler*. 🕗 Men must wear a jacket and tie to get inside the casino.

Staatstheater

The impressive 19C Renaissance-style building lies south of the theatre colonnades. The taste for lavish decoration is evident in its Rococo foyer.

Kurpark★ (Spa Gardens)

A vast park, laid out in 1852, stretches east behind the Kurpark. Sonnenberger Straße *(to the north)* and Parkstraße *(to the south)* are flanked by magnificent villas from the Gründerzeit (late 19C).

WILHELMSTRAßE AND NEROBERG AREA

Museum Wiesbaden

🕗 *Open year-round, Tue 10am–8pm, Wed–Sun 10am–5pm.* 🕗 *Closed Jan 1, May 1, Dec 24–25 & 31.* 🔹 *5€.* ♿ 𝄞 *(0611) 335 22 50. www.museum-wiesbaden.de.*

This museum comprises the **natural sciences collection**, the **collection of Nassau antiquities** and the **art collections**, including the world's largest **Jawlensky collection**★. (The artist lived in Wiesbaden from 1921 until his death in 1941.) Wiesbaden's main street, **Wilhelmstraße**, is lined by elegant shops and the "Warmer Damm" park.

👥 Nerobergbahn★

🕗 *Open May–Aug 9.30am–8pm, Apr and Sept, Wed noon–7pm, Sat–Sun 10am–7pm – every 15min.* 🔹 *3€ round-trip (children 1.50€).* 𝄞 *(01805) 768 46 36. www.eswe-verkehr.de.*

The water-powered funicular railway still runs as smoothly as when it was built in 1888. It leads up the Neroberg, Wiesbaden's local mountain (245m/804ft), which affords panoramic **views**★.

An International Spa Town

The Romans were the first to become aware of the benefits of Wiesbaden's hot sodium chloride springs, and Pliny noted with surprise that the water stayed warm for three days. In the 9C, Wiesbaden was first called "Wisibada" (spa in the meadows) but it was not until the 19C that it evolved into a famous spa town and gathering-spot for the crowned heads and higher nobility. Modern Wiesbaden enjoys an excellent reputation as a spa resort specialising in rheumatism.

Russisch-Orthodoxe Kirche (Russian Orthodox Church)

Christian-Spielmann-Weg 2.
🕗 *Open May–Oct, Sat–Sun 10am–5pm; Nov–Apr, noon–4pm.* 🔹 *1€.* 𝄞 *(0611) 52 84 94.*

Atop the Neroberg, this church (which is also known as the Greek Chapel) was built by Duke Adolf of Nassau in 1847–55 in memory of his wife Elisabeth, a Russian grand duchess who died at age 19. It includes a central building with five gilded cupolas overlooking the city.

ADDRESSES

🛏 STAY

🍽🍽🍽 **Drei Lilien** – *Spiegelgasse 3.* 𝄞 *(0611) 99 17 80. www.dreililien.com. 15 rooms.* In a *Jugendstil* villa, this hotel offers individually furnished rooms mixed with historical details and a high degree of comfort. Lavish breakfast.

🍴 EAT

🍽🍽🍽 **Käfer's Bistro** – *Kurhausplatz 1 (inside the Kurhaus).* 𝄞 *(0611) 53 62 00.* This restaurant is inside the *Kurhaus* and casino constructed in 1907 in Wilhelminian style. Paintings and wood dominate the décor of the beautiful dining room, and there is a sunny terrace for those balmy summer days.

Mainz★

The capital of the federal state of Rheinland-Pfalz, Mainz is Germany's largest and most important wine market and birthplace of Johannes Gutenberg, the inventor of moveable type. Its historic centre was nicely reconstructed after World War II and brims with handsome buildings housing atmospheric taverns.

CATHEDRAL QUARTER

▶ *From Liebfrauenplatz square walk west to Markt and enter the cathedral from the north side.*

Dom★★ (Mainz Cathedral)

Dedicated to Sts. Martin and Stephen, Mainz' Romanesque cathedral is one of the most magnificent in Germany. There are lovely **views**★★ of its complex ridge roof and six towers from the Leichhof square. The adjoining square, the Höfchen, segues into Gutenbergplatz on the south and Markt to the northeast. The cathedral has a double choir linked

▶ **Population:** 197 630
ℹ **Info:** Brückenturm am Rathaus, 55116 Mainz. ℘(06131) 28 62 10. www.info-mainz.de/tourist.
◗ **Location:** Mainz is near the confluence of the Rhine and the Main, across the river from Wiesbaden and not far from Frankfurt. It is the eastern gateway to the Romantic Rhine wine region.
🅿 **Parking:** Garages are located throughout the city. Visit http://wap.parkinfo. com for fees and locations.
⊛ **Don't Miss:** The Dom; Gutenberg Museum.
🕐 **Timing:** Allow up to a day to see Mainz' highlights.

by pillars affixed with **stone funeral monuments**★ honouring 44 of Mainz' 84 archbishops. In the second chapel **(1)** is a moving 15C tomb, and a multicoloured Gothic funerary monument is

MAINZ CATHEDRAL
MARKT
Renaissance Fountain
Liebfrauenplatz
St Gothard's Chapel
Crypt
8
7
West Chancel
TRANSEPT
Crypt
1
Crypt
2
NAVE
3
East Chancel
4
Crypt
6
CLOISTER★
5
Domstraße
Leichhof
N
Nasengäßchen
0   20 m

attached to one of the main pillars (2). In the east crypt, beneath the chancel, is a modern **gold reliquary (3)** of the saints of Mainz. A pillar **(4)** in the east chancel bears another funerary monument surrounded by statuettes of St. Benedict, St. Catherine, St. Maurice and St. Clare. A door in the south aisle leads to the Gothic **cloister**★ *(Kreuzgang)*. Besides the tombstones, note the bas-relief **(5)** of the 14C master-singer Heinrich von Meißen.

Fine statues adorn the doorway **(6)** of the former chapter-house *(Kapitelsaal)*, built in the 15C in an elegant Rhineland style. In the opposite wing is a fine 1328 pewter baptismal font **(7)**. Beyond, a Romanesque doorway **(8)** leads to the Gotthardkapelle.

OLD TOWN

South of the cathedral, the picturesque Kirschgarten square is framed by pretty half-timbered houses. From Augustiner-straße, small side streets lead to ancient houses that used to shelter artisans and craftspeople. Kapuzinerstraße leads to the Church of St. Ignatius past historic houses with sandstone portals and Rococo doors.

Ignazkirche
(Church of St. Ignatius)

Kapuzinerstraße 36. Open year-round, daily 9am–6pm.

Built by Johann Peter Jäger between 1763–75, this church illustrates the transition from Rococo to Neoclassi-cism. Outside is imposing 16C group of the **Crucifixion**★ *(Kreuzigungsgruppe)* by Mainz artist Hans Backoffen (1519), who designed it as his own funerary monument.

Stephanskirche★
(Church of St. Stephen)

Kleine Weissgasse 12. Open year-round, Mon–Sat 10am–5pm, Sun noon–5pm.

This late 13C church is the oldest Gothic hall church on the Middle Rhine. Though severely damaged in World War II, it has been beautifully rebuilt and is one of Mainz' must-see sights thanks to Marc

Chagall's remarkable **stained-glass windows**★★. Created between 1978–85, they depict biblical themes such as the salvation history of the Israelites and the Crucifixion. There are a further 18 colourful windows by Charles Marq, a close friend of Chagall's.

▶ *Along the Ballplatz and the Schillerplatz note the lavish mansions.*

Schillerplatz and Schillerstraße

The Baroque mansions in this square and street house the ministries of the state of Rheinland-Pfalz. The fountain in the centre of Schillerplatz is decorated with carnival scenes.

MUSEUMS
Gutenberg-Museum★★★

Liebfrauenplatz 5. Open year-round, Tue–Sat 9am–5pm, Sun 11am–3pm. Closed public holidays. 5€. (06131) 12 26 40. *www.gutenberg-museum.de.*

The art of the printed word is revered in the Gutenberg Museum as in no other place. Exhibits trace the evolution of printing from the beginnings in Asia but focus primarily on the achievements of native son Johannes Gutenberg. The most prized items are two original **Gutenberg Bibles**★★★ (1452–55).

Pages from Gutenberg Bible, Gutenberg-Museum

Gutenberg-Museum, Mainz

MAINZ
map I

0   300 m

A 643 WIESBADEN

WIESBADEN
↑ A 66 FRANKFURT

MZ-KASTEL

DARMSTADT ↑

ROMAN-GERMANIC MUSEUM

Boelckerstr.

Admiral-Scheer-Str.

Philippsring
Kostheimer
Landstr.

REGIONAL MUSEUM

Deutschhaus-Pl.

MAARAUE

COBLENCE
↑ A 60-E 42 BINGEN

GUTENBERG MUSEUM

RHEIN

CATHEDRAL

see map II

St Steven

St Ignatius

ZITADELLE

SÜD

Salvatorstr.

Weisenauer Str.

Winterhafen

Salvatorstr.

Stadtpark

Am
Stiftswingert

An der
Favorite

Göttelmannstr.

ZALBACH

BINGEN A 60-E 42 ↓ A 63, KAISERSLAUTERN   A 60 ↓

A 60-E 42

A   B

map II

0   100 m

WHERE TO STAY

Stiftswingert.................①

WHERE TO EAT

Geberts Weinstuben....④
Weinhaus Schreiner.....①

REGIONAL MUSEUM

Bauhofstr.

Peter-Altmeier-Allee

Adenauer-

L

Zeughaus-
gasse

CASINO
RHEINGOLDHALLE
CCM

Christofstr.

Karmeliterstr.

Rheinstr.

Uter.

EISERNTURM

Am
Brand

GUTENBERG MUSEUM

Fischtorstr.

Renaissance
fountain

Markt

Liebfrauen-
pl.

ALTE
UNIVERSITÄT

Schöfferstr.

Höfchen

Quintinsstr.

Gutenbergpl.

Leichhof

CATHEDRAL

Schillerstr.

Ludwigsstr.

Weißliliengasse

Domstr.

Kirschgarten

Schillerplatz

Ballpl.

Altstadt

Augustiner-
str.

Other interesting displays include incunabula and 16C–19C books, ancient presses and typesetting machines, and a section on modern book production and paper.

Set up in the basement is Gutenberg's recreated workshop, while at the **Druck-laden** (printshop) you can learn how to print your own books using the ancient technology.

Römisch-Germanisches Zentralmuseum★ (Roman-Germanic Central Museum)

Ernst Ludwig Platz 2. ©*Open year-round, Tue–Sun 10am–6pm.* ©*Closed Dec 24–25 & 31.* ℘*(06131) 912 40. http://web.rgzm.de.*

In the former Electors' Palace (15C–17C), this rambling museum houses collections on European prehistory, the advanced Mediterranean civilisations, and Ancient Roman and early medieval archaeology.

Five original Roman ships are displayed in the nearby **Museum für Antike Schiffahrt** *(Museum of Ancient Shipping; Neutorstraße 2b;* ©*same hours).*

Landesmuseum Mainz★ (State Museum Mainz)

Große Bleiche 49–51. ©*Open year-round, Wed–Sun 10am–5pm, Tue 10am–8pm.* ©*Closed most public holidays.* ⊜*5€.* ℘*(06131) 285 70. www.landesmuseum-mainz.de.*

The Department of Antiquities traces the cultural history of the Rhineland from prehistory to the present.

Of particular interest is the Steinhalle with 300 Roman-era stone memorials, including the **Jupitersäule** (Jupiter's column). The museum's medieval and Baroque sections and its Höchst porcelain and *Jugendstil* glassware are also impressive.

Gutenberg

Johannes Gutenberg (c. 1394–1468), the father of modern printing, is Mainz' most famous son. After honing his skills in Strasbourg as a young man, he returned to Mainz where he devised a groundbreaking printing technique using moveable type. It allowed large volumes of books to be printed at low cost. Gutenberg did not profit from his invention, however. Unable to repay his creditors, he died in poverty in 1468.

ADDRESSES

🛏 STAY

⊜⊜🍽 **Stiftswingert** – *Am Stiftswingert 4.* ℘*(061 31) 98 26 40. www.hotel-stiftswingert.de. 30 rooms.* ⊐. Well managed hotel with cherry-wood furnished guestrooms and modern bathrooms and facilities.

🍴 EAT

⊜⊜ **Weinhaus Schreiner** – *Rheinstraße 38.* ℘*(061 31) 22 57 20. Closed 2 weeks in July and Aug, Sun and public holidays, Jun –Sept Sat eve and Sun.* This classic local wine tavern has rustic décor and a lively atmosphere. The menu features seasonal dishes with a regional flavour.

⊜⊜🍽 **Geberts Weinstuben** – *Frauenlobstraße 94.* ℘*(06131) 61 16 19. www.geberts-weinstuben.de.* Patrons share laughs over a glass of wine or earthy regional fare at this cosy, family-run wine tavern founded in 1887. Sit inside or in the vine-draped inner courtyard.

⊜⊜🍽🍽 **Favorite** – *Karl-Weiser-Straße 1.* ℘*(06131) 801 50. www.favorite-mainz.de. Closed Sun eve and Mon. Reservation recommended.* With its panoramic windows and warm furnishings, this restaurant exudes supreme elegance without being stuffy. The kitchen is expert in putting modern spins on traditional recipes. Nice terrace and separate smokers' lounge.

Mannheim

Mannheim's city layout is a rarity among European towns: its centre is essentially a chessboard of 142 identical blocks *(Quadratstadt)*, each identified by a letter and a number. But it would be wrong to think this is a staid, inflexible city. Local enthusiasm for the arts is and always has been strong. It was at Mannheim's theatre where many of Schiller's plays premiered back in the 18C.

SIGHTS
Kunsthalle Mannheim★★ (Fine Arts Museum)

Friedrichsplatz 4. Open year-round, Tue–Sun 11am–6pm (Wed 8pm). Closed Carnival, Good Fri, May 1, first Tue in May, Dec 24 & 31. 5€. (0621) 293 64 30. www.kunsthalle-mannheim.com.

The museum is undergoing a major facelift until at least 2012. Sections may be closed during this time.

In a 1907 Jugendstil building, this acclaimed art museum concentrates on works of the 19C and 20C. The exceptional **sculpture collection** includes works by Rodin, Lehmbruck, Barlach, Brancusi, Giacometti, Moore, Nam June Paik, Richard Long, Mario Merz and other heavy-hitters. Another focus belongs to such crowd-pleasing **French Impressionists** as Manet, Monet and Cézanne. **German Secession** artists are represented by Slevogt and Corinth; Beckman and Heckel are artists included among the **Expressionists**.

Reiss-Engelhorn Museen★★

Open year-round, Tue–Sun 11am–6pm. Closed 24 & 31 Dec. Permanent collections 2.50€, special exhibits 10€. (0621) 293 31 51. www.rem-mannheim.de.

Mannheim's REM encompasses four museums in different locations. Housed in the former arsenal, the **Museum Zeughaus** (in grid C5) takes you on a journey of discovery through the region's art and cultural history, theatre

▶ **Population:** 308 400

Info: Willy-Brandt-Platz 3, 68161 Mannheim. (0621) 10 10 11. www.tourist-mannheim.de.

◐ **Location:** 23km/14.3mi southeast of Worms, Mannheim sits at the confluence of the Rhine and the Neckar rivers.

ℙ **Parking:** Car parks and garages are located throughout the city. Visit http://wap.parkinfo.com for fees and locations.

❂ **Don't Miss:** The Fine Arts Museum, Reiss-Engelhorn-Museen.

◔ **Timing:** Plan two hours to view the Fine Arts Museum.

and music history, natural history and international photography in modern and playful yet substantial exhibitions. A highlight is the collection of **European porcelain and faïence**★.

The **Museum Weltkulturen** (Museum of World Cultures) is in a modern cube opposite the arsenal (D5). It presents the archaeology collections, including artifacts from the Paleolithic and Mesolithic eras, the Carolingian period, and from ancient Greece and Rome.

The **Schillerhaus Museum** (B5) takes visitors on a multimedia tour of the life of Germany's famous poet and playwright, Friedrich Schiller, who lived in Mannheim from 1783–85. Finally, **ZEPHYR – Room for Photography** (C4) presents outstanding works of contemporary photography.

Schloss Mannheim★ (Palace)

Bismarckstraße 1. Open year-round, Tue–Sun 10am–5pm. 6€, including audioguide. (0621) 292 28 91. www.schloss-mannheim.de.

Construction of this Baroque palace, the biggest in all of Germany (400 rooms, 2 000 windows), lasted from 1720 to 1760 and drew upon the talents of the period's finest artists, including Balthasar Neumann and Cosmas Damian Asam. Today, the building is largely used by the university but the opulent living quarters are accessible to the public. Furniture, paintings, tapestries, porcelain and clocks are among the items reflecting the illustrious lifestyle of the Prince-Electors. A highlight on the ground floor is the Rococo library of Princess Elisabeth Augusta, which is the only room that has been barely altered.

Jesuitenkirche (Jesuit Church)

🕐Open year-round, daily 9am–noon, 2pm–8pm. ℘(0621) 12 70 90. www.jesuitenkirche.de.

Built at the same time as the palace, this massive edifice is said to be the biggest Baroque church in southwest Germany. The façade, though, is Neoclassical.

Technoseum★

Museumsstraße 1. 🕐Open year-round, Tue-Sun 9am–5pm. 🕐Closed Dec 24 & 31. ⊚6€. ♿ ℘(0621) 429 89. www.technoseum.de.

The Technoseum is one of Germany's largest technology museums. The modern presentation chronicles developments in the fields of natural science and technology from the 18C to today and highlights the social and economic changes brought on by Industrialisation. Machines are not merely shown but arranged in context and put through live demonstrations. In one room, for instance, you can gain an insight into the inner workings of a steam engine. Scattered about the floors are several experimentation stations, where you can playfully explore scientific principles.

Heidelberg★★★

A source of inspiration for many poets and artists, each charmed by the town's natural beauty and its castle, Heidelberg symbolises German Romanticism. Hölderlin wrote a famous ode to Heidelberg, and Brentano, Eichendorff and Von Arnim were among the Romantics who gathered here in the early 19C. But this jewel of the Neckar is also a lively university town with a vibrant cultural scene.

A BIT OF HISTORY

The political capital of the Palatinate
– The Pfalz (Palatinate), of which Heidelberg was the political centre, owes its name to the "palatines", the highest officers in the Holy Roman Empire. These functions no longer existed in the 14C, but their vestiges remained with the hereditary family. The governing prowess of these Palatine-Electors (Kurfürsten) made the Palatinate (Kurpfalz) one of the most advanced states of Europe.

▶ **Population:** 143 000

ℹ **Info:** Willy-Brandt-Platz 1 (central station), 69115 Heidelberg. ℘(06221) 194 33. www.cvb-heidelberg.de.

▶ **Location:** Heidelberg is 20km/12.4mi east of Mannheim and reached via the A5 autobahn (Frankfurt–Freiburg).

🅿 **Parking:** Heidelberg has several garages in the old town. Especially convenient are those on Neue Schlossstraße, near the castle, and below Karlsplatz, near the Rathaus.

⊛ **Don't Miss:** Heidelberg Castle, a walking tour of the old city and a panoramic stroll along the Philosophers' Walk.

🕐 **Timing:** Allow half a day for a tour of the castle and another half-day for the rest of the city.

HEIDELBERG CASTLE

0   100 m

Scheffelterrasse

Great Terrace

Burgweg

★ Great Barrel

★ Germany Pharmacy Museum

Well Pavilion

GARDEN ★

Grotto

Rondell

Moat

Elizabeth Gate

NEUE SCHLOSSSTRASSE

Schloß-Wolfsbrunnenweg

N

The "Orléans War" (1688–97) – In the 16C, Elector Karl-Ludwig, hoping to ensure peace, married his daughter **Liselotte** (Elisabeth-Charlotte) to Duke Philip of Orléans, brother of Louis XIV. The marriage alliance proved disastrous to both the Palatinate and to Heidelberg: Political infighting resulted in the town's destruction and the sacking of the castle; total disaster followed in 1693, when it was completely destroyed by fire. Before long the Electors abandoned the partly ruined castle, but today it is precisely this ivy-draped red-sandstone pile that gives Heidelberg its romantic flair.

SCHLOSS★★★

🕐*Open year-round, daily 8am–6pm.* 🎫*5€,* 🎧*guided tour supplement 4€.* 📞*(06221) 65 44 29. www.service-center -schloss-heidelberg.com.*

Looming above the town, Heidelberg Castle is a superb example of a fortress with both Gothic and Renaissance features. For an **overview**★ of the town

and the Neckar Valley, visit the Rondell promontory. Enter the castle through the **Elisabethentor**, a gate built by Friedrich V (allegedly in a single night in 1615) as a surprise for his wife Elizabeth Stuart. Two gates separated by a moat lead to the inner courtyard. The **gardens**★ were laid out under Friedrich V in the 17C. The east face of the castle, with its three towers, is visible from the Scheffel Terrace.

Courtyard and Buildings

The courtyard is on the far side of a fortified bridge guarded by the **Torturm** (**7**; gate tower). The simple residential building, the **Ruprecht**, was built by Ruprecht III who became German king in 1400; above the crown are two little angels, thought to be the architect's twins who died just before completion of the work. The 14C **Apothekerturm** (**1**) tower is even older and forms part of the **Deutsches Apothekenmuseum**★ *(German pharmaceutical museum;*

Heidelberg and its legendary castle

R. Mattes/MICHELIN

🕐 *open year-round, daily 10am–5.30pm; included in general admission),* with 18C–19C apothecaries' equipment and an alchemist's laboratory complete with ancient instruments.

Gothic and Renaissance Additions

Immediately off the courtyard is the Gothic **Brunnenhalle** (Well Wing), whose granite Roman columns came from Charlemagne's palace at Ingelheim. The **Library (6)**, set back from the west wing, is awash with light and was once home to the royals' personal library, art collections and treasure. Only slightly more recent is the **Hall of Mirrors Wing (8**; Gläserner Saalbau). Following a fire, only a shell remains of this tiered, Italian Renaissance building. The **Ottheinrich Wing (9**; Ottheinrichsbau), built by Elector Otto-Heinrich, an enlightened Renaissance ruler, inaugurated the late-Renaissance period in German architecture.

Horizontals predominate in the façade, bearing biblical and mythological ornamentation. The famous sculptor, Alexander Colin of Mechelen (1526–1612), helped design the entrance, a triumphal arch festooned with the Elector's coat of arms.

Transitional Renaissance-Baroque Additions

The **Friedrich Wing**★★ (**10**; Friedrichsbau), whose façade retains the classical Renaissance design, also bears elements pointing towards the coming Baroque. The statues represent the ancestors of Friedrich IV, who added the wing. The rear of the building and views over Heidelberg are best seen from the **Great Terrace** (Altan), accessed via a passageway to the right of the Friedrich Wing.

Grosses Fass★ (Great Vat)

This colossal 18C cask, with a capacity of 221 726l/48 780gal, still serves up wine to visiting customers. The platform above the Fass hosts tastings and occasional dancing. The guardian of this extravagance, an enduring idol of local folklore, is a statue of the dwarf court jester **Perkeo**, celebrated for his astonishing drinking feats.

VIEWS

From the north bank of the Neckar, which you reach either via the Alte or the Karl-Theodor bridges, are **views**★★ of the castle ruins and the old town clustered around the Heiliggeistkirche. Further views of the castle and the town can be seen from the **Philosophenweg**★ (Philosophers' Walk 🕐 *see below*), reached by crossing the Alte Brücke and climbing the Schlangenweg.

⚡ WALKING TOUR
Philosophenweg★
(Philosophers' Walk)

Start your tour of the city by climbing the hill on the north bank of the Neckar to enjoy spectacular views of Heidelberg and its castle. The nicest time to visit is later in the day when the setting sun bathes the city in intense colours.

▷ *Retrace your steps to the Alte Brücke.*

Alte Brücke★

The 18C bridge is flanked by two medieval fortification towers. The west tower contains three prison cells.

▷ *Follow Steingasse to Marktplatz.*

Heiliggeistkirche
(Church of the Holy Spirit)

This late-Gothic church is distinguished by covered market stalls set up between the building's buttresses as they have been for centuries. The galleries in the apses were used for the Biblioteca Palatina, once Europe's finest library, which ended up as war booty at the Vatican in 1623. The chancel was formerly the sepulchre of the Palatine Electors, but only the tomb of Ruprecht III and his wife remains.

Haus zum Ritter★
(Knight's House)

This magnificent bourgeois house owes its name to a bust of St. George in knightly armour on a richly scrolled pediment. Built in 1592 for the Huguenot merchant Charles Bélier, it was the only late-Renaissance masterpiece to survive the devastating Orléans War.

"Homo Heidelbergensis"

In 1907, the jaw of a man who lived some 500 000 years ago was found in Mauer near Heidelberg. Called **Heidelberg Man** (*Homo heidelbergensis*), this hominid is considered to be an ancestor of *Homo sapiens*, the species of modern humankind.

▷ *Follow Hauptstraße to Universitätplatz and the Baroque Old University (Alte Universität).*

Studentenkarzer★
(Student Prison)

Augustinergasse 2. ⏲Open Apr–Sept, Tue–Sun 10am–6pm; Oct 10am-4pm; Nov-Mar Tue-Sat 10am–4pm. ⏲Closed Dec 23–Jan 8. ☞2.50€. ✆(06221) 54 35 54.

One of Heidelberg's most popular tourist attractions, the old student jail was in use from 1712 and 1914. A stint here was practically a rite of passage for male students. Walls are covered in inscriptions and graffiti.

Jesuitenkirche

This 18C Baroque church bears a façade based on the Gesù Church in Rome. The luminous triple nave is supported by pillars decorated with Rococo stuccowork. Accessed via the church is the **Museum of Sacred and Liturgical Art** (*Museum für sakrale Kunst und Liturgie; Richard-Hauser-Platz; ⏲open Jun–Oct, Tue–Sat 11am–5pm, Sun 12.30pm–5pm; Nov–May, Sat 10am–5pm, Sun 12.30pm–5pm; ⏲closed Jan 1, Easter Mon, Pentecost, Dec 25–26; ☞2€; ✆(06221) 16 63 91*). It houses religious artefacts from the 17C–19C, most notably an oversized silver Madonna by J Ignaz Saller (1736).

▷ *Follow Hauptstraße west to the Palais Morass, which houses the Electorial Palatinate Museum.*

Kurpfälzisches Museum★
(Palatinate Museum)

Hauptstraße 97. ⏲Open year-round, Tue–Sun 10am–6pm. ⏲Closed Jan 1, Shrove Tue, Dec 24–25 & 31. ☞3€. ✆(06221) 583 40 20. www.museum-heidelberg.de.

A highlight of this museum is the jawbone of the prehistoric "Heidelberg Man" (500 000 BC). Other key displays are the **Altarpiece of the Twelve Apostles★★** (*Zwölfbotenaltar*) carved by Tilman Riemenschneider in 1509 and several **works from the Romantic Period★★**.

EXCURSIONS
Königstuhl

▶ *5km/3mi southeast, via Neue Schlossstraße, Molkenkurweg and then Gaiberger Weg. Or take the funicular, which stops at four stations: Stadt (near Kornmarkt), Schloss, Molkenkur and Königstuhl.*

🕐 *Funicular: mid-Apr–Oct 9am–8pm, Nov–mid-Apr 9am–5pm.* 🚋 *8€ round-trip from Kornmarkt station.* ✆ *(06221) 513 21 50; www.bergbahn-heidelberg.de.*

The 550m/1 804ft-high Königsstuhl marks the highest point in Heidelberg and can be ascended by funicular-from Kornmarkt via the *Schloss* to the Molkenkur viewpoint. There you switch to the nostalgic Königsstuhlbahn, which rumbles to the top for even more sweeping views of the Neckar Valley. The total trip takes about 20 minutes. Aside from hiking trails, kid-friendly diversions include a **falconry** and a **fairytale-themed amusement park** (🕐 *open May–mid-Nov*).

Schwetzingen★

▶ *10km/6.2mi west via the Friedrich-Ebert-Anlage.*

During the spring asparagus season *(Spargelzeit)*, gourmets flock to Schwetzingen, while music fans descend on this sweet little town during the May and June festival season.

Schwetzingen's **Schloss**★★ (👣 *Guided tour (1hr) Apr–Oct, Tue–Fri on the hour 11am–4pm, Sat–Sun 11am–5pm; Nov–Mar Fri 2pm, Sat–Sun 11am, 2pm & 3pm;* 🕐 *closed Dec 24–25 & 31;* 🚋 *8€;* ✆ *(06221) 53 84 31; www.schloss-schwetzingen.de)* was destroyed in the 17C but rebuilt in 1700–1717 as a Baroque palace. About 40 of the palace rooms are open to the public. The charming 18C **Rococo the-**

atre★ *(Rokokotheater)* is open throughout the summer and hosts concerts and
plays during the Schwetzingen Festival
(🕐 *mid-Jun–early Sept; ☎(06202) 12
88 28).*
The 72ha/178-acre **Schlossgarten**★★,
which blends formal French and English
gardens, is dotted with mock ancient
temples and ruins popular during the
Late Rococo.

DRIVING TOUR

BERGSTRASSE

*From Heidelberg to Darmstadt 58km/36mi
– Allow approx 3hrs.*

The *Bergstraße*, or mountain road, follows an ancient Roman trading route
(strata montana) winding through
gentle forest- and vineyard-covered
hills and sunny escarpments sloping
towards River Rhine. "This is where
Germany starts to turn into Italy", is
how Emperor Joseph II described this
lovely landscape. Dotted with castles
and half-timbered villages, orchards and
wineries, it holds much appeal for hikers, cyclists and others craving outdoor
pursuits.

Weinheim
Sun-splashed Weinheim is the first
town on the *Bergstraße* to see springtime. The 13C agricultural community
has a charming **old town** centred on
a romantic market square with a 16C
Altes Rathaus (old town hall). Nearby,
the Büdinger Hof *(Judengasse 15–17)* is
another attractive building. The **Schloss**
(castle) abuts an English-style park that
segues into the 19C **Exotenwald**★
(exotic forest), with a wonderful variety
of trees. The castle ruins of **Burg Windeck** and **Wachenburg** stand watch over
the town.

Heppenheim
The charming **Marktplatz**★ is framed
by the medieval Liebig pharmacy, the
16C town hall and the vast neo-Gothic
"Bergstraße Cathedral".

Lorsch
A key stop on the *Bergstraße*, tiny Lorsch
is home to **Kloster Lorsch**, an 8C Carolingian abbey that once ranked among the
most important in Europe. In 1991 it was
listed as a UNESCO World Heritage Site,
largely because of the well-preserved 8C
Königshalle★★ (royal hall, also known
as *Torhalle).*
Presumed to be a gatehouse, it sports
arches, an elaborate façade and is one
of the few surviving pre-Romanesque
architectural relics in Germany.
The building opposite houses a trio of
museums *(Museumszentrum Lorsch;
Nibelungenstraße 35;* 🕐*open year-round,
Tue–Sun 10am–5pm;* 🕐 *closed Jan 1,
Shrove Tue, Dec 24;*⊛*4€;* ♿*;* ☎*(06251) 10
38 20; www.kloster-lorsch.de).* One details
the history of the abbey, another presents
Hessian folklore and traditions and the
third focuses on tobacco.
From behind the church you can enjoy
a panoramic view over the Rhine Valley
towards the Odenwald forest region.

Bensheim
This "town of flowers and wine" is proud
of its **old town**.
Quaint half-timbered houses line
the Marktplatz, the Haupstraße and
Wambolterhofstraße. In a sheltered
valley is the **Fürstenlager**★★, once the
summer residence of the landgraves of
Hessen, now surrounded by a park.
To the north, the imposing **Auerbacher
Schloss** (🕐*open year-round, daily
10am–5pm;* ☎*(06251) 729 23; www.
schloss-auerbach.de)* commands a view
of the whole region.

ADDRESSES

🏨 STAY

Hotel-Restaurant Schnookeloch – *Haspelgasse 8. ℰ(06221) 13 80 80. www.schnookeloch.de. 11 rooms. Restaurant.* The Schnookeloch's history is intertwined with the history of this university town, the restaurant having been a traditional student hangout.

Hotel Am Kornmarkt – *Kornmarkt 7. ℰ(06221) 282 18. www. hotelamkornmarkt.de. 20 rooms.* A charming small hotel in the heart of the old city. Staying here entitles you to a discount at the nearby car park 12.

Zum Pfalzgrafen – *Kettengasse 21. ℰ(06221) 204 89. www.hotel-zum-pfalzgrafen.de. 27 rooms.* In a city where rates are rather steep, this mid-size hotel delivers comfortable, reasonably priced rooms. Some have views of the castle.

Weißer Bock – *Grosse Mantel-gasse 24. ℰ(06221) 900 00. www.weisser-bock.de. 23 rooms. Restaurant.* This historic charmer in the old town has one of the best restaurants in the region and is especially known for its hand-picked selection of German and international wines.

Hotel Backmulde – *Schiffgasse 11. ℰ(06221) 536 60. www.gasthaus-backmulde-hotel.de. 25 rooms. Restaurant.* This old sailors' lodging has pleasant rooms dressed in soothing browns and reds with crisp linen and brass chandeliers. Rustic dark wood beams and curtain give the dining room a rustic country flair.

Romantik Hotel Zum Ritter St. Georg – *Hauptstraße 178. ℰ(06221) 13 50. www.ritter-heidelberg.de. 39 rooms. ⬜11€. Restaurant.* Behind the sandstone façade of this 1592 Renaissance building, visitors are welcomed with tradition and history. For fine dining, visit the Restaurant Belier, for an elbows-on-the-table atmosphere the Ritterstube.

Arthotel – *Grabengasse 7. ℰ(06221) 65 00 60. www.arthotel.de. 24 rooms. Restaurant.* This beautifully restored design has an elegant atmosphere and a restaurant renowned for its top-notch cuisine. Unwinding spots include a cocktail lounge and a sunny arched courtyard.

🍽 EAT

Kulturbrauerei Heidelberg – *Leyergasse 6 (between Hauptstraße and Am Hachteufel). ℰ(06221) 50 29 80. www.heidelberger-kulturbrauerei.de.* Though updated, this restaurant exudes old-style charm with coffered ceilings and cast-iron chandeliers. Beer brewed on-site goes down well with the regional specialities. Rooms in the adjacent hotel are spacious and luxurious.

Herrenmühle – *Hauptstraße 239. ℰ(06221) 60 29 09. www.zur-herrenmuehle.de. Reservation recommended.* This lovely spot gets rustic flair from its wooden furniture and beamed ceilings. Enjoy a glass or two of the excellent local wines inside or on the romantic terrace.

Schlossweinstube – *Schlosshof 1. ℰ(06221) 872 70 00. www.moevenpick.com. Closed 1–26 Jan and Mon.* With a to-die-for setting inside the world-famous Heidelberg Castle, this restaurants sprawls across several historic rooms. In summer, the terrace facing the courtyard is also a nice spot.

☕ TAKING A BREAK

Strohauer's Café Alt-Heidelberg – *Hauptstraße 49. ℰ(06221) 18 90 24. www.strohauer.de.* An unhurried ambience envelops this traditional café with its several-metre-long counter of homemade cakes and pastries, complemented by seasonal snacks.

🎭 NIGHTLIFE

Zum Roten Ochsen – *Hauptstraße 217. ℰ(06221) 209 77. www.roterochsen.de. Closed Sun, public holidays and 3 weeks after Christmas.* Once frequented by Bismarck, Mark Twain and John Wayne, this student pub offers rib-sticking German fare served on tables carved with autographs. After 8pm, it becomes a piano-bar and a pleasant place to enjoy a beer or glass of wine.

Pfalz★

The Palatinate is a lovely patchwork of forests (Pfälzer Wald), vineyards, hills crowned with castles and small towns where time seems to move a little slower. The German Wine Route runs through this region, which is blessed with a mild climate that even permits the growth of figs, lemons and exotic fruit.

A BIT OF HISTORY

The wines of the Palatinate – Germany's largest wine-growing region produces almost one-third of the country's total output. The most famous vintages come from the villages of Bad Dürkheim, Deidesheim and Wachenheim.

DRIVING TOUR

FROM WORMS TO BAD BERGZABERN

151km/91mi – Allow one day.

This route runs partly along the German Wine Route (Deutsche Weinstrasse), which connects Schweigen at the French border with Bockenheim.

Worms★

20km/13mi north of Manheim. Neumarkt 14, 67547 Worms. ℘(06241) 250 45. www.worms.de.
Worms is one of Germany's oldest cities and, along with Speyer and Mainz, was an Imperial residence on the banks of the Rhine. Its history is closely associated with the 5C kingdom of the Burgundians whose fate was immortalised in the 12C Nibelungenlied epic (♦see INTRODUCTION: Literature). Surrounded by vineyards, Worms makes a fantastic base for exploring the region.

Dom St. Peter★★ (Cathedral)

◐Open Apr–Oct 9am–6pm; Nov–Mar 10am–5pm. ℘(062 41) 61 15. www.wormser-dom.de.
Worms Cathedral, completed in 1181, is one of the finest Romanesque edifices in Germany. Entering through the

Info: Hetzelplatz 1, 67433 Neustadt an der Weinstraße. ℘(06321) 926 80. www.neustadt.eu, www.deutsche-weinstrasse.de.

Location: The Palatinate Mountains stretch from the Rhine plains to the Vosges. The main access route is the A65 autobahn from Mannheim or Karlsruhe. The German Wine Route starts 15km/9.3mi to the west of Worms (♦see German Wine Route).

Timing: Allow at least one day for the suggested Driving Tour.

south portal, you see a splendid Christ in Judgement statue from the 12C. In the older east chancel note the Baroque **high altar★** by Balthasar Neumann. The elegant west chancel sports rose windows, a chequered frieze and arched blind arcades. The five **Gothic relief sculptures★** in the north aisle represent the Annunciation, the Nativity, the Entombment, the Resurrection and the Tree of Jesse.

Lutherdenkmal (Luther Monument)

Unveiled in 1868, this monument shows Luther before the Diet of Worms surrounded by early Reformers, such John Wycliffe, Jan Hus and Savonarola, as well as Reformist theologians including Melanchthon and Reuchlin.

Museum Heylshof★

Stephansgasse 9. ◐Open May–Sept, Tue–Sun 11am–5pm; Oct–Apr, Sun 11am–5pm and Mon 2–5pm. ⊚3.50€. ℘(06241) 220 00. www.museum-heylshof.de.
This Gründerzeit mansion showcases an important collection of 15C–19C **paintings★**, including works by Rubens, Van Loo and Tintoretto, alongside precious ceramics, glassware and porcelain.

Jewish Sites

Worms was one of Germany's great centres of Jewish culture and is home to Europe's oldest Jewish **cemetery** *(◷open 9am–dusk, July–Aug until 8pm)*, in use since the 11C. The old **synagogue** *(Judengasse; ◷open Apr–Oct, 10am–12.30pm, 1.30pm–5pm; Nov–Mar 10am–noon and 2–4pm)* dates to the same period but was destroyed in World War II and rebuilt in 1961. Steps lead down to the **Mikwe** (bathhouse), while behind the synagogue, the modern Raschi-Haus houses a **Jewish Museum** *(Hintere Judengasse 6; ◷open Nov–Mar, Tue–Sun 10am–12.30am, 1.30pm–4.30pm (Apr–Oct 5pm); ⊜1.50€; ℘(06241) 853 47 01)* which traces Jewish life in the Rhineland.

Museum der Stadt (City Museum)

Weckerlingplatz 7. ◷Open Tue–Sun, 10am–5pm. ◷Closed Jan 1, Good Fri, May 1, Dec 24–26 & 31. ⊜2€. ℘(06241) 94 63 90.

Five thousand years of artefacts are displayed in this former Romanesque monastery. The Ancient Roman section boasts one of Germany's largest collections of glassware from this period.

Nibelungen Museum★★

Fischerpförtchen 10. ◷Open year-round, Tue–Fri 10am–5pm, Sat–Sun to 6pm. ⊜5.50€. ℘(06241) 20 21 20.

This modern multimedia exhibit brings to life the epic Nibelungen legend in two medieval towers and along a section of the old town wall.

▷ *South of Worms, the Rhine plain becomes progressively devoted to viticulture.*

Freinsheim

This large wine town is still encircled by its medieval ramparts. The Baroque town hall, beside a 15C church, has an overhanging roof that protects an outside staircase.

Bad Dürkheim

Sheltered by the Pfälzer Wald, this spa town has thermal springs and enjoys a mild climate in which fig, almond and

---

RhineMain-Danube Canal

Ever since Roman times, emperors, kings, engineers and visionaries have dreamed of linking the Rhine and Danube rivers. Charlemagne took a first stab at this great enterprise, called Charlemagne's Ditch (Fossa Carolina). Bavaria's Ludwig I made another attempt 1 000 years later with the building of the Ludwig Canal. But it would not be until the late 20C that the amazing feat of engineering would finally be completed. In 1992, the inauguration of the 177km/110mi Rhine-Main-Danube Canal created the final link between the North Sea and the Black Sea.

chestnut trees thrive. A couple of miles west *(via Schillerstraße and Luitpoldweg)* is the ruined **Limburg abbey**.

Deidesheim

This is one of the most prosperous and prettiest towns on the German Wine Route with its half-timbered houses, a wine museum and numerous galleries.

Neustadt an der Weinstraße

The commercial hub of the German Wine Route, Neustadt has a pretty **old town**★ that boasts the largest number of historic houses in the region. Its narrow, picturesque lanes surround a pretty market with an 18C town hall.

Hambacher Schloss

◆◆Guided tours (45min) Apr–Oct, daily 11am, noon, 2pm, 3pm and 4pm; Nov–Mar daily 11am, noon, 2pm. ⊜8€. ℘(06321) 92 62 90. www.hambacher-schloss.de.

Founded by the Salian Franks in the 11C, the castle is considered to be "the cradle of German democracy". In 1832, some 30 000 freedom-loving citizens from all parts of Germany demonstrated here for the freedom and unity of Germany. This was when the black, red and gold flag, which was adopted as the German national emblem in 1919 and again in

1949, was first raised. An exhibit commemorates the event.

Kalmit
8km/5mi.
The Kalmit (673m/2208ft) is the highest outcrop in the Rhineland-Palatinate. From the Kalmithaus terrace, there is a **view**★★ of the Rhine plain and Speyer Cathedral. Return to the Wine Route via charming **St. Martin**★.

Schloss-Villa Ludwigshöhe★
Villastraße, 2km/1.2mi from Edenkoben. Historic rooms: ☜visit by guided tour, Apr–Sept, Tue–Sun 9am–5pm; Oct–Nov and Jan–Mar, 9am–4pm. ⊜4€. Max-Slevogt-Galerie: ◷Apr–Sept, 9am–6pm, Oct–Mar 9am–5pm. ⊜2.60€. ℘(06323) 930 16. www.max-slevogt-galerie.de.
Built by Ludwig I of Bavaria, this stately Italianate villa houses a **gallery**★ devoted to the German Impressionist painter Max Slevogt (1868–1932). The apartments are also open to the public. A chairlift goes up to the Rietburg (550m/1804ft), departure point for forest walks.

Trifels★
7km/4.3mi from Annweiler. ◷Open Apr–Sept, daily 9am–6pm; Oct–Mar 9am–5pm. ⊜3€. ℘(06346) 84 70. www.burgen-rlp.de.

Once a Hohenstaufen stronghold, the castle held the crown jewels in the 12C and 13C but is really best known as the place where **Richard the Lionheart** was imprisoned on returning from a crusade in 1193. He was eventually ransomed and returned to England in 1194.

Dahner Felsenland★★
The resort of **Dahn** is surrounded by great hiking terrain through soft mountains and red sandstone outcroppings. The **castle ruins**★ of Altdahn dominate the town. Staircases and guard rooms hewn into the rocks add to the charm of the castle with origins in 1100.

Burg Berwartstein★
Turn off toward Erlenbach (B427). ◷Open Mar–Oct, daily 9am–6pm; Nov–Feb, Sat–Sun, 1pm–6pm. ⊜5€. ℘(06398) 210. www.burgberwartstein.de.
This former robber baron's lair sits 100m/328ft above the village of Erlenbach. Much of the castle is open to the public, including subterranean passages.

Bad Bergzabern★
This charming health resort brims with half-timbered houses. The **Gasthaus zum Engel**★ (1579) is said to be the finest Renaissance building in the region.

ADDRESSES

⌂STAY

⊖⊜🛏 **Hotel Zum Lam** – *Winzergasse 37, Gleiszellen, 5km/3mi north of Bad Bergzabern. ℘(06343) 93 92 12. www.zum-lam.de. 11 rooms. Jan 2–23. ⊠. Restaurant ⊖⊜🛏.* This 18C half-timbered house has a pleasant garden terrace and rooms with all the mod cons.

⊖⊜🛏🛏 **Hotel Deidesheimer Hof** – *Am Marktplatz 1, Deidesheim. ℘(06326) 968 70. www.deidesheimerhof.de. Closed Jan 1–3. 28 rooms. ⊠16€.* This elegant inn has tastefully furnished rooms and a gourmet restaurant serving upmarket regional specialities.

♈/EAT

⊖⊜ **Weinstube Ester** – *Triftweg 21, 67098 Bad Dürkheim. ℘(06322) 98 90 65. www.ester24.de. Closed Mon and Tue.* Many regulars come to this typical Palatinate tavern. Regional dishes, mostly meat and sausage specialities, are on the menu and are a perfect fit with the delicious local wines.

⊖⊜🛏 **Reuters Holzappel** – *Hauptstraße 11, 76889 Bad Bergzabern. ℘(06343) 42 45. www.reuters-holzappel.de. Closed 2 weeks in Sept, Mon and Tue.* This traditional wine cellar occupies a 250-year-old farmhouse with courtyard. Wooden furniture and plenty of trinkets give it a cosy ambience.

Speyer★

The old imperial city of Speyer lies in the Rhine plain and started out around 10 BC as a Roman camp, gaining in importance during the Middle Ages. Its main sight is the magnificent Romanesque cathedral, one of the largest in Europe and burial site of several Holy Roman Emperors.

A BIT OF HISTORY

Imperial city – An episcopal seat since the 4C, Speyer gained in importance from the 11C onwards under the Salian emperors. It was made an Imperial city in 1294 and hosted more than 50 Imperial diets (parliament sessions) until 1570. The city was razed in 1689 by French troops. As a result, the only remaining evidence of Speyer's medieval splendour is the Kaiserdom, fragments of the town wall and the Altpörtel, a former city gate.

KAISERDOM★★

◎ Open Apr–Oct, daily 9am–7pm; Nov–Mar, 9am–5pm. ♿ ℘(06232) 10 21 18. www.dom-speyer.de.
Founded by Konrad II in 1030 and remodelled at the end of the 11C, Speyer's Kaiserdom is the largest Romanesque building in Europe and has been a UNESCO World Heritage Site since 1981.

▶ **Population:** 50 000
🛈 **Info:** Maximilianstraße 13, 67346 Speyer. ℘(06232) 14 23 92. www.speyer.de.
◐ **Location:** South of Heidelberg, Speyer is located between the wooded mountains of the Odenwald and those of the Pfalz.
🅿 **Parking:** Garages are located throughout Speyer. The main train station has a garage convenient for travellers.
◉ **Don't Miss:** The Kaiserdom or the excellent Palatinate Museum.
◕ **Timing:** Allow at least half a day to see the main sights.
👪 **Kids:** Sea Life.

The **interior**★★ is a masterpiece of unity and balance. The **Chapel of the Holy Sacrament** (Afrakapelle, on the left, before the north transept) houses two 15C low-relief sculptures, the Bearing of the Cross and the Annunciation. The two-tier central rotunda contains the **baptistry** (Chapel of St. Emmeram) and, above, a chapel dedicated to St. Catherine.

Kaiserdom

© fab400/Fotolia.com

The Kaiserdom's **crypt**★★ is the finest and largest Romanesque crypt in Germany. Groined vaulting features transverse arches of alternate pink and white sandstone. Four Holy Roman Emperors and four German kings, along with some of their wives, are buried in the **Royal Vault**.

In the gardens south of the cathedral is the 16C **Ölberg**, once the centre of the cloister. A large stone trough, the **Domnapf**, stands in the forecourt. In former times, each time a bishop was installed, it was filled with wine and anyone who wished to do so could drink until he dropped.

SIGHTS
Maximilianstraße

Speyer's main historic thoroughfare runs west from the cathedral to the 12C–13C **Altpörtel**★, a gateway tower. The lively street is lined by ornate Baroque buildings, most notably the **Rathaus** (town hall) and the "Alte Münze" (old mint).

Judenhof
(Jewish Courtyard)

South of the town hall, the Judenhof is at the centre of the medieval Jewish quarter. Remains of the 12C synagogue and a ritual bath (Mikwe) are reminders of this once-vibrant community.

Historisches Museum
der Pfalz★
(Palatinate Museum)

Domplatz. ⏱*Open year-round, Tue–Sun 10am–6pm.* ⏱*Closed Jan 1, Dec 24 & 31.* ☞*4€, more for special exhibitions.* ♿ *℘(06232) 62 02 22. www.museum. speyer.de.*

This excellent museum is filled with treasures that illustrate the region's often-tumultuous history. The rarest and most precious item on view is the gold-plated, cone-shaped **Golden Hat of Schifferstadt**★★ from the 12C BC. In the basement, the **Cathedral Treasury** (Domschatzkammer) houses tomb furnishings of the emperors, notably the funerary crown of Konrad II, the first Salian emperor. Also note the Imperial orb of Heinrich III and the crown worn by Heinrich IV during his penance walk to Canossa. In the cellar, the **Wine Museum** (Weinmuseum) presents 2 000 years of wine history, including a bottle of **Roman wine**★ from the 3C AD, the world's oldest wine in a liquid state.

Technik Museum Speyer★
(Museum of Technology)

Am Technik Museum. ⏱*Open year-round, Mon–Fri 9am–6pm, Sat–Sun 9am–7pm Sat–Sun.* ☞*16€.* ♿ *℘(06232) 670 80. http://speyer. technik-museum.de.* Planes, trains and automobiles make up the bulk of the exhibit at this engaging museum. Highlights include a tour of a U-9 submarine from World War I, the maritime displays and the musical instruments.

🧒👤 Sea Life★

⏱*Open Apr–Oct, Mon–Fri 10am–5pm, Sat–Sun 10am–8pm.* ☞*12.75€.* *℘(062 32) 697 80. www.sealifeeurope.com.* Kids especially love this walk-through aquarium where they get acquainted with marine denizens from the Arctic to the tropical seas.

ADDRESSES

🏠**STAY**

🛏🛏🛏 **Hotel Goldener Engel** – *Mühlturmstraße 5.* *℘(06232) 13260. www.goldener-engel-speyer.de. Closed Dec 23–Jan 7. 46 rooms.* 🚇. This hotel in the centre of town features individually decorated rooms ranging from rustic to modern in style.

♟/**EAT**

🍶🍶🍶 **Kutscherhaus** – *Am Fischmarkt 5a.* *℘(06232) 705 92. www.kutscherhaus-speyer.de. Closed 3 weeks in Aug.* Behind the half-timbered façade of this old house, meals are enjoyed in comfortably furnished dining rooms. The *Biergarten* is one of the most charming in town.

Saarbrücken★

Although pummelled by bombs during World War II, the capital of the Saarland has developed into a regional metropolis infused with subtle French flair, a host of museums and a large number of beautifully restored Baroque buildings by master architect Friedrich Joachim Stengel.

OLD TOWN

Schloss (Palace)

The medieval fortress was replaced in the 17C by a Renaissance castle, which in turn was demolished in 1738 to make way for a Baroque palace designed by Stengel. Since then, the palace has suffered various forms of destruction, including war and fire, but was completely renovated in 1989 by Gottfried Böhm. It now has a modern look and is used by the city administration and as a cultural venue.

The **Historisches Museum Saar** (� year-round, Tue–Sun 10am–6pm (Thu 8pm); ∞5€; &; ℘(0681) 506 45 01; www. historisches-museum.org) adjoins the right wing of the castle. Its permanent exhibition deals with World War I and National Socialism in the Saar region.

Museum für Vor- und Frühgeschichte (Museum of Early and Prehistory)

Schlossplatz 16. ☉*Open year-round, Tue–Sun 10am–6pm (Wed to 10pm).* ☉*Closed Jan 1, Dec 24–25.* & ℘(0681) 95 40 50. www.vorgeschichte.de.

Housed in the neo-Baroque former parliament building, this museum imaginatively presents archaeological items from the beginning of the Stone Age to the early Middle Ages.

A highlight is the **Celtic princess's grave**★★ from Reinheim, which dates to 400 BC. The find is considered one of the most important in Central Europe from the early Celtic period. The princess' jewellery and tomb furnishings, including a gilded bronze jug, are wonderfully preserved.

▶ **Population:** 182 000

ℹ **Info:** Gerberstraße 4 (Rathaus-Carrée), 66111 Saarbrücken. ℘(0681) 93 80 90. www.die-region-saarbruecken.de.

▶ **Location:** Saarbrücken is in the Saar valley, on the French border and at the crossroads of the A6 autobahn to Mannheim and the A4 to Metz, France.

🅿 **Parking:** Garages in the Old City are at Tal- and Reepersbergstraßen and at Roon- and Stengelstraßen.

☺ **Don't Miss:** The Ludwigsplatz and its yellow and red Ludwigskirche.

🕐 **Timing:** Allow three to four hours for all the sights.

Museum in der Schlosskirche

Am Schlossberg 6.
☉*Open Tue–Sun 10am–6pm (Wed to 8pm).* ℘(0681) 954 05 18. www.saarlandmuseum.de.

The renovated palace-church now houses a museum of religious art from the 13C to the 19C. Also of note are the three Baroque tombs of the Saarbrücken princes and the colourful stained-glass windows by Georg Meistermann (1950s).

Ludwigsplatz★★

The square is bordered in the north, south and west by eight magnificent townhouses of various sizes. All with three storeys and mansard roofs, they illustrate the transition from the late Baroque to the Neoclassical style.

Their white and silver-grey colouring enhances the effect of the Ludwigskirche, built in yellow and red sandstone in the centre of the square. The governor of the Saarland has his offices in Ludwigsplatz.

Political Ping-Pong

Today, the Saarland is the smallest and least populous of the 16 German states (not counting the city states of Berlin, Hamburg and Bremen) but long stretches of its 20C history have actually been spent in a veritable tug-of-war over its borders with France. Rich in natural resources, coal in particular, the region fell under French control in the 1920s as part of the reparation payments negotiated at the Treaty of Versailles. However, when the statute ran out in 1935, more than 90 percent of the local population voted in favour of returning to German rule. A similar situation occurred after World War II until another referendum in 1956 once again unified the Saarland with Germany. To this day, though, the French influence is still strongly felt in the local dialect and in the high quality of the regional cuisine.

Ludwigskirche
(Church of St. Louis)

Open year-round, Tue–Sun 10am–5pm. Often closed on Sat afternoons for weddings. 1.50€. *(0681) 525 24. www.ludwigskirche.de.*

After a top-to-bottom restoration, this Baroque Protestant church – a Stengel masterpiece – once again radiates its former glory. The east end exhibits a degree of splendour unusual in a Protestant church, with statues of the Evangelists by Franziskus Bingh.

ADDITIONAL SIGHTS
St. Johanner Markt★

The old town around the market square is the true heart of Saarbrücken.

The focal point is the beautiful fountain (designed by Stengel), with its obelisk and cast-iron railing, built in 1759–60. Life pulses in the crooked, mostly car-free lanes and in the numerous pubs and bistros around here.

Basilika St. Johann★

Open year-round, Sun, Tue & Thu 8.30am–noon, 2–5pm; Fri 8.30am–noon. (0681) 329 64. www.basilika-saarbruecken.de.

This Stengel-designed church with its onion tower and lantern is another jewel of the late Baroque period.

Stadtgalerie
(City Gallery)

St. Johanner Markt 24. Open Tue–Sun 11am–7pm (Wed noon–8pm). (0681) 996 40.

This first-floor gallery displays contemporary and conceptual art, new media, installations, performances and video art. In summer, concerts and exhibitions take over the charming courtyard.

St. Johanner Markt

Kongress- und Touristik Service Region Saarbrücken GmbH

Saarland Museum – Alte Sammlung (Old Collection)

Karlstraße 1. ◷Open year-round, Tue–Sun 10am–6pm (Wed to 10pm).
&♿ ✆*(0681) 95 40 50.*
www.saarlandmuseum.de.
Completely overhauled and expanded, this museum now presents an extensive overview of artworks covering all periods from the Renaissance to the Baroque and into the 19C. Besides paintings, rooms are also filled with a wonderful collection of furniture (including a remarkable Renaissance cabinet from the Abbey of Limburg), sculpture, silver and ceramics.

Saarland Museum – Moderne Galerie (Modern Gallery)

Bismarckstraße 11–15, on the banks of the Saar. ◷Open year-round, Tue–Sun 10am–6pm (Wed to 10pm).
◷Closed Tue after Easter and Pentecost, Dec 24, 25 & 31. ⊚1.50€. ♿ ✆(0681) 996 40. www.saarlandmuseum.de.
The diversity of European art from the late 19C to the 21C is featured in this museum. The collection's particular strengths lie with **German Impressionism**★ (Liebermann, Slevogt, Corinth) and **Expressionism**★ (Kirchner, Jawlensky). Other major artists include Picasso, Léger, Tàpies and Beuys. The museum also owns the estate of the sculptor Alexander Archipenko.

Stiftskirche St. Arnual★ (Collegiate Church of St. Arnual)

In the St. Arnual suburb, via Talstraße and Saargemünder Straße.
Named after 7C bishop Arnual of Metz, this 13C–14C Gothic church was given a Baroque dome in 1746 based on plans by Stengel. As the burial place of the dukes of Nassau-Saarbrücken, the church houses 50 **tombs**★★ dating from the 13C to the 18C, some of them remarkably artistic.

EXCURSION
Völklinger Hütte★

▶ *10km/6.2mi west of Saarbrücken. Rathausstraße 75, Völklingen.*
◷*Open Apr–Oct, daily 10am–7pm; Nov–Mar, 10am–6pm. ◷Closed Dec 24–25 & 31. ⊚12€ (child 3€). ✆(06898) 910 01 00. www.voelklinger-huette.org.*
This iron- and steelworks was established in 1873 and at its peak employed 16 000 people. It remained in operation until 1986 and, in 1994, became the first industrial monument to be included on UNESCO's list of World Heritage Sites. Today it is essentially a giant adventure playground where guides take you on a tour through the labyrinths of blast furnaces and air heaters, coking gas pipes and suspended railways. You can climb to the top of the 30m/98ft-high charging platform where the blast furnace was once fed with coke and ore. High-calibre special exhibitions take place in the blast furnace house, while kids gravitate towards the interactive **Ferrodrom** where exhibits demystify scientific principles.

ADDRESSES

🛏 STAY

⊜⊜ **Hotel Schlosskrug** – *Schmollerstraße 14. ✆(0681) 367 35. www.hotel-schlosskrug.de. Closed Dec 24–early Jan. 20 rooms. Restaurant ⊜⊜.* This traditional, family-run guesthouse in an old townhouse has functional rooms, some with their own bath, as well as larger family rooms with several beds. The restaurant is a good place to try regional home-cooking paired with freshly poured Pilsner.

🍴 EAT

⊜⊜⊜ **Weismüller** – *Gersweiler Straße 43a. ✆(0681) 521 53. www.weissmueller-restaurant-quack.de. Closed Sat lunch, Sun dinner and Mon. Reservation recommended.* This 19C villa delivers modern fine dining on the 1st floor, more casual international fare in the downstairs brasserie and a bar in the basement. In summer, sit on the terrace beneath a canopy of old trees.

THE SOUTHWEST

Germany's southwest covers the *Land* (state) of Baden-Württemberg and embraces one of Europe's top-ranked holiday regions, the Black Forest. Its romantic valleys, fir-clad highlands, crystal-clear lakes and rushing waterfalls weave a magical alchemy of natural beauty. This is great hiking and cycling terrain, of course, punctuated by half-timbered villages, traditional farmhouses and vibrant towns like Baden-Baden and Freiburg. East of here, Lake Constance beckons with a storybook setting characterised by expansive views, a warm climate and stunningly elaborate Baroque churches. Stuttgart, the state capital, exudes cosmopolitan flair and is also the gateway to the thinly populated Swabian Jura region traversed by the Neckar River.

Highlights

1. The narrow medieval streets of **Schiltach** (p343)
2. The stunning view from **Mount Belchen** (p346)
3. A dip in the warm waters of **Baden-Baden** (p354)
4. Glamorous exhibits at the car museums in **Stuttgart** (p386)
5. Celestial architecture along the **Upper Swabian Baroque Road** (p400)

The Black Forest

The Black Forest stretches north–south for about 200km/124mi from Baden-Baden to the Swiss border and east–west for 60km/37mi from France to the Swabian Alps. It is divided into three distinct areas.

In the northern Black Forest streams have carved deep valleys between fir- and pine-studded plateaus. There are plenty of natural mineral springs here, whose healing properties have been cherished since Roman times. Today, the area boasts Germany's highest concentration of spas, health resorts and hotels with beauty and fitness facilities.

The central Black Forest is classic cuckoo-clock country. Don't miss the world's biggest "cuckoo-clocks" in Triberg and Schonach or the German Clock Museum in Furtwangen. Schiltach is a symphony in half-timber, while Gutach has the impressive Vogtbauernhof Open-air Museum, where historic regional houses and farm buildings have been assembled in a mock village. Germany's biggest theme park, Europa-Park Rust, is west of here near the French border.

The gateway to the southern Black Forest is Freiburg, a lively university town with a fantastic brick minster. Be sure to

Half-timbered houses, Schiltach

© Mauritius/Photononstop

Black Forest Treats

The Baden Wine Route cuts through the sun-kissed foothills of the entire Black Forest, with each area specialising in different varietals. Ortenau is famous for its Riesling; the Markgräflerland cultivates mostly Gutedel, while in Breisgau and the Kaiserstuhl the focus is on Grauburgunder (pinot gris) and pinot blanc (Weißburgunder).

Famous throughout the world is the Black Forest ham, which is still smoked in traditional farmhouses and eaten with bread, often as part of a light supper. The region is also home to Germany's most famous cake, the Schwarzwälder Kirschtorte (Black Forest gateau). This waist-expander is a three-layered chocolate sponge cake filled with cream and morello cherries marinated in *kirsch* (cherry) schnapps. With over 14 000, the Black Forest has the world's highest density of distilleries. Aside from cherries, all sorts of other fruit, including pears and plums, are turned into this potent liquor.

drive up Schauinsland (1 284m/4 212ft) for knockout views of the Rhine Valley, the Vosges and the Alps. Further south, the peaks gets higher, culminating in the Feldberg at 1 493m/4 899ft.

Lake Constance

Aside from its size, one of the most remarkable aspects of Lake Constance is its stunning Alpine backdrop. The B31 skirts the northern shore, meandering past orchards, vineyards, golden fields and stunning Baroque churches such as the one in Birnau. Admire the bonanza of plants and flowers on the garden island of Mainau, then hop over to Reichenau Island for an immersion in the early Middle Ages at the 9C UNESCO-protected abbey. Other stops include Friedrichshafen, famous as the birthplace of the Zeppelin airship, and romantic Lindau with its picture-perfect old town.

The Cities

The area described in this chapter is largely rural, but there are four larger cities worth a closer look. The state capital Stuttgart is often undeservedly perceived as all buttoned-up business. Its true that Bosch, Daimler and Porsche all have headquarters here, but Stuttgart also boasts a lively cultural landscape with world-class opera and ballet and a hot hip-hop scene. The locals truly let their hair down during the Cannstatter Volksfest, a festival often compared to Oktoberfest in Munich.

West of Stuttgart, Karlsruhe on the Rhine has a unique fan-shaped city layout and also scores points with its outstanding art museums and a renowned Centre for Art and Media.

Baden-Baden is the northern gateway to the Black Forest and has been one of the most elegant spa resorts since the 19C when the famous, royal and wealthy started to arrive to cure their ailments in the town's warm mineral springs.

In the south, Freiburg is one of Germany's most charming towns. Surrounded by tree-covered mountains, anchored by a medieval centre with its famous minster, and enlivened by 20 000 students, it is a great launch pad for explorations into the southern and central Black Forest.

Tower of Münster, Freiburg im Breisgau

S. Ollivier/MICHELIN

THE SOUTHWEST

0   30 km

EUROPA-PARK	★★★ Highly recommended
Stuttgart	★★ Recommended
Karlsruhe	★ Interesting
Offenburg	Driving Tour showing point of departure

NUREMBERG

BAVARIA

FULDA

Wurtzburg

Romantic

Road

ROTHENBURG

BADEN-WÜRTEMBERG

Großcomburg

Schwäbisch Hall

Kirchheim unter Teck

Stuttgart

Reussenstein Castle

HESSE

Neckar Valley

Hornberg

Guttenberg

Hirschhorn

Neckarsteinach

Dilsberg

Bad Wimpfen

Heilbronn

Maulbronn

Solitude

Bebenhausen

HEIDELBERG

Bruchsal

Karlsruhe

Spire

RHINELAND-PALATINATE

Favorite

Merkur 668

Yburg

Mummelsee

500

Rastatt

Baden-Baden

Alt-Windeck Castle

Saßbachwalden

Dahner Felsenland

FRANCE

SARREBRUCK

METZ

FRANKFURT AM MAIN

Main

Altmühl

Black Forest★★★
Schwarzwald

Although it gets its name from its thick pine forests, the Schwarzwald is actually a delightful pastiche of lakes, pastures, mountains and vineyards. Add to that picturesque villages, ubiquitous cuckoo clocks, excellent food and an abundance of year-round outdoor pursuits and it is easy to see why this mountainous region has long been ranked at the top of Germany's most popular tourist destinations.

A BIT OF HISTORY

Twin sister of the Vosges – The Vosges and the Black Forest ranges both rise from a crystalline base to similar altitudes (the Feldberg at 1 493m/4 899ft and the Grand Ballon at 1 424m/4 672ft). Both drop steeply in the direction of the Rhine, and less abruptly to the Swabian plateau and to Lorraine, respectively.

Varied resources – The region's economy has always been linked to the forest, wood being practically the only construction material in the Middle Ages and the base of all crafts. Trees as long as 50m/164ft were floated along the Rhine all the way to the Netherlands for use by boat-builders. Clock-making, including the famous cuckoo clock, remains a fruitful activity, although today much of the local economy is driven by tourism.

🚗 DRIVING TOURS

1 BLACK FOREST CREST ROAD★★★ (Schwarzwald-Hochstraße)

From Baden-Baden to Freudenstadt. 80km/49.7mi – Allow 4hrs.

Much of the Black Forest Crest Road runs at an elevation approaching 1 000m/3 280ft, skirting villages and ski slopes.

ℹ Info: Ludwigstraße 23, 79104 Freiburg. 📞(0761) 89 64 60. www.blackforest-tourism.com.

Location: In the southwest corner of Germany, the Black Forest stretches for 170km/105.6mi from Karlsruhe to Basel. It is accessible from Stuttgart via the A81, and from Strasbourg or Freiburg via the A5.

Don't Miss: A drive along the Crest Road, driving tour 1 below.

Timing: Allow four hours to travel the Crest Road, driving tour 1, one day each for driving tours 2 and 3.

Kids: Outdoor pursuits throughout the Schwarzwald.

Baden-Baden★★
See BADEN-BADEN.

▷ *Follow signs "Schwarzwald-Hochstraße/B500".*

The road cuts through the Baden wine country and gradually climbs to quiet spa resorts such as Bühlerhöhe.

Mummelsee

This small, dark glacial lake at the foot of the **Hornisgrinde** (1 164m/3 819ft), the highest point of the northern Black Forest, is named after the *"Mümmeln"* (water sprites) that inhabit its icy depths, according to local legend. In former times, Black Forest breweries obtained blocks of ice chopped out of the frozen lake until well into spring.

▷ *At Ruhestein, leave the Hochstraße temporarily for a detour down to the* **Allerheiligen Valley★**, *then climb back from Oppenau to Zuflucht via an extremely steep mountain road.*

Allerheiligen★

The ruins of a 13C church still stand, along with a Gothic chapel. A 1.5km/1mi trail leads from the abbey ruins to the **Allerheiligen-Wasserfälle★**, a celebrated series of seven waterfalls with a total drop of 90m/295ft. Allow about 45 minutes for the round-trip walk.

▶ *Continue along the Hochstraße towards Freudenstadt.*

Freudenstadt★

At the crossing of several tourist routes, this 17C town was destroyed by fire in 1945. It now follows a chessboard plan centred on the **Marktplatz★**, a huge square surrounded by Italianate arcaded buildings. The two naves of the 17C **Stadtkirche** (parish church), built at right angles, form one corner of Marktplatz. Inside, note the carved and painted 12C Romanesque **lectern★★** supported by the Four Apostles. A further treasure is the 12C **baptismal font★** with intricate animal decorations.

2 CENTRAL BLACK FOREST★★

From Freudenstadt to Freiburg.
152km/94.4mi – Allow one day.

The itinerary meanders through the Kinzig and Elz valleys, passing through bustling tourist villages before reaching the Upper Black Forest at Freiburg.

▶ *Drive about 18km/11mi south of Freudenstadt.*

Alpirsbach★

Alpirsbach is worth a stop for its 11C red sandstone **Kloster Alpirsbach★** (▶*open mid-Mar–Oct, Mon–Sat 10am–5.30pm, Sun 11am–5.30pm, Nov–mid-Mar, Thu, Sat–Sun 1pm–3pm; ∞4€; ℘(07444) 510 61; www.schloesser-und-gaerten.de*), a former Benedictine abbey and the oldest Romanesque structure in the Black Forest.

Inside the church note especially the painted apse, the ornate pillars, the Romanesque choir and the late-Gothic high altar. The attached museum showcases 16C objects from daily life at the monastery, unearthed during excavations in 1958.

Schiltach★★

This postcard-pretty town gets its idyllic character from its beautifully restored half-timbered houses and its scenic location at the confluence of the Schiltach and Kinzig rivers.

Schwarzwälder Freilichtmuseum Vogtsbauernhof★★ (Black Forest Open-air Museum)

In Gutach. ▶Open Apr–Oct, daily 9am–6pm (Aug 7pm). ∞6.50€. ℘(07831) 935 60. www.vogtsbauernhof.org.

Landscape of Hochschwarzwald near Bernau

© Brigitte Merz/Look/Photononstop

Of Clocks and Trains

For a unique travel experience, travel the **German Clock Road** (*Deutsche Uhrenstraße*), covering about 320km/198.8mi and taking in various cuckoo-clock sites: museums, factory tours and remarkable clocks (details available from information offices in the region). For railway fans, the **Black Forest Train** (*Schwarzwaldbahn*) negotiates a 670m/2 198ft elevation change following the landscape on a route that avoids bridges. Despite the 39 tunnels required to manage the largest natural obstacles, the journey encompasses magnificent scenery; the most interesting section (27km/16.7mi) is between Hornberg and St. Georgen.

Black Forest construction, craftwork, culture and agriculture are imaginatively presented in this open-air museum in the Gutach Valley. The museum's namesake, the 1612 Vogtsbauern farm, is set amid other farmhouses along with such outbuildings as a bakery, a smithy, a chapel and a granary. All buildings were moved and re-assembled here from throughout the region.

> Continue towards Triberg, enjoying fine **views**★ from the Landwassereck pass. Upstream from Oberprechtal, the beautiful cascades of the Elz parallel the route.

Triberg★

The romantic (if busy) **Waterfall Walk**★ (1hr round trip; ⚭3€) follows the Gutach as it cascades over boulders and past tree-lined mossy banks. Back in town, **Maria der Tannen (Our Lady of the Firs)**★ is one of the most popular pilgrimage churches in the Black Forest. The **Schwarzwald Museum** (Wallfahrtstraße 4; ⚬open May–Sept, daily 10am–6pm, Oct–Apr 10am–5pm, ⚬closed Mon Nov–Easter, Dec 24–25; ⚭5€; ℘(07722) 44 34; www.schwarzwaldmuseum.com) exhibits traditional costumes and local craftwork, including one of Europe's largest collections of barrel-organs. Another attraction is the **World's Biggest Cuckoo Clock** (Schonachbach 27; ⚬open Easter–Oct, Mon–Sat 9am–6pm, Sun 10am–6pm; Nov–Easter, Mon–Sat 9am–5.30pm, Sun 11am–5pm; ⚭2.50€; ℘(07722) 962 20; www.uhren-park.de) which contains a clock shop and is even listed in the Guinness Book of Records. Its claim, however, is disputed

by the world's "other" biggest cuckoo clock about 1km/0.6mi further along in Schonach.

Furtwangen

The **Deutsches Uhrenmuseum** (Robert-Gerwig-Platz 1; ⚬open Apr–Oct, daily 9am–6pm; Nov–Mar, 10am–5pm; ⚭4€; &; ℘(07723) 920 28 00; www.deutsches-uhrenmuseum.de) displays the world's largest collection of Black Forest clocks and explains the ingenuity that artisans brought to the simple telling of time. From here you can visit **Bregquelle** (the source of the Breg), a small stream that eventually feeds into the Danube.

> Soon after leaving Furtwangen, turn right for Hexenloch, a deep wooded gorge enlivened by waterfalls. Between St. Märgen and St. Peter, the twisting road treats you to plenty of fine **views**★★.

St. Peter★

Two onion-domed towers top the splendid Rococo **church**★ of this 18C former Benedictine abbey.
Johann Anton Feuchtmayer carved the marvellous statues representing the Dukes of Zähringen who founded Freiburg. Several hiking trails leave from the car park.

Kandel★

From the viewpoint (30min round-trip walk) is a beautiful **panorama**★ of the Vosges, Feldberg and Belchen.

Waldkirch★

Clustered around the collegiate church of St. Marguerite are pretty 18C houses.

KARLSRUHE

51

FRANCE

★★ BADEN-BADEN ◉

1

Badisches Rebland

500

462

A4

A35

RHIN

A5

1

△ *Hornisgrinde 1164*

▲

Mummelsee

STRASBOURG

Murg

4

28

54

Rench

Ruhestein

Allerheiligen ★

★ *Wasserfälle*

Zuflucht

28

2

Freudenstadt ★

55

Offenburg

Kinzig

Kniebis

28

A5

Wolfach

★ Alpirsbach ✦

2

Kinzig

294

Schiltach ★★

★★ Black Forest Open
Air Museum

▲

Gutach

Landwassereck

Elz

294

Gutach

Triberg ★

▲

500

35

Wasserfall ★

★ Waldkirch †

Bregquelle

▲

Schwenningen

✴ *Kandel* ★
1242

Furtwangen

Villingen

62

Breg

CONSTANCE

31

St Peter ★

Höllental ★

Hexenloch

800

Brigach

3

★★ FREIBURG IM
BREISGAU

Hirschsprung

▲

Donaueschingen

★ *Schauinsland* ✴ *1284*

Titisee

Neustadt

★ Hinterzarten

Titisee ★★

★★ *Feldberg* ✴ *1493*

500

★ *Todnau Falls*

500

Lenzkirch

31

317

1414 ✴

Todtnau

3

N

★★★ *BELCHEN*

Schluchsee

Schluchsee ★

BLACK FOREST

0   20 km

BÂLE   BAD SÄCKINGEN   WALDSHUT

Todtnau Falls

© Christoph Hähnel/Fotolia.com

The **interior**★ of the church has pre-served its original furniture and fittings.

Freiburg★★ – ᕱ *See FREIBURG.*

③ UPPER BLACK FOREST★★★ (Hochschwarzwald)

Round-trip leaving from Freiburg im Breisgau. 142km/88mi – Allow one day.
ᕱ *See maps pp340, 341 and 345.*

This circuit skirts the three main peaks of the Black Forest (Schauinsland, Belchen and Feldberg) and also takes in its two best-known lakes (Schluchsee and Titisee).

Schauinsland★

🚶 An extremely twisty mountain road leads to the upper cable-car station. From the parking lot, follow the signs "Rundweg" and "Schauinsland Gipfel" to the viewing tower *(91 steps)*, which offers a **view**★ across upland meadows to the **Feldberg**★★ *(30min round-trip walk).*

▶ *Follow the road for 1km/0.6mi and take the right fork towards Stohren and the Münstertal. Meandering through meadows, the route finally plunges once more into the forest. At Wiedener Eck, turn right towards the Belchen.*

Mount Belchen★★★

🚶 *30min round-trip walk to the observation platform from the car park.*

Dominating the Wiesenthal, the Belchen rises to a height of 1 414m/4 637ft. When the skies are clear, **views**★★★ extend all across the Rhine plain, the High Vosges and the Alps.

Todtnau Falls★

🚶 *1.5km/1mi from Todtnau,
1hr round-trip walk.*
Climbing through a wooded combe, a trail leads to an impressive series of cas-cades plunging down 97m/318ft.

The Hochkopf Massif
Hochkopf

🚶 *1hr round-trip walk.*
From the parking lot, a trail leads to a look-out with **views**★★ of the barren peaks of the Belchen and the Feldberg and, on clear days, the Alps.

Bernau★

At Bernau-Innerlehen, the **town hall** *(Rathaus)* houses the **Hans-Thoma-Museum** with an exhibition of paintings by this local artist.

The road runs high above the Alb gorges, tunnelling through the cliffs on its way to the Rhine at Albbruck.

Bad Säckingen★

Waldshuter Straße 20, 79713 Bad Säckingen. ℘(07761) 568 30. www.bad-saeckingen.de.
The town sits on the southern edge of the Black Forest, across from the Swiss border. The warm springs at Bad Säckin-gen have cured weary bodies since the Middle Ages. Today the little spa is also known as "Trumpeter's Town" because of the 19C novel "The Trumpeter of Säckingen" by local lad Joseph Victor von Scheffel.

Fridolinsmünster★

Münsterplatz 8. �ᕱOpen year-round, daily 8am–8pm. ℘(07761) 568 190.
Named after St. Fridolin, the Irish mis-sionary who converted the Alemanni and founded a missionary cell here in 522, this twin-towered church dominates the skyline of Bad Säckingen. Although its crypt dates back to the Carolingian era,

the present building is a Gothic basilica built in the 14C and later embellished with Rococo features by JM Feuchtmayer. There is a statue of the saint above the porch alongside Count Ursi of Glarus, one of his converts. The saint's relics are kept in the Fridolinkapelle (chapel) on the right side of the choir in a superb 18C **silver shrine**★ made in Augsburg.

Gedeckte Brücke★ (Covered Bridge)
There has been a wooden bridge in this spot since the 13C, but its stone pillars were not erected until 1575. The bridge is 200m/656ft long, the longest of its kind in Europe, and spans the Rhine, leading to Stein in the Swiss *canton* of Aargau.

Schloss Schönau
The local palace harbours the unusual **Trompetenmuseum** *(Trumpet Museum;* 🕐*open year-round, Tue, Thu & Sun 2pm–5pm (May–Sept also Wed 2pm–5pm);* ✆*2€;* ✆*(07761) 22 17; www.trompeten-museum.de).* It boasts Europe's largest collection of these instruments, the oldest dating back to 1664. Also of interest is an original 1900 trumpet workshop brought here from the town of Oldenburg. From the corner of the park there is a good view of the covered bridge. The palace itself was built c. 1600 by the lords of Schönau and is surrounded by pleasant gardens. It also contains the local history collection, pre- and early history exhibits and several centuries' worth of Black Forest clocks.

Waldshut
Halfway up a wooded slope rising from the Rhine, this small town provided the sparkplug for the Black Forest peasant revolt of 1524. Today it retains two of its fortified 13C gateways: the Lower (or Basle) Gate to the west and the Upper (or Schaffhaus) Gate to the east.
The heart of the historic **old town**★ is **Kaiserstraße**, a street lined by houses with overhanging eaves. Buildings of note include the 18C late-Baroque **town hall;** the **"Wilder Mann"**, a 16C townhouse; and the 16C **"Alte Metzig"** (Butcher's Gateway), now home to the **local museum** *(Heimatmuseum)*.

St. Blasien★
Am Kurgarten, 79837 St. Blasien. ✆*(07672) 414 30. www.stblasien.de.*
The majestic domed church dedicated to St. Blaisen comes into view in the southern part of the Black Forest. It stands in the grounds of a medieval monastery founded in 835 by hermit monks.

Dom★★ (Cathedral)
Inspired by the Pantheon in Rome, French architect Pierre-Michel d'Ixnard pulled out all the stops in designing this early Neoclassical church. Completed in 1772, its central copper dome (33.5m/110ft in diameter) is the third largest in the world after those of St. Peter's in Rome and Les Invalides in Paris. Inside is a splendid Rococo high altar by Christian Wenzinger.

Schluchsee★
This glacial lake became the largest body of water in the Black Forest when it was dammed in 1932.

Feldberg★★
The **Feldbergbahn chairlift** *(*🕐*open Jul-Sept, daily 9am–5pm; May, Jun & Oct 9am–4.30pm;* ✆*8.70€ round trip)* conveys sightseers up the Black Forest's highest mountain, which is crowned by the Bismarck monument. Various 🚶**hiking trails** start near the top, taking in tremendous **views**★ as far as the Alps and down to the Feldsee, a small lake in the hollow of a glacial cirque. In winter, downhill and cross-country skiing are popular outdoor pursuits.

Titisee★★
This clear glacial lake sits at the junction of several tourist routes and is popular for swimming, boating and windsurfing. In winter, cross-country skiing is the main outdoor activity. By the way, the name may sound funny to English-speakers but is actually derived from Roman emperor Titus.
Returning to Frieburg, you travel through **Höllental**★ (Valley of Hell). The route at times is hemmed in by towering cliffs, particularly at **Hirschsprung** (deer's jump), its narrowest point.

ADDRESSES

🏠 STAY

Berggasthaus Gisiboden –
79674 Todtnau-Gschwend. ✆(07671)
99 98 21. www.gisiboden.de. 16 rooms.
Restaurant◠. If you don't mind simple
rooms and shared bathroom facilities,
you will definitely enjoy the peace and
quiet of this rustic mountain inn at an
altitude of 1 200m/3 937ft. It is an ideal
base for hiking and mountain-biking
excursions. The pleasant restaurant
serves rib-sticking regional fare.

Hotel Belchen-Multen –
79677 Schönau-Aitern-Multen.
✆(07673) 209.www.belchen-multen.
de. Closed mid-Nov–mid-Dec. 22 rooms.
Restaurant◠. This well-kept hotel in
the wilds of the Black Forest has simple
rooms and an indoor swimming pool,
which comes in handy on those days
when the sun is a no-show.

Gasthof Gedächtnishaus –
Fohrenbühl 12, 78730 Lauterbach.
✆(07422) 44 61. www.king-gastro.de.
Closed 6 weeks from Jan 6. 7 rooms.
Restaurant ◠◠. Closed Wed dinner and
Thu. An ideal destination for tired hikers,
this historic inn has newly renovated,
modern rooms with a welcome degree
of comfort. The rustic restaurant serves
energy-restoring local fare.

Hotel Sonne – Krumlinden 44, 79244
Münstertal-Obermünstertal. ✆(07636)
319. www.sonne-muenstertal.de. Closed
mid-Nov–mid-Dec. 13 rooms. Restaurant
closed Tue eve and Wed. This pleasant
little hotel snuggles into the romantic
Münstertal valley and gets a high
charm quotient from blond wood
furniture and good-sized balconies.
Regional home cooking beckons in the
traditional restaurant.

Schwarzwaldhaus –
Am Kurpark 26, 79872 Bernau-Innerlehen.
✆(07675) 365. www.sbo.de/schwarz
waldhaus. Closed Nov. 14 rooms.
Restaurant◠◠, closed Thu. Sample
classic Black Forest flair in this cosy
farmhouse covered in wooden shingles
typical of the region. After enjoying a
delicious meal in the former stables,
retire to handsome rooms decorated
either farmhouse- or country-style.

Hotel Alemannenhof –
Bruderhalde 21, 79822 Titisee. ✆(07652)
911 80. www.hotel-alemannenhof.de.
22 rooms. Restaurant◠◠◠. On the
shores of the Titisee, this modern Black
Forest hotel boasts a private beach and
dock. In addition to the comfortable
rooms, the establishment has a pleasant
restaurant and a lakeside terrace.

Hotel Bären – Langestraße 33,
72250 Freudenstadt. ✆(07441) 27 29.
www.hotel-baeren-freudenstadt.de. 25
rooms. Restaurant ◠◠, closed Jan 7–23,
Fri, lunch Mon–Sat. Owned by the same
family since 1878, this central inn has a
homey feel and spacious rooms with
rustic flair. The restaurant will tempt
your tastebuds with creative Black
Forest cuisine. Even vegetarians will
not feel left out.

🍴 EAT

Löffelschmiede – Löffelschmiede 1,
79853 Lenzkirch. ✆(07653) 279. www.sbo.
de/loeffelschmiede. Closed Nov–mid-Dec.
This little family-run restaurant is set in
a small valley near Lenzkirch. Trout and
simple regional dishes are served in the
bright and welcoming restaurant with
its earthenware oven. Also lets out a few
inexpensive rooms.

Jägerstüble – Marktplatz 12,
72250 Freudenstadt. ✆(07441) 23 87.
www.jaegerstueble-fds.de. The rustic
setting and relaxed atmosphere make
this central restaurant a popular choice
with both locals and visitors. Rooms are
decked out in blond-wood furniture
and cheerful colours.

Bareiss – Gärtenbühlweg 14,
72270 Baiersbronn-Mitteltal. ✆(07442)
470. www.bareiss.com. 99 rooms.
Restaurants◠–◠◠◠◠. Charming
décor and creaking wood make this
upscale establishment a delightful
refuge. Restore energies in the on-site
pool and spa or choose from a menu
of activities, including golfing, hunting
and hiking. A farmhouse-style tavern
serves Black Forest specialities, while
the gourmet restaurant is among the
region's best for upscale fare.

Karlsruhe★

Karlsruhe had its genesis in 1715 as the residential retreat of Margrave Karl Wilhelm of Baden-Durlach and evolved into a modern city with a grand palace and fine museums. It is home to the country's oldest school of technology (1825) whose graduates include Heinrich Hertz, discoverer of electromagnetic waves, and pioneering auto engineer Karl Benz. Karlsruhe is also the seat of the *Bundesverfassungsgericht*, **Germany's** highest court.

▸ **Population:** 290 740

▯ **Info:** Bahnhofplatz 6. 𝒫(0721) 37 20 53 83. www.karlsruhe-tourism.de.

▶ **Location:** Karlsruhe is on the right bank of the Rhine, close to the French border and served by the A5 and A65 autobahns.

⊛ **Don't Miss:** Art lovers should head for the Fine Arts Museum and the ZKM.

◔ **Timing:** Allow at least half a day for Karlsruhe's museums.

A BIT OF HISTORY

A star is born – Karlsruhe is one of Germany's earliest masterplanned cities, laid out in the 18C with the palace at its centre and a network of streets radiating away from it. It became the capital of the Grand Duchy of Baden in 1806.

SIGHTS

Staatliche Kunsthalle Karlsruhe★★ (Fine Arts Museum)

◔*Open year-round, Tue–Fri 10am–5pm, Sat–Sun 10am–6pm.* ◔*Dec 24 & 31.* ⊛6€. ⬥ 𝒫(0721) 926 33 59. *www.kunsthalle-karlsruhe.de.*

This is one of Germany's finest and most comprehensive art museums and is particularly famous for its **Old German Masters★★**. Among the displays are an emotionally wrenching *Crucifixion* by Matthias Grünewald, a small tablet depicting *Maria and Child* by Lucas Cranach the Elder and several works by Dürer and his pupil Hans Baldung Grien. The Golden Age of Flemish and Dutch painting is represented by Rubens, Jordaens and Rembrandt.

The 19C collection on the ground floor showcases romantic landscapes by Caspar David Friedrich as well as boldly pigmented canvases by Cézanne.

The adjacent **Orangery** focuses on classical, modern and contemporary art. Paintings by German Expressionists (Marc), Cubists (Léger, Delaunay) and works by Ernst and Dix stand alongside

Staatliche Kunsthalle Karlsruhe

Staatliche Kunsthalle Karlsruhe

sculptures by Barlach, Lehmbruck and Henry Moore. Contemporary artists include Gerhard Richter, Yves Klein and Antoni Tàpies.

Schloss★ (Palace)

The palace served as the grand-ducal residence until 1918 and got a major drubbing in World War II. Only the tall **octagonal tower** (Schlossturm; ⏰open year-round, Tue–Thu 10am–5pm, Fri–Sun 10am–6pm; ✆4€; ✆(0721) 926 65 14) survived and can now be climbed for sweeping views of the city and the Black Forest. The palace park gives access to the **Botanical Garden** (Botanischer Garten; ⏰open year-round, grounds 6am–sunset, greenhouses Tue–Fri 10am–5.45pm, Sat–Sun 10am–5.45pm; ✆(0721) 926 30 08; www.botanischer-garten-karl-sruhe.de), which is a fine place to relax among a profusion of flowers, trees and plants, many of them rare and exotic.

Badisches Landesmuseum★ (Baden Regional Museum)

⏰Open year-round, Tue–Thu 10am–5pm, Fri–Sun 10am–6pm. ⏰Closed Dec 24 & 31. ✆4€. ♿ ✆(0721) 926 65 14. www.landesmuseum.de.

This palace museum covers all major historical periods from the last 2 000 years with paintings, furniture, uniforms, crowns and jewellery, statues and other objects of cultural significance.

Museum beim Markt (Museum by the Market)

Karl-Friedrich-Straße 6. ⏰*Open year-round, Tue–Thu 11am–5pm, Fri–Sun 10am–6pm.* ⏰*Closed Dec 24 & 31.* 🎫*2€.* ♿ ✆*(0721) 926 65 78. www.landesmuseum.de.*
Applied arts since 1900 are the main theme of this museum, which exhibits exceptional collections of **Jugendstil**★ (Art Nouveau) and Art Deco.

Zentrum für Kunst und Medientechnologie★ (Centre for Art & Media)

Lorenzstraße 19. ⏰*Open year-round, Wed–Fri 10am–6pm, Sat–Sun 11am–6pm.* 🎫*5€ per museum or 8€ for both.* ♿ ✆*(0721) 810 00. www.zkm.de.*
This early 20C weapons and ammunition factory now unites research, teaching, workshops and museums revolving around art and electronic media technologies under a single roof.
In the **Museum für Neue Kunst** (Museum for New Art), European and American works since 1960 take centre stage along with rotating shows featuring paintings, graphics, sculpture, photography and installations.
The **Medienmuseum** (Media Museum) is the world's first repository focused exclusively on interactive art. *Access at the level of the blue cube.*

EXCURSIONS
Schloss Bruchsal★★

▶ *20km/12.5mi north of Karlsruhe.* ⏰*Open year-round, Tue–Sun 10am–5pm.* ⏰*Closed Dec 24–25 & 31.* 🎫*5€ for palace and museums.* ♿ ✆*(07251) 74 26 61. www.schloesser-und-gaerten.de.*
Bruchsal was the residence of the last four Prince-Bishops of Speyer. Their huge Baroque palace was commissioned in 1720 by Prince-Bishop Damian Hugo von Schönborn, who brought some of the finest architectural and artistic talent to the Rhine.

Most notable among these was Balthasar Neumann whose magnificent **staircase**★★ (1731), lidded by elaborate stucco ornamentation, is a true Rococo masterpiece. The **state apartments** are filled with original furnishings as well as silver, porcelain and portraits.
The vaulted Gartensaal (Garden Room) with its marble floor opens onto the park that used to extend all the way to the River Rhine 16km/10mi away.

👥♿ Deutsches Musikautomaten Museum★ (German Museum of Musical Instruments)

In the main building. ⏰*Open year-round, Tue–Sun 10am–5pm.*
👂*Guided tours (1hr) with musical demonstrations 11am, 2pm & 3.30pm.*
This fun collection includes 200 musical instruments from the 18C to the 20C, most of them worked by cylinders or perforated cardboard or rolls of paper. It is well worth taking the guided tour to experience the musical recitals. Cinema organs, "Barbary organs" and pianolas (mechanical pianos operated by perforated "piano rolls") are also on view.
Note the "household" organs and orchestrations (in 19C England Aeolian Orchestrelles, machines resembling oversize, upright pianos with manual keyboards and stops). Many instruments hail from Leipzig and the Black Forest.

Museum der Stadt Bruchsal (Local History Museum)

Southern part of the main block.
This local history museum inside the palace presents the city's paleontological collection, including minerals from Bruchsal and the surrounding area.
The prehistoric department brims with fossil finds and excavations from the Stone Age to the Middle Ages.
Finally, there's a sparkling collection of coins and medals, many of them ancient and rare, that is sure to delight numismatists. Another focus is the history of the local penal system from 1848 until the end of World War II. There are also displays about the bombing raids on 1 March 1945 that basically obliterated the town.

Kloster Maulbronn

© Willi Wilhelm/Fotolia.com

Kloster Maulbronn★★
(Maulbronn Abbey)

▶ *38km/23.5mi east of Karlsruhe. Klosterhof 5.*

🕐 *Open Mar–Oct, 9am–5.30pm; Nov–Feb, Tue–Sun, 9.30am–5pm.*

🕐 *Dec 24–25 & 31.* ⊘6€. ♿ 𝄞(07043) 92 66 10. www.klostermaulbronn.de.

Founded in 1147, Maulbronn is considered the most complete and best-preserved medieval monastery complex north of the Alps. The abbey is right in the middle of Salzach Valley, within a small, fortified medieval village that is approached by a rampart walk.

One of the earliest Cistercian foundations in Germany, this enormous abbey remains well preserved with all its outbuildings inside a perimeter wall. The school established here in 1557 has seen the flowering of such diverse talents as Johannes Kepler, Friedrich Hölderlin, Justinus Kerner and Hermann Hesse. The main buildings were constructed between the 12C and 14C in transitional Romanesque-Gothic style. The structure was instrumental in paving the way for Gothic architecture throughout northern and central Europe. The abbey was added to the UNESCO World Heritage list in 1993.

MAULBRONN ABBEY

The Cistercians – This Benedictine order traces its name to the monastery of Cîteaux in Burgundy, France, founded by Robert of Molesmes in 1098. The order grew rapidly and by the 13C maintained 742 monasteries between Ireland and Syria. In Germany, early foundations include the abbeys of Ebrach in Bavaria, Altenberg near Cologne and, well, Maulbronn. Monasteries in Roman Catholic regions got Baroque makeovers in the 18C, while those in Protestant regions, such as Maulbronn, survived unaltered.

Abbey Church★

Consecrated in 1178, the church is entered via a 13C Paradise Porch **(1)**, an early German example of the Romanesque-Gothic transition.

Inside, a Romanesque rood screen **(2)** topped by a dog-tooth frieze divides the nave into separate sections for the monks and the lay brothers.

A large Crucifix (1473), impressively sculpted from a single stone, stands before the screen. Note the richly carved choir stalls, made c. 1450, and the beautiful 14C **Virgin** (to the left of the high altar) **(3)**, probably from the Cologne School.

Cloister★★

The west gallery leads to the **lay brothers' refectory (A)** (rebuilt 1869–70), and to the Romanesque **storeroom (B)**, now a *lapidarium*. The **monks' refectory**★, completed c. 1220–30 and perhaps the most impressive room in the complex, is flanked by the *calefactory* **(C)** and the kitchens **(D)**. Off the east gallery are the **chapter-house** and a **connecting building (E)**.

Monastery Buildings★

Behind the cloister stands a three-storey Gothic palace with the picturesque **Faustturm** (Faust Tower). The famous Doctor Faust, who inspired Goethe, Wagner and many others, was supposedly summoned here in 1516 for alchemy experiments. Back in the main courtyard, the **museum** and information centre are housed in the Frühmesserhaus and on the first floor.

ADDRESSES

🛏 STAY

🍽 **Hotel Betzler** – *Amalienstraße 3.* ℘*(0721) 91 33 60. www.hotel-betzler.de. 34 rooms.* In the heart of Karlsruhe, the Betzler is good value, particularly for easy access to public transport. Rooms are clean and functional. The pedestrian zone and most sights of interest are within walking distance.

🍽🍽 **Am Markt** – *Kaiserstraße 76.* ℘*0721 91 99 80. www.hotelammarkt.de. 38 rooms.* 🚾. This hotel on the market square enjoys a panoramic view of the town. Rooms are simple, modern and comfortable with the usual international-class facilities.

🍽🍽🍽 **Kübler** – *Bismarckstraße 37.* ℘*0721 1440. www.aaaa-hotelwelt.de. 200 rooms.* 🚾. Set in a lush garden in the heart of the city, the Kübler offers a stylish, rustic and intimate atmosphere. Rooms are comfortable and well equipped and some have a traditional faïence oven.

🍴 EAT

🍽 **Alte Bank** – *Herrenstraße 30.* ℘*0721 183 28 18. www.altebank.de.* Pub food is served in this high-ceilinged venue which is particularly suited to lunchtime. Laid-back atmosphere.

🍽 **Lehners Wirtshaus zum Goldenen Kreuz** – *Karlstraße 21a.* ℘*(0721) 249 57 20.* For solid German cuisine, make a beeline for this buzzy brasserie in the town centre. The wooden tables and large bar exude a low-key feel which, in summer, extends to the lively, 300-seat beer garden.

🍽 **Gutenberg** – *Nelkenstraße 27.* ℘*0721 985 15 16. www.gasthaus-gutenberg.de.* This attractive atmospheric rustic restaurant serves regional specialities either indoors, or in its beer garden.

🍽🍽 **Klenerts** – *Reichardstraße 22, Karlsruhe-Durlach (7km/4.5mi east).* ℘*0721 414 59. www.klenerts.de.* Nestled below the Turmberg, this modern bistro-style restaurant offers wonderful views across the city from its terrace. Local and international cuisine.

Baden-Baden★★

From Brahms to Queen Victoria to Bill Clinton, the spa resort of Baden-Baden has long been a favourite playground of the wealthy, famous and powerful. There's plenty to lure them, including an idyllic location on the little Oos River, hot mineral springs that worked miracles on the aching joints of ancient Roman generals and superb cultural institutions. A highlight is the casino, a lavish Belle Epoque extravaganza that inspired Dostoyevski's novel *The Gambler* and Prokofiev's eponymous opera.

▶ **Population:** 54 780
▪ **Info:** Kaiserallee 3, ℰ(07221) 27 52 00. www.baden-baden.de.
▶ **Location:** Wedged into the Oos Valley on the edge of the Black Forest and surrounded by the Baden vineyards, Baden-Baden is 60km/37.3mi from Strasbourg via the A5 Autobahn.
▶ **Don't Miss:** Lichtentaler Allee, the casino or the Museum Frieder Burda.
▶ **Timing:** Allow at least one day to visit the sights and Casino and relax in one of the spas or gardens.

WALKING TOUR
Kurhaus and Casino★

Casino tours (25min, in German) Apr–Oct, daily 9.30am–noon; Nov–Mar, 10am–noon. Closed major holidays. 5€. ℰ(07221) 302 40. www.casino-baden-baden.de. Enquire about tours in English. If you plan to gamble, dress well (men in tie and jacket) and bring a passport.

The majestic 19C Kurhaus hosts balls, festivals, concerts and society events but is really most famous for its elegant casino. A symphony of red velvet and gilded chandeliers, the Belle Epoque venue was designed by Benazét to resemble a French palace.

Spa

Sample the restorative powers of Baden-Baden's mineral springs in two spa complexes: the **Friedrichsbad**, a neo-Renaissance style bathing palace with a Roman-Irish Bath; and the modern **Caracalla-Therme** with pools, saunas, whirlpools, grottoes and other relaxation stations. Both are open daily but the admission price depends on the length of your stay and treatment menu.

GETTING AROUND
Baden-Baden is linked to Karlsruhe by city train line S 4 and regional RE trains. Check ticket prices and schedule with **Stadtwerke Baden-Baden** (ℰ(072 21) 7 71; www.stadtwerke-baden-baden.de) or with **Deutsche Bahn** (www.bahn.de). **Airport** – Karlsruhe/Baden-Baden Airport (10km/6mi west of town) has flights serving Berlin, London, Hamburg and other destinations. ℰ(07229) 66 20 00 or www.baden-airpark.de.

Lichtentaler Allee★★
This riverside promenade has been the place to see and be seen for over a century. Napoleon III, Queen Victoria, Bismarck and Dostoevsky all whiled away the hours here and in the equally enchanting **Gönneranlage**★ nearby.

▶ *The route passes by the Museum Frieder Burda and the State Art Gallery.*

Museum Frieder Burda★
Lichtentaler Allee 8b. Open year-round, Tue–Sun 10am–6pm. Closed Dec 24 & 31. 9€. ℰ(07221) 973 72 22. www.museum-frieder-burda.de.

Baden-Baden.

T. Krieger/MICHELIN

Right in the Kurpark, a stunning building by New York-based architect Richard Meier houses this equally stellar art collection. The focus in on 20C works by Max Beckmann, August Macke, Picasso, Jackson Pollock, Mark Rothko, Georg Baselitz and Gerhard Richter.
The white aluminium facade integrates beautifully with the park and sits next to the **State Art Gallery** (Staatliche Kunsthalle), which also hosts important exhibitions.

Stadtmuseum★ (Town Museum)

Lichtentaler Allee 10. ○*Open year-round, Tue–Sun 10am–6pm (Wed 8pm).* ○*Closed major holidays.* ∞*4€.* ℘*(07221) 93 22 72.*
Two thousand years of town history are engagingly chronicled in this glass pavilion. Keep an eye out for rare coins, gambling paraphernalia, sculpture from across the epochs and an enchanting assortment of historical toys.

Abtei Lichtenthal★ (Lichtenthal Abbey)

Hauptstraße 44. *Guided tours Sun–Wed 3pm by reservation.* ∞*3€.* ℘*(07221) 50 49 10.* *www.abtei-lichtenthal.de.*
Cistercian sisters have run this abbey for more than 750 years. The courtyard and the abbey itself are open to the public. The Princes Chapel (Fürstenkapelle)

contains the tombs of the margraves of Baden.

ADDITIONAL SIGHTS
Neues Schloss (New Castle)

The former hilltop residence of the local margraves is closed to the public but is still a great place to enjoy a signature panorama of the town and surrounding hills.

Stiftskirche (Collegiate Church)

Climb the stairs up to Marktplatz (the market square) to visit the burial place of the Baden margraves from the 14C to the 18C. Several of their epitaphs are remarkable works of art that invite closer inspection. Of particular note is the 5.6m/18ft-high sandstone **Crucifix★**, a 1467 masterpiece by Nicolaus Gerhaert von Leyden and a fine example of late medieval sculpture.

Römische Badruinen★ (Roman Bath Ruins)

Römerplatz 1. ○*Open mid-Mar–mid-Nov, 11am–noon, 3pm–4pm.* ℘*(07221) 27 59 34. www.badruinen.de.*
Excavations beneath the Friedrichsbad have unearthed the remains of baths once used by Roman soldiers, including the ingenious floor heating systems and the well-preserved walls. Computer animation helps you visualise how it all looked originally.

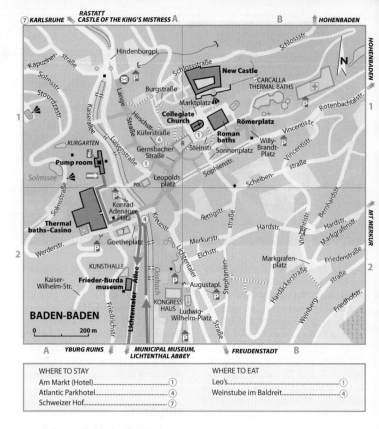

WHERE TO STAY		WHERE TO EAT	
Am Markt (Hotel)	①	Leo's	①
Atlantic Parkhotel	④	Weinstube im Baldreit	④
Schweizer Hof	⑦		

EXCURSIONS

Yburgruinen★ (Yburg Castle Ruins)

▶ 6km/3.5mi southwest via Friedrichstraße.

The tower is all that survives of this 13C castle. From the top there are great **views**★★ of the Rhine plain and the Baden vineyards.

Mount Merkur

2km/1.2mi east via Markgrafenstraße or bus 204 or 205 to Leopoldsplatz. Funicular (Merkurbergbahn): 10am–10pm; ⊖4€ round trip.

From the top of the mountain, you have panoramic **views**★ over Baden-Baden, west towards the Vosges Valley and east to the Murg Valley.

Rastatt★

▶ 19km/12mi north.
Herrenstraße 18, 76437 Rastatt.
✆(07222) 97 24 62. www.rastatt.de.
Less than 10km/6.2mi from the French border, Rastatt straddles the Murg River just before it flows into the Rhine.

Schloss★ (Palace)

↝Guided tour (45min), Apr–Oct, Tue–Sun 10am–5pm; Nov–Mar, Tue–Sun 10am–4pm. ⊙Closed Dec 24–25 & 31. ⊖⊖6€. ✆(07222) 97 83 85. www.schloss-rastatt.de.

This harmonious U-shaped palace was built in 1698–1707 by Italian master architect Domenico Egidio Rossi who was replaced with **Michael Ludwig Rohrer** after Ludwig the Turk's death in 1707. **Royal Apartments** – The margravial apartments are richly embellished with frescoes and stuccowork. The sumptuous **Ahnensaal** (Hall of Ancestors), whose column capitals are decorated with stucco figures representing Turkish prisoners, is especially noteworthy.

Wehrgeschichtliches Museum (Military Museum) – *(access via the south wing)*. Weapons, uniforms and pictures illustrate German military and general history from 1500 to 1918 (*open May–Oct, Tue–Sun 10am–5.30pm; Nov–Apr, Fri–Sun 10am–4.30pm;* *closed Jan 1, Dec 25 & 31; 3€, or 6€ with palace;* *(07222) 342 44; www.wgm-rastatt.de).*

German Freedom Movements Memorial Museum – *(access via the north wing)* displays document German freedom movements from 1500 to the resistance in former East Germany up to 1990 (*open May–Oct, Tue–Sun 1am–5.30pm;*

Nov–Apr Fri 10am–4pm; *closed Jan 1, Dec 24–25 & 31;* *(07222) 77 13 90; www.wgm-rastatt.de).*

Schloss Favorite★★

 5km/3mi southeast of Rastatt.
 Guided tours (1hr) mid-Mar–Sept, Tue–Sun 10am–6pm; Oct–mid-Nov, Tue–Sun 10am–5pm. 7€. *(07222) 412 07. www.schloss-favorite.de.*
Margravine Sibylla Augusta of Baden-Baden commissioned this pleasure palace in 1710, partly to display her famous china, glass and faïence collections. The exterior of this charming 18C Baroque palace is coated with an unusual matrix of gravel and granite chips. The sumptuous **interior**★★ sports floors of brilliant *scagliola* (stucco imitating encrusted marble) as well as mirrors, mosaics and precious chinoiserie collectors' pieces.

ADDRESSES

STAY

 Hotel Am Markt – *Marktplatz 18.* *07221 270 40. www.hotel-am-markt-baden.de. Closed Dec 25. 23 rooms.* This attractive quiet, discreet hotel-pension in the heart of the old town offers lovely bright rooms. Good value.

 Schweizer Hof – *Langestraße 73.* *07 221 30 460. www.schweizerhof.de. 9 rooms.* Set in the city centre, next to the new opera house, this traditional hotel features rooms which are furnished in modern style, some with a balcony, others with a terrace.

 Atlantic Parkhotel – *Goetheplatz 3.* *07 221 36 10. www.atlantic-parkhotel.de. 49 rooms.* *Restaurant*. Dating from 1836 (when it was the Englischer Hof) the Atlantic is a charming historic hotel with large luxurious rooms at reasonable prices. Breakfast can be taken on the pretty terrace.

EAT

 Weinstube im Baldreit – *Küferstraße 3.* *07221 231 36. Open Mon–Sat noon–2pm and 5pm–10pm. Closed Sun.* Tucked away in a dead-end alley in

the old town, this traditional Weinstube serves generous portions of local food with a French accent (the chef comes from just over the Rhine!). Reduced menu at lunchtime.

 Leo's – *Luisenstraße 8–10.* *07221 380 81. www.leos-baden-baden.de. Open 10am–1am (2am Fri–Sat).* Café, restaurant and wine bar in one. Stylish, hip Leo's is the place to eat, drink and be seen in Baden-Baden, particularly as the night wears on. Mediterranean-inspired menu and wine list.

TAKING A BREAK

Café König – *Lichtentaler Straße 12.* *(07221) 2 35 73. www.chocolatier.de.* This legendary coffeehouse has counted Tolstoy and Liszt among its guests and is the best place in town to sample the famous liqueur-laced Black Forest gateau. In summer, sit outside on the lime-tree shaded terrace.

SIGHTSEEING

Tourist bus – City-Bahn trolley tours are offered from March to October (*55min,* *5€).*

Baden Wine Route★★

The **Badische Weinstraße**★★ winds sinuously for 400km/250mi through the vineyards on the lower slopes of the Black Forest, from Heidelberg to the Swiss border, crossing nine wine regions which together comprise the third largest wine-producing area in Germany. Ruby-red Pinot Noir, fruity Riesling, spicy-aromatic Pinot Gris, sweet Muscat and crisp Müller-Thurgau wines all hail from the soils of this diverse region. The tour below travels through the Ortenau district, where vineyards surround charming villages, sheltered from the peaks of the Black Forest. The mild climate, long hours of sunshine and spectacular views of the Rhine Valley and its imposing castle ruins, mean that exploring the Baden Wine Route is a joy.

- **Michelin Map:** 718 and 545 R 12–13 H 58–P62.
- **Info:** www.blackforest-tourism.com.
- **Location:** For a description of the entire Wine Route see the *Green Guide Alsace-Lorraine*. The tour here runs south from Baden-Baden.
- **Don't Miss:** Oberkirche or Durbach.
- **Timing:** Allow a day for the driving tour described which follows minor roads.

DRIVING TOUR

L'ORTENAU
100km/62mi – Allow one day.

▷ *Leave Baden-Baden on the B3 heading for Offenburg.*

The sandstone hills of the northern Black Forest, south of Baden-Baden, allow the vineyards and orchards to flourish.

Steinbach
This charming village lies at the foot of the hills crowned by the ruined castle of Yburg. Note the monument in memory of Erwin von Steinbach, one of the architects of Strasbourg Cathedral.

Neuweier
Set at the foot of the castle, Neuweier vineyard produces a special variety of Riesling known as *mauerwein* (literally, "wall wine" as the ripest grapes come from vines planted next to the wall). The owners are descended from French nobility, who were originally authorised

to bottle the wine by the Prince Archbishop of Würzburg (they also granted this privilege to the villages of Steinbach, and Umweg Varnhalt). A special short-necked, fat bellied *bocksbeutel* distinguishes the wines.

▷ *At Altschweier, turn off the Wine Route in order to visit the little town of Bühl.*

Bühl
This small, busy market town is famous for its dark red plums and its Affental wine. The town's *Zwetschgenfest* (plum festival) takes place every year in September, during which delicious plum tarts and pies are on sale everywhere. The neo-Gothic collegiate church of St. Peter and St. Paul features beautiful modern stained glass (1955–1958) by Albert Burkart.

▷ *Head back towards Altschweier as far as Bühlertal.*

Bühlertal
The surrounding vineyards and forests provide a romantic setting for this small resort town which thrives thanks to its mild climate.

▷ *The road rises to Hof (the residential area of town). Turn right towards Neusatz and its 13C Waldsteg castle.*

BADEN WINE ROUTE

MANNHEIM   KARLSRUHE

Haguenau

Autobahnkirche

Favorite ★ ★

BADEN-BADEN   Yburg

Steinbach   Neuweier

Bühl   Bühlertal

Windeck
Castle ★

Sasbach

Sasbachwalden ★

Kappelrodeck

Oberkirch   Schauenburg

STRASBOURG

Durbach   Lautenbach

Offenburg   Ortenberg

Gengenbach ★

Friesenheim

Erstein

Burgheim

Rhinau

Lahr

Kippenheim   Hausach

Mahlberg

Ettenheim

★ ★ ★ EUROPA-PARK   Ettenheimmünster ★

N

0   20 km

BASEL   FREIBURG   SCHWENNINGEN

Windeck Castle★

This ancient circular castle was built in
1200 but mostly destroyed in the 16C.
Two towers, two rooms and a curtain
wall survive. In the shadow of the towers, in the leafy castle grounds, is the
modern but very charming Burg-Wind-
eck hotel-restaurant *(www.burg-wind-
eck.de)*, which enjoys a lovely **view**★
over the Rhine plain.

▶ *Continue south for 7km/4.5mi to
the L83a.*

Sasbach

🚶 *15min on foot; round trip.*
Leave your car and enter the park.
An obelisk and a stele with inscriptions
in French, German and Latin mark the
spot where, in 1675, the Captain of
Turenne, (one of Louis XIV's commanding officers during the Imperial conquest
of Franche-Comte) died from a bullet
wound.

The Baroque-style parish church, dedicated to St. Bridget, retains some parts
of an older Gothic building.

▶ *Continue southeast via the L86a
then turn left onto the L86.*

Sasbachwalden★

This pretty spa village, which specialises
in the Kneipp form of hydrotherapy, is
a past winner of the national best-kept
village competition. The historic centre
features beautiful flower-decked half-
timbered houses which have been lovingly conserved.
🚶 *Footpaths lead to the* **Mummelsee**
and the **Hornisgrinde***.*

▶ *Retrace your steps then take the
L86a south.*

Kappelrodeck

This small wine-producing village of
beautiful half-timbered houses lies in

the Acher Valley. It can be reached on the **tourist railway** line from Achern to Ottenhöfen. **Schloss Rodeck** (11C, though remodelled in the Renaissance period), is the emblem of the village. According to local legend, in the 14C, the Hex vom Dasenstein (Witch of Dasenstein) lived below the castle. Her name has been adopted by the local wine cooperative – if you get the chance, try a bottle of the local red.

▷ *Continue along the L86a south for 10km/6.5mi.*

Oberkirch★

This charming town, owned by the bishops of Strasbourg from 1303 to 1803, is surrounded by orchards, vineyards and forests. Stroll along the Mühlbach (millstream), to see its quaint half-timbered houses, which go back as far as the 17C. Oberkirch holds two records: the largest strawberry market in Germany and the largest number of distilleries. Its cherry, plum and raspberry brandies have become famous.

The city is dominated by the ruins of Schauenburg Castle which was founded in the 11C by the Dukes of Zähringen; from the castle, there are panoramic views of the Rhine Valley towards Strasbourg.

The Zum Silbernen Stern, now a historic guesthouse (*www.silberner-stern.de*), in Oberkirch-Gaisbach, was the home of the great 17C writer **Hans Jakob Christoffel von Grimmelshausen**, who wrote his famous novel, *Der Abenteuerliche Simplicissimus Teutsch*, here. He also lived in the nearby village of Renchen where he became mayor.

▷ *Follow the B 28 east for 3.5km/2mi.*

Lautenbach

Set among meadows, vineyards and forests in the Rench Valley, Lautenbach is known for its various kinds of stone fruits and strawberries. From the town there are beautiful views from several points over the valleys of the Rhine and the Rench. The late-Gothic **pilgrimage Church of Maria Himmelfahrt** contains one of the few surviving medieval rood screens in Germany. It also has a superb altar, with one of the finest Gothic triptychs in the region.

Created in the late 15C, it is attributed to the Strasbourg School and is a brilliant combination of sculpture and painting. In the central part, the polychrome statues of St. John the Baptist and St. John the Evangelist frame a lovely Madonna on a crescent moon. The two early 16C side altars hold beautiful 15C stained glass from the workshop of Peter Hummel Andlau.

▷ *Return towards Oberkirch then take the K5369 south.*

On the Badische Weinstraße

R. Mattes/MICHELIN

Durbach★

The municipality of Durbach has been growing vines, most notably Traminer and Riesling varieties, since the Middle Ages. Since 1836 they have also been cultivating Sauvignon following an exchange with the owners of the famous Chateau-Yquem vineyards. The village of Durbach enjoys a pretty **location**★ surrounded by vineyards. Its picturesque centre is dominated by the 11C **Schloss Staufenberg** and is a popular tourist destination.

▷ *Continue east on the K5369.*

Offenburg

Originally a Roman settlement, but re-founded in 1148 by the Dukes of Zähringen, Offenburg was raised to the status of Imperial City in 1240 by Emperor Frederick II. Unfortunately its development was abruptly halted in 1689 when the troops of Louis XIV burnt the city down during the War of the League of Augsburg. Today it functions as the administrative and industrial centre of the Ortenau region.

The **Hauptstraße** and adjacent alleyways (in the pedestrian zone) are lined with interesting houses and picturesque squares. Note the Unicorn Pharmacy (Einhornapotheke), a Baroque building from 1720, with its scrolled façade on which stands a unicorn; the Fountain of Neptune dating from 1783; the Fischmarkt (fish market); the Hirschapotheke (Stag Pharmacy) of 1698, and before it the Lion Fountain (Löwenbrunnen) of 1599.

In Pfarrstraße the **Heilig-Kreuz-Kirche**★ (Church of the Holy Spirit) is an elegant if sober Baroque building. It dates from 1700, built on the foundations of a 13C church destroyed by the fire of 1689. The interior exudes a feeling of great harmony. The main altar and side altars are the work of Franz Lichtenauer (1740); the altar table is by Joseph Esperlin (1737). Note the remarkable Neoclassical pulpit of marble and stucco by Johann Nepomuk Speckert (1795), and the superbly carved gate of the Rococo organ loft.

The Baroque **Franziskanerkloster** (Church of the Franciscan Monastery), built in 1702, has a richly decorated altar and Silbermann organ. In the cloister chapel is a beautiful early 16C statue of the Virgin.

In **Spitalstraße**, near the fish market, Sankt-Andreas-Hospital (St. Andrew's Hospital) dates from the 18C. Note on the outside of the adjoining church buildings the 14C Gothic Madonna. Also on the same street is the imposing Old Granary, a large and impressive space, home to exhibitions and cultural events.

The **Rathaus** (town hall) is a beautifully proportioned building dating from 1741. The city coat of arms and the double eagle on the balcony above are a reminder that the city belonged to Austria from the mid-16C until 1706 and, again, from 1771 to 1805. The town hall carillon, which consists of 25 bronze bells, delights both locals and visitors with its repertoire of 100 tunes

▷ *Head southeast on the L99.*

Ortenberg

This "village of wine, flowers and fountains" is dominated by the **Schloss Ortenberg**. Built in the 12C by the Dukes of Zähringen to protect the entrance to the Kinzig Valley, it was destroyed in 1678 by the French and rebuilt in 1838 by Friedrich Eisenlohr who created a building in the Gothic Revival style of the period.

The castle is now home to one of the most modern youth hostels in Germany.

Just outside the village at Ortenberg-Käfersberg, the **Bühlwegkapelle Mariä Ruh** (Mariä Ruh Chapel) dates from 1497 and is renowned for its remarkable early 15C Flamboyant-Gothic style murals.

▷ *Continue on the L99 for 7.5km/4.5mi.*

Gengenbach★

Set on the banks of the River Kinzig, in the heart of the Ortenau district, Gengenbach is a charming, well preserved historic city. Here, the medieval and the Baroque happily rub shoulders, having avoided the ravages of the Thirty Years' War. Gengenbach was raised to the status of Free City in 1360, and became a Protestant stronghold after the Reformation in 1525. However, from 1547, the town, now under Austrian law, again embraced the Catholic faith.

The picturesque streets of the **old town**★ are lined with half-timbered houses and gabled baroque buildings. The Hochtor and the Kinzigtor (city gate) towers are two remnants of the town's medieval fortifications. The late-18C Rathaus stands on the market square. Next to the Old Town, Gengenbach's huge 18C convent conceals an ancient Benedictine foundation, predating it by a thousand years.

The Romanesque early 12C **Church of St. Mary** features a chancel rebuilt in the Gothic period and surmounted by an elegant Baroque tower by Jakob Risch. The interior was remodelled in the Romanesque Revival style between 1892 and 1906 and decorated with many paintings. Note too the beautiful baroque stalls, baptismal font and altar of St. Joseph. Near the church is the old abbey mill and, overhead, the millrace which once supplied it.

Two museums worth a visit are the **Flößerei- und Verkehrsmuseum** (Timber Rafting and Traffic Museum), housed in an old gate-keeper's lodge that is classified as a historical monument, and the **Carnival Museum** in the Niggelturm. The town and its surrounding area are also popular with visitors on account of its mild weather and sports facilities, particularly fishing, horseback riding, hiking and biking.

▷ *Head south out of Gengenbach, on the B 33 and go back (north) in the direction of 'Offenburg. Turn left off the B 33 towards Zunsweier, head south through Diersburg, then turn left onto the B 3.*

Friesenheim and Schuttern

Friesenheim is a small town with beautiful half-timbered houses. Between Friesenheim and Schuttern *(2km/1mi west)*, the remains of a Roman city have been excavated.

At **Schuttern**, visit the Convent Church of Mariä Himmelfahrt. During the Middle Ages Schuttern was home to the very wealthy monastery of **Offoniscella**, founded in 603. It was completely destroyed in the 19C (only the rectory remains), but the site has been excavated to reveal the oldest **mosaic** in Germany; it dates from the 11C, is in the shape of a 3m/20ft diameter medallion and covers the tomb of the abbey founder, an Irish-Scottish monk named Offo.

▷ *Continue south on the B3.*

Lahr

Don't be put off by the industrial suburbs of this city of 42 000 inhabitants. It boasts a fine old historic centre. Highlights are the early 17C **Altes Rathaus** (old town hall) and the **Storchenturm**, a remnant of its 13C castle.

The **Burgheim** church dates back to the Carolingian period, though its belfry is Romanesque. In the nave are frescoes (1463) depicting St. Christopher and the Holy Trinity, while the murals in the choir were completed in 1482.

▷ *Continue south on the B3.*

Kippenheim

The church of St-Maurice was built between the 16C and 18C with a fan-vault ceiling and late-Gothic interior. The town hall is decorated with a stepped gable roof and a Renaissance oriel window. Note the two pretty houses adjacent to it which date from the 16C to 19C.

▷ *Leave the Wine Route and make a 6km/3.5mi-round-trip detour.*

Mahlberg

This small town is home to a 13C castle, a Baroque chapel dedicated to St. Catherine and the interesting **Oberrheinisches Tabakmuseum** (*Museum of Tobacco; 078 25 71 42; open May–late Sept 10am–6pm; 3.50€*).

▶ *Get back on the B3.*

Ettenheim

Ettenheim owes its name to the Duke of Alsace (Etichon II) and until 1803 was part of the bishopric of Strasbourg. The **old town** is separated from the rest of the city by two 18C gates, and spreads around the large parish church. Opposite the town hall rises the gable of the former palace of **Cardinal de Rohan**, one of the main protagonists in the Affair of the Diamond Necklace, a scandal which rocked late 18C France and shook the faith of the people in the monarchy. In the church further along Rohanstraße is the tomb of the Cardinal.

The **Mühlenwanderweg** (*Mills Trail,* 🚶*2hrs 30min*) *goes to the mills of Ettenbach, Ettenheim and Ettenheimmünster.*

▶ *Take the L103 east for 6km/3.5mi.*

ADDRESSES

🛏STAY

FRIESENHEIM

🍴**Mühlenhof** – *Oberweierer Hauptstraße 33, 77948 Friesenheim-Oberweier. ☎078 21 63 20. www.landhotel-muehlenhof.de. 32 rooms. �« .Restaurant ☞☞, closed Tue. Closed last 3 weeks Feb; first 2 weeks Aug.* This hotel-restaurant in a rustic setting serves carefully prepared regional dishes.

SASBACHWALDEN

🍴🍴**Tannenhof** – *Murberg 6, 77887 Sasbachwalden. ☎078 41 66 30 65. www.relaxhotel-tannenhof.de. 21 rooms. �«.* This small, traditional hotel surrounded by vineyards offers attractive, light, modern rooms with traditional wooden furnishings. Wellness centre. Dinner served to residents only.

GENGENBACH

🍴🍴**Hirsch** – *Dorfstraße 9, 77791 Gengenbach-Berghaupten. ☎078 03 939 70. www.hirsch-berghaupten.de. 23 rooms. �«.* Large bedrooms. Regional specialities.

🍴EAT

KAPPELRODECK

🍴**Zum Rebstock** – *Kutzendorf 1, 77876 Kappelrodeck-Waldulm. ☎07842 94 80. www.rebstock-waldulm.de. Closed Mon and Tue lunch.* This quintessential local inn has been family-run since 1750. Tasty regional dishes. Also has rustic, country-style rooms to stay in.

OBERKIRCH

🍴🍴**Haus am Berg** – *Am Rebhof 5, 77704 Oberkirch. ☎078 02 47 01. www.haus-am-berg-oberkirch.de. Closed Tue.* This traditional *Landhaus* enjoys a superb panorama across the vineyards; its terrace has views as far as Strasbourg. International cooking with local flavours in a family atmosphere.

LAHR

🍴🍴**Grüner Baum** – *Burgheimer Straße 105, 77933 Lahr. ☎078 21 222 82. www.gruenerbaum-lahr.de. Closed Wed.* This traditional rural hotel has bright, modern rooms. Regional dishes are prepared according to the season and have a Mediterranean accent. Pleasant courtyard terrace.

Ettenheimmünster★

The town nestles in the picturesque Münster Valley, and was formerly the seat of a Benedictine monastery, dissolved in 1803. Today only its well-proportioned pilgrim church remains. Built between 1687 and 1689, the church of **St. Landelin** was enlarged in the 18C, and its Gothic tower added in the middle of the 19C. The interior, and in particular the altar, is heavily decorated with some notable sculptures, stuccowork and ceiling frescoes. The most precious treasure is a reliquary **bust**★ of the Celtic missionary saint and martyr St. Landelin, created by a Strasbourg silversmith in 1506. It contains the skull of Landelin, who was murdered here in 640.

The splendid **organ**★, built in 1769 by **Johann Andreas Silbermann**, is the best-preserved organ on the whole east bank of the Rhine (concerts during the summer months).

Europa-Park★★★

In this theme park dedicated to Europe, more than 100 attractions and shows take visitors on a tour of 12 European countries: the character of each country, from the architecture to the vegetation and the gastronomy, is brought to life in great detail. In addition, the park, famous for its rollercoasters, offers a great deal of excitement for every member of the family.

Use the map given to you at the entrance to find your way among the various countries. You might also like to get an overall view on board the panoramic EP-Express with main stations in Germany, England, Greece, Russia and Spain. The woodland and lake setting greatly enhances the appeal of the park. There is also the Science House (☜7€, with Europa-Park admission 35€) near the main entrance where you can participate in 80 interactive experiments. Allow about 90 minutes. (☜Note that there may be long queues at the main attractions.)

Germany

Your tour of Europe starts with the host country. Stroll along the German Alley

> **Location:** Europa-Park is on the outskirts of Rust, between Freiburg and Strasbourg: *Europa-Park-Straße 2, 77977 Rust-bei-Freiburg. ✆018 057 766 88. www.europapark.de.*

lined with typical architecture from the different regions of Germany. Enjoy the rose garden of the medieval Balthasar Castle then take a look at a piece of the Berlin Wall.

France

For a breathtaking view of the Park and the Rhine Valley as far as the Vosges and the Black Forest, take a glass lift up the Euro-Tower (75m). The super-fast and high Silver Star rollercoaster offers guaranteed thrills, as does Eurostat, a roller coaster speeding "through space" in the dark. Take a 10-minute break to enjoy a 4D movie experience accompanied by tactile, sound and olfactory effects. Follow up with an easy stroll past the charming bistros and old-fashioned boutiques of the *"quartier français"*.

Switzerland

The Swiss village with its old watermill and wooden chalets sets the scene. Take a thrilling bobsleigh ride down a metal

PRACTICAL INFORMATION

✆ *(0180) 577 66 88. www.europapark.de.* ♿. Hours change daily; call or check the website. Closed Jan–Mar. ☜31€ (child 26.40€), including train; multi-day tickets available.

GETTING THERE

By car from Strasbourg, follow the road to Kuhl and take exit 57b to Rust, or drive along D468 then D5 and take the ferry at Rhinau. Small parking charge. By shuttle from Strasbourg *(Gare routière des Halles)* at 7.50 and 8.20am; return at 6pm from Europapark *(info: ✆03 88 23 43 23).*

VISITING TIP

Three information offices (ATM machines, lost property) located by the lake, at the main entrance (locker and buggy rental) and in Spain. Nestlé Schöller meeting points in every themed area.

WHERE TO STAY

There are several possibilities in Rust including the peaceful, comfortable Pension Kern *(Franz-Sales-Straße 30, 77977 Rust; ✆07822 61 278; pension_kern@web.de; 7 rooms; 50€).*
For accommodation in Europa-Park see the next page.

Poseidon attraction, Europa-Park

© Europa-Park

run at 50km/hr/30mph, then maybe a spinning plane ride or a Wild Mouse ride featuring a vertical lift and a hair-raising nose dive.

Greece

Welcome to Mykonos, one of the Greek islands. At "Cassandra's Curse" you can discover the power of illusions, followed by a thrilling trip on the Poseidon water rollercoaster through Greek mythology. Wrap up by venturing into the legendary world of the sunken city of Atlantis.

Russia

Discover a country full of contrasts from the traditional craftsmen's village to the Mir Space Station and test your nerves on the Euro-Mir ride with spinning gondolas hurtling towards the ground at a speed of 80km/hr/50mph.

Spain

Do not miss the spectacular stunts of the Duel of the Brothers featuring knights on horseback fighting it out in the arena or the flamenco show staged by the "Ballet Español".

Other Countries

Plunge into a gigantic wave in Portugal, experience the famous Venice Carnival in Italy, race along the Silverstone racetrack or book a seat at the Globe Theatre in England, get caught up in a pirates' attack on a Dutch colony in Holland, take a refreshing fjord-rafting ride in Scandinavia or float in a tree trunk down a fast-flowing river in the Austrian Tyrol.

Children's World

Boats, slides, roundabouts, a beach, climbing walls, a Viking ship, the Children's Lighthouse and other attractions keep kids busy here and in the Adventure Land.

Success Story

The Mack family, which has produced fairground vehicles since 1780 and rollercoasters for the largest theme parks in the world since 1921, set up Europa-Park in 1975 as a showcase for its various ride models. The chosen location in the small border village of Rust was a surprise for many, but the grounds of Balthasar Castle (1442) offered 60ha/148acres of beautiful greenery. The European theme adopted in 1982 asserted the originality of the park. Since then, the park has consistently expanded and won many awards. Can we then speak of a model company? Maybe... Today the park sets itself apart from similar ventures by its concern for the environment (use of electric vehicles, solar panels).

ADDRESSES

🛏️STAY

Accommodation inside the park includes themed hotels, a guesthouse, a campsite and a tipi village.
Hotel and guesthouse reservation: ℘01805-86 86 20.

Portugiesisches Kloster – Enjoy four-star plus comforts in the setting of a historical monastery.

Hotel Colosseo – This is one of the largest hotels in Germany; designed in the style of Ancient Rome, it features opulent décor, 324 family rooms and 22 luxury suites, typical Italian restaurants, cafés and bars and a wellness area.

Hotel El Andaluz, Hotel Castillo Alcazar – Both hotels are steeped in Andalusian atmosphere: the first is designed in the style of a Spanish *"finca"* with terracotta floors and arcades, whereas the second suggests the grander style of a Spanish castle at the time of the Reconquista.

Circus Rolando – This guesthouse in the German area is convivial and offers good value for money (23 rooms, swimming pool and sauna).

Campsite – Idyllic location by a lake (200 pitches for camping cars and caravans; vast meadow for tents; playground, breakfast room and boutique; no prior reservation).

Tipi village – Wild West atmosphere; heated tipis, log cabins and covered wagons *(bring sleeping bags and towels – breakfast in the Western Saloon – reservation:* ℘+49 (0) 7822 860 5566, camp-resort@europapark.de*)*.

�/EAT

Inside the park dozens of restaurants and fast food places reflect the diversity of European cuisine: French flavour at Marianne's, Scandinavian-style fish at the Fiskhuset, tapas at the Bodega or Greek specialities at the Mykonos.

Freiburg im Breisgau★★

Sunny Freiburg is one of the most attractive cities in southern Germany. Its 500 year-old university, the old town's cobbled lanes lined by half-timbered houses, a majestic cathedral and an easy-going Mediterranean flair make it a perfect base for exploring the Black Forest. Freiburg is a leader when it comes to alternative energies, especially solar energy and energy-efficient structures.

A BIT OF HISTORY

Freiburg was founded in the 12C by the Dukes of Zähringen who conferred upon it a number of special privileges, hence the town's name which literally means "free town". From 1368 to 1798 the city was under Habsburg rule. In the second half of the 19C, Freiburg won renewed importance as a place of research and learning thanks to its university.

> ▶ **Population:** 219 670
> ℹ️ **Info:** Rathausplatz 2–4 and Rotteckring 14. ℘(0761) 388 18 80; www.freiburg.de.
> ◖ **Location:** Midway between Basel and Stras-bourg, on the Rhine plain.
> 🅿 **Parking:** Garages are located throughout the city.
> 👁 **Don't Miss:** The Münster and Augustinermuseum.
> 🕐 **Timing:** Allow a day for the cathedral and the old town.

SIGHTS
Münster★★ (Cathedral)

Pick up an English-language brochure in the information centre, Herrenstraße 30 (behind the cathedral).

🕐*Open year-round, Mon–Sat 10am–5pm, Sun 1pm–7.30pm.*♿ ℘(0761) 285 37 11. www.freiburger-muenster.info. Work on Freiburg's magnificent cathedral began around 1200 in Romanesque style, but today all that remains from this period is the transept crossing and the two "Cockerel Towers" flanking it. In 1354, work started on a Gothic chancel. The grand design and severity of the times meant that construction was not finished until 1513.

The cathedral's **north side** features an interesting 14C tympanum above the door illustrating the theme of Original Sin. The **West Tower★★★** is surmounted by a delicate spire. Four sharply jutting projections form a star at the foot of the tower house. On the **south side,** statues of the apostles and the Old Testament kings stand on the buttresses of this richly ornate façade.

The cathedral's **west porch and doorway** feature late 13C figures. On the left wall, Satan, disguised as a knight, leads a procession. The doorway itself, guarded by statues representing the Church (left) and the Synagogue (with eyes covered, right) deals with the mystery of the Redemption.

The **nave** is embellished with graceful galleries and statuary: **(1)** the Virgin at the pillar (1270–80); **(2)** a late-Gothic pulpit (1560); **(3)** a statue of Berthold V, last of the Dukes of Zähringen and founder of Freiburg; **(4)** the Holy Sepulchre, from c. 1330; **(5)** 13C stained-glass medallions in the windows; and **(6)** a 1505 group sculpture, the Adoration of the Magi.

The **chancel** includes many more works of note, including **(a)** a Rococo baptismal font and **(b)** a 1521 Oberried altarpiece in the University Chapel. The two side panels, the *Nativity* and *Adoration of the Magi*, are by Hans Holbein the Younger. Also worth closer inspection are: **(c)** in the second Imperial Chapel (*Kaiserkapelle*); an altarpiece depicting Rest during the Flight to Egypt by Hans Wydyz on the central panel; **(d)** a painting of the Crucifixion, in back of the large Hans Baldung Grien altarpiece; **(e)** the Romanesque Locherer Crucifix in beaten silver by Böcklin; and **(f)** an altarpiece in the Locherer Chapel by Sixt von Staufen (1521–24). The carved portion depicts the Virgin. The central panel of the **Hochalter★★** (high altar) by **Hans Baldung Grien** (1512–16) portrays the Coronation of the Virgin.

FREIBURG IM BREISGAU CATHEDRAL

0   20 m

Altar piece ★★

CHANCEL

NAVE

To the Tower

TOWER ★★★

Porch

Ascend the **West Tower** (◷*open year-round, Tue–Sat 9.30am–5pm, Sun 1pm–5pm;* ∞*1.50€;* ☎*(0761) 290 74 47)* along the stairway leading to the tower room. The upper platform beneath the beautiful spire offers **views**★ over the city, with the Kaiserstuhl and the Vosges visible in the distance.

⌁ WALKING TOUR
Allow 1hr 30min not including visits.

Rathausplatz★
The pleasant town hall square has flowered balconies and a fountain featuring Berthold Schwarz, said to have invented gunpowder in Freiburg in 1350.

Haus zum Walfisch (House of the Whale)
Franziskanerstraße 3.
This building (1516) boasts a richly ornamented late-Gothic façade topped by an oriel. It served as the refuge of the Humanist philosopher Erasmus who was one of the key figures of the Reformation.

◐ *Cross Kaiser-Joseph-Straße and follow Marktgasse.*

Münsterplatz
The buildings facing the cathedral across this central square were all designed with municipal or ecclesiastical prestige in mind. They include: the **Erzbischöfliches Palais** (Archbishop's Palace from 1756); the **Historisches Kaufhaus**★ (Historical House of Trade) the centre of commercial life in the Middle Ages; and the **Wentzingerhaus** (1761) with a splendid Rococo staircase. Originally the private residence of renowned local artist Johann Christian Wentzinger, it now houses a local history museum, the **Museum für Stadtgeschichte** (◐ *open year-round, Tue–Sun 10am–5pm;* ◐ *closed Jan 1, Dec 24–25 & 31;* ◉*2€ (includes Augustinermuseum);* ✆*(0761) 201 25 15; www.museen.freiburg.de).*

◐ *Exit the square by the Buttergasse alley next to Wentzingerhaus Kaufhaus*

and then turn left into Schusterstraße to join Konviktstraße, a pleasant shopping street that was rebuilt in the 1960s.

Schwabentor (Swabian Gate)
From the Swabian Gate, which is a rare relic from the medieval fortifications, follow along the *Gewerbekanal* (canal). This "Insel" quarter was home to the artisans who depended on water or watermills to pursue their work: tanners, tailors, gemstone cutters and millers.

◐ *Walking along the canal which, according to legend, hides the head of a crocodile, one passes close by the local modern art museum (Marienstraße 10a) to arrive at Augustinerplatz.*

Augustinermuseum★★
Gerberau 15. ◐*Open year-round, Tue–Sun 10am–5pm.* ◐*Closed Jan 1, Dec 24–25 & 31.* ◉*6€.* ✆*(0761) 201 25 21. www.freiburg.de/museen.*
In a former monastery church, this museum contains a small but exquisite collection of art from the Middle Ages to the 19C. Key attractions include the original stone figures and stained-glass windows from Freiburg's Cathedral, as well as wooden sculptures and panel paintings by Matthias Grünewald, Lucas Cranach the Elder and Hans Baldung Grien. The choir is dedicated to Baroque works while the top floor dis-

19C Gallery, Augustinermuseum

© Augustinermuseum - Städtische Museen Freiburg Photo: Axel Killian/Freiburg
Photo: Axel Killian

plays 19C paintings by such practitioners as Anselm Feuerbach, Franz Xaver Winterhalter and Hans Thoma.

▶ *Follow Grünwälderstraße. At no 2 is the entrance to the market hall (Markthalle). Arriving at Kaiser-Joseph-Straße, continue left to return to the centre.*

ADDITIONAL SIGHTS
♨ Schlossberg★

On this last foothill of the Black Forest (456m/1 500ft), woods have almost completely enshrouded Zähringen Castle. A trail leads from the Schwabentor to the summit where you can enjoy panoramic views from the lookout tower. *(Cable-car service.)*

Archäologisches Museum Colombisschlössle★ (Archaeological Museum at Colombi Palace)

Rotteckring 5.
🕐*Open year-round, Tue–Sun 10am–5pm.* 🕐*Closed Dec 24 & 31.*
👁3€. 📞(0761) 201 25 21.
www.freiburg.de/museen.
This neo-Gothic villa in the heart of town and surrounded by vineyards houses extensive archaeological displays. Female statuettes from the Stone Age, mysterious moon idols from the Bronze Age and treasures from Celtic royal tombs are among the highlights.

369

EXCURSIONS
Kaiserstuhl★

▶ *Around 31km/19mi northwest of Freiburg. Leave Freiburg on Lessing-straße and go to Breisach via Gotten-heim.*

A small volcanic massif rising from the Baden plain, the Kaiserstuhl (the Emperor's Throne; 557m/1 828ft) enjoys a warm, dry climate particularly suitable for orchards and vineyards. In fact, the wines of Achkarren, Ihringen, Bickensohl and Oberrotweil are considered among the finest in the region.

Villages worth a stop include **Endingen★**, with its fine old market square, and **Burkheim★**, in its picturesque spot on the southwest slope of the Kaiserstuhl.

Breisach★ – During the 17C Breisach was at the core of a system of fortifications which were among the most powerful in Europe. However the city was mostly laid waste by French Revolutionaries in 1793 and, during the Allied Invasion in 1945, it was again 85 percent destroyed. The most important building to survive is the **Münster St. Stephan★** (St. Stephen's Cathedral). Its nave, transept and towers are Romanesque; the richly decorated Gothic choir includes an exquisitely carved **altarpiece★** (1526). In the first bay (west), note the late 15C Last Judgement mural by Colmarien Schongauer.

From the **Burgplatz★**, there is a fine view of the peaks of the southern Black Forest, the heights of Sundgau, the Grand Ballon (highest point of the Vosges massif) and the terraces of Kaiserstuhl.

Badenweiler

▶ *36km/22mi south, take the B3 out of Freiburg.*
Ernst-Eisenlohr-Straße 4. ✆07 632 79 93 00. www.badenweiler.de. (ⓒClosed Nov–mid-Dec & Jan–mid-Mar).

This relaxing small Black Forest spa village is set amid orchards and vineyards on a sunny south-facing hillside. As well as its famous spa there are natural hot springs here.

Parc Thermal (Kurpark)★★ – This modern spa enjoys a lovely setting in the grounds of the old castle (Schlosspark), surrounded by tropical plants, cedars, cypresses and huge redwoods. The park includes the remains of Roman baths, once the largest complex north of the Alps, now protected by a large glass tunnel (ⓒ open Apr–Oct 10am–7pm; Nov–Mar 10am–5pm). From the castle ruins are lovely **views★** over the Rhine Valley and the Vosges Mountains.

Blauen★

▶ *45km/28mi southwest of Freiburg and 8km/5mi southeast of Badenweiler.*
Blauen look-out tower offers a remarkable **panorama★★** of the Rhine plain. At a height of 1 165m/3 822ft, this peak of the southern Black Forest provides a sweeping view that takes in the highest point of the Vosges massif to the west, the summit of the Belchen (the third highest mountain in the Black Forest) to the northeast, and on a clear day, the Alps to the south. Down below, the two parallel ribbons of the Rhine and the Rheinseitenkanal (Alsace Grand Canal) are a fine sight.

Schloss Bürgeln★ (Bürgeln Castle)

▶ *46km/28.5mi south of Freiburg, 10km/6mi south of Badenweiler.*
◆⌐Guided visits (1hr) Mar–end Oct daily 11am, 2pm, 3pm, 4pm, 5pm; Nov–Feb Thu–Mon, 2pm, 3pm, 4pm. ◎5€. ✆076 26 2 37. www.schlossbuergeln.de.
Surrounded by neat terraced gardens, this country manor, built in 1762 for the abbots of St-Blasien, dominates the foothills of the Black Forest. The interior features beautiful Rococo plasterwork.

Burg Rötteln (Rötteln Castle)★

▶ *63km/39mi south of Freiburg, at Lörrach; 27km/16.5mi south of Badenweiler.*
ⓒOpen 10am–7pm (5pm Nov–Mar). www.schlossermagazin.de.
Ruins are all that remain of this 14C complex, destroyed during the Palatinate War of Succession. Only the upper parts of the castle – its defensive core – with

ramps and a bridge, are accessible. The Grüner Turm (Green Tower), which now dominates the scene, has been restored and converted into a look-out tower.

ADDRESSES

🏠 STAY

Schwarzwälder Hof – *Herrenstraße 43. ℘0761 380 30. www.shof.de. 42 rooms. Restaurant (closed Sun & Aug 1–15).* This smart hotel marries modern comforts with Black Forest charm and discreet service.

Hotel Am Stadtgarten – *Bernhardstraße 5. ℘0761 28 29 002. www.hotelamstadtgarten.de. Closed Jan. 38 rooms.* A 5-minute walk from the centre, this new design hotel is nothing to look at from the exterior, but inside are chic, fashionable bedrooms (some with a balcony) and stylish public areas.

Hotel Zum Roten Bären – *Oberlinden 12. ℘(0761) 38 78 70. www.roter-baeren.de. 25 rooms. Restaurant .* If you want bragging rights for staying in Germany oldest hotel, book one of the cosy rooms in this gem near the Schwabentor. Don't worry, rooms have all the mod-cons you'd expect, while the cosy restaurant is a fine place to enjoy Swiss-influenced cuisine.

🍴 EAT

Hausbrauerei Feierling – *Gerberau 46. ℘(0761) 24 34 80. www.feierling.de.* This micro-brewery brews its own organic beer in copper vats still visible from the gallery. Regional cuisine is served here and in the beer garden across the road.

Osteria Oporto – *Grünwälderstraße 2. ℘0761 387 00 17. Closed Mon.* Parma hams and strings of garlic hang from the ceiling in this Belle-Epoque decorated informal restaurant. Wash down the excellent antipasti with Italian and Portuguese wines.

Schlossbergrestaurant Dattler – *Am Schlossberg 1 (follow Winterstraße or take the Schlossberg cable-car). ℘(0761) 317 29. www.dattler.de. Closed Tue.* Enjoy fabulous views over Freiburg's rooftops

The view embraces the valley of the Wiese (right up until it disappears into the Basel area); the wooded Blauen Mountains; the gentle hills of the Black Forest; and on the horizon, the Swiss Alps.

from this hilltop fine-dining restaurant. Ask about their value-priced lunch specials.

Gasthaus Kybfelsen – *Schauinslandstraße 49, 79100 Freiburg-Günterstal, 5km/3mi south of Freiburg. ℘0761 294 40. www.gasthaus-kybfelsen.de Closed Mon.* This smart, recently renovated brasserie is a landmark on the main road. Regional specialities are served in its two rustic dining rooms or in its beer garden.

Zur Tanne – *Altgasse 2, 79112 Freiburg-Opfingen, 9km/5.5mi west. ℘766 418 10. www.tanne-opfingen.de. Closed Mon–Tue. 10 rooms, from 49€.* An abundance of carved woodwork and an old tiled oven characterise this typical 100-year old Black Forest restaurant. Its rooms have been simply but tastefully decorated and furnished.

🍴 TAKING A BREAK

Markthalle – *Kaiser-Joseph-Straße 233 (via Grünwälderstraße and Fressgässle). ℘(0761) 38 70 00. www.markthalle-freiburg.de. Closed Sun.* Piles of fruit and vegetables, mountains of bread, buckets of olives – Freiburg's market is a smorgasbord of culinary delights from around the world. Stock up, eat in, take out.

🌙 NIGHTLIFE

Kagan – *Bismarckallee 9 (in the building beside the central station; take the lift). ℘(0761) 7 67 27 66. www.kagan-lounge.de.* At German-American designer Vladimir Kagan's posh party palace, you can sip your cocktails with a view from the 17th floor, then hit the dancefloor on the 18th.

UC Café – *Niemensstr. 7 (between Bertoldstraße and Kaiser-Joseph-Straße). ℘(0761) 38 33 55.* Sit below a shady maple tree at this popular café in Freiburg's pedestrian zone, where visitors stop for coffee and snacks.

Constance★

Konstanz

Presumed to have been founded by Roman Emperor Constantius Chlorus (292–306), Konstanz (Constance) has an enviable location right on the shores of its namesake lake. It has a well-preserved old town and a lively vibe thanks to a large student population. It is also the gateway to the "flower island" of Mainau and charming Reichenau Island with its ancient abbey.

A BIT OF HISTORY

Council of Constance – From 1414 to 1418, a council convened in Koblenz to resolve the Great Schism that had led to the simultaneous existence of three popes. The only conclave ever held north of the Alps concluded in 1417 with the election of Pope Martin V.

Two years earlier this same council had summoned before it the Bohemian religious reformer **Jan Hus**, rector of the University of Prague. Regarded as a threat to the Church's hold on power, his Reformist ideas were categorically rejected, Hus was declared a heretic and burned at the stake. A precursor of Protestantism, he was hailed as a national hero in his native Bohemia.

WALKING TOUR

Allow 90min. Leave from the tourist office, crossing the railway tracks via the underground passageway.

Seeufer★ (Lake Shore)

The easy-going, almost Italianate charm and ambience of Konstanz is particularly evident along its lakeside. Just beyond the boat dock *(near the tourist office)* is the **Konzilgebäude** (council building) the warehouse where the Council of Constance convened in the 15C; it is now used as a concert and congress hall.

At the bottom of the jetty, the 10m/32.8ft-high **Imperia** is a slowly rotating monumental female sculpture created by artist Peter Lenk in 1993. It satirises the influence the Italian courtesan Imperia wielded as the lover of members of

- ▶ **Population:** 82 600
- **Info:** Bahnhofplatz 43. ℰ(07531) 13 30 30. www.konstanz-tourismus.de.
- ▶ **Location:** Bordering Switzerland, Konstanz sits at the point separating Lake Constance (Bodensee in German) from its picturesque prolongation (Untersee). The islands of Mainau *(to the north)* and Reichenau *(to the west)* are linked to the town by a causeway.
- **Don't Miss:** The beautiful islands of Mainau and Reichenau.
- **Timing:** Allow two hours to tour Mainau Island.
- **Kids:** Outdoor activities on Mainau and Reichenau islands (*see Excursions*).

the Council; she was immortalised by Honoré de Balzac in his novel *Ribald Tales (Contes drôlatiques)*.

Across the road, in the municipal gardens *(Stadtgarten)*, is a monument to Count Ferdinand von Zeppelin (1838–1917), the celebrated airship inventor. He was born in Constance on the Insel, a tiny island in the Stadtgarten that is reached via a footbridge. Across the Rheinbrücke (bridge) and along the Rheinsteig are the old **defensive towers** (Rheintorturm, Pulverturm). On the opposite bank, the Seestraße *(to the right)* is lined with Jugendstil villas.

▶ *Follow Rheingasse, which takes you past an elegant early-17C building with a striking red façade housing the cathedral priory. Go left on Inselgasse and right on Brückengasse to return to the cathedral on Münsterplatz. Wedged between the cathedral and the Rhine is the maze-like Niederburg, the town's oldest quarter, where craftsmen and artisans clustered in the Middle Ages.*

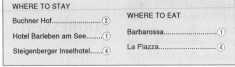

WHERE TO STAY

Buchner Hof........................②

Hotel Barleben am See........①

Steigenberger Inselhotel......④

WHERE TO EAT

Barbarossa..........................①

La Piazza............................④

Münster★ (Cathedral)

Since its construction lasted from the 11C to the 17C, this **cathedral** lacks any architectural unity. The **panels★** *(Türflügel)* of the porch doors in the main façade are decorated with bas-relief sculptures representing scenes from the life of Christ (1470). The 13C Mauritiuskapelle (chapel) houses the most prized piece of sculpture, the **Holy Tomb★**, a vaulted dodecagon containing three statuary groups. It is one of the few examples of its kind from the High Middle Ages, bearing a stylistic resemblance to the sculptures of Bamberg and Naumburg.

In the crypt, four gilded 11C–13C plaques represent Christ in Majesty, the Eagle of St. John, and St. Conrad and St. Pelagius, patrons of the diocese.

They are known as the **Konstanzer Goldscheiben** (gilded plaques of Constance). The tower (◐*open Mon–Sat 10am–5pm, Sun 12.30pm–5.30pm; ⊛2€*) can be climbed for sweeping city and lake views.

▷ *Follow Wessenbergerstraße, a pedestrian zone lined with painted houses. Pass by Obermarkt before turning left into Kanzleistraße.*

Rathaus (Town Hall)

The façade of this Renaissance building is embellished with paintings illustrating the history of Constance.

ADDITIONAL SIGHTS

Archäologisches Landesmuseum (State Museum of Archaeology)

Benediktinerplatz 5. ◐Open year-round, Tue–Sun, 10am–6pm. ◐Closed Jan 1, Dec 24–25 & 31. ◉4€, free 1st Sat of month. ♿ ℘(07531) 980 40. www.konstanz.alm-bw.de.

This museum is housed in the old former Peterhausen Abbey. History comes to life in 3 000sq m/32 291sq ft of exhibition space, spanning an arc from 6 000-year-old stilt buildings to recent industrial activity.

♟ Sea Life

Hafenstraße 9. ◐Open May, Jun, mid-Sept–Oct, daily 10am–6pm; Jul–mid-Sept, 10am–7pm; Nov–Apr, Mon–Fri 10am–5pm, Sat–Sun 10am–6pm. ◉13.95€ (children 9.95€). ℘(01805) 66 69 01 01. www.sealifeeurope.com.

Follow the flow of the Rhine from its source to the North Sea in this imaginatively designed aquarium and encounter some 3 700 aquatic creatures along the way. A 8m/24ft-long tunnel, where sharks, skates and turtles dart around you, is a highlight, as are touch pools where sea anemones and starfish bring big smiles to the faces not only of the youngest visitors.

EXCURSIONS

Insel Mainau★★ (Mainau Island)

▶ 7km/4.3mi north via Mainaustraße. ◐Open Apr–Oct 7am–8pm, Nov–Mar 9am–5pm. ◉15.90€. ♿ ℘(07531) 30 30. www.mainau.de. Allow 2hrs.

Friedrich I, the duke of Baden, quite literally sowed the seeds for this garden island in 1853. Now owned by a Swedish aristocratic family, the Bernadottes, it is a lavish symphony of scent and colour and one of the most popular destinations in the lake region.

The palace, Baroque church and exotic and tropical flowers and plants contribute to the island's magic. ♟The petting zoo, playground, pony rides and butterfly house are magnets for kids.

Insel Reichenau★ (Reichenau Island)

▶ 7km/4.3mi west. Take B33 in the direction of Radolfzell.
℘(07534) 920 70. www.reichenau.de.

Reichenau traces its origins to 724 when St. Pirmin founded the first Benedictine monastery in Germany on this petite island in the Untersee section of Lake Constance. For centuries, it was a renowned centre of learning and arts. Reichenau monks were particularly noted for producing outstanding illuminated manuscripts as well as brilliant frescoes during the Ottonian period (9C).

Thanks to its three ancient churches, Reichenau has enjoyed UNESCO World Heritage Site status since 2000. Note especially the 9C Carolingian church in Oberzell with its wall paintings, and the Romanesque former abbey church in Mittelzell. Here, a wooden vaulted apse, a Gothic chancel and a 1477 altar with relics of St. Mark are among the treasures deserving closer inspection.

ADDRESSES

🏨 STAY

⊜⊜⊜ **Buchner Hof** – *Buchnerstraße 6 (via Mainaustraße). ℘(07531) 810 20. www.buchner-hof.de. 13 rooms. Closed Dec 20–Jan 10.* In a quiet location, this little hideaway near the lake and the old town is run with a personal touch. Rooms are bright and cheerfully furnished in a pleasing palette of colours.

⊜⊜⊜⊜ **Hotel Barleben am See** – *Seestraße 15, 78464 Konstanz-Staad. ℘(07531) 94 23 30. www.hotel-barleben.de. 8 rooms.* This 1872 villa turned boutique hotel draws lots of regulars to its lovely, personalised rooms. The location in the heart of parkland adjacent to the lakeside promenade boosts its appeal as a romantic getaway.

Steigenberger Inselhotel –
*Auf der Insel 1. ℘(07531) 12 50. www.
konstanz.steigenberger.de. 102 rooms.
Restaurant* ☺☺☺☺. Still boasting
details of its former reincarnation as a
monastery, this hotel envelops guests
in a tasteful, upmarket ambience that
moves smoothly from the public areas
to the rooms. Dine in the elegant
restaurant or on the splendid terrace
with lake views.

⚲/EAT

La Piazza – *Marktstätte 2. ℘(07531)
91 79 27. www.lapiazza-kn.de.* A relaxed
atmosphere and a modern setting for
Italian cuisine and outstanding desserts.

Barbarossa – *Obermarkt 8–12.
℘(07531) 12 89 90. www.barbarossa-
hotel.com. 55 rooms. Restaurant* ☺☺☺.
This upstairs dining room decked out
in dark wood delivers attentive service
and a delicate cuisine. A speciality is
locally caught fish, which is sometimes
given an exotic treatment. In winter,
locals get together for wine and tapas
accompanied by live music (*Wed–Sat
6pm–1am*).

Lake Constance★★
Bodensee

**With its expansive horizons
and a climate mild enough
for tropical vegetation, Lake
Constance (*Bodensee* in German)
attracts a multitude of German
holidaymakers who regard it as
their local "Riviera". In addition
to the vistas, which encompass
the Alps to the south in clear
weather, tourists love the lake's
clear waters, medieval towns and
boat cruises.**

GETTING AROUND

FERRY: Between Constance and
Meersburg (20min). Daily departures
every 15min from 6am–8pm (fewer
at other times). ☺7€ with car, 2.50€
per passenger. *℘(07531) 80 30.
www.sw.konstanz.de.*

CRUISES: Hafenstraße 6 (behind
the tourist office). *℘(07531) 346
03 89. www.bsb-online.com.* Trips
available to Mainau, Uhldingen
and the Zeppelin Museum in
Friedrichshafen.

🛈 **Info:** Bahnhofsplatz 13.
℘(07531) 31 13 30 22.
www.konstanz.de/
tourismus.
▶ **Location:** The Rhine
flows into the Bodensee
as it spills out of the
Alps and shares borders
with Switzerland and
Austria. Due to its vast
size, the lake creates
its own microclimate
especially conducive to
fruit cultivation. Boat
services ply the lake's
waters, frequently
linking Constance,
Überlingen, Meersburg,
Friedrichshafen, Lindau
and Bregenz (in Austria).
Don't Miss: Lake cruises
from Constance or
Friedrichshafen.
The Stilt Houses Museum
(see the Driving Tour).
🕐 **Timing:** Allow half a day
for a leisurely boat cruise.
The entire region easily
warrants a full day or two.
Kids: Swimming or
cruising on the lake.

🚗 DRIVING TOURS

FROM ÜBERLINGEN TO LINDAU

56km/35mi – Allow 4hrs.

Überlingen★

Am Landungsplatz 5, 88662 Überlingen.
℘ (07551) 947 15 22.
www.ueberlingen.de.

This former Free Imperial City on Lake Constance was founded around 1180 by Frederick I Barbarossa and achieved great prosperity in the Middle Ages thanks to its vineyards and leading role in the salt and grain trade. Since the mid-19C, the tourist industry has become the local economic engine, especially after Überlingen became an official Kneipp spa resort in 1956.

The town is on the northwest shore of Bodensee (Lake Constance) surrounded by orchards and blessed with a mild climate. West of the centre, a pleasant walk along the ancient moat leads to the **Seepromenade**.

Münsterplatz (Minster Square)

The square is bordered by the Gothic cathedral, the north façade of the town hall and the Renaissance **Alte Kanzlei** (municipal chancellery).

Münster (Minster)★

This Gothic cathedral (1350–1562) is the mightiest in the region. Inside the harmonious five-nave basilica all eyes are drawn to the magnificent wooden high altar carved by local artisan Jörg Zürn (1613–1616). A 16C Swabian work, the Virgin of the Crescent Moon, stands in St. Elizabeth Chapel.

Rathaus (Town Hall)

Münsterstraße 15. Open Mon–Fri 9am–noon, 1pm–4pm (Oct–Apr 5pm) and year-round Sat 9am–noon.
℘ (07551) 99 10 22.
www.ueberlingen.de.

The first-floor Gothic **Ratssaal**★ (council chamber) is beautifully decorated with panelled walls and a carved frieze with 41 statuettes representing members of the Guilds of the Holy Roman Empire. The city council still convenes in this hall today.

Städtisches Museum (Municipal Museum)

Krummebergstraße 30. Open year-round, Tue–Sat 9am–12.30pm, 2pm–5pm (Apr–Oct, also Sun 10am–3pm). 3€. ℘ (07551) 99 10 79. www.museum-ueberlingen.de.

Exhibits in this late-15C mansion with Baroque touches include paintings and sculpture by local artists from the Gothic period to classicism, a collection of 18C crèches *(Krippen)* and 50 dolls' houses from the Renaissance to *Jugendstil*.

Birnau

An important stop on the Upper Swabian Baroque Route, this 18C pilgrimage church overlooks the Bodensee and was an exuberant collaboration of master artists of the day. Peter Thumb designed the building, Gottfried Bernard Göz was responsible for the richly detailed frescoes, while Joseph Anton Feuchtmayr carved the altars, stucco ornamentation and sculptures.

The church's most famous sculpture is the adorable "Honey Sucker", a cheeky cherub caught with his fingers inside a beehive.

Salem★

Founded by the Cistercians in 1137, for over 650 years Klosters Salem (Salem Abbey) was one of the most important abbeys in Germany and its abbot was answerable only to the emperor and the Pope. The abbey reached its apogee under Abbot Anselm II (1746–1778), builder of the pilgrimage church of Birnau. In 1802 it passed to the Margrave (Counts) of Baden and is still under their ownership.

Today the 7ha/17acre abbey complex is a striking architectural ensemble which combines the Gothic, Renaissance, Baroque and classical. It resembles a small village, complete with private college, craftworkers, a café-restaurant and shop. Seek out the pharmacy, in the Untertor-Haus, an elegantly designed Baroque pavilion.

Boats on the lake with Überlingen in the background

T. Krieger/MICHELIN

Münster★ (Cathedral) – Construction of this fine Gothic building began in 1297, though it was not consecrated until the Council of Constance in 1414. The splendid Gothic windows are pierced by gables east and west. The interior is typical of Cistercian architecture, with its large choir and high arches. It owes its splendid alabaster decoration to Abbot Anselm II.

Schloss★ (Castle) – (℘07 553 81 437; www.schloesser-magazin.de; open Apr–Nov Mon–Sat 9.30am–6pm, Sun and hols 10.30am–6pm; ⬚7€). The highlight is the old refectory which has retained its beautiful stucco ceiling, executed by the Schmuzer brothers. The same artists are also responsible for the superb vaulting in the library. Also worth a visit are the Bernhardusgang (Bernard Gallery), the Kaisersaal (Emperors' Hall) completed in 1707 – the first large reception room in a Baroque abbey in Germany – and the Rococo study of Abbot Anselm II.

In the old convent part of the castle, the Feuerwehr Museum (Firemen's Museum) is a reminder that this section was constructed after the devastating fire of 1697 (by Franz Beer, from the school of Vorarlberg). Its size and decoration reflect the wealth of the Abbey at that time.

▷ *Return to the B 31 and head in the direction of Uhldingen to reach the lakeside village of Pfahlbauten.*

👤👤 Pfahlbaumuseum★★ (Stilt Houses Museum)

Strandpromenade 6, 88690 Uhldingen-Mühlhofen. ℘07 556 85 43. www. pfahlbauten.de. ⏰*Open Apr–Sept 9am–7pm; Oct and after Easter 8am–5pm; Nov–Mar weekends 9am–5pm; Feb Sun 10am–4pm.* 👣*Guided tours (in German)* ⬚*7€ (children 4.50€).*

This spectacular open-air Lake Village museum, constructed in 1922 near the original excavation site, comprises 20 stilt houses which vividly evoke the Bronze Age period (between 4000 and 1000 BC.). The architectural reconstructions (the most recent were added in 2002), are wholly convincing, as are the costumed actors who play out the daily lives of the village inhabitants. Even if you don't understand the German tour, both parents and children will enjoy pretending to be archaeologists, or having a go at stone carving, or perhaps making fire, using only the primitive techniques of our ancestors.

Meersburg★

A former residence of Prince-Archbishops, Meersburg is now a picturesque village on a rocky outcrop overlooking the lake and surrounded by vineyards and orchards. The historic upper town (Oberstadt) centres on the **Marktplatz**★, from which the **Steigstraße**★, bordered by half-timbered houses, offers delightful views.

Meersburg

© BasleB/iStockphoto.com

Dominating the Unterstadt (lower town) from its perky perch is the massive medieval **Burg Meersburg** (*Meersburg Castle;* ○*open Mar–Oct, daily 9am–6.30pm; Nov–Feb, daily 10am–6pm;* ✆*8.50€;* 📞*(07532) 800 00; www.burg-meersburg.de*). For seven years until her death in 1848, this was the home of **Annette von Droste-Hülshoff**, a poet born in Westphalia in 1797 and famous for the 1842 novella *Die Judenbuche (The Jew's Beech)*. Annette's rooms are among the 28 that can be seen on a self-guided tour. Others include the kitchen, baths, private and representational rooms. The prison, the torture chamber and the treasury, however, can only be seen on guided tours (included in admission).

▶ *The itinerary continues along the Grüne Straße (Green Route), famous for its apple orchards, whose fruit is exported throughout Europe.*

Friedrichshafen

Friedrichshafen is a lively if industrial port town and the birthplace of the dirigible at the turn of the 20C.

Aside from the Zeppelin Museum described below, the Baroque **church** (*Schlosskirche*) near the castle (still occupied by the ducal family of Württemberg) is worth a visit. Designed by

Christian Thumb between 1695 and 1701, it features a richly detailed ceiling and fanciful choir stalls.

Friedrichshafen is the departure point for boat excursions to the Rhine falls in Schaffhausen, to the "flower island" of Mainau and to the stilt houses in Unteruhldingen (⌖*see Überlingen*).

🚹🚺 Zeppelin Museum

Seestraße 22. ○*Open Jul–Sept, daily 9am–5pm; May–Jun & Oct, Tue–Sun 9am-5pm; Nov–Apr, Tue–Sun 10am–5pm; last entry 30min before closing.* ○*Closed Dec 24–25 & 31.* ✆*7.50€.* ♿📞*(07541) 380 10. www.zeppelin-museum.de.*

In a converted railway station on the eastern promenade of Lake Constance, the Zeppelin Museum is a must-see for technology buffs. In six major departments, it presents the entire history of airships first developed in Friedrichshafen by Count Ferdinand Zeppelin at the turn of the 20C. Among the museum's main attractions is a 33m/108ft-long reconstructed walk-through section of the *LZ 129 Hindenburg* that tragically crashed in New Jersey in 1937. Upstairs, an art exhibition demonstrates regional works from the Middle Ages to today. Look for works by Otto Dix, Max Ackermann and Karl Caspar.

Wasserburg

Often deluged by day-trippers, this village is wedged into a narrow spit of land jutting into the lake. Walk to the tip for beautiful views over the river banks with the Alps as a backdrop.

Lindau★★

(&see LINDAU IM BODENSEE)

ADDRESSES

🏠 STAY

⊖ **Gasthof Auer** – Stockacher Straße 62, 78359 Orsingen-Nenzingen. ℘(07771) 24 97. www.auer-nenzingen.de. Closed 1 week in late July. 5 rooms. Restaurant⊖. Simple but welcoming, this inn combines a rustic restaurant serving seasonal, regional cuisine with a few basic but nicely decorated rooms.

⊖ **Landgasthof Sternen** – Schienerbergstraße 23, 78345 Bankholzen-Moos. ℘(07732) 24 22. www.zum-sternen. de. 18 rooms. Restaurant⊖⊖. This congenial country inn is a great place to lay low in well-proportioned, charmingly furnished rooms. The restaurant is justly popular for its fresh fish and meat dishes sourced from regional suppliers.

⊖⊖ **Bodensee-Hotel Kreuz** – Grasbeurer Straße 2, 88690 Uhldingen-Mühlhofen. ℘(07556) 92 88 90. www.bodensee-hotel-kreuz.de. 43 rooms. Restaurant⊖⊖. This family-run hotel on a quiet side-street offers rooms in a historic main building and a modern annex. In either, the interior is warm and traditional with spacious, homey rooms, many with balcony.

⊖⊖ **Gästehaus Schmäh** – Kapellenstraße 7, 88709 Hagnau. ℘(07532) 62 10. www.gaestehaus-schmaeh.de. 17 rooms. This well-maintained guesthouse is situated in a quiet residential area and sports spotless, balconied rooms furnished in simple, rustic oak. Sun-worshippers will love relaxing with a book on the lawn behind the house.

⊖⊖⊖ **Villa Seeschau** – Von-Laßberg-Straße, 88709 Meersburg. ℘(07532) 43 44 90. www.hotel-seeschau.de. 18 rooms. This pretty villa is surrounded by lush gardens and has elegant, good-sized rooms in neutral hues and with balcony views of the lake. The panorama terrace is the perfect spot for breakfast.

🍴 EAT

⊖ **Pfälzer Hof** – Lindenplatz 3, 88142 Wasserburg. ℘08 382 98 85 30. www.pfaelzer-hof-wasserburg.de. Closed Jan–Mar, Nov–Dec & Wed throughout the year. This family-run hotel-guesthouse has a friendly atmosphere. Simple rustic cooking.

⊖⊖ **Winzerstube zum Becher** – Höllgasse 4, 88709 Meersburg. ℘(07532) 90 09. www.winzerstube-zum-becher.de. Closed 3 weeks in Jan and Mon. This rustic establishment has been welcoming thirsty visitors since 1610 and been run by the same family for the past 120 years. The kitchen specialises in regional cuisine with international accents.

⊖⊖ **Bürgerbräu** – Aufkircher Straße 20, 8862 Überlingen. ℘07551 927 40. www.buergerbraeu-ueberlingen.com. Closed Wed. This charming half-timbered historic lakeside inn serves high-quality local and regional dishes in a cosy rustic dining room.

🚃 TAKING A BREAK

Strandcafé – Strandbadstraße 102 78315 Radolfzell. ℘(07732) 16 50. www.strandcafe-mettnau.de. This modern glass pavilion has an enviable lakeside location with first-rate views from all tables. Come for coffee or pre-dinner sunset drinks.

🏃 SPORTS AND LEISURE

Swimming – There are numerous beaches with swimming pools around the lake, most notably at Überlingen and Meersburg.

Cruises – Bodensee-Schiffsbetriebe, 88045 Friedrichshafen. ℘07 541 9238 389. www.bsb-online.com. Cruises cover several parts of the lake: Überlingen See cruises depart from Meersburg (3hrs 15min, 14.10€) allowing guests to enjoy the lakeside village, Birnau church and Mainau Island. Evening cruises depart from Friedrichshafen, Immenstaad, Hagnau, Meersburg and Radolfzell.

Lindau im Bodensee★★

Bavaria's westernmost town, Lindau's old town sits on an island in Lake Constance and exudes a casual, almost Mediterranean flair. Its lanes brim with fine gabled burghers' houses reflecting its past prosperity as a trading partner with Italy. Alas, its lanes are often deluged with visitors, but simply wander off into a quiet side-street or hidden courtyard and the magic of Lindau will quickly reveal itself.

🐾 WALKING TOUR
OLD TOWN★★

Marktplatz (Market Square)
A large circular fountain anchors Lindau's handsome market square, which is dominated by two churches. The Baroque **Haus zum Cavazzen**★, on the west side, houses the **Town Museum** (Stadtmuseum; ⏱open year-

- ▶ **Population:** 24 700
- ℹ **Info:** Alfred-Nobel-Platz 1, opposite the train station. ℘(08382) 26 00 26. http://lindau-tourismus.de.
- ◐ **Location:** Lindau is on the far eastern edge of Bodensee (Lake Constance). Ferries link the town to Konstanz and Bregenz (Austria) several times daily (www.bsb-online.com).
- ✋ **Don't Miss:** A stroll through the old town.
- ⏱ **Timing:** Allow one hour for a walking tour of the old town.

round, Mon–Fri 11am–5pm, Sat 2pm–5pm, Sun 11am–5pm; ⏱closed Nov–Mar Mon; ⊛3€; ℘(08382) 94 40 73).

◐ Follow **Maximilianstraße★★**, the old town's picturesque main artery, then turn right into the Zeppelinstraße.

LINDAU IM BODENSEE

Lindau harbour

©Gillet Luc/iStockphoto.com

Schrannenplatz

The landmark Brigands' Tower *(Diebsturm)* is part of the medieval fortifications. The nearby **Peterskirche**, the oldest church in town (AD 1000), serves as a war memorial and is adorned with **frescoes** (15C) by Hans Holbein the Elder.

ADDRESSES

STAY

⊖⊖⊖ **Hotel Lindauer Hof** – *Seepromenade. ℘(08382) 40 64. www.lindauer-hof.de. 30 rooms. Restaurant* ⊖⊖⊖. This hotel is a winning marriage of history and modern sophistication and is pleasantly close to the lake. Meals are served on the first floor or on the pretty terrace.

⊖⊖⊖ **Hotel Vis à Vis** – *Bahnhofplatz 4–5. ℘08 382 39 65. www.visavis-lindau.de. 51 rooms.* Opposite the station, this smart new hotel offers spacious rooms with warm colours and light airy contemporary designs, plus a bistro.

⊖⊖⊖⊖ **Hotel Bayerischer Hof** – *Seepromenade. ℘(08382) 91 50. www. bayerischerhof-lindau.de. 97 rooms. Restaurant* ⊖⊖⊖. Sporting a classical

▶ *Backtrack on Zeppelinstraße.*

Hafen★ (Harbour)

This is the departure point for boat trips on Lake Constance. Contact Bodensee-Schiffsbetriebe *(Schützingerweg 2; ℘(08382) 275 84 10; www.bsb-online.com).*

façade, this elegant hotel has plush yet traditional décor and flair. Views of the harbour channel are a major perk of the stylish restaurant.

EAT

⊖⊖ **Alte Post** – *Fischergasse 3. ℘08 382 934 60. www.alte-post-lindau.de Closed Nov, late Dec–Mar. 11 rooms.* Traditional local cooking with attention to detail is served either in the *Biergarten*, on the terrace in the square or in the formal dining room of this long-established city centre hotel.

⊖⊖ **Zum Sünfzen** – *Maximilianstraße 1. ℘08 382 58 65. www.suenfzen.de.* The restaurant in this beautiful 14C historic house is something of a local institution. In summer you can dine out, under the sunshades, on its pretty terrace on the pedestrianised street.

Stuttgart★★

The capital of Baden-Württemberg is a city in transition. No longer purely defined by its urbanity, it is gradually becoming increasingly green and pedestrian-friendly and more in sync with the forested hills surrounding it. As the hub of Mercedes Benz, Stuttgart is naturally associated with cars, but fans of art and modern architecture will also have plenty to see and explore. Originally called "Stutengarten", the name derives from a seigniorial 10C stud farm. In the 14C Stuttgart became the home of the dukes and kings of Württemberg and centuries later hit its full stride during the Industrial Revolution.

A BIT OF HISTORY

Two auto pioneers – An engineer born in Bad Cannstatt, **Gottfried Daimler** (1834–1900) invented the internal combustion engine needed to power vehicles. **Karl Benz** (1844–1929) envisaged an entire motor vehicle, which he elaborated in every detail at Mannheim. Soon he was able to start manufacturing cars in larger numbers; in 1899 he sold his 2 000th vehicle and thus became the world's leading automobile manufacturer.

▶ **Population:** 600 000
▪ **Info:** Königstraße 1a. ✆(0711) 222 80. www.stuttgart-tourist.de.
◐ **Location:** Stuttgart lies in a valley surrounded by vineyards and wooded hills opening onto the Neckar. The finest city **view**★ is from the upper platform of the 400m/1 312ft-high **Fernsehturm** (TV tower).
▣ **Parking:** There is ample parking throughout Stuttgart. Visit http://wap.parkinfo.com for fees and locations.
⊚ **Don't Miss:** The world-class fine arts gallery. Car buffs should make time for the Mercedes-Benz and Porsche museums.
▲▪ **Kids:** Wilhelma Park and Zoo.

In 1901, Daimler's company marketed the **Mercedes**, a name that would make an automotive dynasty as well as no small fortune. Today, the night sky over Stuttgart blazes with the illuminated three-point-star within a circle, the firm's world-famous trademark.

Mercedes-Benz Museum

©Olaf Loose/istockphoto.com

Urban landscape – The only remnants of Stuttgart's medieval core are apparent on **Schillerplatz**, flanked by the **Stiftskirche** (Collegiate Church) and the **Altes Schloss** (Old Castle). The statue of Schiller in the centre of the square is the work of the Danish sculptor Thorwaldsen (1839). The Baroque **Neues Schloss** (New Palace) is now the home of regional ministerial departments.

WALKING TOUR
TRAIN STATION TO SCHLOSSPLATZ
Allow 2hrs.

▶ *From the tourist office take Schillerstraße to the train station. Built between 1917 and 1924, it has a tower topped with a Mercedes star (free access). From here, have a look down Königstraße.*

Schlossgarten (Castle Gardens)
A lovely spot for a picnic, these gardens are crisscrossed by more than 11km/8mi of walkways and form part of the vast green belt cinched around the central city. The original "Stutengarten" was located here.

▶ *Keep right to get to the Staatstheater (State Theatre), then hook a left after the opera house to go through a subway to emerge onto Konrad-Adenauer-Straße.*

Kulturmeile Konrad-Adenauer-Straße
Stuttgart's main cultural institutions conveniently line up along an 800m/2 625ft stretch of Konrad-Adenauer-Straße in what has come to be known as the "Boulevard of Culture" (*Kulturmeile*). On your left looms the vast Staatsgalerie (state gallery), the vast art museum that displays its fine collections in the original Neoclassical 19C building and in modernist additions by Sir James Stirling (1984) and Wilfrid and Katharina Steib (2002).
Walking south on Konrad-Adenauer-Straße takes you past the **Conservatory of Music and Dramatic Arts** and the

House of History (*Haus der Geschichte*) to the **Wilhemspalais**, where the last king of Württemberg, William II, lived until his abdication in 1918. A statue of the monarch and his little dog stands in front of the Neoclassical building.

▶ *Cross Konrad-Adenauer-Straße, then walk past the New Castle on your right to Schlossplatz (Castle Square).*

Schlossplatz (Castle Square)
This green square is the heart of the city. It is dominated by the **Neues Schloss** (New Castle), a royal residence built between 1746 and 1807 and now the seat of the Baden-Württemberg state parliament. Opposite, the Classical columns of the **Königsbau** (Royal Pavilion) conceal a vast new shopping centre called Königsbau-Passagen. The glass cube on the left houses the **Kunstmuseum Stuttgart** (Museum of Art).

▶ *Head south from Schlossplatz to Schillerplatz.*

Altes Schloss (Old Castle)
The most prominent building flanking Schillerplatz is the Old Palace, a largely 16C Renaissance ducal residence which consists of four wings flanked by round towers. Its **courtyard**★ (*with access to the Schlosskirche church*) is surrounded by three floors of arcaded galleries. It now houses the regional history museum (*see next*).

Landesmuseum Württemberg★ (Württemberg State Museum)
Schillerplatz 6, inside Altes Schloss.
Open year-round, Tue–Sun 10am–5pm. 4.50€. (0711) 89 53 51 11. www.landesmuseum-stuttgart.de.
This museum chronicles regional history from prehistoric times to today. Its collections from the Bronze and Iron Ages include important finds from a from mid-6C BC Celtic **royal tomb**★ excavated near Ludwigsburg.
Upstairs Roman artefacts mingle with southern German **religious statuary** ★★. Funerary objects (weapons, jewels

and household items) are displayed in the **Franks and the Alemanni Section**, tribes that dominated wide parts of Europe between the 3C and 8C.

Additional exhibits include a coin gallery; collections of furniture, clocks, scientific instruments and weapons; and the crown jewels of the kings of Württemberg.

A fine collection of musical instruments is on display in a nearby building, the Fruchtkasten on Schillerplatz.

Stiftskirche (Collegiate Church)

Also on Schillerplatz, the Collegiate Church strikes a fine silhouette and combines architectural elements from the Romanesque (base of the south tower, 12C), early Gothic (chancel, 14C) and late Gothic (the nave, 15C). A **memorial**★ to the Dukes of Württemberg stands in the chancel.

Kunstmuseum Stuttgart (Stuttgart Fine Arts Museum)

Kleiner Schlossplatz 1. ⏰*Open year-round, Tue, Thu–Sun 10am–6pm, Wed & Fri 10am–9pm.* ⏰*Closed Jan 1, Good Fri, Dec 24–25 & 31.* 🎫*5€.* ☎*(0711) 216 21 88. www.kunstmuseum-stuttgart.de.* North of Schillerplatz, this gallery possesses prized canvasses by famous artists from the classical, Modern and contemporary periods. Pride of place goes to *Neue Sachlichkeit* artist **Otto Dix**★ who was famous for the ferocity of his social critique and anti-war sentiment. The museum building itself is in an impressive glass cube that glows from within at night. The mobile out the front is by Alexander Calder.

SIGHTS
Staatsgalerie★★ (Fine Arts Gallery)

Konrad-Adenauer-Straße 30–32. ⏰*Open year-round, Wed–Sun 10am–6pm (Tue and Thu 8pm).* ⏰*Closed Good Fri, Dec 24 & 25.* 🎫*5.50€, special exhibitions 10€.* ♿ ☎*(0711) 47 04 00. www.staatsgalerie.de.* Stuttgart's state gallery consists of three parts. The 19C Alte Staatsgalerie (Old

State Gallery) presents a world-class collection of European painting from medieval times to late 19C Impressionism. Highlights include the 14C–16C **Old German Masters Section**★★ and the **Herrenberg Altar** by Jerg Ratgeb (1519), which portrays the Last Supper, the Crucifixion and the Resurrection. Venetians and Florentines from the 14C dominate the Italian section, while Dutch Old Masters range from Memling to Rembrandt, Ruisdael to Rubens.

Since 1994, 20C works have found a home in the Neue Staatsgalerie (New State Gallery), a Postmodern building by Sir James Stirling. Look for Fauvists and French Cubists (Matisse, Braque, Juan Gris), Expressionists (Kokoschka), the artists of *Neue Sachlichkeit* (Dix, Grosz) and artists of the Bauhaus. Contemporary art is represented by Dubuffet, and Giacometti as well as Baselitz, Beuys and Kiefer and such American Pop Artists as Andy Warhol.

A separate annex is linked to the Old State Gallery by glass bridges. Designed by the Basel architectural team of Wilfrid and Katharina Steib, it opened in 2002 and harbours a prized graphics collection.

Linden Museum★★

Hegelplatz 1. ⏰*Open year-round, Tue–Sun 10am–5pm (Wed 8pm).* ⏰*Closed Mon before Mardi Gras, Good Fri, May 1, Dec 24–25 & 31.* 🎫*4€.* ♿ ☎*(0711) 202 23. www.lindenmuseum.de.* Take a journey back in time and around the world at this ethnographic museum with artefacts from the Americas, the Pacific, Africa, the Middle East, the Far East and southern Asia.

EXCURSIONS
Höhenpark Killesberg

▶ *4km/2.5mi north via Heilbronner Straße.*

Part of the greenbelt around the inner city, Höhenpark features cascades, fountains and flowerbeds, as well as **miniature train** rides and a look-out tower with views over the entire city.

Wilhelma Park, Wiessenhoff Museum-
Killesberg Park, Porsche Museum | Le Corbusier House | LUDWIGSBURG

STUTTGART

WHERE TO STAY

Abalon	①	
Bellevue	④	
Der Zauberlehrling	⑦	
Cube	⑦	
Kern's Pastetchen	⑨	
Weinstube Kochenbas	⑬	
Weinstube Schellenturm	⑮	

WHERE TO EAT

Augustenstüble .... ①

Conservatory of Music and
Dramatic Arts .... **P**

House of History .... **R**

Württemberg State
Museum .... **T**

Royal Pavillon and
Königsbau Passagen .... **V**

385

Weissenhofsiedlung and Museum★ (Weissenhof Estate and Museum)

Rathenaustraße 1. ◷*Open year-round, Tue–Fri 11am–6pm, 10am–6pm Sat & Sun.* ◷*Closed Jan 1.* ⬭*4€.* ✆*(0711) 257 91 87. www.weissenhof.de.*

This housing estate is the outcome of a 1927 building exhibition and regarded as a milestone in modern architecture. It drew 17 leading architects, including Le Corbusier, Walter Gropius and Mies van der Rohe.

Most buildings can only be seen from the outside, but two semi-detached homes by Le Corbusier now house an exhibition on the estate's genesis and history and a restored interior to reflect the original 1927 floorplan, colours and furnishings.

⚇ Wilhelma Park and Zoo★

▶ *4km/2.5mi northeast via Heilbronner Straße.*
◷*Open May–Aug, daily 8.15am–6pm; Mar–Apr & Sept–Oct 8.15am–5pm.* ⬭*12€.* ♿ ✆*(0711) 540 20. www.wilhelma.de.*

Considered among Europe's finest botanical and zoological gardens, Wilhelma was laid out in the 19C. Don't miss the **aquarium**, **terrarium** and **Amazonian house**.

Mercedes-Benz Museum★★

▶ *Mercedesstraße 100, 6km/3.5mi east.*
◷*Open year-round, Tue–Sun 9am–6pm.* ◷*Closed Jan 1, Dec 24–25 & 31.* ⬭*8€.* ♿. ✆*(0711) 173 00 00. www.mercedes-benz-classic.com.*

This new museum sits mere paces from the garage where Gottlieb Daimler first developed the gasoline engine some 120 years ago.

Exhibits are in a spectacular building designed like a giant double helix wrapped around a towering, triangular atrium. Visitors descending from the top take a journey through time, encountering their gull-wing, prototype, racing and luxury car fantasies along the way.

Porsche Museum★★

▶ *Porscheplatz 1, Zuffenhausen. 8km/5mi north via Heilbronner Straße.*
◷*Open year-round, Tue–Sun 9am–6pm.* ◷*Closed Jan 1, Dec 24–26 & 31.* ⬭*8€.* ♿ ✆*(0711) 91 12 09 11. www.porsche.com/museum.*

Porsche stands for glamorous sports cars, but did you know it was Daimler-Benz engineer Ferdinand Porsche who also invented the Volkswagen Beetle in 1934? Since 2009, a futuristic "temple of torque" pays homage to the man and the brand. The building itself is stunning: a gravity-defying triangle hovering on concrete stilts. Behind its gleaming white walls await 80 of the company's most dazzling legends of prowess and style, including the legendary Roadster 356.

Schloss Solitude★

▶ *9km/5.6mi southwest via Rotebühlstraße.*
⬗*Guided tours (30–45min), Apr–Oct, Tue–Sat 10am–noon & 1.30pm–5pm, Sun 10am–5pm; Nov–Mar, Tue–Sat 1.30pm–4pm, Sun 10am–4pm.* ◷*Closed Dec 24 & 31.* ⬭*3.50€.* ✆*(0711) 69 66 99. www.schloss-solitude.de.*

This 18C royal summer residence wraps around a domed oval pavilion with the lower outbuildings spreading out in a wide arc. The palace interior is mostly Neoclassical, although a few apartments are French Rococo. The most opulent room is the White Hall *(Weisser Saal)* whose ceiling fresco depicts Duke Carl Eugen.

Schloss Solitude

©Olaf Loose/istockphoto.com

ADDRESSES

🛏 STAY

Hotel Abalon – *Zimmermannstraße 7 (access via Olgastraße 79). ℘(0711) 217 10. www.abalon.de. 42 rooms.* This modern building is in the city centre but has comparatively quiet rooms that are spacious and functionally furnished. Views are great from the leafy rooftop terrace.

Bellevue – *Schurwaldstraße 45. ℘0711 48 07 60. www.bellevue-stuttgart.de. Closed Tue–Wed and all Aug.* This traditional 100-year-old family-run hotel-restaurant will give you a warm welcome. Ask for a bedroom with a view.

Der Zauberlehrling – *Rosenstraße 38. ℘0711 237 77 70. www.zauberlehrling.de. 17 rooms.* Restaurant. Rooms are spacious and modern in this chic design hotel, and carefully decorated in every detail. Each has its own flair and atmosphere.

🍴 EAT

Weinstube Kochenbas – *Immenhofer Straße 33. ℘0711 60 27 04. www.kochenbas.de. Closed Mon; last week Aug; first week Sept.* This is one of the oldest wine bars in the city. Enjoy its rustic atmosphere and hearty Swabian dishes.

Weinstube Schellenturm – *Weberstraße 72. ℘0711 236 48 88. www.weinstube-schellenturm.de. Closed Mon and Dec 24–Jan 6. Open dinner only.* Housed in a fortified tower that originally dates from the 16C (though it has been twice rebuilt) this atmospheric restaurant serves fine Swabian food and wines including homemade *Maultaschen* ("Swabian ravioli") and *käsespätzle* (cheese noodles). In summer, dine on the lovely terrace.

Cube – *Kleiner Schlossplatz 1. ℘0711 280 44 41. Closed Sun evening. Reservation advised.* This light and airy dining room, on the top floor of the Kunstmuseum (Museum of Art), serves excellent international cuisine; very good value at lunchtime. Extensive wine list.

Augustenstüble – *Augustenstraße 104. ℘0711 62 12 48. Open dinner only.* This bistro-style restaurant serves regional cuisine, accompanied by an extensive wine list, right up until midnight.

Kern's Pastetchen – *Hohenheimer Straße 64. ℘0711 48 48 55. www.kerns-pastetchen.de. Closed Sun and 3 weeks in Jun.* This elegant rustic-style restaurant serves top-quality regional and international cuisine with French and Austrian influences.

🍽 TAKING A BREAK

Weinhaus Stetter – *Rosenstraße 32 (south of and parallel to Charlottenstraße). ℘(0711) 24 01 63. www.weinhaus-stetter. de. Closed Sun, Dec 25–Jan 8, 2 weeks between late Aug and early Sept.* For over 100 years this rustic establishment has been offering an excellent choice of mainly regional wines to accompany its small selection of hearty local dishes.

🌙 NIGHTLIFE

USEFUL TIPS

The **Bohnenviertel** between Charlottenstraße and Pfarrstraße brims with charming restaurants and bars. The mainly cobbled streets are pedestrian friendly.

EVENTS

PUBLICATIONS

The annual *Highlights* brochure lists events taking place year-round. Pick it up at the tourist office or download it as a free PDF file from www.stuttgart-tourist.de. The monthly magazines *Lift Stuttgart* and *Prinz* highlight current happenings and are on sale in bookshops and newspaper kiosks.

🛍 SHOPPING

USEFUL TIPS

Stuttgart's main shopping district centres on Königstraße and its side streets. The main department store is *Breuninger* (on Marktplatz). South of the Altes Schloss, the *Markthalle* is an Art-Deco covered market. Craft shops and antique dealers are found in the *Bohnenviertel* (between Charlottenstraße and Pfarrstraße).

Bad Wimpfen★★

This small fortified town with its web of half-timbered houses along narrow streets overlooks the River Neckar. Buttressing the hill are the Ludwigshalle saltworks, which once brought prosperity to the entire region.

🐾 WALKING TOUR
WIMPFEN AM BERG★★ (UPPER TOWN)
Start on Marktplatz.

Kaiserpfalz (Imperial Palace)

Behind the Rathaus (town hall) are remains of the Kaiserpfalz with the **Blauer Turm** (blue tower) from which views extend over the town and the Neckar Valley. Further on is the 16C Romanesque **Steinhaus** (stone house), where a museum traces the history of Bad Wimpfen since Roman times.

▶ *Continue along the wall to the staircase on the right, which leads to the spur on which the town is built, below the* **Roter Turm** *(red tower) – the fortress'*

▶ **Population:** 6 900
🛈 **Info:** Carl-Ulrich-Straße 1. ℰ(07063) 972 00. www.badwimpfen.de.
◖ **Location:** Bad Wimpfen is a short distance from the A6 (Mannheim–Nurremberg). From Heidelberg, travel along the Neckar via the scenic B37.
◔ **Don't Miss:** The suggested driving tour through the Neckar Valley.
◕ **Timing:** Allow one and a half hours for the walking tour, four hours for the excursions.

final defensive point. Follow Schwibbogengasse to Hauptstrasse and then Klostergasse.

Historic Streets

Klostergasse is lined by half-timbered houses, including the former bathhouses, easily recognisable by their exterior galleries. You can explore more

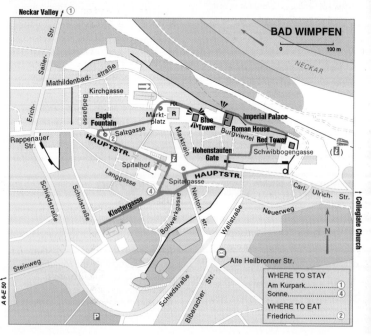

of the town's streets via Langgasse, which leads to **Hauptstraße**★ by way of a narrow alley *(Spitalgasse)*, which runs past a former hospital *(Spitalhof)* whose cluster of half-timbered houses is among the oldest buildings in town. It is now a gallery.

▷ *Continue west along Hauptstraße, with its picturesque, elaborate signs, past the 1576* **Adlerbrunnen** *(eagle fountain) before returning to Marktplatz via Salzgasse.*

WIMPFEN IM TAL (LOWER TOWN)

The Gothic **Stiftskirche St. Peter und St. Paul** (parish church) has retained a strikingly plain west façade from an earlier Romanesque building. The **cloister**★★ shows the evolution of the Gothic style.

The north gallery (c. 1350), already more angular in design, marks the transition to the Renaissance. ▶ *Guided tour (1hr) by prior appointment.* 𝄞*(07063) 970 40.*

🚗 DRIVING TOUR

NECKAR VALLEY★

74km/46mi – Allow 4hrs.

▷ *Leave Bad Wimpfen on the B27 N.*

Downstream from Bad Wimpfen, the **Neckartal** cuts through the sandstone massif of the Odenwald, many of whose hills are crowned by castles.

Burg Guttenberg (Guttenberg Castle)

9km/5.6mi north of Bad Wimpfen.
🕐*Open Apr–Oct, Apr–Oct, daily 10am–6pm; Mar & Nov weekends by request.*
⊙*5€.* 𝄞*(06266) 910 22.*
www.burg-guttenberg.de.
A massive defensive wall protects this castle, which shelters rare collections of **objets d'art**★ and archives. Note the 18C "Library-Herbarium" in which plants are encased in 92 "wooden books".

▷ *Drive towards Neckarzimmern, then 1.5km/1mi to Burg Hornberg.*

Burg Hornberg

🕐*Open year-round daily 10am–5pm.*
⊙*3€.* ♿. 𝄞*(06261) 50 01.*
www.burg-hornberg.de.
Crowning a vine-covered hill, this **castle** is easily recognised from afar by its tall keep. A **museum** features the armour of Götz von Berlichingen, who died here in 1562. This knight, popularised in German folklore as a Robin Hood figure, was immortalised in a play by Goethe.

▷ *Return to the B27 and continue towards Neckarzimmern, skirting Eberbach.*

Hirschhorn am Neckar★

38km/23.6mi northwest of Burg Hornberg.
The castle stands on a fortified spur. From the terrace and tower *(121 steps)* the **view**★ encompasses the wooded slopes of the Neckar Valley.

▷ *Follow the B37 southwest.*

Neckarsteinach

Four castles stand on a narrow ridge overlooking the village: the Vorderburg and Mittelburg castles are privately owned. Hinterburg Castle (c. 1100) is the oldest and is now in ruins. Burg Schadeck, also in ruins, is a small 13C castle known as "swallow's nest".

▷ *Continue on the B37.*
After 4km/2.5mi hook a left over the bridge at Neckargemünd. Follow the K3200 for 4.5km/3mi.

Dilsberg

Dilsberg is noteworthy for its romantically ruined castle reached by following the signs to *Burgruine*.
From the **tower**★ (97 steps) unfolds a fantastic panorama of the Neckar. The route ends with a scenic approach to Heidelberg (🕐*see HEIDELBERG).*

ADDRESSES

🏠 STAY

🍴🍴 **Am Kurpark** – *Kirschenweg 16, Bad Wimpfen. ℘(07063) 977 70. www.amkurpark.de. Closed mid-Dec–mid-Jan. 9 rooms.* This hotel-guesthouse has a quiet location near the spa park. You will find comfortably furnished guestrooms (including six double rooms with balcony) and a friendly welcome.

🍴🍴 **Sonne** – *Langgasse 3, 74206 Bad Wimpfen. ℘(07063) 245. www.sonne-wimpfen.de. Closed 21 Dec–18 Jan. 18 rooms. Restaurant*🍴🍴🍴. This old town hotel delivers modern comforts in historic surroundings. The rustic but comfortable rooms occupy two handsome half-timbered buildings. The restaurants Friedrich and Feyerabend are on the premises.

🍴 EAT

🍴🍴🍴 **Friedrich** – *Hauptstraße 74, Bad Wimpfen. ℘(0706) 32 45. Closed Mon, Tue.* This bright and convivial restaurant at the beginning of the pedestrian zone serves international fare.

Schwäbisch Hall★★

This town, built in tiers up the steep flank of the Kocher Valley, grew up around salt springs already known in Celtic times. In the Middle Ages, it was famous for the *Heller*, the Imperial silver coins, minted here. The town's well-preserved half-timbered houses and tranquillity make it a pleasant stopping point.

▶ **Population:** 36 800

ℹ **Info:** Am Markt 9. ℘(0791) 75 12 46. www.schwaebischhall.de.

▶ **Location:** Schwäbisch Hall is tucked into the Kocher Valley, south of the Hohenlohe plain, in northeastern Baden-Württemberg.

SIGHTS

Marktplatz★★ (Market Square)

This sloping central square is dominated by the monumental stone steps of the **Michaelskirche** (Church of St. Michael), which hosts a popular open-air theatre festival in summer. It is flanked by houses in a variety of architectural styles from Gothic to Baroque.

Dating from 1509, the **Marktbrunnen** (fountain) stands against a decorative wall adorned with statues of Samson, St. Michael and St. George (copies, originals are in the Hällisch-Fränkisches Museum). The rectangular design, unusual in a Gothic work, incorporates the old pillory post. The elegant 18C Late Baroque **town hall**★ and its beautiful clock-tower stand opposite the church.

The two parallel streets of **Obere** and **Untere Herrengasse**, linked by stone stairways, are bordered by numerous 15C and 16C half-timbered houses.

Michaelskirche

Originally Romanesque, this church was transformed into a Gothic hall-church in the 15C and is reached via 53 steps. The Flamboyant chancel was added in the 16C.

Hällisch-Fränkisches Museum (Regional Museum)

Keckenhof 6. ⏱Open year-round, Tue–Sun 10am–5pm. ⏱Closed Good Fri, Dec 24-25 & 31. ⏺2.50€. ♿ partly. ℘(0791) 75 12 89. www.schwaebischhall.de.

This museum is housed in seven historical buildings, one of which is the eight-storey **Keckenturm** (tower) from the 13C. Collections concentrate on the

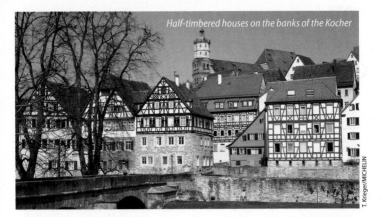
Half-timbered houses on the banks of the Kocher

T. Krieger/MICHELIN

art, culture and everyday life of the townspeople, delving into the history of the *Heller* coins and the region's role in the salt trade. Highlights include the hand-painted wainscoting from a 18C synagogue and ivory carvings created during the Thirty Years' War.

Kunsthalle Würth (Fine Art Museum)

Lange Straße 35. ⓘ *Open year-round, Tue–Sun 10am–6pm.* ⓘ *Closed Dec 25 & 26.* ☏ *(0791) 94 67 20. www.kunst.wuerth.com.*
Open since 2001, this ultra-modern art temple created from a 19C brewery presents often exemplary changing exhibitions of works created after World War II.

Along the Banks of the Kocher★

Attractive views of the half-timbered buildings across the river unfold from the **Henkersbrücke** (Hangman's Bridge). The view is perhaps even better from the junction of Am Spitalbach lane and the Salinenstraße quay from where you can also spot the Church of St. John. **Views★** of the stepped silhouette of the old town lorded over by the Michaelskirche are especially appealing from Unterwöhrd Island. Attractive roofed wooden bridges span the river.

EXCURSION
Benediktinerkloster Großcomburg★ (Benedictine Abbey of Grosscomburg)

▶ *3km/1.8mi south.*
↪ *Guided tours (30min) only, Apr–Oct, Tue–Fri 11am, then hourly 1pm–4pm; Sat–Sun hourly 3pm–5pm.* ⓘ *3€.* ☏ *(0791) 93 81 85.*
Dating from 1130, the crown-shaped **chandelier★★** in the church is made of copper-plated and gilded iron. In front of the high altar is an **antependium★** of the same period, showing Christ surrounded by the apostles. The supporting framework is treated with *cloisonné* enamel and filigree work.

The White Gold of Hall

The word Hala means "salt" in old German. The Celts found a salt-water spring here and were using it as long ago as 500 BC. Rediscovered in AD 800, the saltworks quickly brought fame and fortune to the town of Hall. Green brine was pumped from a well that was dug where Hallplatz now stands, then processed by "distillers" who fed huge wood fires to evaporate the water. The resulting salt, said to be very white, very fine and of high quality, was used until 1924. The town was renamed Schwäbisch Hall in 1934.

Tübingen★★

Tübingen escaped World War II with nary a shrapnel wound and is therefore a 3D history textbook from the Middle Ages to the 19C. The maze of narrow sloping lanes lined with ancient half-timbered houses and its animated student life create a delightful atmosphere.

⚬WALKING TOUR
OLD TOWN★★

Eberhardsbrücke (Bridge)

This bridge gives a scenic **view**★ over the Neckar with the Hölderlin Tower rising behind weeping willows. The **Platanenallee** is a beautiful walkway along the Neckar. Gondolas travel from Hölderlin Tower past the riverfront.

▷ *Right after crossing the bridge, take the staircase down to the riverbank.*

Hölderlinturm (Tower)

Bursagasse 6. ◐*Open year-round, Tue–Fri 10am–noon, 3pm–5pm, Sat–Sun 2pm–5pm.* ◔*3€.* ✆*(07071) 220 40.* Once part of the fortifications, this tower was the residence of Friedrich Hölderlin from 1807 until his death in 1843. Now a museum, it has displays on the life and work of the poet.

▷ *Turn right at the front of the tower, then left on Bursagasse. The route skirts*

▶ **Population:** 85 350
ℹ **Info:** An der Neckarbrücke 1 ✆(07071) 913 60. www.tuebingen-info.de.
◑ **Location:** Tübingen is near Stuttgart, on the banks of the Neckar and Ammer rivers, between the slopes of Schlossberg and Österberg.
🅿 **Parking:** Garages are located throughout Tübingen. Visit http://wap.parkinfo.com for fees and locations.
⊛ **Don't Miss:** A walking tour of the old town.
◔ **Timing:** Allow a full day to absorb the history of Tübingen.

Tübingen's first university hospital (Burse) with its double staircase. Also here is the protestant seminary (Evangelisches Stift), where Hegel, Hölderlin and Schelling once studied. Climb up to the palace via Burgsteige and note the interesting fraternity house at no 20.

Schloss Hohentübingen (Palace)

The present Renaissance building was constructed on the foundations of an 11C fortress built by the archdukes of Tübingen.

Neckar riverfront

© Jens Hilberger/Fotolia.com

TÜBINGEN

200 m

STUTTGART, Bebenhausen Abbey

STUTTGART

ROTTENBURG

WHERE TO STAY	WHERE TO EAT	
Am Schloss..................①	Brinkmann..................②	Schwärzlocher Hof..................④
Metropol..................④	Casino..................①	Weinstube Forelle..................⑦
	Museum..................③	

It is now a **museum**★ (🕐 open May–Sept, Wed–Sun 10am–6pm; Oct–Apr to 5pm; 🕐 closed Jan 1, Dec 24 & 25; 🖮 4€; 📞(07071) 297 73 84; www.uni-tuebingen.de/museum-schloss) on pre- and early history. A favourite exhibit is the tiny "**Vogelherdpferdchen**"★, an ivory horse figurine named for the cave near Ulm where it was discovered in 1931. It is one of the oldest works of art from the New Paleolithic Age.

There are also outstanding exhibits from Classical Antiquity, Ancient Egypt and the Ancient Orient.

Note in particular the **religious chamber**★ from an Old Kingdom tomb (third millennium BC), completely covered in bas-relief sculptures.

There is a good **view**★ of the Neckar and the roofs of the old town from the castle terrace.

▷ *Backtrack, then turn left on Wienergäßle towards Marktplatz.*

Marktplatz★ (Market Square)

This charming historic square is surrounded by half-timbered houses and accented by a Renaissance fountain and a statue of Neptune. It comes alive on market days (*Mon, Wed and Fri*). The 19C graffito decoration on the 15C **Rathaus** (town hall) depicts the allegories of Justice, Agriculture and Science. The astronomic clock dates from 1511.

393

The University

They say that rather than having a university, Tübingen *is* a university, so closely linked are the town and its *alma mater*. It all began in 1477, when Count Eberhard founded the institution in a town of only 3 000. Tübingen University now has 16 faculties and 24 000 students registered in 74 different fields of study. The university and the Protestant seminary of 1536 have educated such important figures as the poets Hölderlin, Mörike and Uhland, the philosophers Hegel and Schelling, the astronomer Kepler, the theologian Melanchthon, and Swiss biologist, Friedrich Miescher – discoverer of DNA. It has also produced nine Nobel Prize winners, most in the field of chemistry.

Wilhelmsstift

At Collegiumgasse 7, this late 16C stone building was once home to a renowned academy for young Protestant noblemen who came here from throughout Europe. Note the coat of arms of Baden-Württemberg above the portal.

▶ *Continue via Hafengasse, then turn right into Pfleghofstraße and enter the old hospital through the arched porch.*

Bebenhausener Pfleghof (Bebenhaus Hospice)

The Bebenhausen Hospice was erected in the 15C and served as the tithes barn for the abbey. Jutting out from the tall, steep roof is a three-storey dormer through which the grain was passed.

▶ *Go around the building, then descend via Schulberg to arrive at Holzmarkt.*

Holzmarkt

This square owes much of its attractiveness to the fountain of St. George. In the old Heckenhauer bookshop the writer and poet Hermann Hesse spent his apprenticeship from 1895 to 1899. At the northern end of the church, note the sculpture of St. George, who was martyred on the wheel. It inspired John Heartfield, an artist famous for his photomontages denouncing Nazism.

Stiftskirche (Collegiate Church)

Am Holzmarkt. ◷*Open from Easter to Oct; Fri and Sat, 11.30am–5pm, Sun, 1pm–5pm; during local school summer holidays, Tue–Sun, 11.30am–5pm.* ⊚1€. ✆(07071) 44 01 86. *www.stiftskirche-tuebingen.de.*
This 15C Gothic hall-church boasts a Flamboyant rood screen and pulpit. The chancel was for centuries the burial place of the Württemberg princes. Note the funerary monument of university founder Eberhard the Bearded and the **Renaissance tombs★★** of Duke Ludwig and his wife, adorned with fine alabaster relief work. There is also an altar created by a student of Dürer (1520) and choir stalls adorned with Bible figures. Climb the tower for sweeping views over the Neckar, castle and the Swabian Jura.
West of the church is the **Cottahaus**, the former home of Johann Friedrich Cotta (1764–1832). A leading publisher during the Enlightenment, he was the first to print the works of Goethe and Schiller.

EXCURSION
Kloster Bebenhausen★

▶ *6km/3.7mi north via the Wilhelmstraße.* ◷*Open Apr–Oct, Mon 9am–noon and 1pm–6pm, Tue–Sun 9am–6pm; Nov–Mar, Tue–Sun 10am–noon, 1pm–5pm.* ◷*Closed Jan 1, Dec 24–26 & 31.* ⊚5€. ✆(07071) 60 28 02. *www.kloster-bebenhausen.de.*
Along with Maulbronn and Eberbach, this 12C abbey ranks among the best preserved Cistercian monasteries in Germany. Located in the tranquil Schönbuch Forest, it is an interesting example of Romanesque-Gothic architecture. The landmark roof **turret★** dates from the monastery's 15C heyday. Also note the Flamboyant-style cloister (1475–1500) with its beautiful net-vaulted ceiling.

Friedrich Hölderlin in Tübingen

Friedrich Hölderlin was born at Lauffen am Neckar in 1770. He studied theology at Tübingen'sn Protestant seminary, where he befriended philosophers Hegel and Schelling, in preparation for the ministry. Poetry continued to interest him in Tübingen, a craft he began while studying in Maulbronn. Finally rebelling against a career in the church, he worked as a tutor in Frankfurt, Switzerland and Bordeaux. The first sign of mental illness (thought to be schizophrenia) manifested itself in 1802. In 1806, he returned to Tübingen where he was promised recovery under the care of medical professor Autenrieth at a residential home. When treatment failed, Hölderlin resided in the tower room at the home of the Zimmers, a family of carpenters, at Bursagasse 6, for the remainder of his life.

Schloss Bebenhausen

Guided tours (45min) Apr–Oct, Tue–Sun hourly 10am–noon, 2pm–5pm; Nov–Mar, Tue–Sat 11am, 2pm, 3pm and 4pm, Sun also noon. Closed Jan 1, Dec 24–26 & 31. 4€.

On the monastery grounds, this palace is the former hunting lodge of King Charles of Württemberg. This is where the last king of Württemberg, Wilhelm II, retired after his abdication. His widow, Charlotte, lived here until her death in 1946.

ADDRESSES

STAY

Hotel Metropol – *Reutlinger Straße 7. (07071) 910 10. 12 rooms. Restaurant.* This little hotel is on the edge of town within walking distance of the historic centre. Rooms are rather basic but clean and modern.

Hotel Am Schloss – *Burgsteige 18. 07071 92 940. www.hotelamschloss. de. 37 rooms. Restaurant.* Housed nextdoor to the castle in two old wooden houses, this cosy restaurant serves national and Swabian specialities. In summer dine on the terrace and enjoy the view.

EAT

Casino – *Wöhrdstraße 25. 07071 65 07 50. www.casino-am-neckar.de. Open daily from 11am, closed Sun at 9pm.* This smart, modern, lively brasserie on the banks of the River Neckar specialises in fish and Swabian dishes. Dine in the *Biergarten* in summer.

Schwärzlocher Hof – *Schwärzloch 1 (2.5km/1.5mi west of town, via Schwärzlocher Straße between Schleifmühleweg and Burgholzweg).*

(07071) 433 62. www.hofgut-schwaerzloch.de. Closed Dec 25–mid-Feb. The chancel of a 12C church has been incorporated into this farm inn. There is a beautiful view of the surrounding area from the terrace, shaded by lime trees. Sample the *Most* (dry cider) with traditional dishes.

Weinstube Forelle – *Kronenstraße 8. (07071) 240 94. www.weinstube-forelle.de.* This restaurant is popular with students and tourists in the evenings for its friendly staff and creatively updated Swabian dishes.

Museum – *Wilhelmstraße 3. 07071 228 28. www.restaurant-museum.de. 11am–3pm, 6pm–midnight.* The elegant main restaurant serves fresh, light, creative Mediterranean-inspired cuisine. Or you can dine informally downstairs in the *Weinstube*.

Brinkmann – *Belthlestraße 13. 07071 44 09 39. www.brinkmann-restaurant.de. Closed Tue.* This small, chic, minimalist restaurant, decorated in warm colour tones, serves regional, national and international dishes.

Swabian Jura★
Schwäbische Alb

East of the Black Forest, between Stuttgart and Lake Constance, the Swabian Jura region is a paradise for walkers, cyclists and history buffs. From the highest point at Lemberg (1 015m/3 330ft), the Jura plateaus drop 400m/1 312.3ft to the Neckar basin in the northwest. Mountain outcrops form natural fortresses; some were chosen as castle sites by such famous dynasties as the Hohenstaufens and Hohenzollerns.

🚗 DRIVING TOURS

1 FROM KIRCHHEIM UNTER TECK TO BURG HOHENZOLLERN

125km/77.6mi – Allow one day.

Kirchheim unter Teck
The tower of the 18C half-timbered Rathaus (town hall) overlooks the central crossing in town.

▶ *Drive E on the L 1200 to Holzmaden.*

ℹ Info: Marktplatz 1, 72574 Bad Urach. ℘(07125) 94 81 06. www.schwaebischealb.de.

Location: East of the Black Forest, between Stuttgart and Lake Constance, the Swabian Jura is punctuated by caves, dry valleys and steep-sided gorges.

Don't Miss: Burgruine Reußenstein and Burg Hohenzollern.

🕐 Timing: Allow one day for driving tour 1 and half a day for driving tour 2.

Kids: Urwelt-Museum Hauff, Bärenhöhle caverns.

Holzmaden
Urwelt-Museum Hauff★
Aichelberger Straße 90. Open year-round, Tue–Sun 9am–5pm. Closed Jan 1, Dec 25 & 31. 5€. ℘(07023) 28 73. www.urweltmuseum.de.
This prehistoric collection showcases fossilised dinosaur bones, fish, sea lilies and ammonites found locally in the 180 million-year-old Jurassic slate strata.

Burg Hohenzollern

© Björn Schick/Fotolia.com

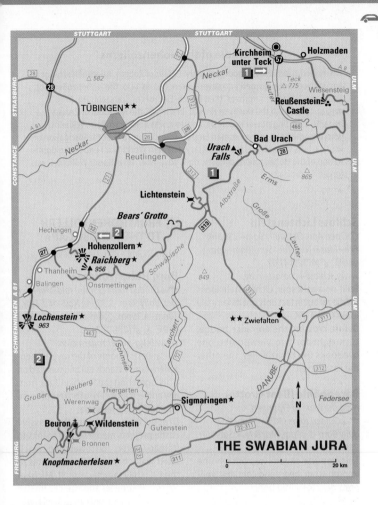

THE SWABIAN JURA

Burgruine Reußenstein (Castle Ruins)

🚶 *45min round-trip walk.*

Head for the edge of the escarpment to appreciate the **setting**★★ of Reußenstein as it dominates the Neidlingen Valley. From the look-out point built into the castle ruins there is a **view**★ of the whole valley and, beyond it, the plain of Teck.

▶ *After Wiesensteig, which is characterised by its many half-timbered houses, the route follows the Schwäbische Albstraße, marked by blue-green arrows.*

Bad Urach

This is a pretty town, enclosed deep in the Erms Valley, with half-timbered houses surrounding the picturesque central **Marktplatz** (market square).

Uracher Wasserfall (Urach Falls)

🚶 *15min round-trip walk.*
Leave from the parking area marked "Aussicht 350m".

At the end of the walk you will be rewarded with an impressive **view**★ of the valley and the waterfall (flow reduced in summer).

The Cradle of the Hohenzollerns

The Hohenzollern dynasty goes back to the Counts of Zollern, rulers of Hechingen and subsequently divided into several branches. In 1415, the Hohenzollerns of Franconia became margraves, then Prince-Electors of Brandenburg. In 1618 they succeeded to the Duchy of Prussia. In the 18C the Kingdom of Prussia became a leading power in Europe, and so it was a Hohenzollern, Wilhelm I, who became head of the German Empire, founded in 1871 at the instigation of Prussia. Less than 50 years later, military defeat in World War I ended the domination of the Hohenzollern dynasty: on 9 November 1918, Kaiser Wilhelm II was forced to abdicate.

Schloss Lichtenstein

◷*Open Apr–Oct, daily 9am–5.30pm; Feb–Mar & Nov, Tue–Sun 10am–4pm.* ◉*6€.* ℘*(07129) 41 02. www.schloss-lichtenstein.de.*

Built on a rock spur, Lichtenstein looks medieval but in fact only got its fairytale looks in the 19C.

Before crossing the entrance bridge, turn right for two viewpoints: one overlooks the Echaz Valley, the other the castle itself.

Bärenhöhle (Bear Grotto)

Near the town of Erpfingen. •⌒•*Guided tours (30min) Apr–Nov, daily 9am–5.30pm, Mar & Nov, Sat–Sun 9am–5pm.* ◉*3€.* ℘*(07128) 925 18.*

This popular cavern was once home to prehistoric bears and contains well-preserved fossilised bones.

◐ *At Onstmettingen, follow the signs Nädelehaus and Raichberg.*

Raichberg★

⚑ *30min round-trip walk.*

Park at the hotel and walk past a stone tower, across the fields to the lip of the plateau. From here **views**★ extend over the downward sweep of the Jura. In the distance, you can spot the turrets of Burg Hohenzollern.

◐ *Continue to BURG HOHENZOLLERN (◐see BURG HOHENZOLLERN) via Tannheim and Hechingen.*

2 FROM HOHENZOLLERN TO THE DANUBE GAP★

89km/55.3mi – Allow half a day.

Burg Hohenzollern★

•⌒•*Guided tours (35min) mid-Mar–Oct, daily 9am–5.30pm; Nov–mid-Mar, 10am–4.30pm.* ◷*Closed Dec 24 & 31.* ◉*9€.* ♿ ℘*(07471) 24 28. www.burg-hohenzollern.com.*

The ancestral home of the royal Hohenzollern family stands tall and turreted on a hill bordering the Swabian Jura; from any angle, it looks like a fortress plucked straight from a fairytale.

Draped over a hillside, the massive castle projects medieval flair thanks to its many turrets and towers and crenellated walls, but actually only dates to the 19C. Only the chapel of **St. Michael** *(Michaeliskapelle)* and the casemates survived from the old castle, which was built between the 11C and 15C and fell into disrepair in the 18C. The chapel's stained-glass windows are considered to be the oldest in southern Germany. Another chapel held the coffins of Friedrich-Wilhelm I, the Prussian Soldier King, and his son Frederick the Great from Potsdam from 1952 to 1991 when they were returned to Potsdam.

•⌒•Guided tours provide access to the castle **treasury** *(Schatzkammer),* a treasure chest of crowns and gowns, uniforms, snuff boxes, flutes and porcelain. Before leaving the castle, tour the ramparts *(start on the left, after the drawbridge)* and enjoy the **panorama**★ of the Swabian Jura and the Upper Neckar Valley.

Lochenstein★

🚶 *30min round-trip walk.*

Park at the Lochenpaß saddle and climb to the Lochenstein summit (alt 963m/3 159.4ft) topped by an iron cross. From here a **view**★ of the Balingen–Hechingen depression, and, in the distance, Hohenzollern Castle, is possible.

▶ *Beyond the pass, the road corkscrews downhill and then crosses the bare, rolling uplands of the Großer Heuberg plateau.*

Knopfmacherfelsen★

Below the car park, make your way to a **viewpoint**★ over the Danube Valley as far as Beuron Abbey and, on the right, Schloss Bronnen.

Kloster Beuron (Beuron Abbey)

🕐 *Open year-round, daily 6am–8pm.*
♿ ☎(07466) 170.
www.erzabtei-beuron.de.

This flourishing Benedictine congregation contributed to the revival of monastic life, the liturgy and the use of the Gregorian chant in Germany. The **Gnadenkapelle** (chapel of mercy), added in 1898, is decorated in the so-called "Beuron style" inspired by a 19C Byzantium-influenced school of sacred art.

Burg Wildenstein

7km/4.3mi from Beuron via Leibertingen.
This small citadel commanding the Danube has a defence system made up of two moats and two towers linked by a fortified wall.

▶ *Below Beuron, the road follows the Danube Valley★ past Wildenstein and Werenwag castle, towards Sigmaringen. Approaching the town, the cliffs give way to whimsical rock pinnacles between Thiergarten and Gutenstein.*

Sigmaringen★

🚶 *Schwabstraße 1.* ☎*07571 106 224. www.sigmaringen.de. Apr–Sept 10am–1pm, 2pm–6pm, weekends and hols 10am–1pm; Oct–Mar Mon–Fri 10am–noon, 1pm–4pm.*

Thanks to its strong natural defensive site, Sigmaringen prospered as the capital of the small principality of Hohenzollern-Sigmaringen. The castle, perched on the cliff above, dominates the town.

Schloss (Castle)

☎*07 571 72 90. www.hohenzollern.com.*
🚶*Guided visit (1hr) May–Oct 9am–5pm; Mar–Apr 9.30am–4.30pm; Nov and Feb 10am–3.30pm.* 🕐*Closed Dec–Jan.* ⊚*6.50€.*

The oldest parts of the castle date back to 1200 though many alterations and rebuilding took place during the 17C and 19C. In fact the rooms are decorated in 16C style with coffered ceilings and tapestries and contain valuable furniture and large paintings. The Armoury is home to one of the largest weapons collections in Europe, dating from the 15C to the 19C.

Museum Marstall

Carriages, sleighs and sedan chairs are on display, alongside a fine collections of 15C and 16C Swabian paintings and sculptures.

Kath. Pfarramt St. Johann (Catholic Parish Church of St. John)

Standing fast on the castle rock, the church boasts bright stuccowork. Note in the transept chapel *(to the left)*, the alleged cradle of St. Fidelis of Sigmaringen (1577–1622), who was the first martyr and patron of the Capuchin order, as well as patron saint of Hohenzollern.

Upper Swabian Plateau★★

The enormous prosperity and cultural influence of the Benedictine abbeys of the 18C resulted in a flurry of beautiful Baroque churches scattered across the Upper Swabian Plateau. Some of the finest artists of the period were brought in to create magnificent buildings whose fluid decorations harmonise with their surroundings "so that God may be glorified in all things", according to the inscription on the Weingarten façade.

Info: Klosterhof 1, 88427 Bad Schussenried. ℘(07583) 33 10 60. www.oberschwaben-tourismus.de.

Location: Between Ulm and Bodensee (Lake Constance), this tour crosses the Upper Swabian Plateau through gentle hills and soft light.

Don't Miss: The abbey churches in Weingarten, Steingaden and Oberschwäbische Barockstraße.

🚗 DRIVING TOUR

RAVENSBURG TO ZWEIFALTEN
85km/52.8mi – Allow half a day.

Ravensburg
This ancient Swabian town, and one-time Free Imperial City, still hides behind a city wall of towers and forti-fied gateways. The road from Wangen passes beneath the Obertor, a gateway with stepped gables. At the end of Marktstraße is a block of old buildings comprising the **Rathaus** (town hall, 14C–15C) and the weigh-house with the Blaserturm, a 15C–16C tower. Another stone tower, the **Mehlsack** (sack of flour), originally whitewashed, looms 50m/164ft above the southern part of the old town. A steep staircase *(240 steps)* leads up to the Veitsburg for even more spectacular views.

▶ *Follow the B30 towards Weingarten.*

Weingarten★★
Consecrated in 1724, the abbey church in Weingarten rivals Ottobeuren as the largest Baroque sanctuary in Germany, 102m/334.6ft long and 44m/144.3ft wide at the transepts. Various architec-tural elements reflect an Italian influence transmitted by way of Salzburg. The interior is a collaboration of the masters of the day. The frescoes on the vaulted ceiling by Cosmas Damien Asam are full of virtuosity, as are the choir stalls carved by Joseph Anton Feuchtmayer. The **organ**★★ was crafted by Joseph Gabler (1700–1771) and fits perfectly with the rest of the decoration: its 6 666 pipes follow the line of the windows and blend with the pink marble.

▶ *The tour continues along the Upper Swabian Baroque Road (signposted "Oberschwäbische Barockstraße") via the B30 until Bad Waldsee. Turn left onto the L 275.*

Bad Schussenried
🕐*Museum & Church: Easter–Oct, daily 1.30pm–5.30pm, Sat also 9.30am–11.30am. Library: Apr–Oct, Tue–Fri 10am–1pm, 2pm–5pm, Sat–Sun 10am–5pm; Nov–Mar, Sat–Sun 1pm–4pm.*
🕐*Closed Jan 1, Dec 24, 25 & 31.* 🎫*5€.* ℘(07383) 22 40. www.schloesser-magazin.de.

This pleasant town's **abbey buildings** (now partly used as a psychiatric hospi-tal and for art and cultural events) and abbey church owe their sumptuous Baroque appearance to Premonstra-tensian abbots. In the church, the upper panels of the intricately decorated choir stalls (1717) are separated by 28 statu-ettes representing men and women who founded religious orders. The most spectacular part of the complex is the light-flooded Baroque **library**★ with two storeys of bookcases canopied by a ceiling fresco by Franz Georg Herrmann depicting the Apocalypse, Scholarship, Education and Craft.

Steinhausen★

Designed by Dominikus and Johann Zimmermann, this hamlet's beautiful little pilgrimage church comprises a single nave and a small chancel, both oval. Capitals, cornices and window embrasures are adorned with birds, insects or flowers. Also note the 1415 Pietà above the altar.

▶ *Follow the L275 until Riedlingen, then join the B312 to Zwiefalten.*

Zwiefalten★★

This village has a remarkable 18C **church**, built by **Johann Michael Fischer and** considered a late Baroque masterpiece. Behind a comparatively plain façade lurks a lavish interior accented by a profusion of colours, exuberant details and artistic virtuosity. The eye finally settles on the details: ceiling paintings of the Virgin Mary by Franz Joseph Spiegler, a pulpit decorated by Johann Michael Feuchtmayer (uncle of the sculptor and stuccoworker, Joseph Anton Feuchtmayer), angels and cherubs galore.

▶ *Go back to Riedlingen, then take the B311 to the left.*

The Devil to Pay

Of the 66 stops (sets of pipes) of the Weingarten organ, the 46th is called "Vox Humana". Joseph Gabler's ambition was to build an organ combining man and machine in resounding praise of God. After countless attempts to recreate a human sound, he is said to have sold his soul to the devil, who supplied him with a piece of metal which he melted down to make the pipes. The monks were so enthralled by the beauty of the organ's song that they were unable to pray, whereupon the abbot ordered an enquiry. Gabler was found out, confessed and sentenced to death. But since the only sounds produced by the organ now resembled wailing, Gabler was reprieved.

Obermarchtal

🚗 *Tour on request.* ☏ (07375) 95 91 00. Built by Michael Thumb, Christian Thumb and Franz Beer, this 17C **abbey church** is an example of the early Baroque and filled with such treasures as white Wessobrunn stuccowork, numerous altars, the elaborate carved choir stalls by Paul Speiegger and a famous organ.

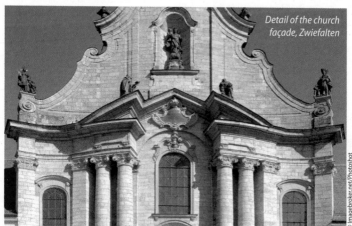

Detail of the church façade, Zwiefalten

© Imagebroker.net/Photoshot

Ulm★★

The royal palace of "Hulma", recorded for the first time in 854, was one of Europe's most important medieval cities. Blessed with an exceptional cathedral and walks along the Danube, the old city delights visitors. Ulm's most famous local figure is Albert Einstein, born here in 1879.

MÜNSTER★★★

Open Jul–Aug, daily 9am–7.45pm; Apr–Jun & Sept to 6.45pm; Mar & Oct to 5.45pm; Nov–Feb to 4.45pm (tower closes one hour earlier). Tower 4€. www.muenster-ulm.de.

At a height of 161m/528ft, Ulm's cathedral spire is the tallest in the world and the most distinctive feature of the city skyline. Although the foundation stone was laid in 1377, the two towers and spire were only added in 1890.

The minster's **interior** also draws the eye skyward. The chancel arch bears the largest fresco north of the Alps, a 1471 work depicting the Last Judgement. To the right on the chancel arch stands the 15C *Man of Sorrows*, an early work by native Ulmer, Hans Multscher.

The Iconoclasts

Konrad Sam, a virulent preacher, brought the Swiss Reformation to Ulm in 1530, advocating the destruction of religious imagery. Following a referendum approved by 87 percent of the population, he made the cathedral Protestant. Private donors removed their altars and sealed the cathedral's central door, the stalls and the tabernacle. Some altars were given to neighbouring villages, where they remain today. The full rage of the iconoclasts was unleashed on 21 June 1531 when the remaining cathedral icons (60 altars, numerous statues, altarpieces and hangings) were destroyed.

- ▶ **Population:** 121 650
- **Info:** Münsterplatz 50. (0731) 161 28 30. www.tourismus.ulm.de.
- **Location:** Ulm is separated from Neu-Ulm by the river Danube and is about midway between Munich and Stuttgart on the A8 autobahn.
- **Parking:** Garages can be found near the main train station and the town hall.
- **Don't Miss:** Ulm's cathedral and the suggested walking tour.
- **Timing:** Allow at least an hour to tour Ulm's cathedral, including a climb up the world's tallest church spire.
- **Kids:** Ascending Ulm Cathedral's spire (older children).

The pulpit is canopied by a splendid wooden sounding board from 1510, the work of Jörg Syrlin the Younger. There is a second pulpit in the late-Gothic style further up that is intended for the Holy Spirit, the invisible preacher. The four side aisles feature fine late-Gothic fan vaulting.

Left of the entrance to the chancel is the **tabernacle**★, at 26m/85ft the tallest in Germany. This masterpiece (c. 1460–70) was chiselled out of limestone and sandstone. Three rows of wooden figures depict the prophets and lawmakers. Note the small figures of people and animals carved into the handrail of the banister on which the artist has allowed his imagination to run riot.

The **choir stalls**★★★ are a marvellous example of wood carving, executed by Jörg Syrlin the Elder between 1469 and 1474. Two series of characters, from the Bible and from pagan Antiquity, face one another. Men are grouped on the left, women on the right, the upper gables being devoted to the Church's apostles

Nave, Münster

© Reinhold Mayer/Ulm/ Neu-Ulm Touristik GmbH

and martyrs, and the high backs of the stalls to Old Testament figures.

For many cathedral visitors, the highlight is a 768-step **ascent of the spire**. The structure resembles stone lacework in its upper reaches, revealing a **panorama**★★ not only of the town and the Danube but as far as the plateaux of the Swabian Jura and the Alps.

SIGHTS

Stadthaus (Town Hall)

Ulm's white-and-glass town hall is a daring design by avant-garde architect Richard Meier. A modern counterpoint to the venerable cathedral, it generated a lot of controversy upon its completion in 1993. However, it does actually lend a casual air to the Münsterplatz and has since been accepted as an attractive link between the past and the present.

Ulmer Museum★

Marktplatz 9. ⟳Open year-round, Tue–Sun 11am–5pm, Thu to 8pm (special exhibit only). ⟳Closed Dec 24, 25 & 31. ⸛3.50€, Fri free, combination ticket with Kunsthalle Weishaupt 8€. ✆(0731) 161 43 12. www.museum.ulm.de.

This rambling museum has some great works by local masters. Note especially the *Virgin Mary of Bihlafingen* by Hans Multscher and the charming 13C *Mary of Sorrows*, edged in blue and gold, by a master from the Lake Constance area. The archaeological department boasts the 30 000-year-old Stone Age "Lion Man" statuette, masterfully carved from a mammoth tusk.

Also part of the museum is the late-Renaissance **Kiechelhaus**, which is the only suviving Patrician mansion from the 16C–17C and provides insight into the lifestyle of a wealthy merchant family. A new modern building makes a suitable setting for the **Kurt Fried Collection** of 20C art, including works by Klee, Kandinsky, Kirchner and Rothko.

Kunsthalle Weishaupt

Hans-und-Sophie-Scholl-Platz 1. ⟳Open year-round, Tue–Sun 11am–5pm, Thu until 8pm. ⸛6€ or 8€ in combination with Ulmer Museum. ✆(0731) 161 43 60. www.kunsthalle-weishaupt.de.

A spectacular, modern glass-and-steel building, designed by Richard Meier

WHERE TO STAY
Pension Rösch.............①
Schiefes Haus.............④

WHERE TO EAT
Weinkrüger.................①
Zunfthaus.....................④

STREET INDEX
Krampgasse 1
Kronengasse 3
Schwörhausgasse 5

Olympic Designs

Pictograms representing each
of the Olympic disciplines were
designed at the Ulm School of
Design by German designer Otl
Aicher for the Olympic Games
in Munich in 1972. They have
been used at each games and are
reproduced on the medals, to the
great pride of the city.

student Wolfram Wöhr, houses one
of Germany's most important private
collections of 20C art. Feast your eyes
on Concrete art (Albers, Richard Paul
Lohse), American Colour Field paintings (Rothko, Kenneth Noland), Pop
Art (Warhol, Rauschenberg) as well as
sculptures and installations by such
high-profile practitioners as Keith Har-
ing and the late Nam June Paik.

Altes Rathaus (Old Town Hall)

This elegant Gothic and Renaissance
building features painted façades and
an astronomical clock on its west façade.
It borders the market square with the
Fischerkasten fountain, thus named
because fishermen would cool their
wares in it. The spiral pedestal was fashioned by Jörg Syrlin the Elder in 1482.

Museum der Brotkultur★ (Bread Museum)

*Salzstadelgasse 10. ⏰Open year-round,
daily 10am–5pm (Wed to 8.30pm).
⏰Closed Good Fri and Dec 24. ⊚3.50€.
♿ ☎(0731) 699 55. www.museum-
brotkultur.de.*
The cultural and social history of 8000
years of bread is explored in this unique
museum. Exhibits range from ovens,
models, guilds, coins and stamps, to spe-
cially selected works of art (by Brueghel,
Corinth, Kollwitz and Picasso), all related

404

Museum der Brotkultur

Museum der Brotkultura

to grain or bread. The world's food supply is also critically examined.

Fischerviertel★ (Fishermen's Quarter)

Ulm is most lovely in the narrow alleys emanating from the little Blau River in the quarter once inhabited by millers, fisherfolk and tanners. From Fischerplätzle, a small, lime-tree-shaded square, turn left into a narrow street and pass over the little bridge, which leads to the so-called mid-15C **Schiefes Haus** (crooked house) on the banks of the Blau. The tiny alley opposite is known as the **Kußgasse** (kissing alley) because the roofs of the houses touch one another. In the nearby 17C **Schwörhaus** (house of oaths) the town mayor swears allegiance to the 14C constitution and renews his oath of office on the first Monday of July.

The town **walls** afford a wonderful close-up of the gables of the old houses. The crooked **Metzgerturm** (butcher's tower), erected in 1349, stands out since it stands nearly 2.05m/6.7ft off-centre. Go through the rose garden to reach the **Adlerbastei** (eagle bastion), where the unfortunate "Tailor of Ulm" attempted to fly in 1811.

South Bank of the Danube★

In fine weather, take a stroll along the pretty *Jahnufer* (the south bank of the Danube) to take in enchanting views of ornately gabled houses, the Metzgerturm and the cathedral.

ADDRESSES

STAY

Pension Rösch – *Schwörhausgasse 18.* *(0731) 657 18. 16 rooms.* This simple little hotel provides good value and clean rooms at the entrance to the picturesque fishermen's district.

Schiefes Haus – *Schwörhausgasse 6. (0731) 96 79 30. www.hotelschiefeshausulm.de. 11 rooms.* This restored medieval house harmoniously marries historic and modern touches. Some beds even sport water-filled mattresses.

EAT

Weinkrüger – *Weinhofberg 7. (0731) 649 76.* Enjoy regional specialities in the comfortable ambience of this former tannery. Dark wood and whimsical, handpicked décor give the dining room a cosy country feel.

Zunfthaus – *Fischergasse 31. (0731) 644 11. www.zunfthaus-ulm.de. Reservation recommended.* Set in the heart of the old town, this 600-year-old half-timbered building once served as the guild of the fishermen and ship builders. Today its three floors house a country-style restaurant serving regional cuisine, including locally caught fish.

TAKING A BREAK

Café Ströbele – *Hirschstraße 4. (0731) 637 79. Shop closed Sun.* This beloved café makes habit-forming cakes (try the *Schwarzwald Torte* – Black Forest gateau), deliciously roasted coffee, and 40 types of chocolate.

NIGHTLIFE

Barfüßer – *Paulstraße 4, 89231 Neu-Ulm (0731) 97 44 80. www.barfuesserbrauhaus.de.* On balmy summer days, there are few places more idyllic than this riverside beer garden. Sample the homemade brews along with tasty nibbles and traditional dishes.

Germany's southernmost region bewitches visitors with gorgeous scenery, quaint villages, ancient traditions and art-filled cities. Whether you want to raise a mug of beer at Munich's Hofbräuhaus, cheer on the famous local football team, FC Bayern München, ski the slopes above Garmisch-Partenkirchen, soar to the "top of Germany", the Zugspitze, or go underground in a Berchtesgaden salt mine, Munich and southern Bavaria has it all. A more sober visit can also be made to confront the darkest chapter in German history at Dachau concentration camp memorial site.

Highlights

1 The science and technology **Deustches Museum** (p417)

2 Beer and bratwurst in a beer hall on Platzl Square in **Munich** (p421)

3 The fantasy castle of **Neuschwanstein** (p448)

4 Gazing into four countries from the peak of the **Zugspitze** (p451)

5 Views of Berchtesgaden National Park from the **Eagle's Nest** (p457)

Capital of Bavaria

The magic of Munich and southern Bavaria best unfolds when the Föhn blows in from the mountains. A warm and gusty wind, it creates crystal-clear air and generates the illusion that the Alpine peaks are actually within arm's reach when, in fact, they are over 90km/56mi away! Locals claim the wind makes them cranky, but photography enthusiasts will have a field day. Just climb up any tower to see for yourself.

City for All Seasons

Any time of year is a fine time to visit Munich. Springtime brings longer days, raucous carnival celebrations, potent beers and traditional dancing during the *Starkbierzeit* (strong beer festival). Summer is best for carousing in beer gardens or listening to live music at the Tollwood Festival against the backdrop of the landmark Olympic Stadium. The biggest lure in autumn is, of course, Oktoberfest, the world's biggest drink-up. Winter, too, is lovely with its aromatic Christmas markets, a busy cultural calendar and cosy beer taverns serving hearty fare.

Munich Museum Mania

Museums are in season year-round, naturally, and there's truly something for everyone. Art fans could spend days feasting on canvasses from Tintoretto to Twombly by just touring the three Pinakothek museums. Sculpture vultures should steer towards the Glyptothek

Bavaria's "Dark Ages"

If Berlin was the head of the Nazi government (1933–45), its heart beat in Bavaria. After Hitler came to power in January 1933, Munich became the official "Capital of the Movement" and Nuremberg was chosen for staging the Nazi party's mass rallies. In Dachau, north of Munich, Germany's first concentration camp was built in 1933. In 1935 the party brass ushered in the systematic repression of the Jews by passing the notorious Nuremberg Laws. Many leading Nazis were Bavarian, including Heinrich Himmler and Hermann Göring. Hitler himself was born just across the border, in Austria's Braunau. The Alpine resort of Berchtesgaden served as the southern party headquarters, and the Winter Olympic Games of 1936 were held in Garmisch-Partenkirchen. Although the Nazis enjoyed almost universal support in Bavaria, there were also some pockets of resistance, most notably from the Munich-based student group, Die Weisse Rose (The White Rose).

and the Antiquity Collection, while technology lovers should put the German Museum, the Transport Museum and the BMW Museum at the top of their list. Those who are interested in the history of the German royal family will want to make the pilgrimage to the Residence and its many treasures as well as the Wittelsbach's summer retreat, Nymphenburg Palace, with its expansive and lushly landscaped gardens.

Legacy of Ludwig II

The most famous Wittelsbach ruler was Ludwig II, the late 19C fairytale king whose life ended young, tragically and mysteriously in Lake Starnberg, just south of Munich. An idealist and a dreamer, Ludwig quite literally built his legacy in stone. The palaces he conceived – Neuschwanstein, Herrenchiemsee, Linderhof – are as lavish as they are theatrical and thus a perfect reflection of the king's fantasies and longings for a time long gone.

Bewitching Scenery

What all three of Ludwig's palaces have in common is their stunning locations: surrounded by forest, in a romantic valley and on an island in a huge lake. But then it's hard to find any less than breathtaking scenery in southern Bavaria. The rugged peaks of the mighty Alps give way to rolling foothills, thick forests, rippling mountain streams, moody moorland and majestic lakes

Schloss Linderhof

© Bergfee/Fotolia.com

that are havens for water-rats. Through it all run rivers like the Isar and the epic Danube which has captured the imagination of poets, painters and composers and delivered power and prosperity to the region.

Roman Metropolises

When Munich was created in the 11C, Passau, Augsburg and Regenburg had already been on the map for over 1,000 years. Founded by the Romans, they reached their zenith in the Middle Ages, especially Augsburg, where the Fugger family financed European wars, and Regensburg, whose UNESCO-listed old town is still an enticing blend of medieval architecture and 21C vitality fuelled by a sizeable student body.

Königssee, Berchtesgaden National Park

© Stefan Baum/Bigstockphoto.com

MUNICH AND SOUTHERN BAVARIA

MUNICH AND SOUTHERN BAVARIA

0   30 km

MUNICH	★★★	Highly recommended
Regensburg	★★	Recommended
Füssen	★	Interesting
Kempten		If you have time
		Driving Tour showing point of departure

WURTZBURG   BAMBERG   BAYREUTH

Nuremberg

Canal

Main

Danube

Altmühl

Ingolstadt

Donauwörth

STUTTGART

BADEN-WÜRTTEMBERG

Ulm

DANUBE

RIEDLINGEN

Upper Swabian Plateau

HERBERTINGEN

Weingarten

Ravensburg

Iller

Ottobeuren

Kempten

Allgäu

Hindelang

CONSTANCE

Lindau

Lake Constance

Paradies

GERMAN

Nebelhorn △2224

ST. GALL

SWITZERLAND

Breitachklamm

CHUR   ST. ANTON

Kleinwalsertal

Oberstdorf

Kansel

Lech

ST. ANTON

Augsbourg

Lech

A 96

MUNICH

Dachau

Stade Allianz Arena

Ammersee

Andechs

Dießen

Starnberger See

Buchheim Museum

Isar

Rottenbuch

Steingaden

Wies

Oberammergau

Hohenschwangau

Ettal

Füssen

Linderhof

Wank 1780

NEUSCHWANSTEIN

ZUGSPITZE

2962

ALPINE

Garmisch-Partenkirchen

Innsbruck

Inn

BOLZANO

A 13

408

Munich★★★

München

"Lederhosen and laptops" is the motto of Bavaria's vibrant and prosperous capital and it beautifully encapsulates the city's knack for blending tradition with innovation. Beer halls, gardens and Baroque churches, fantastic shopping, and world-class art and culture galore make it easy to fall in love with Munich.

A BIT OF HISTORY

The foundation of the town – Munich's origins hark back to the 9C when a small village was established near a Benedictine abbey. The name München was derived from the German word for monk: *Mönch*. Ever since, the town's emblem has been a little monk *(Münchner Kindl)*. In 1158 Henry the Lion, Duke of Saxony, built a local bridge across the Isar River, forcing all traders to pass through Munich. This stratagem marked the beginning of the city's long and flourishing career as an economic power player.

The rise of the Wittelsbachs – In 1180 Henry the Lion was stripped of his titles, banished from southern Germany and replaced with Count Otto von Wittelsbach. The House of Wittelsbach governed Bavaria without interruption until the demise of the monarchy 1918.

The Kings of Bavaria – In 1806 Duke Max IV Joseph was promoted by Napoleon to King Maximilian I. His son, **Ludwig I** (1825–48), an enlightened and art-minded fellow, welcomed to his court the best of Europe's architects and artists, eventually enriching Munich with the Alte Pinakothek, the university, the

▶ **Population:** 1 326 800

Info: Bahnhofsplatz 2 and Marienplatz 8, 80335 München. ℘(089) 23 39 65 00. www.muenchen.de.

Location: Munich is the largest city in southern Germany and the third largest in Germany. Served by the A9 (Berlin) and the A8 (Salzburg) autobahns, it also has a huge and modern international airport.

Parking: Garages are located throughout this city. Visit http://wap.parkinfo.com for fees and locations.

Don't Miss: Pinakothek art museums, German Museum, English Garden, beer halls, Viktualienmarkt, Residenz, Marienplatz.

Timing: You will want to spend at least two, preferably three, days in this fascinating city.

Kids: German Museum, Museum of Human and Natural History, Hellabrunn Zoological Gardens, SeaLife Munich, Flugwerft Schleissheim.

Glyptothek and the Propylaea. **Maximilian II** (1848–64) continued the artistic traditions of his father by founding the Bavarian National Museum in 1855. A special place in Bavarian history is reserved for **Ludwig II** (1864–86). This tormented romantic, a passionate admirer of Wagner, succeeded to the throne at the age of 18. Beloved

Simplicissimus

A satirical literary journal created in Munich in 1896, *Simplicissimus* became famous throughout Germany for its caricatures and audacity. Writers Thomas Mann and Frank Wedekind took an active part in it, as did some avant-garde and Expressionist artists. In the 1930s, the Nazis took over this weekly publication and turned it into an instrument of propaganda. It disappeared, along with the Nazis, in 1945.

PRACTICAL INFORMATION

TELEPHONE AREA CODE: ✆089

TOURIST INFORMATION

Tourist Offices: *Bahnhofsplatz 2 (main train station);* Neues Rathaus *(Marienplatz 8).*

PUBLICATIONS

Several publications publish listings of current events. Check out the freebies *München im...* (followed by the month) and *In München* and the glossy for-purchase *Prinz*. Thursdays *"SZ-extra"* supplement of the *Süddeutsche Zeitung"* newspaper also has listings.

TICKETS

Book tickets well in advance by phone, online or in person from the tourist offices or at commercial ticket vendors such as www.muenchenticket.de.

POST OFFICES WITH LATE HOURS

Bahnhofsplatz 1, Mon–Fri 8am–8pm, Sat 9am–4pm; Postfiliale 24 at the airport *(central area level 3)* in McPaper, Mon–Sat 7.30am–9pm.

DAILY PAPERS

Süddeutsche Zeitung, Münchner Merkur.

INTERNET

www.munich-online.de; www.munich-info.de; www.muenchen. de; www.munichfound.de.

AIRPORT

✆*(089) 975 00. www.munich-airport.de.* Munich International Airport, 34km/ 21mi north, is linked to the city by S-Bahn lines S1 and S8 *(departures around the clock, 9.60€)*, and by the Lufthansa Airport Bus *(www.airportbus-muenchen.de; departure every 20min from 5.10am to 7.50pm, 10.50€).*

GETTING THERE AND AROUND

Central Munich is compact and large sections of it are pedestrianised. Many sights are within walking distance; the city's main museums can be reached by tram or U-Bahn, e.g. from Karlsplatz, Marienplatz or Hauptbahnhof (main railway station).

Public Transport – Munich and its surroundings are divided into four ring-shaped price zones. The network consists of subways (U-Bahn), buses and trams *(Straßenbahn)*, and light rail (S-Bahn). The main local transportation authority is **MVV** *(Münchner Verkehrs-und Tarifverbund; ✆(089) 41 42 43 44; www.mvv-muenchen.de)*. Information by phone, online or at the MVV office on the mezzanine level of the main train station, Mon–Sat 9am–6pm. Tickets are available from vending machines at any U-Bahn or S-Bahn rail station and in trams and from bus drivers. Tickets must be stamped on the station platform or aboard buses and trams in order to be valid. The fine for riding without a valid ticket is 40€.

Tickets for the central zone *(Münchner Innenraum)*, which includes Munich city centre: single tickets *(Einzelfahrt)* 2.50€; strip card *(Streifenkarte)* 12€ consists of 10 strips, stamp two strips for rides within the central zone, more strips for longer trips, card can be used by more than one person and transfers are allowed. Single day tickets *(Single-Tageskarte)* 5.40€, and group day tickets for up to five people 9.80€, are valid from when they are stamped to 6am the following day.

CityTourCard – There are four versions: one-day single *(Single 1 Tag)* 9.80€, three-day single *(Single 3 Tage)* 18.80€, one-day "Partner" (for five adults – two children between six and 14 years old equal one adult) *(Partner 1 Tag)* 16€; three-day "Partner" *(Partner 3 Tage)* 29€. The ticket entitles you to unlimited use of public transport in the central city and to discounts between 10 percent and 50 percent for about 30 sights, museums, castles, tourist attractions, city tours and bicycle hire. It is available from MVV offices, U-Bahn and S-Bahn ticket vending machines and in some hotels.

Bicycle rental – Munich is a bicycle-friendly city. *Radius Bike Tours (Arnulf-straße 3; ✆(089) 59 61 13; www.radius munich.com)* rents bikes for 17€ per 24hrs (50€ deposit) and also conducts bike and walking tours. The office is opposite track 32 of the Hauptbahnhof and is open mid-Mar-Oct, 9.30am–6pm.

March Beer

The March "strong beer" season originated in the 17C when Franciscan monks began brewing high-alcohol beer to provide them with energy and sustenance during the Lent fasting period. Although drinking was permitted during Lent, they still took a barrel to the Pope to make doubly sure. He readily assented, believing that such a "bad" beer (it was very strong and probably ruined during the journey) was punishment enough. These spring beers traditionally end in "ator".

by his subjects, he was a restless and emotional young man prone to deep depression. Craving solitude and living in a fantasy world, Ludwig largely withdrew from society and dedicated himself to castle building: Neuschwanstein, Linderhof and Herrenchiemsee all sprang from his fevered brow. Declared mentally unstable, Ludwig II was deposed in 1886 and confined to Schloss Berg, on the shores of Lake Starnberg. He was found drowned there shortly afterwards. His uncle Luitpold was appointed prince regent. Luitpold's son, **Ludwig III**, was made the last king of Bavaria in 1912, but under pressure from a workers' revolutionary movement after World War I, he was forced to abdicate in 1918.

Between two wars – In 1919, **Adolf Hitler**'s German Workers' party was formed and its platform proclaimed at the Munich Hofbräuhaus. In 1923, Hitler fomented an uprising (the Munich Putsch, or Beer Hall Putsch). It was unsuccessful, the party was dissolved and Hitler imprisoned.

During imprisonment he penned his infamous manifesto *Mein Kampf (My Struggle)*. Upon his release, Hitler reorganised the group as the National Socialist (Nazi) Party and, by 1933, had risen to chancellor of Germany. In 1938, he chose Munich as the venue for a meeting with Chamberlain, Daladier

and Mussolini at which the annexation of the Sudetenland was agreed.

Munich today – Munich was heavily bombed in World War II, but recovered rapidly to become a key economic zone in southern Germany. It is now a prime purveyor of cars, electronics, insurance services, information technology and other industries. Microsoft, BMW and Siemens all have headquarters here and the trade fair grounds attract some 2 million visitors each years. Tourism is another major economic factor.

KUNSTAREAL (ART QUARTER)★★★

Munich's famous Art Quarter encompasses the Alte Pinakothek (14C to 18C), the Neue Pinakothek (19C), the Pinakothek der Moderne (early 20C) and – since 2009 – the Museum Brandhorst (late 20C and 21C) (&see page 417).

ALTE PINAKOTHEK★★★

Barer Straße 15. ○*Open year-round, Tue 10am–8pm, Wed–Sun 10am–6pm.* ○*Closed Shrove Tue, May 1, Dec 24, 25 & 31.* ∞*7€, Sun 1€.* &*⌂(089) 23 80 52 16. www.pinakothek.de.*

The **Alte Pinakothek**, a colossal building designed by Leo von Klenze in the early 19C, houses paintings amassed by the House of Wittelsbach.

German School

The most extensive section is devoted to German Old Masters. Alongside sacred 15C paintings are works by painters inspired by the Italian Renaissance. Masterpieces include **Albrecht Dürer**'s *Four Apostles* (1526); **Albrecht Altdorfer**'s *Landscape* (1528); and **Hans Holbein the Elder**'s *St. Sebastian Altarpiece* (1516).

Dutch and Flemish Schools

Among the most important works in this section are *The Land of Milk and Honey* (1566) by **Pieter Brueghel the Elder** and *The Last Judgement* (c. 1614–16) by **Peter Paul Rubens**. Early Dutch masterpieces include the *Altarpiece of the Three Magi* (1455) by **Rogier Van der**

Alte Pinakothek

Weyden; *Seven Joys of Mary* (c. 1480) by **Hans Memling**; and *Last Judgment* by **Hieronymus Bosch**. Finally, **Rembrandt**'s Passion Cycle constitutes the heart of the collection of 17C Dutch paintings.

Italian School

Here the spotlight is on the great Renaissance masters: **Sandro Botticelli**'s *Lamentation of Christ* (post 1490); three major works by **Raphael** including the *Madonna Tempi* (1507); *The Crowning of Thorns* (1560) by **Titian**; **Tiepolo**'s the *Veneration of the Holy Trinity* by Pope Clemens (1739) and the *Adoration of the Magi* (1753); and several works by **Antonio Canaletto** and **Francesco Guardi**.

French School

French Classicism is represented by **Claude Lorrain**'s *Sea Port at Sunrise* (1674) and paintings by **Nicolas Poussin**, who takes his subjects from Ovid's *Metamorphoses* (1627). Among the 18C painters, **François Boucher**'s *Madame Pompadour* is on display, commissioned by her in 1756.

Spanish School

This school is notably represented by **Murillo**'s lively genre paintings alongside epic canvases by **El Greco** and **Velázquez**.

NEUE PINAKOTHEK★★

Barer Straße 29, enter from Theresienstraße.
🕐*Open year-round, Wed 10am–8pm, Thu-Mon 10am–6pm.* 🕐*Closed May 1, Dec 24, 25 & 31.* 💶*7€, Sun 1€.*
♿ 📞*(089) 23 80 51 95.*
www.pinakothek.de.

The **Neue Pinakothek** is a well-proportioned Postmodernist work by Alexander von Branca, completed in 1981. It replaced the original building by Friedrich von Gärtner that suffered irreparable damage during World War II. The collection focuses on works from the 19C and early 20C.

Early 19C

Galleries **1, 2 and 2a** are devoted to European art from around 1800. Canvasses worth focusing on include: **Thomas Gainsborough**'s portraits and landscapes, works by **Jacques-Louis David**, including the *Marquise de Sorcy*, **Joshua Reynolds** *(Captain Pownall)*, **William Turner** *(Ostend)* and **Francisco Goya** *(Marquesa de Caballero)*.

😊 A Bit of Advice 😊

A Day Pass pass to all four Kunstareal museums is 12€. Combination tickets valid for visits on separate days are 29€.

The Collection

The Pinakothek collection was started in the 16C by Duke Wilhelm IV, who commissioned historical scenes from the most eminent painters of his time, Altdorfer and Burgkmair. In the 17C, the Elector Maximilian I founded the Kammergalerie which, under King Ludwig I, developed into the finest exhibition of art in the whole of Europe. The building suffered severe damage in 1943, but the paintings had already been moved to a safe location.

Early 19C German painters

On display in Galleries **3 and 3a** are early-Romantic works from Dresden, Berlin and Munich, including the highly spiritual landscapes of **Caspar David Friedrich**. Johann Christian **Dahl** (*Frederiksholm Canal in Copenhagen*, 1817) and Karl **Blechen** (*View of Assisi*, 1830) are also represented. Ludwig I of Bavaria was a great patron of the arts who commissioned many paintings, including those on display in Galleries **4 and 4a**. Galleries **5 and 5a** are devoted to the German Neoclassicists in Rome, including a well-known landscape by **Ludwig Richter**, *The Night-Watchman* (*Watzmann*, 1824).

The following galleries focus on two early 19C trends: the spiritual Nazarenes, who sought to reconcile northern and southern painting by hearking back to Raphael and Dürer; and artists of the **Biedermeier** style.

From Romanticism to Realism

Pride of place is given to French painters in Galleries **10 and 10a**. The Romantics are represented by **Théodore Géricault** and his admirer **Eugène Delacroix**. In Galleries **11 and 11a**, Andreas Achenbach and **Carl Spitzweg** (*The Hussar*, *The Poor Poet*, 1839, *The Writer*, 1850) represent late German Romanticism.

Late 19C German painters

Gallery **15** is entirely devoted to **Hans von Marées** (1837–1887), a great portrait painter inspired by Renaissance art. Gallery **16** contains works by a group of German painters who went to live and work in Rome: Arnold Böcklin, Hans Thoma, **Anselm Feuerbach** and **Wilhelm Leibl**.

Impressionists, post-Impressionists and Symbolists

Galleries **18 and 19** contain paintings by German Impressionists, notably *Summer Holiday* by Friedrich von Uhde and *Portrait of the Writer Eduard Graf von Keyserling* (1901) by **Lovis Corinth**.

Symbolism and *Jugendstil* provide the theme of Galleries **20 and 21a**. *Margarethe Stonborough-Wittgenstein*, the philosopher's sister, was the subject of a famous portrait by **Gustav Klimt** (1905). **Auguste Rodin**'s marble bust of *Helene von Nostitz* is surrounded by several works of Ferdinand Hodler *(Disappointed)*, Egon Schiele (*Agony*, 1912) and Giovanni Segantini (*Ploughing*, 1890).

Post-Impressionists Toulouse-Lautrec, Vuillard and Ensor share Gallery **21** with **Claude Monet**'s large-scale *Waterlilies* (1918). Galleries **22** and **22a** are devoted to such French Impressionists as **Paul Gauguin, Camille Pissarro, Edgar Degas**, and **Paul Cézanne**. Also on display is a painting from **Vincent Van Gogh**'s *Sunflowers* series (1888).

PINAKOTHEK DER MODERNE★★

Barer Straße 40. 🕐*Open year-round, Tue–Sun 10am–6pm (Thu 8pm).* 🕐*Closed Shrove Tue, May 1, Dec 24, 25 & 31.* ⊚*10€, Sun 1€.* ♿ ✆(089) 23 80 53 60. www.pinakothek.de.

The building, designed by Munich architect Stephan Braunfels, is known as the "Cathedral of Light" because of its glass rotunda and glazed saw-tooth roofs. It unites four museums with collections of 20C paintings, sculpture, graphics, design and architecture under a single roof.

Staatsgalerie Moderner Kunst (State Gallery of Modern Art)

3rd floor. The question of form and content in modern art is the underlying theme of the permanent exhibition, arranged in chronological order and by cross-influence.

"Classic" Modern Art (Galleries 1–17) – A large section is devoted to German Expressionism. The artist group *Die Brücke (The Bridge)*, which was led by **Ernst Ludwig Kirchner** and whose tortured subjects set them apart from the Fauves, is well represented. So are members of *Der Blaue Reiter (The Blue Rider)*, who focused on abstraction and spiritualisation of form; Franz Marc and **Wassily Kandinsky** were at the visionary helm of this group. Another Expressionist, **Max Beckmann**, is represented by the *Temptation of St. Anthony.*

The Cubists and Futurists moved towards autonomous art, as illustrated in numerous works by **Pablo Picasso** (including *Madame Soler*) and **Georges Braque**. Surrealism is represented by Max Ernst, René Magritte and Salvador Dalí, and Bauhaus by Feininger and Paul Klee.

Modern Art (Galleries 20–36) – Important themes in art during the second half of the 20C – informal art, celebration of the trivial, rise of pop culture, etc. – are broached in artists' monographs. One can thus follow the works of **Joseph Beuys**, **Francis Bacon** *(Crucifixion)* and Willem de Kooning. The museum also displays some remarkable works by American artists, with paintings by **Andy Warhol**, photographs by Jeff Wall and videos by Bruce Nauman.

Other Departments

Neue Sammlung (New Design Collection, basement) – In addition to objects of industrial design, accessories, cars and computer equipment, the museum presents prototypes of items designed since the industrial revolution up to the 1960s.

Selections from the **Grafische Sammlung** (State Graphic Arts Collection) are shown in temporary exhibitions on the

A Bit of Advice

Two other museums exhibit works by German Expressionists: The Lenbach Collections in Munich (*Blaue Reiter* movement) and the Buchheim Museum in Bernried (*Die Brücke* movement).
See INTRODUCTION: Art.

ground floor owing to their great sensitivity to light.

Finally, the **Architekturmuseum** (Architecture Museum) is the largest of its kind in Germany with a rich collection of models, photographs, blueprints and computer prints dating from the 16C to today. The focus is on architecture in Germany in the 19C and 20C with particular attention given to the genius of Leo von Klenze, Le Corbusier and Peter Zumthor.

MUSEUM BRANDHORST★★

Open Tue–Sun 10am–6pm (Thu 8pm). Closed Shrove Tue, May 1, Dec 24–25 & 31. 7€ (Sun 1€). (089) 238 05 22 86. www.museum-brandhorst.de.

In a stunning, eco-friendly building by the Berlin architectural firm Sauerbruch Hutton, the Museum Brandhorst has enriched Munich's cultural landscape since 2009. It presents masterpieces by key contemporary artists, including the largest collection of works by Cy Twombly outside of Houston. The artist's 12-canvas *Lepanto* cycle, which is displayed in its own, polygonal room, is especially stunning. Pop-Artist Andy Warhol also gets plenty of wall space alongside groundbreaking German practitioners Joseph Beuys, Mario Merz, Sigmar Polke, Georg Baselitz and Gerhard Richter. Select works by Damien Hirst, Dave LaChapelle and Bruce Nauman complete the collection.

DEUTSCHES MUSEUM★★★

Museumsinsel 1. Open year-round, daily 9am–5pm. Closed 1 Jan, Shrove Tue, Good Fri, May 1, Nov 1, Dec 24, 25 & 31. 8.50€. (089) 217 91. www.deutsches-museum.de.

Deutsches Museum

Deutsches Museum/Munich City Tourist Office

Founded in 1903, this museum – one of the most important in the world for scientific and technical matters – is built on an isle in the Isar **(Museumsinsel)**. It traces the history of science and technology from the beginning of time to the present and explains physical processes and phenomena. Besides a large number of original items and reconstructions are dioramas and scale models. According to the wishes of founder and Bavarian electricity pioneer **Oskar von Miller**, the displays invite visitors to enquire, touch and discover.

⊙This is a huge museum, so be selective and don't expect to see everything on a single visit.

Ground Floor

Oil and gas, electricity, metallurgy and civil engineering are among subjects addressed on the ground floor.

The Aeronautical Section exhibits early planes, including the Messerschmitt Me-262 – the first fighter jet made on a production line – helicopters, gliders and vertical take-off machines. The bulk of flying machines, though, are at the

---

⊙ A Bit of Advice ⊙

Combination tickets for the three Deutsches Museum branches (Museumsinsel, Flugwerft und Verkehrszentrum) cost 17€ and are valid on separate days.

---

museum's branch in Schleissheim, the **Flugwerft Schleissheim** (⊙ *see below*). An Elbe sailing ship (1880) and an Italian steam tug (1931) stand at the entrance to the Navigation Department *(continued in the basement)*. There's also a nifty collection of model trains, although to see the big engines, you have to visit the museum's **Verkehrszentrum** near Theresienhöhe (⊙ *see below*). Also on this floor is an exhibit on bridges that will remain closed until at least 2012.

Basement

Among many other displays, the Navigation Section highlights naval construction, warships (including U-1, the first German submarine, built in 1906), methods of navigation, fishing techniques, and Jacques Picard's 1958 bathysphere. This is followed by an exhibition on mining techniques that includes a model salt mine.

Children aged three to eight will be stimulated and entertained in the **Kinderreich**, an educational play zone.

First Floor

This floor is dominated by the Physical Science Section (optics, mechanics, nuclear physics, electronics, etc.). The Old Aeronautics Hall presents pioneering flying machines, such as gliders built by Otto Lilienthal (c. 1885) and a 1917 Fokker Dr I Triplane, made famous by Baron von Richthofen's "circus" in World War I. Note also the Wright

Brothers' Type-A Standard (USA, 1909), a Blériot Type XI (1909) and a Junkers F-13 (the first successful commercial airliner, 1919). Note that the Chemistry section is being overhauled and will remain closed until at least 2012.

Second Floor

The main draw here is the re-created Altamira Cave with its famous Stone Age paintings, but there is plenty more to keep your brain engaged: glass and ceramics, printing techniques, photography (Daguerre's apparatus, 1839), space travel, textiles and environmental science.

Third Floor

Exhibitions on weights and measures, telecommunications, agriculture, microelectronics and computer science fill this floor.

Fourth to Sixth Floor

The upper floors are dedicated to astronomy and present everything from ancient equipment to solar system models. **Tickets** (∞2€) for shows in the sixth-floor Planetarium must be purchased at the information booth in the entrance foyer.

♿♟ Verkehrszentrum (Transport Museum)

Theresienhöhe 14a. ○*Open year-round, daily 9am–5pm.* ○*Closed Jan 1, Shrove Tue, Good Fri, May 1, Nov 1, Dec 24, 25 & 31.* ∞*6€ (child 3€).* ♿. ℘*(089) 5008065 01. www.deutsches-museum.de.*

Housed in the former exhibition centre near Theresienwiese, this museum traces the evolution of mobility in three large halls. Historical coaches and steam locomotives take you back to the beginning, while exhibits such as the ultra-speedy Transrapid train offer a glimpse of the present.

Flugwerft Schleißheim★

Effnerstraße 18, 85764 Oberschleißheim, next to Schloss Schleißheim. ○*Open year-round, daily 9am–5pm.* ○*Closed Jan 1, Shrove Tue, Good Fri, May 1, Nov 1, Dec 24, 25 & 31 Dec.* ∞*6€ (child 3€).*

♿. ℘*(089) 315 71 40. www.deutsches-museum.de.*

A 1920s Bavarian air corps hangar now houses the aviation department of the Deutsches Museum. Aside from gliders, helicopters and small planes, it also has several military aircraft from the Cold War era, including a 1959 Lockheed F-104F Starfighter and a Soviet MiG-23BN from 1980. Behind a glass wall, engineers are busy restoring historical craft. Children can even get their own "pilot's license".

RESIDENZ★★ (THE RESIDENCE)

Combined ticket for the Residenzmuseum and Schatzkammer ∞*9€. With Altes Rezidenztheater 11€.*

After the ruling Wittelsbachs had outgrown their original residence *(Alter Hof, on Burgstraße)*, construction of a new royal palace began in 1385. The complex was expanded considerably in subsequent centuries and today consists of seven structures enclosing eight inner courtyards.

Schatzkammer★★ (Treasury)

○*Open Apr–mid-Oct, daily 9am–6pm; mid-Oct–Mar 10am–5pm; last entry 1hr before closing.* ○*Closed Jan 1, Shrove Tue, Dec 24, 25 & 31.* ∞*6€.* ℘*(089) 29 06 71. www.residenz-muenchen.de.*

Bavarian rulers had a passion for collecting precious things, as you will see on a tour of the treasury which brims with gold works, enamels, crystalware, carved ivories and other fanciful items. Among the highlights are an 11C cross made for Queen Gisela of Hungary, Heinrich's crown from 1280 and dazzling jewellery inlaid with precious stones.

Residenzmuseum★★

○*Open Apr–mid-Oct, daily 9am–6pm; mid-Oct–Mar, 10am–5pm, last entry 1hr before closing.* ○*Closed Jan 1, Shrove Tue, Dec 24, 25 & 31.* ∞*6€.* ℘*(089) 29 06 71. www.residenz-muenchen.de.*

Allow at least two hours to visit this vast museum. An audioguide, available in multiple languages, is included in the admission price.

On your tour you will see **Die Reichen Zimmer** (state rooms, 1730–37), which illustrate early Rococo style. Highlights include the **Königlichen Appartements** (royal apartments) in the **Königsbau** (king's wing), which were built under Ludwig I between 1826 and 1835. One of the most important rooms is the **Antiquarium** (c. 1570). Inlaid with marble and embellished with ceiling frescoes, it is a treasure trove of original and copied statues from ancient Greece. Also noteworthy are the **Special Collections** with porcelain masterpieces from Meissen, Nymphenburg, Frankenthal and Sèvres.

The 17C **Hofkapelle** (court chapel) is dedicated to the Virgin Mary, patron saint of Bavaria.

The **Reiche Kapelle** (ornate chapel, 1607) was the private chapel of Duke Max I and is a lavish kaleidoscope of coloured marble and gilded reliefs.

Altes Residenztheater (Cuvilliéstheatre)★★

Enter via Brunnenhof courtyard.
Open mid-Jun–mid-Sept, daily 9am–6pm; Apr–mid-Jun & mid-Sept–mid-Oct 2pm–6pm Mon–Sat, 9am–6pm Sun; mid-Oct–Mar, Mon–Sat 2pm–5pm, Sun 10am–5pm, last entry 1hr before closing. 3€.

This enchanting red-and-gold Rococo theatre was masterminded by **François de Cuvilliés**, built in 1750s and recently restored. The Prince-Elector's box is set apart by the elegance of its hangings, marble and stuccowork.

WALKING TOUR
OLD TOWN★★

See itinerary on the city map – Allow half a day.

Marienplatz★ (St. Mary's Square)

This square is the heart of Munich and centres on the **Mariensäule**, a column erected in 1638 by Prince-Elector Maximilian in honour of Mary, patron saint of Bavaria. On the square's north side looms the fantastic neo-Gothic **Neues Rathaus** (new town hall, 1867–1908) with the tourist office on the ground floor. Its enchanting **carillon** (*Glockenspiel*) has tourists craning their necks daily at 11am and noon (*Mar–Sept, also 5pm*) when brightly coloured figurines emerge accompanied by merry chimes. Two scenes are represented: the upper level shows a knights' tournament held

in 1568 in celebration of the marriage of Duke Wilhelm V to Renata of Lothringia; the lower half re-enacts the **Schäfflertanz** (Dance of the Coopers), first held to celebrate the end of the plague in the 16C.
The **Altes Rathaus** (old town hall) on the square's eastern side is decorated with stepped gables and bell turrets and now houses the **Spielzeugmuseum** (toy museum).

Peterskirche
(Church of St. Peter's)
This 13C three-aisle Gothic church acquired a Baroque look in the 17C and 18C. Note Erasmus Grasser's statue of St. Peter (1492) in the centre section of the high altar. The bell-tower – affectionately nicknamed "Old Pete" – can be climbed *(306 steps, ☞1.50€)* for splendid city views.

▷ *Continue via Burgstrasse, which follows the route of the medieval town wall.*

Weinstadel
Burgstraße 5.
Munich's oldest surviving building (1552) used to be the office of the Clerk of the Court and sports a colourful *trompe-l'œil* façade.

▷ *At the end of Burgstraße, the route passes under the tower of the Old Castle.*

Alter Hof
(Old Castle)
This building was the official Wittelsbach residence from 1253 to 1474. The south wing has an elegant tower with half-timbered corbelling (late 15C), known locally as the *Affenturm* (monkey tower). In recent times, sections of the building have been controversially turned into apartment and office buildings.
The complex also contains a **central information office** about Bavarian castles and palaces and a free **multimedia exhibition** *(☉open Mon–Fri 10am–6pm, Sat 10am–1pm; ☎(089) 21 01 40 50)* about the Alter Hof and general Munich history.

▷ *Exit Alter Hof to the east and continue on Münzstraße.*

Hofbräuhaus
Munich's best-known beer hall has stood on **Platzl Square** since 1589. Every day, servers deliver virtual rivers of beer in one-litre (1.75 pint) tankards *(Maßkrug)* to a thirsty crowd cheering on raucous brass bands performing popular songs. The huge vaulted **Bierschwemme**, on the ground floor, is the rowdiest section. Head to the beer garden if you like it quieter.

▷ *From Platzl head north to Hofgraben, turn left and continue to Max-Joseph-Platz.*

Nationaltheater
(National Theatre)
Built between 1811 and 1818 by Leo von Klenze, the national theatre is home to the Bavarian State Opera and can seat up to 2 100 people.

Residenz★★ *(☞See above)*
For an exterior tour of the Residence, you can walk from courtyard to courtyard. Coming from either Residenzstrasse or Max-Joseph-Platz, the first one you enter is the Königsbauhof, followed by the Grottenhof (grotto courtyard), the Kapellenhof (chapel courtyard), Brunnenhof (fountain courtyard), Apothekenhof (apothecary courtyard) and the Kaiserhof (Imperial courtyard).

▷ *Follow Residenzstraße north along the west side of the Residenz.*

Odeonsplatz
(Odeon Square)
On the west side of this square stands the 19C Leuchtenberg-Palais, built for Eugène de Beauharnais, Count of Leuchtenberg, and now home to the Bavarian Finance Ministry.
To the south, the **Feldherrnhalle** (1840–44) by Andreas Gärtner marks the southern terminus of grand Ludwigstraße built under Ludwig I; the northern end culminates in a triumphal arch *(Siegestor).*

View of Munich with the Alps – Siegestor, Theatinerkirche and Frauenkirche in the foreground

Rudolf Sterflinger/Munich City Tourist Office

Theatinerkirche★

A fine example of Baroque architecture, this church was built between 1663 and 1688, first under the direction of the Italian Agostino Barelli and later by Enrico Zuccalli from Graubünden, Switzerland. The particularly lavish interior stucco ornamentation is primarily by Nicolo Petri. Several Bavarian rulers, including King Max I and Crown Prince Ruprecht are buried in the south transept.

◯ *Follow Theatinerstraße south until to see the entrance to the Fünf Höfe arcades on your right.*

Fünf Höfe (Five Courtyards)

The Fünf Höfe is a beautifully designed shopping complex consisting of arcades linking five interior courtyards. Each passageway is lined with high-end boutiques, cafés and restaurants.

The glass-and-steel complex was designed by Herzog & de Meuron and completed in 2003. Do not miss the **Kunsthalle der Hypo-Kulturstiftung**, an exhibition space that hosts changing high-calibre art shows (◯*open year-round, daily 10am–8pm;* ◯*closed Dec 24; admission varies;* ℘ *(089) 22 44 12; www.hypo-kunsthalle.de).*

◯ *Exit the Fünf Höfe via the Pranner passageway to emerge on Kardinal-Faulhaber-Straße.*

Erzbischöfliches Palais (Episcopal Palace)

Kardinal-Faulhaber-Straße 7.
Cuvilliés' finest palace was built between 1733–37 and still serves as the residence of the local archbishop. It boasts a magnificent pink-and-white façade with a rounded balcony supported by cherubs.

Palais Portia

Kardinal-Faulhaber-Straße 12.
This pink-and-grey mansion was originally designed by Enrico **Zuccalli** (1694), with a façade by **Cuvilliés**, for one of Karl Albrecht's favourites, Countess Portia.

◯ *Take the alley at the end of Kardinal-Faulhaber-Straße.*

Frauenkirche★★ (Church of Our Lady)

Altes Rathaus architect **Jörg von Halspach** also designed this vast late Gothic hall-church (1468–88). The two onion-domed towers were added in 1525 and are a city landmark.

In striking contrast to the austere, red-brick façade, the **interior** is brilliant white and makes a stunning impression. Eleven pairs of octagonal pillars support the reticulated vaulting. Seen from the entrance, the perspective of these columns forms a continuous line, effectively hiding the aisles.

In the south aisle is a monumental black marble **cenotaph**★ to Emperor Ludwig of Bavaria, by Hans Krumper (1619–22). All the chapels contain high-quality paintings and altarpieces, and those off the ambulatory sport extraordinary 15C **stained-glass windows**. A lift in the south tower whisks you to a **viewing platform**★ (○*open Apr–Oct, Mon–Sat 10am–5pm; ○3€*).

○ *Follow Liebfrauenstraße, then turn right into the Kaufingerstraße which becomes Neuhauserstraße.*

Deutsches Jagd- und Fischereimuseum (German Hunting and Fishing Museum)

Neuhauserstraße 2. ○Open year-round, daily 9.30am–5pm (Thu 9pm). ○Closed Shrove Tue, Dec 24 & 31. ○3.50€. ℘(089) 22 05 22. www.jagd-fischerei-museum.de.

The museum, housed in a former Augustinian church, displays three floors of ancient and modern arms, trophies, paintings and drawings of hunting scenes, along with a veritable zoo's worth of stuffed animals.

○ *Walk a few steps west on Neuhauserstraße to the Michaelskirche.*

Michaelskirche★ (Church of St. Michael's)

This 16C Jesuit sanctuary is considered the oldest Renaissance church north of the Alps. The façade is decorated with pilasters, bands of script and a statue of the church's patron, the Archangel Michael.

The single nave inspired many Baroque builders in southern Germany. The pulpit and seven side altars date from 1697. Thirty of the Wittelsbach rulers, including King Ludwig II of Bavaria, are buried in the crypt (*Fürstengruft*).

○ *Head south on Eisenmannstraße which turns into Damenstiftstraße. After crossing Brunnstraße, take the Asamhofpassage on your left to Sendlinger Straße. Turn right and the Asam Church will be on your right.*

Asamkirche★ (Church of St. Johannes Nepomuk)

The church, built in 1733, is usually referred to by the name of the men who constructed it, the **Asam Brothers**: the painter Cosmas Damian Asam and the sculptor Egid Quirin Asam. The church's remarkable unity of style is due to the fact that the brothers not only drew up the plans but also supervised every stage of the building process. The result is Rococo artistry run amok with colour, stuccowork, gilding, statuary and embellishments of every sort covering every single square inch of wall space.

○ *Turn left on Sendlinger Straße as you exit the church, then turn right on Hermann-Sack-Straße, then cut across Oberanger.*

St. Jacobsplatz

Munich's **Jewish Museum**★ (○*open year-round, Tue–Sun 10am–6pm; ○closed Jan 1, Shrove Tue, Rosh Hashanah, Yom Kippur, Dec 24, 25 & 31; ○6€; ℘(089) 23 39 60 96; www.juedisches-museum-muenchen.de*). Opened in 2007 and is part of an architectural ensemble on St. Jakobsplatz that also includes a **community centre** and a **synagogue**. The small permanent exhibit in the basement delivers impressions of the city's Jewish history and cultural contributions, while the upper floors are taken up by changing presentations.

Münchner Stadtmuseum★ (City Historical Museum)

St. Jakobsplatz 1. ○Open year-round, Tue–Sun 10am–6pm. ○Closed Shrove Tue, Dec 24 & 31. ○4€, Sun free. ℘(089) 23 32 23 70. www.stadtmuseum-online.de.

In the stables of the old arsenal, this museum illuminates all aspects of the

Beer garden by the Chinese Tower, Englischer Garten

P. Scarlandis/Munich City Tourist Office

Heiliggeistkirche
(Church of the Holy Spirit)

This Gothic hall-church at the top of Viktualienmarkt went Baroque in the 1720s and got a neo-Baroque façade in 1888. The mid-15C Virgin in the north aisle, said to be by Hammerthal, hails from the Benedictine abbey at Tegernsee.

▷ *Turn left on Im Tal to return to Marienplatz.*

ADDITIONAL SIGHTS
NORTH OF THE OLD TOWN
Englischer Garten★
(English Garden)

Just north of the historic centre, in the district of Schwabing, this vast park was designed in the late 18C and is characterised by broad, tree-bordered lawns, streams and lakes. It is particularly popular in summer for sunbathing, strolling, playing and picnicking. There are also several beer gardens, most notably the one below the **Chinese Tower** (*Chinesischer Turm*) which seats up to 7 000. Enjoy a view of Munich's old town from the **Monopteros**, a circular temple built by Klenze.

A Little Exercise

The people of Munich enjoy all kinds of sports in the English Garden: jogging, cycling, basketball playing and... surfing. Yes, surfing! Go to the bridge on Prinzregentenstraße at the southern tip of the park and see them "hang ten" on an artificial wave.

Propyläen

West side of Königsplatz.

This imposing gateway by Leo von Klenze (1784–1864) was inspired by the Acropolis in Athens and completed two years before the architect's death. The frieze represents the Greek war of liberation against the Turks.

city's cultural history. Themes covered include musical instruments, puppetry, photography and film. A separate exhibition chronicles Munich during the Third Reich. The most important artistic item is a sculpture ensemble by Erasmus Grasser called the *Moriskentänzer* (morris dancers).

▷ *Continue to Sebastiansplatz and walk past the Schrannenhalle, a former granary turned event-location, to the central food market.*

Viktualienmarkt
(Food Market)★

Fruit and vegetables, meat and fish have been sold on this market daily except Sunday since 1807. Stalls, kiosks and a beer garden *(in suitable weather)* crowd around a colourful maypole, ensuring a lively atmosphere and making for a fun lunch spot. Two of the six fountains recall local comedian Karl Valentin and his partner Liesl Karlstadt.

Glyptothek★
(Antique Sculpture Collection)

Königsplatz. ◯Open year-round, Tue–Sun 10am–5pm (Thu 8pm). ◯Closed Shrove Tue, Nov 1, Dec 24, 26 & 31. 3.50€, Sun 1€. ⚷(089) 28 61 00. www.antike-am-koenigsplatz.mwn.de.

One thousand years of Greek and Roman sculpture are gathered under the roof of this museum, buttressed by a colonnaded Neoclassical porch. The **Tenea Apollo** (*Gallery I*), with his handsome, smiling face, is among the more memorable pieces, as is the **Barberini Faun** (c. 220 BC) *(Gallery II)*, which appears sated with drink and half asleep. Also note the **bas-relief by Mnesarete** *(Gallery IV)*, which is said to have adorned the tomb of Socrates' daughter, and the statue of *Irene*, the Goddess of Peace *(Gallery V)*.

Antikensammlungen★ (Collection of Antiquities)

Opposite the Glyptothek. ◷*Open year-round, Tue–Sun 10am–5pm (Wed 8pm).* ◷*Closed Jan 1, Shrove Tue, Good Fri, Nov 1, Dec 24, 25 & 31.* ⊜*3.50€, Sun 1€. ℘(089) 59 98 88 30. www.antike-am-koenigsplatz.mwn.de.*

Greek, Etruscan and Roman art is what you will find at this famous collection. Displays on the ground floor trace the evolution of pottery in Greece, which reached its zenith during the 6C and 5C BC. Geometric decoration was succeeded by the representation of black figures on a red background (illustrated by an amphora and a goblet by the painter Exekias). The transition towards the use of red figures against a background of varnished black can be seen on another amphora, where a single subject – Hercules' banquet in the presence of Athena – is treated in the two styles *(Gallery III, showcase 6)*. **Bronzes** on the first floor and **Etruscan jewellery** in the basement *(Galleries VII and X)* testify to the enormous craftsmanship of these metalworkers.

Städtische Galerie im Lenbachhaus★ (Lenbach Collections)

Luisenstraße 33. ◷*Open year-round, Tue–Sun 10am–6pm.* ◷*Closed Shrove Tue, Dec 24.* ⊶*Closed until at least 2012.* ⊜*5–10€, depending on exhibitions.* ♿ ℘*(089) 23 33 20 00. www.lenbachhaus.de.*

Housed in a 19C villa, the Lenbach collections are devoted primarily to the works of **19C Munich painters**. The landscapes of EB Morgenstern and portraits by FA von Kaulbach and F von Defregger stand out, as do the powerful portraits created by **Franz von Len-**

bach himself *(King Ludwig I, Bismarck, Wagner)*.

But the gallery's international reputation is built, above all, on the avant-garde **Blaue Reiter** collection. Born in the tumultuous period just before World War I, the movement is represented by its founding members, Kandinsky and Marc, as well as by paintings of Jawlensky, Klee and Macke. **Contemporary art**, including works by Joseph Beuys and Anselm Kiefer, are usually shown in the Kunstbau annex.

EAST OF THE OLD TOWN Bayerisches Nationalmuseum★★ (Bavarian National Museum)

Prinzregentenstraße 3. ◷*Open year-round, Tue–Sun 10am–5pm (Thu 8pm).* ◷*Closed Shrove Tue, May 1, Pentecost, Nov 1, Dec 24, 25 & 31.* ⊜*5€. ♿ ℘(089) 211 24 01. www.bayerisches-national-museum.de.*

Maximilian II created this museum in 1885 with the aim of preserving Bavaria's artistic and cultural heritage. The rooms on the ground floor offer a survey of Bavarian arts and crafts from **Romanesque to Renaissance** *(Galleries 1–19)*, including silver and gold plate and religious statuary. The interior of an **Augsburg weaver**'s studio is in Gallery 9; the **Renaissance and Baroque** periods are represented by tapestries *(Gallery 22)*, medieval town representations and Italian bronzes *(Gallery 25)*. The first floor houses musical instruments, board games, silverware and porcelain, while the basement is dedicated to folklore exhibits.

Museum Villa Stuck

Prinzregentenstraße 60. ◷*Open year-round, Tue–Sun 11am–6pm.* ◷*Closed Shrove Tue, Dec 24.* ⊜*9€. ℘(089) 455 55 10. www.villastuck.de.*

Franz Stuck (1863–1928) was a professor at the Munich Academy of Fine Arts from 1895 and a founding member of the Munich Secession. He personally drew up the plans for this exquisite *Jugendstil* villa along with its custom-made furniture, panelling, bas-reliefs, sculptures and coffered ceilings. Today the rooms house temporary art exhibitions.

Staatliches Museum für Völkerkunde (State Ethnology Museum)

Maximilianstraße 42. ○*Open Tue–Sun 9.30am–5.30pm.* ○*Closed Shrove Tue, Good Fri, May 1, Nov 1, Dec 24–25 & 31.* ⊕*4€.* ♿*. ℘(089) 210 13 61 00. www.voelkerkundemuseum-muenchen.de.*

Amassed by the Bavarian royal family, this collection of over 200 000 objects from the Americas, India, Middle East and Oceania was first displayed in 1836 and has taken up this museum since 1868. It is considered the second largest of its kind in Germany.

SCHLOSS NYMPHENBURG★★ (NYMPHENBURG PALACE)

6km/3.7mi west of the city centre. ○*Open mid-Apr–Oct, daily 9am–6pm; Oct–mid-Apr, 10am–4pm.* ○*Closed Jan 1, Shrove Tue, Dec 24, 25 & 31.* ⊕*5€. ℘(089) 17 90 80. www.schloss-nymphenburg.de.*

A combination ticket to all palaces and exhibitions in and around Nymphenburg Palace is 10€.

The oldest part of this former summer residence of the Bavarian rulers is the 17C five-storey central pavilion, built in the style of an Italian palazzo. Prince-Elector Max Emmanuel (1679–1726) added two side wings, while his successors Karl-Albrecht (1726–45) and Max III Josef (1745–77) commissioned various outbuildings.

From 1701 onwards, the surrounding park was enlarged with formal French gardens and several park pavilions: the Pagodenburg (1719), Badenburg (1721), Magdalenenklause (1728) and Amalienburg (1739).

Schloss★★ (Palace)

The splendid **banqueting hall** *(Steinerner Saal*, or Stone Hall*)* is a symphony of white, gold and pale green and was richly adorned with coloured stuccowork and frescoes by Johann Baptist Zimmermann and his son, Franz. The panelled rooms in the north wing are decorated with tapestries and paintings. One of the most fascinating rooms is devoted to

NYMPHENBURG PALACE

View of Oktoberfest

© fotoman_65/Fotolia.com

Munich Festivals

Waitresses at Oktoberfest

Wilfried Hösl/Munich City Tourist Office

Oktoberfest – The world's biggest public party is held on the Theresienwiese from mid-September to the first Sun in October. It originated in 1810 as part of the celebrations surrounding the marriage of Crown Prince Ludwig I of Bavaria to Princess Therese of Saxe-Hildburghausen. Each year, 6 or 7 million locals and visitors flock to the huge beer halls and the thrill rides on the midway. The party kicks off on Saturday with the Brewer's Parade, followed by the Costume Procession on Sunday. But mostly Oktoberfest is about beer drinking: visitors consume around 7 million l/1 850 000 gal of *Wiesenbier*, brewed especially for the event and delivered by horse-drawn drays. It is served in a 1l/0.2gal tankards called a *Mass*. For sustenance, revellers gorge on roast chicken and beef (two oxen are cooked on a spit each day). Hotels usually fill up, so book as early as a year in advance. If you show up during Oktoberfest, hope for cancellations but expect to pay top-Euro.

Fasching – Carnival is celebrated with high spirits and much merriment and ends with the traditional market women's dance at the Viktualienmarkt.

Corpus Christi – The religious festival of *Fronleichnam* involves a procession of clergy, Roman Catholic personalities, Catholic student organizations and guild representatives through streets garlanded with young birch branches.

Other festivals – *Starkbierzeit* ("strong beer" festival) in March; *Auer Dult* (local festival) in late Apr/early May, late Jul and mid-Oct; *Tollwood Festival* (global music and theatre) from late Jun to mid-Jul and in Nov; *Opernfestspiele* (opera festival) in Jul; and the *Christkindlmarkt* (Christmas market) in December.

Cultural activities in Munich are listed in *Offizielles Monatsprogramm* (in German) and *Munich Found* (in English), both available at the tourist office.

Chinese lacquer. In the south pavilion, the apartments of Queen Caroline contain the famous **Schönheitengalerie** (Gallery of Beauties). King Ludwig I commissioned Joseph Karl Stieler (1781–1858) to immortalise the epoch's most beautiful women on canvas.

Park★

From the top of the palace steps you have a sweeping view over the formal flower gardens and the Grand Canal ending in a waterfall in the far distance.

Amalienburg★★ – This charming Rococo hunting lodge is one of **Cuvilliés**' most accomplished designs. The simplicity and sobriety of the exterior contrasts vividly with the extraordinarily elaborate interior. The **Hall of Mirrors** is a case in point: the combination of blue walls and ceiling, silver-plated stucco and wood-framed glass forms a marvellous ensemble.

Badenburg – A luxurious heated swimming pool, its ceiling decorated by mythological motifs, is the centrepiece of this 18C bathhouse.

Pagodenburg – The 18C fascination with Asia is exemplified in the design of this octagonal tea house where a drawing room, a Chinese room and a boudoir occupy the first floor.

Magdalenenklause – A "hermitage" built in the popular mock-ruin style, this pavilion is dedicated to St. Mary Magdalene.

Marstallmuseum und Porzellansammlung (Museum of Carriages and Sleighs and Porcelain Collection) – The museum is housed in the palace's former stables. Besides superb 18C and 19C harnesses, the Wittelsbachs' broughams, coaches, sledges and sedan chairs are on display. Note especially the coronation coach of Emperor Karl VII, and the state coach and personal sleigh of Ludwig II.

Upstairs, a series of rooms houses the **Bäuml Collection of Nymphenburg Porcelain**. Painted figurines by Franz Anton Bustelli, factory master from 1754 to 1763, are particularly stunning. The **reproductions in porcelain★** – miniature copies of paintings in the Alte Pinakothek – were commissioned by King Ludwig I.

Botanischer Garten München-Nypmhenburg★★ (Botanical Gardens)

Menzinger Straße 65. ○*Open Jan, Nov, Dec, daily 9am–4.30pm; Feb, Mar, Oct until 5pm; Apr, Sept until 6pm; May–Aug, until 7pm.* ○*Closed Dec 24 & 31.* ∞*4€.* ⌖ ℘*(089) 17 86 13 10. www.botmuc.de.*
Next to Schloss Nymphenburg, this is one of Europe's finest botanical gardens with over 14 000 plant species. The Scmuckhof *(opposite the main building)*, Spring Garden and Rose Garden are particularly memorable. Rhododendrons brighten the Alpine Garden; orchids and sub-tropical beauties bloom in the greenhouses.

OLYMPIAPARK QUARTER
Olympiapark

5km/3mi north of the city centre via Dachauer Straße. ⌖*Guided tours late Mar–Oct, including: Olympic Stadium tour at 11am (6€), park tour aboard miniature train at 2pm (8€). Olympic Stadium:* ○*open Apr–mid-May & mid-Sept–Oct 8.30am–6pm, mid-May–mid-Aug 8.30am–8pm, mid-Aug–mid-Sept 8.30am-7pm, Oct–Mar 9am-4.30pm, closed on events days.* ∞*2€.* ⌖ ℘*(089) 30 67 24 14.*
www.olympiapark-muenchen.de.
Munich hosted the 20th Olympic Games in 1972 and the grounds continue to be used for sporting events, festivals and concerts. They can be explored on guided tours or by renting an audio-guide from the Info Pavilion *(∞7€).*
A highlight is the lift ride up the 290m/951ft-high **Olympiaturm** *(television tower;* ○*open 9am–midnight; ∞4.50€)* where you can take in a scenic **panorama★★** with views often extending as far as the Alps.

Your ticket also lets you take a spin around the small and private **Rock 'n' Roll Museum** at the tower level. It features guitars, letters, fan mail and photographs of such giants as Jimi Hendrix and Jim Morrison.

SeaLife München

⏱Open Apr–Sept, daily 10am–7pm, Oct 6pm, Nov–Mar 5pm. ⏱Closed Dec 24. ⬤15.50€ (child 9.95€). ✆(089) 45 00 00. www.sealifeeurope.com.

This child-oriented and partly interactive aquarium is home to some 10 000 marine and freshwater creatures. The order of the tanks simulates the habitats encountered if following the flow of the Isar into the Danube, which itself flows into the Black Sea before spilling into the Mediterranean.

BMW-Museum

Petuelring 130. Northeast corner of Olympiapark. ⏱Open year-round, Tue–Sun 10am–6pm. ⏱Closed Jan 1, Dec 24, 25 & 31. ⬤12€ (child 6€). ♿✆(089) 38 22 56 57. www.bmw-museum.de.

The famous car maker's flagship museum is housed in a giant silver bowl docked to a new pavilion. Inside, floating ramps lead visitors on a dynamic multimedia journey past shiny cars and motorcycles, from vintage wheels to concept cars and the latest production models.

The museum sits next to the BMW headquarters, plant and stunningly designed **BMW Welt** car pick-up centre, which also has free exhibits that are open to the public.

A tour of the **BMW plant** is 8€ and only available by pre-registering at ✆ +49 (0)1802-11 88 22.

EXCURSIONS

Dachau Concentration Camp Memorial Site★

▶ 19km/11.8mi northwest. Alte Römerstraße 75, Dachau. Follow signposts to Dachau Ost and "KZ-Gedenkstätte".

⏱Open year-round, Tue–Sun 9am–5pm. Audioguide recommended (⬤3€). ♿✆(08131) 66 99 70. www.kz-gedenkstaette-dachau.de.

Allow at least two hours to visit Nazi Germany's first concentration camp, built in March 1933 near the pleasant town of Dachau on the orders of Heinrich Himmler. Originally designed for the detention of German political opponents of the Nazi regime, the camp was soon flooded by tens of thousands of deportees, mostly Jews of diverse nationalities. More than 35 000 people died there, plus at least 6 000 Russian prisoners-of-war killed on the nearby SS firing range. Whether on a guided tour or independent, visitors are sobered by the **ruins and commemorative monuments**. Two prisoner barracks have been faithfully reconstructed and the foundations of 32 others are still visible. They offer a glimpse of a camp which was designed for 5 000 prisoners-of-war but was crammed with 30 000 people by 1944. At the rear camp entrance one can still read the inscription "Arbeit macht frei" (Freedom Through Work). A Jewish memorial, a Protestant commemorative sanctuary and a Catholic chapel have been built within the precincts of the old camp. Just beyond its borders are the crematorium and a gas chamber, although the latter was apparently never used.

A **museum** presents (in English and German) a sobering and comprehensive look at life in the camp. Exhibits deal with the organisation of the KZ system and use photographs and documents to illustrate the Dachau camp's history, daily life, medical experiments, mass executions, and its liberation.

Allianz Arena Stadion★

▶ 10km/6.5mi north near intersection of A9 and A99.

🚶Guided tours (1hr 15min, minimum 11 people) daily except on game days 10.15am–5.30pm (Nov–Mar 4.30pm), English tour at 1pm. ⬤9€ (children under 12, 5€). ✆(01805) 155 51 01. www.allianz-arena.de.

Built for the FIFA World Cup 2006, this gigantic 66 000-seat stadium is an architectural stunner designed by Herzog & de Meuron. Each of the 2 760 transparent inflatable panels can be lit up in a particular colour: white for international games, blue for local club 1860 München, red for Bayern Munich.

🚗 DRIVING TOUR

AROUND AMMERSEE
Round trip of 116km/72mi – Allow half a day.

Ammersee★
This glacial lake sits framed by wooded hills at an elevation of 533m/1749ft and is popular for swimming, sailing and boating.

▷ *Follow the western lakeshore.*

Dießen
Built in 1730, Diessen's Rococo **Marienmünster**★ (St. Mary's Minster) was a collaboration between architect **Johann Michael Fischer**, the Asam brothers and Cuvilliés.

▷ *The road climbs from Fischen to Andechs, offering fine lake views.*

Kloster Andechs★ (Andechs Abbey)
Guided church tour (30min), mid-Apr–Oct, Mon–Sat noon, Sun 12.15pm. ℘(08152) 37 60. www.andechs.de.
This 10C abbey overlooks the Ammersee. Its Gothic **church**★★ got a Rococo remodel in 1750 by Johann Baptist Zimmermann. Bavarian composer Carl Orff (of *Carmina Burana* fame) is buried in the Chapel of Suffering. Still an active abbey, the monks brew their own beer, which can be sampled in the beer garden and beer hall.

▷ *Return to Munich via Herrsching and Seefeld or detour to Bernried.*

Buchheim Museum★
45km/28mi southwest. Am Hirschgarten 1, Bernried. ⏱Open Tue–Sun 10am–6pm (Nov–Mar 5pm). ⏱Closed Dec 24 & 31. ⊙8.50€. ♿. ℘(08158) 99 70 20. www.buchheimmuseum.de.
This museum on the shores of Lake Starnberg presents the private art collection of *Das Boot* author Lothar-

Günther Buchheim. Its main strength is in German Expressionism, with members of *Die Brücke*, such as Kirchner, Heckel, Pechstein and Schmidt-Rottluff being particularly well represented.

ADDRESSES

🛏STAY

🛏 **Motel One** – *Orleansstraße 87; Landsberger Straße 79; Michael-Haslbeck-Straße 26a; Herzog-Wilhelm-Straße; 28, Tegernseer Landstraße 161. www.motel-one.com/de/hotels/hotels-muenchen.* Modern chain hotel that provides good value for money.

🛏 **Creatif Hotel Elephant** – *Lämmerstraße 6. ℘089 55 57 85. www.creatif-hotel-elephant.com. 45 rooms. (Lowest rates Jul–Aug).* Close to the Hauptbahnhof, this colourful, bright and buzzy budget design hotel was renovated in 2006 and features hypoallergenic rooms and English TV channels.

🛏🛏 **Hotel Müller** – *Fliegenstraße 4. ℘(089) 232 38 60. www.hotel-mueller-muenchen.de. Closed Dec 23–Jan 6. 44 rooms.* In a quiet spot in the happening Glockenbachviertel, steps from the historic centre, this hotel includes such perks as free Wi-Fi and a generous breakfast buffet in its room rates.

🛏🛏 **Mariandl** – *Goethestraße 51. ℘089 534 108. www.mariandl.com. 30 rooms. Restaurant🛏🛏.* Close to the station, but away from the bustle, this grand late-19C castle-like building houses a charming hotel with Belle Époque and Art Nouveau furniture and décor. It has a restaurant and a popular *Konzertcafé* which regularly hosts live classical musicians and which adds to the likeable atmosphere.

🛏🛏 **Am Viktualienmarkt** – *Utzschneiderstraße 14. ℘089 231 10 90. www.hotel-am-viktualienmarkt.com. Closed Dec 20–Jan 7. 30 rooms.* Ideally located in the city centre, this welcoming family-run hotel offers bright, modern, minimalistic designer-style rooms in beiges, creams and browns. Some of the rooms are small but all offer good value for money.

⊜⊜ **Hotel Uhland** – *Uhlandstraße 1* *(089) 54 33 50. www.hotel-uhland.de. 25 rooms.* Run by a multi-generational family, this charming hotel is in a century-old neo-Renaissance mansion on a quiet side street near the Oktoberfest grounds. It has rooms that suit all tastes; some with modern water beds, some with rustic furniture. Service is bend-over-backwards friendly.

⊜⊜ **Hotel Drei Löwen** – *Schillerstraße 8. (089) 55 10 40. www.hotel3loewen.de. 97 rooms. Restaurant⊜⊜.* This welcoming hotel near the main train station has bright, colourful and modern cosy rooms, whimsically decorated two-room suites and a wood-panelled lobby.

⊜⊜⊜ **Hotel Schlicker** – *Tal 8. (089) 242 88 70. www.hotel-schlicker.de. Closed Dec 23–Jan 7. 69 rooms.* In the heart of the old quarter, this hotel in a 16C building offers personalised service and neat, well-kept and spotlessly clean rooms. Some have views of the new town hall with its world-famous carillon, but those in back are quieter.

⊜⊜⊜ **Hotel Platzl** – *Sparkassen-straße 10. (089) 23 70 30. www.platzl.de. 167 rooms. Restaurants⊜⊜–⊜⊜⊜.* Tradition marries modern comforts in this Bavarian-style hotel within staggering distance of the famous Hofbräuhaus and Munich's main historic sights. Dining options include the elegantly vaulted Pfistermühle restaurant with its leafy terrace and the modern beer-hall-style Wirtshaus Ayinger.

⊜⊜⊜⊜ **Hotel Bayerischer Hof** – *Promenadenplatz 2. (089) 212 00.www. bayerischerhof.de. 373 rooms. 25.50€. Restaurant ⊜⊜⊜.* Hospitality doesn't get more luxurious than at this traditional grand hotel which has kept an illustrious guest list since 1841. The rooftop pool and spa offers the ultimate in relaxation with a view of the Frauenkirche.

⍓/EAT

REGIONAL SPECIALITIES

The most famous local specialities include the veal sausages known as *Weißwurst*, roast knuckle of pork *(Schweinshaxe)* and *Leberkäs*, a meat loaf. At beer festivals, a favourite offering is *Steckerlfisch*, which are small fish grilled on a skewer. *Pretzels* and white radishes *(Radi)* are often served with beer. And speaking of beer: Munich is Germany's beer capital. Five and a half million hectolitres (110 000 000 gal) of beer are brewed every year, most of it consumed in the beer halls and gardens *(Biergarten)* within Munich.

⊜ **XXXLUTZ** – *Theresienhöhe 5. 089 51 050. www.xxxlutz.de.* Go up to the second floor of this modern furniture shop and you'll find an airy restaurant with bargain prices. You'll probably be the only tourist there!

⊜ **Pasta e Basta** – *Fraunhoferstraße 19. 089 1393 9446. www.pastaebastaweb. de.* Good-value budget Italian food.

⊜ **Spektakel** – *Pfeuferstraße 32, Sendling. 089 76 75 83 59. www. spektakel-muenchen.de.* Typical Bavarian pub-restaurant popular with the locals.

⊜ **VaPiano** – *Salvatorpassage, Fünf Höfe, Theatinerstraße 15. 089 20 60 658. www.vapiano.de. No reservations.* Enjoy top-quality all-fresh fast food, such as made-to-order fire-roasted pizzas, fresh homemade pasta and gourmet salads in smart-casual surroundings. Swipe the card they give you when you take your dish and pay at the end. Other city addresses: *Franzstraße 5; Richard-Strauss-straße 80, Hackerbruecke 4, Viktualienmarkt 15.*

⊜ **Café Voilà** – *Wörthstraße 5. 089 48 91 654. www.cafe-voilà.de.* This popular locals' place is perfect for brunch, or a beer or two.

⊜ **Ratzkeller** – *Marienplatz 8. 089 21 99 89 30.* This popular, stylish, huge labyrinthine tavern lies beneath the Gothic arches of the town hall and is a real city institution. Pig out on a dish of crispy pork hock, or on its trademark tasty sausages, tucked away in a cosy wooden cubicle.

Dürnbräu – *Dürnbräugasse 2. (089) 22 21 95.* Oozing traditional Bavarian flair from every nook and cranny, this inn is a great spot for hearty meals and cool brews. Enjoy the terrace or courtyard garden in fine weather.

Karawanserei – *Pettenkoferstraße 1. (089) 54 54 19 54. www.karawanserei-muenchen.de. Reservation required.* No need to ride a camel through the desert to enjoy a fine meal at this exotically decorated Persian restaurant in a little palace in the city centre. The menu includes plenty of vegetarian options.

Spatenhaus an der Oper – *Residenzstraße 12. 089 290 70 60. www.kuffler.de.* This beautifully designed traditional-modern-rustic restaurant is famous for its game dishes. The upstairs room is more formal. Lovely bedrooms.

Käfer Schänke – *Prinzregentenstraße 73. (089) 416 82 47. www.feinkost-kaefer.de. Closed Sun and public holidays.* This fine-food emporium blends a delicatessen shop, a catering service and a pleasant warren of a restaurant with stylish but relaxed décor. The globally-inspired menu is likely to contain a favourite for everyone.

Lenbach – *Ottostraße 6 (089) 549 13 00. www.lenbach.de. Closed Sun. Reservation necessary.* Conceived by star designer Sir Terence Conran, this trendy restaurant's décor was inspired by the Seven Deadly Sins but the creative, contemporary food is considerably more down-to-earth.

Bogenhauser Hof – *Ismaninger Straße 85. (089) 98 55 86. www. bogenhauser-hof.de. Closed Dec 24–Jan 8, Sun and public holidays.* This former 19C hunting lodge is now a modern gourmet restaurant with inspired seasonal cuisine. The idyllic summer garden is ideal for lounging over leisurely dinners on balmy summer nights.

🍴 TAKING A BREAK

Café Arzmiller – *Theatinerstraße 22. (089) 29 42 73.* A good place to relax and forget the stress of the tourist track. Coffee, cakes and daily specials are served in the lovely, peaceful Theatinerhof. The house speciality, *Strudel*, is not to be missed.

Café Luitpold Palmengarten – *Brienner Straße 11. (089) 242 87 50. www.cafe-luitpold.de. Closed public holidays.* This café offers a choice of more than 300 different cakes and tarts. The house speciality is *Luitpoldkuchen*, which can be enjoyed beneath a glass dome in the palm-filled inner courtyard or on the terrace facing Maximilianplatz.

Confiserie Rottenhöfer – *Residenzstraße 25/26. (089) 22 29 15. www.rottenhoefer.de. Closed Sun and public holidays.* Founded in 1825, this chocolate shop was once official purveyor to the Bavarian court. It sells over 160 kinds of the sweet stuff and also operates a café.

Viktualienmarkt – *Viktualienmarkt. (089) 23 39 65 00. www.viktualien markt.de. Closed Sun.* This traditional market dates back to 1807 and offers a wide variety of delectable victuals, including handmade sausages, artisanal cheeses, smoked fish, fine olive oils and hearty loaves of bread.

🎭 NIGHTLIFE

USEFUL TIPS

Beer gardens are an integral part of Bavarian life, especially in Munich. Many of these chestnut tree-shaded gardens and terraces open at the slightest ray of spring sunshine. Although prices can be high and the service limited, people enjoy the unique atmosphere.

Munich's best-known café and bar scene is in **Schwabing**. Around the university is a plethora of student bars, while south of the Münchner Freiheit U-Bahn station, Leopoldstraße is lined by posh establishments where people go to "see and be seen". Other parts of town with good nightlife are Haidhausen (around

Pariser Platz and Weißenburger Platz) and the Gärtnerplatzviertel quarter. For online information: www.munig.com, www.nightlife-munich.de and www.munichx.de.

SIGHTSEEING

WALKING TOURS

The tourist office organises tours with English-speaking guides for groups, on request (℘(089) 233 32 34). **Stattreisen** (℘(089) 54 40 42 30; www.stattreisen-muenchen.de) also offers dozens of themed walking tours (beer, architecture, on foot, tram or bike) in German. Regular guided tours in English are offered by **New Munich Tours** (www.newmunich.com), **Radius Bike Tours** (⌚see p411) and from **Munich Walk Tours** (℘(089) 24 23 17 67; www.munichwalktours.de).

BUS TOURS

SIGHTseeing Gray Line

(Schützenstraße 9 ℘(089) 54 90 75 60, www.stadtrundfahrten-muenchen.de) – Hop-on, Hop-off Express Circle: Buses depart every 20 minutes and follow a one-hour loop taking in all major sights. You are free to get on and off as often as you wish. Tickets cost 13€ (child 7.50€). An extended route (Grand Circle) taking in Nymphenburg Palace and the Olympic Park is 19€. Buses depart from Bahnhofplatz (in front of Karstadt department store). Tickets available aboard.

FINDING YOUR WAY

The liveliest part of Munich is in the pedestrianised old town around Marienplatz and Karlsplatz (or "Stachus") via shop-lined Neuhauser Straße and Kaufingerstraße. Elegant boutiques cluster in Maffeistraße, Pacellistraße, Maximilianstraße and Brienner Straße; antique dealers in Ottostraße near Maximilianplatz; art galleries under the arcades of Hofgartenstraße. Schwabing, around Leopoldstraße, enjoyed its fame as the city's artistic and intellectual hub at the turn of the 20C and remains one of Germany's buzziest after-hours destinations.

🛒 SHOPPING

USEFUL TIPS

Many consider Munich Germany's best city for shopping. The old town has numerous arcades and boutiques catering to all budgets. *Beck am Rathauseck* and other department stores line Neuhauser Straße and Kaufingerstraße between Marienplatz and Karlsplatz (Stachus). Another good shopping district is Schwabing (along Leopoldstraße and smaller side streets such as Türkenstraße), which is home to small and funky boutiques. International labels are found in Residenzstraße, Brienner Straße and Maximilianstraße. The *Fünf Höfe* shopping centre is a visual stunner in stylish Theatinerstraße and is also filled with high-end boutiques and shops. Independent designers cluster in the charming Gärtnerplatzviertel along such streets as Reichenbachstraße and Hans-Sachs-Straße.

Art galleries – Most of Munich's key galleries are in Maximilianstraße and the nearby streets, in Residenzstraße and on Odeonsplatz. In the old artists' district of Schwabing, the most interesting drags are Türkenstraße, Schellingstraße and Franz-Joseph-Straße.

Antiques – Munich antiques range from the elegant, exclusive dealers to bargain-basement bric-à-brac shops. Schwabing boasts a wealth of antique shops as does the city centre around Maximilianplatz, Lenbachplatz and Promenadenplatz.

Antique shop in Munich

© Manfred J. Bail /Westend 61/Photoshot

Augsburg★★

Bavaria's third-largest city (after Munich and Nuremberg) and a stop on the Romantic Road, Augsburg has long been associated with luminaries, including 16C artist Hans Holbein the Younger, Mozart's father Leopold (1719–1787) and the dramatist Bertolt Brecht (1898–1956). Today, the Renaissance city continues to enchant visitors with its artistic beauty and lively cultural scene.

A BIT OF HISTORY

Roman origins – Founded in 15 BC by Drusus and Tiberius, stepsons of Emperor Augustus, Augsburg is, along with Trier and Cologne, one of Germany's oldest cities.

It became a trading centre en route to Italy and, at the fall of the Roman Empire, an episcopal see. By the late 13C it was a Free Imperial City and the seat of the Diet.

The Fuggers – Augsburg reached its historical peak at the end of the 15C, when it became a European financial centre thanks to two wealthy merchant families, the Fuggers and the Welsers. History has preserved the name of Jakob Fugger the Rich (1459–1529), renowned as the Empire's banker and the financier of the Habsburgs. He was powerful enough to rebuke Charles V, reminding him: "It is well known that, without my help, Your Majesty would no longer wear the crown of the Holy Roman Empire" The unpaid debt of the Habsburgs to their Augsburg bankers has been estimated at 4 million ducats.

SIGHTS
Rathausplatz
(Town Hall Square)
Augsburg's hulking **town hall** ranks among the most important secular Renaissance buildings north of the Alps. Built by Elias Holl between 1615 and 1620, its two onion-domed towers frame a pediment adorned with the traditional pinecone. Inside, the Golden

▶ **Population:** 263 300
🛈 **Info:** Rathausplatz. 𝒫(0821) 50 20 70. www.augsburg-tourismus.de.
◐ **Location:** Augsburg is one hour west of Munich by the A8 and 30 minutes by train. The river Lech, a tributary of the Danube, crosses the town and feeds into a canal in the lower town.
🅿 **Parking:** Public car parks and garages are located throughout the city, including near the main train station and the Rathaus. Electronic signs indicate car park locations and space availability.
👁 **Don't Miss:** Maximilianstraße and the cathedral.
🕐 **Timing:** Allow about one day to see Augsburg.

Hall *(Goldener Saal;* 🕐*open year-round, daily 10am–6pm;* ✎*2€),* with its restored coffered ceiling, can be visited. The **Perlachturm** was originally a Romanesque watchtower and can be climbed in summer. A yellow flag is flown when views extend all the way to the distant Alps.

Rathausplatz

T. Krieger/MICHELIN

AUGSBURG

0 ____ 300 m

St. Anna-Kirche

Fuggerstraße 8. ℘(0821) 34 37 10.
When Luther came to Augsburg in 1518 to defend his reformed thesis, he stayed at what was then a Carmelite monastery. The rooms, accessed via a flight of wooden stairs (Lutherstiege) now house a small exhibition about the man and his times. The **Fugger Chapel**★ (Fuggerkapelle), where Jakob Fugger and his brothers are buried, is a prime example of Renaissance architecture. Note the three works by Lucas Cranach the Elder in the east chancel.

Fuggerei★

Enter via Jakoberstraße. ⊙Open Apr–Sept, daily 8am–8pm; Oct–Mar, daily 9am–6pm. ⊛4€. ⅃℘(0821) 31 98 81 14. www.fugger.de.
Known as the "town within the town", the Fuggerei was founded in 1516 by Jakob Fugger the Rich and is the world's oldest social housing compound. To this day it provides simple but permanent housing for impoverished local Catholics in exchange for a symbolic annual rent of 0.88€ and a daily prayer for the souls of the founders.

435

Dom St. Maria (St. Mary's Cathedral)

Hoher Weg. ℘*(0821) 316 63 53.*
Augsburg's cathedral has origins in the
10C but didn't get its Gothic shape until
the 14C. Noteworthy features include the
Jungfrauenportal★★ (Virgin's Door),
as well as 11C Romanesque bronze door
Türflügel★ (panels). Four of the nave
altars are adorned with **paintings**★ by
Holbein the Elder. Outside the cathedral
look for remains of the Roman city.

Maximilianstraße★

Elegant Maximilianstraße is flanked
by the mansions of wealthy Renaissance-era Augsburgers (including the
Fuggers at no 36) and punctuated by
two monumental 16C fountains depicting Mercury and Hercules. The latter is
outside the **Schaezlerpalais** at no 46,
which is Augsburg's most important
Rococo building and home to several
art collections as well as a grand **Festsaal**★★ (ballroom) canopied by a lush
ceiling fresco and stuccowork.

Städtische Kunstsammlungen★ (Municipal Art Collection)

Maximilianstrasse 46. ⏱*Open Tue
10am–8pm, Wed–Sun 10am–5pm.*
⏱*Closed Good Fri, Dec 24–25 & 31.*
9€. ℘ *(0821) 324 41 02. www.kunst-
sammlungen-museen.augsburg.de.*
The beautifully restored Schaezlerpalais
harbours several art collections, most
importantly the **German Baroque Gallery** (Deutsche Barockgalerie), which
presents painters who have worked and
lived in Augsburg, such as Josef Heintz,
Johann König and Matthäus Günther.
The same building also houses the
Collection Haberstadt, which was
amassed over decades by a local art
dealer and his wife. The collection
includes paintings by Paulo Veronese,
Giovanni Battista Tiepolo, Antonius van
Dyck, Jacob Ruisdael und Lucas Cranach
the Elder.
Many more famous canvases grace
the walls of the **State Gallery of Old**

Masters in the nearby Church of St.
Catherine (Katharinenkirche). Highlights
include a portrait of Jakob Fugger the
Rich by Albrecht Dürer and Hans Holbein's world-famous series of paintings
of Roman basilicas.

Basilika St. Ulrich und Afra★

Ulrichsplatz 19. ℘*(0821) 34 55 60.*
This former Benedictine abbey was built
in 1474 in late-Gothic style with Renaissance and Baroque additions. It boasts
the shrines of the town's patron saints
as well as three lavishly gilded Baroque
altars and a bronze Crucifixion (1607).
St. Simpert's chapel features a lovely
gallery topped by terracotta **Statues
of the Saints**★.
The Catholic basilica hugs the much
smaller Protestant **Ulrichkirche** in
reflection of the religious compromise
achieved at the Peace of Augsburg.

ADDRESSES

🏠STAY

⊖ **Unterbaarer Hof** –
Ulmer Straße 218. ℘*(0821) 43 13 00.
www.unterbaarer-hof.de. 6 rooms.
Restaurant*⊗. This good-value hotel has
modern if fairly basic rooms and a huge
self-catering apartment. The restaurant
specialises in specialities from Swabia
and Bavaria served in a cosy ambience
with plenty of wood and curtained
windows.

⊖⊖ **Ost am Kö** – *Fuggerstraße 4.* ℘*089
50 20 40. www.ostamkoe.de. 49 rooms.*
⊿. Set in the centre of Augsburg,
300m/330yd from the station, the
bedrooms of this smart traditional-
modern hotel are well equipped and
most look onto a tranquil courtyard.
Facilities include a sauna.

⊖⊖ **Dom Hotel** – *Frauentorstraße 8.*
℘*0821 34 39 30. www.domhotel-
augsburg.de. Closed mid-Dec–early
Jan. 57 rooms.* Elegant rooms and
apartments in a historic townhouse
near the cathedral. In summer,
breakfast is served under the
chestnut trees.

♈/EAT

⊖☺ **Zur alten Feuerwache** – *Zeugplatz 4. ℘(0821) 51 16 85.* Dine beneath the vaulted ceilings of the 16C former armoury. A large *Biergarten* offers a relaxing respite at the front.

⊖☺ **Die Ecke** – *Elias-Holl-Platz 2. ℘(0821) 51 06 00. www.restaurant-die-ecke.de.* This historic restaurant once hosted such luminaries as Mozart and Bertolt Brecht and ingeniously melds rustic and modern styles in an elegant setting. Great for special occasions.

⊖☺☺ **Haupt im Prinz Karl Palais** – *Schertlinstraße 23. ℘0821 589 84 75. www.restaurant-haupt.de. Closed Sun–Mon.* Housed in a former barracks, with vaulted ceilings, and a garden, this modern restaurant serves delicious local and international dishes.

⊖☺☺☺ **August** – *Frauentorstraße 27 ℘0821 352 79. Dinner only. Closed Sun–Tue, 1st week Jan, Easter Week and late Aug–mid Sept.* Michelin two-star chef Christian Grünwald lives up to his reputation with carefully selected dishes that reflect his very individual style of creative cuisine. In summer dine out on the lovely roof terrace.

Ottobeuren★★

The Benedictine abbey of Ottobeuren, founded in 764 under the patronage of Charlemagne, was transformed into the Baroque style in the 18C. The abbey church is undoubtedly one of the most stunning churches in Germany.

SIGHTS
Abbey Church★★

🕐*Open year-round, daily 9am–sunset, 8.30pm at the latest. ♿ ℘(08332) 79 80. www.abtei-ottobeuren.de.*
In 1748, **Johann Michael Fischer**, the great architect of southern Germany, put the finishing touches on this jewel

▸ **Population:** 8 000

▪ **Info:** Marktplatz 14. ℘(08332) 92 19 50. www.ottobeuren.de.

◯ **Location:** Ottobeuren is a charming village surrounded by forests and pastureland. The A96 autobahn (Memmingen–Munich) is 11km/6.8mi north.

⊛ **Don't Miss:** The abbey church.

🕐 **Timing:** Allow at least two hours to view the church and other buildings.

Abbey church

T. Krieger/MICHELIN

Baroque decoration inside the abbey church

F. Zaninotto/MICHELIN

of German Baroque, which was to be his masterpiece. He was assisted by equally gifted Rococo masters when it came to the church's interior ornamentation: Johann Jakob Zeiller and Franz Anton Zeiller for the frescoes, Johann Michael Feichtmayr for the stuccowork, and Johann Joseph Christian for the figurative sculptures.

The church's astonishing dimensions are only evident once inside. The impression of space is enhanced by the unusual amount of light, a result of the church's north–south orientation. The architecture of the entire church is focused on the flattened central dome, amid a proliferation of paintings, stuccowork and sculptures with wonderfully depicted cherubs, draperies and lighting.

The four altars, of St. Michael – patron saint of the Ottobeuren area and the Empire – of the Holy Guardian Angels, of St. Joseph and of St. John the Baptist, are remarkable features, as are the outstanding **pulpit** and, opposite, the representation of the **Baptism of Christ** in red and marble stucco.

On the altar of the Holy Sacrament stands a much venerated **crucifix** dating from 1220, the Ottobeurer Gnadenheiland (Merciful Redeemer). The **high altar**, with paintings of the Holy Trinity by Zeiller and larger-than-life figures of the Apostles and saints is outstanding. The walnut **choir stalls**★★ (1764) are masterpieces of the woodcarver's art. The high backs to the stalls are decorated with gilded lime-wood reliefs by Joseph Christian.

Karl Joseph Riepp, a pupil of the famous organ builder Silbermann, built the **chancel organs** ★★ in 1766.

Abbey Buildings

⊙*Open Palm Sun–Oct, daily 10am–noon, 2pm–5pm; limited hours rest of the year.* ⊜*4€.* ☎*(08332) 79 80.*

The abbey's buildings were constructed between 1711 and 1725. Inside the **museum**★ admire the superb decoration which echoes the splendour of the church.

⊙Note the magnificent **library**, the theatre and the **Kaisersaal** (Emperor's Hall), with a frescoed ceiling depicting the coronation of Charlemagne. The museum also houses interesting medieval artworks and 15C–17C paintings.

German Alpine Road★★★
Deutsche Alpenstraße

Splendid mountain scenery combined with such landmarks as the Wieskirche and the castles of Ludwig II of Bavaria make the Alpenstraße an unforgettable journey. When passing through the region's villages, where life goes on much as it has for centuries, stop to sample local culinary and cultural traditions, or head off for a walk in the woods or across alpine meadows.

🚗 DRIVING TOURS

1 THE ALLGÄU★
From Lindau to Füssen 112km/69.6mi – Allow half a day.

The Allgäu is home of the Swabians, an Allemanic tribe that settled in the area around the 2C AD. It is a fairytale landscape where lazy cows graze on steep mountain pastures and farmers still produce wonderful artesanal cheeses.

Lindau★★ – ℓ*See LINDAU.*

▶ *Leave Lindau on the A96 (towards Memmingen), then join the B308.*

Paradies
Engineers gave this name to a viewpoint between Oberreute and Oberstaufen, along a sweeping curve, from which the distant Swiss Appenzell Alps can be seen.

Oberstaufen
This charming ski resort sits at the foot of the Hochgrat massif (1 832m/6 010ft). From the mountain station at 1 708m/5 600ft, you'll have a 360-degree **view**★★ across the Allgäu, Lake Constance and into Switzerland.

▶ *The road now climbs the alpine valley of the Iller, which runs to the foot of Grünten.*

Info: Deutsche Alpenstraße, Radolfzeller Straße 15, 81243 Munich. ℓ(089) 829 21 80. www.deutsche-alpenstrasse.de.

▶ **Location:** Running from Lindau on Lake Constance (Bodensee) to Berchtegaden near the Austrian border, this 450km/279.6mi scenic route traverses spectacular high mountain country accented by pristine Alpine lakes. It meanders along the foothills of the Allgäu and the Bavarian Alps, parallelling the southern German border and linking world-famous ski resorts, bucolic villages, onion-domed churches, royal castles and the lofty peaks of the Zugspitze (2 964m/9 724.4ft) and the Watzmann (2 712m/8 897.6ft).

Don't Miss: Beautiful panoramas appear around every corner, but the best lie atop the Wendelstein and along the final part of tour 4 below.

Timing: Allow at least three days to explore this alpine region.

Kids: Hohenschwangau and Neuschwanstein castles; cable-car rides up the Wendelstein.

Bad Hindelang★
Together with its immediate neighbour, Bad Oberdorf, this romantic flower-decked village is a popular spa and holiday resort perfectly suited for mountain walks in summer and skiing in winter. Above Bad Hindelang, climbing the **Jochstraße**★ delivers idyllic views over the jagged summits of the Allgäu Alps. From the **Kanzel**★ viewpoint, near the summit, take in the splendid panorama

Bad Hindelang seen from the Jochstraße

T. Krieger/MICHELIN

embracing the Ostrach Valley and surrounding mountains.

On it descent, the road crosses the Wertach valley, skirts the Grüntensee and passes near the sprawling Pfronten ski resort before arriving at Füssen.

Füssen★
Kaiser-Maximilian-Platz 1.
℘ (08362) 938 50.
www.stadt-fuessen.de.

Tucked into the *Königswinkel* ("royal corner") in the Allgäu mountains, Füssen is surrounded by the lakes of Forggensee, Hopfensee and Weißensee.
This historic town is like the dot of the exclamation mark at the end of the Romantic Road (Romantische Straße) and enjoys a spectacular setting in the Alpine foothills. Most visitors use it as a base from which to visit Ludwig II's fairytale palace of Neuschwanstein and his ancestral home of Hohenschwangau,

but the town is actually worth a stop in its own right. Attractions include an ancient abbey, art museums and the surrounding lakes.

Museum der Stadt Füssen im Kloster St. Mang★ (Local History Museum at Abbey of St. Mang)

🕘*Open Apr–Oct, Tue–Sun 11am–5pm, Nov–Mar, Tue–Sun 1pm–3pm.* 🎫*2.50€.* 📞*(08362) 90 31 46.*

This ancient Benedictine **abbey** looks back on more than 1 000 years of history. It honours the work of St. Magnus, an 8C missionary who founded a monk's cell here and is buried in the church's crypt. In the 18C, the medieval complex got a complete Baroque makeover reflecting the skill and vision of Johann Jakob Herkomer who had learnt his craft in Venice. The monastery was secularised in 1802.

The southern wing, with *trompe l'œil* paintings in the cloister, now houses a modern **museum** containing exhibits on the history of the abbey, Füssen's violin-making tradition and milestones from the town's past. Perhaps even more impressive are the richly decorated rooms themselves, most notably the festive **Kaisersaal**★★ (Imperial Hall), a large banquet hall embellished with fanciful frescoes and stucco ornamentation. In

summer it hosts classical concerts. Also of note is the **Annakapelle**★ (St. Anna Chapel) from 850 with its macabre Dance of Death fresco from 1602, which vividly depicts the ravages of the Black Plague.

Stadtpfarrkirche (Parish Church)

🕘*Open year-round, daily 8.30am–6pm.* Herkomer's Baroque design displays astonishing harmony and rich décor that encompasses an elaborate fresco cycle with scenes from the life of St. Magnus. An artistic and spiritual highlight is the high altar with statues by Anton Sturm. Various reliquaries of the saint, including his staff, are dotted around the church.

Hohes Schloss (High Palace)

The ramp up to the castle entrance starts behind the parish church.
🕘*Open Apr–Oct, Tue–Sun 11am–5pm; Nov–Mar, Fri–Sun 1pm–4pm.* 🕘*Closed Dec 24 & 31.* 🎫*2.50€.* 📞*(08362) 90 31 64.*

Looming above the town, the fortified late-Gothic palace became the summer residence of the Prince-Bishops of Augsburg in the late 15C. Today, the former apartments house two collections. The **Staatsgalerie** (Bavarian State Gallery) is on Swabian art from the 15C and 16C. The most impressive room is the octagonal **Rittersaal**★ (Knights'

Hall), which is lidded by a sumptuous coffered ceiling.

On the lower floor, the **Städtische Gemäldegalerie** (Municipal Picture Gallery) presents paintings by Spitzweg, Lier, Defregger and other Munich School members working around 1900.

This is supplemented by a rotating selection of graphics by Franz Graf von Pocci (1807–1876). For a dazzling **panorama**★ climb up the clock-tower which is accessible via the gallery. Surrounding the castle is a public park called the Baumgarten.

Lechfall (Lech Gorge)
500m/547yd south.
The river Lech leaves the Alps in Füssen and cascades down a small, rocky gorge spanned by a footbridge.

Forggensee (Lake Forggen)
Boats depart from Füssen landing docks, Jun–mid-Oct, daily 10am–5.30pm. Commentary. ⊗8€ (50min tour), ⊗11€ (2hr tour). Forggensee Schiffahrt ℘(08362) 92 13 63. www.schiffahrt.fuessen.de.
The Forggensee is a 12km/7.4mi long and up to 3km/1.8mi wide reservoir created in 1954 to regulate the waterflow of the Lech River. In summer it is swarmed by watersports enthusiasts and bicyclists enjoying the paved trails around its perimeter.

Cruise boats ply its waters, allowing breathtaking views of the mountains, Neuschwanstein Castle and historic Füssen. In winter, the lake is drained and you can walk on the dry bottom to look for remnants of Stone Age and Roman settlements.

2 THE AMMERGAU★
From Füssen to Garmisch-Partenkirchen. 95km/59mi – Allow one day.

The road bypasses the Ammergau Alps to the north, then crosses countryside seamed and broken by the moraines deposited by the ancient Lech glacier. This rolling land is punctuated by villages with onion-domed churches.

Hohenschwangau and Neuschwanstein★★★
See NEUSCHWANSTEIN.

Steingaden★
Long before reaching the village of Steingaden, the distinctive onion-domed silhouette of its 12C Premonstratensian abbey church rises from the misty horizon. Numerous alterations have all but obscured its Romanesque origins. The Gothic entrance bears a painted genealogy of the Welf family who founded the abbey in 1147. But first and foremost it is luxuriant Baroque flourishes that now give the interior its dynamic and uplifting character. Ten gleaming pillars guide

Interior of Wieskirche, Steingaden

the eye towards the pastel-coloured ceiling fresco depicting the ascension of Mary and enhanced with breathtaking stuccowork. Only the cloister, where the architect Dominikus Zimmermann is buried, retains its comparatively austere 13C Romanesque columns.

Wieskirche★★

Wies 12, 86989 Steingaden. ○*Open May–Oct, daily 8am–7pm; Nov–Apr to 5pm.* ○*Donations appreciated.* ⟨*(08862) 93 29 30. www.wieskirche.de. To avoid the worst crowds, visit early in the morning or at the end of the day and avoid Sundays.*

The Wieskirche, whose full name is Pilgrimage Church of the Scourged Saviour, is a masterpiece of Bavarian Rococo masterminded by the architect Dominikus Zimmermann in the 18C. It has been on UNESCO's World Heritage list since 1983.

Exterior and Interior – The elegantly understated church exterior leaves visitors unprepared for the splendour of the interior. Gilded stucco, wood carvings and vivid frescoes stand out from the white walls, bathed in subtle light entering the windows. The lower parts of the interior are sparsely decorated to symbolise the Earth. The upper reaches (the heavens) vibrate with a profusion of frescoes, stucco and gilded work. The immense **cupola fresco** represents the Second Coming, the Gates of Paradise (still closed) and the Last Judgement. The decoration of the **choir** is unparalleled: columns, balustrades, statues, gilded stucco and frescoes form a glorious symphony of colour.

In the centre of the church is a figure of the flagellated Christ. In 1738, a local farmer noticed tears in the eyes of the statue. This prompted such a pilgrimage rush that the local abbot commissioned this magnificent church to accommodate everyone. To this day, up to 1 million people visit every year.

Rottenbuch

First built as an Augustinian monastery, the **Mariä-Geburts-Kirche**★ (Church of

the Nativity of the Virgin) was remodelled in Baroque and Rococo styles in the 18C. The School of Wessobrunn, of which Joseph and Franz Schmuzer were masters, crafted the magnificent stucco. Matthäus Günther's ceiling fresco depicts the death of St. Augustine in perfect visual harmony with the extravagantly sculpted décor. The pulpit, organ loft and altars by Franz Xaver Schmädl are heavily adorned with statues and giltwork in pure Rococo tradition.

Echelsbacher Brücke (Echelsbacher Bridge)

Opened in 1929, this was Germany's first bridge made of reinforced concrete. Almost 90m/295.3ft long, it spans the deep Ammer Gorge. Walk to the middle of the bridge for an impressive view.

Oberammergau★

This small town of farmers and craftspeople, encircled by the wooded foothills of the Ammergau, is internationally famous for its Passion Play, staged every ten years (next in 2020) by hundreds of local amateur actors. The tradition derives from a vow made by the inhabitants in 1634 after being spared by a plague epidemic. Performances are held at the **Passionstheater** (○○*guided tours (45min) Apr–Oct 10am–5pm, Dec Sat–Sun 11am and 3pm;* ○*6€;* ⟨*(8822) 923 10),* where tours give you insight into the play's history, meaning and production.

Oberammergau is also renowned for its *trompe l'œii* facades painted in a style called *Lüftlmalerei* (roughly "air painting"). These are colourful frescoes depicting both secular and religious themes, from fairytales to Biblical scenes.

Linderhof★★

⟨*See Schloss LINDERHOF.*

Ettal★

A blossoming of the Benedictine tradition and the local veneration of a Virgin statue explain the vast dimensions of **Ettal Abbey**★, founded by Emperor Ludwig the Bavarian in 1330. The origi-

Der Blaue Reiter

The symphony of nature in the Tölzer Land – a pastiche of glassy lakes, muscular mountains and soft meadows – greatly inspired key members of the artists' group *Der Blaue Reiter* (The Blue Rider), founded in 1911 by Wassily Kandinsky and Franz Marc. Along with fellow artists Gabriele Münter, Paul Klee, August Macke, Alex Jawlensky and others, they spent summers here and Kandinsky and Marc eventually ended up buying houses in Murnau on the Staffelsee and Kochel am See, respectively. Blue Rider artists may have developed different artistic styles but all shared a desire to translate emotion and spirituality onto canvas. The clear, reflective light of the Alpine foothills, the intensity of the colours (especially the blue of the sky and the lakes) and the harmony of the landscape were all conducive to their vision. The group disbanded at the outbreak of World War I in 1914. Both Marc and Macke died on the battlefield.

nal Gothic church succumbed to a fire in 1774 after which it was rebuilt by Baroque star architect Enrico Zuccalli and Joseph Schmuzer of the Wessobrunner School. The dazzlingly detailed dome **fresco** showing St. Benedict and his followers is a masterpiece by Johann Jakob Zeiller.

The monastery is still active today with several dozen monks keeping busy running a hotel, a brewery, a distillery and other ventures.

▷ *The road rejoins the Loisach Valley. To the south, the cragged Wetterstein range reveals the peaks of the Zugspitze, Alpspitze and Dreitorspitze. Continue to Garmisch-Partenkirchen.*

Garmisch-Partenkirchen★★★
♿*See GARMISCH-PARTENKIRCHEN.*

③ THE UPPER ISAR VALLEY AND THE LAKE DISTRICT★
From Garmisch-Partenkirchen to Schliersee. 105km/65mi – Allow 1 day.

The first part of the route traverses the upper Isar Valley, which here runs wide and wild. It is among the most scenic stretches of road in the Alps.

▷ *From Garmisch-Partenkirchen, take the B2 (E533) towards Mittenwald, then follow signs to Krün and Wallgau. On leaving Wallgau, turn right on Risserstraße, a small road that runs through the upper Isar Valley, continuing as the*

B307 past Vorderriss and skirting the Sylvenstein reservoir. Continue on the B307 over the Achenpass all the way to Tegernsee.

Tegernsee
Splendidly embedded in forested Alpine foothills, Tegernsee has long been popular with the rich, famous and powerful. It is surrounded by four villages, each with its own flair.

Bad Wiessee on the western shore is a fashionable spa resort with a sparkling casino. Rottach-Egern in the south is the ritziest enclave and has the best restaurants and posh houses. On the eastern shore, the village of Tegernsee is the most historical with origins as a Benedictine monastery founded in 746. It has a famous beer hall, the Bräustüberl. Finally, **Gmund** in the north is the most low-key village and popular with families.

▷ *Continue on the B307 to Schliersee.*

Schliersee
Beside the lake of the same name, this small community – together with Fischhausen, Neuhaus and Spitzingsee (♿*see itinerary below*) – offers interesting day trips. The **St. Sixtus Parish Church**★ (Pfarrkirche) was styled Baroque between 1712 and 1714. The interior frescoes and delicate stucco were executed by Johann Baptist Zimmermann (1680–1758), brother of the architect of the Wieskirche (♿*see WIESKIRCHE*).

4 THE SUDELFELD AND THE CHIEMGAU MOUNTAINS★

From Schliersee to Berchtesgaden.
172km/107mi – Allow one day.

▶ *Continue on the B307 until Neuhaus to catch the road climbing up to Spitzingsee (10km/6.2mi round-trip).*

Spitzingsee

Less than 0.6km/0.4mi from the summit, the steep access road offers views of the Fischhausen–Neuhaus plain and Schliersee. Soon after, the road stops at the Spitzingsee.

▶ *Continue on B207. About 3km/1.8mi before Bayrischzell, the road passes the cable-car terminal to the Wendelstein summit.*

Wendelstein★★

🕐*Cable-car: daily 9am–5pm (Nov–Apr 4pm);* 🚡*round-trip 24.50€. Cogwheel train: daily 9.15am–4pm (Nov–Mar 4pm).* 🕐*Closed late Nov–Dec 20.* 🚡*Round-trip 25€.* ✆*(08034) 30 80. www.wendelsteinbahn.de.*
👥 To ascend the Wendelstein, take either the **cable-car** from Bayrischzell-Osterhofen *(7min)*, or the **cogwheel train** *(Zahnradbahn)* from Brannenburg *(25min)*.
From the mountain station at 1 738m/5 702ft, a trail leads another 100 vertical metres (328ft) to the peak. Crowned by a solar observatory and an 18C chapel, it offers an unforgettable **panorama**★★ and access to four trails (Geo-Wanderwege). The Gipfelweg circles the summit in about 2hrs 30min.

▶ *From Wendelstein follow the A8 Munich–Salzburg autobahn to the shore of Lake* **Chiemsee**★. *Turn south onto the B305 which winds through the Chiemgau, a delightful region of lakes, moors, valleys and lakes with top skiing, hiking and mountain biking in the villages of Reit im Winkl, Inzell and Ruhpolding.*

Ruhpolding★

This popular cross-country skiing resort also has a famous art work: a 12C Romanesque statue of the Virgin Mary in the twin onion-domed parish church of **St. George**.

▶ *The Schwarzbachwacht pass reveals the contrast between the austere wooded Schwarzbach Valley and the open pastures on the Ramsau slopes. The drive offers* **panoramas**★★ *of the Watzmann peak and the Hochkalter with its Blaueis glacier. The German Alpine Road ends at Berchtesgaden.*

Berchtesgaden★★

👁*See BERCHTESGADEN.*

View from Wendelstein towards Munich

© Alexander Mertz/iStockphoto.com

ADDRESSES

🛏 STAY

THE CHIEMGAU

🍴 Gästehaus Weißes Rössl – *Dorfstraße 19, 83242 Reit im Winkl. ☎(08640) 982 30. www.weissesroessl-riw.de. 20 rooms.* This low-key inn in the Chiemgau Alps offers self-catering apartments perfect for families along with comfortable rooms, all with balconies. Cool off in the outdoor pool or wrap up your day in the sauna or gym.

THE AMMERGAU

🍴 Gasthaus Zum Fischerwirt – *Linderhofer Straße 15, 82488 Ettal. ☎(08822) 63 52. www.zum-fischerwirt. de. Closed Nov–mid-Dec and 2 weeks at Easter. 10 rooms. Restaurant (🍴🍴).* A traditional, pleasant hotel with charmingly decorated sparkling rooms and a restaurant serving reasonably-priced regional favourites.

🍴 Alpengasthof Winklmoosalm – *Dürrnbachhornweg 6, 83242 Reit im Winkl. ☎(08640) 974 40. www.winklmoosalm. com. Closed Nov–Dec. 18 rooms. Restaurant (🍴🍴).* You'll sleep well in the fresh mountain air of this well-maintained inn in a famous ski area. Enjoy panoramic views and organic dishes in the cheerfully decorated restaurant.

THE ALLGÄU

🍴🍴 Alpenlandhotel Hirsch – *Kurze Gasse 18, 87541 Bad Oberdorf. ☎(08324) 308. www.alpengasthof-hirsch. de. Closed 3 weeks in Nov. 25 rooms. Restaurant (🍴).* Tradition meets modern comforts at this family-run hotel with spotless rooms, some with kitchenette or sitting area. There's a playroom for kids, a spa for grown-ups and a restaurant for everyone to enjoy.

🍴🍴 Hotel Eiskristall – *Birkstraße 3. ☎(08362) 50 78 12. www.hotel-eiskristall.de. 32 rooms. Restaurant (🍴🍴).* Expect a hearty welcome when checking into this family-run hotel on the town outskirts, close to the ice rink. The Alpine décor with lots of wood, thick carpets and carved crafts is inviting, the rooms spacious and pleasantly rustic and the restaurant topnotch.

🍴🍴 Hotel Geiger – *Uferstraße 18, 87629 Füssen-Hopfen am See. ☎(08362) 70 74. www.hotel-geiger.de. Closed Nov–mid-Dec. 24 rooms. Restaurant 🍴🍴🍴.* Newly renovated, this long-standing family hotel on the lakeside promenade features chic designer décor, a small spa with Finnish sauna and mint steam room and two restaurants one rustic, one à la carte.

🍴🍴🍴 Hotel Sonne – *Reichenstraße 37 ☎(08362) 90 80. www.hotel-sonne.de. 50 rooms.* Champagne breakfast and free fitness centre passes are among the extra perks at this central hotel with cheerful, spacious and modern rooms, many with balconies.

THE UPPER VALLEY OF THE ISAR

🍴🍴Hotel Lederer am See – *Bodenschneidstraße 9, 83707 Bad Wiessee. ☎(08022) 82 90. hotel@lederer. com. Closed Nov–mid-Dec. 89 rooms. Restaurant (🍴🍴🍴).* Four traditional-style houses make up this appealing hotel complex with a popular country-style restaurant overlooking the lake.

🍴 EAT

THE CHIEMGAU

🍴🍴 Schlosswirt – *Kirchplatz 1, 83098 Brannenburg. ☎080 34 707 10. www. schlosswirt.de. Closed Tue; 3rd week Nov; Tue–Wed mid-Oct–Apr.* The meat couldn't be fresher at this family-run restaurant which runs its own butcher's and delicatessen.

THE AMMERGAU

🍴🍴 Moosbeck-Alm – *Moos 38, 82401 Moos. ☎08867 912 00. www.moosbeck-alm.de. Closed mid-Nov–mid Dec and Tue.* Dine either in the rustic König-Ludwig-Stube or in the conservatory of this Landhaus with outdoor pool and wellness facilities.

THE ALLGÄU

🍴 Zum Schwanen – *Brotmarkt 4. Closed Mon, Sun dinner, mid-Jan–mid-Mar. ☎(08362) 61 74.* The welcoming hosts serve specialities from the Allgäu in a well-kept setting with a muted, rustic flair.

Oberstdorf★★

A well-known mountain, skiing and spa town in the Allgäu Alps of southern Germany, this charming resort is lorded over by the Fellhorn and Nebelhorn peaks and is the departure point for walking and hiking tours. Vehicles are banned from the centre of town.

▶ **Population:** 9 900

Info: Prinzregenten-Platz 1. ℘(08322) 70 00. www.oberstdorf.de.

Location: Midway between Bodensee (Lake Constance) and the castles of Ludwig II, deeply incised into the Allgäu Alps, and seven other valleys, the town lies at the junction of the valley of the Iller River.

Don't Miss: A trip to the Nebelhorn or the Fellhorn.

Timing: Allow a full day to explore this Alpine resort.

Kids: Riding the cable-car up the Nebelhorn or Fellhorn.

SIGHTS
Nebelhorn★★

🚶 *Take the Nebelhorn cable-car (45min) via three stations: Seealpe (1 280m/ 4 200ft), Höfatsblick (1 932m/6 338.5ft), Summit (2 224m/7 296.5ft).*
⏱*Operates daily 8.30am–4.50pm (4.30 in winter), every 10min.* ⏱*Closed for 4 weeks in Apr/May and Nov5–mid-Dec. Round trip summer ⊛16.50€ Seealpe, 23€ Höfatsblick, 26.50€ summit; ski day pass 32.50–36.50€. ℘(08322) 960 00. www.das-hoechste.de.*
The highest cable railway in the Allgäu leads to the 2 224m/7 300ft-high summit of the Nebelhorn. In clear weather, the **panoramic view**★★ extends over more than 400 Alpine peaks, from the Zugspitze in the east to the Säntis in the west. Laced by numerous hiking trails, the Nebelhorn is also the departure point for the demanding "Hindelang climb". In winter, it morphs into a popular ski resort.

Fellhorn★★

🚶 *Take the Fellhorn cable-car in two stages to the summit (2 037/6 683ft).*
⏱*Operates late May–late Jun, 9am– 4.15pm, late-Jun–Oct 8.30am-4.50pm; Dec–Apr (depending on snow) 8.30am– 4.30pm or 5pm. Round trip summer ⊛23€, ski day pass 33–36€. ℘(08322) 960 00.*
There is a wonderful **view**★★ over the Allgäu, the Austrian and Swiss Alps, from the 2 037m/6 683ft-high summit of the Fellhorn. The mountain has an easily accessible network of hiking paths, including an interesting **Blumen-und Wanderlehrpfad** (flower walk) with rare Alpine blooms all the way to the peak.

EXCURSIONS
Breitachklamm★★

▶ *6.5km/4mi southwest, plus 1hr 30min round-trip walk.*
⏱*Open May–Sept, daily 8am–5pm; Oct–Apr, 9am–4pm.* ⏱*Closed Nov, Dec and during snowfall. ⊛3€. ℘(08322) 48 87. www.breitachklamm.de.*
In the lower gorge, galleries lead into sheer, polished walls, where the turbulent mountain creek has carved a course 100m/328ft deep into the bedrock. You can return via a series of stairways taking you to Walserschanze, on the Kleinwalsertal road, from where there is a frequent bus service back into town.

Kleinwalsertal★

▶ *17km/11mi southwest.*
A high valley of the Breitach River, this mountain area was settled in the 13C by the **Walsers**, Germanic emigrants from the Upper Valais. Today the Kleinwalsertal has Austrian police, German customs, a German postal service and Austrian stamps. (Adopting the Euro simplified money matters.) **Riezlern**, **Hirschegg** and **Mittelberg** are the most popular resorts.

Schloss Neuschwanstein★★★

With its forest of playful towers and turrets, Neuschwanstein is the quintessential fairytale castle and a product of the imagination of King Ludwig II of Bavaria (1845–1886). Set against the splendid backdrop of the Alps, it is a top tourist attraction in Germany and is deluged with visitors every day. A friend and sponsor of the composer Richard Wagner, Ludwig II regarded this palace as a tribute to his operas and German heroic legends in general. Escape the crowds by hitting the forest trails surrounding the castle.

- **Info:** Neuschwanstein-straße 20, 87645 Schwangau. ℘(08362) 93 98 80. www.neuschwanstein.com.
- **Location:** About 5km/3mi east of Füssen, the castle is on a rocky ridge 200m/656ft above the Pöllat Gorge, making an impressive sight.
- **Don't Miss:** The view of the castle from the Marienbrücke.
- **Timing:** Allow half a day for your visit, including waiting time.

A BIT OF HISTORY

The construction – King Ludwig II found the ideal location for "Neu-Hohen-schwangau" (the name "Neuschwanstein" only came in 1890) not far from Hohenschwangau Castle, where he had spent part of his childhood and youth. Ludwig came up with the design of the new palace himself. To some extent it was inspired by the medieval Wartburg in Thuringia (*see EISENACH*), which he had visited in 1867.

The end of a dream – Ludwig II only lived at Neuschwanstein for 170 days.

The palace construction had put a serious strain on the royal coffers and the king's increasingly eccentric behaviour led a government commission from Munich to bring him news of his dethronement on 10 June 1886. Just three days later, he was found floating dead in Lake Starnberg. The true circumstances of his death, and that of his doctor who had accompanied him on a walk that fateful evening, remain a mystery to this day.

Schloss Neuschwanstein and Schloss Hohenschwangau on the left

© photo75/iStockphoto.com

VISIT

Guided tours (35min) Apr–Sept, daily 9am–6pm; Oct–Mar, 10am–4pm. Ticket booths open 1hr prior. Closed Jan 1, Shrove Tue, Dec 24, 25 & 31. www.neuschwanstein.de. *9€, same-day combination ticket with Schloss Hohenschwangau 17€.*

*Buy tickets at the **Ticketcenter** (Alpseestraße 12, Hohenschwangau; (08362) 93 08 30; www.ticket-center-hohenschwangau.de) in Hohenschwangau village before embarking on the 30min walk up to the castle (horse-drawn carriage rides available, 5€ uphill, 2.50€ downhill). Advance tickets (1.80€ booking fee) available by phone and online.*

The interior, with its profusion of gilded panelling and wall paintings, reflects Ludwig's fertile imagination and fantasies. The most distinctive chambers are on the third floor: the **throne room**★ (unfinished), the **bed chamber**★ furnished with Gothic pieces, the **living room**★ with its Lohengrin-inspired decorations, and the artificial stalactite cave with the adjacent winter garden, evoking the Tannhäuser legend. The design of the **Sängersaal** *(minstrels' hall)* is based on the Wartburg, where the legendary poetry contest featured in the Wagner opera *Tannhäuser* was said to have taken place in the early 13C. For dreamy **views**★★ of the castle, take the short but steep 10-minute trail up to Marienbrücke bridge above the cascading Pöllat River.

SCHLOSS HOHENSCHWANGAU★

Guided tours (35min) Apr–Sept, daily 9am–6pm; Oct–Mar, 10am–4pm. Closed Jan 1, Shrove Tue, Dec 24, 25 & Dec. 9€, same-day combination ticket with Schloss Neuschwanstein 17€. For advance tickets, see Schloss Neuschwanstein above.

In the 1830s, when **Maximilian II** of Bavaria was still crown prince, he commissioned this castle as a summer residence; it stands atop the foundations of a 12C fortress. The flamboyant neo-Gothic style was in accord-

Ludwig II's Castles

The term *Königsschlösser* generally refers to Ludwig's ancestral home of Hohenschwangau and his romantic fantasy castle of Neuschwanstein. But the king's passion for palaces didn't end here. His favourite retreat was actually the comparatively intimate Schloss Linderhof, in an idyllic valley near Garmisch-Partenkirchen. By contrast, Herrenchiemsee Palace in Chiemsee was less a residence than a tribute to his idol, French King Louis XIV. No surprise then that Ludwig only spent 10 days living here.

ance with current taste and reflected Maximilian's predilection for chivalric romance. Ludwig II spent most of his largely unhappy youth in this castle, which stands in a picturesque setting on a wooded hill overlooking the pretty Alpsee. It is about a 15-minute walk to the castle from Hohenschwangau village.

In comparison with Neuschwanstein – and in spite of the almost compulsive repetition of the swan motif – Hohenschwangau has retained a romantic, comfortable feel. Queen Maria, Ludwig II's mother, spent much time here, which explains the welcoming, lived-in atmosphere.

After the maniacal decoration of Schloss Neuschwanstein, the clean lines of the maple and cherrywood Biedermeier furniture here may come as a relief. Still, some rooms also sport elaborate wall paintings, usually depicting scenes from German history or mythology.

One of Ludwig II's favourite rooms was the upstairs music room where he would listen to Richard Wagner playing the piano, still in situ today. Don't miss the king's bedchamber, where the ceiling is painted to represent night stars.

Follow your visit of the castle with a stroll to a beautiful **viewpoint**★ on a shaded rocky spur of the **Pindarplatz** on the Alpsee.

Garmisch-Partenkirchen★★

Germany's most famous winter sports resort snuggles against the massive peaks of the Wetterstein chain, most notably the Zugspitze which soars to a lofty 2 962m/9 717ft and is the highest mountain in the country. The twin town hosted the fourth Winter Olympics in 1936 and the World Alpine Ski Championships in 1978.

SIGHTS
Alte St. Martin-Kirche (Old Church of St. Martin)
Garmisch's original parish church is a 13C Gothic pile in a picturesque neighbourhood with carefully preserved chalets on the west bank of the River Loisach. Several of its medieval murals have been uncovered and restored, most notably a 7m/22ft-high image of St. Christophorus and scenes depicting the Crucifixion and the Last Judgement.

Neue St. Martin Kirche (New Church of St. Martin)
Garmisch's "new" parish church is an 18C work by the famous Wessobrunn architect Josef Schmuzer with ceiling frescoes by Matthias Günther and a chancel carved by Frank Hosp.

LOCAL WALKS
Wank★★
🏃 *20min cable-car ride, operates May–Oct, daily 8.45am–5pm at least half-hourly; Nov-Apr 9am-4.30pm. 18€ round-trip. (08821) 79 70. www.zugspitze.de.*
From the summit (1 780m/5 840ft) of sunny Wank mountain **views**★★ open up across the entire Wetterstein range and the Zugspitze peak, extending all the way to Munich on clear days. Enjoy varied vistas while following the two easy and bench-lined panoramic trails along the top.

Philosophenweg (Philosophers' Way)
🏃 The early 18C church of St. Anton is the departure point for this easy and

- ▶ **Population:** 26 000
- ℹ **Info:** Richard-Strauß-Platz 2. ℘(08821) 18 07 00 www.garmisch-parten kirchen.de.
- ▶ **Location:** Garmisch-Partenkirchen is a highlight on the Deutsche Alpenstraße and less than 15km/9.3mi from the Austrian border.
- ✦ **Don't Miss:** A trip up the Zugspitze and Linderhof Palace.
- 👥 **Kids:** Snow sports, cable-car ride up the Wank, Leutasch Ghost Gorge.

panoramic walk along the icy Loisach River. Enjoy clear **views**★ of the surrounding massifs, including the Zugspitze looming behind the Waxenstein.

Partnachklamm★★
🏃 *About 90min round-trip. Bring rain gear. ⏰Open summer, daily 8am–6pm, winter 9am–5pm. 3€. ℘(08821) 31 67. www.partnachklamm-info.de.*
The splendour of this 800m/2 624ft-long deep, narrow gorge carved by a rushing creek into solid rock will probably etch itself into your memory forever.
The route passes two spectacular bottlenecks amid the thunder of falling water and clouds of frothy spray. In winter it is decorated with icicles. The trailhead is about 2km/1.2mi south of the Olympic ski stadium.

Kramerplateauweg
🏃 *Upon leaving Garmisch, cross the Loisach River.*
At the foot of the Kramerspitz, this almost entirely flat trail leads to the mountain restaurant Almhütte *(45min)* and the Pflegersee lake *(90min)*, which is great for swimming.

WHERE TO STAY		WHERE TO EAT		
Gästehaus Brigitte	(1)	Arnspitze	(2)	Joseph Naus Stub'n ..... (3)
Gasthof Fraundorfer	(4)	Kurpark Pavillon	(1)	Zur Schranne ..... (4)

EXCURSIONS

Mittenwald★

▶ *20km/11.8mi east.*

Mittenwald is intensely popular thanks to its gorgeous location below the Kranzberg and Karwendel massifs and the beauty of the town itself.

Its biggest claim to fame is its abundance of intricately frescoed **house façades★★** in a style called *Lüftlmalerei* (ℓ*see cover photo*). The ones on Obermarkt are especially spectacular.

ZUGSPITZE★★★

ℓ*(08821) 79 70. www.zugspitze.de.*

The Zugspitze is the northwest pillar of the Wetterstein limestone massif, a rocky barrier enclosing the valley of the Loisach and on the border with Austria. With a summit at 2 964m/9 724ft above sea level, the Zugspitze is the highest peak in Germany.

Its matchless panorama and extensive ski slopes keep the mountain well supplied with tourist facilities. On clear days

you have views extending to Germany, Italy, Switzerland and Austria.

🚶 Summit Ascent

🖐*Appropriate (warm) clothing should be worn.*

Getting to the Zugspitze summit involves riding either a cogwheel train, followed by a short cable-car ride, or a steep cable-car ride straight up from the Eibsee lake. Many people ascend the summit on the cogwheel train and return by cable-car, or vice versa.

Coming from Ehrwald on the Austrian side, use the **Tyrolean Zugspitz Railway** *(www.zugspitzbahn.at).*

From Garmisch-Partenkirchen

Duration 1hr 15min by cogwheel train and cable-car. Departs hourly from 8.15am to 2.15pm. ⊗47€ round-trip in summer, 38€ in winter. Last train to Garmisch 4.30pm. ℓ(08821) 79 70. www.zugspitze.de.

The high-tech cogwheel trains depart from their own station behind the main train station in Garmisch and travel along the foot of the mountain past the Eibsee lake before starting their steep ascent through a 4.6km/2.8mi tunnel to the Zugspitzplatt station. From here, a cable-car *(Gletscherbahn)* ascends the last 350m/1 148ft to the summit in 4min.

From the Eibsee

Duration 10min by cable-car. Departs at least every 30min from 8am to 4.45pm (4.15pm in winter). ⊶*47€ round-trip (38€ in winter).* ℘*(088 21) 79 70. www.zugspitze.de. Service reduced or suspended in bad weather.*

This intensely steep cable-car makes the trip straight to the summit in a mere ten minutes and is not really suited for those suffering from fear of heights.

Zugspitzgipfel★★★ (Summit)

The upper terminals of the *Gletscherbahn* and the Eibsee cable-car are on the German side, while the Tyrolean Zugspitzbahn terminates on the Austrian side.

The **panorama**★★★ to the east reveals the Kaisergebirge, the Dachstein and the Karwendel, the glacial peaks of the Hohe Tauern, the High Alps of the Tirol

Steep ride to Zugspitzgipfel
©Adam Bukolt/Bigstockphoto.com

and the Ortler and the Bernina massifs. Nearer are the mountains of the Arlberg before the Säntis in the Appenzell Alps; further away, to the west and northwest, are the Allgäu and Ammergau ranges. To the north, the Bavarian lowlands are visible, along with the Ammersee and Starnberger See lakes. On good days, you can even spot Munich in the distance.

In fine snow conditions (usually from October to May), the lower Zugspitzplatt offers a **skiing** area and a a terrain park with half-pipes, kicker and rail areas.

View of Zugspitze from Eibsee
©Vadim Shtral/Bigstockphoto.com

SCHLOSS LINDERHOF★★ (LINDERHOF PALACE)

▶ 27km/16.7mi north of Garmisch-Partenkirchen. ✎Guided tours Apr–mid-Oct, daily 9am–6pm; mid-Oct–Mar, 10am–4pm. 🕙Closed 1 Jan, Shrove Tue, 24, 25 & 31 Dec. Outbuildings closed Apr–Sept. ✍Summer 8€, winter 7€. ✆(08822) 920 30. www.linderhof.de. Allow at least two hours and prepare for long waits in high season.

Ludwig II's most whimsical palace is tucked deep into the forest in one of the most secluded and idyllic valleys of the Ammergau Alps. Though not particularly large, it was the young king's favourite retreat and beautifully reflects his romantic fantasies.

Schloss★★(Palace)

Ludwig II had this intimate palace built between 1874 and 1879 in a style blending Italian Renaissance and Baroque elements and inspired by his idol, French King Louis XIV. The lavish **state bedchamber** surpasses even the luxury of Versailles, while the dining room has a table that disappears into the floor.

Park★★

The Italianate terraced gardens complement the landscape's natural slopes. Views from the **Temple of Venus** rotunda are especially enjoyable when the fountains are in action.

🕤 Do not miss the **Moorish Kiosk**, an exotic extravaganza of stained glass, feathers, painted wood and even an enamel throne. The **Venus Grotto** is just as lavish and features an artificial lake complete with waterfall and a gilded shell-shaped boat. The setting was inspired by the Wagner opera Tann-häuser.

ADDRESSES

🛏STAY

🍽**Gästehaus Brigitte** – St. Martin-Straße 40. ✆(08821) 739 38. www.hotel brigitte.de. 11 rooms. This spotless guest-house is near the cable-car station and just around the corner from trails and the Olympic skating rink.

🍽🍽**Gasthof Fraundorfer** – Luswigstraße 24. ✆08 821 92 70. www.gasthof-fraundorfer.de. Closed Nov. 31 rooms. ☕16€. Some of the bedrooms may be small here but the balconies, with views over the Waxenstein, help to compensate. Expect oompah music, yodelling and folk dancing at its convivial Bavarian restaurant.

MITTENWALD

🍽 **Hotel Garni Edlhuber** – Innsbrucker Straße 33, 82481 Mittenwald. ✆08 823 13 89. www.edlhuber-mittenwald.de. 6 rooms. ☕. This traditional wooden family-run hotel, at the foot of the Karwendel mountain, is an idyllic location for outdoors holidays. Comfortable, pretty rooms and a warm welcome await.

🍴EAT

🍽 **Zur Schranne** – Griesstraße 4. ✆(08821) 16 99. Closed Tue. Sample feel-good Bavarian food, served in particularly belt-loosening portions, at this typical regional eatery. Sit inside or on the covered terrace.

🍽 **Kurpark Pavillon** – Richard-Strauss-platz 1. ✆08 821 31 79. Regional specialities are served in this attractive glass pavilion in the centre of Garmisch; ideal for dinner after an evening at the casino or the theatre.

🍽🍽 **Arnspitze** – Innsbrucker Straße 68. ✆08 823 24 25. www.arnspitze-mittenwald.de. Closed Tue–Wed and Apr (open Easter). This typical Bavarian Alpine gasthof serves fine regional cooking.

🍽🍽 **Joseph-Naus Stubn** – Klammstraße 19. ✆(08821) 90 10. For a more refined, modern take on local cuisine, grab a table at this graciously rustic restaurant named for the man who first reached the Zugspitze summit in 1820.

MITTENWALD

🍽**Postkeller und Alte Braustub'n** – Innsbrucker Straße 13. ✆08 823 17 29. www.postkeller-mittenwald.de. Closed Mon. This cheerful modern establishment is a mix of restaurant and brewhouse, with regional cuisine and home-brewed beer that you can enjoy outside on the terrace.

Chiemsee★

Known as the "Bavarian Sea", the Chiemsee is the largest of the province's lakes. Its calm waters offer plenty of recreation options, including swimming, boating and windsurfing. The lake's two islands are both worth a visit: steer towards Herreninsel (Gentlemen's Isle) to tour King Ludwig II's extraordinary palace and to the Fraueninsel (Ladies' Isle) to view its ancient Benedictine abbey. In the background are the Chiemgau Alps, a popular winter sports area.

THE ISLANDS

Ferries to Herreninsel and Fraueninsel leave from the docks in Prien-Stock (exit the A8 at Bernau). The trip to Herreninsel takes about 15min, round trips cost 6.70€; combination tickets for Herreninsel and Fraueninsel (25min) are 7.80€. Boat tours around the lake are 12.40€. ℘(08051) 60 90. www.chiemsee-schifffahrt.de.

Herreninsel

The parks, woods and forests of the "Gentlemen's Isle" are ideal for a leisurely amble. King Ludwig II of Bavaria bought this island in 1873 to save it from deforestation and ended up building a sumptuous palace.

Schloss Herrenchiemsee★★

20min walk from the dock. Guided tours (30min) only, Apr–mid-Oct, daily 9am–6pm; mid-Oct–Mar 9.40am–4.15pm. Closed Jan 1, Shrove Tue, Dec 24, 25 & 31. 7€. ℘(080 51) 688 70. www.herrenchiemsee.de.

It was to be the grandest of Ludwig II's palaces: a glorious edifice modelled on Versailles in honour of his idol, the French monarch Louis XIV.

Ludwig poured considerable funds into the construction of the **Neues Schloss** (New Palace) on Herreninsel but when he died in 1886 it was still only partly finished. The resemblance to Versailles is quite striking: the Latona fountain stands amid formal French gardens,

📋 **Info:** Felden 10, 83233 Bernau. ℘(08051) 96 55 50. www.chiemsee.de.

▶ **Location:** Prien, on the western shore, is the busiest and most central of the Chiemsee resorts. The A8 autobahn (Munich–Salzburg) skirts the lake's southern shore.

👁 **Don't Miss:** Schloss Herrenchiemsee, the view of the Alps from the northern lake shore between Rimsting and Seebruck.

🕐 **Timing:** Allow at least half a day to visit Schloss Herrenchiemsee.

👪 **Kids:** Lake activities.

while the façade is adorned with columns and crowned by a flat roof in the Italian style.

Tours of the apartments start in the entrance hall with its splendid **double state staircase** *(Prunktreppenhaus)* and proceed to a succession of lavish and pompous rooms. The **state bedroom★** and the 77m/252ft-long **Hall of Mirrors★** are especially dazzling.

The south wing houses the **König Ludwig II Museum** *(entrance included in Schloss ticket)*, which documents the fairytale king's life through portraits, busts, historical photographs and original clothing. Spend some time here before the start of the guided tour.

Augustinian Monastery at Altes Schloss (Old Palace)

The first Augustinian monastery was founded on the island in 1130 but the current incarnation dates back to the Baroque era. The four wings enclose a large, almost rectangular courtyard with an idyllic rose garden. Also known as Altes Schloss (Old Palace), it is now partly a **museum** tracing 1 200 years of Bavarian history. Highlights include the Baroque library designed by Johann Baptist Zimmermann and King

Chiemsee at Seebruck

T. Krieger/MICHELIN

Ludwig II's private quarters, including the Blue Bedroom. Almost as impressive are the state rooms in the Princes' Tract, especially the Imperial Hall and the Garden Room.

Fraueninsel

This small islet is home to the Benedictine **Frauenchiemsee Monastery**, founded in 782 by Duke Tassilo III. It is one of the oldest women's abbeys in Germany. Secularised in 1803, it was revived in 1837 by King Ludwig I of Bavaria.

The three-aisled church is Carolingian at its core but sports Romanesque frescoes as well as Gothic and Baroque touches. Copies of its ceiling frescoes now grace the upper chapel of the nearby **Torhalle** (gatehouse), which is now a museum presenting a thorough survey of early sacred art in Bavaria.

ADDRESSES

STAY

Gruber-Alm – *Almweg 18, 83370 Seeon-Seebruck. ℘(08667) 696. www.gruber-alm.de. 19 rooms. Restaurant.* This pleasant hotel on a little hill affords views of the Chiemgau Alps. The "Wedding Room" has a handpainted ceiling, while others brim with rustic Bavarian hospitality. The restaurant serves tummy-filling regional dishes.

Alter Wirt-Bonnschlößl – *Kirchplatz 9, 83233 Bernau am Chiemsee. ℘(08051) 965 69 90. www.alter-wirt-bernau.de. 41 rooms. Closed mid-Mar–mid–Apr and late Nov–mid-Dec. Restaurant, closed Mon except Aug.* Match your mood or comfort needs to these twin properties. The half-timbered Alter Wirt inn has rustic charm and country furnishings, while the Bonnschlössl offers modern rooms in a turreted 15C miniature palace with its own park.

Inselhotel Zur Linde – *on the Fraueninsel. 5min boat ride from Gstadt. ℘(08054) 903 66. www.inselhotel-zurlinde.de. 14 rooms. Restaurant.* A romantic island getaway, this inn dates from 1396 and was once the haunt of artists and writers. Rooms and public areas ooze unhurried charm, while the dining room, still with its original layout, adds yet more character to the place.

ᛒ/ EAT

Kloster-Wirt – *Frauenchiemsee 50, Frauensinsel. 5min boat ride from Gstadt. ℘(08054) 77 65. www.klosterwirt-chiemsee.de.* Part of the island's Benedictine abbey, this dockside restaurant is nice spot for a hearty meal or just coffee and cake. In fine weather, there's no better place to sit and relax than the beer garden with its chestnut trees.

Berchtesgaden★★

Journey's end of the German Alpine Road (Deutsche Alpenstraße), Berchtesgaden has a sublimely beautiful setting embraced by half a dozen mountain ranges and anchored by the painterly Königssee lake. Much of the landscape is protected as the Berchtesgaden National Park and is a year-round outdoor playground. The only stain on the region's legacy came during the Nazi years when Adolf Hitler chose the Obersalzberg as the site of his southern headquarters.

SIGHTS
Schlossplatz★

This triangular square is the heart of Berchtesgaden. On the western side is the Getreidekasten, the former granary furnished with an arcade in the 16C. Lombard influence is evident in the façade of the **Church of St. Peter and St. John** (*Stiftskirche St. Peter and Johannes*), decorated with multi-coloured stones.

Schloss (Palace)

Guided tours (1hr) mid-May–mid-Oct, Sun–Fri 10am–noon, 2pm–4pm; rest of the year Mon–Fri 11am-2pm. 7€. (08652) 94 79 80. *www.haus-bayern.com.*
Once a monks' priory, this sumptuous palace is still owned – and sometimes used – by the Wittelsbachs, Bavaria's former royal family. The palace museum displays weapons, religious art, French tapestries and Nymphenburg porcelain. A **guided tour** allows a closer look at the palace. Visit the highest terrace for unforgettable views of the Watzmann.

♣♣ Salzbergwerk (Salt Mines)★★

Bergwerkstraße 23. Guided tours (2hrs) May–Oct, daily 9am–5pm; Nov–Apr, daily 11am–5pm. Closed Jan 1, Good Fri, Pentecost, Dec 24,25 & 31. 14.90€. (08652) 60 02 20. *www.salzzeitreise.de.*

- ▶ **Population:** 7 670
- **Info:** Königsseer Straße 2, (08652) 96 70. www.berchtesgaden.de and www.berchtesgadener-land.de.
- ▶ **Location:** Berchtesgaden is the main town of the Berchtesgadener *Land* (region), which also includes the Schönau on Königssee 5km/3mi south of town, Obersalzberg 4km/2.5mi east, Marktschellenberg 9km/6mi north, Ramsau 9km/6mi west, and Bischofswiesen 5km/3mi north.
- **Don't Miss:** Königssee, Eagle's Nest, Roßfeld-Höhenringstraße.
- **Timing:** Allow a full day, preferably two, to enjoy this region's outstanding natural beauty.
- ♣♣ **Kids:** The salt mines.

The Berchtesgaden salt mines, which started operating in 1517, brought prosperity to a once very poor region. The salty rock is washed by water and the resulting brine *(Sole)* is piped to Bad Reichenhall to be refined. On the **tour**, visitors get to dress in miner's overalls, take a small train, whoosh down wooden slides and raft across an illuminated underground lake.

Dokumentationszentrum Obersalzberg★★

Salzbergstraße 41. Open Apr–Oct, daily 9am–5pm; Nov–Mar, Tue–Sun 10am–3pm; Closed Jan 1, Nov 1, Dec 24, 25 & 31. 3€. (08652) 94 79 60. *www.obersalzberg.de.*
After the American military handed the Obersalzberg back to the Bavarian government in 1996, the decision was made to document the area's sinister past in a multi-lingual, multimedia exhibition centre. Open since 1999, it stands

Obersalzberg

Adolf Hitler first visited and fell in love with the Obersalzberg area in 1923 and began spending summers in the Wachenfeld House in 1928. After seizing power in 1933, he had the property enlarged and turned into the elegant Berghof chalet. Many of the party brass built their own estates, including Martin Bormann and Hermann Göring, thus gradually turning the Obersalzberg into the southern Nazi party headquarters alongside Berlin. Most of the compound was destroyed by British and American bombs in April 1945. The Bavarian government demolished the remaining ruins in 1952; a year later the American military made the area a recreation zone.

on the foundations of the former Nazi guesthouse "Hoher Göll". A visit here is an essential, if disturbing, experience.

EXCURSIONS
Kehlsteinhaus★★
(Eagle's Nest)

▶ *4km/2.5mi east.*

🕐 *Buses operate mid-May–Oct, daily 8.55am–4pm, every 25min. ⬡15.50€. (08652) 2969. www.kehlsteinhaus.de.*

One of the region's most impressive **panoramas**★★ unfolds from the Eagle's Nest lodge atop Mount Kehlstein at 1 834m/6 020ft. A restaurant today, it was originally a gift from the Nazi party to Hitler on his 50th birthday and is the only remaining Third Reich-era building. It took 3 000 workers 13 months to build the steep **road**★★★ leading all the way up the mountain. Today, special shuttle buses make the vertigo-inducing ascent from the parking lot at Hintereck. At the end of the road, a lift hewn

straight through the rock ascends the final 100m/328ft. **Views**★★★ extend across the German and Austrian Alps, while the Königssee shimmers below like an emerald jewel.

Königssee★★

▶ *5km/3.1mi south.*

🕐 *Boats leave year-round approx every 30min. Allow 1hr 45min round trip, plus at least 1hr for short walks ashore. ⬡12.80€ to St. Bartholomä, 15.80€ to Salet. 𝄞(08652) 963 60; www.seenschifffahrt.de.*

This long, narrow lake is one of the most romantic sites in Bavaria and the heart of the Berchtesgaden National Park. With the Watzmann, Germany's second-highest mountain (2 713m/8 900ft) looming above, the lake narrows at St. Bartholomä, where you can visit the onion-domed pilgrimage **Chapel of St. Bartholomä**. From here, an easy to moderate trail *(1hr)* leads to the **Eiska-**

Chapel of St. Bartholomä by Königssee

©Sándor Kelemen/istockphoto.com

pelle★★, an ice grotto formed by avalanches and constantly changing shape and size (😊 *do not enter – dangerous!*). More trails leave from the final boat stop at Salet, including the easy 15min trek to the **Obersee** and the 400m/1 312ft Röthbach Falls.

For birds eye-views of the lake and the surrounding peaks, take the Jennerbahn **cable-car** up the 1 800m/5 900ft Mount Jenner (🚠20.80€ round-trip).

Maps and information can be picked up at the **Nationalpark-Haus** (*Franziskanerplatz 7;* 🕐 *open Mon–Sat 9am-5pm;* 🖉 *(08652) 643 43; www.nationalpark-berchtesgaden.de*) in central Berchtesgaden.

Hintersee★
▶ *12km/7.4mi west via B305.*
The road climbs the narrow Ramsau Valley to reach this lake framed by the domes of the Reiteralpe and the teeth of Hochkalter. The eastern shore, the "enchanted forest" (*Zauberwald*) bordering it, and the shady lakeshore make this a popular destination for hikers, especially families.

Almbachklamm (Almbach Gorge)★★
▶ *5km/3mi north via the B305.*
Considered one of the prettiest gorges in the Bavarian Alps, this one is carved into the cliffs behind a traditional inn and 17C marble mill that still grinds big chunks of rocks into smooth balls.

A trail follows the creek past waterfalls and pools, crossing more than two dozen iron footbridges along the way. From the top of the gorge, return either the same way or continue via a steepish trail to the village of Ettenberg with its lovely pilgrimage chapel. Allow about 90min for the gorge only or 2hrs 30min for the trek to Ettenberg.

🚗 DRIVING TOUR

ROSSFELD PANORAMASTRAßE★★
Round-trip of 29km/18mi east of Berchtesgaden (anticlockwise) 1hr 30min. Toll 🚗 *4.60€ car & driver, 1.90€ per passenger.* 🖉 *(08652) 574 10, www.rossfeldpanoramastrasse.de.*

The **Rossfeld Panoramic Road** (*open year-round*) ascends the crest of the Austrian valley of the Salzach and overlooks the Tennengebirge. The Dachstein with its glittering glaciers fills the background. On the other side of the ridge is a view over Berchtesgaden, Salzburg and the peaks of Hoher Göll, Kehlstein and Untersberg. From the Hennenkopf car park, it is only a few minutes' climb to Hennenkopf Cross at 1 551m/5 089ft. The road plunges down from the crest after the Rossfeldhütte (inn) and winds through the charming valleys of the Oberau region.

Almbachklamm

© Rainer Schmidt/Bigstockphoto.com

Regensburg★★

Regensburg is among the most delightful towns in eastern Bavaria with a history going back 2 000 years. Its remarkably well-preserved medieval centre is punctuated by a stunning cathedral, an ancient stone bridge and Italianate patrician towers. In 2006, it made UNESCO's list of World Heritage Sites.

A BIT OF HISTORY

Preserved by time – Regensburg began in 179 AD as a Roman garrison guarding the empire's natural frontier of the Danube at its most northerly point. The town was converted to Christianity in the 7C, and St. Boniface founded a bishopric there in 739, making it a centre of religious life in the Middle Ages. As the seat of the Bavarian dukes (6C–13C), the town developed into an important trading post. It became part of Bavaria in the 19C and lost influence to Munich, a circumstance that spared it from bombardment during World War II. Today its city centre is one of the best-preserved medieval towns in Germany.

The city of diets – Once a Free Imperial City, Regensburg hosted plenary sessions of the Imperial Diet charged with responsibility for the internal peace and external security within the Holy Roman Empire. From 1663 to 1806 the city was the seat of a permanent diet, which drew representatives from 70 states to Regensburg.

WALKING TOUR
OLD TOWN
Allow half a day.

Kathedrale St. Peter★
Domplatz 1. ○*Open Apr–Oct, daily 6.30am–6pm; Nov–Mar, 6.30am–5pm.* ℰ*(0941) 597 10 02.* *www.bistum-regensburg.de.*
Construction of this cathedral began after 1260 but was essentially brought to a halt in 1525; the spires were not added until the 19C. The **Eselsturm** (Donkey Tower), above the northern transept is

- **Population:** 133 500
- **Info:** Altes Rathaus. ℰ(0941) 507 44 10. www.regensburg.de.
- **Location:** Regensburg is located in eastern Bavaria and spans the Danube at the crossroads of the A3 and A93.
- **Parking:** Garages are located throughout Regensburg. Visit http://wap.parkinfo.com for fees and locations.
- **Don't Miss:** The cathedral, the view from the left bank.
- **Timing:** Allow at least a full day for this lovely city.

all that remains of the original Romanesque sanctuary. The **west front**, richly decorated, is the work of a local family of sculptors named Roritzer. The main entrance, flanked by two neo-Gothic towers, is unusual, with a triangular, jutting porch. A statue of St. Peter can be seen on the pier.
Inside, the huge late-Gothic nave houses two 13C masterpieces of local Gothic statuary: the archangel Gabriel and, opposite, Mary at the Annunciation. The three chancel windows are adorned with beautiful 14C stained **glass**★★. The

The Gorges of the "Donaudurchbruch"

Between Kelheim and Kloster Weltenburg, the Danube narrows as it "breaks through" steep, narrow limestone cliffs in a series of meanders. The best way to view this beautiful gorge is on a boat cruise. Up to 20 tours depart from Kelheim daily from mid-March to October. Drop by the tourist office or visit www.schiffahrt-kelheim.de for a timetable. The round-trip is 7.80€.

Detail of Kathedrale St. Peter

M. Hertlein/MICHELIN

cathedral is home to a famous boys' choir, the Regensburger Domspatzen.

Domschatz
(Cathedral Treasury)
Krauterermarkt 3. In the south wing of the bishops' residence (Bischofshof), entrance via the courtyard.
○Open Apr–Oct, Tue–Sat 10am–5pm, Sun noon–5pm, Dec–Mar, Fri–Sat 10am–4pm, Sun noon–4pm.
○Closed Jan 1, Nov 2–30, Dec 24–Jan 6. ☞2€. ℘(0941) 576 45.
www.bistumsmuseen-regensburg.de.
The cathedral's treasury displays liturgical items, reliquaries and vestments from the 11C to the 18C.

Kreuzgang (Cloister)
Access via the cathedral garden.
Inside the cloister, traces of ancient frescoes adorn the walls of the Romanesque **Allerheiligenkapelle** (All Saints Chapel). The old 11C Stefanskapelle is another highlight with an altar reliquary thought to date from the 5C–8C.

▶ *Move towards the apse of the cathedral for a closer look at the stonemasonry.*

Museum St. Ulrich★
Domplatz 2. ○Open Apr–Oct, Tue–Sun 10am–5pm. ☞2€. ℘(0941) 516 88.
www.bistumsmuseen-regensburg.de.

The museum in the early-Gothic **Ulrichskirche** presents religious art from the 11C to the 20C, including bishops' crosses, reliquaries and paintings. The church itself is decorated with murals from the 13C to the 16C.

▶ *Make your way to Alter Kornmarkt via the Romanesque Römerturm (Roman Tower), which is connected to the ducal residence (Herzogshof).*

Alte Kapelle★
(Old Chapel)
St.-Kassians-Platz 7.
The Basilica of Our Lady associated with this chapel stands on the south side of Alter Kornmarkt. Originally Carolingian, the Alte Kapelle was completely transformed in the Rococo style in the 18C. The splendid reredos, the painted ceiling and the gilded stuccowork are beautifully accented by the light penetrating the tall windows. It is only open during services but you can see the interior through a glass pane.

Porta Praetoria
On your left are remnants of the ancient wall and the north gate of the 2C Roman camp, which covered almost 25 ha/ 62 acres.

▶ *Turn right and go down to the Danube.*

Steinerne Brücke
(Stone Bridge)

This 310m/1 017ft-long bridge from the 12C rests on 16 arches and for many centuries was the only crossing across the Danube for a long distance.

From the middle, there is a fine **view**★ of the old town. In the foreground is the 14C Brückturm gateway, flanked by the huge roof of the 17C Salzstadel (salt loft). Beside this building, on the quayside, is the **Historische Wurstküche**, the oldest sausage kitchen in Germany.

Goliathstraße

Goliath House, with its monumental 16C frescoes, stands out among several interesting houses flanking this street. At Watmarkt 4 stands a fine Gothic patrician tower with a private chapel on the ground floor (now a restaurant), a first-floor balcony and a residential wing.

Altes Rathaus and Reichstagsmuseum★ (Old Town Hall and Imperial Diet Museum)

Guided tours (1hr), Apr–Oct 9.30am–4pm, every half-hour (3pm tour in English); Nov, Dec & Mar 10am, 11.30am, 1.30pm, 2pm, 3pm and 3.30pm (2pm in English); Jan–Feb 10am, 11.30am, 1.30pm and 3pm. Closed Jan 1, Shrove Tue, Dec 24 & 25. 7.50€. (0941) 507 34 40. *www.museen-regensburg.de.*

The eight-storey tower of the old town hall dates from 1250. The Gothic western section was built c. 1360. The façade includes a gabled doorway and a pedestal supporting a charming oriel window. Tours include a stop in the *Reichssaal* (Imperial Hall) where the delegates of the permanent diet once gathered.

Haidplatz★

This square is surrounded by historic buildings, including the Zum Goldenen Kreuz inn (at no 7) with a stone tower and façade. In the centre of the square is the 1656 **Justitiabrunnen** (Justice Fountain).

Schottenkirche St. Jakob
(Scottish Church of St. Jacob)

Protected by a glass roof, the portal of this ruined church, founded by Irish Benedictine monks in 1090, is a Romanesque masterpiece (1183).

Its complex iconography is still not fully understood, although it is possible to identify scenes from the Last Judgement: note the representations of the good deeds on the left and the bad deeds on the right.

Bismarckplatz

In Roman times and also in the Middle Ages warehouses stood on this lively square on the edge of the city centre. Today, it is dominated by two 19C Neoclassical buildings. Sporting a columned portico, the Präsidialpalais (Presidential Palace) at the southern end was home to the French delegation in town for the Imperial Perpetual Diet. The imposing building on the square's north side is the municipal theatre (*Stadttheater*).

The former embassy of Württemberg stands at the corner of Gesandtenstraße (street of the envoys). Further down this street, the Trinity Church (Dreieinigkeitskirche) is surrounded by ornate Baroque epitaphs of several of these ambassadors.

▶ *From Gesandtenstraße, turn left on Rote-Hahnen-Gasse, then right on Hinter der Grieb.*

Hinter der Grieb

This alley and the surrounding lanes are flanked with patrician houses from the Middle Ages. At the bottom is a beautiful view of the cathedral.

☺ A Bit of Advice ☺

Nothing goes better with Bavarian *Bratwurst* than *Händlmaier's süßer Hausmachersenf*, the sweet, smoky mustard: a Regensburg speciality concocted by Johanna Händlmaier in 1914 to sell in her butcher's shop as the perfect accompaniment to her husband's sausages.

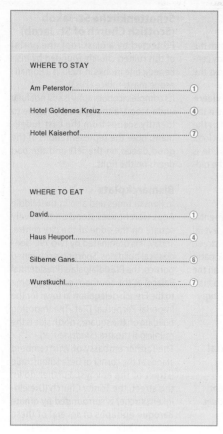

WHERE TO STAY

Am Peterstor..①

Hotel Goldenes Kreuz................................④

Hotel Kaiserhof..⑦

WHERE TO EAT

David...①

Haus Heuport...④

Silberne Gans...⑥

Wurstkuchl...⑦

⊳ *Upon arriving in Untere Bachgasse, head down an alleyway at no 7 which leads to Wahlenstraße 16. Turn right to get to Kramgasse alley that leads back to the cathedral.*

ADDITIONAL SIGHTS
Kunstforum Ostdeutsche Galerie (Art Forum East German Gallery)
Dr. Johann-Maeir-Straße 5. ⏰*Open year-round, Tue–Sun 10am–5pm (Thu 8pm).* ⏰*Closed Jan 1, Shrove Tue, 1 May, 1 Nov, Dec 24–25 & 31.* ⊜*6€.* ☏*(0941) 29 71 40 .*
www.kog-regensburg.de.
Smartly presented in 15 bright galleries organised by style or subject matter, this collection presents a thorough survey of Eastern European art from the 19C (Romantic period) to the late 20C. Artists represented include the Impressionist Lovis Corinth, German expressionists and Secession artists Otto Dix and Oskar Kokoschka as well as Käthe Kollwitz who is famous for her emotionally charged bronze sculptures.

AROUND ST. EMMERAM SQUARE
Basilika St. Emmeram
Emmeramsplatz 3. ⏰*Open year-round, daily 10am–4.30pm.* ☏ *(0941) 510 30.*
This was once the abbey church of an 8C Benedictine monastery. A Gothic gateway on **Emmeramsplatz** leads to the huge Romanesque porch (12C) and the double doors at the church entrance whose 11C sculptures (depicting Jesus Christ, St. Emmeram and St. Dionysius) are among the oldest in Germany.

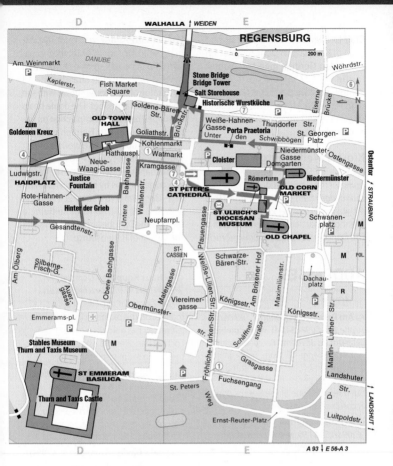

Schloss Thurn und Taxis (Thurn and Taxis Castle)

Emmeramsplatz 5. Guided tours (80min), Apr–Oct, Tue–Fri 11am, 2pm, 3pm, 4pm, Sat–Sun also 10am; Nov–Mar Sat–Sun 10am, 11am, 2pm, 3pm. Closed Dec 24 &25. 11.50€. (0941) 504 81 33. www.thurnundtaxis.de.

The Thurn and Taxis princes held the German postal monopoly until the 19C. As compensation for losing the monopoly, they were given the St. Emmeram abbey buildings, which the family has occupied since 1816. Tours take in the state apartments, lavishly decorated in Historicist style, as well as the cloister of the Basilica St. Emmeram.

Fürstliche Schatzkammer (Treasury)

Open Apr–early Nov, Mon–Fri 11am–5pm, Sat–Sun 10am–5pm, early Nov–late Mar Sat–Sun 10am–5pm. 4.50€. (0941) 504 81 33. Closed Dec 24–25.

The north wing of the Neoclassical former stables contains a branch of the Bavarian National museum. Displays include furniture, porcelain and weapons from leading workshops in Europe.

EXCURSIONS
Walhalla★

11km/6.8mi east.
Open Apr–Sept, daily 9am–5.45pm; Oct 9am–4.45pm; Nov–Mar, 10am–11.45am, 1pm–3.45pm. Closed Shrove Tue, Dec 24, 25 & 31. 4€. (09403) 96 16 80. www.walhalla-regensburg.de.

Built between 1830 and 1842 by Ludwig I of Bavaria, this Doric temple honours great German men and women. Inside are 127 marble busts and 64 commemorative plaques of famous soldiers, artists and scientists, politicians, musicians and other movers, shakers and thinkers.

Kloster Weltenburg★

◗ *33km/20.5mi southwest, on the banks of the Danube.* ◷*Open year-round, daily 8am–6pm.* ♿♬*(09441) 20 40. www.klosterschenke-weltenburg.de.* Right on a particularly scenic stretch of the Danube Gorge *(Donaudurchbruch)*,

Weltenburg Abbey was built by Cosmas Damian Asam in 1718. Its impressive church boasts an oval narthex and nave as well as a high altar dominated by a statue of St. George shown with the dead dragon at his feet. The dome bears a *trompe-l'œil* Asam composition on the theme of the Church Triumphant.

The abbey operates the world's oldest monastic brewery (since 1050) and has an enchanting beer garden. The nicest way to get here is by boat *(operates late Mar–Oct, 40min to abbey, 20min back; ⊕8.20€ round-trip)* from Kelheim, a town on the Danube about 30km/18.5mi southwest of Regensburg.

ADDRESSES

🏠STAY

⊜**Am Peterstor** – *Fröhliche-Türken-Straße 12.* ℰ*0941 545 45. www.hotel-am-peterstor.de. 36 rooms. Reception open 7am–11am, 4pm–10.30pm.* There are few facilities at this basic but comfortable hotel, located 5min from the centre, but it remains one of the best budget accommodations in town.

⊜⊟**Hotel Kaiserhof** – *Kramgasse 10.* ℰ*(0941) 58 53 50. www.kaiserhof-am-dom.de. 30 rooms.* Welcoming guestrooms all offer views of the cathedral's twin towers. The breakfast room is set in a former 14C chapel with a high vaulted ceiling.

⊜⊟⊟**Hotel Goldenes Kreuz** – *Haidplatz 7.* ℰ*0941 558 12. www.hotel-goldeneskreuz.de. 9 rooms. Café open daily 7am–7pm, Sun and hols 9am–7pm.* This has been the city's most famous hotel since the 16C and it has recently re-opened its doors. In contrast with the beams, ancient stone and frescoes, bedrooms are light and modern.

🍴/EAT

⊜**Wurstkuchl** – *Thundorferstraße 3.* ℰ*0941 466 210. www.wurstkuchl.de. Open 8am–7pm.* 500-year-old tavern by the Old Stone Bridge. Try the homemade sausages cooked on the charcoal grill, accompanied by sauerkraut and *Wurstkuchl* mustard.

⊜⊟**Haus Heuport** – *Domplatz 7* ℰ*(0941) 599 92 97. www.heuport.de. Closed 2 weeks in Jan.* This beautiful 13C mansion in the old town (opposite the cathedral) has a small restaurant and cocktail bar. Simple cuisine is served in the dining room or on the terrace.

⊜⊟⊟**Silberne Gans** – *Werftstraße 3.* ℰ*0941 280 55 98. www.silbernegans.de. Closed Mon and first fortnight Jan.* This ultra-modern restaurant occupies a beautifully renovated historic house on the Danube. Pretty summer terrace.

⊜⊟⊟⊟**David** – *Watmarkt 5.* ℰ*(0941) 56 18 58. Closed carnival week, 2 weeks in Aug, Sun and Mon.* Accessed by lift, this 5th-floor restaurant in a historic mansion serves Mediterranean cuisine in a romantic atmosphere. A covered terrace offers views of the town.

🍵TAKING A BREAK

Café Goldenes Kreuz – *Haidplatz 7.* ℰ*(0941) 5 72 32.* This elegant café is in a historic building with abundant Gothic design details. In summer enjoy the people-watching from the terrace facing vibrant Haidplatz.

🍸 NIGHTLIFE

Brauhaus Joh. Albrecht – *Schwarze-Bärenstraße 6.* ℰ*(0941) 510 55. www.brauhaus-joh-albrecht.de.* This lively micro-brewery serves delicious beers that pair up exceptionally well with the hearty regional dishes dominating the menu.

Eichstätt★★

Eichstätt, a small episcopal town and seat of a Catholic university, owes its Baroque character to its reconstruction after the Thirty Years' War; only the cathedral survived the burning of the town by the Swedish army. But Eichstätt is also a centre of contemporary architecture with dazzling buildings designed by Karljosef Schattner, Karl Frey and Günther Behnisch.

▶ **Population:** 13 100

🗎 **Info:** Domplatz 8.
  ℘(08421) 600 14 00.
  www.eichstaett.info.

◑ **Location:** Eichstätt lies in the midst of the Altmühl Valley natural park.

🐾 **Don't Miss:** The cathedral and the Residenzplatz.

🕐 **Timing:** About half a day to take in Eichstätt's highlights.

SIGHTS
Dom★ (Cathedral)
Like so many churches in Germany, the 14C cathedral is characterised by a mix of architectural styles. The east tower is Romanesque, the Gothic main portal is decorated with Biblical figures and scenes, while the west face was crafted by Baroque masters Jakob Engel and Gabriel de Gabrieli.

The Gothic **cloister**★ was a 15C addition to the cathedral.

As you enter, turn left towards the late 15C **Pappenheim Altar**★★ in the north transept. Carved from Jura limestone, it rises almost 9m/29.5ft high. On the other end, in the Gothic west choir, is a famous 1514 statue by Loy Hering depicting Eichstätt's first 8C bishop **St. Willibald**. Willibald's relics are housed in the elaborate canopied Baroque altar by Matthias Seynold behind the statue.

Leaving the cathedral via the eastern exit takes you to the **Mortuarium**★, a late-Gothic funerary chapel paved with elaborate **tombstones**. The four **stained-glass windows** on the east wall depicting the Last Judgement are by Hans Holbein the Elder (c. 1500).

The **Diözesanmuseum** (cathedral treasury; ◑open Apr–Oct, Wed–Fri 10.30am–5pm, Sat–Sun, 10am–5pm; ⊛3€, Sun 1€; ℘(08421) 502 66) is located in historical rooms above the cloister that were turned into a modern exhibition space by Karljosef Schattner. Its 12 rooms are filled with outstanding examples of ecclesiastical art. Highlights include a gold and jewel-encrusted finger reliquary of St. Jacob (12C), intricately

woven Baroque tapestries, lavish monstrances and late medieval sculpture.

Residenzplatz★
Next to the cathedral, Residenzplatz is framed by lavish Rococo townhouses, including the bishop's palace, that are the legacy of master builders Gabriel de Gabrieli and Maurizio Pedetti. An 18m/59ft-high column of the Virgin Mary rises from a cherub-festooned fountain in front of the bishop's palace.

Willibaldsburg (Willibald Castle)
Burgstraße 19.
This 14C hilltop castle is largely the work of Augsburg Renaissance architect Elias Holl. Within its confines are two museums, a garden with fantastic **views**★★ of the river and town and a hand-carved **well** *(Tiefer Brunnen)* that is an astonishing 76m/249.3ft deep.

The **Jura-Museum**★ (◑open Apr–Sept, Tue–Sun 9am–6pm; Oct–Mar, Tue–Sun 10am–4pm; ◑closed Jan 1, Shrove Tue, Dec 24, 25 & 31; ⊛4€; ♿ ℘(08421) 29 56) has a fabulous collection of locally found fossils that should get even amateurs excited. Pride of place goes to an extremely rare fossilised skeleton of an archeopteryx, the creature that constitutes the evolutionary link between reptiles and birds.

Upstairs, the **Museum of Pre-History and Early History** (◑see Jura-Museum; ⊛4€; ℘(09141) 894 50) chronicles regional history from the Stone Age to the early Middle Ages and counts a mammoth skeleton, Celtic weapons and Roman measuring devices among its possessions.

EXCURSION
Schloss Ellingen (Elligen Palace)

▶ *29km/18mi northwest of Eichstätt.*
🚌 *Guided tours, hourly, Apr–Sept, Tue–Sun 9am–6pm; Oct–Mar, Tue–Sun 10am–4pm.* 🕐 *Closed Jan 1, Shrove Tue, Dec 24, 25 & 31.* 🎫 *4€.* 📞 *(09141) 974 790.*

ADDRESSES

🏨 STAY

🛏 **Hotel Zum Hirschen** – *Brückenstraße 9, 85072 Eichstätt-Wasserzell.* 📞 *(08421) 96 80. www.hirschenwirt.de. Closed Jan–mid-Feb. 40 rooms. Restaurant* 🍽. Family-owned and family-friendly, the Hirschen is a good base for Altmühltal explorations. Rooms are timeless and functional with country-style décor. Enjoy robust regional dishes in the restaurant with winter garden.

Ellingen served as the regional seat of the Teutonic Knights from the 13C until Napoleon's dissolution of the order in 1806. The **palace** *(Schloss)* was designed by Franz Keller (1718–25) and is largely Baroque infused with Neoclassical elements. The chapel has frescoes by Cosmas Damian Asam and stuccowork by Franz Roth. The huge twin-flight **main staircase**★ is worth seeing, as is the small museum on the history of the Teutonic Order.

🛏🍽 **Hotel Adler** – *Marktplatz 22.* 📞 *(08421) 67 67. www.adler-eichstaett.de. Closed Dec 18–Jan 10, Feb 1–7, Oct 30–Nov 5. 28 rooms.* This restored Baroque building has good-sized rooms with cherrywood furnishings. No smoking throughout.

🍴 EAT

🛏🍽 **Gasthof Krone** – *Domplatz 3.* 📞 *(08421) 44 06. www.krone-eichstaett.de. Closed Wed.* In the heart of the old town, this pleasant brewery-owned tavern is great for winding down and enjoying fresh, rib-sticking Bavarian food.

Burghausen★★

Right on the border with Austria, Burghausen has a lovely, well-preserved old town crowned by the longest hilltop fortress in Germany. The dukes of Bavaria, who became rulers of Burghausen in the 12C, converted its medieval castle into this formidable defence system that stretches for an impressive 1 043m/3 420ft atop a narrow, rocky spur.

SIGHTS
Burg★★ (Castle)

Leave your car in the Stadtplatz and walk along the circular cliff road. Beneath the Wöhrenseeturm and beyond the lake, a steep path leads to the outer fortifications. From here, the ramparts are visible, stepped up the Eggenberg hill. The Georgstor, or **St. George's Gate**, is set

- ▶ **Population:** 18 250
- ℹ **Info:** Stadtplatz 112. 📞 (08677) 88 71 40. www.tourismus.burghausen.de.
- ▶ **Location:** Burghausen lies within a curve of the River Salzach, which forms the border between Germany and Austria.
- ▶ **Don't Miss:** The Burg from which Burghausen takes its name.
- 🕐 **Timing:** Allow two to three hours to visit the Burg and its museums.

in the innermost ring of battlements, which protect the last small medieval courtyard at the castle's centre. Inside are two museums worth visiting.

Staatsgalerie in der Burg
(Bavarian Picture Gallery)
🕐*Open Apr–Sept, daily 9am–6pm, Oct–Mar, daily 10am–4pm.* 👓*3€.* 📞*(08677) 46 59. www.pinakothek. de/zweiggalerien/burghausen.*

The former ducal apartments in the main castle building house this small branch of the famous Munich Pinakothek art museum. The focus is on 15C and 16C paintings, sculpture and tapestries made in Austria and Bavaria.

From the observation **platform** *(62 steps, access from the second floor),* enjoy splendid panoramic **views**★ of Burghausen, the Salzach and the surrounding hills. The Gothic **chapel** *(in the same wing)* has elegant star vaulting.

Stadtmuseum
(Municipal Museum)
🕐*Open mid-Mar–Apr & Oct, daily 10am –4pm; May–Sept, daily 9am–6pm.* 👓*2€.* 📞*(08677) 651 98. www.burghausen.de/stadtmuseum.*

The duchess' former private quarters *(main castle, last door on the right)* now tell the history of Burghausen through an eclectic collection of tools, weapons, folk art, furniture, town models, paintings and sculpture spread over four floors. ⊶The museum will be closed for renovation from late 2010 to 2012.

EXCURSIONS
Raitenhaslach
▶ *6km/3.7mi south.*
Red marble tombstones commemorating 15C–18C abbots are a key feature of this 12C Cistercian church, modified in the Baroque style in the late 17C. The life of St. Bernard of Clairvaux is illustrated in the fine **ceiling frescoes** (1739) by Johannes Zick of Lachen.

Tittmoning
▶ *16km/10mi south.*
On the west bank of the Salzach, Tittmoning preserves the remains of its medieval fortifications and a castle, a former residence of the Prince-Bishops of Salzburg. Two fortified gateways give access to the broad **Stadtplatz.** Brightly painted façades, some deco-

rated with gilded figures, wrought iron signs, oriel windows and emblazoned fountains make this town a charming place to stop.

Altötting
▶ *21km/13mi northwest.*
Each year, Altötting draws more than a million pilgrims who come to see the "Miraculous Virgin", a black Madonna, housed in the tiny, octagonal 8C **Gnadenkapelle**★ (Chapel of Mercy). Its walls are decorated with silver urns containing the hearts of Bavarian rulers.

The most famous item in the treasury of the **Gothic Collegiate Church** *(Stiftskirche)* across Kapellplatz square is the 15C **Goldenes Rössl**★★ (golden horse), an exquisitely-detailed portable gold altar given to Charles VI of France by his wife, Isabella of Bavaria.

Marktl am Inn
▶ *10km/6.2mi north.*
This riverside village was thrust into the world's spotlight in 2005 when local boy Joseph Ratzinger (b. 1927) became Pope Benedikt XVI.

The pontiff's **Birth House** *(Marktplatz;* 🕐*open Easter Mon-Oct, Tue–Fri 10am–noon, 2pm–6pm, Sat–Sun 10am–6pm;* 👓*3.50€;* 📞*(08678) 747 680)* has been turned into a small museum. It is opposite the church, **Pfarrkirche St. Oswald,** where he was baptised.

ADDRESSES

🛏STAY
⊜⊜ **Hotel Post** – *Stadtplatz 39.* 📞*(08677) 96 50. www.hotelpost.de. 24 rooms. Restaurant* ⊜⊜. This central inn has rooms that range from rustic to elegant and a restaurant serving modernised Bavarian home-cooking.

⊜⊜ **Bayerische Alm** – *Robert-Koch-Straße 211.* 📞*(08677) 98 20. www.bayerischealm.de. 23 rooms. Restaurant* ⊜⊜. Enjoy views of the Burg from your private balcony at this family-run inn on the town outskirts. The bi-level restaurant and beer garden serve fresh, light and healthy fare.

Passau★★

Passau enjoys an enchanting setting at the confluence of the Inn, the Danube (Donau) and the little Ilz rivers. The old town, with its Baroque churches and patrician houses, crowds onto the narrow tongue of land separating the Inn and the Danube. The Oberhaus fortress looms above town on a wooded bluff on the northern bank of the Danube. Right on the border with Austria and close to the Czech Republic, Passau also makes a good base for explorations of Bohemia and Upper Austria.

A BIT OF HISTORY

The Passau bishopric was founded in the 8C by St. Boniface, the English-born "Apostle of Germany". By the late 10C it had become extraordinarily powerful and, until the 15C, encompassed the entire Danube Valley, including Vienna. From the Middle Ages on, river trade (especially of salt, also called the "white gold") played an important role in Burghausen's prosperity. Today, it is a popular river cruise stop en route to Vienna and Budapest.

▶ **Population:** 50 000
▯ **Info:** Rathausplatz 3, 94032 Passau. ☎(0851) 95 59 80. www.passau.de.
◖ **Location:** Passau is in eastern Bavaria, right on the border with Austria, and consists of three quarters: Ilzstadt to the north, Innstadt to the south, and the peninsula of Altstadt.
🅿 **Parking:** Find parking on the Domplatz and south of the Schanzlbrücke.
🅐 **Don't Miss:** Views from the Veste Oberhaus, Dom St. Stephan, the Three Rivers Point.
🕓 **Timing:** Allow a day to enjoy Passau at leisure.

SIGHTS
OLD TOWN
Dom St. Stephan

Most of this late-Gothic **cathedral** was destroyed by fire in the 17C and rebuilt in the Baroque style.

The cavernous sanctuary is richly decorated with frescoes and stuccowork.

Old Town by the River Inn

© Daniel Hermann/Dreamstime.com

Four **lateral chapels** feature paintings by the Austrian artist JM Rottmayr (1654–1730). From the Residenzplatz, visitors can admire the cathedral's **east end**★★, a remarkable late-Gothic work. The cathedral also houses the world's largest **organ**★★ with 17 774 pipes and 233 stops.

Residenzplatz

The square is bordered on the south by the early Neoclassical bishops' **New Palace**. The surrounding streets are still lined by arcaded houses with corbelling and concealed ridge roofs.

Rathausplatz

The 14C **Rathaus** (town hall) with its painted façade dominates this picturesque square. The tower dates to the late 18C.

Glasmuseum★★

Am Rathausplatz, in the Hotel "Wilder Mann". ⃝*Open year-round, daily 1pm–5pm.* ⃝*5€.* ⃝*(0851) 350 71. www.glasmuseum.de.*
Glassware from Bohemia, Bavaria and Austria from 1700 to 1950 makes up the bulk of this precious collection of 30 000 pieces. The most important display comes from **Bohemia** (*Biedermeier, Historicism, Jugendstil*); note especially the Lobmeyr state goblet depicting the Marriage of Neptune with Amphitrite, which is considered a key glasswork of the 19C.

Dreiflüsseeck★ (Three Rivers Point)

From St. Michaels-Kirche, go down to the Inn quayside.
The fast-flowing Inn River runs past the Schaiblingsturm (1481), once used to store salt. At the confluence of the three rivers, the greenish current of the Inn can be spotted running alongside the brown Danube waters and dark water of the Ilz before they mingle.
From the Danube bank, on the far side of the promontory, there is a fine viewpoint.

THE LEFT BANK OF THE DANUBE
Veste Oberhaus (Fortress)

This imposing citadel was built in 1219 as a refuge for the bishops against rebellious burghers. It is linked with the Veste Niederhaus by a fortified road. From the belvedere marked *Zur Aussicht*, near the parking lot, and from atop the tower *(142 steps)*, there are magnificent **views**★★ over the Inn, the Danube and Passau itself. The town's history, art and religious roots, including some paintings from the Danube School, are traced in the small **Oberhausmuseum**.

EXCURSION
Bayerischer Wald★ (Bavarian Forest)

The Bavarian Forest includes low, rounded mountains, wild rock bastions and isolated river valleys, and a protected national park area. The natural woodland draws a wide variety of animal species. Together with the Bohemian Forest on the Czech side, it forms the largest contiguous forest in Europe. The area is known for its glass industry with many studios, factories and shops.

🚗 DRIVING TOURS

SOUTHERN MOUNTAINS: FROM FREYUNG TO ZWIESEL★

Freyung to Zwiesel. 70 km/43.5mi – Allow 2hrs. To get to Freyung from Passau, take the B 12. Continue north to Mauth, then turn left towards Weidhütte.

🚶 Hans-Eisenmann Haus

Neuschönau. ⃝*08 558 96 150. www.nationalpark-bayerischer-wald. de. Open 9am–5pm (4pm from mid-Jan–mid-Mar). Closed mid-Nov–Christmas. Treetop Walk 8€, children 6€.*
Seemingly lost in the heart of the woods, this Bavarian Forest National Park Information Centre is the best place to organise your excursion into the region. There are exhibition rooms

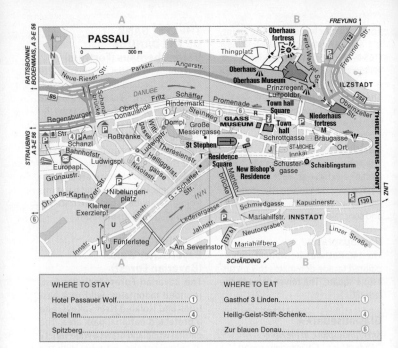

WHERE TO STAY		WHERE TO EAT	
Hotel Passauer Wolf	①	Gasthof 3 Linden	①
Rotel Inn	④	Heilig-Geist-Stift-Schenke	④
Spitzberg	⑥	Zur blauen Donau	⑥

(in German only) and a waymarked footpath *(7km/4mi, 3hrs)* that takes you into the large Tierfreigelände (Wildlife Enclosure) where you can see lynx, bison, wolves, brown bears, wild cats and deer; there are aviaries too. You can also drive here. A major new attraction added to the park in 2010 is the world's longest **tree-top walk** (1 300m/1 422yd) where you can observe the woods as you go, from a height of between 8m/26ft and 25m/82ft off the forest floor.

◐ *Go back to Spiegelau, famous for its glassworks, to continue on to Frauenau.*

Glasmuseum (Glass Museum)★

Am Museumpark 1, Frauenau. 𝒞09 926 941 020. www.glasmuseum-frauenau.de. Open Mon–Fri 9am–5pm, Sat–Sun and hols 10am–4pm. Closed mid-Nov to around Dec 20. ⊜5€.

Reopened in 2005, this museum traces man's 3 000-year love affair with glass and its link between art and industry. On display are many works by American and German 20C artists. Look out for the striking Pop Art exhibits.

NORTHERN MOUNTAINS: AROUND THE GROßER ARBER★

This circular tour departs from Bodenmais (70km/43.5mi north of Passau) and covers about 65km/40mi (allow 3hrs).

◐ *To get to Bodenmais from Passau, take the B85 (Bayerische Ostmarkstraße) to Regen, then turn right.*

Bodenmais★

This town with a healing climate lies in a pastureland at the southern foot of the forest's highest mountain, the Großer Arber (1 456m/4 775ft).

Lam

The charming winter-sports resort of Lam is located at the bottom of a broad valley. The valley rises gradually, to meadows and woods, and to the Lamer Winkel, which marks the start of the valley. A scenic road runs along the mountainside, with views of the Großer Arber, and rises to the pass known as the Brenner Sattel at 1 030m/3 379ft.

Hindenburg-Kanzel★

A **look-out point**★ offers a fine view of the Lamer Winkel and the Arber.

Großer Arber★★

From the lower cable-car terminal, 1hr round trip, including 20min walk. ○*Operates May–first snow, 9am–4.30pm, first snow–mid-Jan, 8.30am–4pm, mid-Jan–Apr 8.30am–4.30pm.* ○*9.50€ round-trip.* ○(09925) 941 40. www.arber.de.

From the upper terminal, a path leads to two rocky crags, one overlooking the **Schwarzer Regen depression**★★, and another (surmounted by a cross) with views of the Lamer Winkel and the forest to the north.

The **Großer Arbersee**★ lake sits to the right as the road winds down through the forest. On the way are several **views**★ of the Zwiesel basin, the Falkenstein and the Großer Rachel.

ADDRESSES

⌂STAY

○ **Rotel Inn** – *Donauufer, 50m/55yd from the main train station (Hauptbahnhof).* ○(0851) 951 60. www.rotel-inn.de. *Closed Oct–Apr. 93 rooms.* This hotel on the bank of the Danube has single and double rooms, but bathrooms are down the hall.

○○ **Hotel Passauer Wolf** – *Rindermarkt 6.* ○(0851) 931 51 10. *40 rooms. Restaurant*○○. This traditional establishment is mid-way between the Danube and the *Altstadt*'s pedestrian zone. Each room is furnished uniquely and the restaurant delivers rustic meals with beautiful river views on the side.

○○○ **Spitzberg** – *Neuburger Straße 29.* ○0851 95 54 80. www.hotel-spitzberg.de. *35 rooms.* ○. This striking modern 4-star hotel is very close to the old town and has attractive bedrooms.

⍟ EAT

○ **Gasthof 3 Linden** – *Steinweg 6.* ○0851 756 83 83. www.3linden-passau.de. Traditional and modern cuisine is served in a trendy setting in this beautiful ancient stone *gasthof.* House specialities include *Krustenschweinbraten* (baked pork) and *Käsespätzle* (cheese noodles).

○○ **Heilig-Geist-Stift-Schenke** – *Heiliggeistgasse 4.* ○(0851) 26 07. *Closed Jan 6–31 and Wed.* This establishment built in 1358 has a cosy, rustic atmosphere. Expect beautiful vaulted ceilings, open fires and a charming vine-covered garden.

○○○ **Zur blauen Donau** – *Höllgasse 14 (Fritz-Schäffer Promenade).* ○0851 490 86 60. www.blaue-donau-passau.de. Dinner only. Closed Sun–Mon & hols; 1 week mid-Jan; 1st 3 weeks Aug.* This highly regarded and friendly restaurant on the banks of the Danube serves excellent regional cuisine.

⍟ NIGHTLIFE

Café Duft – *Theresienstraße 22.* ○(0851) 346 66. www.cafeduft.de. A former stable, this café also features a terrace on the pedestrian zone. Regional and *tapas* dishes also served, at night in cosy candlelight.

Don't expect *lederhosen* lads or raucous oompah bands – the charms of northern Bavaria go far beyond the tourist brochure clichés. This is a region whose cultural landscape was shaped by some of the world's finest artists, Albrecht Dürer, Tilman Riemenschneider and Balthasar Neumann among them. Germany's most popular holiday route, the fabled Romantic Road, links enchanting villages and proud castles with spirit-lifting scenery. The region's biggest city is Nuremberg, which played special roles during both the Holy Roman Empire and the Third Reich and today is especially famous for its Christmas market. Nearby romantic Bamberg is also steeped in history and suffered hardly any wartime damage.

Highlights

1 The dazzling Riemenschneider altar in **Creglingen** (p475)

2 The Grand Staircase in the Residence in **Würzburg** (p479)

3 Sunset views of the Tauber Valley from **Rothenburg** old town (p485)

4 Tucking into an original **Nuremberg** sausage (p496)

5 Artistic masterpieces in the interior of **Bamberg** Cathedral (p497)

Tripping Romantic

A trip along the Romantic Road is a wonderfully rewarding experience. Leaving Würzburg with its vineyard-ribboned hills and show-stopping Residence, the road carves through the idyllic Tauber Valley where you should stop at the palace of the Teutonic Order in Weikersheim and at the Riemenschneider altar in Creglingen before losing yourself in the tangle of medieval alleyways of Rothenburg ob der Tauber. Further on, Dinkelsbühl is almost as evocative but gets smaller crowds, while Nördlingen has a unique location inside a meteorite crater. Both are still encircled by their ancient town walls. *(For destinations further south see MUNICH AND SOUTHERN BAVARIA.)*

Triumph & Trauma

South of Rothenburg, the A6 runs east to Nuremberg, a city that has certainly seen its historical ups and downs. It soared to political prominence in 1356 with the passage of the Golden Bull, reached its artistic zenith in the Renaissance under Albrecht Dürer and launched Germany's first railway in 1835. Alas, such glory was tainted in the 20C when the Nazi brass passed the anti-Semitic Nuremberg Laws in 1935 and held its mass party rallies here.

In 1945–46, the Allies chose the city to hold the Nazi war crime trials. Reminders of all these histories remain scattered throughout the town.

Canoeing in the Wiesent valley, Franconian Switzerland

© Alexander Rochau/Fotolia.com

Map Legend

NORTHERN BAVARIA

0 — 30 km

N

Places and Labels

- CZECH REPUBLIC
- SAXONY
- THURINGIA
- HESSE
- BAVARIA
- Fichtelgebirge Nature Park
- Luisenburg
- Eremitage
- Bayreuth
- Neuhaus a. d. Pegnitz
- Gößweinstein
- Hersbrücker Alb
- Franconian Mountains
- Döbraberg 795 173
- Kronach
- Sanspareil
- Franconian Switzerland
- Tiergarten
- Nuremberg
- Playmobil Funpark
- Pilgrimage Church
- Cobourg
- Bamberg
- Volkach
- Dettelbach
- Sulzfeld
- Marktbreit
- Ochsenfurt
- Creglingen
- Detwang
- Feuchtwangen
- Dinkelsbühl
- Wallerstein
- Nördlingen
- Harburg
- Donauwörth
- Regensburg
- DANUBE
- Canal Main-Danube
- Altmühl
- Wurtzbourg
- Sommerhausen
- Veitschöchheim
- Romantic
- Weikersheim
- Bad Mergentheim
- ROTHENBURG
- Route
- Frankfurt am Main
- Fürstenlager
- HEIDELBERG

Directions
- PLZEŇ
- PASSAU
- CHEMNITZ
- LEIPZIG
- ERFURT
- DORTMUND
- MAYENCE
- MANNHEIM
- ULM
- AUGSBOURG
- MUNICH

Key
- ★★★ Highly recommended
- ★★ Recommended
- ★ Interesting
- If you have time
- Driving Tour showing point of departure

- ROTHENBURG
- Wurtzbourg
- Bayreuth
- Sulzfeld

Off the Beaten Track

North of Nuremberg, tourist crowds get thinner despite some key destinations. Bamberg is famous for its beer and its neatly preserved ensemble of architectural gems, which garnered it UNESCO World Heritage listing. Bayreuth is usually mentioned in one breath with Richard Wagner, although it owes its most beautiful palaces to a woman, the Margravine Wilhelmine.

Outdoor types, meanwhile, should steer to Franconian Switzerland, a fabulous playground of narrow valleys carved by sprightly streams and rock formations pockmarked with hundreds of caves. Canoeing, hiking, biking, caving and rock-climbing are all popular here.

473

Romantic Road★★

Romantische Straße

By way of river valleys and an idyllic, rolling countryside, the "Romantic Road" recalls at every stage some aspect of uniquely German history. As the route unfolds, it evokes medieval city life (Rothenburg), the religious sensibility of artists like Tilman Riemenschneider, German chivalry (Bad Mergentheim), Baroque episcopal courts and Imperial towns like Würzburg.

- **Info:** Marktplatz, Dinkelsbühl. ☎(09851) 902 71. www.romantische strasse.com.
- ▶ **Location:** Germany's most popular tourist route stretches from the Main Valley to the foot of the Bavarian Alps, passing river valleys, fields, forests, orchards and pretty little towns.
- **Don't Miss:** Rothenburg ob der Tauber, Dinkelsbühl.
- **Timing:** Allow four hours for suggested driving tour ①; five hours for driving tour ②; and a full day for driving tour ③.

🚗 DRIVING TOURS

FROM WÜRZBURG TO ROTHENBURG

100km/62mi – Allow 4hrs.

▶ Leaving **Würzburg★★**

(&*see WÜRZBURG), the B 27 descends towards the Tauber Valley.*

Bad Mergentheim★

Marktplatz 3, 97980 Bad Mergentheim. ☎(07931) 571 31. www.bad-mergentheim.de.
Bad Mergentheim was chosen as headquarters for the Knights of the Teutonic Order in the 16C and today is a popular

GETTING AROUND

The entire route is signposted Romantische Straße. From April to October, the Europabus travels the route in both directions once a day. Deutsche Touring (*☎01805) 79 03 03; www.deutsche-touring.com).*

stop on the Romantic Road set among the forested hills of the charming Tauber

Deutschordenschloss, Bad Mergentheim

© F1 Online/Tips Images

The Teutonic Order

The Teutonic Order was founded as a Germanic Hospitaller community in the Holy Land; it became a religious order in 1198 when the knights returned home after the fall of Jerusalem. They became princes of sizeable territories and estates, either by conquering them or by accepting them as gifts.

In 1525 the Grand Master of the order, Albrecht von Brandenburg-Ansbach, adopted Luther's teaching and suppressed the order's religious role. The community's territory of Prussia also became secular. Dispossessed of its seat, the Teutonic Order elected as its new headquarters Schloss Mergentheim, which the order had controlled since 1219. The castle remained the Teutonic residence for three centuries. In 1809 Napoleon abolished the order.

Today it has reconstituted itself as a religious and charitable body and has its headquarters in Vienna.

valley. It is celebrated for its historic old town, its castle and grounds and the healing qualities of its mineral springs.

Deutschordenschloss und Museum (Castle and Museum of the Teutonic Order)

Schloss 16. Open Apr–Oct, Tue–Sun 10.30am–5pm; Nov–Mar, Tue–Sat 2pm–5pm, Sun 10.30am–5pm. Closed Dec 24, 25 & 31. 5€. *(07931) 522 12.* www.deutschordensmuseum.de.

This 12C castle was extended in the mid-16C to become the residence of the Teutonic Order and its Grand Master. The museum occupies three floors and has an eclectic collection that ranges from historic dolls' houses to medieval sculpture and panel painting, faïences, alabaster and marble reliefs from the Renaissance and Baroque, as well as ivory carvings.

On the second floor, the **New State Rooms** take you through the audience chamber, the "State Bedroom" and the assembly hall *(Kapitelsaal)*. Exhibits on the third floor trace the history of the Teutonic Order.

Weikersheim

Guided tours (1hr) Apr–Oct, daily 9am–6pm, Nov–Mar, daily 10am–noon and 1pm–5pm. Closed Dec 24 & 31. 5.50€. *(07934) 99 29 50.* www.schloss-weikersheim.de.

Once the seat of the counts of Hohenlohe, this town's castle (1580–1680)

on the banks of the Tauber has scant Baroque influences. The magnificent **Rittersaal**★★ (Knights' Hall) is typical of the transition between the Renaissance and Baroque styles. **Formal gardens** (1710), accented with grotesque statues in the Franconian style, end in a charming orangery.

The narrow Tauber Valley begins above the town of Bieberehren. The road rises and falls over slopes covered alternately by woodland, orchards and willow-fringed riverbanks.

Creglingen★

The isolated **Herrgottskirche** (open Apr–Oct, daily 9.15am–6pm; Nov–Dec, Feb–Mar Tue–Sun 1pm–4pm; 2€; www.herrgottskirche.de), 1.5km/1mi along the road to Blaufelden, contains the **Altarpiece of the Virgin Mary**★★ carved by Tilman Riemenschneider. Note how this exquisite artist channelled his own sensibilities into the expression of the Madonna at the Assumption. Opposite the church is a **Fingerhutmuseum** (thimble museum) – the only one of its kind in Germany.

Detwang

In the church at Detwang another **Riemenschneider altarpiece**★ depicts the Crucifixion.

Rothenburg ob der Tauber★★★

See ROTHENBURG OB DER TAUBER.

FROM ROTHENBURG TO DONAUWÖRTH
105km/64mi – Allow 5hrs.

Feuchtwangen
Once a Free Imperial City, this town was also the birthplace of medieval minstrel Walther von der Vogelweide. An attractive market square sits surrounded by pretty houses and overlooked by a parish church with an altarpiece of the Virgin by Michael Wolgemut. Installed in a 17C burgher's house is a **Fränkisches Museum** (Museum of Franconian Folklore) displaying a collection of furniture and regional pottery and costumes.

Dinkelsbühl★
Ramparts and watchtowers still surround this idyllic medieval town which, every July, hosts a colourful festival *(Kinderzeche)* commemorating how the town was spared destruction in the Thirty Years' War *(see Calendar of Events)*. The **Georgskirche**★ has retained its Romanesque tower. Other highlights include the **Deutsches Haus**★ *(Am Weinmarkt)* and the Hezel-hof *(Segringer Straße 7)*.

Wallerstein
From atop a promontory in the heart of town *(Wallersteiner Felsen, access via the Fürstlicher Keller)*, you can enjoy the vast panorama of the Ries.

Nördlingen★
 Marktplatz 2. *090 81 84 116.*
www.noerdlingen.de.
The former Free Imperial City of Nördlingen lies in the middle of the Ries basin created by a giant meteorite about 15 million years ago. First recorded in 898, it is only one of three German towns still surrounded by a medieval town wall.

St. Georgskirche★ (St. George's Church)
This late 15C hall-church is surmounted by a majestic, 90m/295.3ft-high, copper-domed bell-tower, affectionately dubbed **"Daniel"** *(open Apr–Oct, daily 9am–7pm; Nov–Mar, 9am–5pm; 1.50€)*. It is well worth braving the 350 steps to the top in order to fully appreciate Nördlingen's near-circular shape and the crater within which it was built. A watchman still lives up here and calls out every half hour between 10am and midnight. Originally, this was intended to make contact with the guards holding watch on the town gates.
The church interior is canopied by graceful fan vaulting. The pulpit (1499) is reached via a corbelled staircase with only three steps. Note the curious little **organ** on the finely worked baldaquin *(on the right side)*. The main altar is Baroque in style but incorporates five statues created in Gothic times. They

Dinkelsbühl

T. Krieger/MICHELIN

depict Jesus on the cross, St. Mary, St. John and two angels and were created by Niclaus Gerhaert von Leyden.

Stadtmauer★
(Town Walls)

The Nördlingen town walls are completely preserved and fully accessible. The ramparts, which for the most part are covered, extend over a length of 2 632m/2 878yd and are punctuated by five gates and 14 towers.

One of the most attractive sections is along the battlements from the Berger Gate via the Alte Bastei, or old bastion, to the Reimlinger Gate.

In order to learn more about the fortifications and their role in the history of Nördlingen, swing by the small but excellent **Stadtmauermuseum** (open Apr–Oct, daily 10am–4.30pm; 2€; ℘09081 91 80) in the Löpsinger gate tower. Exhibits include cannon and uniforms from the Thirty Years' War.

Stadtmuseum★
(City Museum)

Vordere Gerberstraße 1.
Open mid-Mar–Oct, Tue–Sun 1.30pm–4.30pm. Closed Nov–mid-Mar, Good Fri. 3€. ℘(09 081) 273 82 30. www.stadtmuseum-noerdlingen.de.

Housed in a former hospital, this engaging museum has four floors of displays covering the pre- and early history of the Ries basin, along with the political and economic influence Nördlingen enjoyed as a Free Imperial City. Art fans will be drawn to the collection of 19C painting and altar panels by Old German masters. A highlight here is the altar wings from the St. Georgskirche painted by Friedrich Herlin in 1462.

Not only kids will get a kick out of the huge model featuring around 6 000 tin figures in a recreation of a famous Thirty Years' War battle that took place outside the town walls.

Rieskrater-Museum★

Eugene-Shoemaker-Platz 1. Next to Stadtmuseum. Open May–Oct, Tue–Sun 10am–4.30pm, Nov–Apr, Tue–Sun 10am–noon, 1.30pm–4.30pm.

Closed Jan 1, Shrove Tue, Good Fri, Dec 24–26. 3€. ℘(09081) 273 82 20. www.rieskrater-museum.de.

The Ries meteorite crater was formed approximately 15 million years ago. Just imagine it – a giant stone sphere, 1km/0.6mi in diameter, hits the earth at a speed of c. 70 000kph/43 496mph, penetrating up to 1km/0.6mi into the rock! The energy of 250 000 nuclear atom bombs (such as that used in Hiroshima in Japan, 1945) is released, and a wave of pressure and heat extinguishes all life within a range of 100km/62mi. A crater 14km/9mi in diameter forms, which eventually extends to 25km/16mi because of all the rock that subsequently caves in.

The crater, which was originally 4km/2.5mi deep, was gradually filled in over the course of millions of years, but was later partially excavated and opened up again.

The Rieskrater-Museum, which is housed in a carefully restored barn (1503), does a fine job of giving the layperson an understanding of this mindboggling phenomenon.

Neresheim Abtei (Abbey)★

19km/12mi southwest on the B466.
Guided tours Easter–Oct, Mon–Sat 11am and 3pm, Sun 11.15am and 3.15pm. Donations appreciated. ℘(07326) 85 01.
www.abtei-neresheim.de.

The abbey church was the last major commission designed by **Balthasar Neumann** and was built between 1745 and 1792. Inside, the seemingly weightless ceiling decoration is a work of Martin Knoller and was painted between 1771 and 1775.

Schloss Harburg

Guided tours (50min), mid-Mar–Oct, Tue–Sun 10am–5pm. 5€. ℘(09080) 968 60.

This large fortified castle looks down on a picturesque village along the banks of the Wörnitz. Tours take in the church, the watertower, the prison tower, the private quarters, the well and the festival hall.

▶ *Leave via Mündlingerstraße, to the left, and take the Romantic Road to Mündling for Kaisheim.*

Kaisheim

The former Cistercian abbey church was built at the end of the 14C in the full flower of the Gothic era. (The abbey itself is now a penal institution). Around the chancel is a 12-sided **ambulatory**★ *(to visit, apply at the presbytery).* The 18C emperor's room in the Imperial foundation is open to the public *(on request).*

Donauwörth

This Free Imperial City is proud of its pastel historic buildings along the Reichsstraße; the most impressive are the town hall and the *Fuggerhaus* (1543). The 18C Baroque pilgrimage church of Heilig Kreuz boasts Wessobrunn stuccowork. The Gothic Liebfrauenmünster has beautiful 15C murals. Parts of the town's fortifications still stand.

ADDRESSES

🏨STAY

DINKELSBÜHL

🍴 **Zum Goldenen Anker** – *Untere Schmiedgasse 22. ✆(09851) 578 00. www.goldener-anker-dkb.de. 18 rooms. Restaurant* 🍴. This old inn has spacious country-style rooms and traditional cooking.

🍴 **Hotel Kunst-Stuben** – *Segringer Straße 52, 91550 Dinkelsbühl. ✆(09851) 67 50. www.kunst-stuben.de. 5 rooms.* This small, welcoming property is managed by an artist couple happy to offer tours of their studio. Each room is individually furnished and immaculate.

WEIKERSHEIM

🍴 **Laurentius** – *Marktplatz 5. ✆(07934) 910 80.www.hotel-laurentius.de. 11 rooms. Restaurant* 🍴. Behind the cheerful yellow façade await immaculate rooms with Italian furnishings. The restaurant is in a beautiful vaulted cellar.

FEUCHTWANGEN

🍴 **Romantik Hotel Greifen-Post** – *Marktplatz 8. ✆(09852) 68 00. www.greifen.de. 35 rooms. Closed 1–7 Jan. Restaurant* 🍴, *closed Sun dinner, Mon.* This 600-year-old establishment knows the true meaning of hospitality. Rooms are elegantly furnished in Renaissance, Romantic, 19C or country-house style and the dining room drips with historic charm. Indoor pool and sauna.

NÖRDLINGEN

🍴 **Hotel Sonne** – *Marktplatz 3. ✆(090 81) 50 67. www.kaiserhof-hotel-sonne.de. Closed 2 weeks in Nov. 29 rooms. Restaurant* 🍴. This traditional hotel in the heart of town dates from 1477. It has comfortable rooms and a country-style dining room with a neat vaulted ceiling.

🍽/EAT

BAD MERGENTHEIM

🍴 **Bundschu** – *Milchlingstraße 24. ✆(07931) 93 30. www.hotel-bundschu. de. Closed Mon.* This Mediterranean-style restaurant with garden terrace serves regional cuisine and also has a few attractive, modern rooms.

🍴 **Zirbelstube** – *Poststraße 2. ✆(07931) 59 36 07. www.victoriahotel.de. Closed Jan, Aug, Sun.* The pine-coated walls and attractive paintings form an elegant backdrop for the richly nuanced classical fare created with regional ingredients whenever possible.

NÖRDLINGEN

🍴 **Meyer's Keller** – *Marienhöhe 8. ✆(09081) 44 93. www.meyerskeller.de. Closed Mon, Tue lunch.* This pleasant brasserie serves tasty regional dishes in a dining room accented by modern artworks and contemporary décor. In fine weather, sit under a canopy of shady old trees.

Würzburg★★

Würzburg lies at the northern terminus of the Romantic Road. Although much of the city centre was destroyed by bombs in just 22 minutes on 16 March 1945, the main sights have been meticulously rebuilt. This includes the splendid Prince-Bishops' Residence, which has been a UNESCO World Heritage Site since 1981. It was in Würzburg that Wilhelm Conrad Röntgen discovered X-rays in 1895.

A BIT OF HISTORY

The master of Würzburg – Flamboyant Gothic sculptor and woodcarver **Tilman Riemenschneider** (c. 1460–1531) was born in Heiligenstadt im Eichsfeld, Thüringia. He worked in Würzburg from 1483 and became town mayor in 1520–21. His work was always more than purely decorative and largely centred on expressing human emotions.

➤WALKING TOUR
THE OLD TOWN AND MARIENBURG FORTRESS

Residenz★★

& ℘(0931) 35 51 70.
www.residenz-wuerzburg.de.
The residence of the rich and powerful Prince-Bishops, this superb 18C Baroque palace is one of the largest in Germany and was built under the direction of the architectural genius **Balthasar Neumann**.

Schloss★★ (Palace)

Open Apr–Oct, daily 9am–6pm; Nov–Mar 10am–4.30pm; ticket office closes 1hr before closing.
Some sections by guided tour only, offered throughout the day (11am and 3pm in English) Closed Jan 1, Shrove Tue, Dec 24,25 & 31. ⊛7€.
The monumental **Treppenhaus★★** (Grand Staircase) occupies the whole northern part of the vestibule and is one of Neumann's masterpieces. The huge **fresco★★** decorating the vaulted ceiling is by the Venetian **Giovanni**

▶ **Population:** 132 700
Info: Am Congress Centrum and Marktplatz, 97070 Würzburg. ℘(0931) 37 23 35. www.wuerzburg.de.
Location: Former capital of the Duchy of Franconia, Würzburg lies on the banks of the Main, at the northwest border of Bavaria.
Parking: You'll find parking garages throughout Würzburg. Visit http://wap.parkinfo.com for fees and locations.
Don't Miss: The Residenz.
Timing: Allow a couple of hours for the Residenz and its gardens and a full day for the suggested driving tour.

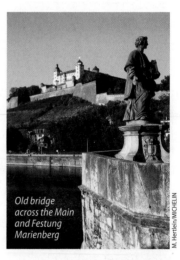
Old bridge across the Main and Festung Marienberg
M. Hertlein/MICHELIN

Tiepolo (1753) and illustrates the four then-known continents. In the **Weißer Saal** (White Room), between the Grand Staircase and the Imperial Hall, the brilliant **stucco ornamentation** is the work of Italian artist Antonio Bossi.
The oval **Kaisersaal★★** (Imperial Hall) on the first floor is also splendidly adorned with **frescoes by Tiepolo**.
The **Paradezimmer** (Imperial Apartments) are a luxurious suite of restored

WÜRZBURG
map I

WHERE TO EAT
Schützenhof.............④

WÜRZBURG
map II

WHERE TO STAY

Hotel Amberger......................................	①
Hotel Rebstock.......................................	④
Strauss..	⑨

WHERE TO EAT

Alte Mainmühle......................................	③
Backöfele..	⑤
Bürgerspital...	①
Weinhaus zum Stachel...........................	⑦

rooms with Rococo stuccowork, tapestries and German furniture. The residence also houses a picture gallery with some fine **17C and 18C Italian paintings**, among them works by Bellucci, Canaletto and the Veronese school.

Hofkirche★ (Court Church)

The Residenz church is another work of Balthasar Neumann. Marble, gilding and warm ceiling frescoes by court painter Rudolf Byss all combine to form an exuberant composition. Two more **Tiepolo** paintings hang above the side altars: *The Assumption* and *The Fall of the Angels*.

Hofgarten★ (Court Gardens)

Astute use of old, stepped bastions has produced a layout of terraced gardens. From the eastern side, the whole 167m/545ft of the palace façade, with its elegant central block is visible. The stucco is by Johann Peter Wagner.

Martin von Wagner Museum★

South wing. ◷*Picture Gallery: open year-round, Tue–Sat 10am–1.30pm; Collection of Antiquities: Tue–Sat 1.30pm–5pm; Graphics Collection: Tue, Thu 2pm-4pm.* ◷*Closed Jan 1, Good Fri, May 1, Oct 3, Nov 1, Dec 24 & 31.* ℘*(0931) 31 22 88. www.museum.uni-wuerzburg.de.*

The university-affiliated museum houses two grand collections as well as graphic works. On the second floor is the **Gemäldegalerie★** (Picture Gallery) with 14C–20C German and European works. Key works are altar paintings by the masters of Würzburg (14C–16C) alongside Franconian sculpture, especially that of Riemenschneider. Dutch and Italian painters from the 16C to the 18C are well represented too (Tiepolo). The **Antikensammlung★** (Collection of Antiquities) on the third floor presents works from around the Mediterranean dating as far back as the third millennium BC. Pride of place goes to an internationally renowned collection of **Greek vases★★** (6C–4C BC), but objects from Etruscan, Roman and Egyptian civilisations are also on display.

▶ *From April to October, a bus shuttles between the Residenz and Marienberg fortress. To continue this tour, take either bus 9 from Residenzplatz or walk down Hofstraße to the cathedral.*

Dom St. Kilian (Cathedral of St. Kilian)

◷*Open Mon–Sat 10am–5pm, Sun 1pm–6pm.*

This columned basilica anchored by four towers was rebuilt after 1945 but has retained its original 11C–13C silhouette. The modern **Altar of the Apostles** holds three 16C **sculptures★** by Riemenschneider. The 18C **Schönborn Chapel** by Balthasar Neumann off the left transept contains the tombs of the Prince-Bishops from the Schönborn dynasty.

Museum am Dom (Cathedral Museum)

◷*Open Apr–Oct, Tue–Sun 10am–6pm; Nov–Mar to 5pm.* ⊜*3.50€.* ℘*(0931) 38 66 56 00. www.museum-am-dom.de.*

This museum presents religious art from the 11C to the 21C, including a fantastic Crucifixion by Riemenschneider. Following a modern curatorial concept, it is organised by such themes as "Hoping", "Admonishing" and "Testifying" in order to encourage reflection and interaction on the visitors' part.

Neumünster (New Cathedral)

The imposing Baroque **west façade** of this church (1710–16) is attributed to Johann Dientzenhofer. In niches below the cupola are a Riemenschneider *Virgin and Child* and a Christ figure in an unusual pose with arms folded below the chest (14C). In the west crypt is the **tomb of St. Kilian**, the missionary who was martyred in Würzburg in 689 and has since become the patron of the Franconians. The exit to the left of the chancel leads to the idyllic **Lusamgärtlein**, a small garden where the 13C troubadour-poet Walther von der Vogelweide was buried.

▶ *Go north on Kürschnerstraße, then left on Eichhornstraße to arrive at Marktplatz.*

Marienkapelle (St. Mary's Chapel)

This fine Gothic chapel was financed by the town burghers in the 14C and 15C and boasts an attractive Annunciation on the tympanum of the north doorway. Inside the western front is the 1502 tombstone of Konrad von Schaumberg, carved by Riemenschneider and, on the north side, a **silver Madonna** made by the Master of Augsburg, J Kilian, in 1680.

▷ *Cross Marktplatz and head down Schustergasse . At the end, turn right on Domstraße.*

Rathaus (Town Hall)

The 13C town hall boasts a painted façade from the 16C and a charming interior courtyard. The western part, the **Roter Bau** (red building), is in late Renaissance style, while the Baroque **Vierröhrenbrunnen** (fountain) in front dates from 1765.

▷ *Continue straight to the bridge.*

Alte Mainbrücke★ (Old Main Bridge)

The Alte Mainbrücke was built between 1473 and 1543 and was embellished with a dozen monumental stone statues of saints in 1730. From the bridge, you can spot the baroque Alter Kranen (old crane) on the bank of the Main River. A town landmark, they were built by the son of Balthasar Neumann, Franz Ignaz, around 1770.

The old Customs House now contains the House of Franconian Wine (Haus des Frankenweins) where you can sample the local vintages.

▷ *The most direct way to Marienburg fortress is signposted from the end of the bridge. A more scenic route goes through the vineyards (Weinwanderweg) hugging the slopes below the fortress. This pleasant walk (30min) offers lovely viewpoints, especially of St. Mary's Chapel.*

Festung Marienberg★ (Marienberg Fortress)

⏰Guided tours Apr–Oct, Tue–Sun 11am, 2pm, 3pm and 4pm, Sat also 10am (3pm tour in English). ⊛3€, combination ticket with Fürstenbaumuseum 5€. ♿, ✆(0931) 35 51 70. www.schloesser.bayern.de.

From 1253 to 1719, this stronghold was the home of the Prince-Bishops of Würzburg. Built above the west bank of the Main, the original 13C castle was enlarged in the late Middle Ages and fortified after being stormed by Swedish troops in 1631 during the Thirty Years' War. The first-floor Prince-Bishops' apartments now house the **Fürstenbaumuseum** (Princes' Building Museum; ⏰open mid-Mar–Oct, Tue–Sun 9am-6pm; ⊛4€), richly furnished and hung with paintings and tapestries, including one from 1564 depicting the family of Prince-Bishop Julius Echter of Mespelbrunn.

Mainfränkisches Museum★★ (Regional History Museum)

Second floor of Festung Marienberg, enter on the right in the first courtyard. ⏰Open Apr–Oct, Tue–Sun 10am–5pm, Nov–Mar to 4pm. ⏰Closed Shrove Tue, Dec 24, 25 & 31. ⊛4€, combination ticket with Fürstenbaumuseum 5€. ✆(0931) 20 59 40. www.mainfraenkisches-museum.de.

Housed in the former arsenal, the most important section of this collection of Franconian arts and crafts is the around 80 **sculptures by Tilmann Riemenschneider** (first floor), including *Adam and Eve*, *Virgin Mary and Child* and *The Apostles*. The vaulted galleries of the **Echterbastei** form a backdrop for statues, gold and silver religious plate, Gothic paintings and Franconian folk art. Also duck down into the old cellar to admire the historic winepresses.

Käppele (Chapel)

⏰Open Apr–Oct, daily 6.45am–6pm, Nov–Mar, Mon–Sat 6.45am–5pm, Sun 8.30am–6.30pm.

A monumental Way of the Cross leads to this Baroque pilgrimage church built by Balthasar Neumann in 1748. The adjoin-

A Masterpiece in 210 Days

Disappointment with other painters led Prince-Bishop Carl Philipp von Greiffenclau to commission the best fresco artist of the day, Giovanni Battista Tiepolo, to embellish the palace. The painter arrived with his two sons on 12 December 1750. Tiepolo wanted for nothing; he was served eight courses at lunch and seven in the evening. In addition, he received three times the pay he earned in Venice. Tiepolo had a reputation for painting with great speed, but the artist surpassed all estimates during his short three years in Würzburg. He created frescoes in the Imperial Hall and Residenz staircase, two altars for the Würzburg court church and one for Schwarzach Abbey (now in Munich's Alte Pinakothek) while also completing private commissions for local families. Unable to paint during the winter, Tiepolo worked day and night for the rest of the year. It took him only 210 days to complete the vast and hugely intricate staircase fresco in the Residenz.

ing chapel of mercy is connected via a "miracle passage". A superb **view**★★ unfolds from the chapel terrace, with the fortress of Marienberg rising from the vineyards.

EXCURSION
Schloss Veitshöchheim★
◗ *7km/4.3mi northwest.*
Echterstraße 10. ◷*Open Apr–Oct, Tue–Sun 9am–6pm.* ⊛*4€.* ✆*(0931) 915 82.*
www.schloesser.bayern.de.
The 17C summer residence of the Prince-Bishops was enlarged in 1753 by Balthasar Neumann. Rooms brim with shiny Rococo and Empire furniture and are festooned with stucco ornamentation by Antonio Bossi. The lavish **park**★ is a maze of shaded walks and arbours dotted with over 200 statues.

🚗 DRIVING TOUR

FRANCONIAN WINE ROUTE★
(Bocksbeutelstraße)
87km/55mi – Allow 1 day.

◗ *Leave Würzburg on the B13 in the direction of Ansbach or Ochsenfurt.*

Medieval monks introduced viticulture to Franconia, which enjoys a mild climate and hot, dry summers. The main varietals are mainly dry white **Müller-Thurgau** and slightly fruitier **Silvaner**.

Ochsenfurt
Encircled by ancient **ramparts**★, Ochsenfurt's centre is a hodgepodge of half-timbered houses adorned with wrought-iron signs. A mechanical clock in the lantern turret strikes the hours at the 15C **Neues Rathaus**. The **Stadtpfarrkirche St. Andreas** built between the 13C and the 15C, has a fanciful interior.

◗ *Turn left off the B13 and drive alongside the Main.*

Marktbreit
The town hall and city gate form a fine Renaissance ensemble (1579), complemented by two Baroque houses festooned with corner bay windows.

Sulzfeld
A highlight of this pretty wine-growing village is the Renaissance **Town Hall** with its scrolled gables.

◗ *Pass through Kitzingen and Mainstockheim (on the east bank of the Main) and head for Dettelbach.*

Dettelbach★
Dettelbach clings to the northern slopes of the Main Valley and sports a late-Gothic (c. 1500) town hall and 15C parish church, whose principal tower is linked by a wooden bridge to a smaller one. Northeast of the upper town is the 17C **pilgrimage church "Maria im Sand"**.

▶ *Between Dettelbach and Neuses am Berg, the road runs through a plateau of vineyards, then drops back down into the Main Valley and crosses the river.*

Volkach★

This delightful wine-growing town lies on the eastern side of a wide oxbow in the Main. Of the original medieval enclave only two gates bookend the main street: the **Gaibacher Tor** and the **Sommeracher Tor**. The 16C Renaissance **town hall** on the Marktplatz (with the tourist office) is fronted by a 15C fountain topped by a Virgin statue. Slightly further south is the **Bartholomäuskirche** (Church of St. Bartholomew), a late-Gothic building with Baroque and Rococo flourishes. At the northwestern edge of town *(about 1km/0.6mi in the direction of Fahr)*,

the 15C **pilgrimage church "Maria im Weingarten"** enjoys an idyllic vineyard setting. Inside is the famous limewood **Rosenkranzmadonna**★ (Virgin with Rosary), a late Riemenschneider work (1512–24).

▶ *Return to Würzburg via Schwarzach, turning right onto the B22. If continuing to Nuremberg via the B8, make a stop in Iphofen.*

Iphofen

Half-timbered Iphofen is a popular stop for clued-up gourmets. The refined cuisine of Zehntkeller (✆*(09323) 84 40; www.zehntkeller.de*) and the creative fare made with locally sourced ingredients at Deutscher Hof (✆*(09323) 33 48; www.deutscher-hof-iphofen.de;* ⏱*closed Wed–Thu*) are both stand-outs.

ADDRESSES

⌂ STAY

⊜⊜ **Hotel Amberger** – *Ludwigstraße 17–19.* ✆*0931 35 100. www.hotel-amberger.de. 70 rooms.* ⚏. This centrally located hotel features spacious modern rooms and a fine breakfast buffet.

⊜⊜ **Hotel Rebstock** – *Neubaustraße 7.* ✆*(0931) 309 30. www.rebstock.com. 70 rooms. Restaurant* ⊜⊜*, closed Aug and Sun.* Behind the Rococo façade of 1737, a range of rooms from elegant and modern to rustic and traditional awaits. The charming restaurant and bistro-style winter garden deliver continental cuisine.

⊜⊜ **Strauss** – *Juliuspromenade 5.* ✆*0931 305 70. www.hotel-strauss.de. 74 rooms.* ⚏*9€.* Close to the Old Town station, rooms are modern and functional.

♟/EAT

⊜⊜ **Alte Mainmühle** – *Mainkai 1.* ✆*0931 167 77. www.alte-mainmuehle.de.* Next to the Alte Mainbrücke this charming rustic restaurant serves regional and international dishes.

⊜⊜ **Backöfele** – *Ursulinergasse 2.* ✆*0931 590 59. www.backoefele.de. Closed Dec 24–Jan 1.* A city institution, this historic house is famous for its cosy rustic atmosphere.

⊜⊜ **Bürgerspital** – *Theaterstraße 19.* ✆*(0931) 35 28 80.* This mood-lit wine tavern with its cross-vaulted ceiling is operated by the Bürgerspital wine estate. Franconian specialities, including fish, accompany the excellent variety of local wines.

⊜⊜⊜ **Weinhaus zum Stachel** – *Gressengasse 1 (near Marktplatz).* ✆*(0931) 527 70. www.weinhaus-stachel.de. Closed Sun. Reservations recommended.* This traditional *Weinstube* with an idyllic courtyard dates to the 15C. Excellent Franconian wines and regional cuisine. In the evening, a small menu of refined dishes is available.

⍟ NIGHTLIFE

USEFUL TIPS

Try the bars along Juliuspromenade north of the city centre and Sanderstraße, south of the city centre.

Rothenburg ob der Tauber★★★

One of the oldest towns on the "Romantic Road," Rothenburg overlooks the winding course of the Tauber River from its rocky crag. Once behind the ramparts in the pedestrian-only medieval centre, visitors revel in the 16C among ancient houses, fountains and narrow, cobbled lanes.

A BIT OF HISTORY

A long drink *(Meistertrunk)* – During the Thirty Years' War, Protestant Rothenburg was unable to withstand the Catholic siege by General Tilly's army. After 40 000 victorious merceneries had pillaged the town for three months, Tilly decided to raze it unless, he declared, some local could empty in a single draught a tankard (a 3.4l/6-pint tankard) of wine. The town mayor, a man named Georg Nusch, volunteered and miraculously succeeded: Rothenburg was saved. Ever since Rothenburgers have recreated the event annually at Pentecost.

Saved again – Rothenburg stagnated throughout the 17C and 18C, too poor to expand beyond its own walls. In the 19C, however, the town's steep-roofed houses with their gables, staircase turrets and corner oriels were rediscovered

▶ **Population:** 11 000

Info: Marktplatz 2, 91541 Rothenburg. ℘(09861) 404 800. www.rothenburg.de.

Location: The old town stands on a steep promontory overlooking the Tauber River.

Don't Miss: A stroll through the old town.

Timing: Allow 4hrs for the suggested walking tour.

Kids: The mechanical clock on the Ratstrinkstube and a walk along the ramparts.

by Romantic painters, and Rothenburg has since became a major tourist attraction.

WALKING TOUR
OLD TOWN★★★

Starting at Marktplatz, follow the itinerary marked on the town map. Allow half a day.

Rathaus★ (Town Hall)

This 14C structure has seen a number of architectural additions over the centuries. Visitors can inspect the **Historiengewölbe** (historic vaults), now a history museum, or climb the tower for a **view**★ of the fortified town. North of Marktplatz is the gable of the 1446

Herrngasse in Rothenburg

©Angela Jones/Bigstockphoto.com

ROTHENBURG
ob der Tauber

0 ——— 200 m

Ratstrinkstube (now the tourist office) with a **mechanical clock** from 1910 that re-enacts the Long Drink *(on the hour, 11am–3pm, 8pm–10pm)*.

Baumeisterhaus

With its elaborate Renaissance façade and pretty courtyard, this former private home is one of the most beautiful build-ings in Rothenburg. Statues on the first floor represent the seven virtues, those on the second the seven deadly sins.

Mittelalterliches Kriminalmuseum (Medieval Justice Museum)

Burggasse 3–5.

🕐 *Open May–Oct, daily 10am–6pm; Nov & Jan–Feb, 2pm–4pm; Mar & Dec, 10am–4pm.* 💶4€. 📞*(09861) 53 59. www.kriminalmuseum.rothenburg.de.*
Punishment was swift and brutal, as you will learn at this museum which displays documents and instruments of public humiliation, torture and execution.

Plönlein

A picturesque corner of half-timbered houses, often photographed: one street is level, another ascending to the Siebers Tower, another descending. The fountain once supplied the fish stock used by Tauber fishermen.

▷ *Go past the Siebersturm (tower) and take Spitalgasse, named after the old hospital down the street, which is our next stop. Enter on your right.*

Spital (General Hospital)

Most of the buildings of this hospital date back to the 16C and 17C. There are some fine art works in the Gothic chapel (Spitalkirche). The best viewpoint from which to appreciate the silhouette of the Hegereiterhaus, a pavilion with a pointed roof and turreted staircases topped by a lantern-shaped roof, is from the centre of the courtyard. In former times, the kitchens and servants' quarters were located here. The half-timbered old cellar and bakery are now a youth hostel. To the west, the former tithing barn has morphed into the Reichsstadthalle, a congress and event centre. Views from the top of the Kalkturm extend across the entire town . A walkway links the two towers, Stöberleinsturm au Sauturm.

▷ *Backtrack on Spitalgasse.*

The southern entrance into the city is via the Spitaltor (Hospital Gate), a mighty 17C bastion wrapped around two oval inner courtyards. It has seven gates, a moat and a drawbridge and warrants thorough exploration inside and out.

▷ *Backtrack to Plönlein, turn left on Burggasse and leave the town centre via*

Kobolzeller Gate. Turn right and follow the trail below the ramparts. At the bottom of the valley, a double bridge (Doppelbrücke) straddles the Tauber River.

Burggarten (Castle Gardens)

All that remains of the double fortress erected on this promontory is a chapel, the Blasiuskapelle, which has been turned into a war memorial, and a fortified gateway, the Burgtor. The area is now a large public garden with magnificent **views**★.

▷ *Return to the town via the Burgtor; assailants unaware of the grimacing mask above the second gate risked being drenched in boiling oil here.*

Herrngasse★

The mansions of medieval burghers line this busy commercial street. In the **Franziskanerkirche**, note the 15C and 16C sculptures and the Creglingen Madonna (1400).
Back in Herrngasse, check out the hidden courtyards. Number 15 features a half-timbered gallery on embossed wooden pillars.

▷ *Turn left into Kirchgasse after the round fountain.*

St. Jakobskirche★

Klostergasse 15. 🕐*Open Apr–Oct, daily 9am–5.15pm; Nov, Jan–Mar 10am–noon, 2pm–4pm; Dec 10am–5pm.* 💶2€.
This 14C Gothic church shelters Tilman Riemenschneider's masterful **Heiligblutaltar★★ (Altarpiece of the Holy Blood)** (1504). Note the tense, perplexed expressions conveyed in the scene, as well as Jesus' compassion. The stained glass windows in the east chancel are also worth closer inspection.

ADDITIONAL SIGHTS
Stadtmauer★ (Ramparts)

Constructed in the 13C and 14C, these ramparts, complete with gates and towers, are still perfectly preserved. Long stretches are open to the public.

St. Wolfgangskirche

Open Apr–Sept, Wed–Mon 10am–1pm, 2.30pm–5pm, Oct to 4pm. ↔1.50€.
North of the Klingentor, this curious 15C Gothic church, fortified and incorporated into the barbican, doubled the defences of the gateway.

Reichsstadtmuseum (Imperial City Museum)

Open Apr–Oct, daily 9.30am–5.30pm; Nov–Mar, 1pm–4pm. Closed Shrove Tue, Dec 24 & 31. ↔4€. (09861) 93 90 43. www.reichsstadtmuseum. rothenburg.de.
A Dominican monastery from 1258 to 1554, this building is now a local museum showing, among other collections, the Rothenburg Stations of the Cross (1494).

Also on view is the tankard reportedly drained by Mayor Nusch in front of General Tilly. Its design depicts the Emperor and the seven Electors and was made in 1616.

Puppen-und Spielzeug Museum (Doll and Toy Museum)

Hofbronnengasse 13. Open Mar–Dec, daily 9.30am–6pm; Jan–Feb, daily 11am–6pm. ↔4€. (09861) 73 30.
For more than a quarter-century, this privately run museum has enchanted kids and anyone young at heart with its amazing collection of dolls, model, trains, marionettes, stuffed animals and other toys spanning more than two centuries.

ADDRESSES

STAY

Hornburg – *Hornburgweg 28, 91541. 09861 8 480. www.hotel-hornburg.de. Closed 1 week Nov & Dec 24–26. 10 rooms.* This small hotel, decorated in Art Nouveau style, has bags of charm and a lovely garden.

Mittermeier – *Vorm Würzburger Tor 9. (09861) 945 40. www.mittermeier. rothenburg.de. 27 rooms. Restaurant , closed 2 weeks in Jan & Aug, Sun and Mon.* Friendly and dedicated staff as well as individually decorated themed rooms (e.g. "Africa" or "Spain") give this pretty sandstone villa an edge. The restaurant serves an upscale menu with a youthful, fresh style.

Hotel Spitzweg – *Paradeisgasse 2. (09861) 942 90. www.hotel-spitzweg.de. 9 rooms.* This 16C hotel has comfortable, rustic rooms and plenty of memorabilia of Romantic painter Carl Spitzweg, a Rothenburger.

EAT

Altfränkische Weinstube – *Klosterhof 7. 098 61 64 04. www. altfraenkische-weinstube-rothenburg.de. Dinner only. Closed Tue & Jan–Mar.* Dine on hearty traditional cooking in this cosy, atmospheric 650-year old inn.

Baumeisterhaus – *Obere Schmiedgasse 3. (09861) 947 00.* This 1596 Renaissance gem opposite the town hall serves hearty Bavarian cuisine on two floors adorned with beautiful paintings. The courtyard is surrounded by half-timbered galleries.

Reichs-Küchenmeister – *Kirchplatz 8–10. 09861 9 700. www.reichskuechenmeister.com. Closed Jan–Mar & Mon–Tue.* This beautiful historic house includes a wine bar, a lovely garden restaurant and main dining room, off which are two, more cosy, small areas. The menu combines international and local specialities.

Die Blaue Sau – *Vorm Würzburger Tor 9. 09861 945 40. www.blauesau.eu. Dinner only except Mon. Closed Sun.* Delicious Italian cuisine is served in this vaulted cellar in this atmospheric *enoteca*.

TAKING A BREAK

USEFUL TIPS

Many cafés sell the locally famous *Schneeballen* (snowballs), which are cakes made with shortbread pastry and traditionally covered with icing or cinnamon.

Nuremberg★★
Nürnberg

Thanks to being in the crosshairs of two major trade routes, Nuremberg prospered in the Middle Ages and also enjoyed political standing as the frequent host city of the Imperial diets. In the 15C and 16C, it experienced a cultural flourishing that involved some of the finest artists of the day, including Albrecht Dürer. Although badly bombed in World War II, the city still preserves medieval flair, best experienced during the world's most famous Christmas market held every December. The Nazi leadership regarded Nuremberg as so quintessentially "Germanic" that they chose to stage their huge party rallies here.

A BIT OF HISTORY

The golden age – Nuremberg reached its political and economic heyday during the 15C and 16C. On the crossroads of major trade routes and a mainstay for Franconian craftsmanship, the city once rivalled Augsburg in importance and wealth. The first German scientific university was founded in Nuremberg in 1526. Sculptors **Veit Stoß** (c. 1445–1533) and **Adam Krafft** (c. 1460–1508/09);

▶ **Population:** 493 000
▪ **Info:** Hauptmarkt 18, Königstraße 93 and Frauentorgraben 3, 90403 Nürnberg. ✆(0911) 233 61 35. www.tourismus. nuernberg.de.
◖ **Location:** The second-largest city in Bavaria after Munich, Nuremberg is served by the A9 and A3 autobahns.
▣ **Parking:** Garages are located throughout the city. Visit http://wap.parkinfo. com for fees and locations.
⊛ **Don't Miss:** The German National Museum and the old town.
◷ **Timing:** Allow a day for the German National Museum and for taking in all the sights.
▴▵ **Kids:** A walk along the city's medieval ramparts.

bronze caster **Peter Vischer the Elder** (c. 1460–1529); **Michael Wolgemut** (1434–1519), painter of altarpieces, and above all, his pupil **Albrecht Dürer** (1471–1528) were all based in this city and profoundly influenced the artistic

Pegnitz River and Heilig-Geist-Spital, in the heart of old Nuremberg

M. Hertlein/MICHELIN

489

landscape throughout central Europe. From the 13C, **Hans Sachs** and the *Meistersänger (see INTRODUCTION: Music)* brought new life to a German poetic form and provided the inspiration for Richard Wagner's 1868 opera *Die Meistersänger von Nürnberg (The Mastersingers of Nuremberg).*

The Nuremberg Trials – It was in Hitler's "ideological capital" of the Third Reich that the notorious anti-Semitic laws were promulgated in 1935. And it was no coincidence that the Allies chose Nuremberg to bring high-ranking Nazi officials before an international military tribunal to face charges of war crimes. The trials took place between November 1945 and October 1946 in the **Justizpal-ast** (Palace of Justice) on Fürther Straße, now a civil court. About two dozen of the accused were condemned to death by hanging.

GERMAN NATIONAL MUSEUM★★★ (GERMANISCHES NATIONALMUSEUM)

Kartäusergasse 1. Open year-round, Tue–Sun 10am–6pm (Wed 9pm). Closed Shrove Tue, Dec 24, 25 & 31. 8€. (0911) 133 10. www.gnm.de. The museum, founded in 1852, possesses the largest collection of art and antiquities in Germany, although only 20 000 of its millions of items can be displayed at any given time. In fact, since the museum is so vast, keep the overwhelm-factor at bay by studying the plan available upon entering and limiting your time to the sections that interest you most.

Upper Floors

The **picture gallery** *(first floor, Section B)* displays works by **Albrecht Dürer**, Hans Baldung Grien, Hans Holbein the Elder, Albrecht Altdorfer and Lucas Cranach the Elder. There are also some later works, including a *Self-portrait* by Rembrandt. Works by **Veit Stoß**, Tilman Riemenschneider and Ignaz Günther stand out within the sculpture collection.

The most noteworthy among the **scientific instruments (Section A)** is the so-called **Behaim terrestrial globe** (c. 1493), the oldest surviving depiction of the earth in globe form.

Also on view are medical instruments **(Section C)**, a collection of dolls and dolls' houses (one from 1639) and folkloric galleries **(Section D)** with farmhouse furnishings, clothing and religious art. The second-floor galleries include an excellent exhibition of 19C and 20C art and design **(Section E)**, notably Ernst Ludwig Kirchner's Expressionist *Self-portrait* (1914).

Ground Floor

The impressive collection of medieval religious art **(Section C)** illustrates the work of craftsmen from the Carolingian period (9C) to the early Renaissance. Many types of decorative arts are rep-

Adam Krafft

Born in Nuremberg around 1460, Krafft left his mark on every church in the city. His early works – typical of the late-Gothic style – portrayed very expressive figures with tumultuous draperies, and rich decorative reliefs. He then moved towards greater clarity and his later, more monumental, works assume more rounded and restrained poses (see the Stations of the Cross from St. John's Cemetery, dating from 1505, in the Germanisches Nationalmuseum).

resented, including glass, ceramics, furniture and textiles. The gold- and silversmiths' work should not be missed. The section on ancient musical instruments (**Section D**) boasts the world's largest collection of historical pianos. There is also an extensive prints and drawings section and a numismatic collection (**Section F**).

✽₊WALKING TOUR
OLD TOWN★★

This tour begins at a ruined church, a site that perfectly illustrates the extent of destruction sustained during World War II. It also puts into perspective the enormous reconstruction effort undertaken by the town and its citizens.

Katharinenkirchenruine (Ruin of St. Catherine's Church)

Peter-Vischer-Straße.

Once part of a Dominican convent, St. Catherine's became the home of Nuremberg master singers from 1620 to 1778. It burned down in 1945 and was never reconstructed. Today, the partially roofed ruin hosts a popular summer concert series.

▶ *Turn right on Oberer Bergauerplatz, then left on Pfarrgasse.*

Lorenzkirche★ (St. Lawrence Church)

Lorenzer Platz 10. ◷*Open year-round, Mon–Sat 9am–5pm, Sun 1pm–4pm.* ℘*(0911) 244 69 90.*

This pretty church, two Gothic choirs, one from the 13C, the other from the 15C. A magnificent rose window enlivens the west façade. Enter via the south door to admire Veit Stoß's 16C carved wooden masterpiece, **Annunciation★★**. Stoß also created the Crucifix above the high altar. The **tabernacle★★** (1493–96), crafted from limestone by Adam Krafft, stands left of the main altar. It features more than 100 figurines.

▶ *As you head north on Königstraße, note the Nassauer Haus at the corner of Karolinenstraße. With its fortified tower, it is the oldest residential building in Nuremberg.*

Heilig-Geist-Spital (Hospice of the Holy Spirit)

The general hospital is in a 14C–15C building, spread over two wide arches, spanning a branch of the Pegnitz. The covered part of the bridge, known as the **Crucifixion Courtyard** on account of Krafft's Crucifixion Group, used to be a home for the elderly.

▶ *Continue going straight after the bridge to get to Hauptmarkt.*

Frauenkirche★ (Our Lady's Church)

Hauptmarkt 14. ◷*Open year-round, Mon–Thu & Sat 9am–6pm, Fri 9am–5pm, Sun 12.30pm–6.30pm.* ♿. ℘*(0911) 20 65 60.*

Dominating the Hauptmarkt, this Gothic church was built between 1355 and 1358 on the site of the synagogue destroyed in 1349. The main architect is believed to have been Peter Parler. The gable, with its pinnacles and niches, was designed by Adam Krafft (early 16C) and crowns the beautiful façade, one of the only original parts. The clock above the balcony, created in 1509 by Sebastian Lindenast and Georg Heuss, attracts visitors each day at noon for the *Männleinlaufen* (running of the little men). Colourful metal figurines representing the seven Electors are shown swearing allegiance to Emperor Karl IV after the Golden Bull was issued in Nuremberg in 1356.

Inside, the **Tucher Altar** in the chancel is a masterpiece of the pre-Albrecht Dürer Nuremberg School of painting: the triptych (c. 1445–50) represents the Crucifixion, Annunciation and Resurrection. Note the depiction of Jesus on his way to school, in the chancel.

Schöner Brunnen★ (Beautiful Fountain)

The 14C Gothic four-tiered **fountain**, comprising 40 figures *(copies)* dominates the northwest corner of the central Hauptmarkt square. At the top of the 19m/62ft-high pyramid, Moses is surrounded by the prophets; depicted around the base are the seven Electors and nine Old Testament and medieval heroes: three forefathers, three Jews and three Christians. A seamless gold ring hangs from a railing *(on the upper part)*, where an apprentice locksmith is said to have placed it in the 17C. It has been polished by millions of hands touching it for good luck.

The hustle and bustle of the Hauptmarkt, particularly during the Christmas market, masks its grisly origins: the Jewish quarter stood there until 1349, when it was razed to the ground and its occupants murdered by the locals.

Stadtmuseum Fembohaus (Fembo Municipal Museum)

Burgstraße 15. ◷*Open year-round, Tue–Fri 10am–5pm, Sat–Sun 10am–6pm.* ◷*Closed Jan 1, Shrove Tue, Good Fri, Dec 24–26 & 31.* ⊛*5€.* ♿ ℘*(0911) 231 25 95. www.fembohaus.de.*

The museum occupies a 16C Renaissance mansion, the only patrician house to survive in its entirety. Exhibits cover the history of Nuremberg in traditional fashion and through a multimedia journey "narrated" by Albrecht Dürer and Hans Sachs *(⊛4€).*

Kaiserburg (Imperial Castle)

➳*Guided tours (1hr 30min); Apr–Sept, daily 9am–6pm; Oct–Mar, 10am–4pm.* ◷*Closed Jan 1, Shrove Tue, Dec 24, 25 & 31.* ⊛*6€.* ℘*(0911) 2 00 95 40.*

This city landmark perches on a sandstone outcrop in the northern part of the old town. Between 1050 and 1571, all Holy Roman Emperors spent at least some time in residence here.

Tours take in the **Palas** (main palace) with richly furnished rooms, the Romanesque double chapel, the Deep Well and an extensive collection of tools and weapons.

Kaiserburg

Stadtbefestigung★ (Fortifications)

Completed in the mid-15C, Nurenberg's fortifications have survived remarkably well. They consist of an inner and an outer ring *(Zwingermauer)*, the ramparts of the former being topped by a covered parapet walk. A wide, dry moat (in which modern roads now run) was outside the latter. No fewer than 67 defensive towers still exist, including the four 16C **Great Towers:** Frauentor, Spittlertor, Neutor and Laufertor.

The most interesting section extends between the Kaiserburg and the Spittlertor and is easily explored on a 30min walk starting in the castle garden *(Burggarten, below the Kaiserburg)*. From the ramparts walk to the watch-path, which can be followed as far as the Neutorzwinger. Continue inside the ramparts, then cross the suspension footbridge over the Pegnitz River before concluding the stroll.

Tiergärtnerplatz

The half-timbered houses around the picturesque square by the Tiergärtner-tor (gate) suffered the least damage during World War II.

Albrecht-Dürer-Haus★ (Dürer House)

Albrecht-Dürer-Straße 39. ⏰*Open year-round, Tue, Wed & Fri 10am–5pm, Thu 8pm, Sat & Sun 6pm.* ⏰*Closed Dec 24, 25 & 31.* ⬤*5€.* ✆*(0911) 231 25 68.*

The house where **Dürer** lived with his family from 1509 until his death in 1528 now houses a memorial exhibition shedding light on the life and times of this Renaissance giant. Watch a multimedia show to learn more about his work, then peruse original graphics and visit the recreated workshop where live printing demonstrations are held. Audio tours "narrated" by Agnes Dürer are spiked with personal anecdotes and provide insight into the family's daily life.

Sebalduskirche★

Albrecht-Dürer-Platz 1. ⏰*Open Jun–mid-Sept, daily 9.30am–8pm, Jan–Mar to 4pm, Apr–May & mid-Sept–Dec to 6pm.* ♿ ✆*(0911) 214 25 00.*

Nuremberg's oldest parish church was built around 1215 as a three-nave Late Romanesque basilica with two chancels, but was Gothicised shortly thereafter. To the right of the entrance, at the far end of the first chancel, the **St. Peter Altarpiece** (1485) takes pride of place, painted on a gold background in Michael Wolgemut's studio. In the centre, the richly decorated **baptismal font★** (c. 1430) is the oldest bronze religious work in Nuremberg. In the nave, on the inner side of the great left pillar, is the painted statue of St. Sebald (1390) and on the next column, the **Virgin Mary in Glory★** made of pear wood. The magnificent **reliquary shrine of St. Sebald★★** dominates the west chancel. The Gothic tomb was cast in bronze by Peter Vischer (1519) and his sons and is supported by dolphins and snails and adorned with a host of statuettes.

Spielzeugmuseum★ (Toy Museum)

Karlstraße 13–15. ✆*0911 231 31 64. www.museen.nuernberg.de. Open Tue–Fri 10am–5pm, (weekends 6pm) & Mon during Christmas markets 10am–5pm. Closed Dec 31 & Jan 1.* ⬤*5€, children 3€.*

Nuremberg has been famous for making toys since the Middle Ages and both old and new playthings are on display. There is a special play area for children.

▶ *Follow Karlstraße; turn right onto Henkersteg (Executioner's Bridge), which makes a fine sight alongside the beautiful half-timbered Weinstade (wine store), one of Nuremberg's most beautiful buildings. Hutergasse (opposite) will take you to Ludwigsplatz. Turn right to the foot of the Weisserturm (White Tower).*

The bizarre Ehekarrussel (Marriage Carousel) fountain, completed in 1984 by sculptor Jürgen Weber, illustrates the poem by Hans Sachs: "Bittersweet married life".

▷ *Return via Breite Gasse or Karolinenstraße, two shopping streets.*

The Mauthalle (Tollhouse) was built between 1498 and 1502 as an Imperial corn and salt store. Since 1572 it has served as a customs house and a local brewery.

ADDITIONAL SIGHT
Reichsparteigelände ★★ (Former site of the Nazi Party Congress)

Bayernstraße 110 (at Luitpoldhain), exit Nuremberg on the B4 in the direction of Fischbach. ℘0 911 231 56 66. www.museums.nuremberg.de. Open Mon–Fri 9am–6pm, weekends 10am–6pm. ⊙5€, audioguide included. Allow 2–3hrs.

Few German cities were confronted so directly with the face of National Socialism as Nuremberg. The city was promoted by Hitler as the ideological capital of the Third Reich and it was here that the Allies chose to establish the international military tribunal which would judge and condemn leading Nazis. The buildings that stand on the site where the Nazi Party rallies were held stand as witness to the megalomania of the regime. Its Dokumentationszentrum (Documentation Centre) was opened in 2001 and uses diverse modern educational media to help visitors understand the foundations of the Nazi party and its development, as well as the history of the Congress site and the Nazi era in the city. A fascinating visit.

EXCURSIONS
♠♣ Playmobil Funpark

▷ *16km/10mi west of Nuremberg. Leave the city heading towards Ansbach.*
⊙Open daily 9am–6pm. ⊙2.50€–10€ according to the season. ℘0911 9666-1700. www.playmobil-funpark.de.

Created by the Playmobil company, next to its headquarters at Zirndorf, this is a fine year-round theme park.

♠♣ Zoo (Tiergarten)

Am Tiergarten 30. ℘0911 54 546. www.tiergarten.nuernberg.de. Leave town via Bahnhofstraße go as far as the station, then take Kressengartenstraße and Ostendstraße. ⊙Open Apr–Sept 8am–7.30pm, Oct–Mar 9am–5pm. ⊙9€, children 4.50€.

Covering 63 ha/156 acres, this is one of the biggest zoos in Europe and is home to the only dolphinarium in southern Germany. From Easter to October, you can ride the *Adler*, a scale model replica of Germany's first ever train. Take a stroll too in the Hesperides Gardens, landscaped in the 17C and 18C on top of gardens that belonged to medieval peasants.

🚗 DRIVING TOUR

HERSBRUCKER ALB

109km/67.7mi round trip – Allow half a day.

▷ *Follow Sulzbacher Straße, then take the A9 towards Bayreuth.*

Neuhaus an der Pegnitz★

This charming locality, dominated by the tower of Burg Veldenstein, comes into view after a bend in the road.

▷ *Continue following the Pegnitz towards Hersbruck.*

Hersbruck

An attractive little town, Hersbruck has stately burghers' houses and the remains of medieval fortifications. The **Deutsche Hirtenmuseum** (*German Shepherds' Museum, Eishüttlein 7*) contains a folk art collection. Continue towards Happurg over the Pegnitz bridge, from which, looking back, there is a fine view of the Wassertor (fortified gate).

▷ *Return to Nuremberg via the B14.*

ADDRESSES

🏨 STAY

🍽🍺 Hotel Am Jakobsmarkt –
Schottengasse 5. ☎(0911) 200 70. www.hotel-am-jakobsmarkt.de. 72 rooms. Rooms here are either modern and functional or rustic and traditional and spread over the main building and a half-timbered annex reached via an inner courtyard.

🍽🍺 Hotel-Restaurant Jägerheim –
Valznerweiherstraße 75, 90480 Nürnberg-Zerzabelshof. ☎(0911) 94 08 50. www.hotel-jaegerheim.de. 33 rooms. Restaurant 🍽🍺. This quiet hotel near the exhibition grounds is well served by public transport and has smart rooms with pale wooden furniture and a traditional restaurant.

🍽🍺🍺🍺 Le Méridien Grand-Hotel –
Bahnhofstraße 1. ☎(0911) 232 20. www.grand-hotel.de. 186 rooms. ⌖20€. Restaurant 🍽🍺🍺. This palatial hotel has welcomed guests since 1896. Next to the central train station, it has luxurious rooms, the nicest of which have Art Nouveau furnishings. The restaurant exudes refinement with marble floors and slender pillars.

🍴 EAT

USEFUL TIPS

The city's culinary speciality, *Nürnberger Rostbratwürste* is often offered as *Drei im Weckla* (three sausages in a roll) at stalls and in traditional restaurants.

🍽 Historische Bratwurstküche Zum Gulden Stern –
Zirkelschmiedsgasse 26. ☎(0911) 205 92 88. www.bratwurstkueche.de. The oldest sausage kitchen in town occupies a historic house of 1419, with woodsy, country-style wooden décor. Nuremberg sausage straight from the beech-wood grill is the specialty.

🍽 Quo Vadis – *Elbinger Straße 28.*
☎0911 51 55 53. www.ristorante-quovadis.de. Closed Mon. Delicious Italian dishes are served up in a rustic Mediterranean atmosphere.

🍽 Zum Sudhaus – *Bergstraße 20. ☎0911 20 43 14. www.sudhausnuernberg.de.*
This is a Nuremberg institution; its décor evokes Bavaria's grand country houses.

🍽🍺 Sebald – *Weinmarkt 14. ☎(0911) 38 13 03. www.restaurant-sebald.de. Closed Sun.* This charming house in the old town harbours a modern restaurant and bistro with a relaxed ambience. Sun-yellow walls and warm colours give it Tuscan flair.

🍽🍺🍺🍺 Essigbrätlein – *Weinmarkt 3. Closed Dec 24–Jan 1, 2 weeks in Aug and Sun–Mon. ☎(0911) 22 51 31.* Innovative, modern cooking in the elegant old-world style of a 16C inn at a top-rated restaurant near Hauptmarkt.

🍸 NIGHTLIFE

Altstadthof – Braustüberl "Schwarzer Bauer" – *Bergstraße 19–21. ☎(0911) 22 72 17. www.altstadthof.de.* This old-style micro-brewery near the castle is a nice spot to kick back at the end of the day. Sit in the small bar or in the beer garden.

Blauer Adler – *Bahnhofsplatz 5 (in the west wing of the central station). ☎(0911) 242 62 90. www.blaueradler.com. Open daily from 9am.* Match your mood to one of five levels of this buzzy establishment which presents an interesting contrast to the station's historic architecture.

CULTURE
USEFUL TIPS

Events are listed in the monthly magazines *Plärrer* and *Prinz*, available at bookshops and newspaper kiosks. The free monthly listings magazine *Doppelpunkt* can be picked up in bars, restaurants and shops.

Online resources: www.kubiss.de, www.events-nuernberg.de, www.congressing.de.

🛒 SHOPPING
USEFUL TIPS

Karolinenstraße, Breite Gasse and Königsstraße are the city's busiest shopping streets, with department stores and a variety of specialist shops. If you're looking for small gifts, *Lebkuchen* are ideal. Traditionally made during Advent, these spicy gingerbread cookies are now available year-round and often come in attractive metal boxes.

Bamberg★★

Established in the Middle Ages, transformed in the 17C and 18C and spared wartime bomb-raids, Bamberg is one of Germany's most delightful towns with 2 300 well-preserved buildings in styles ranging from the Romanesque to the Baroque. UNESCO honoured Bamberg's old town by giving it World Heritage status in 1993. Foodies should try such local gastronomic delights such as traditionally prepared carp *(Karpfen)*, and smoked beer *(Rauchbier)* which tastes like bacon.

KAISERDOM★★ (IMPERIAL CATHEDRAL)

🕐 *Open Apr–Oct 9.30am–6pm, Nov–Mar 5pm.*

Dominating Bamberg's skyline with its four towers, the Cathedral of St. Peter and St. George was completed in 1237 in a transitional style bridging the Romanesque and the Gothic. The older of its two apses, the eastern Georgenchor, stands upon a raised terrace, while the western Peterschor is entirely Gothic.

The finest of the cathedral entrances is the **Fürstenportal** (Princes' Gate) facing the Domplatz.

It comprises 10 receding arches supported by fluted, ribbed columns decorated with apostles and prophets with

▶ **Population:** 70 000

ℹ **Info:** Geyersworthstraße 3. ℘(0951) 87 11 61. www.bamberg.info.

▶ **Location:** Bamberg was built on seven hills. The River Regnitz and the Rhine-Main-Danube Canal bisect the town, with the historic centre in the upper part of town.

🅿 **Parking:** Garages are in the old town, at Geyersworthstraße 5; on the south side at Schützenstraße 2; and on the north side at Am Georgendamm and Hornthalstraße.

👁 **Don't Miss:** The Old Town, especially the Kaiserdom and the Rathaus.

🕐 **Timing:** Plan on spending a full day to properly sample Bamberg's treasures (and beers).

Christ propped up in the tympanon. The **Adamsporte** (Adam's Door) features diamond and dog-tooth carving.

The interior brims with artistic masterpieces including the celebrated 13C statue of an equestrian knight only known as **Bamberg Rider★★★ (1)** *(Bam-*

Kaiserdom

© Frank/Fotolia.com

BAMBERG CATHEDRAL

berger Reiter), and the statuary group, **The Visitation (2)**. At the centre of the nave is the **tomb**★★★ **(3)** of Emperor Henry II and his wife Kunigunde. It took native son Tilman Riemenschneider 14 years to complete the tomb. The **Christmas Altar**★ **(4)** depicting the Nativity is a stellar 1523 work by Veit Stoß. The funerary statue **(5)**, statue representing the Christian church **(6)**, and another symbolising the Jewish Faith (in the form of a blindfolded woman, **(7)** are also worthy of closer inspection.

☙WALKING TOUR
OLD TOWN
Allow 4hrs.

▶ *Leave from the Obere Brücke bridge which links the old town with the modern city centre.*

Altes Rathaus★
(Old Town Hall)
Standing alone on an islet in the river, Bamberg's unusual medieval town hall is Gothic at its core but got a Baroque makeover in the 18C. Its charms include vividly painted *trompe l'œil* façades, a bridge tower and a small half-timbered annex, known as the Rottmeisterhaus.

▶ *Climb Karolinenstraße up to Domplatz square framed by the cathedral, the New Residence and the Old Residence. Make a short detour through adjoining streets, especially Judenstraße, to admire beautiful façades (e.g. Böttingerhaus Palace at no 14). Also note the statues of the Virgin affixed to the corners of the buildings.*

Alte Hofhaltung
(Old Residence)
⏲*Open May–Oct, Tue–Sun 9am–5pm and for special exhibits.* ⊜*3.50€.* ℘*(0951) 87 11 42.*
Near the dome stands the 16C episcopal palace whose ornate doorway – called the **Schöne Pforte** (beautiful gate) leads to a delightful inner **courtyard**★★ *(Innenhof)* framed by half-timbered Gothic buildings. Inside, the moderately interesting Historical Museum chronicles Bamberg's cultural history.

▶ *Cross the square.*

Neue Residenz
(New Residence)
Domplatz 8. ☙*Guided tours (45min), Apr–Sept, daily 9am–6pm; Oct–Mar, daily 10am–4pm.* ⏲*Closed Jan 1, Shrove*

Tue, Dec 24, 25 & 31. ∞*4€.* ☺ ✆*(0951) 51 93 90. www.schloesser.bayern.de.*
This palace, the largest building in Bamberg, includes two early 17C Renaissance wings *(on Obere Karolinenstraße)*; and two late 17C Baroque wings *(on the Domplatz)*, by local architect Leonard Dientzenhofer.
On the first floor you can peruse paintings by Lucas Cranach the Elder and other Old German Masters, while on the second floor the Imperial apartments wow with intricate parquet floors, Baroque furniture and authentic Gobelins tapestries.
The **Emperors' Hall** *(Kaisersaal)* has outstanding portraits and allegorical frescoes.

▶ *Turn right on Obere Karolinenstraße.*

Kloster St-Michael (St. Michael Abbey)
Franziskanergasse 2. ⏰*Open year-round, Mon–Sat 9am–6pm, Sun from 10am.*
This historic Benedictine abbey on the Michaelsberg hill was commissioned in 1015 by Henry II and rebuilt in neo-Gothic style after a fire in 1610, then remodelled again under the direction of the brothers Dientzenhofer in the 18C. Inside, all eyes go to the ceiling frescoes depicting the "Heavenly Garden" with 578 flowers and herbs. From the terrace behind the church, enjoy a magnificent view over the city.

Fränkisches Brauereimuseum (Franconian Brewery Museum)
⏰*Open Apr–Oct, Wed–Sun 1pm–5pm.* ∞*2.50€.* ✆*(0951) 530 16. www.brauereimuseum.de.*
With its nine breweries, Bamberg is the beer capital of Franconia. This museum in the vaulted cellars of the former Benedictine brewery displays some 1 300 objects that engagingly explain the process of beer making.

▶ *Head back down into town through the terraced gardens. At the foot of the New Residence, pick up Dominikaner-straß to arrive at Untere Brücke bridge.*

The Bamberg Christmas Crèche Tour

During Christmas-time, Bamberg is deluged by visitors eager to follow the city's enchanting Crèche Trail *(Bamberger Krippenweg)*. Dozens of churches, museums and squares are decorated with splendid, handcrafted Nativity scenes.
The route kicks off in the cathedral with Veit Stoß's famous 1523 Nativity altar as well as a modern crèche that tells the famous story in eight enchanting scenes. Other tour highlights include multiple crèches in the peaceful *Maternkapelle* and an exhibit in the *Obere Pfarre* featuring more than 200 individual movable figures averaging 45cm/1.5ft in height. But each of the 33 stations is an artwork in itself, from the enormous manger in Schönleinsplatz with life-size figures in traditional local garb to the tiny crib in the church of St. Gandolf, seen through a special viewer.

From the **Untere Brücke** there is a wonderful view of the half-timbered houses of the old fishermen's quarter along the Regnitz River. It was nicknamed "Little Venice" (Klein Venedig) by Bavarian King Maximilian II. With their balconies and small gardens, sometimes with boats moored alongside, these medieval houses present a romantic and much-photographed setting. Every August, it forms the picturesque backdrop for the "Sandkerwa", a festival revolving around fishermen's jousting competitions *(Fischerstechen)* and an Italian night.

E.T.A. Hoffmann House
Schillerplatz 26. ⏰*Open Apr–Oct Tue–Fri 3pm–5pm, Sat–Sun 10am–noon.* ∞*2€. www.etahg.de.*
Ernst Amadeus Theodor Hoffmann (1775–1822) was one of the pre-eminent writers of the Romantic Age. His stories and novels had a profound influence on other European writers, French ones in

particular. The house where Hoffmann lived between 1809 and 1813 still has some of the original furnishings as well as an exhibition on the man and his accomplishments.

EXCURSIONS
Schloss Weissenstein★
◔ 21km/12mi south in Pommersfelden. Guided tours (1hr) Apr–Oct, daily 10am–5pm (last tour 4pm). 6€. ℘(09548) 981 80. www.schoenborn. de/weissenstein.html.
This palace, designed by Dientzenhofer and Hildebrandt in the 18C, is one of Germany's finest Baroque palaces with a stunning **double staircase**★.
On the ground floor, an artificial grotto opens onto the garden, while the marble hall on the first floor features frescoes by Rottmayr. You'll also get to peek at

the Elector's apartments, a gallery with paintings by Rubens, Titian and Cranach, and the dizzying hall of mirrors.

Walfahrtskirche (Pilgrimage Church) Vierzehnheiligen★★
◔ 30km/18.6mi northeast in Bad Staffelstein. Open Mar-Oct, daily 6.30am–6.30pm, Nov–Feb 7.30am–5.30pm. ℘(09571)950 80. www.vierzehnheiligen.de.
On an open hillside overlooking the Upper Main Valley, this pilgrimage church dedicated to the 14 Auxiliary Saints is a marvel of Baroque architecture created by the era's master builder Balthasar Neumann.

The Pilgrimage – In 1445 and 1446, a shepherd on this hillside reported repeated visions of the infant Jesus accompanied by the "14 Holy Helpers". The worship of this group of saints, actively encouraged by German Dominicans and Cistercians, occurred in the early 15C, when Mysticism prevailed. Visions and voices were commonplace (those heard by Joan of Arc, born in 1412, were of St. Catherine and St. Margaret, themselves members of the Auxiliary Saints). Devotion to the Holy Helpers remained alive for many years, attracting crowds of pilgrims to a chapel which was superseded, in the 18C, by this sumptuous Rococo church.

Exterior

The ochre sandstone basilica was built between 1743 and 1772 following designs by Balthasar Neumann. The west façade is framed by domed towers, while the ornately decorated gables are adorned with a statue of Christ flanked by allegorical figures of Faith and Charity.

Interior

The interior layout is organised as a succession of three oval bays framed by colonnades and covered by low inner domes. The Rococo decoration features outstanding colour combinations inside the domes, delicate stuccowork, rich gold outlines defining the woodwork of the galleries, and graceful cherubs.

Nothelfer-Altar★★
(Altar to the "Auxiliary Saints")

The true heart of the church is the bay containing the altar to the Auxiliary Saints. A Rococo pyramid with a pierced baldaquin, this remarkable work was designed by Johann Michel Küchel, a student of Balthasar Neumann, and executed by Johann Michael Feuchtmayr and his fellow stucco-workers from the prestigious Wessobrunn School in 1764. It was placed in the physical centre of the church, right where the shepherd's visions were believed to have occurred. Artistic representations include:

◆ **Balustrade: 1)** St. Denys
2) St. Blaise **3)** St. Erasmus
4) St. Cyriacus (delivery from the Devil at the final hour).

◆ **Altar niches: 5)** St. Catherine, patron saint of the learned, of students and girls wishing to marry (signifying the model of Christian wisdom) **6)** St. Barbara, patron saint of miners, artillerymen and prisoners (signifying the grace of a noble death).

◆ **Buttresses: 7)** St. Acacius (the agonies of death) **8)** St. Giles, the only intercessor not to suffer martyrdom **9)** St. Eustace (converted by the vision of a stag with a Cross between its antlers) **10)** St. Christopher (patron saint of travellers).

◆ **Atop the baldaquin: 11)** St. Vitus **12)** St. Margaret (intercession for the forgiveness of sins) **13)** St. George, patron saint of peasants and their possessions **14)** St. Pantaleon.

After exploring the abbey, trek up the slopes above the church for inspiring views of the edifice itself, the nearby fortress-like yellow sandstone abbey of Banz across the Main River, and the surrounding countryside.

Coburg★

◗ *46km/29mi north.*
Dominated by a mighty fortress, Coburg was once the capital of the dukes of Saxe-Coburg. It has beautiful façades, especially around the Marktplatz.

Veste Coburg (Fortress)★★

◷*Open Apr–Oct, daily 9.30am–5pm, Nov–Mar, Tue–Sun 1pm–4pm.* ◷*Closed Shrove Tue, Dec 24, 25 & 31.* ◉*5€.* ℘*(095 61) 87 90. www.kunstsamm lungen-coburg.de.*

The Noble Dynasty of Saxe-Coburg

In a history of intrigue and diplomacy spanning centuries, the noble dynasty of Saxe-Coburg was related either directly or through marriage to nearly every royal family of Europe: Belgian, Portuguese, Russian, Swiss and Bulgarian. The marriage between Edward, the Duke of Kent, and the Coburg Princess Victoire produced Queen Victoria; she, in turn, married a cousin: Prince Albert of Saxe-Coburg.

Going back to the 11C, this well-preserved fortress is guarded by a triple ring of fortified walls. In 1530 Martin Luther famously sought refuge here while defending his faith at the Diet of Augsburg; the rooms where he stayed are now a museum. The precious **art collections**★, include paintings by Dürer and Cranach and the largest Venetian glassware collection in Europe.

Schloss Ehrenburg

🚪 *Guided tours (50min), Apr–Sept Tue–Sun 9am–5pm; Oct–Mar 10am–3pm.* ⏰ *Closed Jan 1, Shrove Tue, Nov 1, Dec 24, 25 & 31.* 💶 *4€.* ✆ *(095 61) 80 88 32. www.sgvcoburg.de.*
This castle was the residence of the Dukes of Coburg from 1547 to 1918. Today the Renaissance palace features a Baroque interior with an early 19C English neo-Gothic façade. Castle rooms house sumptuous Empire and *Biedermeier* furniture. An art gallery contains works by German and Dutch masters.

ADDRESSES

🏨 STAY

😐 **Brasserie Fässla** – *Obere Königsstraße.* ✆*0951 26516. faessla@t-online.de. 26 rooms.* 🍴. These simple rooms above the brewhouse are ideal for sleeping off a beer or two!

😐 **Arkaden Hotel im Kloster** – *Karmelitenplatz (entrance on the road behind the church).* ✆*0951 8410. www.arkaden-hotel-im-kloster.de. 23 rooms.* 🍴*5€.* This gorgeous, peaceful hotel close to the historic centre offers excellent value for money.

😐 **Hotel IBIS am Schillerplatz** – *Theatergassen 10.* ✆*0951 980 480. www.ibishotel.com. 50 rooms.* The main advantage of staying in this chain hotel is its location in the historic centre.

😐 **Wilde Rose** – *Kesselerstraße (in the pedestrianised zone).* ✆*0951 981820. www.hotel-wilde-rose.de. 29 rooms.* Located in the heart of the city.

😐 **Barock-Hotel am Dom** – *Vorderer Bach 4.* ✆*(0951) 540 31. www.barockhotel.de. Closed Feb. 19 rooms.* Next to the cathedral, this sweet hotel occupies a building with an elegant 18C Baroque facade. Design details abound and breakfast is served beneath a Gothic vault.

😐😐 **Romantik Hotel Weinhaus Messerschmitt** – *Lange Straße 41.* ✆*(0951) 29 78 00. www.hotel-messerschmitt.de. 67 rooms. Restaurant* 😐😐. This hotel is the ancestral home of aviation pioneer Willy Messerschmitt. A recent expansion has added a modern annex to the historic building. The restaurant has a charming terrace.

🍴 EAT

😐 **Gasthaus Zum Sternla** – *Lange Straße 46.* ✆*0951 28750. www.sternla.de. Open 10am–11pm.* Right in the heart of town, this is Bamberg's oldest inn. It has a small garden and serves local Franconian specialities.

😐 **Brauerei Klosterbräu** – *Oberer Mühmbrücke 1–3.* ✆*0951 522 65. 10.30am–10pm.* Set in the historic watermills quarter of town, this brasserie serves local Franconian specialities. In summer dine out on the terrace beside the Regnitz.

😐 **Historischer Brauereiausschank Schlenkerla** – *Dominikanerstraße 6.* ✆*0951 560 60. www.schlenkerla.de. Closed Tue. 9.30am–11.30pm.* In the shadow of the cathedral, this half-timbered establishment serves local Franconian specialities and *Rauchbier* (smoked beer), brewed on the premises.

Bayreuth★

Bayreuth is the Holy Grail to Wagner fans who flock to town in August for the prestigious Bayreuth Festival. But Wagner was not the only one to leave his mark on the town. In fact, it was one of the most cultivated women of the 18C, the Margravine Wilhelmina, who transformed the town into the cultural centre it remains to this day.

A BIT OF HISTORY

Princess Wilhelmina – Wilhelmina, sister of Prussian King Frederick the Great, had the great misfortune to be paired with a rather dull husband: Margrave Friedrich of Brandenburg-Bayreuth. A gifted artist, writer, composer and patroness, she turned her energy towards transforming Bayreuth into an artistic and cultural hub and surrounding herself with clever personages of the age. Some of Bayreuth's finest buildings date back to her lifetime (1709–1758).

Wagner and the festival – Wagner moved to Bayreuth in 1872 along with his wife Cosima, the daughter of the Hungarian composer **Franz Liszt**. Wagner's music was stimulated by admiration for his father-in-law, who is said to be indirectly responsible for many of Wagner's masterworks. The writer and composer of *Parzival* and *Tannhäuser*, Richard Wagner searched far and wide for the ideal music venue. With the support of King Ludwig II of Bavaria, he designed his own Festival Hall *(Festspielhaus)*, revolutionary in its

- ▶ **Population:** 74 400
- **Info:** Luitpoldplatz 9, 95444 Bayreuth. ℘(0921) 885 88. www.bayreuth.de.
- **Location:** Between the wooded heights of the Fichtelgebirge and the desolate landscape of Swiss Franconia, the A9 autobahn linking Munich and Berlin runs near the town.
- **Parking:** There are plenty of parking garages.
- **Don't Miss:** The Bayreuth Festival if you're an opera fan.
- **Timing:** Allow half a day.
- **Kids:** Cave explorations in tours ① and ③.

day for its generous audience space as well as its outstanding acoustics.
The first festival took place in 1876. After his death in 1883, the tradition continued under his daughter, Cosima and, subsequently, his son Siegfried, then his grandsons Wieland (d. 1966) and Wolfgang, who retired in 2008, passing on the torch to his daughters Eva Wagner-Pasquier and Katharina Wagner.

SIGHTS
Markgräfliches Opernhaus (Margravial Opera House)★

Opernstraße 14. ◷*Open Apr–Sept, daily 9am–6pm; Oct–Mar, daily 10am–4pm.* ◷*Closed Jan 1, Shrove Tue, Dec 24, 25 & 31.* ⊛*5€.* ⚇. ℘*(0921) 759 69 22. www.bayreuth-wilhelmine.de.*

Bayreuth Festival

From 25 July until 28 August, Bayreuth reverberates to the sound of Wagner. But don't think you can just show up and buy a ticket: you have to apply for one. Each year, more than half a million opera fans vie for the 60 000 tickets, which are allocated by lottery. Wait times of seven years or more are not uncommon. Applications can only be made in writing and need to be sent no later than mid-September for the next year's festival to: **Bayreuther Festspiele – Kartenbüro – Postfach 100262, 95402 Bayreuth, Germany**. Returned ticket are sometimes available on performance day, but you need to get up early: people start queuing around 6am. For the full scoop, see www.bayreuth-festspiele.de.

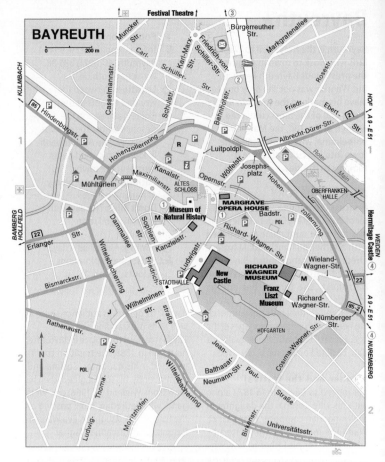

BAYREUTH

0 ——— 200 m

WHERE TO STAY

Goldener Anker.....................①
Grunau Hotel.........................④

WHERE TO EAT

Bayerischer Hof....................②
Bürgerreuth Ristorante...........③

Oskar - Das Wirtshaus
    am Markt............................①
Zur Sudpfanne.....................④

Margravine Wilhelmina commissioned this gorgeous Baroque theatre in 1748 as a venue for the opera and ballet.

The austere façade gives no clue to the exuberance of the **interior decoration**★ by Giuseppe Galli Bibiena of Bologna. The reds, greens and browns harmonise perfectly with the gilded stuccowork on the columns; the interior is constructed entirely of wood. Visitors are treated to a 45-minute sound and light show about the theatre and its patroness.

Neues Schloss (New Palace)

🕐Open Apr–Sept, daily 9am–6pm; Oct–Mar, Tue–Sun 10am–4pm.
🕐Closed Jan 1, Shrove Tue, Dec 24, 25 & 31. ᦉ5€. ᦉ. ☎(0921) 75 96 90.

After a fire destroyed their old residence, Wilhelmina directed the construction of this palace and even designed some its most memorable features, including the **Broken Mirrors Cabinet**★ (Spiegelscherbenkabinett). Elsewhere the lavish **decorations**★ reflect the masterful Rococo flourishes of stucco artist Jean Baptiste Pedrozzi. Wilhelmina's private quarters were on the first floor of the north wing. On the ground floor are a small exhibition about this remarkable woman and a collection of Bayreuth porcelain. Elsewhere you can admire 18C Dutch and German paintings, including the *Four Seasons* cycle by Jan Brueghel the Elder.

Richard-Wagner-Museum★

Richard-Wagner-Straße 48.
⊶ *Closed for renovation until at least 2013.* ℰ *(0921) 75 72 80.*
www.wagnermuseum.de.
Wagner's private mansion, built with funds supplied by Ludwig II and called **Haus Wahnfried**, is a key stop on any Wagnerian pilgrimage, even though the only remaining original feature of the house is the façade.

Displays including furniture, manuscripts, pianos and Wagner's death mask evoke the maestro's life and work as well as the history of the Bayreuth Festival. The composer and his wife Cosima lie buried in the garden.

Franz Liszt Museum

Wahnfriedstraße 9. ◔*Open Jul–Aug, 10am–5pm, Sept–Jun 10am–noon & 2pm–5pm.* ◔*Closed Jan 1, Dec 24, 25 & 31.* ◒*2€.* ℰ *(0921) 516 64 88.*
www.bayreuth.de.
The house where the piano virtuoso spent his final years is now a museum dedicated to his life and work. The exhibition is an engagingly presented assembly of portraits, letters, his piano and other objects. Liszt is buried in the town cemetery *(Stadtfriedhof – entrance on Erlanger Straße).*

Festspielhaus (Festival Hall)

Festspielhügel 1–2 (enter via Karl-Marx-Straße). ⊶*Guided tours Sept–Oct, Tue–Sun 10am, 11am, 2pm, 3pm; Dec–Apr, Tue–Sun 10am and 2pm.* ◒*5€.*
ℰ *(0921) 787 80. www.bayreuther-festspiele. de.*
The Festival Hall on the Grüner Hügel (green hill) was inaugurated in 1876 with a performance of the *Ring of the Nibelungen* cycle. It ranks among the world's most important opera stages (although

it does not have a resident ensemble). It is only used for the Wagner Festival. Famous for its exceptional acoustics, the opera house incorporates many design elements that were revolutionary for the time. The orchestra, for instance, was hidden below the stage so that the audience could focus entirely on the performance. The amphitheatre layout results in excellent sight lines. The wooden seats, however, are infamous for their lack of comfort!

Urwelt-Museum Oberfranken (Museum of Prehistory)

Kanzleistraße 1. ◔*Open year-round, Tue–Sun 10am–5pm (Jul–Aug also on Mon).* ◒*2€.* ℰ *(092151) 12 11.*
www.urwelt-museum.de.
This museum presents the natural history of Upper Franconia over the last 500 million years.

EXCURSION

Schloss Eremitage (Hermitage Palace)★

▶ *4km/2.5mi east via Wieland-Wagner-Straße.* ◔*Open Apr–Sept 9am–6pm; Oct 1–15 10am–4pm.*
◔*Closed mid-Oct–Mar.* ◒*2.50€.*
♿ ℰ *(0921) 759 69 37.*
This summer palace was a gift from her husband to the Margravine Wilhelmina, She also built the **New Palace** *(Neues Schloss)* and created the magnificent English-garden-style **Schloßpark★** with its pavilions, follies and fountains, most famously the **Lower Grotto**, a vast basin with sculpture fountains whose jets blend with water gushing from the surrounding arcade.

🚗 DRIVING TOURS

1 FRANCONIAN SWITZERLAND★★ (Fränkische Schweiz)

Round-trip tour of 105km/65mi – Allow one day.

Tüchersfeld

This charming village is dramatically framed by jagged rocks.

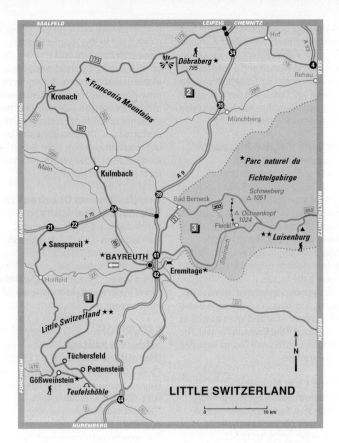

LITTLE SWITZERLAND

Pottenstein

The castle, a former residence of the Prince-Bishops of Bamberg, overlooks the town. Natural wonders, like gorges and caves, dot the local countryside.

🕯🕯 Teufelshöhle (Devil's Cave)

🕯🕯Guided tours (45min) Apr–Oct, daily 9am–5pm; Nov–Feb, Tue & Sat–Sun 10am–3pm. Last tour half hour before closing. ⊘Closed Dec 24 & 25. ⊛3.80€. ℘(09243) 208. www.teufelshoehle.de.
Explore an ethereal wonderland of stalactites and stalagmites in Germany's largest caverns. The Barbarossadom (Cathedral of Barbarossa) is especially impressive.

Gößweinstein★

This tiny village is dominated by a huge and richly decorated basilica designed

between 1730 and 1739 by Balthasar Neumann. A 45min loop trail starting at the castle above town leads to several fine **vistas**★★ over the Wiesent valley.

Sanspareil★

After completion of Bayreuth's Eremitage, Margravine Wilhelmina and Margrave Friedrich converted an old hunting estate into an impressive **rock garden**★ named Sanspareil ("without equal" in French).

Burg Zwernitz

⊘Open Apr–Sept, Tue–Sun 9am–6pm; 1–15 Oct 10am–4pm. ⊛2€. ♿. ℘(0974) 909 89 06.
From 1338, this 12C fortress was the property of the Hohenzollern margraves before falling to Bavaria in 1810. Reopened in 2011, the fortress contains furnishings and a selection of 16C–18C weapons. The keep offers good **views**.

2 THE FRANCONIAN FOREST★ (Frankenwald)

Round-trip of 125km/78mi – Allow 5hrs.

Döbraberg★

🚶 *45min round-trip walk. Climb to the look-out tower (795m/2 608ft).*

The majestic **panorama**★ extends as far as the Thuringian Mountains in the north and the Fichtelgebirge in the south.

Kronach

Festung Rosenberg (16C–18C), one of the largest medieval fortresses in Germany, towers over the small town of Kronach and the wooded heights of the Frankenwald. Inside, the Franconian Gallery displays works by medieval and Renaissance artists, including sculptor Tilman Riemenschneider and paintings by Kronach-born **Lucas Cranach the Elder** (⌖ *see INTRODUCTION: Art).*

Kulmbach

Once the seat of the Hohenzollern margraves, Kulmbach is famous today for its strong beers *(Kapuziner, Mönchshof).*

The **Plassenburg**★ (🕐 *open Apr–Sept daily 9am–6pm; Nov–Mar daily 10am–4pm;* 🕐 *closed Jan 1, Dec 24, 25 & 31;* ⟶4€; ♿ 𝒫 *(09221) 822 00; www.schloesser.bayern.de),* another well-preserved medieval fortress, melds a strong, defensive exterior with an elegant **Renaissance courtyard**★★. Displays include 300 000 **tin soldiers**★ from the Deutsches Zinnfigurenmuseum (German Tin Figure Museum).

3 FICHTELGEBIRGE NATURE PARK★

Loop trip of 92km/57mi – Allow 5hrs.

The **panoramic route**★ follows the Steinach Valley into the granite massif of the Fichtelgebirge. Above Fleckl, a cable-car climbs the **Ochsenkopf** *(alt.1 024m/3 360ft).*

Luisenburg★★

This labyrinth of enormous granite boulders makes for a pleasant hike along a pine-shaded, hilly path *(blue arrows indicate the way up, red the way down).* Several look-out points along the way afford views of the Fichtelgebirge.

ADDRESSES

🏨 STAY

🍽🍽 **Grunau Hotel** – *Kemnather Straße 27 (east of Wieland-Wagner-Straße and Königsallee). 𝒫 (0921) 798 00. www.grunau-hotel.de.* On the top floors of a shopping centre, this modern hotel has spacious and quiet rooms. Guests get discounted access to a fitness centre.

🍽🍽🖫**Goldener Anker** – *Opernstraße 6. 𝒫 (0921) 650 51. www.anker-bayreuth.de. Closed Dec 24–mid-Jan. 35 rooms. Restaurant*🍽🍽🖫. Owned by the same family since the 15C, each room at this venerable hotel has its own style, but all are spacious. The intimate restaurant serves upscale French cuisine.

🍴 EAT

🍽 **Oskar – Das Wirtshaus am Markt** – *Maximilianstraße 33. 𝒫 (0921) 516 05 53. www.oskar-bayreuth.de.* This restaurant in the former town hall has a pretty winter garden and a terrace. Bavarian specialities (great dumplings!) make up the bulk of the earthy menu.

🍽🍽 **Zur Sudpfanne** – *Oberkonnersreuther Straße 6, 95448 Bayreuth-Oberkonnersreuth (southeast along Nürnberger Straße) 𝒫 (0921) 528 83. www.sudpfanne.de.* This popular restaurant in a former brewery building is well known for its creative international cuisine infused with local touches. Leafy beer garden.

🍽🍽 **Bürgerreuth Ristorante** – *An der Bürgerreuth 20. 𝒫 0921 784 00. www.buergerreuth.de. Closed Mon in winter.* Excellent classic and home-style Italian cuisine.

🍽🍽 **Bayerischer Hof** – *Bahnhostraße 14. 𝒫 0921 786 00. www.bayerischer-hof.de. Closed 2–11 Jan.* Stylish French bistro near the station.

CENTRAL GERMANY

After travelling around Germany's heartland, it is easy to understand why the country is often called the "land of poets and thinkers". Martin Luther studied in Erfurt, posted his "95 Theses" in Wittenberg and translated the Bible from Greek into German at Eisenach's Wartburg Castle. Nearby Weimar drew an entire cast of intellectual and creative giants, from Cranach to Bach, Goethe to Schiller, Herder to Liszt. The Bauhaus movement was born here, later peaking in Dessau. Architectural gems abound, from medieval cathedrals to Neoclassical palaces and fantastical Hundertwasser buildings. Those looking for nature should head for the trails of the Thuringian Forest or take a leisurely stroll around the richly landscaped gardens at Wörlitz.

Highlights

Touring Central Germany

A tour could begin in Marburg, a bustling university town about 100km/60mi north of Frankfurt. Its landmark church is dedicated to St. Elizabeth (1207–32), who was buried here after her short life of caring for the sick and poor while living at Wartburg in nearby Eisenach (incidentally the birthplace of Johann Sebastian Bach). From this hilltop castle, take in the verdant expanse of the Thuringian Forest, which is bisected by the 168km/104mi-long Rennsteig, Germany's oldest (since the 14C) and most popular long-distance hiking trail. It skirts postcard-pretty villages, including Goethe's old haunt, Ilmenau.

The town most closely associated with Germany's literary giant, though, is Weimar, where Goethe lived for 57 years. His authentically preserved home is now a place of pilgrimage, as is the one of his friend and colleague Friedrich Schiller. Along with a dozen other sites, the buildings were UNESCO-listed in 1999. Meanwhile, north of Weimar, you can connect with the darkest chapter in German history at chilling Buchenwald concentration camp memorial.

Travelling east for 24km/15mi takes you to Erfurt, capital of the state of Thuringia and a university town since 1392. Its medieval centre is one of the best-preserved anywhere in Germany

Dom St. Marien and Severi-Kirche, Erfurt

© Wasiseven/Dreamstime.com

with plenty of lovingly restored buildings and the unique Merchants' Bridge (Krämerbrücke). The cathedral is another showstopper. And don't miss a stroll around the tangled old town.

Like Weimar, Jena too was an intellectual centre during the Enlightenment but since the 19C it is primarily known as a city of science and optics. A tour of the Optical Museum is a must. If you have the kids in tow, make a quick detour down the scenic Saale Valley to the Feengrotten (Fairy Grottoes) in Saalfeld.

Alternatively, steer north and pay your respects to Georg Friedrich Händel in his birth town of Halle and to Martin Luther, a native of Eisleben. Wittenberg, where Luther posted his "95 Theses" against Church corruption, is further north, near the Bauhaus city of Dessau and the fabulous Wörlitz gardens. Finally, follow the Elbe up to Magdeburg where a key stop is the early-13C Dom, Germany's oldest Gothic cathedral and the burial site of Otto I, who was crowned first Holy Roman Emperor in 962.

Magdeburg★★

Magdeburg developed on an important trade crossroads and was one of the key cities in the Middle Ages until the Thirty Years' War brought the glory years to an end. During World War II, Magdeburg was almost completely destroyed by fire-bombing and in GDR days became a model city of socialist architecture. In 1990, it beat Halle to become capital of the federal state of Sachsen-Anhalt.

A BIT OF HISTORY

A steadfast merchant city – Magdeburg was founded by Emperor Otto I, who built his favourite palace here and raised the town to the status of archbishopric in 968. The early success of this commercial centre, which declared its support for Martin Luther in 1524, was brought to an end in 1631 when imperial troops laid siege to the town before destroying it and killing most of its 20 000 inhabitants.

Famous local figures include Baroque composer Georg Philipp Telemann (1681–1767).

DOM★★★
(CATHEDRAL)

Open May–Sept, 10am–6pm; Apr & Oct, 10am–5pm; Nov–Mar, 10am–4pm. Sun from 11.30am.
(0391) 541 04 36.
www.magdeburgerdom.de.

Begun in 1209 and the burial site of Otto I, Magdeburg's Dom is considered the oldest Gothic house of worship in Germany and, at 120m/393.7ft long, is also one of the largest. The towers, though, were only completed in 1520. The light-flooded if rather austere interior is an artistic treasure trove.

The most precious works are the famous early-Gothic sandstone sculptures of the Five Wise and Five Foolish Virgins (1250). Also of note are the intricately carved choir stalls (1363) and the emotional war memorial by 20C artist Ernst Barlach.

> **Population:** 230 500
> **Info:** Ernst-Reuter-Allee 12. (0391) 194 33. www.magdeburg-tourist.de.
> **Location:** Magdeburg is in the heart of Sachsen-Anhalt and is served by the A2 (Berlin–Hannover) and A14 motoways (Leipzig).
> **Parking:** Garages are near the Johanniskirche and on the Elbuferpromenade.
> **Don't Miss:** A walk through the old town.
> **Kids:** Elbauenpark.
> **Timing:** Magdeburg can be appreciated in one day.

OLD TOWN
Kloster Unser Lieben Frauen★★
(Our Lady Abbey)

Regierungsstraße 4-6. Open year-round, Tue–Sun 10am-5pm.
2€. (0391) 56 50 20.
www.kunstmuseum-magdeburg.de.

Magdeburg's oldest surviving building is a harmonious 12C Romanesque design converted into a concert hall and an art museum. On display are contemporary works by Giovanni Anselmo, Mario Merz, Siegfried Anzinger, Leiko Ikemura, Enrico Castellani and others, as well as a survey of sculpture from antiquity to the present.

Rathaus (Town Hall)

On Markt, outside the Italian Renaissance-style town hall, stands a gilded replica of the famous equestrian statue of the Magdeburg Knight (1240). The original is in the Kulturhistorisches Museum (Cultural History Museum).

Grüne Zitadelle★
(Green Citadel)

Breiter Weg 9. Guided tours (1hr) year-round, Mon–Fri 11am, 3pm and 5pm, Sat–Sun hourly 10am–5pm. Tours leave from the Citadel Infopoint.

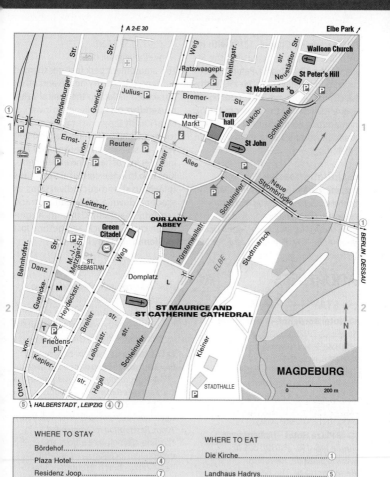

↑ A 2–E 30

Elbe Park ↗

↗ BERLIN, DESSAU

MAGDEBURG

N

0   200 m

⑤ ↘ HALBERSTADT, LEIPZIG ④ ⑦

WHERE TO STAY		WHERE TO EAT	
Bördehof	①	Die Kirche	①
Plaza Hotel	④	Landhaus Hadrys	⑤
Residenz Joop	⑦		

⌖6€. ℘(0391) 620 86 55.
www.gruene-zitadelle.de.
Close to the Dom, this whimsical pink
building was the final work of Austrian
cult artist and architect Friedensreich
Hundertwasser (1928–2000). Completed
in 2005, it perfectly reflects his design
philosophy of wanting to create "a natural oasis for humanity within a sea of
functional spaces".

Construction of this unusual building in
the heart of town engendered considerable controversy. It contains flats, offices,
shops and a hotel as well as a permanent
exhibition showcasing Hundertwasser's
work and vision.

Johanniskirche
(Church of St. John)

🕑Open Mar–Oct, Tue–Sun 10am–6pm;
Nov–Feb, 10am–5pm. No visits on
event days. ℘(0391) 593 44 50.
www.mvgm-online.de.
Magdeburg's oldest parish church (941),
in which Martin Luther preached (see
the memorial in front of the church), was
all but destroyed during World War II. It
is now used as an events and exhibition
venue.

Petriberg (St. Peter's Hill)

North of the town hall, on the banks of
the Elbe, three churches crown St. Peter's hill. The small Magdalenenkapelle

(St. Madeleine Chapel, 1315) with its intricate Gothic net vaulting; the St. Petrikirche (Church of St. Peter), a three-aisled Gothic hall-church (14–15C) with a handsome Gothic red-brick south porch; and the Church of the Walloons (1285), named for a community of protestant Walloon refugees who settled here in 1694.

♿♿Elbauenpark★

Tessenowstraße 5a. Access from the city centre via Schleinufer and Markgrafenstraße. ◐*Open May–Sept, daily 9am–8pm; Mar–Apr 10am–6pm, Oct 9am–6pm, Nov–Feb 10am–4pm.* ◉*3€.*

♿ ☎*(0391) 59 34 50.*
www.elbauenpark.de.
This amusement park features themed gardens, a butterfly house and other attractions including the conical **Jahrtausendturm**★★ (millennium tower), at 60m/196.8ft the world's tallest wooden tower. Inside, an exhibit traces 6 000 years of science and technology and includes lots of hands-on experiments. Kids also love the colourful **Spielhaus** (playhouse) and such diversions as scooting down a tobogganing track, tackling the 25m/82ft-high Angerfelsen climbing rock, and getting lost and found in a leafy labyrinth.

ADDRESSES

🏨 STAY

☞ **Hotel Bördehof** – *Magdeburger Straße 42, 39179 Magdeburg-Ebendorf.* ☎*(039203) 515 10. www.boerdehof.de. 42 rooms.* Near the autobahn, this converted farmhouse has cheerful, modern rooms. Cap off a day on the tourist track with a relaxing sauna or by watching the pretty birds fluttering around the on-site aviary.

☞☞ **Plaza Hotel** – *Halberstädter Straße 146–150.* ☎*(0391) 605 10. www.12plaza.de. 104 rooms. Restaurant*☞☞. This hotel is on the outskirts of town and well served by public transport. Behind its modern, white façade await comfortable rooms tastefully decorated in English country style. The restaurant serves classic German food.

☞☞ **Residenz Joop** – *Jean-Burger-Straße 16.* ☎*(0391) 626 20. www.residenz joop.de. 25 rooms.* This villa hotel is in a quiet residential district. From 1903 until World War II it was the Swedish consulate. Rooms are spacious, comfortable and tastefully furnished.

🍴 EAT

☞–☞☞ **Le Frog – Brasserie am See** – *Heinrich-Heine-Platz 1 (in the Rotehorn public park on the right bank of the Elbe).* ☎*(0391) 531 35 56. www.lefrog-md.de.* This glass pavilion occupies a pretty lakeside spot in the sprawling Rotehorn

park. Whether it's coffee and cake, a Mediterranean meal or a late-night cocktail, there's something for everyone here. If the weather permits, you can sit in the pleasant *Biergarten*.

☞☞ **Die Kirche** – *(on the right bank of the Elbe, cross the two arms of the river and follow Cracauer Straße, Genthiner Straße and Pechauer Straße south).* ☎*0391 535 33 52. www.kirche-prester.de. Open Mon–Fri from 5pm, weekends from 10am. Reservation recommended.* This fine-dining place enjoys an exceptional location in an ancient neo-Gothic church. In summer, you can sit on the beautiful terrace at the water's edge.

☞☞☞ **Landhaus Hadrys** – *An der Halberstädter Chaussee 1, Ottersleben. www.landhaus-hadrys.de.* ☎*0391 662 66 81.* This bright, modern restaurant is set in a lovely old villa with a nice lounge. A pleasant terrace looks onto the garden.

🌙 NIGHTLIFE

Alex – *Ulrichplatz 2 (southeast of the roundabout between Ernst-Reuter-Allee and Otto-von-Guericke-Straße).* ☎*(0391) 59 74 90. www.alexgastro.de.* This hotspot for the young and young-at-heart bustles all day long. In the morning, crowds come for the big breakfast buffet, at night for cocktails. A good place to watch the sun set over the Ulrichplatz fountain.

Wörlitzer Park★★

Wörlitz Park is the oldest landscaped park on the European mainland and part of the Garden Realm created by Prince Leopold III around Dessau between 1764 and 1800. Retaining all its original magic, the park has enchanting canalside trails, voluptuous hedges and lakes with small islands reached by ferry or gondola. In 2000, the gardens' special appeal was recognised by UNESCO, which placed Wörlitz on its list of World Heritage Sites.

- **Info:** Förstergasse 26, 06786 Wörlitz. ℘(034905) 202 16. www.wbticket.de.
- **Location:** Wörlitz Park is 17km/10.5mi west of Dessau. From the A9 (Leipzig–Berlin), take exit 10 and follow the B185 to Orienbaum, then the B107 to Wörlitz.
- **Don't Miss:** A leisurely stroll through the gardens.
- **Timing:** Allow at least half a day to see the grounds and buildings.
- **Kids:** Exploring the lake and small islands by boat.

A BIT OF HISTORY

Prince Leopold III Friedrich Franz von Anhalt-Dessau (1740–1817), known as "Father Franz" to his subjects, was an enlightened ruler to whom the welfare of his small state was paramount (🕯️ see DESSAU). His endeavours extended far beyond material matters; he sought to link the beautiful with the practical, promoting literature, music, architecture and garden design.

A number of trips to England provided him with food for progressive thought and paved the way for his planned reforms. It was also in England that he saw his first landscaped parks and was inspired to create such a park environment of his own. Master builder **Friedrich Wilhelm von Erdmannsdorff**, who had accompanied him on his trips, acted as his assistant and like-minded adviser. The gardens were completed around 1800.

VISIT

Schloss★ (Palace)

🚣 Guided tours (1hr), May–Sept, Tue–Sun 10am-6pm, Apr & Oct 10am–5pm. ⌖4.50€. ℘(034905) 40 90. www.gartenreich.com.

Built by Erdmannsdorf between 1769 and 1773, this is the earliest Neoclassical

Admiring the scenery on board a gondola

©World Pictures/Photoshot

palace outside of England; it replaced an earlier Baroque hunting lodge.

The two-storey yellow-and-white building sits dignified against a backdrop of mature trees. Erdmannsdorff made ingenious use of the many technical innovations of the day, including water pipes, lifts, cast-iron stoves, folding beds and cupboards, all of which vastly improved the living standard of the ruling family.

The original interior has survived virtually intact and sports ceiling frescoes and murals inspired by antiquity. Most sculpture and carpentry work was undertaken by local people.

The elegant **Speisesaal** (dining room) with its elaborate stucco decoration and slim Corinthian pillars, and the great **Großer Festsaal** (banqueting hall) are striking. The **library** is richly hung with paintings (Snyders, Van Ruysdael, Antoine Pesne) and fitted with furniture, the highlight of which is the suite of Roentgen pieces.

Gotisches Haus★ (Gothic House)

Guided tours (1hr), Apr & Oct Tue–Sun 10am–5pm; May–Sept, Tue–Sun, 10am–6pm. 4.50€. (034905) 40 90. www.gartenreich.com.

One of the earliest neo-Gothic buildings in Germany, the Gothic House was erected between 1773 and 1813. The canal-facing main façade was inspired by the Church of Maria dell' Orto in Venice. While the palace served official purposes, this structure was the prince's private refuge. Through Swiss scholar Johann Caspar Lavater he acquired an outstanding **Swiss stained glass★** collection from the 15C to the 17C, which has intact. All rooms feature 16C–18C paintings by Dutch, German and Italian masters, including Tintoretto and Lucas Cranach the Elder.

Wörlitz Park by Gondola★

Boats depart from the pier (Gondolastation) Apr–Oct , daily 11am–4pm; May–Sept, daily 10am–6pm. 45min. 6€. www.woerlitz-information. de or www.gartenreich.com. Phone ahead to book gondola tours for groups (034905) 3 10 09.

An enchanting way to experience the charms of this extensive garden landscape is being poled around in a romantic gondola. Tours travel across Lake Wörlitz, glide through a canal and pass the Gothic House. Each boat seats up to 15 people comfortably.

EXCURSION
LUTHERSTADT WITTENBERG

23km/14mi east of Wörlitz.
Schlossplatz 2. (03491) 49 86 10. www.wittenberg.de.

Wittenberg enjoys a pleasant location between the wooded hills of Fläming and the Elbe. The town was the centre of Martin Luther's work and the place where, on 31 October 1517, he posted his famous "95 Theses" against Church corruption. This was a key step towards the Reformation and a new era in the religious and political history of the Western world. Sites related to Luther and his fellow reformer Philipp Melanchton were inscribed on UNESCO's list of World Heritage Sites in 1996. A historic university town, Wittenberg also attracted many other talented people, including the master painter, Lucas Cranach the Elder.

A key town in the Reformation – Summoned by the Elector Friedrich the Wise (1502) to teach philosophy at his newly founded university, **Martin Luther** was at the same time appointed the town preacher. In 1547, a year after Luther's death, **Emperor Charles V** seized Wittenberg and reputedly meditated over the tomb of the great Reformer. The "Lutherstadt" prefix was added to Wittenberg in 1938.

Schlosskirche★ (Castle Church)

Am Schlossplatz. Open Good Fri–Oct, Mon–Sat 10am–6pm, Sun 11.30am–6pm; Nov–Good Fri to 4pm. Tower: Good Fri–Oct, Mon–Fri noon–4pm, Sat–Sun 10am–5pm; 2€. (03491) 40 25 85. www.schlosskirche-wittenberg.de.

The original castle church burnt down in 1760, destroying the original doors on which Luther pinned his famous "95 Theses" condemning the abuses of the Church. The text, though, is engraved in the new bronze door from 1858. Luther's tomb is below the pulpit; next to his is that of his dear friend and supporter, Philipp Melanchthon. Also note Peter Vischer's bronze epitaph of Friedrich the Wise to the left of the main altar.

Markt★ (Market Square)

Wittenberg's central square is bordered by gabled houses, including the birthplace of Lucas Cranach the Elder at no 4 who lived and worked at Schlossstraße 1 from 1513–50. In front of the late-Gothic (1440) town hall stand 19C statues of Luther and Melanchthon.

Stadtkirche St. Marien (Parish Church of St. Mary)

On Kirchplatz, east of the market square. ⏱*Open Easter–Oct, Mon–Sat 10am–6pm, Nov–Easter to 4pm, Sun year-round from 11.30am.* ✆*(03491) 628 30. www.stadtkirchengemeinde-wittenberg.de.*

Luther himself preached and was married to Katharina von Bora in this triple-aisle Gothic (14C–15C) church that got a neo-Gothic makeover in the 18C. The key piece of artistry is Lucas Cranach's

1547 **Reformation Altar**★★. Cranach also crafted the elaborate epitaphs in the chancel. Older still is the **baptismal font**★ created by Hermann Vischer of Nurenberg in 1457.

Lutherhaus★

Collegienstraße 54. ⏱*Open Apr–Oct, daily 10am–6pm; Nov–Apr, Tue–Sun 10am–5pm.* ✆*5€.* ✆*(03491) 40 20 30. www.martinluther.de.*

Luther's former home (1508–46), a converted monastery, presents a comprehensive and engaging exhibit about the man, his life and the impact of his teachings on the world. Aside from instructive explanatory panels, there are top-notch paintings (including Ludwig Cranach's *Ten Commandments*), period artefacts (Bibles, garments, coins) and a room furnished by Luther himself in 1535.

Melanchthonhaus

Collegienstraße 60. ⟳*Closed for renovation until at least November 2011.* ✆*(03491) 40 20 30. www.martinluther.de.*

Luther's companion lived and died in this elegant gabled Renaissance home. The author of the Confession of Augsburg-was a man of moderate temperament who dedicated himself to reconciling the different factions of the Reformation. His study and documents relating to his work can be seen in this house.

Twin towers of Stadtkirche St. Marien over the houses of Markt

©Thomas Röske/Fotolia.com

Dessau-Rosslau

Dessau-Rosslau is indelibly associated with the Bauhaus School, which was based here from 1925 to 1932. Having the greatest concentration of Bauhaus structures garnered Dessau-Rosslau UNESCO World Heritage Site status in 1996. Although the town was heavily war-damaged and rebuilt in socialist style, it is not devoid of charm. Along with the Bauhaus buildings, Prince Leopold III's landscaped gardens are most enjoyable.

> ▶ **Population:** 78 500
> 🛈 **Info:** Zerbster Straße 2c, 06844 Dessau. ✆(0340) 204 14 42. www.dessau-tourismus.de.
> ◐ **Location:** Flanked by the Elbe and the Mulde rivers, Dessau is just off the A9 autobahn linking Berlin and Munich.
> ✍ **Don't Miss:** The Bauhaus buildings that put the city on the cultural map. Note: A 24hr pass for all Bauhaus buildings is 15€.
> ◔ **Timing:** Allow three hours to explore the Bauhaus sites.

BAUHAUS SITES
Bauhausgebäude★ (Bauhaus Building)

Gropiusallee 38. ◔*Open year-round, daily 10am–6pm.* ◔*Closed Dec 24 & 31.* ◆*Guided tours (1hr) daily 11am and 2pm, also noon and 4pm mid-Feb–Oct. General access free, exhibit ☷6€, tours 4€.* ✆*(0340) 650 82 51. www.bauhaus-dessau.de.*

The "Design Academy", built according to plans by Walter Gropius, opened in 1926 and displays key features of the Bauhaus style: cubic blocks, lack of visible supports and glazed façades. Gropius and Mies van der Rohe served as its successive directors. You are free to walk around, but in order to see Gro-

pius' office, the auditorium and other rooms not generally open to the public you need to join a guided tour. Some rooms are once again used as a school.

Meisterhäuser★ (Master Houses)

Ebertallee 59–71. ◔*Open mid-Feb–Oct, Tue–Sun 10am–6pm; Nov–mid-Feb, Tue–Sun 10am–5pm.* ☷*7.50€.* ◆*Guided tours (1hr) Tue–Sun 12.30pm and 3.30pm, Sat–Sun also 1.30pm.* ☷*11.50€. Tours leave from the Bauhausgebäude.* ✆*(0340) 661 09 34. www.meisterhaeuser.de.*

Walter Gropius masterplanned this row of houses for himself and his Bauhaus professors (built 1925–26).

Destroyed in the war, three of them have been rebuilt and are open to the public: the **Kandinsky-Klee-Haus**, the **Muche-Schlemmer-Haus** and the **Feiningerhaus**. The latter houses a centre dedicated to the Dessau-born composer Kurt Weill.

Törtenensiedlung

The Bauhaus-designed Törten housing estate south of the centre was built between 1926 and 1928 to relieve a housing shortage and to give workers a shot at owning their own homes. Although few of the 314 terraced houses

Bauhausgebäude

Martin Brück 2005, Stiftung Bauhaus Dessau

The Bauhaus Movement

One of the seminal aesthetic movements of the 20C, the Bauhaus School was founded by architect Walter Gropius in Weimar in 1919. He was joined by Paul Klee, Ludwig Mies van der Rohe, Wassily Kandinsky and other top talents of the day who taught architecture, design, painting and sculpture in an interdisciplinary approach. As the political climate in Weimar turned conservative, the school moved to Dessau in 1925 where they moulded a new style of living in Bauhaus workshops. In 1932, they moved again, this time to Berlin, only to be closed down for good by the Nazis in 1933. Their design concepts, however, survived, and in fact it is hard to imagine 20C and 21C architecture without the Bauhaus.

have remained unchanged, the unmistakable Bauhaus style is still clearly in evidence.

ADDITIONAL SIGHT
Georgium

⏱Open year-round, Tue–Sun 10am–5pm. ⏱Closed Dec 24 & 31. ◎3 €. ✆(0340) 61 38 74. www.georgium.de. Surrounded by the richly landscaped English-style Georgengarten park, this 18C Neoclassical palace houses a prized art collection of Old Masters (Cranach, Grien), 18C Frankfurt paintings and Dutch artists from the 16C and 17C.

ADDRESSES

🛏STAY

🛏 **City-Pension** – Ackerstraße 3a. ✆(0340) 882 30 76. www.city-pension-dessau.de. 24 rooms. This central hotel has functionally furnished, light and airy rooms. The generous breakfast buffet is great for getting the day kick-started.

🍴EAT

🍴 **Das Pächterhaus** – Kirchstraße 1, 06846 Dessau-Ziebigk. ✆(0340) 650 14 47. www.paechterhaus-dessau.de. Closed Mon. This nicely restored 1743 half-timbered house delivers seasonal dishes and excellent wines in its cosy rooms or the lovely garden at the back.

Halle★

Halle must balance its heritage as an old university town and birthplace of Georg Friedrich Händel with its legacy as the centre of the chemical industry in GDR days. Since 1990, the town has progressed and cleaned up in leaps and bounds and is again ready for its close-up – and not only during the biannual Händel Festival!

SIGHTS
Marktplatz★

This huge square is dominated by the belfries of the Marktkirche and by the **Roter Turm** (red tower), built in the 15C and almost 80m/262.4ft high. An 1859 statue of Händel surveys the square.

- ▶ **Population:** 240 000
- ℹ **Info:** Marktplatz 13, 06108 Halle. ✆(0345) 122 99 84. www.halle-tourist.de. Contact or visit the tourist office for a **Halle Welcome Card**.
- ▷ **Location:** Halle is on the Saale River, some 30km/18.6mi northwest of Leipzig.
- 🅿 **Parking:** Händelhauskarree garage on Hallorenring.
- 👁 **Don't Miss:** Moritzburg Art Museum, Händel-Haus.
- 🕐 **Timing:** Allow about half a day for Halle, plus another half a day for the excursions.

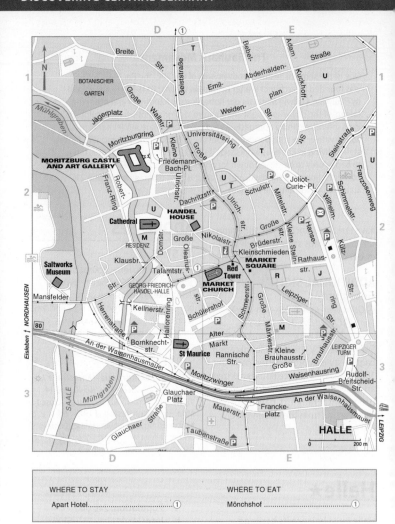

WHERE TO STAY

Apart Hotel............................①

WHERE TO EAT

Mönchshof ....①

Marktkirche (Market Church)★

🕐Open year-round, Mon–Sat 10am–5pm, Sun 3pm–5pm. 📞(0345) 517 08 94. www.marktkirche-halle.de.

This three-aisled 16C Gothic hall-church was wedged between two existing towers belonging to different Romanesque churches whose naves had been torn down. The **reredos**★ of the high altar carries a Virgin and Child painted by a pupil of the Cranach School. The most important exhibit, though, is Luther's death mask on display in its own room in the northwest tower (👛2€). The tower can be climbed Monday to Saturday at 3.30pm and Sun at 11.30am (👛6€, including guided church tour).

Kunstmuseum Moritzburg★★ (Moritzburg Art Gallery)

Friedemann-Bach-Platz 5. 🕐Open Tue 10am–7pm, Wed–Sun 10am–6pm. 🕐Closed Dec 24 & 31. 👛5€, half-price after 5pm. 📞(0345) 21 25 90. www.kunstmuseum-moritzburg.de.

Moritzburg castle was built in the 15C as a residence of the archbishops of Magdeburg and partly converted into a museum in the early 20C. It now houses a significant collection of **19C and 20C German art**, presenting a sweeping survey of various periods, including Romanticism, Impressionism and Expressionism. Sections of the palace that had been ruined since the Thirty Years' War were recently covered, nearly doubling the exhibition space.

Händel-Haus★

Grosse Nikolaistraße 5. ⏲*Open Apr–Oct, Tue–Sun 10am–6pm, Nov–Mar 10am–5pm (Thu 7pm).* 🎫*4€.* ♿ ☎*(0345) 50 09 01 03. www.haendel-in-halle.de.*

One of the world's most famous composers, **Georg Friedrich Händel** (1685–1759) was born in this big half-timbered house in 1685. Exhibits trace major stations in his life and career as well as regional music history. An adjacent building presents two floors of precious historical musical instruments.

Moritzkirche (St. Maurice)

Hallorenring.

This three-nave church, built between 1388 and 1511, has reticulated and star-vaulted ceilings typical of the Flamboyant Gothic style. Inside are naively expressive sculptures by Conrad Einbeck, most notably the *Man of Sorrows*, the statue of St. Maurice (1411) and a Pietà (1416).

Dom (Cathedral)

Am Domplatz.
⚠*Closed for restoration.*

This three-aisled Gothic abbey church (14C) was transformed by Cardinal Albert of Brandenburg in 1520. The statues of Christ, the apostles and saints that decorate the pillars were created around 1520 in the workshop of the gifted sculptor Peter Schroh and foreshadow the Renaissance stylistically.

👥 Technisches Halloren- und Salinemuseum (Salt Museum)

Mansfelder Strasse 52. ⏲*Open Tue–Sun 10am–5pm.* ⏲*Closed 1 Jan, 24–25 & 31 Dec.* 🎫*2.10€.* ☎*(0345) 209 32 30. www.salinemuseum.de.*

The Saltworks Museum has displays on the history of salt mining in the region.

EXCURSIONS
Doppelkapelle Landsberg (Double Chapel)

▶ *In Landsberg, 19km/12mi east.*
🚶*Guided tours (1hr), May–Oct, Sat 3pm, Sun 11am and 3pm or by appointment.* 🎫*2€.* ☎*(0346 02) 206 90.*

The Romanesque double chapel of **St. Crucis** sits atop a rocky spur and is one of only 30 chapels in Germany where common people celebrated Mass in the lower chapel while the nobility sat upstairs. The **capitals**★ on the columns are richly adorned with figures and plant and animal motifs. From the balcony, there is a superb **view**★.

Eisleben

▶ *34km/21mi west of Halle.*

Memories of **Martin Luther**, who was born – and died – in this small mining town are evoked at a number of sites. Both his **birthplace** (*Luther-Geburtshaus, Seminarstraße 16*) and the house where he died (**Luther-Sterbehaus**, *Andreaskirchplatz 7*) are now museums and are included on UNESCO's list of World Heritage Sites.

Luther pilgrims might also want to stop by the Church of St. Peter and St. Paul where he was baptised, St. Andreas Church where he gave his last sermon, and Marktplatz, anchored by a 1883 Luther statue.

ADDRESSES

🛏STAY

🍴🍴 **Apart Hotel** – *Kohlschütterstraße 5.* ☎*0345 525 90. www.apart.halle.de. 48 rooms.* 🚗. Formerly a privately owned grand villa, with high ceilings and stucco decoration, the rooms and bar have a 1920s theme and the hotel has theatrical connections. Sauna.

🍴/EAT

🍴 **Mönchshof** – *Talamtstraße 6.* ☎*0345 202 17 26. www.moenchshof-halle.de. Closed Sun dinner.* Next to the cathedral, this traditional dark wood-panelled restaurant serves reliable regional dishes.

Quedlinburg★

Lorded over by a rock pinnacle crowned by a castle and an abbey church, half-timbered Quedlinburg is one of the most picture-perfect towns in the Harz region. More than 700 houses in the historic centre are classified as historical monuments, which elevated the town to UNESCO's World Heritage List status in 1994.

OLD TOWN★
Markt★
(Market Place)

The early 17C Renaissance **Rathaus** borders the northern side of the market place. On the left of the façade is a statue of Roland (c. 1440). Houses built in the 17C and 18C frame the other three sides of the square.

Historic Streets★

Circle St. Benediktkirche via Marktstraße and Kornmarkt to explore the cobbled lanes behind the **Rathaus** (town hall), then return to the Markt along Breitstraße, with several picturesque alleyways opening off it. On the far side of the square, stroll towards the castle by way of Wordgasse, Hohe Straße and Blasiistraße. On one side of the charming **Schlossbergplatz★**, at no 12, stands

▶ **Population:** 23 200

ℹ **Info:** Markt 2.
℘(03946) 90 56 24.
www.quedlinburg.de.

◐ **Location:** Quedlinburg is near the A14 autobahn (Leipzig–Magdeburg), and an ideal base for exploring the Harz Mountains.

☺ **Don't Miss:**
The Schlossberg.

◐ **Timing:** Allow half a day for a leisurely tour of the old town and the Schlossberg.

the late 16C **Klopstockhaus** (◐*open Apr–Oct, Wed–Sun 10am–5pm; Nov–Mar, Wed–Sun 10am–4pm;* ◐*closed Jan 1, Dec 24-25 & 31;* ∞*3.50€;* ℘*(03946) 2610)* in which the poet Friedrich Gottlieb Klopstock was born in 1724. Today it contains exhibits chronicling his life and work.

Lyonel-Feininger-Galerie★

Behind the Klopstock Museum, Finkenherd 5A. ◐*Open Apr–Oct, Tue–Sun 10am–6pm; Nov–Mar, Tue–Sun 10am–5pm.* ◐*Closed Jan 1, Dec 24 & 31.* ∞*6€.* ♿. ℘*(03946) 22 38. www.feininger-galerie.de.*

This gallery houses works by Expressionist painter Lyonel Feininger. Born in New

Schlossberg

© 3quarks/Dreamstime.com

York City, Feininger trained in France and Germany, where he exhibited with the *Blaue Reiter* group in 1913. After World War I he joined the Bauhaus.

SCHLOSSBERG★
Stiftskirche★★ St. Servatius (Collegiate Church)

On the site of the original 9C church, the present basilica was begun in 1070 and ranks as one of the most important Romanesque houses of worship in Germany.

Beneath the chancel, the **crypt★★** is divided into three aisles with diagonal rib-vaulting decorated by **frescoes★** depicting scenes from the Bible.

The **Domschatz★★** (treasury) – manuscripts, a 10C Gospel, and, above all, the **Quedlinburg Knotted Carpet★** – is kept in the sacristy.

Enjoy a beautiful **view★** over the city from the large terrace near the church.

Schloss (Palace)

The 16C–17C palace formed part of the abbey, and took on its irregular floor plan due to the rocky base on which the castle was built.

The **Schlossmuseum★** (Ⓛopen Apr–Oct, daily 10am–6pm, Nov–Mar, Sat–Thu 10am–4pm; Ⓛclosed Jan 1, Dec 24 & 31; ⊚4€; ℘(03946) 90 56 81) presents the history of Quedlinburg. The Abbess' Reception Room, the Throne Room and the Princes' Hall (mid-18C) can be visited.

Lyonel Feininger (1871–1956)

Born in New York to musicians, Feininger was fascinated from a young age by the visual universe of the American metropolis. At the age of 16 he was sent to Germany to study music, but quickly became interested in sculpture and started a career drawing picture books. Over time, Feininger became a painter known for melding Expressionism and Cubism, and focusing on apparently banal subjects (factories, boats, ports and buildings). In 1919 Walter Gropius invited Feininger to join the Bauhaus, where he taught until the closure of the school by the Nazis.

EXCURSION
Gernrode

▶ *7km/4.3mi south.*

Gernrode's collegiate church of **St. Cyriacus★**, first documented in 961, is another fine example of Ottonian-period Romanesque architecture with a typical three-aisle nave, flat ceiling and upper galleries.

The hall crypt is among the earliest of its type in Germany. Upstairs is the **Holy Sepulchre group★**, a rare example of Romanesque sculpture.

ADDRESSES

⌂STAY

⌂⊜⊜⊟ **Romantik Hotel Theophano** – *Markt 14. ℘(03946) 963 00. www.hotel theophano.de. 22 rooms. Closed Jan 7–Feb 28. Restaurant⊜⊜⊟, closed Sun and Mon.* The rooms in this hotel are particularly charming, with tasteful pastel tones; some have four-poster beds. The restaurant is in the vaulted wine-cellar of this half-timbered building.

⌂⊜⊟⊟ **Schlosshotel Zum Markgrafen** – *Weingarten 30. ℘(03946) 811 40. www.schlosshotel-zum-markgrafen.de. 12 rooms.* This beautiful 1898 villa was completely renovated in the 1990s after stints as a Soviet military command post and a textile factory. Surrounded by a small park, it has elegant rooms with stucco ornamentation, coffered ceilings and murals.

Erfurt★

Erfurt, the state capital of Thuringia, is a peaceful, captivating university town with an enchanting silhouette of steeples and bell-towers. The cobbled lanes of its lively old town are lined with carefully restored centuries-old buildings. It is the main city closest to the geographical centre of reunified Germany.

A BIT OF HISTORY

A trading town – Erfurt was founded as a bishopric by the English missionary St. Boniface in 742. Its strategic location along the important trade route linking the Rhineland with Russia – the Via Regia – greatly contributed to the town's prosperity in the Middle Ages. So did the production of a much sought-after blue pigment derived from the woad plant. In the 15C, Erfurt joined the Hanseatic League.

Spirituality and Humanism – Nicknamed "Thuringian Rome" because of its roughly 90 churches and chapels, Erfurt has long attracted religious thinkers. The influential Christian mystic **Master Eckhart** was born in nearby Gotha and in 1298 became prior of Erfurt's Dominican convent and vicar-provincial of Thuringia.

Two centuries later **Martin Luther** shook the religious world with his "95 Theses" protesting church corruption posted on the church door in Wittenberg. Luther studied at Erfurt university between 1501 and 1505, entered the Augustinian monastery and was ordained as a priest before setting off for Wittenberg in 1511.

AROUND THE DOMPLATZ

The Domplatz is dominated by two imposing houses of worship: the Mariendom (St. Mary's Cathedral) and the Severikirche (Church of St. Severus). In the square's centre, an obelisk commemorates a visit in 1777 by the Archbishop of Mainz.

▶ **Population:** 200 800

Info: Benediktsplatz 1, 99084 Erfurt. ✆(0361) 664 00. www.erfurt-tourismus.de.

◐ **Location:** Erfurt is off the A4 autobahn, between Gotha and Weimar.

Parking: Garages near the Dom, the main train station and throughout town.

Don't Miss: Mariendom, Severikirche.

Timing: Spend about one day seeing the main sights.

Dom St. Marien★★ (St. Mary's Cathedral)

Erfurt's most prominent landmark, the cathedral was completed in the 14C and stands on top of several predecessors dating back to the 8C.

Its richly ornamented **triangular portals**★★ at the north entrance consist of two doors set obliquely and supporting elegant statuary groups depicting the Apostles and the Wise and Foolish Virgins.

The church's **interior** boasts several important artworks: the Romanesque altar of the Virgin (1160); the **bronze candelabrum**★ shaped like a man and known as "Wolfram" (1160); the melodious Gloriosa bell (1497); and the intricately worked choir stalls (14C). The stained-glass **windows**★ above the choir (c. 1370–1420) depict episodes from the Old and New Testaments as well as from the lives of various saints. Luther was ordained as a priest here in 1507 and held his first lectures in the *Auditorium Coelicum* below the church.

Severikirche★ (Church of St. Severus)

Linked to the cathedral by a sprawling, 70-step open staircase, St. Severi is a five-nave early-Gothic hall church that also harbours its share of treasures. The saint's remains were brought to Erfurt from Ravenna, where he served as a bishop, in 836 and have been enshrined in an elaborate **sarcopha-gus**★ since the 14C. Also note the stone Madonna (1345) and the 15m/45ft-high baptismal font (1467)

AROUND THE FISCHMARKT
Fischmarkt (Fish Market)

Inside the imposing neo-Gothic **Rathaus** (town hall; ⏱ open year-round, Mon, Tue, Thu 8am–6pm, Wed 4pm, Fri 2pm, Sat–Sun 10am–5pm) are **frescoes**★ illustrating the lives of Luther, Faust and Tannhäuser. The square is framed by magnificent townhouses that reflect the wealth of the one-time woad traders. Standouts include the buildings known as "Zum Breiten Herd" and "Zum Roten Ochsen".

Krämerbrücke★ (Merchants' Bridge)

This bridge across the little Gera River, built in 1325, is the only one north of the Alps with houses built on it. Most are narrow, half-timbered structures dating from the 16C to the 19C. The bridge is 18m/59ft wide and 120m/393.7ft long.

Angermuseum★

Anger 18. ⏱Open year-round, Tue–Sun 10am–6pm. ◉5€, with special exhibit 7.50€. ℘(0361) 554 56 11. www.angermuseum.de.

This museum presents medieval art from Thuringia in a Baroque building from 1706. Among its highlights are 14C and 15C **altarpieces**★★; a **Pietà**★★ by the Master of St. Severinus; and sarcophagi and paintings by Hans Baldung Grien. The focus of the picture gallery is on 18C–19C German landscape painting.

Augustinerkloster (Augustinian Monastery)

🔊Guided tours hourly, Mon–Sat 10am–5pm (Nov–Mar to 4pm), year-round Sun 11am, 2pm and 4pm. ◉3.50€, or 5€ with Luther cell. ℘(0361) 576 600. www.augustinerkloster.de.

This austere monastery is an important stop for Martin Luther pilgrims. The Reformer stayed here as an Augustinian monk from 1505–11. Tours take in the

room where Luther lived and exhibits about his life and accomplishments.
🔊 Admission to the church, where he held his first mass, is free.

Zitadelle Petersberg (Petersberg Citadel)

⏱Open Apr–Oct, daily 11am–6pm; Nov–Dec, 11am–4pm. ⏱Closed Jan 1, Dec 24, 25 & 31. ◉3.50€. 🔊Guided tours (1hr) Apr–Dec several times daily; ◉3.50€). ℘(0361) 439 11 73. www.petersberg.info.

One of the best-preserved Baroque fortifications in central Europe, this citadel was built between 1665 and 1707 atop the foundations of a Benedictine monastery. It contains a museum on military history, but to explore the subterranean defensive tunnels you must join a guided tour.

EXCURSION
Gotha★

▶ 25km/15.5mi west via the B7.

One of the oldest settlements in Thuringia (775), Gotha prospered as an important trade-route stop in the Middle Ages. After the Thirty Years' War, the local dukes built the first and largest Baroque palace in Thuringia: the U-shaped **Schloss Friedenstein** (⏱open Tue–Sun 10am–5pm (Nov–Apr 4pm); ◉7€; ℘(03621) 82 34 51; www.stiftungfriedenstein.de), now home to several museums. If you have limited time, focus on the **Schlossmuseum**, whose extravagant rooms are a perfect backdrop for an eclectic collection of coins, sculpture, antiques, etchings and even objects from Ancient Egypt. Walls are graced with paintings by such masters as Cranach the Elder and Rubens, although top billing actually goes to the famous Gotha Lovers by an anonymous artist. The **Kunstkammer** (art chamber) boasts such exotic items as engraved ostrich eggs, carved ivory and decorated coconut shells.

The other museums deal with local folk art and nature, but considerably more unique is the Baroque **Ekhof-Theater** (separate admission ◉2.50€). It has lavish décor and ingenious mechanics.

Weimar★★

Many non-Germans associate Weimar with the ill-fated Weimar Republic which existed uneasily between World War I and the Hitler years. But in fact, the town's claim to fame in European history rests unerringly on the extraordinary flowering of intellectual and artistic talent there, attracting Luther, Cranach, Bach, Wieland, Schiller, Liszt and, perhaps most importantly, Germany's greatest classical poet, Johann Wolfgang von Goethe.

A BIT OF HISTORY

An intellectual and cultural hotbed – Weimar's heyday coincided with the succession, in 1758, of Duchess Anna Amalia. It was during her reign that the town's intellectual reputation grew, largely because of **Goethe** (1749–1832). He was appointed minister of the small, provincial capital and produced here the majority of his life's work, including his dramatic masterpiece, *Faust*.

Goethe's success went hand-in-hand with that of **Friedrich von Schiller**, who moved permanently to Weimar in 1799. The work produced by these two close friends, along with the writings of the theologian **Johann Gottfried Herder** (1744–1803), a disciple of Kant, raised Weimar's literary reputation to that of "home of German Classicism".

▶ **Population:** 64 400

▌ **Info:** Markt 10. ✆(03643) 74 50. www.weimar.de.

◖ **Location:** Set on the banks of the Ilm, Weimar is in the heart of Thuringia, around 20km/12.4mi from the state capital Erfurt. The A4 autobahn links the town with Dresden to the east and Frankfurt to the southwest (via the A5).

🅿 **Parking:** Convenient central parking is in a garage near the Goethe House.

⊘ **Don't Miss:** The suggested walking tour, Buchenwald.

🕐 **Timing:** Allocate a full day to truly sample Weimar's legacy, especially if visiting Buchenwald.

A couple of centuries earlier, from 1552 until his death a year later, **Lucas Cranach the Elder** had worked in Weimar on his final masterpiece: the altarpiece triptych for the Parish Church of St. Peter and St. Paul. **Johann Sebastian Bach** was organist and choirmaster here from 1708 to 1717.

In 1848 **Franz Liszt** took the position, and became the driving force behind Weimar's School of Music, which still bears his name today.

Statue of Goethe and Schiller

© Ellen Ebenau/Fotolia.com

In 1860, Grand Duke Alexander founded the **Weimarer Malerschule** (Fine Arts Academy), where a numerous late 19C artists studied, including Hans Arp, Max Liebermann and Christian Rohlfs.

It was under the influence of such celebrated graduates as **Arnold Böcklin** (1827–1901) that painters spearheading the contemporary avant-garde movement developed the "Weimar School". Under Walter Gropius, the institution spawned the Bauhaus, the influential college of architecture and design.

The Weimar Republic (1919–33) – The constitution of the Weimar Republic was drafted and adopted in 1919 by the German National Assembly as delegates convened at the Deutsches Nationaltheater (German National Theatre). The government itself, however, was never based in Weimar as members returned to Berlin just one week after adopting the text. The humanist tradition of Goethe's town had merely provided the budding democracy with a welcome counterpoint to the politically oppressive atmosphere of postwar Berlin.

◥◞ WALKING TOUR
HISTORIC CENTRE★★

Weimar's chief highlights – mostly related to heroes of the German Renaissance or Enlightenment – cluster within a compact area in the bustling pedestrian city centre. The main squares are Theaterplatz, with the National Theatre and Bauhaus Museum, and the neighbouring Marktplatz.

Goethes Nationalmuseum and Wohnhaus★★ (Goethe National Museum and Private Residence)

Frauenplan 1. ◷*Open Apr–Sept, Tue–Sun 9am–6pm (Sat to 7pm); Oct, Tue–Sun to 6pm; Jan–Mar to 4pm.* ◷*Closed Dec 24.* ◉*8.50€.* ℘*(03643) 54 53 47. www.weimar-klassik.de.*

Germany's greatest man of letters lived in this 1709 Baroque mansion for 50 years, first as a tenant, then, after 1792, as owner until his death in 1832. The interior is largely the way he left it. The

living room, study, library and bedroom are all furnished with paintings and sculptures from Goethe's times.

Tickets also give access to a permanent exhibition next door that is concerned less with the man himself than with the period of the Enlightenment and all the great minds that shaped it, including Wieland, Herder, Schiller, Anna Amalia and her son, Duke Carl August.

▷ *Exit the museum and follow Ackerwand to Frau von Stein House.*

Haus der Frau von Stein
Ackerwand 25.

Charlotte von Stein, lady-in-waiting to Anna Amalia and Goethe's longtime muse, lived in this house for 50 years until her death in 1827. For now, the building is still home to the Goethe Institute language school and cultural centre. However, in 2008 the city sold the building to a Spanish art collector who promised to pay for its badly needed restoration. Eventually it may become an art museum.

▷ *Continue to the end of Ackerwand, which leads to Platz der Demokratie.*

Platz der Demokratie

The equestrian statue of Grand Duke Carl August dominates this square. On the south side, the former palace (1757–74) is occupied by the **Franz Liszt Hochschule für Musik**. The 16C–18C **Grünes Schloss** (Green Palace) houses the **Duchess Anna Amalia Library** (◷*open year-round, Tue–Sun 10am–3pm;* ◉*6.50€;* ℘*(03643) 54 54 01*) with medieval manuscripts, early printed works, rare 16C–17C documents and 18C volumes. The library re-opened in late 2007 after being partially destroyed in a devastating fire three years earlier.

▷ *Leave Platz der Demokratie, and head for the Markt and Cranach-Haus.*

Cranach-Haus

The famous painter spent the last years of his life in this Renaissance house (1547–49) at Markt 12, adorned with

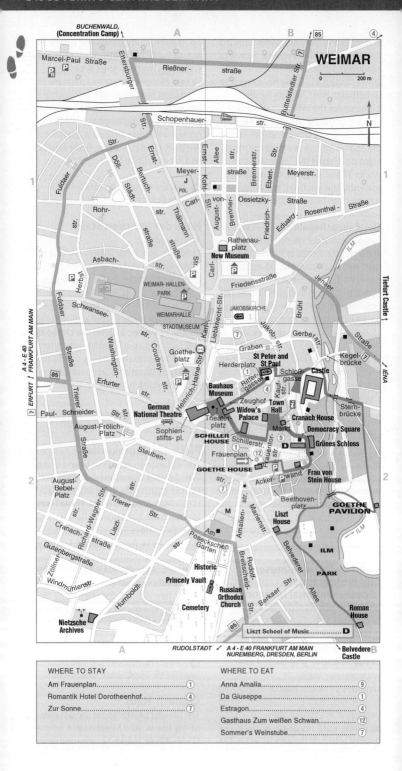

BUCHENWALD,
(Concentration Camp)

Marcel-Paul Straße

Rießner - straße

WEIMAR

0   200 m

Etersburger Str.

Schopenhauer- str.

N

Meyer-J
POL

straße

Meyerstr.

Rohr-

str.

Ossietzky- Straße   Straße

Asbach-

str.

Eduard - Rosenthal - Straße

Rathenau-
platz
New Museum

P

Friedensstraße

WEIMAR-HALLEN-
PARK

P
WEIMARHALLE

STADTMUSEUM

JAKOBSKIRCHE

Graben

(7)

Gerber str.

Straße

Schwansee-

Coudray-

str.

Goethe-
platz

Herderplatz

Ritter-
gasse

Schloß-
gasse

**St Peter and
St Paul**

Kegel-
brücke

Castle

P

Erfurter

str.

Washington-

**Bauhaus
Museum**

Zeughof

Kauf- str.

**Widow's
Palace**

**Town
Hall**

Cranach House

Stern-
brücke

August-Frölich-
Platz

**German
National Theatre**

Theater-
platz

Markt

Democracy Square

Sophien-
stifts- pl.

**SCHILLER
HOUSE**

Schillerstr.

(1)

**Frau von
Stein House**

Steuben-

Frauenplan

(12)

GOETHE HOUSE

str.

Acker-

(7)

**GOETHE
PAVILION**

August-
Bebel-
Platz

Trierer

Str.

Beethoven-
platz

**Liszt
House**

ILM

Am
Poseckschen
Garten

str.

M

PARK

**Historic
Princely Vault**

**Russian
Orthodox
Church**

Belvederer

Str.

Allee

**Roman
House**

Windmühlenstr.

Cemetery

85

Liszt School of Music.................D

**Nietzsche
Archives**

RUDOLSTADT   A 4 - E 40 FRANKFURT AM MAIN
NUREMBERG, DRESDEN, BERLIN

Belvedere
Castle

WHERE TO STAY		WHERE TO EAT	
Am Frauenplan	①	Anna Amalia	⑨
Romantik Hotel Dorotheenhof	④	Da Giuseppe	①
Zur Sonne	⑦	Estragon	④
		Gasthaus Zum weißen Schwan	⑫
		Sommer's Weinstube	⑦

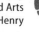

scrolled gables. His studio was on the third floor.

The **Rathaus** (town hall), opposite, was built c. 1500 but was heavily remodelled in the mid-19C.

▶ *Take Schillerstraße direction Theaterplatz.*

Schillers Wohnhaus★ (Schiller's Private House)

Schillerstraße 12. ◑*Open Apr–Sept, Tue–Sun 9am–6pm (Sat to 7pm); Oct, Tue–Sun 9am–6pm; Nov–Mar, Tue–Sun 9am–4pm.* ◑*Closed Dec 24.* ◉*5€.* ℘*(03643) 54 53 50. www.klassik-stiftung.de.*

Schiller moved here in 1802 to be near his great friend Goethe, and in this house wrote *William Tell* and *The Bride of Messina*. The museum examines his life and work.

▶ *Continue on Schillerstraße to Theaterplatz.*

Deutsches Nationaltheater (German National Theatre)

Theaterplatz 2. www.nationaltheater-weimar.de.

The present 1907 structure was built on the site of a 1779 Baroque building. It was in this previous theatre that Schiller's great plays were staged and directed by Goethe, and it was here, in 1850, that Richard Wagner's *Lohengrin* was first performed. In 1919 the German National Assembly adopted the constitution of the Weimar Republic here. In front of the present building stand the **statues**★★ of Goethe and Schiller, sculpted in 1857 by Ernst Rietschel.

Bauhaus-Museum

Theaterplatz. ◑*Open year-round, daily 10am–6pm.* ◉*4.50€.* ℘*(03643) 54 59 61. www.klassik-stiftung.de.*

The Bauhaus School was founded in 1919 Weimar by Walter Gropius and cohorts and occupied this building until the group was forced to move to Dessau in 1925. The small permanent collection introduces the major players, their innovative approach to architec-

ture and design and their impact on the modern aesthetic. Exhibits also pay homage to the School of Applied Arts founded in Weimar in 1908 by Henry Van de Velde.

Wittumspalais

Theaterplatz. ◑*Open Apr–Oct, Tue–Sun 9am–6pm; Nov–Dec, Tue–Sun 10am–4pm; Jan–Mar Wed–Mon 10am–4pm.* ◑*Closed 24 Dec.* ◉*5€.* ℘*(03643) 54 53 77. www.klassik-stiftung.de.*

After her husband's death, Anna Amalia moved to this Baroque palace where she held her illustrious salons with Goethe, Schiller, Herder and Wieland in attendance. Rooms are representative of the late 18C for a person of her standing. Note the Neoclassical ballroom and the late Baroque ceiling frescoes.

▶ *Go to Herderplatz via Zeughof, then Rittergasse.*

Stadtkirche St. Peter und Paul (or Herderkirche)

Am Herderplatz.

This triple-nave Gothic hall-church was built between 1498–1500 but turned Baroque-style in the 18C. It is also known as the Herderkirche, in memory of the sermons preached here between 1776 and 1803 by the philosopher, Johann Gottfried Herder, who is buried here. The famous **Cranach Triptych**★★, begun by Lucas Cranach the Elder and finished by his son in 1555, represents the Crucifixion on its central panel and is surrounded by scenes from the Old and New Testaments. Luther and Cranach the Elder are depicted on the right.

▶ *Follow Schloßgasse to the square.*

Schlossmuseum (Palace Museum)

◑*Open Apr–Oct, Tue–Sun 10am–6pm, Nov–Mar to 4pm.* ◉*6€.* ℘*(03643) 54 59 60. www.klassikstiftung.de.*

Built under Duke Carl August, the early 19C city palace (*Stadtschloss*) features some of Germany's finest Neoclassicist apartments and important Weimar artworks. Highlights include a **Cranach**

collection★★; Flemish and Italian paintings; and work by Hans Baldung Grien, Albrecht Dürer and Bartholomäus Bruyn the Elder. The Weimar School and German Impressionists and Expressionists (Max Beckmann, Max Liebermann) are also represented.

Ilm Park★★
"Weimar is in fact a park in which they happened to build a town," wrote Adolf Stahr in 1851. Expansive green spaces continue to shape modern Weimar. This magnificent riverside park parallels both banks of the Ilm River from the palace of Tiefurt to the Belvedere, yet is steps from the town centre.

Goethes Gartenhaus★★
Open Apr–Oct, Wed–Mon 10am–6pm, Nov–Mar to 4pm. 4.50€. (03643) 54 53 75. www.klassik-stiftung.de.
Duke Carl August gave this summer residence as a gift to Goethe and the great man liked it so much that he frequently used it a retreat until the end of his life. *Wilhelm Meister's Theatrical Mission*, major parts of *Iphigenia*, and early drafts of *Egmont* and *Torquato Tasso* were written in this humble cottage.

> Cross the park in the direction of the Belvederer Allee.

Liszt-Haus
Marienstraße 17. Closed until at least March 2011. (03643) 54 54 00. www.klassik-stiftung.de.
The great composer lived and taught in this converted garden house between 1869 and 1886. The period rooms are preserved so neatly it feels as though Liszt could be returning at any moment. His study, living, dining and bedrooms are filled with personal items; note the Bechstein grand piano.

ADDITIONAL SIGHTS
Neues Museum
Rathenauplatz. Open Apr–Oct, Tue–Sun 11pm–6pm, Nov–Mar to 4pm. 3.50€. (03643)54 50 63. www.klassik-stiftung.de.

This 19C neo-Renaissance building presents art by the international avant-garde since 1960, with emphasis on German art, Italian *Arte Povera*, and American Minimal and Conceptual Art. During the Third Reich it was the headquarters of Thuringia's Nazi administration.

Fürstengruft
(Ducal Tomb)
Historischer Friedhof.
Johann Wolfgang von Goethe is buried alongside Grand Duke Carl August and Weimar's other ducal rulers in a **mausoleum** (*open Apr–Oct, daily 10am–6pm, Nov–Mar to 4pm; 3.50€; (03643) 54 54 00; www.klassik-stiftung.de*) in the 19C **Historischer Friedhof** (historical cemetery). A 2006 investigation found that other remains, believed to have been those of Schiller, were not.
The **Russian Orthodox Church** nearby was built in the 19C for Maria Pavlova, Grand Duchess and daughter-in-law of Carl August. Goethe's muse, Frau von Stein, is also buried in this cemetery.

Nietzsche Archiv
(Nietzsche Archive)
Humboldtstraße 36. Open Apr–Oct, Tue–Sun 1pm–5pm. 2.50€. (03643) 54 51 59. www.klassik-stiftung.de.
Philosopher Friedrich Nietzsche (1844–1900) spent the last three years of his life in this house. Suffering from mental illness, he was nursed by his sister Elizabeth.
After his death, she moved the Nietzsche Archive, which she had founded in 1894, to this building and hired Henry Van de Velde to turn the ground floor into an exhibition space. In her role as self-appointed caretaker of her brother's intellectual property, Elizabeth contributed to the philosopher's anti-Semitic and pro-nationalist image which inspired the ideology of the Third Reich. The most beautiful part of the archive is the library.
Notice the bust of Nietzsche by Max Klinger. Documents chronicle the life and work of the philosopher.

EXCURSIONS
Buchenwald Museum and Memorial
▶ *8km/5mi northwest.*
🕐 *Open Apr–Oct, Tue–Sun 10am–6pm; Nov–Mar to 4pm. Grounds open until dusk.* 🕐 *Closed Jan 1, Dec 24–26.* ♿
📞 *(03643) 43 02 00. www.buchenwald.de.*
Near Weimar, in the Ettersberg Forest, stood one of the largest Nazi concentration camps. Some 250 000 people were deported to Buchenwald; over 50 000 died there before the camp was liberated by Americans on 11 April 1945.

The **Gedenkstätte Buchenwald** (memorial centre) shows a film tracing the history of the camp. A tour of the camp starts at the gatehouse, still bearing the chilling slogan: *"Jedem das Seine"* ("You get what you deserve").

Each residential barrack is outlined on the ground; at the far end a building used for storing the inmates' possessions is now a museum. Outside the camp, a road leads to the quarry where prisoners were worked to death.

From 1945 to 1950, the Soviet occupation force set up **Special Camp 2**, in which Nazi criminals, officials and political prisoners were interned. Over 7 000 are believed to have died here. From the entrance *(1km/0.6mi towards Weimar)* the Steles' Way leads to the **Avenue of Nations**, which links three mass graves. The last of these brings you to the **Buchenwald Memorial**.

In 1943, some 20 000 prisoners were sent to Camp Dora, north of Nordhausen *(see Harz map)*, to convert underground shafts into a manufacturing plant for V-2 rockets. It too is a memorial today.

ADDRESSES

🛏STAY

🍽 **Hotel Zur Sonne** – *Rollplatz 2. 📞(03643) 862 90. www.thueringen. info/hotel-zur-sonne.html. 21 rooms. Restaurant🍽.* This neat brick house is in the heart of the old town. Modern, attractively furnished rooms and a no-nonsense tavern-style restaurant.

🍽🍽 **Hotel Am Frauenplan** – *Brauhausgasse 10. 📞03643 494 40. www.hotel-am-frauenplan.de. 41 rooms.* Opposite Goethe's former home, this was once the palace of the Countess von Bernstoff. Bedrooms are comfortable and cosy. Breakfast is served in the courtyard when warm.

🍽🍽🍽 **Romantik Hotel Dorotheenhof** – *Dorotheenhof 1, 99427 Weimar–Schöndorf. 📞(03643) 45 90. www.dorotheenhof.com. 60 rooms. Restaurant 🍽🍽🍽.* This pretty hotel, in an idyllic park location above the town, used to belong to a 19C cavalry captain and now delights guests with cosy country-style rooms. The elegant restaurant is canopied by a charming vaulted ceiling.

🍽/EAT

🍽 **Sommer's Weinstube Restaurant** – *Humboldtstraße 2. 📞(03643) 40 06 91. www.wein-sommer.com. Closed Sun.* Family-run restaurant with an old-fashioned charm. The wine list complements Thuringian specialities.

🍽 **Estragon** – *Herderplatz 3. 📞03 643 90 85 99.* Opposite the Church of St. Peter and St. Paul, this is a good little find; the menu is based on simple, flavoursome organic soups and salads.

🍽 **Trattoria Da Giuseppe** – *Eisenfeld. 📞03 643 81 48 38. Closed all day Sun, and Mon and Tue evenings.* The locals come to Giuseppe's charming trattoria for his pizzas, fresh tagliatelle and red wines, sourced direct from Italy.

🍽🍽🍽 **Gasthaus zum Weissen Schwan** – *Frauentorstraße 23. 📞(03643) 90 87 51. www.weisserschwan.de. Closed Jan–Feb, Mon and Tue.* This inn was a favourite with Goethe. Thuringian food.

🍽🍽🍽🍽 **Anna Amalia** – *Markt 19. 📞03 643 80 20. www.luxurycollection. com/elephant.* This sophisticated restaurant is a perfect setting in which to enjoy Marcello Fabbri's classic Mediterranean-influenced cuisine. Special lunchtime menu and terrace.

Jena

Jena has developed steadily since the foundation of its university in 1548, drawing numerous scientists and intellectuals over the centuries, including Wilhelm von Humboldt, Schiller and Hegel. Goethe worked on his philosophical treatise while French and Prussian armies battled outside the gates in 1806. Jena is also famous for its optics, established in the mid-19C by Carl Zeiss and Ernst Abbe, inventors of the scientific microscope.

▶ **Population:** 102 500

▪ **Info:** Johannisstraße 23, 07743 Jena. ℘(03641) 80 64 00. www.jena.de.

◉ **Location:** Jena is northeast of the Thuringian Forest, just off the A4 autobahn and about 23km/14.3mi east of Weimar.

⊙ **Don't Miss:** Zeiss Planetarium and Optical Museum.

◷ **Timing:** Jena can be explored in a day.

👥 **Kids:** Zeiss Planetarium.

SIGHTS

Johannistor (St. John's Gate)

Along with the Pulverturm on the other side of the Marktplatz (market square), this gate is all that remains of the 14C fortifications.

Stadtmuseum and Kunstsammlung (City Museum and Art Collection)

◷*Open year-round, Tue, Wed & Fri 10am–5pm, Thu 2pm–10pm, Sat–Sun 11am–6pm.* ◷*Closed Jan 1, Dec 24 & 31.* ⊛*4€.* ℘*(03641) 49 82 61. www.stadtmuseum.jena.de.*

This museum presents regional art and milestones in Jena's history in a beautiful, partially half-timbered building.

Stadtkirche St. Michaelis

This collegiate church of the Cistercians got a Gothic facelift in the 15C. Note the canopied porch on the south side.

Goethe-Gedenkstätte (Goethe Memorial)

Fürstengraben 26. ◷*Open Apr–Oct, Wed–Sun 11am–3pm.* ◷*Closed May 1, Ascension Day, Oct 3 & 31.* ⊛*1€.* ℘*(03641) 93 11 88.*

Exhibits in this former inspector's house at the Botanical Gardens, where Goethe stayed while in Jena, focus mostly on his accomplishments as a politician and natural scientist.

Schillers Gartenhaus (Schiller Museum)

Schillergässchen 2. ◷*Open Tue–Sun 11am–5pm (Nov–Mar, Tue–Sat).* ◷*Closed public holidays.* ⊛*2.50€.* ℘*(03641) 93 11 88. www.uni-jena. de/gartenhaus.html.*

Schiller wrote several of his famous works *(Wallenstein, Maria Stuart)* while spending the summers of 1797 to 1799 in this garden house. Ground-floor exhibits track his life in Jena, while upstairs are the family's private quarters, including his study and bedroom.

Stadtkirche St. Michaelis

© Volker Lissner/Fotolia.com

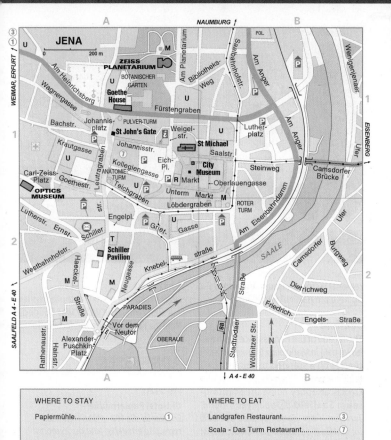

WHERE TO STAY

WHERE TO EAT

👥 Zeiss Planetarium★

🕐Open Tue–Sun, showtimes vary.
👛8€ (child 6.50€). ♿ 📞(036 41) 88
54 88. www.planetarium-jena.de.
This state-of-the-art planetarium
presents celestial shows geared towards
both adults and children.

Optisches Museum★ (Optics Museum)

Carl-Zeiss-Platz 12. 🕐Open year-round,
Tue–Fri 10am–4.30pm, Sat 11am–5pm.
🕐Closed on public holidays. 👛5€. ♿
📞(03641) 44 31 65.
www.optischesmuseum.de.
The museum retraces 500 years of the
history of optics with a collection of
spectacles, telescopes and photographic
equipment. Also visit a workshop
from 1866.

🚗 DRIVING TOUR

UPPER SAALE VALLEY★

From Rudolstadt to Saalburg. 61km/38mi
– Allow 4hrs.

The winding Saale River forms a natural
link between towns like Jena and Halle,
masterpieces of sacred architecture like
Merseburg and Naumburg, and numerous riverside castles.

Rudolstadt

Once the seat of the princes of Schwarz-
burg-Rudolstadt, this town is dominated
by the fine silhouette of 18C **Schloss
Heidecksburg**★ (🕐 open Tue–Sun
10am–6pm (Nov–Mar 5pm); 👛6€;
📞(03672) 429 00; www.heidecksburg.de).
Several magnificent Rococo **rooms**★★
are open to the public, and there's also a

Feengrotten

© bfflv/Fotolia.com

regional history museum. **Views**★ from up here are particularly delightful.

Saalfeld

The façade of the Renaissance **Rathaus** (town hall) in Marktplatz (market square) centres on a stepped tower with two oriel windows. The historic rooms of a Franciscan abbey house the **Stadtmuseum Saalfeld** (◷ open year-round, Tue–Sun 10am–5pm; ◷ closed Dec 24 & 31; ◉ 4€; ♿; ℘ (03671) 59 84 60; www.museumimkloster.de), with collections on local history and folklore.

☙ **Feengrotten**★ (Fairy Grottoes)

◖ 1km/0.6mi southeast of Saalfeld on the B281. ◖ Guided tours (45min), Apr–Oct, daily 9.30am–5pm; Nov–Mar 10.30am–3.30pm; ◉ 8€. ℘ (03671) 550 40. www.feengrotten.de.

The subterranean grottoes of this abandoned slate mine are a whimsical wonderland with stalactite and stalagmite formations sparkling in a myriad of fantastic colours.

◖ Leave Saalfeld on the B85. Cross the Saale at the Hohenwarte Dam and drive along the Hohenwarte reservoir (Talsperre) for 10km/6.2mi via Drognitz and Remptendorf to the Bleiloch reservoir. Driving across the dam, you arrive back at the river's east bank.

Saalburg

Now a lakeside town, Saalburg lost its outskirts when the valley was flooded. Note the remains of the 16C fortifications.

ADDRESSES

☙ STAY

◖ **Hotel Papiermühle** – Erfurter Straße 102. ℘ 03 641 45 980. www.papiermuehle-jena.de. 25 rooms. ◘. Two pretty brick houses make up this family-run hotel and inn. Bedrooms are decorated with dark-wood furnishings. The inn dates from 1737 and brews its own beer.

☙ EAT

◖◖ **Landgrafen** – Landgrafenstieg 25. ℘ 03 641 50 70 71. www.landgrafen.de. Known as "The Balcony of Jena" because of its breathtaking views over the city, this restaurant immediately beneath the town's landmark tower offers homemade Thüringer cuisine. The hotel is very popular as a wedding venue.

◖◖◖ **SCALA – Das Turm Restaurant** – Leutragraben 1. ℘ 03 641 35 66 66. www.scala-jena.de. International fine dining with panoramic views through floor-to-ceiling windows, at this modern restaurant set on the 28th floor of Germany's largest office building.

Naumburg★

Pretty Naumburg lies on the edge of the Thuringian basin, surrounded by terraced vineyards and wooded hillsides topped by castles. Lordly townhouses, sturdy fortifications and, above all, the exceptional cathedral still reflect the town's heritage as a wealthy medieval trading centre. The philosopher Friedrich Nietzsche spent a lot of time in the town at various stages of his life.

▶ **Population:** 30 000
🛈 **Info:** Markt 12, 06618 Naumburg. ℘(03445) 27 31 12. www.naumburg-tourismus.de.
◖ **Location:** Naumburg is in the heart of the Saale-Unstrut wine-growing region, about 50km/31mi south of Halle.
😊 **Don't Miss:** Cathedral St. Peter and St. Paul.
🕐 **Timing:** Allow half a day to see Naumburg.

A BIT OF HISTORY

Important trading centre – The seat of a bishopric since 1028, Naumburg started developing as a civic entity in the 12C, becoming an important trading centre in the late Middle Ages. The "Peter-Pauls-Messe" held here was a serious rival to the trade fair in Leipzig.

A model town – Largely spared damage during World War II, in 1991 Naumburg was one of five cities in the former East Germany to be selected as a model for restoring historic city centres.

SIGHTS

Dom Sts. Peter und Paul★★ (Cathedral of Saints Peter and Paul)

Domplatz 16/17. 🕐*Open Mar–Oct, daily 9am–6pm (Sun from noon); Nov–Feb, 10am–4pm (Sun from noon).* ⊚*4€.* ℘*(03445) 23 01 10.*

This double-chancel cathedral is a perfect example of the stylistic evolution from late Romanesque to early Gothic. The Romanesque nave was built in the early 13C; by the late 13C the western section was completed with early-Gothic features. The eastern chancel is separated from the central nave by the only remaining hall-church rood screen in Germany.

The western chancel is bathed in ethereal light thanks to extraordinarily luminous stained-glass windows. It features another magnificent **rood screen**★★. This one is by the artist known only as the Master of Naumburg and depicts poignant, lifelike scenes of the Passion. The splendid central portal shows a Crucifixion group, surmounted by the Majesty of God as a fresco in a quatrefoil. The same master also created the famous **statues**★★★ of the cathedral's benefactors, Uta and Ekkehard.

Marktplatz (Market Square)

The large market square is framed by 16C–17C houses as well as the **Town Hall**. A late-Gothic building, it has a beautiful portal from 1612 and boasts six transverse gables with tracery decoration. The same façade design is repeated on the Schlösschen (1543), behind which towers the church of St. Wenceslas. The Hohe Lilie (municipal museum), with its late-Gothic corbie gable and traced transom, stands at the entrance to Herrenstraße.

St. Wenzel-Kirche★ (Church of St. Wenceslas)

A church on this site was first recorded in 1228. The present building was constructed in the 15C as a late-Gothic hall-church. Features added during the Renaissance include five tribunes built between 1610 and 1618. In the 18C, though, the interior got its Baroque makeover resulting in a mirror-vaulted ceiling, and a magnificent carved altar and pulpit.

The organ is one of the largest surviving ones built by **Zacharias Hildebrand** and was put through its paces by

Joys of the Grape

Two lovely rivers give Germany's northernmost wine-growing region its name: the Saale and the Unstrut. Only 665ha/1 643 acres in size, this area has a viticultural heritage going back 1 000 years and considers Freyburg as its unofficial capital.

Some 30 grape varieties grow in these limestone and red sandstone soils, on vineyards clinging to steep riverside terraces that are drenched by up to 1 600 hours of sunshine a year. Most varietals are dry, fresh and white, with Müller-Thurgau leading the pack, followed by Weissburgunder (pinot blanc), Silvaner and Riesling. Only a quarter is dedicated to red wines, mostly Dornfelder and red Burgundy.

none other than the famous composer Johann Sebastian Bach himself. Inside the church are also two fine paintings by **Lucas Cranach the Elder**: *The Adoration of the Magi* (1522) and *The Blessing of the Children* (1529).

Townhouses

In Jakobstraße note the **Alte Post** (1574) with its three-storey oriel. Houses in **Marienstraße** sport extravagantly ornate portals that reflect the burghers' one-time prosperity. **Herrenstraße** features some fine oriels, including the town's oldest house at no 1. The Lorbeerapotheke, an old pharmacy next door, also boasts a splendid oriel, as does the house at no 8 (1525).

Marientor (St. Mary's Gate)

This is the only one of the five original town gates to have survived. It is a rare example of a double gate with gatehouses, a curved courtyard to trap intruders, and a watchpath. It is 14C at its core but was extended in the 15C.

Nietzsche-Haus

Weingarten 18. ○*Open mid-Mar–Oct, Tue–Fri 2pm–5pm, Sat–Sun 10am–4pm.* ⊕*2.50€.* ℘ *(03445) 20 16 38.*
From 1890 until 1897, during his collapse into mental and physical decline, Nietzsche was cared for in this house by his mother. Photos and documents evoke the intellectual life and body of work created by this controversial philosopher.

Organ, St. Wenzel-Kirche

©Milan Systemtechnik/istockphoto.com

Eisenach★★

The history of Eisenach is closely linked with the reformer Martin Luther who went to school here and later translated the New Testament into German while in hiding at Wartburg castle. Eisenach is also the birthplace of the composer Johann Sebastian Bach and a gateway to the Thuringian Forest.

▶ **Population:** 44 100
🛈 **Info:** Markt 9, 99817 Eisenach. ℘(03691) 792 30. www.eisenach.de.
◐ **Location:** Eisenach is on the northwestern edge of the Thuringian Forest, just off the A4 autobahn.
🌀 **Don't Miss:** The Wartburg.
🕐 **Timing:** Allow at least three hours for the Wartburg.

A BIT OF HISTORY

At the heart of Germany – At the beginning of the 13C, the *Minnesänger* (*see INTRODUCTION: Music*) held legendary singing contests in the Wartburg, a custom that inspired Wagner's opera *Tannhäuser*.

Martin Luther attended school in Eisenach and sought refuge at the Wartburg in 1521–22 while under papal ban. This is where he translated the New Testament from the Greek into the German vernacular (*see INTRODUCTION: History*). Eisenach is also the 1685 birthplace of composer **Johann Sebastian Bach**.

WARTBURG★★

Allow 2hrs. Park in the pay car park below the castle and walk about 15min or take bus 10 from the train station or Karlsplatz. Guided tours (1hr); Apr–Oct, daily 8.30am–5pm (English tour 1.30pm); Nov–Mar, daily 9am–3.30pm. 8€. ℘(036 91) 25 00. www.wartburg-eisenach.de.
Built between 1155 and 1180, Wartburg castle is one of the best-preserved and most imposing Romanesque structures, despite later alterations in other architectural styles.
It has been on UNESCO's list of World Heritage Sites since 2000. Perched on a rocky spur, the castle welcomes visitors through a 12C entrance leading into a 15C–16C **outer courtyard** (*Erster Burghof*) framed by half-timbered buildings. Inside the fortified complex is the **Palas**★, where the landgraves resided. Enjoy sweeping **views**★ of Eisenach, the Thuringian Forest and the Rhön

Wartburg
J. Bouraly/MICHELIN

foothills from the ramparts and south tower.
Tours take in the **Hall of the Troubadours** (Sängersaal) where Moritz von Schwind's monumental fresco illustrates the *Minnesänger* contest. Tours end in the **museum** and the **Lutherstube**, the austerely furnished room where Martin Luther stayed while working on his translation.

ADDITIONAL SIGHTS
Markt

The market place is bordered by administrative buildings and townhouses surrounding a fountain with a statue of Eisenach's patron saint, St. George.

Martin Luther in the Wartburg

After refusing to renounce his reformist views at the Diet of Worms on 18 April 1521, Martin Luther (👁 *see INTRODUCTION: History*) was excommunicated, declared an outlaw and placed under papal ban. To prevent his arrest, his protector Frederick III, the Elector of Saxony, spirited Luther to the Wartburg where he spent the next 10 months living as an anonymous knight named Junker Jörg. He spent his days translating the New Testament from Greek into German: a major linguistic achievement that helped unify the many German dialects into a common language. More profoundly, though, it made the Bible more accessible to ordinary people, which contributed greatly to the success of the Reformation movement.

Schloss (Castle)

Markt 24. ⏰*Open year-round, Tue–Fri 10am–6pm, Sat–Sun 10am–5pm.* ◉*2€.* ☏*(036 91) 67 04 50.*
The former residence of the local dukes houses the **Thüringer Museum**, a collection of porcelain, paintings and folk art from the 18C–20C.

Rathaus (Town Hall)

Eisenach's three-storey 16C town hall was built on the site of an old tavern and blends Baroque and Renaissance elements. It was remodelled after a fire in 1636. Note that the tower is slightly tilted.

Georgenkirche

Markt. ⏰*Open year-round, daily 10am–noon, 2pm–4pm.* ☏*(03691) 21 31 26.*
This triple-aisled 16C church contains the tombs of several landgraves of Thuringia. Luther preached here in 1521 despite his being officially banned from the Holy Roman Empire. Johann Sebastian Bach was baptised here in 1685.

Predigerkirche

The late 13C early-Gothic church houses the **wooden sculpture collection**★ formerly in the Thuringian Museum. Carvings date from the 12C–16C.

Lutherhaus

Lutherplatz 8. ⏰*Open year-round, daily 10am–5pm.* ◉*3.50€.* ☏*(03691) 298 30. www.lutherhaus-eisenach.de.*
Martin Luther lived in this half-timbered house between 1498 and 1501 while studying at the Latin School. A modern exhibition uses paintings, documents and multimedia terminals to tell the story of his life and accomplishments.

Bachhaus (Bach Museum)

Frauenplan 21. ⏰*Open year-round, daily 10am–6pm.* ◉*7.50€.* ♿ ☏*(03691) 793 40. www.bachhaus.de.*
The actual house where Johann Sebastian Bach first saw the light of day no longer exists but it looked very much like the 600-year-old half-timbered structure that now holds a museum dedicated to the composer.
Recently expanded and modernised, it traces his life and accomplishments through manuscripts, scores and portraits of the prolific Bach family. Visits include a live concert played on period instruments. A new annex has listening stations.

Automobile Welt Eisenach

Friedrich-Naumann-Straße 10. ⏰*Open year-round, Tue–Sun 11am–5pm.* ◉*3€.* ♿ ☏*(03691) 772 12.*
Vehicle manufacturing has been part of Eisenach's history since 1896 and car buffs and nostalgic types should make a beeline to this automobile museum housed in the original 1935 plant. A 1907 Wartburg Dixi, boxy GDR-era vehicles, cool sports cars and eccentric prototypes are all among the collections.

🚗 DRIVING TOUR

THURINGIAN FOREST★★

Eisenach to Ilmenau. 110km/68mi –
Allow 1 day.

The Thuringian Forest is one of the most beautiful natural regions in Germany and is hugely popular with hikers, cross-country skiers and outdoor types of all stripes. The mid-level massif is littered with charming villages where traditional skills and craftsmanship are kept alive. The delightful forest road mainly parallels the **Rennsteig**, a 168km/104mi-long 🚶 hiking trail that keeps to the forest's higher elevations, crossing the Großer Inselsberg (916m/3 005ft) and Großer Beerberg (983m/3 225ft) peaks.

▷ *Leave Eisenach in the direction of Gotha.*

Großer Inselsberg
🚶 *1hr round-trip walk.*
The **views**★★ from the summit take in much of the forest.

👥 Marienglashöhle★
🔦*Guided tours (45min), Apr–Oct, daily 9am–5pm; Nov–Mar, 9am–4pm.*
💶*6€.* ✆*(03623) 31 16 67.*
www.schauhoehlen.de.
This natural **mine** produces crystalline gypsum, a mineral used in the decoration of church altars and the protection of pictures of the Virgin Mary. This watery gypsum was named *Marienglas* (Mary's glass) in the Middle Ages.

▷ *The road cuts across the Rennsteig and twists between the Regenberg and the Spießberg. Consider a hike through the Ebertswiese, a marsh- and meadowland. Steinbach is overlooked by the Hallenburg ruins. The road continues towards Oberhof via the grasslands of the Kanzlergrund.*

Oberhof★
At 800m/2 625ft, Oberhof is the forest's most important winter sports centre and the host of annual biathlon and nordic combined (cross-country skiing and ski-jumping) world cups. More than 4 000 plant species grow In the **Rennsteiggarten** botanical park. Follow the B247 to the car park lot of the **Ohratalsperre** reservoir which supplies water to Weimar, Jena, Gotha and Erfurt.

▷ *Leave Oberhof towards Schmücke.*

Ilmenau
On the forest's northern fringe, Ilmenau has always been associated with Goethe, said to have been particularly fond of its natural beauty. A plaque in his memory adorns the wall of the *Amtshaus* in Marktplatz, which now features a small Goethe museum. 🚶 The **Goethewanderweg** (hiking trail) links sites associated with the great writer.

Exploring around Oberhof

© FAN Travel Stock/AWL Images

WHERE TO STAY

Auf der Wartburg...........................①

Göbel's Sophien Hotel..................⑥

Kaiserhof.....................................⑨

Villa Anna....................................④

WHERE TO EAT

Turmschänke...............................②

Villa Antik...................................⑤

ADDRESSES

🏨 STAY

Villa Anna – *Fritz-Koch-Straße 12.* *℘03691 239 50. www.hotel-villa-anna. de. 15 rooms.* A warm welcome awaits at Villa Anna, which offers a winning combination of historic atmosphere and modern elegance.

Göbel's Sophien Hotel – *Sophienstraße 41. ℘03 691 25 10. www.sophienhotel.de. 60 rooms.* This family-owned international-style modern establishment, in the centre of town, offers high quality rooms. Spa and sauna.

Kaiserhof – *Wartburgallee 2.* *℘03 691 888 90. www.kaiserhof-eisenach.de. 60 rooms.* A large welcoming reception area and spacious comfortable rooms are the hallmarks of this traditional old hotel in the heart of town. Beautiful dining room with vaulted ceiling.

Auf der Wartburg – *In the Wartburg fortress, limousine shuttle available from the station if requested. ℘03 691 79 70. www.wartburghotel.de. Closed Jan 6–Feb 6. 35 rooms.* A night in this beautifully restored, very atmospheric medieval hotel, perched on a mountaintop, surrounded by

forest, is an unforgettable experience.
Its restaurant enjoys an equally
impressive setting.

⑂/ EAT

◯◉◉ **Villa Antik** – *Wartburgallee 55.*
℘*03 691 72 09 91. www.villa-antik.de.*
This charming 19C villa near the city
centre is home to an elegant restaurant
with stucco decoration and antique
furniture; it serves regional cuisine.

◯◉◉ **Weinrestuarant
Turmschänke** – *Karlsplatz 28.*
℘*03 691 21 35 33. www.turmschaenke-
eisenach.de.* The rustic charm of the
medieval Nicolaiturm is an ideal setting
for the inspired regional cuisine of
Ulrich Rösch.

Kassel★

Once the seat of landgraves, Kassel is renowned for the romantic Wilhelmshöhe park, with its follies, grottoes and waterfalls as well as a lovely palace now brimming with paintings by Dürer, Rembrandt, Rubens and other Old Masters. Kassel's postwar reconstruction has not always been done in the best taste, but the town's various sights make it an interesting stop nonetheless. Every five years, the art world focuses its attention on Kassel when it hosts the renowned international contemporary art exhibition called Documenta.

A BIT OF HISTORY

The Brothers Grimm – Jakob (1785–1863) and Wilhelm Grimm (1786–1859) lived in Kassel from 1805 to 1830, working as court librarians. Fascinated by legends and folklore, the brothers collected a wealth of stories published under the title *Kinder und Hausmärchen*, known in English as *Grimms' Fairy Tales*.

Documenta – Internationally, Kassel is often associated with the Documenta, an international exhibition of contem-

▶ **Population:** 194 000

▤ **Info:** Obere Königstraße 8. ℘(0561) 70 77 07. www.kassel-tourist.de.

◑ **Location:** Kassel hugs the Fulda River *(boat tours from Fuldabrücke)* and is surrounded by two nature parks, the Habichtswald and the Naturpark Meißner-Kaufungen Wald. The town is also at the crossroads of the A7 (Fulda–Hannover) and the A44 (to Dortmund) autobahns.

◷ **Timing:** Allow half a day for a visit of the Wilhelmshöhe park.

porary art held for 100 days every five years since 1955. The next one is in 2012.

WILHELMSHÖHE★★
Park★★

This sprawling Baroque park boasts nearly 800 tree species and, in the late 18C, was transformed into an English style garden. **Löwenburg**, a mock medieval castle built around 1800, is a fine example of the era's Romanticism.

Wilhelmshöhe park

Ch. Bastin & J. Evrard/MICHELIN

The park is lorded over by the 72m/236ft-tall **Hercules★** *(Herkules)*, emblem of Kassel and highlight of the park. **Views★★** from up here are predictably fabulous. Below here, a **water staircase** *(Kaskadentreppe)* shoots an enormous **cascade★** of water into the Neptune and Fountain pools.

Schloss Wilhelmshöhe (Palace)

🕐*Open year-round, Tue–Sun 10am–5pm (Thu 8pm).* 🕐*Closed Jan 1, Dec 24-25 & 31.* ⊜*6€.* ♿ ✆*(0561) 31 68 00. www.museum-kassel.de.*

Completed in 1803, the palace now houses a prized **Antikensammlung★** (collection of antiquities) from Greece and Rome. There are plenty of Greek vases, the 2C **Kassel Apollo**, a series of busts, a sarcophagus, urns and other precious objects.

If time is limited, head straight to the outstanding **Gemäldegalerie Alter Meister★★★** (Old Masters picture Gallery). Important works by German painters include Altdorfer's *Crucifixion*, a triptych *(Reisealtar)* by Cranach the Elder, Dürer's *Portrait of Elizabeth Tucher* and *Hercules at Antioch* by Hans Baldung Grien. The Dutch and Flemish Schools are represented by Rembrandt's *Portrait of Saskia van Uylenburgh*; Rubens' *Crowning of a Hero* and Jordaens' *The Painter's Betrothal*. Also on display here are landscapes by Jan Brueghel, Jacob van Ruisdael and Jan Steen. Works by Italians (Tintoretto, Titian, Bassano), Spanish (Ribera, Murillo) and French (Poussin) artists complete the collection.

ADDITIONAL SIGHTS
Karlsaue Park★

The most popular sections of this 18C riverside park are the gardens below the Schöne Aussicht terrace, and the Siebenbergen Fulda island. The Baroque orangery is home to the **Astronomisch-Physikalisches Kabinet** (🕐*open year-round, Tue–Sun 10am–5pm (Thu 8pm);* 🕐*closed May 1, Dec 24, 25 & 31;* ⊜*3€;* ✆*(0561) 31 68 05 00)* with a rich collection of astronomical instruments and clocks as well as an attached planetarium. Models demonstrate observable scientific phenomena and there area displays explaining the evolution of technology since antiquity.

Hessisches Landesmuseum★ (Hessian State Museum)

Brüder-Grimm-Platz 5. ✆*(0561) 31 68 00. www.museum-kassel.de.* ⌐*Closed for renovation.*

This sprawling museum displays artefacts and objects related to the cultural history of the Hesse region dating from prehistory to the present. Its extensive collections range from Stone Age tools to medieval sculpture and precious 17C porcelain, to centuries' worth of decorative objects. Pride of place goes to a major collection of coloured Bohemian crystal and locally forged silverware. There are also hundreds of items tracking the evolution of wall coverings from the 18C to the 20C (Deutsches Tapetenmuseum).

EXCURSION
Göttingen

▶ *47km/29.2mi north on the A7.*

Along with Heidelberg, Tübingen and Marburg, Göttingen is a town defined by its university, which was founded in 1734. Some 44 Nobel Prize winners have either studied, taught or conducted research here.

The charming old town bustles with students on bicycles and is filled with Gothic churches and Neoclassical university buildings.

The 13C–15C **Altes Rathaus** (old town hall) harbours the tourist office. It is perhaps best known for what lies beneath it: the **Ratskeller** (wine cellar), a rustic tavern that is probably the most fun and lively spot in Göttingen. At the front is the **Gänselieselbrunnen** (goosegirl fountain), the city's emblem. Newly anointed PhDs must give her a kiss.

One of the city's most impressive views is the **Vierkirchenblick**, with a church on each point of the compass if viewed from the southeast corner of the market: east, St. Albanikirche; south, St. Michael-

WHERE TO STAY

WHERE TO EAT

Town centre, Göttingen

© Charles Mahaux/Tips Images

skirche; west, St. Johannis; and north, St. Jakobi with the tallest tower in town. The eastern part of the old town is dotted with **half-timbered houses**. One of the biggest beauties is the **Junkernschänke★** (*Barfüßerstraße 5*), a 16C Renaissance inn with a stunning multicoloured façade.

Finally, a visit to Göttingen should include a stop at the 🔺🔺**Städtisches Museum** (*municipal museum; Ritterplan 7/8;* 🕐*open year-round, Tue–Fri 10am–5pm, Sat–Sun 11am–5pm;* 🕐*closed major public holidays;* 👓*1.50€ (child 1€)* 📞*(0551)400 28 43. www.museum.goettingen.de*), housed in a well-preserved, half-timbered Renaissance building. It contains comprehensive exhibits on Göttingen's historical and cultural development. Art fans are drawn to the rooms housing religious works, paintings by regional artists and contemporary glass art. Children cherish the collection of old toys from as far back as the 19C and can participate in a wide variety of activities, including interactive guided tours.

ADDRESSES

🏨 STAY

🍽️🍽️ **Hotel Astoria** – *Friedrich-Ebert Straße 135.* 📞*0561 728 30. www.adessohotels.de. 40 rooms.* This turn-of-the-20C house near the town hall offers quiet, contemporary bedrooms.

🍽️🍽️ **Stadthotel** – *Wolfsschlucht 21.* 📞*0561 78 88 80. www.stadthotelkassel.de. 42 rooms.* This plain modern hotel is conveniently situated between the Hauptbahnhof and the theatre, opposite the main shopping area. Spacious rooms.

🍽️🍽️ **Hotel Chassalla** – *Wilhelmshöher Allee 99.* 📞*0561 927 90. www.hotelchassalla.de. 44 rooms.* This friendly family-owned hotel in the town centre offers simple but comfortable rooms.

🍴 EAT

🍽️🍽️ **El Erni** – *Parkstraße 42.* 📞*0561 71 00 18. www.el-erni.de.* New Spanish cuisine is the order of the day at this elegant modern-rustic restaurant.

🍽️🍽️ **L'Orangerie** – *An der Karlsaue 20.* 📞*0561 286 103 18. www.orangeriekassel.de.* Set in a very elegant early-18C Baroque building, the Orangery restaurant has a magnificent terrace equally suited to a candlelit dinner, or just a drink.

🍽️🍽️🍽️ **Park Schönfeld** – *Bosestraße 13.* 📞*0561 220 50. www.schlossschoenfeld.com.* In a parkland setting, this restaurant is set in part of an 18C manor house.

Fulda

Fulda is closely linked to Christian history in Germany. Its Baroque core, with the cathedral, palace and mansions of the nobility, recall a time when Prince-Bishops guarded the tomb of English missionary St. Boniface.

SIGHTS
Dom (Cathedral)

Fulda's cathedral got its Baroque looks in 1704 under Johann Dientzenhofer. St. Boniface is buried in the crypt below the high altar. The alabaster bas-relief at the base of the 18C **funerary monument**★ represents the saint.

His reliquaries are at the **Dommuseum** (◐open Apr–Oct, Tue–Sat 10am–5.30pm, Sun 12.30pm–5.30pm; Nov–Mar, Tue–Sat 10am–12.30pm, 1.30pm–4pm, Sun 12.30pm–4pm; ◐closed mid-Jan–mid-Feb. ◎2.10€; ⋋;℘(0661) 872 07; www.bistum-fulda.de).

Michaelskirche★

Built around an eight-columned 9C rotunda with a stout, square tower, this church overlooks the cathedral forecourt. The vaulted crypt is Carolingian.

EXCURSIONS
The Rhön
◐ 104km/65mi southeast of Fulda.

▶ **Population:** 63 500
🛈 **Info:** Bonifatiusplatz 1. ℘(0661) 102 18 14. www.tourismus-fulda.de.
◐ **Location:** Fulda is the economic and cultural centre of eastern Hessen and is close to Thuringia and Bavaria.

The remnants of an enormous extinct volcano, the Rhön's craggy peaks rise up to 1 000m/3 280ft above bleak moorlands. Strong winds make the area popular with gliders.

Gersfeld
◐ 31.5km/19.5mi southeast of Fulda.
The most central resort in the Rhön, Gersfeld has a Protestant **church** (1785) where the placement of organ, altar and pulpit liturgically symbolises the Lutheran reform.

The Kreuzberg★

At the end of a steep climb awaits a splendid **view**★ from the second-highest peak in the Rhön (Calvary; 928m/3 045ft). The highest – the Wasserkuppe – can be seen to the north (950m/3 117ft).
The **panorama**★★ extends as far as Fulda and the Vogelsberg.

Marburg★★

Marburg is distinguished by a great castle and an imposing Gothic church. The latter is dedicated to St. Elizabeth, the Hungarian princess who retired here to care for the sick and poor. For centuries, her relics made Marburg a major pilgrimage centre, but after the Reformation it became a hub of Protestant scholarship and theology, largely due to its prestigious 16C university. Today, Marburg is still a busy student town and has some of the liveliest nightlife in the region.

▶ **Population:** 78 000
🛈 **Info:** Pilgrimstein 26, 35037 Marburg. ℘(06421) 991 20. www.marburg.de.
◐ **Location:** Marburg is on a rocky outcrop above the Lahn River and at the centre of a triangle formed by Frankfurt, Kassel and Cologne.
◉ **Don't Miss:** St. Elizabeth's Church.
◔ **Timing:** Allow 2–3 hours.

A BIT OF HISTORY

St. Elizabeth (1207–31) – Princess Elizabeth, daughter of the King of Hungary and intended bride of Landgrave Ludwig of Thuringia, was brought under the care of the Thuringian court to Wartburg castle near Eisenach (⚘ *see EISENACH*) at the age of four. Early in her life she became known for her kindness towards the sick and unfortunate. She married Ludwig in 1221, but after he died of the plague in 1227 Elizabeth was heartbroken and withdrew to Marburg. Here she dedicated her life to helping the sick and the poor. She died, most likely of exhaustion or a disease, at the age of 24.

A place of pilgrimage – Elizabeth was canonised only four years after her death (1235). Her remains were exhumed the following year to be immortalised in the superb Gothic church built in her honour. A steady stream of pilgrims flocked here to pay her respects, making Marburg one of the largest centres of pilgrimage in Western Christianity.

Seat of the Reformation – In 1529 Elizabeth's descendant, **Philip the Magnanimous**, abolished the cult of relics and re-buried Elizabeth's remains in a local cemetery. Philip later invited reformers Martin Luther and Hyldrych Zwingli to the famous "Marburg Religious Discussion" (1529).

ELISABETHKIRCHE★★ (CHURCH OF ST. ELIZABETH)

🕓*Open Apr–Sept, daily 9am–6pm; Oct 10am–5pm; Nov–Mar, 10am–4pm. Shrine:* ⊛*2.50€.* ♿; ✆ *(06421) 654 97. www.elisabethkirche.de.*

The first truly Gothic church in Germany was built between 1235 and 1283. It is also considered the country's first hall-church and is filled with important art treasures.

As you amble around, pay special attention to the following: **(1)** a statue of St. Elizabeth (c. 1470) wearing an elegant court gown, in the nave; **(2)** an openwork Gothic rood as well as a modern Crucifix by Ernst Barlach; **(3)** an altarpiece of the

ST ELIZABETH'S CHURCH

Pietà (1360); **(4)** the tomb of St. Elizabeth (after 1250); **(5)** the remains of 14C–15C frescoes in the niches; and **(6) St. Elizabeth's Shrine**★★ *(Elisabethschrein)* in the old sacristy.

This masterpiece in gold was completed by craftsmen from the Rhineland c. 1250. Other highlights: **(7)** St. Elizabeth's Window assembled from 13C medallions; **(8)** a 1510 statue of St. Elizabeth personifying Charity, by Ludwig Juppe; **(9)** *The Landgraves' Chancel*, the necropolis of the descendants of St. Elizabeth.

ADDITIONAL SIGHTS

▶ *Leaving the church, climb up to the old town by way of the Steinweg – an unusual ramp with three levels. It continues as the Neustadt and then the Westergasse. Turn right into Marktgasse.*

Marktplatz★ (Market Square)

The upper market *(Obermarkt)* is still framed by historic buildings. Particularly outstanding examples include nos 14 and 21, from 1560; no 23; and no 18, a stone house of 1323, the oldest preserved house still inhabited. The fountain, dedicated to St. George, is a popular meeting spot.

Rathaus (Town Hall)

Marburg's town hall is a 16C Gothic building much beloved for its mechanical cockerel that crows reliably on the hour every hour. It sits in a lofty perch atop the Renaissance tower, which was added in 1581 because the original building was considered too modest.

▷ *Take Nikolaistraße to Marienkirche.*

Marienkirche (Church of St. Mary's)

This late 13C church sits adjacent to a Gothic former ossuary. From the terrace, there is a fine view over the roofs of the old town to the valley beyond. Past the church, you can glimpse the castle above. At the end of the esplanade, a passage leads down to the **Kugelkirche** (late 15C; ○ *open year-round, daily 9am–6pm*), a fine small church in the late-Gothic style.

▷ *Climb some more steps, this time to the top of the Kugelgasse. Before the Kalbstor fortified gate, turn right on Ritterstraße.*

The house at Ritterstraße 15 once belonged to legal historian Friedrich Karl von Savigny (1779–1861), one of the founders of the "Historical School" of the study of law. He was also a key member of the "Marburg Romantics" group that also included Clemens von Brentano, Achim and Bettina von Arnim and Jakob and Wilhelm Grimm.

Schloss★ (Palace)

From the 13C to the 17C, the landgraves of Hessen resided in this hilltop castle, which treats you to sweeping views of the Lahn Valley from the terrace. Surviving buildings (13C–15C) include the Gothic Princes' Hall with its double nave, the west hall which reveals excavations of the previous fortress (9C and 11C), the south hall, with its memorials of the founding of the university (1527) and of the religious debates that took place in Marburg in 1529, and finally the castle chapel with its medieval ceramic floor.

Museum für Kulturgeschichte★ (Museum of Cultural History)

○ *Open Apr–Oct, Tue–Sun 10am–6pm; Nov–Mar, Tue–Sun 10am–4pm.* ○ *Closed Jan 1, Dec 25-26 & 31.* ⊛ *4€.* ✆ *(06421) 282 23 55. http://web.uni-marburg.de/uni-museum.*

After touring the historical palace rooms, proceed to the 15C Wilhelmsbau wing, which houses this sprawling museum. It has five floors of exhibits spanning the period from the Bronze Age to the present day. Of particular note are findings from a 5C Merovingian warriors' grave, Celtic coins, Romanesque crucifixes, fragments of stained glass from the St. Elisabethkirche, a 15C tapestry depicting the story of the Prodigal Son, and a collection of medieval shields and armour.

On the two top floors, the spotlight is on daily life in the 18C and 19C.

Assembled are a hodgepodge of glass, porcelain, dolls' houses and costumes as well as fully decked-out *Biedermeier* and *Jugendstil* period rooms.

Museum für Bildende Kunst (Fine Arts Museum)

Ernst-von-Hülsen-Haus, Blegenstraße 11 (next to the Stadthalle performance hall). ○ *Open year-round, Tue–Sun 11am–1pm, 2pm–5pm.* ○ *Closed Jan 1, Dec 25-26 & 31.* ⊛ *4€.* ✆ *(06421) 282 23 55. http://web.uni-marburg.de/uni-museum.*

Four centuries of paintings, graphics and sculpture grace the rooms of this museum in a 1927 building that blends Neoclassical and Art Deco elements.

Key canvases include *Adam and Eve* by Flemish painter Louis Finson (1610) and Carl Spitzweg's *Der Briefbote im Rosenthal* (*The Letter Carrier in Rosenthal*, ca. 1858). There are fine examples of Expressionism (Lovis Corinth's *Bacchanal*, 1921) and New Objectivity (Carlo Mense's *Mother with Children*, 1925).

The arc of art spans all the way to more contemporary works, such as examples of new figurative painting (Bernard Schultze, Dieter Krieg, Hans-Hendrik Grimmling) and installations by such practitioners as Hannsjörg Voth.

WHERE TO STAY

WHERE TO EAT

ADDRESSES

🛏 STAY

⊝⊜ **Dammühle** – *Dammühlenstraße 1, 35041 Marburg-Wehrshausen-Dammühle (6km/3.7mi west along Barfüßertor).* ℘*(06421) 935 60. www.hotel-dammuehle. de. 26 rooms. Restaurant*⊝⊜. This small half-timbered 14C mill, in a charming location, has prettily decorated, comfortable rooms, some of them very modern and spacious. There's country-style dining and a large *Biergarten*, and for children, crazy golf and a playground.

⊝⊜ **Village Stadthotel** – *Bahnhofstraße 14. www.village-hotels.de.* ℘*06421 68 58 80. 20 rooms.* ⛧. This small, well-run hotel in the city centre has modern, stylish, comfortably furnished rooms.

⊝⊜ **Welcome Hotel** – *Pilgrimstein 29.* ℘*06421 91 80. www.welcome-hotel-marburg.de. 146 rooms.* ⛧. This welcoming hotel, set at the foot of the Schlossberg, features simple but stylish rooms and apartments plus a restaurant with a terrace and a pleasant bar.

⊝⊜⊜⊜ **Vila Vita Hotel Rosenpark** – *Rosenstraße 18. www.rosenpark.de.* ℘*06421 600 50. 138 rooms.* ⛧. *Restaurant*⊝⊜⊜⊜. This luxurious hotel beside the Lahn is an oasis of calm, known for its wellness and spa facilities. Seasonal cuisine with Mediterranean influences is served in the elegant Bel Etage restaurant.

🍴 EAT

⊝ **Weinstube Weinlädele** – *Schlosstreppe 1.* ℘*06421 142 44. www.weinlaedele.com.* This historic inn puts a contemporary twist on favourite regional dishes. *Flammkuchen* are a speciality.

⊝⊜ **Zur Sonne** – *Markt 14.* ℘*(06421) 171 90.* Cosy dining rooms spread across several floors of this 16C half-timbered gem serving classic German cuisine, pasta dishes and inspired specials.

⊝⊜⊜⊜ **Bel Etage** – *Rosenstraße 18. www.rosenpark.de.* ℘ *06421 600 50.* The menu at this elegant and atmospheric Mediterranean restaurant changes with the season.

THE EAST

This chapter covers Saxony, which has been for centuries one of the country's most prosperous and culturally sophisticated states. Two cities of very different character dominate: no-nonsense Leipzig with its traditions as a trading town and centre of music and the arts; and playful Dresden, nicknamed "Florence on the Elbe" for its Baroque looks and extraordinary art collections. Dresden is also the gateway to Saxon Switzerland, the region's most dramatically beautiful area where nature has moulded sandstone into bizarre columns, battered cliffs, tabletop mountains, and deep valleys and gorges. Upriver from Dresden, Meissen is the birthplace of European porcelain and home to one of the world's most famous china brands.

Highlights

A State of the Arts

A journey through Saxony is an encounter with a rich musical and artistic legacy. In Leipzig you can walk in the footsteps of Johann Sebastian Bach, who worked as cantor of the St. Thomas Church, whose famous boys' choir (Thomanerchor) has delighted music-lovers since 1212. Felix Mendelssohn-Bartholdy founded Germany's first conservatory in Leipzig in 1843, where Robert Schumann signed up as a professor. Two years later, Mendelssohn became music director of the prestigious Gewandhaus Orchestra. All of these institutions still exist to this day, but of late Leipzig has also made its mark in the contemporary fine arts. In fact, the New Leipzig School is the most important artistic movement to come out of Germany since reunification, and paintings by many of its leading practitioners, especially Neo Rauch, are sought after by collectors world-wide.

Although not as trendsetting as Leipzig, Dresden also has a strong artistic heritage, measured more by the size, depth and quality of its art collections, as well as by the inspiration it provided to such famous painters as Canaletto and Caspar David Friedrich. How many of the artworks have survived is all the more astonishing given Dresden's near total devastation in World War II. Since then, the city has risen phoenix-like from the ashes.

Making an intricate teapot, Museum of Meissen Art

MEISSEN/A&C Media Community e.K.

Map legend:

- ★★★ Highly recommended
- ★★ Recommended
- ★ Interesting
- Driving Tour showing point of departure

DRESDEN ★★★

Königstein ★★

Leipzig ★

Hermhut

0   30 km

Unique Souvenirs

Shopping in Saxony means one can buy unique handmade gifts. A popular souvenir from Dresden is the original *Stollen*, a fruit-filled cake enjoyed at Christmastime. Gorgeous Christmas ornaments and decorations are still produced in the Ore Mountains in the southern part of the state. In Meissen, you can buy the famous hand-painted porcelain straight from the factory. The town is also the hub of the Saxon Wine Region, one of the northernmost in Europe. Although the vineyards may be relatively few in number, wine has been cultivated here for nearly 850 years thanks to more than 1 500 hours of sunshine in an average year.

Dresden★★★

Risen from the ashes of World War II and relative neglect during the Cold War years, Dresden has made a full-on comeback and can rightly reclaim its seat in the pantheon of European capitals of arts, culture and architecture. One night of carpet fire-bombing in February 1945, just weeks before the armistice, laid waste to centuries of vision and cash expended by a series of Saxon rulers, most notably August the Strong. At least 35 000 people died in the conflagration. Since reunification, reconstruction has proceeded at a steady pace, with the re-opening of the Frauenkirche, the Green Vault (the priceless treasure-chamber of the Saxon dukes) and the Albertinum art collection being the most headline-catching accomplishments.

▶ **Population:** 504 795

🛈 **Info:** Prager Straße 2, 01069 Dresden. ✆(0351) 49 19 21 00. www.dresden-tourist.de.

◐ **Location:** Dresden sits in the heart of Saxony, on the banks of the Elbe and is served by the A4, A13 and A14 autobahns.

🅿 **Parking:** Garages abound, especially near the Frauenkirche and the Zwinger.

◈ **Don't Miss:** The old town, Frauenkirche, Zwinger, Grünes Gewölbe.

🕐 **Timing:** Allow at least a couple of days for this amazing city.

A BIT OF HISTORY

"Florence on the Elbe" – Dresden's major development took place in the early 18C during the reigns of Electors **August the Strong** and his son Augustus III. These powerful patrons of the arts enticed scores of craftsmen and artists from Italy to build such magnificent Baroque edifices as the Zwinger, the Japanese Palace and the Hofkirche (court church). They also amassed outstanding collections of paintings and objets d'art.

A Line of Organ Builders

Gottfried Silbermann (1683–1753) apprenticed in Strasbourg with his brother Andreas, famous for creating the Alsace organs of Ebersmunster. In 1710, Gottfried settled in Freiberg, designing instruments with remarkable tone. Of the 51 organs attributed to him, those in Freiberg are the best. Gottfried's nephew Johann Andreas followed suit, and designed 54 organs in the Upper Rhine region.

The Night of the Apocalypse – A few months before the end of World War II, on the night of 13–14 February 1945, Dresden was the target of one of the Allies' most destructive air raids. Three successive waves of Lancaster bombers left the blackened skeletons of houses and monuments emerging from a waste of smoking ruins. In all, 75 percent of the city was destroyed. Restoration of Dresden's historic sites and the rebuilding of residential quarters have given the town a special quality that marries urbanism with heritage.

ZWINGER★★★

Commissioned by August the Strong, master architect **Matthäus Daniel Pöppelmann** (1682–1737) designed and realised this stunning Baroque palace between 1711 and 1728. Sculpture was provided by Balthasar Perlmoser. Painstakingly reconstructed, the complex now houses several museums (most famously the Old Masters Picture Gallery), and is one of Dresden's key attractions.

◈ *The best view of the complex is from the entrance through the Carillon Pavilion.*

PRACTICAL INFORMATION

TELEPHONE AREA CODE: ✆035
TOURIST INFORMATION
For **ticket reservations**, call Dresden Tourism at ✆(0351) 49 19 22 33; for room reservations the number is ✆(0351) 49 19 22 22 and for general information, dial ✆(0351) 49 19 21 00. Mon–Fri 8am–6pm, Sat 9am–4pm, Sun 9am–2pm. Or visit www.dresden.de. Dresden Tourism also has two information offices: one across from the Hauptbahnhof (main train station) at Prager Straße 2, *Mon–Sat 10am–7pm*; the other at Schinkelwache on Theaterplatz near the Semperoper, *Mon–Thu 10am–6pm, Fri 10am–7pm, Sat–Sun 10am–5pm*.

City magazines *SAX* (www.cybersax.de), the freebies *BLITZ!* (www.blitz-stadt magazin.com) and *Frizz* (www.frizz-magazin.de) provide complete listings information. *SAX* is sold at newspaper kiosks and bookshops, while the other two are found in bars, boutiques and tourist offices, as is the monthly *Dresdner Kulturmagazin* (www.dresdner.nu).

TOURIST CARDS
Available at tourist offices and DVB service centres – The **Dresden-City-Card** (21€ valid 48hrs) lets an adult (plus any children under six) use all buses, trams and Elbe ferries, plus free entry to 12 museums of the State Art Collections and discounts for other museums.

The **Dresden-Regio-Card** (32€ valid 72hrs) includes free rides on the S-Bahn trains along the Elbe to e.g. Meissen, Pirna and Königstein, discounts for rides on various narrow-gauge trains, and discounts at the region's main museums.

POST OFFICES WITH LATE HOURS
Altmarkt-Galerie (Webergasse 2, inside shopping centre; Mon–Sat 9.30am–9pm) and **Königsbrücker Straße 21–29** (Mon–Fri 9am–7pm, Sat 10am–1pm).

DAILY PAPERS
Sächsische Zeitung; *Dresdner Neueste Nachrichten*.

INTERNET
www.dresden-tourist.de; www.dresden-online.de; www.dresden.de.

GETTING THERE AND AROUND

AIRPORT
Drivers coming from Leipzig should take the A14 east to the A4 *(114km/70mi)*; from Berlin, follow the A113 south to the A13 *(190km/118mi)*. **Dresden Airport** (DRS; ✆(0351) 881 33 60; www.dresden-airport.de) is less than 10km/6.2mi north of the city centre. S-Bahn trains (S2) run into town from the airport throughout the day.

RAIL
There is also direct **Deutsche Bahn** train service to and from Leipzig, Berlin, Meissen, Frankfurt and other cities. Note that Dresden has two railway stations: *Dresden-Hauptbahnhof* south of the old town and *Dresden-Neustadt* (Schlesischer Platz 1). Most trains stop at both stations.

PUBLIC TRANSPORT
Dresden's largely pedestrianised historic centre contains most sights and museums and is compact enough for walking. The city is served by a network of trams and buses operated by Dresdner Verkehrsbetriebe (DVB; ✆(0351) 857 10 11; www.dv-bag.de). There are service centres at the Hauptbahnhof, *Mon–Fri 7am–7pm, Sat 8am–6pm, Sun 9am–6pm*; Postplatz, *Mon–Fri 7am–8pm, Sat 8am–6pm, Sun 9am–6pm*; Pirnaischer Platz and Albertplatz, *Mon–Fri 7am–6pm, Sat 9am–4pm*.

Tickets are available at station vending machines, aboard and at service centres. The basic fare is 1.80€. One-day passes *(Tageskarte)* cost 4.50€ and are worthwhile if you plan on multiple trips. One-day family/group tickets *(Familientageskarte)* start at 6€.
The DVB is integrated into the Verkehrsverbund Oberelbe *(VVO; ✆(0180) 22 66 22 66, Mon–Fri 9am–6pm, Sat 9am–4pm; www.vvo-online.de)*, which also covers "Swiss Saxony" *(Sächsische Schweiz)*, the eastern Erzgebirge Mountains and parts of the Oberlausitz area.

DRESDEN

Moritzburg Castle
(A 13-E 55) BERLIN
(A 4-E 40) BAUTZEN

HOYERSWERDA

0   300 m

Zwinger
© Frank Exss/Bildagentur RM/Tips Images/Photononstop

The huge rectangular courtyard is bookended by the **Wallpavillon**★★ (Rampart Pavilion) to the north and the **Glockenspielpavillon** (Carillon Pavilion) on the opposite end. It is in the former that the Zwinger's harmonious marriage of sculpture and architecture best expresses itself. Crowning the pavilion is August the Strong's idol, **Hercules**, carrying the world on his back. The Wallpavillon leads to a terrace and the **Nymphenbad**★★ (Bath of the Nymphs).

The southwest side of the complex, the elegant **Zwinger Gallery**, is best seen from the outside passing beneath the gorgeous **Kronentor** (Crown Gate). Opposite, the **Semperbau** (Semper Building) is a 1847 work of Gottfried Semper with sculpture by Ernst Rietschel.

Gemäldegalerie Alte Meister★★★ (Gallery of Old Masters)

Semperbau, west wing. ◷*Open year-round, Tue–Sun 10am–6pm.* ◷*Closed Dec 25.* ◉*10€.* ✆*(0351) 49 14 20 00. www.skd.museum.*

Assembled by Augustus the Strong and Augustus III, the Gallery of Old Masters is one of the largest and most prestigious of its kind. The most important masters from the Italian Renaissance and the Baroque period are represented, as are Dutch and Flemish painters from the 17C.

The admission ticket price also includes access to the **Armory** and the **Porcelain Collection**.

Italian paintings are hung on a red background, Dutch and Flemish paintings on a green background and Spanish and French paintings on a blue background.

Ground Floor

Galleries 1–4 contain tapestries after sketches by Raphael and numerous townscapes by Bernardo Bellotto, otherwise known as Canaletto, who painted Dresden and Pirna with such extraordinary precision that many paintings were used as blueprints during the postwar reconstruction.

Galleries 5–6 house paintings by Dresden masters.

1st Floor

Galleries 101–102: Works by Silvestre and Canaletto.

Galleries 104–106 and 108–111: Flemish and Dutch painting from the 16C–17C. Rembrandt's *Self-portrait with Saskia* (**Gallery 106**), Rubens' *Bathsheba* and Vermeer's *Girl Reading a Letter by the Window* (**Gallery 108**).

Gallery 107: Paintings by the early Netherlandish (Jan van Eyck) and early German (masterpieces by Holbein, Cranach the Elder and Dürer) schools.

Gallery 112: 17C French painting (Claude Lorrain, Nicolas Poussin).

Galleries 113–121: 16C Italian painting. Works by Veronese, Tintoretto, Giorgione *(Sleeping Venus)*, Titian, in **galleries 117–119**. A highlight is Raphael's portrayal of the Virgin and Child, the *Sistine Madonna,* in **gallery 117**.
Gallery 116: Paintings by Botticelli, Mantegna and Pintoricchio *(Portrait of a Boy)*.

2nd Floor:
Gallery 201: Pastel painting. Jean-Étienne Liotard's *Chocolate Girl*, world's largest collection of works by Rosalba Carriera (75 pastels).
Gallery 202: 18C French painting.
Galleries 203–207: 18C Italian painting with works by Tiepolo and Crespi.
Galleries 208–210: Spanish painting (El Greco, Murillo, Zurbarán, Velázquez).
Galleries 211–216: 17C and 18C German painting.

Porzellansammlung★★ (Porcelain Collection)

East Asia Gallery, via Glockenspielpavillon.
◷*Open year-round, Tue–Sun 10am–6pm.* ◷*Closed Dec 25.* ◉6€.
& ℘(0351) 49 14 20 00.
www.skd.museum.
This gallery displays porcelain from the famous manufactory at **Meissen**, as well as rare and precious imports from Japan and China. Do not miss the "dragoon vases" for which the Elector paid with 600 dragoon soldiers in 1717, or the life-size porcelain figures from Meissen (early 18C). For background, visit the exhibition devoted to Johann Friedrich Böttger (1682–1719), the man credited with inventing European porcelain in 1708.

Rüstkammer★★ (Armoury)

Semperbau, east wing.
◷*Open year-round, Tue–Sun 10am–6pm.* ◉3€. ℘(0351) 491 420 00.
www.skd-dresden.de.
Even dedicated pacifists should be able to appreciate the artistry of this precious collection of hand-crafted ceremonial weapons. The inventory includes 1 300 objects from the 15C to 19C hailing from places throughout Europe and the Middle East.
There is also a collection of child armour, worn during tournaments held in the court of Saxony.

Mathematisch-Physikalischer Salon★★ (Salon of Mathematics and Physic)

◷*Closed for renovation.* ℘(0351) 49 14 20 00. www.skd.museum.de.
The inventive genius of scientists is documented in the clocks and instruments of the 16C to 19C, including sun, sand, oil, artistic and automatic timepieces.

NEUSTADT★ (NEW TOWN)

Reached via Augustusbrücke, Dresden's Neustadt spreads across a medieval city quarter destroyed by fire in 1685 and subsequently rebuilt in stone. It was spared from total devastation in 1945.
Just beyond the bridge, Neustädter Markt is dominated by the gilded **equestrian statue**★ of Augustus the Strong. Stroll along the pedestrianised **Hauptstraße** to reach Albertplatz square, which is graced by two fountains.
Königstraße, which radiates southeast from Albertplatz, is one of Dresden's most elegant streets and is lined with beautifully restored Baroque, Neoclassical and Gründerzeit townhouses.
From Albertplatz, follow Alaunstraße north into the lively student quarter teeming with bars, cafés, pubs, clubs and restaurants and accented by the **Kunsthofpassage**.

⟿ WALKING TOUR

The Elbe divides Dresden into two distinct parts. South of the river, the old town *(Altstadt)* is dominated by the Zwinger, Semperoper and Frauenkirche; in the north, the new town *(Neustadt)* is anchored by Albertplatz.

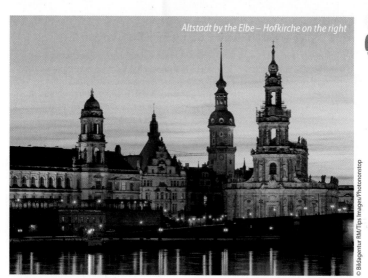
Altstadt by the Elbe – Hofkirche on the right

© Bildagentur RM/Tips Images/Photononstop

HISTORIC CENTRE★★★ (ALTSTADT)

▶ *Kick off your tour on Theaterplatz, which is flanked by the Zwinger, the Semper Opera House and the Hofkirche cathedral.*

Semperoper★★ (Semper Opera House)

Theaterplatz 2.

Guided tours daily. 8€.

(0351) 796 63 05. www.semperoper-erleben.de, www.semperoper.de.

Numerous operas premiered at this famous venue, including *Der Rosenkavalier* by Richard Strauss. Designed by Gottfried Semper in Italian Renaissance style, it first opened in 1841 but had to be rebuilt a mere three decades later after being devastated by a fire.

Six sculptures surviving from the original structure were incorporated into this modern replica, open since 1985. They represent Schiller and Goethe *(above the entrance)*, Shakespeare and Sophocles *(on the left)* and Molière and Euripides *(on the right)*.

Tours are only available on rehearsal- and performance-free days. The 3pm tour is in English.

▶ *Cross Theaterplatz and head to the Hofkirche.*

Ehemalige Katholische Hofkirche★★★ (Former Court Cathedral)

Open year-round, Mon–Tue 9am–6pm, Wed–Thu 9am–5pm, Fri 1pm–5pm, Sat 10am–5pm, Sun noon–4pm.

(0351) 484 47 12.

This enormous 18C basilica is the largest church in Saxony and was strongly influenced by the Italian Baroque. It is dominated by an 86m/282ft bell-tower and decorated with statues of the saints and apostles. Above the high altar, a painting (1765) by Anton Raphael Mengs depicts the Ascension. The Baroque pulpit was executed by Balthasar Permoser in 1722, while the organ was the last work (1750–55) of the master craftsman **Gottfried Silbermann**. Several kings and princes of Saxony are buried in the crypt, as is the heart of August the Strong, whose body lies in Cracow Cathedral.

Residenzschloss (Castle)

After a top-to-bottom makeover, Dresden's Renaissance palace now houses the dazzling Historical Green Vault and the New Green Vault, both brimming with hand-crafted *objets d'art* assembled by Augustus the Strong.

*Note that admission to the **Historical Green Vault** is by timed ticket only and*

Dresden-Hellerau: Germany's First Garden City

Ebenezer Howard's late-19C "Garden City Movement" inspired German entrepreneur Karl Camillo Schmidt to found a similarly progressive community in Hellerau in 1909 *(www.dresden-hellerau.de)*. Top architects Heinrich Tessenow, Hermann Muthesius and Curt Frick collaborated on what would become Germany's first Garden City. The community and its annual festival attracted artists and visionaries from throughout Europe. Under the National Socialists and in the postwar years it served military purposes but now it is slowly being returned to its former glory.

limited to 120 people per hour. Advance reservations are highly recommended and available online (www.skd.museum – payment by MasterCard or Visa) or by calling ℰ (0351) 49 14 20 00.

▷ *Follow Sophienstraße around the palace.*

Historisches Grünes Gewölbe★★★ (Historical Green Vault Collections)
Residenzschloss, enter via Sophienstraße. ◷Open year-round, Wed–Mon 10am–7pm. ⊚10€. ♿. ◷Closed 25 Dec. ℰ (0351) 49 14 20 00. www.skd.museum.

The recreated Historical Green Vault is a veritable walk-in treasure chest consisting of nine rooms sheathed in mirrors, ivory, amber, marble, gold and silver. They are a perfect setting for the unique items, displayed without protective glass just as they would have been during the times of Augustus the Strong. Cut-stone vessels, rhinoceros-horn goblets and astronomical table clocks are among the more unique treasures to be admired.

Neues Grünes Gewölbe★★★ (New Green Vault Collections)
Residenzschloss, enter via Sophienstraße. ◷Open year-round, Wed–Mon 10am–6pm. ◷Closed 25 Dec. ⊚10€. ♿ ℰ (0351) 49 14 20 00. www.skd.museum.

In a modern setting on the palace upper floor, the New Green Vault features some of the collection's most stunning objects. Highlights include a cherry pit engraved with 185 faces (16C), a boat fashioned entirely from ivory (1620), a

sculpture of a moor carrying a plate of emeralds by Balthasar Perlmoser (1724) and a hat clasp with a 41-carat green diamond (1769).

Tickets to the Neues Grünes Gewölbe are also good for the **Türckische Cammer** (Turkish Chamber) in the same building. On view again for the first time in 70 years, it is one of the oldest and most important collections of Ottoman art anywhere in the world outside Turkey.

▷ *Backtrack to the Hofkirche, continue to Schlossplatz and turn right onto Augustusstraße.*

Fürstenzug★ (Procession of the Princes)
Augustusstraße is parallelled by a stunningly detailed 102m/335ft-long ceramic mural hand-painted onto 24 000 Meissen porcelain tiles. It depicts Saxon rulers from 1123 to 1904.

▷ *Follow Augustusstraße to Neumarkt.*

Frauenkirche★ (Church of Our Lady)
◷Open year-round, Mon–Fri 10am–noon, 1pm–6pm, limited hours at weekends. ♿ ℰ (0351) 6560 6100, tickets (0351) 656 60 67 01. www.frauenkirche-dresden.de.

Designed by Georg Bähr and first consecrated in 1726, this landmark lingered as a postwar ruin for decades but after reunification, funds poured in from around the world to finance its resurrection. An exact replica opened in 2005, once again topped by the striking 95m/312ft-high dome that so characterises the town silhouette. **Views**★★

from the top are stupendous (🕐open Mar–Oct, Mon–Sat 10am–6pm, Sun 12.30pm–7pm (Nov–Feb daily to 4pm).

Verkehrsmuseum (Transport Museum) at Johanneum
Augustusstraße 1, enter from Neumarkt. 🕐*Open year-round, Tue–Sun 10am–5pm.* 🕐*Closed Jan 1, Dec 24, 25 & 31.* 🎫*4.50€.* 📞*(0351) 864 40.* *www.verkehrsmuseum-dresden.de.*
The Renaissance-era **Johanneum** once housed the royal stables and is now a transport museum with a big collection of vintage cars, model trains and original planes.

▶ *Pick up Brühlsche Gasse off Neumarkt and walk towards the river.*

Brühlsche Terrasse (Brühl Terrace)
The so-called "Balcony of Europe", this riverside promenade was built onto the ancient fortifications and offers fantastic **views**★ of the Elbe and the Neustadt.

▶ *Follow the Brühlsche Terrasse east to the Albertinum.*

Albertinum★★
Enter from Brühlsche Terrasse or Georg-Treu-Platz. 🕐*Open year-round, daily 10am–6pm.* 🎫*8€.* 📞*(0351) 49 14 20 00. www.skdmuseum.*
This stunning art collection presents paintings and sculpture from the Romantic period to the present. It reopened in 2010 after extensive renovation due to 2002 flood damage.

▶ *Head south on Schiessgasse to Wilsdruffer Straße via Landhausstraße.*

Stadtmuseum (City Museum)
Wilsdruffer Straße 2. 🕐*Open year-round, Tue–Sun 10am–6pm (Fri 7pm).* 🎫*4€.* 📞*(0351) 65 64 80.* *www.stmd.de.*
Built between 1770 and 1775 for the Saxon government, this Baroque building has exhibits detailing Dresden's history from its founding in the 13C. Special emphasis is placed on the 19C and 20C.

▶ *Follow Gewandhausgasse to Kreuzstraße.*

Neues Rathaus (New Town Hall)
This early 20C neo-Renaissance building is surmounted by a golden statue of Hercules. Trips up the 100m/328ft **tower** *(partly by lift)* are available (🕐open May–Oct, daily 10am–6pm; 🎫2.50€).

Kreuzkirche (Holy Cross)★
🕐*Open Mon–Sat 10am–6pm, Sun noon–6pm. Tower* 🎫*2.50€.* 📞*(0351) 496 58 07. www.kreuzirche-dresden.de.*
Just west of the town hall, Dresden's oldest church has origins in the early 13C and has been home to the famous Kreuzchor boys' choir for nearly as long. The current structure is a neo-Baroque beauty from 1900 with more than 3 600 seats, making it one of the largest Protestant churches in Germany.

ADDITIONAL SIGHTS
👥Deutsches Hygiene-Museum (German Hygiene Museum)
Lingnerplatz 1. 🕐*Open year-round, Tue–Sun 10am–6pm.* 🎫*7€.* ♿ 📞*(0351) 48 46 40 00. www.dhmd.de.*
The name may be odd, but the exhibits are intriguing. Using glass and wax figures, anatomical models and interactive stations, this museum looks at human existence from a biological, social and cultural perspective.

Asisi Panometer
Gasanstalstraße 8b. 🕐*Open Tue–Fri 9am–7pm, Sat–Sun 10am–8pm.* 🎫*10€.* 📞*(0351) 860 39 40. www.asisi.de.*
This space uses a 360-degree panorama and advanced technology to take you on a virtual journey back to Dresden's 18C Baroque heyday during the reign of Augustus the Strong.

EXCURSIONS
Schloss Moritzburg★
▶ *14km/8.7mi northwest, via Hansastraße.* 🕐*Guided tours (1hr) Apr–Oct, daily 10am–5.30pm; Feb–Mar and Nov–Dec Tue–Sun 10am–4pm; Jan Sat–*

Sun 10am–4pm. ◐Closed Dec 24 & 31. ✆6.50€. ✆(03207) 87 30. www.schloss-moritzburg.de.

Built in the 16C by Duke Moritz of Saxony, this hunting lodge has an idyllic island location and was turned into a Baroque pleasure palace under Augustus the Strong in the 18C.

Schloss and Park Pillnitz★

◐ 15km/9.3mi southeast via Bautzener Straße. ◐Open Apr–Oct, Tue–Sun 10am–5pm; Nov–Mar visit by guided tour only, Sat–Sun 11am, noon, 1pm and 2pm. ◐Closed Dec 24 & 25. ✆4€. ✆(0351) 261 32 60; www.schloesser-dresden.de.

This Baroque riverside summer palace with Chinese flourishes is surrounded by a lush garden and vine-covered slopes. It's a popular day trip from Dresden and is easily reached by boat or bike.

Aside from strolling and picnicking, you can learn about court life in the museum in the Neues Palais (New Palace). Augustus the Strong's throne and decorative arts are displayed in the Bergpalais and Wasserpalais outbuildings (◐open May–Oct, Tue–Sun 10am–6pm; ✆4€).

Freiberg★

◐ 37km/23mi south.

At the foot of the Erzgebirge mountain range, Freiberg once pegged its wealth to an abundance of silver, copper and various minerals. The key sight is the 15C **Cathedral**★★ (❧guided tour (45min), May–Oct, Mon–Sat 10am, 11am, 2pm, 3pm & 4pm, Sun 11.30am, 2pm, 3pm & 4pm; Nov–Apr, 11am (Sun 11.30am), 2pm and 3pm; ✆3.50€; &; ✆(03731) 30 03 40. www.freiberger-dom.de).

It is filled with important religious artworks, including the **tulip pulpit**★★, a masterpiece by sculptor Hans Witten (c. 1505); the **Gottfried Silbermann organ**★★; and the Romanesque **golden entrance portal**★★ from 1230.

Schloss Augustusburg★

◐ 75km/46.5mi southwest. ✆(037291) 380 18. www.die-sehenswerten-drei.de.

Elector Augustus I built this castle as a hunting lodge in 1570 atop the Schellen-

berg hill (515m/1 690ft). The chapel has an altar painting by Lucas Cranach the Younger (1571) that shows the elector surrounded by his 14 children.

The castle houses several exhibitions, most importantly a comprehensive motor-cycle museum.

🚗 DRIVING TOUR

SAXON SWITZERLAND★★★

78km/49mi – Allow one day.

Saxon Switzerland is one of Germany's most striking natural wonders, an area of craggy sandstone cliffs, rock outcrops, whimsical pinnacles and deep gorges carved by the Elbe River.

The valley can be explored by road, following the itinerary below, or by river on one of the "Weiße Flotte" boats linking Dresden and Bad Schandau.

◐ Leave Dresden to the east via Pillnitzer Landstraße.

Schloss Pillnitz★

◐See DRESDEN: Excursions.

Bastei★★★

Perched on a rocky outcrop, the Bastei was the site of a 13C wooden castle and today is most famous for its sweeping **views**★★ across the Elbe and the almost otherworldly rock formations that form the heart of the Saxon Switzerland National Park.

Only a few foundations survive from the original castle, which is reached via the photogenic 76m/249.3ft-long stone **Basteibrücke** (bridge). From here, a series of narrow footbridges (◐not suitable for the vertigo-prone!) take you through the ruined fortress and to ever more spectacular views.

To avoid the worst crowds, arrive early or late in the day. Sunset is especially nice.

◐ Follow the S165 (Basteistraße) east, then turn right onto the S163 to Bad Schandau via Waltersdorf.

Bad Schandau★

This spa town renowned for its iron-rich waters is the region's main tourist centre. The **Nationalparkhaus** *(Dresdner Straße 2b;* Oopen Apr–Oct, daily 9am–6pm; Nov–Mar, Tue–Sun 9am–5pm; Oclosed Jan; ☎4€; ℘(035022) 502 40; www.lanu.de)* has interpretive and interactive exhibits about the national park's flora, fauna and history and makes for a good introduction to the region and its unusual natural charms.

At the town exit, towards Schmilka, the **Personenaufzug** *(lift;* Oopen Apr & Oct, daily 9am–6pm, May–Sept, 9am–7pm, Nov–Mar, 9am–5pm; ☎2.50€)* whisks you up a 50m/164ft-high tower for great views of the surrounding countryside. From here a trail leads to another viewpoint over the Schrammsteine rock massif in about one hour.

These formations are especially popular with rock climbers. If you want less exertion, board the nostalgic **Kirnitzschtalbahn**★ railway, which trundles through a canyon alongside a creek and eventually arrives at a waterfall.

> Cross the Elbe at Bad Schandau and turn right along the B172 to Königstein.

Festung Königstein★★ (Königstein Fortress)

OOpen Apr–Sept, daily 9am–8pm; Oct, 9am–6pm; Nov–Mar, 9am–5pm. ☎6€. ℘(035021) 646 07. www.festung-koenigstein.de.

A great sweep of the Elbe arrives at the tabletop mountain called **Königstein** (360m/1 181ft) which is crowned by a formidable fortress. Built between the 13C and the 16C, it served at one time as a prison whose list of famous inmates included porcelain inventor JF Böttger *(see MEISSEN);* August Bebel, co-founder of the Social Democrat party; and Fritz Heckert, co-founder of the Spartacists and a prominent German Communist. From the rampart walk, you will have far-reaching **views**★★ of the Liliental tabletop mountain across the Elbe and as far as Bohemia.

Barockgarten Großsedlitz★

OOpen Apr–Sept, daily 8am–8pm; Oct 8am–6pm; Nov–Mar, 8am–4pm. ☎3€. ℘(03529) 563 90. www.barockgarten-grosssedlitz.de.

This French-style garden was commissioned in 1719 by Count Wackerbarth and is considered a prime example of Baroque landscape gardening.

> Return to Dresden on B172.

ADDRESSES

🏠STAY

🛏 **Backstage** – *Prießnitzstraße. 12.* 𝒫*0351 888 77 77. www.backstage-dresden.de. 11 rooms.* 🚪*6.50€.* This trendy new budget hotel is set in an old dairy, just a few minutes' walk from the centre of town. Rooms are large, light and comfortable, decorated by young local artists and craftspeople.

🛏 **Gästehaus Mezcalero** – *Königsbrücker Straße 64.* 𝒫*(0351) 81 07 70. www.mezcalero.de. 23 rooms.* 🚪*6€.* Artistically decorated with a Mexican–Aztec theme, this upscale hostel-hotel puts you equally close to nightlife and the sights. The cheapest beds are in dorms and some rooms share baths.

🛏 **Kangaroo-stop Hostel & Backpacker** – *Erna-Berger Straße. 8–10 (300m/330yd from Neustadt station).* 𝒫*0351 314 34 55. www.kangaroo-stop.de. 24 rooms.* 🚪*5€.* The main advantage of this basic friendly hostel is its price and central location. BBQs and campfires are organised on the outside terrace.

🛏🛏 **Gasthof Coschütz** – *Kleinnaundorfer Straße 1.* 𝒫*(0351) 401 03 58. www.gasthof-coschuetz.de. 11 rooms. Restaurant* 🛏🛏. Four generations have run this well-furnished, comfortable hotel on the city outskirts. The restaurant features regional cuisine, select wines and seating on two terraces in summer.

🛏🛏 **Landhaus Lockwitzgrund** – *Lockwitzgrund 100.* 𝒫*(0351) 271 00 10. www.landhaus-lockwitzgrund.de. 9 rooms. Restaurant* 🛏🛏. The former stables of a noodle factory have been ingeniously converted into a romantic country estate. Rooms pair modern conveniences with historic features and the upscale restaurant enjoys a fine reputation with guests and locals alike.

🛏🛏 **Ibis Hotels** – *Prager Straße.* 𝒫*0351 48 56 20 00. www.ibis-dresden.de. 918 rooms (in three buildings).* 🚪*10€.* Occupying three huge Soviet-era buildings, along Prager Straße, this chain hotel wins few marks for aesthetics, but its rooms offer standard international-style comforts and are just a few steps away from the town's historic monuments.

🛏🛏 **Martha Hospiz** – *Nieritzstraße 11.* 𝒫*(0351) 817 60. www.martha-hospiz.de. Closed Dec 22–27. 50 rooms. Restaurant* 🛏🛏. Affiliated with a non-profit Christian organisation, this hotel has a superb central location, nice new rooms with classic furniture, some in *Biedermeier style*, and a cosy restaurant specialising in potato-based dishes in the vaulted cellars.

🛏🛏🛏 **Schloss Eckberg** – *Bautzner Straße 134.* 𝒫*(0351) 809 90. www.hotel-schloss-eckberg.de. 84 rooms. Restaurant* 🛏🛏 🛏🛏. A dreamy riverside park filled with artworks surrounds this unique estate. Choose from antique-filled rooms in a neo-Gothic palace or modern ones in the Kavaliershaus, which also has three saunas. All guests enjoy breakfast at the palace which also has a superb restaurant with views of the city skyline across the river.

🛏🛏🛏🛏 **Hotel Taschenbergpalais** – *Taschenberg.* 𝒫*0351 12 812. www.kempinski.com/dresden. 214 rooms.* 🚪*26€.* This imposing Baroque palace, linked to the castle by a passage, was built in 1705 by Augustus the Strong for his mistress, the Countess Cosel. Largely destroyed during World War II, it has been splendidly rebuilt by Kempinski hotels in a "modern-with-Baroque-nuances" style to reflect its former glory. Rooms and suites have been carefully refurbished with wooden inlay, marble and many period touches.

🍽/EAT

🍴 **Aha Ladencafé** – *Kreuzstraße 7.* 𝒫*0351 496 06 73. www.ladencafe.de.* 🍴. The arty New World-style Aha Café serves soups, salads and vegetarian dishes at very reasonable prices. The building also features exhibitions and a craft shop.

🍴 **Historisches Fischhaus** – *Fischhausstraße 14 (5km/3mi northeast of city centre via Bautzner Straße.)* 𝒫*(0351) 89 91 00. www.fischhaus-dresden.de.* In business since 1573, this atmospheric restaurant in a leafy setting on the city outskirts specialises in the fresh catch of the day. It is also a great place to try the local beer and wine.

⊜⊜ **Capetown's** – *Weisse Gasse 1.*
ℰ0351 497 62 80. www.capetowns.de.
Set on a pleasant pedestrianised street,
very close to Notre Dame, this is a good
place to try South African cooking, or
simply to relax with a beer or cocktail.

⊜⊜ **Kurhaus Kleinschachwitz** –
*Berthold-Haupt-Straße 128, 01259
Dresden-Kleinschachwitz. ℰ(0351) 200
19 96. www.kurhaus.net.* Right next to
the ferry landing for Pillnitz Palace, this
restaurant is noted for its beautiful
architecture and good food. With its
riverside beer garden, it makes a perfect
refreshment break, especially if you're
cycling along the Elbe River.

⊜⊜ **Luisenhof** – *Bergbahnstraße 8,
01324 Dresden-Weißer Hirsch. ℰ(0351)
214 99 60. www.luisenhof.org.* Set in a
historic 19C building, this restaurant
is called "Dresden's balcony" for its
sweeping town views. Only fresh,
seasonal ingredients are used and the
cakes are homemade and delicious.

⊜⊜⊜ **CoselPalais** – *An der
Frauenkirche 12. ℰ0351 496 24 44.
www.coselpalais-dresden.de.* Next to
Notre Dame, the 18C baroque palace
of Count Cosel, bodyguard of Frederick
Augustus, is now home to a courtyard
restaurant and café; the latter serves
pastries on Meissen plates, the former
serves light Franco-German cuisine and
excellent wines from Saxony.

⊜⊜⊜⊜ **Caroussel** – *Rähnitzgasse 19.
ℰ(0351) 800 30. www.buelow-residenz.de.
Closed Mon–Tue. Reservation recommended.* Meals are celebrations in this
elegant dining room presided over by
chef Dirk Schröer. His contemporary
culinary concoctions use the best the
region has to offer – from venison to
lamb to mushrooms and fruit. In fine
weather, enjoy your meal alfresco in the
glass-covered inner courtyard.

⊜⊜⊜⊜ **Gourmetlounge** –
*Merbitzer Straße 53 (5km/3mi west of
the Theaterplatz). ℰ0351 425 50.
www.gourmetlounge.de. Closed 2 weeks
Jan; 2 weeks Jul–Aug; Sun and Mon.
Dinner only.* The romantic Art Nouveau-
style Hotel Pattis is a distinguished
setting for this gourmet restaurant, set
in the old ballroom which now boasts
sumptuous 21C lounge-style fittings.

🍽 TAKING A BREAK

Café Schinkelwache – *Theaterplatz 2.
ℰ(0351) 490 39 09. www.restaurant-
dresden.de.* A stately old guardhouse
designed by Karl Friedrich Schinkel has
been reborn as a classic café where you
can relax from sightseeing over fresh
pastries or a light meal.

Café Toscana – *Schillerplatz 7 (5km/3mi
east of old town on the Elbe). ℰ(0351)
310 07 44.* This popular coffeehouse
with winter garden and terrace boasts
views of the *Blaues Wunder* bridge and a
12m/39ft-long cake buffet.

Dresdner Molkerei Gebrüder Pfund –
Bautzner Straße 79. ℰ(0351) 810 59 48.
Possibly the world's most famous
dairy shop, Pfunds is decorated with
a kaleidoscope of hand-painted tiles
and comes with a café and restaurant
specialising in cheese-based dishes. It is
hugely popular with coach tourists.

🎭 ENTERTAINMENT

Cafés, bistros and restaurants
abound in the old town around the
Frauenkirche and on **Weisse Gasse**
near Altmarkt. In the **Neustadt**,
upscale places concentrate on
Königstraße, while a lively, more
youthful scene dominates north
of **Albertplatz**, especially on
Alaunstraße and **Louisenstraße**.

Ballhaus Watzke – *Kötzschenbroder
Straße 1 (corner of Leipziger Straße).
ℰ(0351) 85 29 20. www.watzke.de.*
This brew-pub is set in a former
dancehall with picture-perfect views
of the old town from the riverside beer
garden. Enjoy them while quaffing a
glass of cold unfiltered house lager
and tucking into a plate of hearty *Haxe*
(roasted pork knuckle).

Brauhaus am Waldschlösschen –
*Am Brauhaus 8b (2km/1.2mi east
of Albertplatz; follow Bautzner
Straße). ℰ(0351) 652 39 00.
www.waldschloesschen.de.* At this
attractive brew-pub you can enjoy
a delicious *Dunkel* or a refreshing
Hefeweizen along with cocktails and
traditional dishes. There's live music
Mon–Sat and splendid views across
the Elbe from the beer garden anchored
by a seven-tiered bronze fountain.

italienisches Dörfchen – *Theaterplatz 3. ℘(0351) 498 160. www.italienisches-doerfchen.de.* This gastro complex includes a fine Italian restaurant, a café, a beer garden and a riverside terrace. Some rooms have magnificent exposed beams, stuccowork and ceiling frescoes.

Winzerstube Zum Rebstock – *Hauptstraße 17. ℘(0351) 5 63 35 44. www.winzerstube-zum-rebstock.de.* This sweet little wine tavern overlooks a quiet courtyard accented with a fountain and herb garden. Glasses of wine from Saxony and the Nahe region can be paired with nibbles or a full meal.

Fährgarten Johannstadt – *Käthe-Kollwitz-Ufer 23b. ℘(0351) 459 62 62. www.faehrgarten.de. Closed Nov–Mar.* Kick back in this leafy beer garden and watch the Elbe steamers pass by, preferably at sunset. If the aroma of wood-fired steaks doesn't tempt you, perhaps the delicious beers and wines will. There is a big playground for children.

Semperoper – *Theaterplatz. ℘(0351) 491 17 05. www.semperoper.de.* An evening at this illustrious opera house will not be soon forgotten. The busy performance schedule includes not only full-length operas but also ballet, jazz, classical concerts and contemporary dance. Book early or hope for last-minute cancellations.

🛒 SHOPPING

Dresden's main shopping streets are **Prager Straße** (department stores) and **Wilsdruffer Straße**. The best and most central all-purpose shopping centre is the **Altmarkt-Galerie**. In the new town, steer towards **Königstraße** (elegant boutiques), **Hauptstraße** (chains) and **Alaunstraße** (funky boutiques).

Kunsthofpassage – *enter from Alaunstraße 70 or Görlitzer Straße 21. www.kunsthof-dresden.de.* This series of five courtyards, each designed by a different local artist, brims with independent boutiques selling everything from ceramics to jewellery, fashion to home accessories.

Neustädter Markthalle – *Metzer Straße 1. ℘(0351) 810 54 45. www.markthalle-dresden.de.* This restored 1899 market hall has been reborn as a gourmet shopper's nirvana. Pick up fresh produce and local specialities along with toys and teas, flowers and Freiberg porcelain on the ground floor and in the basement, or check out the fashions on the upper floor.

Markets – Altmarkt, Mon–Sat from 8am. The Spring Market (*Frühlingsmarkt*) is held here in May, the Autumn Market (*Herbstmarkt*) in September and the *Striezelmarkt* in December.

SIGHTSEEING

CITY TOURS BY COACH

Stadtrundfahrt Dresden – *℘(0351) 99 56 50, www.stadtrundfahrt.com,* 1hr 30min tours, every 15 to 30min. First departure 9.30am, last one 5pm. Day tickets cost 🚌20€ and are valid for unlimited stops, basic tours around the Zwinger, Frauenkirche, Pfunds Molkerei and the Fürstenzug, an evening city tour, and admission to Schloss Pillnitz. Departure Augustusbrücke/Schlossplatz and 21 other stops such as Königstraße, Dr. Külz-Straße and the Frauenkirche. *Combination tickets with the Grünes Gewölbe cost 35€.*

WALKING TOURS

Themed walking tours are organised by igeltours ℘(0351) 804 45 57; www.igeltour-dresden.de.

BOAT TOURS

Sächsische Dampfschiffahrt, ℘(0351) 86 60 90, www.saechsische-dampfschiffahrt.de, offers 90min Elbe cruises in faux paddle-wheel steamers for 🚌11€. Trips depart daily (11am, 1pm, 3pm & 5pm) from the Terrassenufer. Other otpions include trips to Schloss Pillnit, Meißen and "Swiss Saxony".

TRABI SAFARI

℘(0351) 899 00 60, www.trabi-safari.de, from 20€. Climb behind the wheel of an authentic GDR Trabant car and follow your guide who narrates the tour while driving a separate vehicle.

Bautzen★

Crowning a rocky outcrop skirted by the Spree River, Bautzen has managed to retain its old-fashioned charm despite wars and the deprivations under the East German regime. It has been the cultural and political capital of the Sorbs, Germany's only ethnic minority, for over 100 years. Sorbs descended from a Slavic people and speak a language related to Czech and Polish. Signs are bilingual and women still wear folkloric headdresses during traditional festivals such as the symbolic *Hexenbrennen* (witches' burning) on 30 April.

☛ WALKING TOUR

OLD TOWN
Hauptmarkt (Main Market Square)

The old market square is surrounded by nicely restored Baroque houses and a three-story 18C town hall built by Johann Christoph Naumann. Reichenstraße leads east from the market square to the **Reichenturm** (Tower of the Rich; ⏱open Apr–Oct, daily 10am–5pm; ₪1.40€; ℘(03591) 46 04 31; www.bautzen.de), a 56m/179ft severely leaning tower that offers an excellent view of the city.

- ▶ **Population:** 42 000
- ℹ **Info:** Hauptmarkt 1, 02625 Bautzen. ℘(035 91) 420 16. www.bautzen.de.
- ▶ **Location:** Bautzen is on the A4 autobahn linking Dresden and Görlitz.
- ⏱ **Timing:** Allow at least four hours to see the cathedral, Ortenburg Castle and to wander along the ramparts.

Dom St. Peter★

This hall-church (1213–1497) is shared by Roman Catholics and Protestants *(Catholic Masses in the chancel; Protestant services in the main nave)*. Construction began early in the 13C, with the southern section enlarged in the 15C.

In 1664, the 85m/279ft tower was crowned with a Baroque cupola. Inside the cathedral, note the large **Crucifix** (1714) by Balthazar Permoser; the **Baroque high altar** (1722–24) by G Fossati in the chancel; an **altar painting** by GA Pellegrini; and the Princes' Loggia (1674) in the Protestant section.

▶ *Follow the road that runs past the cathedral as far as the monastery.*

Remnants of the **monastery** date back to 1683, while the southern façade with its imposing portal is from 1755.

View of Bautzen with Alte Wasserkunst on the left

© Ines Gesell/iStockphoto.com

▶ *Now follow Schloßstraße.*

This charming street with restored Baroque houses leads to Ortenburg castle.

Schloss Ortenburg

Where Ortenburg stands today was once a fortified complex completed c. AD 600 and expanded in 958 by Heinrich I. Two 15C fires destroyed the original, but in the late 15C, when the region fell under Hungarian rule, Hungarian king Matthias Corvinus had it rebuilt in late-Gothic style. A relief portrait of the king graces the tower of the north wing. The Thirty Years' War left profound scars, removed by renovations after 1648. In 1698, three Renaissance gables were added.

Sorbisches Museum/ Serbski Muzej

🕒*Open Apr–Oct, Mon–Fri 10am–5pm, Sat–Sun 10am–6pm; Nov–Mar, Mon–Fri 10am–4pm, Sat–Sun 10am–5pm.* 🕒*Closed Dec 24 & 31.* 👁*2.50€.* ♿. 📞*(03591) 270 87 00. www.museum.sorben.com.*

In the former Salt House, an annex added to Ortenburg palace in 1782, the **Sorbian Museum** illustrates the history, culture and way of life of the Sorbs from the 6C to the present.

Town Ramparts★

The 17 surviving medieval fortification towers give Bautzen its distinctive silhouette. A walk along the ramparts is like travelling back centuries in time. En route, you'll pass the enchanting ruins of the **Nikolaikirche** and its historic cemetery with ornate headstones that are veritable works of art.

Alte Wasserkunst★

🕒*Open daily Apr–Oct 10am–5pm; Feb, Mar, Nov & Dec 4pm; Jan, Sat–Sun 10am–4pm.* 👁*2€.* 📞*(03591) 415 88.* This formidable defensive and watertower has been standing since 1558 and supplied the town's water until 1965. Recently restored, it houses a fascinating technological exhibition and treats visitors to sprawling views over the town and surroundings from the top.

ADDRESSES

🛏STAY

🛏 **Villa Antonia** – *Lessingstraße 1.* 📞*(03591) 50 10 20. www.hotel-villa-antonia.de. 13 rooms. Restaurant* 🍴🍴. This charming little hotel in a late 19C villa has bright and timelessly furnished rooms. The restaurant specialises in Austrian cuisine.

🛏 **Dom Eck** – *Breitengasse 2.* 📞*(03591) 50 13 30. www.wjelbik.de. 12 rooms.* Over-shadowed by the cathedral, this artist-decorated and family-owned hotel delivers Sorbian hospitality in modern and comfortable rooms.

🛏🛏 **Goldener Adler** – *Hauptmarkt 4.* 📞*(03591) 486 60. www.goldeneradler.de. 30 rooms. Restaurant* 🍴🍴. Right in the heart of the historic centre, this upscale hotel occupies a lovingly restored 16C building. Rooms lack no mod-cons, while the restaurant sports a romantic cross-vaulted ceiling.

🍴EAT

🍴 **Mönchshof** – *Burglehn 1.* 📞*(03591) 49 01 41. www.moenchshof.de.* Time-travel back to the Middle Ages at this congenial inn where you'll be eating without utensils amid historical vaults or on the terrace with sweeping views.

🍴🍴 **Wjelbik** – *Kornstraße 7.* 📞*(03591) 420 60. www.wjelbik.de.* Sample Sorb culinary specialities such as elderberry soup or braised beef with horseradish at this historic restaurant. Dishes often use locally sourced ingredients.

🍴🍴 **L'Ambiente** – *Innere Lauenstraße 1.* 📞*(03591) 442 63. www.l-ambiente.de. Closed Sun–Mon.* If you are in the mood for Mediterranean, steer the compass to this restaurant right on the market square. It serves gourmet-level creations (including fresh lobster) alongside inspired pizza and pasta.

Görlitz★

Germany's easternmost city rose to prosperity during the 15C and 16C through textile manufacture and trade in woad (blue dye). World War II miraculously spared the town's more than 4 000 historic houses and today it is a veritable 3D textbook of architecture with fine examples of Renaissance, Baroque, Neoclassical and Art Nouveau buildings. Görlitz sits right on the border with Poland, from which it is separated by the Neisse River. The town on the other bank is called Zgorzelec.

> ▶ **Population:** 58 500
> ℹ **Info:** Brüderstraße 1, 02826 Görlitz. ℘(03581) 475 70. www.europastadt-goerlitz.de.
> ◐ **Location:** Görlitz stretches along the west bank of the Neiße River, which has formed the border with Poland since 1945.
> ⊛ **Don't Miss:** The old town.
> ⊕ **Timing:** Görlitz can be seen in a day.
> ▲▲ **Kids:** Outdoor recreation in the Zittauer Gebirge (⸙see Excursions).

OLD TOWN★
Most of Görlitz's sights are concentrated in the historic town, which is anchored by two central squares, the Obermarkt and the Untermarkt.

Obermarkt
Fine Baroque houses line up along the north side of Görlitz' largest square, while its western flank is punctuated by the **Reichenbacher Turm** (◐ open late May–Oct, daily 10am–5pm; ⊚1.50€; ℘(03581) 67 13 55; www.museum-goerlitz.de), a fortified 52m/170.6ft-high tower first mentioned in 1376. 165 steps lead to a viewing platform for wonderful **views**★.
The nearby **Kaisertrutz** (⊶ closed for renovation until at least May 2011; ℘ (03581) 67 13 55; www.museum-goerlitz.de) is a massive late-Gothic keep (1490) that was once part of the medieval town fortifications. It houses changing regional history.

Dreifaltigkeitskirche (Holy Trinity Church)
◐Open May–Sept, Mon–Sat 10am–6pm, Sun noon–6pm; Oct 10am–5pm. ♿℘(03581) 428 70 00.
Dating from the 13C, this church boasts exquisite **choir stalls**★ (1484) and two valuable altars: the Baroque high altar (1713) by Caspar Gottlob von Rodewitz, a student of Permoser, and the late-Gothic winged **Golden Maria altar**★ in the Barbara chapel. Its skinny bell-tower is nicknamed "*Mönch*" (monk).

Barockhaus (Baroque House)
Neißstraße 30. ⊶Closed for restoration; call for updates. ℘(03581) 67 13 55. www.museum-goerlitz.de.
Southeast of the square, this imposing Baroque mansion (1727–1729) houses the city's fine art collection as well as decorative objects from the 16C–19C, beautiful Renaissance and Baroque furniture and precious glass. Also note the elaborately painted 18C **armoires**★ on the second floor and the engravings section with works from the 16C–20C.

Untermarkt★
This historic square is framed by gorgeous buildings attesting to Görlitz's one-time wealth: the 14C *Rathaus* (town hall); the Baroque Alte Börse (old stock exchange; 1706–14), now a hotel; and the 1706 Alte Waage (weigh-house).

Schlesisches Museum (Silean Museum)
Untermarkt 4. ◐Open year-round, Tue–Sun 10am–5pm. ⊚4€. ♿℘(03581) 879 10. www.schlesisches-museum.de.
The imposing Renaissance-era Schönhof mansion is home to this modern museum detailing the cultural and political history of the region of Silesia.

WHERE TO STAY	
Börse...	②

WHERE TO EAT	
Lucie Schulte..................................	②
Tuchmacher...................................	⑤

The emphasis is on arts and crafts of the 17C–19C. Important items include geographical views of Silesia, objects from tourism and art from the local mountains. Industrial culture, town life and the art of the classical modern movement are also included.

"Silesian Heaven"

"He who doesn't know 'heaven' hasn't lived," goes a Silesian saying. Perhaps that is why their national dish is the *Schlesisches Himmelreich*. Prepared from pickled pork and dried fruit, it is served with a light lemon sauce and white bread dumplings.

St. Peterskirche★

🕐 Open Apr–Oct, daily 10am–6pm; Nov–Mar 4pm. ♿ 𝄢 (035 81) 428 70 00.
A city landmark, this mighty twin-towered church resides on a hilltop high above the Neiße.

It was completed in the late 15C and contains a magnificent 17C **pulpit** with gilded acanthus leaves and a **great organ** by Eugenio Casparini (1703).

Karstadt-Warenhaus

An der Frauenkirche 5–7.
Fairly plain on the outside, this steel-framed department store (1912–13) is an Art Nouveau jewel beyond its heavy doors. The most eye-popping feature is its kaleidoscopic glass ceiling.

ADDRESSES

🛏️STAY

Börse – *Untermarkt 16.* ☎*03581 764 20. www.boerse-goerlitz.de. 27 rooms.* 🛌*.* This ancient exchange hall, right in the city centre, has a splendid Baroque façade (1714) and has been expertly converted into a luxury hotel. Bedrooms are large, stately, comfortable and tastefully furnished with beautiful, out-of-the-ordinary antiques.

🍽️/ EAT

Lucie Schulte – *Untermarkt 22.* ☎*03581 41 02 60. www.goerlitz-kocht. de.* This pretty, stylish restaurant is tucked away in a narrow alleyway by the market. International and regional cuisine is served in an attractive vaulted dining room.

Tuchmacher – *Peterstraße 8.* ☎*03581 473 10. www.tuchmacher.de. Closed Mon lunch.* Set in an attractive Renaissance bourgeois townhouse (now a hotel). Fine local and regional cuisine and a pleasant courtyard.

Annaberg-Buchholz★

After the discovery of silver and tin ore in 1491 and 1496, Annaberg and Buchholz experienced an economic boom; at its peak, 600 mines enriched the people in the capital of the Erzgebirge (Ore) Mountains. In the 16C, as the silver petered out, lace production became Annaberg's most important industry. Today the town's principal attraction is its Gothic cathedral.

> 🛈 **Info:** Adam-Ries-Straße 16, 09456 Annaberg-Buchholz. ☎(03733) 18 80 00. www.erzgebirge-tourismus.de.
>
> ▶ **Location:** The mountains follow the border of Germany and the Czech Republic for about 150km/93mi.
>
> 🕐 **Timing:** Allow at least three hours for the suggested driving tour.

SIGHTS

St. Annen-Kirche★★

🕐*Open Mon–Sat 10am–5pm (Jan–Apr 4pm), Sun noon–5pm (Jan–Apr 4pm).* ☎*(03733) 231 90. www.annenkirche.de.* Built between 1499 and 1525, St. Anna's is one of the most important late-Gothic hall-churches in Germany. Twelve slender pillars support the vaulted ceiling, each yoke covered by a "blossom baldaquin". The gallery parapets feature scenes from the Old and New Testaments. Especially noteworthy are the **Schöne Tür**★★ (beautiful door), a multi-coloured portal designed in 1512 by Hans Witten, one of this region's most accomplished wood carvers of the late-Gothic period. He also created the church's Madonna sculpture and the delicate baptismal font. References to Annaberg's mining past are evident in the **pulpit**★★ (1516), which is decorated with the relief figure of a miner.

Also note the painted panels behind the **Miners' Altar**★ (Bergmannsaltar, c. 1520), depicting various stages of mine work in that period.

The tower, which is still inhabited by the keeper, can be climbed from May to September.

Erzgebirgsmuseum mit Besucherbergwerk

Große Kirchgasse 16. 🚶*Guided tours (1hr) year-round, daily 10am–5pm.* 🕐*Closed Dec 24.* 💰*5.50€ (museum and mine).* ☎*(037 33) 234 97. www.annaberg-buchholz.de.* This museum retraces local history with an emphasis on mining and has some endearing examples of local folk art. Annexed to the museum is the

Im Gößner mine, which opened at the height of Annaberg's prosperity c. 1498. *The entrance shaft is in the museum courtyard.*

Technisches Museum-Frohnauer Hammer (Frohnau Forge Technical Museum)

Sehmatalstraße 3. *Guided tours (1hr) daily year-round 9am–noon, 1pm–4.30pm. Closed Jan 1, Dec 25. 3€. (037 33) 220 00. www.annaberg-buchholz.de/hammer.*

This 15C mill complex south of the old town started out as a flower mill, then housed a coin mint and in the 17C was converted into an iron forge.

On tours you get to see close-ups of the historic hydraulic bellows and the power-hammers, some of them massive in size. Upstairs is a wide array of objects produced at the forge, while the gallery opposite presents artistic woodcarvings.

Visits wrap up in the former miller's mansion where you can observe a lace-maker at work.

DRIVING TOUR

THE ORE MOUNTAINS★

81km/50.3mi (93km/57.7mi via Schwarzenberg). Follow the B95 from Annaberg-Buchholz to Oberwiesenthal.

For centuries, the Ore Mountains coughed up silver, tin, cobalt, nickel and iron in sumptuous amounts, bringing great prosperity to this remote region of Saxony. When the mines petered out, locals turned to craftmaking as a source of income. Many of Germany's finest Christmas ornaments and decorations are still produced here, often by hand, to this day.

Fichtelberg

The highest peak of the Erzgebirge, the Fichtelberg soars 1 214m/3 983ft above the ski resort of Oberwiesenthal. Ride the chair-lift to the top for a sweeping **panorama**★.

○ *A pretty forest road winds from Oberwiesenthal to Ehrenzipfel. Optional detour to Schwarzenberg.*

Schwarzenberg

Resting on a crag, this historic town boasts a 12C fortress that became the Elector's hunting lodge in 1555–58 and the adjacent Baroque **St. Georgen-kirche**★ (1690–99).

○ *The road reaches the Sosa Talsperre, a pretty reservoir and a nice spot for taking a break. The route then climbs along the winding valley of the Zwickauer Mulde to Klingenthal.*

Klingenthal

This former mining community is best known for the musical instruments made here since the mid-17C. The Baroque church **Zum Friedenfürsten**, which features an unusual octagonal floor-plan, makes a pleasant stop for stretching your legs.

ADDRESSES

STAY

Wilder Mann – *Markt 13. 03733 14 40. www.hotel-wildermann.de. 71 rooms. Restaurant, closed Sun–Mon.* This fine hotel occupies a Gothic Flamboyant-style building dating from 1509, one of the oldest houses in the city, complete with vaulted entrance hall. Bedrooms are modern and there is a sauna. Its Silberbaum restaurant occupies the atmospheric, vaulted Kartoffelkeller *(potato cellar)*, which specialises *(natürlich...)* in potato-based dishes.

EAT

Zum Hammer – *Tannenberg, 6km/4mi north of Annaberg-Buchholz. Untere Dorfstraße 21. 03733 529 51. www.zumhammer.de. Open lunch and dinner weekends; dinner only Mon–Fri.* Dark wooden beams, tiled floors and rustic furniture give this restaurant a rustic atmosphere.

Meissen ★

Meissen is famous for its porcelain, distinguished by its logo showing a pair of crossed swords in blue. At the heart of Germany's second-most northerly wine growing region, it also produces pleasantly fruity dry white wines. Meissen's historic centre, which is remarkably well preserved, is dominated by the flamboyant Albrechtsburg and the cathedral.

▶ **Population:** 28 500
▪ **Info:** Markt 3, 01662 Meissen. ℘(03521) 419 40. www.tourist info-meissen.de.
▶ **Location:** Meissen lies in the picturesque Elbe Valley, near Dresden.
🅰 **Don't Miss:** The Burgberg and the Porcelain Museum.
🕐 **Timing:** It takes about half a day to explore Meissen.

A BIT OF HISTORY

The porcelain of Saxony – It was in 1708, during the reign of Augustus the Strong, that **Johann Friedrich Böttger** (1682–1719) discovered the formula for creating the white hard-paste porcelain until then made only in China. In 1710 Augustus the Strong founded the Royal Saxon Porcelain Factory.

OLD MEISSEN

The old town has plenty of Gothic and Renaissance charm. **Marktplatz** is dominated by the late-Gothic **Rathaus** (town hall, 1470–86), the late-15C Bennohaus, the Renaissance **Marktapotheke** (pharmacy; 1555–60) and the Hirschhaus with a fine 1642 doorway.

Frauenkirche (Church of Our Lady)

This late-Gothic hall-church with its fine star-vaulting cuts a commanding presence on the Marktplatz. Its carillon bells are made of Meissen porcelain. For nice views of the town and the river, climb up the **tower** (🕐 open Apr–Oct, daily 10am–noon, 1pm–5pm; ⊜2€).

BURGBERG ★★

On a hilltop above the old town, the **Albrechtsburg★** (🕐 open Mar–Oct, daily 10am–6pm; Nov–Feb, daily 10am–5pm; 🕐 closed Jan 1, Dec 24, 25 & 31; ⊜4€, special exhibitions 8€. ℘(03521) 470 70; www.albrechtsburg-meissen.de) is one of the finest civic examples of the late-Gothic (1521–24) style. An exhibition on the ground floor illuminates the historical and technical aspects of

porcelain making, while the second floor boasts a stunning collection of medieval sculpture. Two rooms tell the story of when the castle was home to Europe's first porcelain factory.

Next door, the **Dom★** is a Gothic hall church built from 1250 atop a Romanesque sanctuary and completed in the late 15C. Note the **funerary plaques★** in the **Fürstenkapelle** (Dukes' Chapel) and the **lay brothers' altar★** (Laienaltar) in front of the rood screen, which can be traced to Lucas Cranach the Elder. The **Stifterfiguren★★** (benefactors' statues) in the chancel represent Emperor Otto I and his second wife, Empress Adelaide.

Museum of Meissen Art★

Talstraße 9. 🕐 Open May–Oct, daily 9am–6pm; Nov–Apr 5pm. 🕐 Closed Dec 24–26. ⊜8.50€. ℘(03521) 46 82 33. www.meissen.com. In 1865, the studios and workshops of the Meissen factory were transferred from the Albrechtsburg, where they had been for 150 years, to this site about 1km/0.6mi southwest of the town centre.

Start your visit by joining a guided tour of four **demonstration workshops★★**, where the processes of manufacturing, decorating and firing porcelain can be observed (expect long queues).

This is followed by a spin around the **Schauhalle** (exhibition room), which displays the world's largest collection of Meissen porcelain from 1910 to today.

MEISSEN

0   300 m

LEIPZIG

A4 · E 40 CHEMNITZ
FREIBERG ↑ A 14 LEIPZIG

A 13 · E 55 BERLIN
A 4 · E 40 BAUTZEN
DRESDEN

ALBRECHTSBURG
CATHEDRAL
Our Lady
NATIONAL PORCELAIN FACTORY
NICOLAIKIRCHE
ST-AFRAKIRCHE
Markt

FREITAL

WHERE TO STAY	
Am Talkenberger Hof	①
Burgkeller	④
Ross	⑦

WHERE TO EAT	
Romantik Restaurant Vincenz Richter	①
zenSuR	④

ADDRESSES

🏨 STAY

🛏 **Hotel Am Talkenberger Hof** –
*Am Talkenberger Hof 15, 01640 Coswig,
near Meissen.* ℰ*(03523) 743 17.
www.talkenberger-hof.de. 9 rooms.*
A warm atmosphere reigns at this
charming inn draped in vine leaves and
flowers. It's right on the Saxon Wine
Road and has clean, well cared-for
rooms with country-style furnishings.
From the terrace you can enjoy superb
views over the Elbe Valley.

🛏🛏 **Ross** – *Großenhainer Straße 9.
℘03521 75 10. www.hotelrossmeissen.de.
41 rooms.* This centuries-old coaching
inn, opposite the station, has been
converted into a modern hotel by the
Eichholz family.

🛏🛏🛏 **Burgkeller** – *Domplatz 11.
℘03521 414 00. www.meissen-hotel.de.
10 rooms.* �. The elegant bedrooms of
this charming small hotel (est. 1881)
look onto the cathedral.

🍴 EAT

🛏 **Romantik Restaurant Vincenz
Richter** – *An der Frauenkirche 12.
℘03 521 45 32 85. www.vincenz-richter.de
Closed last 3 weeks Jan and Mon.*
This charming picture-book historic
property began life as a draper's
business in 1523. It now serves regional
cooking. In summer, dine in the
delightful inner courtyard.

🛏🛏 **zenSuR** – *Heinrichplatz 6.* ℘*03 521
722 50. www.goldener-loewe-meissen.de.
Closed Tue & Thu lunch, & mid-Jan–mid-
Feb.* The main restaurant serves creative
international cuisine in an elegant
setting. The Weinstube serves excellent
value regional dishes.

Leipzig★

Leipzig has been renowned as a
place of commerce since the Middle
Ages, but the city also has a proud
musical heritage. Bach, Wagner
and Mendelssohn-Bartholdy all
lived here, and its orchestras and
musical institutions still enjoy a
fine reputation throughout Europe.
In the late 1980s, Leipzig was a
leading centre of the peaceful
protests that led to the downfall of
the German Democratic Republic,
paving the way for the reunification
of the two Germanies in 1990 (ℰ*see
INTRODUCTION: History)*.

A BIT OF HISTORY

The Leipzig Fairs – The first mention
of Leipzig was in the chronicle of Bishop
Thietmar of Merseburg (975–1018), who
noted the death of the Bishop of Meissen
in "Urbs Lipzi". The township of "Lipzk"
was granted a city charter around 1165,
which was also roughly the year when
it held its first trade fair. It is still held
today, making it the oldest in the world.

▸ **Population:** 497 500
🛈 **Info:** Richard-Wagner-
Straße 1, 04109 Leipzig.
℘(0341) 710 42 60.
www.lts-leipzig.de.
▸ **Location:** Leipzig is in the
far west of Saxony, at the
confluence of the Weiße
Elster and Pleiße rivers.
🅿 **Parking:** Garages are
plentiful, especially near
the main train station.
👁 **Don't Miss:** Bach Museum,
St. Thomas Church and
the Musical Instrument
Museum; a concert at
the Gewandhaus.
🕐 **Timing:** Allow a full day to
explore Leipzig's musical
and political heritage.

City of books and music – One of the
world's earliest books, the *Glossa Super
Apocalipsim*, was printed in Leipzig in
1481. These days, Leipzig nurses its literary heritage with an annual book fair,

Gewandhausorchester Leipzig

Many orchestras were founded as court orchestras, but not the Leipzig Gewandhaus Orchestra, which got its start in 1843 thanks to donations from wealthy burghers. The orchestra got its unusual name ("cloth-hall orchestra") because its first performance space in 1781 was in the converted Clothworkers' Guildhall. Famous composers and performers appeared here over the centuries, and Beethoven's *Triple Concerto*, Schubert's *Symphony in C major*, Mendelssohn's *"Scottish" Symphony* and Brahms' *Violin Concerto in D major* all premiered here. In 1884, the orchestra finally got its own purpose-built concert hall. Bombed in 1944, it was rebuilt in modern fashion in 1981. Famous Gewandhaus directors have included Felix Mendelssohn-Bartholdy, Arthur Nikisch and Kurt Masur. Since 2005 it has been helmed by Riccardo Chailly.

Germany's second-largest after Frankfurt. Leipzig also enjoys a fine reputation musically, thanks to the Choir of St. Thomas (Thomanerchor), the Gewandhaus Orchestra and the Felix Mendelssohn-Bartholdy University of Music and Theatre.

A prosperous city – The discovery in the 16C of silver in the Erzgebirge Mountains ensured Leipzig's prosperity. Today the city is still an important economic centre with corporate investors including Porsche and BMW.

OLD TOWN★

The historic centre of Leipzig, south of the impressive central station *(Hauptbahnhof)* with its huge shopping centre, is encircled by a ring road tracing the town's medieval fortifications.

Altes Rathaus★
(Old Town Hall)

On Markt, this long, low building with its decorated façade and dwarf gables is a typical example of German Renaissance architecture. It was completed in 1556 after plans by Hieronymous Lotter. The tower features a balcony for town pipers or heralds.

Today the building houses the local history museum, the **Stadtgeschichtliches Museum** (🕐open year-round, Tue–Sun 10am–6pm; 🕐closed Dec 24, 25 & 31; ⚭4€; 🕭; 𝒫(0341) 965 13 20; www.stadtgeschichtliches-museum-leipzig.de).

Zeitgeschichtliches Forum★
(Forum of Contemporary History)

Grimmaische Straße 6. 🕐*Open year-round, Tue–Fri 9am–6pm, Sat–Sun 10am–6pm.* 𝒫*(0341) 222 20. www.hdg.de.*

This modern and engaging museum chronicles the history of the GDR, the daily lives of its citizens and the peaceful movement that led to its downfall.

Alte Börse★
(Old Exchange)

On the Naschmarkt.

This former commodities market (built 1678–87) was Leipzig's first Baroque edifice. Today it is a splendid venue for receptions, concerts and other events. The statue outside (by Carl Seffner, 1903) shows Goethe as a student.

Katharinenstraße

North of the Alte Börse.

Of the Baroque houses on the west of Katharinenstraße, the finest is the **Romanushaus** *(at the Brühl)*, built in 1701 by Johann Gregor Fuchs. The neighbouring houses *(nos 21 and 19)* were built in the mid-18C. The Fregehaus *(no 11)*, also by Fuchs, belonged to the wealthy banker Christian Gottlob Frege whose trade emporium stretched across Europe and to America.

Museum der Bildenden Künste★★
(Fine Arts Museum)

Katharinenstraße 10. ◷*Open Tue, Thu–Sun 10am–6pm, Wed noon–8pm.* ☞*5€.* ♿ *(0341) 21 69 90. www.mdbk.de.*

A striking 34m/111.5ft-high glass cube is the modern home of a fantastic art collection with works from the late Middle Ages to the present. Highlights include rooms dedicated to native sons Max Beckmann and New Leipzig School representative Neo Rauch.

Notable **German Old Masters** include works by Master Francke, Lucas Cranach the Elder and Hans Baldung Grien. **Flemish Old Masters** are represented by disciples of van Eyck and Rembrandt, van der Weyden, Frans Hals and van Ruisdael. **Italian Masters** include Conegliano, Francia and Tintoretto.

German 19C painters receive ample space, with works by Anton Graff, Tischbein, CD Friedrich, Spitzweg, Böcklin, Liebermann, Klinger and Leibl.

In the Sculpture Department there are works by, among others, Permoser, Thorvaldsen, Rodin and Klinger. The collection of prints and drawings offers a virtually unbroken survey of graphic art from medieval times to the present.

Nikolaikirche★
(Church of St. Nicholas)

Nikolaistraße. ◷*Open year-round, daily 10am–6pm.* ℘*(0341) 960 5270.*

This 12C church played a key role in the peaceful revolution of 1989. Dedicated to St. Nicholas, the patron saint of merchants, it was originally Romanesque in style but saw several Gothic modifications, including the 14C chancel and west towers and the 16C triple nave and central tower. Its impressive Neoclassical **interior**★, by Carl Dauthe, dates back to the late 18C. Pale, fluted pillars end in light green palm leaves, while the vaulting is coffered in rose with stucco flowers. 30 paintings hang in the narthex and chancel.

The late-Romanesque wooden crucifix in the chancel is believed to be the oldest work of art in town.

Mädlerpassage
© Mauritius/Photononstop

Arcades

Leipzig's glass-roofed arcades are remarkably well restored and now make an attractive setting for a great variety of shops, cafés and bars.

Mädlerpassage – *Opposite Naschmarkt.* This is the grandest and best known of the arcades, home to Auerbachs Keller, where Goethe set scenes in *Faust.*

Specks Hof – *Schuhmachergäßchen.* The restoration of this 1911 trade hall preserved its best old features while modernising the whole.

Strohsack – This modern arcade links Nikolaistraße with Ritterstraße. Check the time on the glass-covered clock in the floor.

Steibs Hof – *Between Brühlstraße and Nikolaistraße.* This 1907 trade fair house appeals with its blue-and-white tiled courtyards.

Jägerhofpassage – *Between Hainstraße and Grosse Fleischergasse.* This 1914 *Jugendstil* arcade with ivory-tiled walls now houses a cinema.

WHERE TO STAY		WHERE TO EAT		Niemans Tresor..................⑥
Am Bayrischen Platz...........①		Auerbachs Keller...............①		Stadtpfeiffer......................⑨
Fürstenhof.........................④		Barthels Hof.....................④		Zill's Tunnel.......................⑦
Michaelis..........................⑦		La Cachette......................⑤		Statue of Goethe as a student.............A

Thomaskirche★
(Church of St. Thomas)

Thomaskirchhof. ⊙*Open year-round,
daily 9am–6pm.* ℘*(0341) 22 22 40.
www.thomaskirche.org.*
First documented in 1212, this late-
Gothic triple-aisle church took on its
present appearance in the late 15C.

Johann Sebastian Bach was cantor
here for 27 years and is buried opposite the altar.
The church is also renowned for the **St.
Thomas Boys' Choir** (Thomanerchor)
once directed by Bach, which occasionally performs during concerts and
church services.

Thomaskirche where Bach was cantor

Bachmuseum

Thomaskirchhof 16. ○*Open year-round, Tue–Sun 10am–6pm.* ○*Closed Dec 24, 25 & 31.* ⊛*6€.* & *(0341) 913 72 02. www.bach-leipzig.de.*

The newly revamped and expanded Bach Museum introduces visitors in interactive fashion to the great composer, his family and his times. Aside from perusing documents and instruments, you get to customise the instrumentation of a chorale and learn how to date a Bach manuscript. The museum occupies the 16C home of the Bose merchant family, who were good friends with the Bachs.

Ägyptisches Museum★ (Egyptian Museum)

Goethestraße 2. ○*Open year-round, Tue–Sat 1pm–5pm, Sun 10am–1pm.* ○*Closed Jan 1, May 1, Dec 24 & 31.* ⊛*5€.* & *(0341) 973 70 10. www.uni-leipzig.de/~egypt/.*

The 9 000 exhibits in this museum range from antiquity to the Christian era.

THE RING ROAD AND AROUND
Augustusplatz

This vast square is ringed by some of Leipzig's most important cultural institutions. The entire north side is taken up by the monumental **Opernhaus**

(opera house) from the 1960s. Behind it is a pleasant park with a duck pond and a statue of Richard Wagner. On the square's west end looms Leipzig's first skyscraper, the **Krochhaus** (1928–29), which in 1970 was bested by the MDR Hochhaus next to the Neues Gewandhaus concert hall. Leipzig University is here as well.

Neues Gewandhaus

This famous concert hall was inaugurated in 1981 and is home of the famous Gewandhausorchester. The massive auditorium has seats for up to 1 900 music fans. The bust of Beethoven (1902) in the foyer is a work by Leipzig-born Max Klinger. The neo-baroque Mendebrunnen Fountain (1886) outside the Gewandhaus is anchored by an 18m/ 59ft granite obelisk ringed by figures from Greek mythology symbolising the importance of water for humankind.

Mendelssohn-Haus

Goldschmidtstraße 12. ○*Open year-round, daily 10am–6pm.* ⊛*4€.* *(0341) 127 02 94. www.mendelssohn-stiftung.de.*

This house was the last residence (1845–47) of the famous composer Felix

---

Musicians in Leipzig

Johann Sebastian Bach worked and composed in Leipzig from 1723–1750 as cantor of St. Thomas and as music director for all the town's churches. Bach had faded into obscurity when **Felix Mendelssohn-Bartholdy** became director of the Gewandhaus orchestra in 1835. He turned Leipzig into a city of musical renown, established Germany's first musical conservatory and composed numerous original musical works. **Clara Wieck** and **Robert Schumann** lived in a Neoclassical house at Inselstraße 16, which now contains a memorial exhibit. The *Spring Symphony* was composed here.

Mendelssohn-Bartholdy, who moved to Leipzig in 1835 to head the prestigious Gewandhaus orchestra. The museum in his first-floor apartment uses letters, compositions, original furniture, watercolours that he painted himself and other memorabilia to illustrate his life, times and accomplishments. *Concerts are held in the Musik Salon every Saturday at 11am.*

Neues Rathaus
(New Town Hall)

The 19C town hall was built on the foundations of Pleißenburg Castle, best known as the scene of a famous argument between Luther and Eck in 1519.

ADDITIONAL MUSEUMS
Museen im Grassi★

Johannisplatz 5–11.
www.grassimuseum.de. Combination ticket to two Grassi museums are 8€, to all three 12€.

The Grassi museums complex was built between 1925 and 1929 in the Expressionist style, with echoes of Art Deco, by Carl William Zweck and Hans Voigt. It comprises three museums organised around four inner courtyards.

Museum für Angewandte Kunst★
(Museum of Applied Arts)

Open year-round, Tue–Sun 10am–6pm. Closed Dec 24 & 31. 5€. (0341) 222 91 00. www.grassimuseum.de.

This collection covers European arts and crafts from the Middle Ages to the early 20C. Exhibits include furniture (e.g. Nuremberg hall cabinet, 16C), porcelain (Meissen), glassware (Venetian, Bohemian) and valuable *Jugendstil* pieces (Gallé, Lalique).

Museum für Völkerkunde★
(Museum of Ethnography)

Open year-round, Tue–Sun 10am–6pm. Closed Dec 24 & 31. 6€. (0341) 973 19 00. www.mvl-grassimuseum.de.

One of the oldest and most important ethnographic museums in Europe, this institution explores the history and culture of the peoples of Asia, Africa, America and Oceania.

Museum für Musikinstrumente★
(Museum of Musical Instruments)

Open year-round, Tue–Sun 10am–6pm. Closed Dec 24 & 31. 5€. (0341) 973 07 50. www.mfm.uni-leipzig.de.

One of Europe's finest of its kind, this museum displays 5 000 instruments from five centuries and from around the world, as well as an interactive sound laboratory.

Museum in der Runden Ecke
(Stasi Museum)

Dittrichring 24. Open year-round, daily 10am–6pm. Closed Jan 1, Dec 23–26 & 31. 3€. (0341) 961 24 43. www.runde-ecke-leipzig.de.

In the former *Stasi* headquarters, this exhibition provides a look at the machinations and methods used by the infamous East German Ministry for State Security to spy on its own people.

ADDRESSES

STAY

Hotel Am Bayrischen Platz – *Paul-List-Straße 5.* (0341) 14 08 60. *32 rooms.* Karl Marx slept here in 1874, and you can stay in the same room. Others rooms at this villa-style hotel are smaller and less fancy but still tastefully furnished.

Hotel Michaelis – *Paul-Gruner-Straße 44.* (0341) 267 80. www.hotel.michaelis.de. *59 rooms. Restaurant , closed Sun.* Built in 1907 and now a listed building, this hotel has been renovated with an eye for detail. Rooms are harmonious, elegant and individually styled, while the restaurant is modern and tastefully decorated.

Hotel Fürstenhof – *Tröndlinring 8.* (0341) 14 00. www.starwoodhotels.com. *92 rooms.* 22€. *Restaurant , closed Sun.* Behind the façade of this classic mansion (1770) awaits a luxuriously elegant interior. Service is impeccable and the Mediterranean-style spa complex an oasis of relaxation. Refined restaurant.

♀/EAT

"Zill's Tunnel" Restaurant – *Barfußgässchen 9. ℘(0341) 960 20 78. www.zillstunnel.de.* This restaurant-cum-tavern has been doling out German and Saxon dishes since 1841.

Barthels Hof – *Hainstraße 1. ℘(0341) 14 13 10. www.barthels-hof.de.* At this carefully restored 18C restaurant you can match your mood to one of the three dining rooms: the elegant white-linen Webers Speisestube, the cross-vaulted Barthels wine tavern and the historical cellars. Two courtyards beckon in good weather. All in all, a fine establishment to sample classic Saxon cuisine.

Niemans Tresor – *Thomaskirchhof 20. ℘0341 21 61 00. www.niemannstresor.de. Open Tue–Sun (weekends dinner only). Closed Mon & 1–6 Jan; 3 weeks Jul–Aug.* Opposite the church of St. Thomas, this high quality restaurant occupies a beautiful Art Nouveau-style former bank building.

Auerbachs Keller – Historische Weinstuben – *Grimmaische Straße 2 (Mädler-Passage). ℘(0341) 21 61 00. www.auerbachs-keller-leipzig.de. Closed Sun.* A Leipzig institution, this wine tavern and restaurant has been in business since 1525. It was a favourite hangout of Goethe and reportedly provided inspiration for a scene from *Faust*. The cuisine is classic and traditional.

La Cachette – *Pfaffendorfer Straße 26. ℘0341 562 98 67. www.restaurant-la-cachette.de. Closed Sun, Mon.* Near the zoo, this fine restaurant is decorated with Art Nouveau paintings by Alfonse Mucha. The cuisine is Mediterranean and fresh oysters are a speciality.

Stadtpfeiffer – *Augustusplatz 8. ℘0341 217 89 20. www.stadtpfeiffer.de. Dinner only. Closed Sun–Mon and Jul–Aug.* Petra and Detlef Schlegel go to great lengths to welcome their guests and serve faultless seasonal cuisine. There is a tasting menu (7 courses 108€, 4 courses 98€, 3 courses 88€) plus à la carte dishes.

☞TAKING A BREAK

USEFUL TIPS

Leipziger Lerchen ("Leipzig larks") are a local speciality found in all cake shops. The actual bird once contributed to the town's culinary reputation, but when the king of Saxony banned lark hunting in 1876, bakers transferred the name to a new pastry, made of shortbread and almond paste.

NIGHTLIFE

USEFUL TIPS

Lively bars cluster in the city centre between the Brühl and the Neues Rathaus. The most animated lane is the Barfußgässchen in the pedestrian zone, which is chock-a-block with bars, restaurants and cafés. West of here, Gottschedstraße draws scores of night owls and students. For alternative flair, head south to Karl-Liebknecht-Straße, locally known as "Karli".

PUBLICATIONS

The monthly calendar of events, *Leipzig im…* is available at the tourist office for 0.50€, while the monthly listings magazine *Prinz* can be bought at kiosks.

☞ SHOPPING

USEFUL TIPS

Leipzig is a great place to shop. Many of the finest shops are in such glass-roofed arcades as the Mädlerpassage, Specks Hof, Strohsack, Steibs Hof and Jägerhofpassage. The biggest shopping centre is in the main train station.

INDEX

INDEX

580

INDEX

INDEX

INDEX

STAY

EAT

MAPS AND PLANS

Sight

Highly recommended ★★★
Recommended ★★
Interesting ★

Selected monuments and sights

	Tour - Departure point
	Catholic church
	Protestant church, other temple
	Synagogue - Mosque
	Building
■	Statue, small building
	Calvary, wayside cross
◎	Fountain
	Rampart - Tower - Gate
	Château, castle, historic house
	Ruins
	Dam
✿	Factory, power plant
☆	Fort
∩	Cave
	Troglodyte dwelling
	Prehistoric site
▼	Viewing table
Ⅶ	Viewpoint
▲	Other place of interest

Sports and recreation

	Racecourse
	Skating rink
	Outdoor, indoor swimming pool
	Multiplex Cinema
	Marina, sailing centre
	Trail refuge hut
	Cable cars, gondolas
	Funicular, rack railway
	Tourist train
◆	Recreation area, park
	Theme, amusement park
	Wildlife park, zoo
	Gardens, park, arboretum
	Bird sanctuary, aviary
	Walking tour, footpath
	Of special interest to children

Special symbols

	Park and Ride
	Covered parking
19	Federal road (Bundesstraße).

Map Legend continued overleaf

Additional symbols

🛈		Tourist information
═══	══	Motorway or other primary route
❶	❶	Junction: complete, limited
▭	══	Pedestrian street
Ɪ═══Ꞽ	══	Unsuitable for traffic, street subject to restrictions
▭▭▭	----	Steps – Footpath
🚆	🚆	Train station – Auto-train station
🚌	S.N.C.F.	Coach (bus) station
──●──		Tram
Ⓜ		Metro, underground
🅿		Park-and-Ride
♿		Access for the disabled
✉		Post office
☎		Telephone
✉		Covered market
⋅✕⋅		Barracks
△		Drawbridge
⛏		Quarry
✕		Mine
🅱	🅵	Car ferry (river or lake)
⛴		Ferry service: cars and passengers
⛴		Foot passengers only
③		Access route number common to Michelin maps and town plans
Bert (R.)...		Main shopping street
AZ **B**		Map co-ordinates

Abbreviations

J	Law courts (Justizgebäude)
L	Provincial government (Landesregierung)
M	Museum (Museum)
POL.	Police (Polizei)
R	Town hall (Rathaus)
T	Theatre (Theater)
U	University (Universität)

The German letter ß (eszett) has been used throughout this guide.

You know
the Green Guide

...Do you really know **MICHELIN**?

• Data 31/12/2009

The world No.1 in tires with 16.3% of the market

A business presence in over **170 countries**

A manufacturing footprint
at the heart of markets

In 2009 **72** industrial sites in **19** countries produced:

- **150** million tires
- **10** million maps and guides

Highly international **teams**

Over **109 200** employees* from all cultures on all continents

including **6 000** people employed in R&D centers in Europe, the US and Asia.

*102 692 full-time equivalent staff

The Michelin Group
at a glance

Michelin competes

At the end of 2009

Le Mans 24-hour race
12 consecutive years of victories

Endurance 2009
- 6 victories on 6 stages in Le Mans Series
- 12 victories on 12 stages in American Le Mans Series

Paris-Dakar
Since the beginning of the event, the Michelin group has won in all categories

Moto endurance
2009 World Champion

Trial
Every World Champion title since 1981 (except 1992)

Michelin, established close to its customers

○ **72 plants in 19 countries**

- Algeria
- Brazil
- Canada
- China
- Colombia
- France
- Germany
- Hungary
- Italy
- Japan
- Mexico
- Poland
- Romania
- Russia
- Serbia
- Spain
- Thailand
- UK
- USA

● **A Technology Center spread over 3 continents**

- Asia
- Europe
- North America

● **Natural rubber plantations**

- Brazil

Our mission

To make a sustainable contribution to progress in the mobility of goods and people by enhancing freedom of movement, safety, efficiency and the pleasure of travelling.

Michelin committed to environmental-friendliness

Michelin, world leader in low rolling resistance tires, actively reduces fuel consumption and vehicle gas emission.

For its products, Michelin develops state-of-the-art technologies in order to:
- Reduce fuel consumption, while improving overall tire performance.
- Increase life cycle to reduce the number of tires to be processed at the end of their useful lives;
- Use raw materials which have a low impact on the environment.

Furthermore, at the end of 2008, 99.5% of tire production in volume was carried out in ISO 14001* certified plants.

Michelin is committed to implementing recycling channels for end-of-life tires.

*environmental certification

**Passenger Car
Light Truck**

Truck

Michelin
a key mobility enabler

Earthmover

Aircraft

Agricultural